Religious Responses to Violence

RELIGIOUS
RESPONSES TO
VIOLENCE

Human Rights in Latin America Past and Present

Edited by
ALEXANDER WILDE

University of Notre Dame Press

Notre Dame, Indiana

Copyright © 2016 by University of Notre Dame Press
Notre Dame, Indiana 46556
www.undpress.nd.edu

Manufactured in the United States of America

Library of Congress Cataloging-in-Publication Data

Wilde, Alexander.
Religious reponses to violence : human rights in Latin America
past and present / edited by Alexander Wilde.
Includes bibliographical references and index.
ISBN 9780268044312 (pbk. : alk. paper)
ISBN 0268044317 (pbk. : alk. paper)
Human rights—Latin America. Human rights—
Latin America—Religious aspects. Civil rights—
Latin America. Freedom of religion—Latin America.
JC599.L3 R475   2015
261.7098—dc23
2015034485

∞ *The paper in this book meets the guidelines for permanence and durability*
of the Committee on Production Guidelines for Book Longevity of
the Council on Library Resources.

CONTENTS

PART II

Contemporary Ministries Responding to Violence

LIST OF ABBREVIATIONS

ABI	Associação Brasileira de Imprensa (Brazilian Press Association)
ACIB	American Committee for Information on Brazil
ACR	Asociación Columbiana para la Reintegración (Colombian Agency for Reintegration, formerly the High Commissioner for Reintegration)
AFDD	Agrupación de Familiares de Detenidos Desaparecidos (Association of Relatives of Disappeared Detainees, Chile)
APAC	Associação de Proteção e Assistência aos Codenados (Association for the Protection and Assistance of Prisoners, Brazil)
AUC	Autodefensas Unidas de Colombia (United Self-Defense Forces of Colombia)
BNM	*Brasil: Nunca mais* (Brazil: Never Again)
CAH	Consejo Aguaruna y Huambisa (Awajun-Wampis Council, Peru)
CEAS	Comisión Episcopal de Acción Social (Episcopal Commission for Social Action, Peru)
CEBs	Comunidades eclesiales de base (Christian base communities)
CELAM	Consejo del Episcopado Latinoamericano (Conference of Latin American Bishops)
CELS	Centro de Estudios Legales y Sociales (Center for Legal and Social Studies, Argentina)
CEPA	Comité Evangélico de Promoción Agraria (Evangelical Committee on Agricultural Development, Nicaragua)

CEPAD	Comité Evangélico Pro-Ayuda al Desarrollo (Evangelical Committee for Pro-Development Aid, Nicaragua)
CESE	Coordenadoria Ecumênica de Serviço (Ecumenical Coordination Service, Brazil)
CINEP	Centro de Investigación y Educación Popular (Center for Research and Popular Education, Colombia)
CNBB	Conferência Nacional dos Bispos do Brasil (National Conference of Brazilian Bishops)
CNDH	Comisión Nacional de Derechos Humanos (National Human Rights Commission, Mexico)
CNRR	Comité Nacional de Reparación y Reconciliación (National Commission for Reparation and Reconciliation, Colombia)
CONADEP	Comisión Nacional sobre la Desaparición de Personas (National Commission on the Disappearance of Persons, Argentina)
CONAR	Comité Nacional de Ayuda a los Refugiados (National Committee for Aid to Refugees, Mexico)
CUC	Comité de Unidad Campesina (Committee for Peasant Unity, Guatemala)
CyR	Cristianismo y Revolución (Christianity and Revolution, Argentina)
DDR	Desarme, desmovilización y reintegración (Disarmament, demobilization, and reintegration, Colombia)
EGP	Ejército Guerrillero de los Pobres (Guerrilla Army of the Poor, Guatemala)
ELN	Ejército de Liberación Nacional (National Liberation Army, Colombia)
EPICA	Ecumenical Program for Inter-American Communication and Action
EPL	Ejército Popular de Liberación (Popular Liberation Army, Colombia)
EZLN	Ejército Zapatista de Liberación Nacional (Zapatista Army of National Liberation, Mexico)
FALN	Fuerzas Armadas de Liberación Nacional (Armed Front for National Liberation, Venezuela)

FAR	Fuerzas Armadas Rebeldes (Rebel Armed Forces, Argentina and Guatemala)
FARC	Fuerzas Armadas Revolucionarias de Colombia (Revolutionary Armed Forces of Colombia)
FMLN	Frente Farabundo Martí para la Liberación Nacional (Farabundo Martí National Liberation Front, El Salvador)
IACHR	Inter-American Commission on Human Rights
ICJ	International Commission of Jurists
IDL	Instituto de Defensa Legal (Institute for Legal Defense, Peru)
MAPU	Movimiento de Acción Popular Unitario (Unitary Movement for Popular Action, Chile)
MIR	Movimiento de la Izquierda Revolucionaria (Movement of the Revolutionary Left, Chile)
MSTM	Movimiento de Sacerdotes para el Tercer Mundo (Movement of Priests for the Third World, Argentina)
NCC	National Council of Churches
PDPMM	Programa de Desarrollo y Paz del Magdalena Medio (Development and Peace Program for Magdalena Medio, Colombia)
PRN	Proceso de Reorganización Nacional (National Reorganization Process, Argentina)
REMHI	Proyecto Interdiocesano de Recuperación de la Memoria Histórica (Inter-Diocesan Recovery of Historical Memory Project, Guatemala)
SERPAJ	Servicio Paz y Justicia (Service for Peace and Justice, Argentina)
STM	Superior Tribunal Militar (Superior Court of Military Justice, Brazil)
TSN	Tribunal de Segurança Nacional (Tribunal for National Security, Brazil)
UDHR	Universal Declaration of Human Rights
UNCHR	United Nations Commission on Human Rights
UNDPKO	United Nations Department of Peacekeeping Operations

UNHCR	United Nations High Commissioner for Refugees
URNG	Unidad Revolucionaria Nacional Guatemalteca (Guatemalan National Revolutionary Unity)
USCC	United States Catholic Conference
USO	Unión Sindical Obrera de la Industria del Petróleo (Labor Union of Petroleum Industry Workers, Colombia)
USP	Universidad de São Paulo (University of São Paulo)
VPR	Vanguarda Popular Revolucionária (People's Revolutionary Vanguard, Brazil)
WCC	World Council of Churches
WLF	World Lutheran Federation
WOLA	Washington Office on Latin America

LIST OF ILLUSTRATIONS

FIGURES

TABLE

PREFACE
AND
ACKNOWLEDGMENTS

This book is the fruit of a two-year project at the Center for Latin American and Latino Studies at American University in Washington, DC. It is based on fresh research about active religious responses to violence that have had social impact over the past half century. We wanted to explore how churches and individuals were motivated by their religious beliefs, particularly in the form of constructive agency to mitigate violence. Struck by the contrast between the visibility of church responses during Latin America's authoritarian era and the lower profile today, we adopted a diachronic perspective of "past" and "present," hypothesizing differences in religious responses to political and criminal violence. We also wanted to examine a range of societies throughout Latin America, to identify commonalities as well as contrasts. Finally, we believed that a multidisciplinary approach would be appropriate for such an exploratory project. The participants were scholars in anthropology, history, sociology, and political science whose current research reflects affinities with our central questions and approach. This volume is richer for the perspectives of their different disciplines—and for the individual authorial voices they bring to their chapters—on our core analytical questions.

How the churches relate to "human rights" was from the inception a natural crosscutting theme of the project's research. We sought fresh historical perspective on how the different churches viewed and contributed to the human rights movement when it emerged in the 1970s. The religious dimensions of that movement were, we believed, ripe for reappraisal, in order to understand better what led the churches of that era to defend human rights (or not) and the nature of the legacy of their responses to violence in Latin America today. The resulting research offers a range of illuminating insights into questions about both the past and the present of human rights. This book's second major theme—pastoral "accompaniment"—emerged as a project focus through discussion of ongoing research and is engaged in virtually every chapter.[1] Our initial conceptualization emphasized institutional and structural factors conditioning religious responses to violence. In examining the dynamic between church-linked actors and context, however, project participants were drawn particularly to interactions and relationships at the pastoral level. The research addressing this pastoral level proved an illuminating lens for our central questions and constitutes a major contribution of this volume.

The subject of violence itself is present in every chapter of this book. Following an interpretation of contemporary scholarship on the subject, authors examine *violencias* in many forms and the ways in which churches have responded in particular settings, both historical and contemporary. While political transitions from dictatorship to democracy ended generalized and systematic state violence in Chile and Argentina, Latin America's broad processes of democratization have not diminished levels of violence in many places examined in this book. Our research affirms the importance of distinguishing political and state violence from criminal violence—but also points to the need for better conceptualization if contemporary violence is to be addressed more effectively. This book suggests more generally that religious pastoral ministries, with their insights into the lived experience of violence, offer potentially significant new perspectives and perhaps remedies.

The chapters in this book all demonstrate careful attention to context—the specific circumstances to which the churches were responding. But they all also share a common perspective in first understanding those responses *in religious terms*, "from within." They take religion seriously because it has significant social consequences, because it provides a lens for understanding larger processes of social and political change, and because, at base, it is a way in which many human beings attempt to make sense of their lives and the experience of violence. This book's contributors attempt to see the world through the eyes of believers and then "translate" their perceptions, justifications, and rationales for response into the secular language of scholarly analysis. In this sense the book provides a religious perspective on Latin America's violence that we believe enlarges understanding of its character, causes, and potential antidotes, beyond the explanations of the social sciences as such.

LIKE ANY COLLECTIVE endeavor, this volume has benefited from many minds, hands, and spirits. I am immensely grateful for the opportunity to have worked through many stages with each of its authors. In sharing their research passions and talents, they made this joint exploration a genuinely creative process. I was initially drawn to the study of religion and violence in Latin America in the 1960s, a period of extraordinary energy in a new field, and it has been a deep pleasure to uncover such energy today in different places, thanks to the work of subsequent generations. Two of our contributors deserve special thanks: Dan Levine, an old friend and major force in this field for a half century, and Bob Brenneman, a new friend whose research shines with originality and passion. Both lent indispensable support to critical aspects of this enterprise.

This volume also reflects the ideas and experience of other participants in our project workshops (March 2012 and January 2013) and several panels at professional meetings, as well as valuable counsel in uncounted bilateral exchanges: Karina Kosicki Bellotti, Evan Berry, Phillip Berryman, John Burdick, Miguel Carter, Cath Collins, Steven Dudley, Joe Eldridge, Daniel Esser, Tom Getman, Henri Gooren, Frances Hagopian, Elizabeth Lira, Juan Méndez, Kevin O'Neill, Tom Quigley, Catalina Romero, Cynthia Sanborn, Timothy Steigenga, and Jon Wolseth. Thanks to you all.

A three-day meeting in Guatemala in July 2013 on the topic "The Role of the Church in Facing Violence in Mesoamerica" powerfully affirmed the present-day vitality of religion in that deeply troubled region. Three dozen participants with grassroots ministries in Mexico, Colombia, and all the countries of Central America demonstrated remarkable willingness to share their real-world pastoral experiences and think collaboratively across the wide spectrum of their different faith traditions. My deep gratitude to Willi Hugo Pérez, rector of the Semilla Seminary and co-convener and organizer of the meeting, and to Bob Brenneman,

Claudia Dary, Joe Eldridge, Amelia Frank-Vitale, Pedro Pantoja, Alejandro Solalinde, and Dennis Stinchcomb.[2]

I owe a particular debt to my colleagues at American University who have accompanied this project for two years: Joe Eldridge, university chaplain and a legendary advocate for human rights and dear friend; Bill Gentile, producer of a three-part video series on evangelical churches and gang violence in Guatemala (available on YouTube as *God and Gangs: Criminal Violence and Religion in Guatemala*); Dennis Stinchcomb, who combined great enthusiasm for our research with exemplary management skills; Jacquelyn Dolezal, who shepherded the English and Spanish manuscripts into publication with patience and meticulous care; Inés Luengo de Krom, chief administrator of the Center for Latin American and Latino Studies (CLALS); Meredith Glueck; Phil Chamberlain; and Amanda Sheldon.

Thanks also to Patrick Breslin, who provided superb editing skills and acute understanding of our issues in revising all the chapters, and Andrew McKelvy, for his excellent translation of María Soledad Catoggio's chapter.

There are several people without whom this book would have not been possible. Eric Hershberg, director of CLALS and an old and valued friend, brought his broad scholarly intelligence, exceptional professional experience, and encouraging collegial counsel to every step of this project, from its inception to the end. Toby Alice Volkman, program director of the Henry R. Luce Initiative on Religion and International Affairs, gave us enthusiastic support from the very beginning and allowed us space to develop our project creatively. My deep gratitude to them both and to the Luce Foundation for its two-year project grant.

Much more could be said, but the last word of thanks is to Anne Pérotin-Dumon, for her consistent *esprit critique* and unfailingly generous faith.

Alexander Wilde
Washington, DC, USA
September 2014

Notes

1. In project workshops in 2012 and 2013 and panels in the annual meetings of the Society for the Scientific Study of Religion in 2012 and Latin American Studies Association in 2013.

2. A rapporteur's report by the Guatemalan anthropologist Claudia Dary, "Las iglesias ante las violencias en Mesoamérica," may be downloaded at www.american.edu/clals/Religion-and-Violence-Documents.cfm.

INTRODUCTION

Alexander Wilde

I see the church as a field hospital after battle. [We must]
heal the wounds, heal the wounds. . . . And you have to
start from the ground up.
                    —Pope Francis, Rome, September 2013

We live in a country at war. . . . So much pain, so many
loved ones dead! These young men live in armed groups,
so how to take them out of the conflict? *There has to be
a way out.* . . . This is our work . . . to transform the person. We reach out to the person right where they are.
                    —Pastor José C., Urabá, Colombia, June 2013

Modern Latin America is both notably violent and notably religious.
During the past half century it has evolved from a region of political instability and frequent dictatorships into one of elected governments,
while its societies and economies have undergone sweeping changes and
high levels of violence have remained a persistent problem. During this

1

same period, religion has shown remarkable dynamism as a force in society. This book was stimulated by the desire to understand better the striking coincidence of these phenomena and the relationship between them. It is the fruit of a two-year collaborative research project on how active religious responses to violence have had social impact.[1] The chapters reveal a range of responses in the Christian churches and individuals inspired by faith, but the book aims particularly to illuminate religious vitality directed to constructive agency, with action meant to mitigate violence rather than employ or justify it.

Violence was a defining dimension of Latin America's history in the 1970s and 1980s, and the region remains today, by many measures, one of the most dangerous in the world. Contemporary statistics on homicide, assault, police violence, and kidnapping are alarming; crime tops all other issues of concern in public opinion surveys. Beyond the indicators lies a more pervasive sense of insecurity that for many frames daily life. During this same span religion has undergone an extraordinary renewal as a dimension of Latin American life and society. Following the Second Vatican Council (1962–65), the Catholic Church adopted an active social mission, new pastoral ministries, and original, influential, and controversial theologies. In many places it publicly defended human rights against repressive regimes. Evangelical and Pentecostal churches grew at historically unprecedented rates across the region, challenging centuries of Catholic cultural dominance. Their *templos* have become a distinctive and pervasive grassroots presence in Latin America's modern cities and countryside. Together these sweeping changes in Catholic and Protestant Christianity suggest something of the vitality of religion as a social force.

From the late 1960s through the 1980s—a period of repressive governments and violent civil conflict—the Catholic Church was a major public actor in many Latin American countries. Violence was then seen largely in political terms: as violence wielded by authoritarian regimes to remain in power, in many cases against guerrilla movements employing arms to overturn them. The international Cold War environment and frequent U.S. intervention in the region were the backdrop for these conflicts, and both sides invoked political ideologies to legitimate their use of violence. In this context Catholics were also divided. They had different views about the legitimacy of those employing violence. Progressive Catholics sympathized with revolutionary guerrillas aiming to overthrow dictatorships representing entrenched power. Conservatives supported existing authorities and justified state repression. But for most Catholics who took action, the human suffering wrought by violence—whether exercised in the name of national security or national revolution—became the primary concern. Over time, many found in human rights a new basis to affirm a Christian commitment to nonviolent defense of human life and to denounce the "state violence" of repressive regimes.

Since the 1980s elected governments have replaced authoritarian regimes across Latin America. Violence persists in the more open, fragmented context of today's "real existing democracies" (Schmitter 2009; see also O'Donnell 2004),[2] but it is largely seen in social rather than political terms. Criminal mafias and youth gangs are the most identifiable sources of widely felt insecurity. Elected governments are often blamed for corruption and for complicity with these actors, but the state itself is generally not perceived as the central source of violence, in contrast to the period of authoritarian rule. In part for this reason, religious responses today lack the high drama of the past, and the churches are less visible in political life. Similarly, scholarship on religion is more diverse and scattered in comparison to work on the earlier period (framed by debates, for example, about liberation theology).

But in fact the churches are addressing contemporary violence in many different ways, and their efforts are important. As this volume demonstrates, their approaches and perspectives may complement—or contradict—those of governments, international agencies, civil society actors, and the general public. The new studies presented here examine the specifically *religious* character of their responses—how they relate their mission and faith to violence in different contexts—to understand better how and why they have taken action. This approach also throws light on dimensions scanted in other perspectives on violence and suggests other potential strategies to mitigate its causes and effects.

This volume raises four core analytical issues that appear throughout this introduction and inform the research in this book:

1. How and why have religious responses to violence changed or demonstrated continuity over time? And particularly, what are the main factors that appear to motivate constructive social action?

2. How are the responses of church-linked organizations and individuals distinctively religious? How do they illuminate the moral dimensions of violence?
3. How have the characteristics of violence itself changed over time, as perceived by the churches?
4. When do religious responses to violence have the greatest impact?

In addressing these issues, the contributors draw on several scholarly literatures. The most important is modern study of religion in Latin America, which has developed in several phases over the past half century to become a significant and sophisticated field of research. Its initial growth was stimulated by the dynamism of Catholicism in the 1960s and the emergence of a progressive Church and liberation theology. This research on the authoritarian era was dominated by questions about the character of Christian base communities and their impact within the Church and by the changing relationship of the institutional Church and religiously linked actors to politics and political violence (see, e.g., Berryman 1984; Dodson and O'Shaughnessy 1990; Levine 1980, 1981, 1986; Lowden 1996; MacLean 2006; Mainwaring 1986; Mainwaring and Wilde 1989; Mallimaci and Villa 2007; Mignone 1988; Smith 1982; Tovar 2006). One body of recent research, particularly on Argentina, has thrown additional light on pre-Conciliar Catholic elements that justified repressive violence (e.g., Serbin 2000; Verbitsky 2005, 2006, 2007, 2008, 2009; Vidal 2005).

The remarkable rise of Evangelical and Pentecostal churches drew a new generation of scholars concerned with their specific character and appeal in a kind of religious competition with Catholicism. Themes of their research included a theological emphasis on personal conversion, personal spirituality, gender roles, and congregational ecclesiology—and the consequences of these distinctive new forms of religiosity for society, politics, and violence. Although Evangelicals have increased in number everywhere in Latin America, their rapid increase in societies that suffered extreme violence, such as Guatemala, has drawn particular interest (see, e.g., Brenneman 2011; Chesnut 1997, 2003; Cleary and Steigenga 2004; Freston 2008; Garrard-Burnett 1998, 2010; Garrard-Burnett and Freston 2014; O'Neill 2010; Smilde 2007; Steigenga 2001; Steigenga and Cleary

2007; Stoll 1991; Wolseth 2011). At the same time, retrenchment in the Catholic Church under Popes John Paul II and Benedict XVI sparked research on the legacies of progressive Catholicism and liberation theology within the Church itself and for social movements in Latin American democracies. Other important lines of work addressed the increased emphasis on institutional concerns, doctrinal orthodoxy and traditional family morality, and the "competition" with Evangelicals through new spiritualities such as Opus Dei and Charismatic Catholicism (see, e.g., Burdick 1993, 2004; Cleary 2011; Cleary and Stewart-Gambino 1992; Drogus and Stewart-Gambino 2005; Fleet and Smith 1997; Hagopian 2009; Levine 1992). The dynamism of both Catholic and Protestant churches over the past half century and the range and depth of this field of research are captured in Daniel H. Levine's impressive synthesis, *Politics, Religion, and Society in Latin America* (2012).

The contributors to this volume have drawn creatively on many parts of this larger literature to address our specific focus on religious responses to violence, in ways touched on in the two following sections of this introduction. These studies share the careful attention to context and multidimensional analysis of religious actors characteristic of the best research in this field. At the same time, it should be made clear that most of them are shaped by our particular interest in exploring constructive religious agency with social impact. This means that pietistic spirituality as such—which has been such a significant and dynamic strain in Catholic as well as Evangelical and Pentecostal religiosity—is drawn on selectively. Similarly, the more conservative elements in both traditions (but especially Catholicism) are less represented in this volume than in Latin American reality. Conservative prelates and pastors—and their faithful—are more characteristic in both the past and the present than the social ministries analyzed in our research. The chapters by Catoggio and Morello do analyze religious legitimation of state violence, for example, but the broad influence of more conservative Catholic hierarchies shaped by Popes John Paul II (1979–2005) and Benedict XVI (2005–13)—exemplified most notoriously today by Cardinal Archbishop Juan Luis Cipriani of Lima—falls largely outside our scope.

The remainder of this introduction considers the themes of human rights and pastoral accompaniment that run through the chapters of this book. Each has served as an important lens to understand social ministries responding to violence. Each appears in scholarly literatures, but we believe that bringing them together here offers a host of fresh insights and gives the book its coherence and integrity.

Human Rights

The cause of human rights bridges past and present. In the 1970s and 1980s, human rights gave the churches a new way to understand and address violence. Latin America was an important focus for the international human rights movement, and churches in the region were significant actors in legitimating the idea and establishing emerging practices. In today's real existing democracies, issues of human rights remain present and significant. They constitute an ongoing referent in politics, although competing with many other issues on public agendas (Wilde 2013). For Catholic pastoral ministries addressing conflict and violence, human rights remain a touchstone. This was also true historically for mainstream Protestant churches (see chapter by Kelly) but appears less so for the Evangelical churches, at least in explicit form (see chapter by Brenneman). The place the churches give human rights is an important way to judge continuities and changes in religious responses to violence over time—and to ask about how differences between Catholic and Evangelical theologies, doctrines, and practices affect those responses.

When human rights are an established concern, as they are today, it is easy to underestimate their sheer novelty in the 1970s, when they became the basis for a new form of moral resistance to violence in Latin America. During World War II the Allies had evoked human rights as an ethical ground for their war aims and made them a founding principle for the new United Nations, which approved the Universal Declaration of Human Rights in 1948. But during the early decades of the Cold War, they remained a marginal factor in the bifurcated logic of global ideological struggle. Only in the 1970s did the idea of human rights become a social cause and real factor in national politics and international diplomacy. Latin America, under harsh authoritarian rule, was a major focus for the emerging global human rights movement, and the region in turn greatly influenced the human rights "regime" then in formation.

The churches—the Catholic Church in particular—were major actors in this development. One of their most important contributions was coming to accept that such rights—certain values fundamental to human life, universal and inherent in the human condition—should be enshrined in law. Historically the churches had made theological and moral appeals, but for religious advocates of human rights, law and legal institutions offered a new and concrete means to protect them. This commitment also opened up the possibility of alliances with other actors in civil society, such as the bar association in Brazil and democratic politicians in Chile (see chapters by Queiroz and Wilde). Where an activist (but potentially catalytic) minority of religious actors took this step, they embraced a basically secular idea that resonated with the religious and nonreligious alike (see chapters by Levine and Kelly). Acceptance of universal human rights also moved beyond the "rights of the Church" claimed for the ecclesiastical institution (although that historical perspective remained strong in Argentina; see chapters by Catoggio and Morello). When the Church defended human rights, it redefined its relationship with the state. It continued to assert its autonomous religious mission but now denounced violent acts of state agents as violations of fundamental human rights. Indeed, it argued that the state had an intrinsic, positive responsibility in law to protect such rights.

The grounding of human rights in law carried with it an implicit commitment to nonviolence. How Catholic support for human rights made that commitment explicit and active was a complex process that scholars are only beginning to examine (see, e.g., Green 2010; Keck and Sikkink 1998; Méndez and Wentworth 2011; Moyn 2010; Neier 2012; Stites Mor 2013).[3] As noted, the Church was divided in its responses to the political and state violence of the authoritarian period. Fundamental biblical tenets of Christian faith that pointed to nonviolence—"thou shalt not kill," "blessed are the peacemakers"—had to be interpreted in a particular context of violence (as indeed they had been for two thousand years). In the 1970s and 1980s, violent conflict in Latin America was to an unusual degree understood and justified in terms of warring secular political ideologies—of Marxist class revolution and of the National Security Doctrine—heavily shaped by the Cold War. The period was also characterized by what seems in retrospect a strikingly prevalent belief in the *efficacy* of violence to achieve or prevent fundamental social change.

Armed revolutionaries in Central and South America were encouraged by the overthrow of corrupt dictatorships in Cuba (1959) and Nicaragua (1979); reactionaries, by the success of military coups in Brazil (1964), Chile (1973), and Argentina (1976) and by frequent support from U.S. policy. In this regional context, appeals to human rights, law, and non-violence appeared quixotic. But it was the setting in which the churches struggled to define their responses to violence in light of their own religious values.

The Second Vatican Council initiated fundamental theological developments that challenged the Catholic Church to *aggiornamento*—to rethinking its religious mission in the modern world. It called the faithful to consider how timeless truths, doctrines, and practices should be understood and applied in human history as it was unfolding, what the Council called interpreting "the signs of the times." At Medellín, Colombia, in 1968 the Latin American bishops urged more active engagement with secular social forces to remove obstacles holding back fuller, freer lives for the majority of the region's people. Adopting the phrase of the global head of the Jesuit order, Pedro Arrupe, they adopted "a preferential option for the poor" that gave the Council's broad new social direction a more specific focus in the region. Medellín also famously spurred the development of liberation theology—an original body of religious thought about how Christians should respond to a context of historical injustice, inequality, and poverty that in that period was defined by opposing political projects employing violence. Liberationists extended the concept of sin beyond individual lives to social analysis—interpreting the existing arrangements of Latin American societies as "institutional sin." They were influenced by the social sciences then emerging in the region, particularly Marxist analysis but—it is worth noting—also by non-Marxist thinking at the time, which was strongly oriented toward identifying "structural" obstacles to "development."

These theological trends all challenged Christians to social action or, in religious terms, to active witness in a violent world. The remarkable growth and influence of liberation theology, in particular, catalyzed religious debate about violence. At the time much attention was given to whether it encouraged or even legitimated church support for guerrilla insurgencies. Two groups of Catholics, with widely divergent positions, agreed that that was the core message of liberation theology. These were religiously inspired laypeople and clerical revolutionaries who took up arms (of whom the most famous was Camilo Torres; see chapters by Garrard-Burnett and Levine) *and* their theological opposites, reactionary, "antisecular" lay Catholics and clerics (see chapter by Morello) who rejected Conciliar reforms and justified violent state repression.[4] But in retrospect it is clear that the vast majority of the Church—leaders and followers—lay between these two groups, occupying a spectrum of political sympathy for one kind of violence or the other but tending to coalesce over time for varied reasons around the idea of human rights and, in some circumstances, their active defense.

Today we can see better both how liberation theology contributed to human rights and how it differed from them, in concept as well as praxis. Liberationists legitimated the belief that faith should be lived through social action and that it was right for Christians to collaborate with secular progressive forces. More broadly, liberation theology led to acceptance of social conflict as an inherent dimension (and even engine) of needed change. It did not, however, unambiguously embrace nonviolence as principle and method, nor did it see law as an instrument for attaining greater social justice—both of which were foundation stones of the human rights movement. Liberation theology also reflected the dominant sociological thinking of the 1970s and 1980s, emphasizing social structures and social forces rather than the rights and experience of the human individual, a perspective central to the movement for human rights that was emerging.

For the Catholic Church, the cause of universal human rights became a clear way to separate its pastoral mission from political involvement. "Human rights" were, of course, "political" in a broad sense: they involved political legitimacy and power both nationally and internationally. But during the 1970s and 1980s the Church could embrace them as a cause transcending politics in the usual partisan sense. The focus of the human rights movement on the state violence of the authoritarian era facilitated the religious distinction between "pastoral" support for human rights and partisan "political" involvement (see chapters by Levine, Queiroz, and Wilde).[5] This distinction was reinforced by the Church's experience in these years, when its primordial commitment to bind up the wounds of human suffering led Christians to share that suffering. These included thousands persecuted and hundreds martyred for their faith—most famously Salvadoran Archbishop Óscar Romero, an outspoken advocate of nonviolence—whose sacrifice inspired deep commitment to the Church's social pastoral ministry (see chapters by Levine, Garrard-Burnett, and Morello).

The religious embrace of human rights during the authoritarian period left a real but limited legacy for today's churches and democracies. Critics argue that "rights" conceived in terms of law and individual protections are weak instruments to combat everyday forms of violence; that contemporary violence is "inchoate" and "ambiguous," preventing the apparently clear distinctions of the past between victims and victimizers; and even that the concept "victims" employed by the human rights movement is "dehistoricized," reducing them to a legal category. It is notable that, as this volume illustrates, there is substantial overlap between critics from both social science and religious perspectives (see chapters by Albro and Theidon). At base their critique suggests some of the limits of the liberal concepts—foundational for the human rights movement—in confronting the realities of violence as it is experienced in Latin America today. Public opinion nowhere conceives criminal violence, for example, as a "human rights" issue. Indeed, to the extent that human rights involve protecting the rights of criminals (see chapters by Brenneman and Johnson), it strongly supports harsh policies.

"Human rights" is less a focus for religious advocacy today than in the past, for reasons both of context and of the churches themselves. Human rights had greater saliency when regimes ruled through "state violence" than they do in the more open politics of today's electoral democracies. Within the religious sphere itself, advocacy based on human rights also appears limited by the more socially conservative hierarchies that have come with institutional retrenchment in the Catholic Church and in the Evangelical and Pentecostal churches, by theologies, ethics, and spiritualities less oriented to social action. And yet human rights remain an important referent for Catholic activists in post-transitional settings (see chapters by Queiroz and Wilde) and in contemporary social conflicts, ranging from violence against Central American migrants in Mexico (see chapter by Frank-Vitale) to mixed political and criminal violence in Colombia (see chapters by Tate and Pachico) to emblematic struggles between local communities and corporations over natural resources (see chapter by Arellano-Yanguas). Church-linked actors, often in ecumenical efforts, continue to educate people—particularly rural populations, women, and indigenous communities—about the rights due them by law (see, e.g., Burdick 2004; Cleary 2007; Cleary and Steigenga 2004; Tate, this vol.).

In a spectrum of active involvement, the churches have also promoted "human rights" as a broad ideal, encompassing social, economic, and cultural dimensions within the panoply of rights necessary, as they see it, to the fuller life that God intended for humanity (see chapters by Levine and Wilde). Basic civil and political rights, and the rights to physical integrity and life itself, were the primary focus of the human rights cause in the 1970s and 1980s—and unfortunately remain relevant concerns in Latin America today. The broader, more holistic scope of human rights has endured as a notable principle in the Catholic Church, visible in its public proclamations but more limited in its practice. In certain circumstances social conflict has spurred theological developments that give religious legitimation to the defense of human rights in emerging issues, such as the environment, as Arellano-Yanguas demonstrates so insightfully in his chapter on Peru. Conflicts between local communities and extractive industries are occurring in many places in Latin America today, and a wider, religiously linked concept of human rights has promise of finding allies and shaping public agendas through their social pastoral ministries (see Levine and Wilde 1977).

How human rights became an element of the churches' religious mission is an important focus for this book, but our research led us to the significance of another dimension of their life as faith communities: their self-understanding in taking violence into account through pastoral action. Those ministries represent more than the incorporation of the secular idea of human rights. They are the direct interface of lived faith in a violent world.

Pastoral Ministries and Accompaniment

Traditionally understood as the "care of souls," pastoral ministry took a decidedly social turn in the early twentieth century in both Catholic and

Protestant churches. Responding to the dramatic social and economic changes brought about by industrialization and urbanization, new theologies evoking the goal of "social justice" pointed toward more active religious engagement with values and structures of the secular world. They stimulated the creation of new church social ministries such as Catholic Action (influential primarily in Europe and Latin America) and progressive Protestant church participation in movements of social reform (particularly in the United States). This new social justice orientation in the first half of the twentieth century prepared the way for the developments in the churches in the historical period studied in this book.

The concept and practice of pastoral "accompaniment" grew out of changes spurred by Vatican II and the pastoral guidelines that Latin American bishops issued at regionwide meetings in Medellín, Colombia (1968), and Puebla, Mexico (1979). In 1971 the Colombian bishops—considered among the most conservative in the hemisphere—proclaimed active pastoral ministry crucial to the Church's religious mission: "unless the Christian message of love and justice *shows its effectiveness through action in the cause of justice in the world*, it will only with difficulty gain credibility with the people of our times" (quoted by Pachico, this vol.; emphasis added). Liberation theology—though frequently at odds with bishops everywhere in the region—also embraced the idea that, as Levine puts it in his chapter, "authentic faith requires believers (and the church) to share the experience of the poor and powerless, to side with and empower victims, and to build the kingdom starting now." In broad terms, for the Church to accompany the poor implies its presence in the specific circumstances of their lives. As Garrard-Burnett and Arellano-Yanguas usefully elucidate, a pastoral relationship with them is not politically partisan clericalism: clergy should support but not lead the community. The nature of the Church's accompanying presence should be one of witness (and when circumstances involve extreme violence, Tate's term *compassionate witness* seems particularly apposite).

As it is used in this book, in chapters on the past as well as the present, "accompaniment" designates an active pastoral policy in the churches to be present among the poor. "The poor" include those living in poverty but are also understood to be those who lack other resources—social, cultural, institutional, spiritual—needed for more fully human lives. Beyond physical presence, pastoral "accompaniment" also implies *movement at the side of the poor through time.* It interprets the charge of the Lord's Prayer—"Thy kingdom come, Thy will be done"—in historical terms, a commitment to realizing God's purposes for humanity in the world by reading the "signs of the times" and acting on them in the light of faith.

The emergence of pastoral accompaniment in this period has had enduring consequences. Where the church has brought priests, nuns, and lay workers in direct, face-to-face contact with poor, marginal populations, it has shared their changing experience of violence. This willingness to be present in dangerous settings is found in pastoral ministries today, as it was in the past—and in Evangelical churches (see chapters by Johnson, Brenneman, and Theidon) as well as the Catholic Church (see chapters by Wilde, Morello, Arellano-Yanguas, Frank-Vitale, Pachico, and Tate). The fact that it occurs in both Protestant and Catholic churches strongly suggests a common foundation in Christian thought and practice: shared beliefs in divine love and in the worth of human life that should be made manifest in their ministries. Both evoke the need to recognize and defend individual "dignity"—a recurrent term that resonates deeply with the churches as a moral category. It is reflected in the willingness of these ministries to side with society's underdogs—whether prisoners in Brazil and former gang members in Central America or beleaguered peasant communities in Colombia and indigenous groups in Peru. This commitment, which may set them against authorities and public opinion, is a reminder of the distinctiveness of faith communities.

There are also, to be sure, differences between the two Christian traditions. Catholic pastoral practice, for example, tends to be directed toward communities as a whole—believers and nonbelievers alike—while Evangelical and Pentecostal practices are focused on those who have undergone personal religious conversion or might be motivated to do so. Differences in theology are important, but the new studies in this book, which examine different faith traditions on the ground, challenge simplistic contrasts and present an array of insights and implicit hypotheses bearing on alternative approaches to social pastoral ministries. Some examples:

- The broader Catholic focus can allow clergy to negotiate and mediate between different parties in conflict, aiming to achieve peaceful solutions by engaging all relevant actors, including the violent ones.

This inclusiveness and mediation role are highlighted by Pachico in her chapter on Colombia's Magdalena Medio, in which she cites the director of the Jesuit project: "We want this to be the region where everybody talks." Theidon, in contrast, finds personal religious conversion a foundation for the fruitful evangelical work with FARC and former paramilitary combatants—also in Colombia—in "rebuilding the intimate sphere of social relationships and individual subjectivities."

- Frank-Vitale suggests the useful concept of *blindaje social* (social armor) to describe how a Mexican priest's legitimacy in his local community and full trust from his parish allow him to survive and protect Central American migrants from violence. It is a notion that clearly applies to Catholic pastoral ministries in other violent settings. But at the same time, something similar seems to be at work in the trust Johnson finds that Pentecostal pastors possess in their prison ministries in Rio de Janeiro.

- Tate, Pachico, Frank-Vitale, and Arellano-Yanguas all demonstrate how contemporary Catholic pastoral ministries are able to draw on national and international resources, facilitated by linkages with other levels in the developed structures of the Church. By contrast, the more congregational character of Evangelical churches—and a certain pattern of competition between their pastors noted by several authors—seem a limitation (certainly when compared to the historically significant international Protestant support for human rights analyzed by Kelly).

Various contributors analyze the specifically *spiritual* dimension of Catholic social ministries, which bears on fundamental questions concerning religious leadership against violence. Arellano-Yanguas insightfully examines what he calls "the spirituality of grassroots agency" in accompaniment that entails a religious commitment to empower local communities and respond to their views. Tate illuminates how that spirituality has evolved over various decades of pastoral practice in response to changes in the sources and levels of violence. And Wilde identifies a fruitful dynamic between initiatives taken within the "civil society of the Church" (see chapter by Levine) and responsive ecclesiastical leaders in the defense of human rights in Chile. In all these cases and others, one can identify a specifically religious interaction inherent in direct lived contact between the clergy and marginalized populations—giving these pastoral ministries a social presence with potentially greater impact. They are not in themselves a panacea: larger forces of political and economic change clearly shape the scope and complexity of violence in Latin America, as Pachico and Tate remind us. Their presence, rather, is a stubborn reminder of the everyday *violencias* of lives in urban slums and marginal spaces, populations wounded and left aside by the large processes of change. These ministries illuminate truths about violence beyond their modest scale—that enduring solutions must encompass dimensions of human life that lie beyond secular and material forces. With their roots in the authoritarian past, they remain a vital part of the Church's presence in today's real existing democracies, in which they are called to heal the wounds, starting from the ground up.

Overview of This Book

Chapters 1 and 2—on rights and violence—provide analytical and historical depth to subjects central to this book that are addressed in more specific ways by its other authors. Daniel H. Levine, whose work has contributed in so many different ways to the study of religion in Latin America, provides a magisterial treatment of how Catholicism came to embrace "rights" in both theory and practice. His analysis, which is both synthetic and subtle, offers a rich background for understanding the religiously linked dimensions of the human rights movement, the importance of liberation theology and social Catholicism, and of the real ways that faith can inspire social action. It illuminates a host of factors shaping pastoral ministries addressing violence—such as the church's "legitimacy" and "trust," its "critical resources, both material and moral," and the consequences of its presence among the poor—that are reflected in subsequent chapters. Robert Albro's thematic chapter examining past and present violence draws from a substantial body of contemporary scholarship and offers important insights into debates about its causes and character. Describing the "pervasive reality of violence" that is "embedded in

Latin America's democratic societies," he emphasizes the importance of understanding the different ways that violence is *experienced* in everyday life. The limitations of liberal concepts and institutions—beginning with those of Latin American states themselves—to address these realities are evident in subsequent chapters on contemporary violence.

The following six chapters, making up Part I, reexamine church responses to violence in the 1970s and 1980s through the defense of human rights. They bring fresh perspectives and new sources to what have been familiar narratives in more than a generation of scholarship. Broadly speaking, they are all "revisionist," taking historical distance to illuminate factors or dynamics only partially understood in the heat of events, or utilizing new analytical frameworks that throw light on the contemporary relevance of the churches' human rights legacy. They examine how human rights and violence were perceived at the time within the churches; how different communities and levels within those churches (including the international) understood their faith and framed active responses. These chapters deal less with theology or ideology (which predominated in earlier studies of liberation theology) than with how ideas may have been reflected in behavior and action. Finally, taking violence as a focus, these six chapters begin to bring together two scholarly literatures—on religion and on human rights—that developed rather separately.

Appropriately, two chapters by historians lead off this part. Patrick William Kelly draws on substantial research in original sources to reexamine the historical role of international Church activism for human rights. In an analysis framed by the emerging field of transnational history, he carefully demonstrates how religious advocates moved beyond humanitarian concerns to employ explicit human rights concepts and practices in the 1970s. He persuasively argues that their efforts addressing the military dictatorships in Brazil and Chile—each examined in subsequent chapters—mark a key turning point. Virginia Garrard-Burnett historicizes religious responses to violence in Central America in the two decades under consideration, providing an insightful and nuanced examination of tensions between religious sympathies for armed insurgencies and Christian nonviolence. With an analysis of different national trajectories in the period, she argues strongly for the antecedents of human rights defense in liberation theology and the pastoral strategies of accompaniment that led to sharing the experiences of the poor. She also incorporates an insightful interpretation of religious actors in regional peace processes in the 1990s, encompassing both those in the region and those internationally.

The next four chapters, by historically minded social scientists, analyze national cases of highly visible Church defense of human rights (Chile and Brazil) and another of notorious complicity with a repressive dictatorship (Argentina). Alexander Wilde throws fresh light on how religious beliefs and practices led the Chilean Catholic Church to relative unity in defending human rights during the Pinochet dictatorship. He identifies a distinctive dynamic between initiatives taken by religiously linked groups and their acceptance and legitimation by a responsive hierarchy. He also argues that in Chile concepts of liberation theology were given a new grounding by the Church's pastoral strategies of accompaniment—by action that fostered "values of tolerance, respect, solidarity, and agency"; led to notable tactics of active nonviolence; and helped legitimate democratic transition. María Soledad Catoggio's chapter exemplifies a new generation of scholarship on the Catholic Church and political violence in Argentina. In a synthetic analysis of Argentina's twentieth-century political history, she skillfully reexamines how different responses to Peronism led to internal divisions in the Church that, in a cycle of failed elected governments and military coups, further frayed its "corporate solidarity." Reactionary Catholic elements supported many of the political goals and violent tactics of the military dictatorship of the 1970s, and clergy, nuns, and lay activists suspected of leftist sympathies were persecuted. In stark contrast to Chile, the institutional Church did not accept them as martyrs or offer meaningful public protection but did intervene in many of their cases; Catoggio provides a useful, original classification of eight different strategies.

Gustavo Morello contributes further fresh perspectives on an Argentine context in which political violence was widely considered legitimate in his valuable chapter examining four different ways that Catholics responded in one region. These encompass the "committed," who embraced pastoral accompaniment; the "revolutionary," who sought transformation of the Church and society; the "institutional," who wanted the Church to be an apolitical mediator between state and society; and the "antisecular," who resisted both religious and political change. As he shows on the basis of original data from interviews with torture survivors, the latter group actively employed pre-Conciliar Catholic doctrines and rituals to justify state violence. In contrast, Rafael Mafei Rabelo Queiroz examines Brazil and the religious and legal underpinnings of the important movement for human rights that emerged during the dictatorship. His chapter provides an original and illuminating analysis of the processes by which leaders from the Church and the Brazilian Bar came together and made human rights based in law a foundation for democratic opposition. Drawing on original interview data, he argues that the alliance between the two groups was based less on common values than shared experience. He concludes with a suggestive argument that their efforts laid the groundwork for post-transitional prison reforms and official policies for justice and truth.

Part II examines religious responses to violence in contemporary democracies. The defense of human rights appears as one element of those responses but now within a changed political and religious landscape. In contrast to Part I, where human rights are a dimension of national-level church-state conflict, these seven chapters focus on local and regional realities, with secondary reference to national and international factors. This emphasis reflects the leading edge of scholarship today and is appropriate, I think, to efforts to understand our quite different contemporary context. It also brings us much closer to more immediate (even intimate) experiences and processes underlying religious responses to violence than those analyzed in most existing research on the earlier revolutionary/authoritarian period. This part is almost evenly balanced between Catholic and Evangelical/Pentecostal cases, reflecting the significant new presence of the latter in Latin America today. The seven chapters are arranged to stimulate thinking about common and contrasting elements in faith traditions and practice as well as varieties of violence in different contexts.

Elyssa Pachico's chapter is a powerful introduction to these themes. The first of three chapters on Colombia, a country with a half century of experience of multiple forms of violence, it is framed by a deep-focus historical view of the sustained, long-term Jesuit presence in one highly conflicted region. Pachico provides an original analysis of an innovative fifteen-year pastoral program linking peace to development and illuminates the ways in which this social ministry is both spiritually based and practically oriented. She examines an array of pastoral strategies that address root causes of poverty and violence, encourage economic development through community empowerment, and engage all stakeholders, including violent actors, to build peace "from the ground up." Although aspects of this program have been replicated in other Colombian regions, her analysis is clear about its limitations. Peru—which unlike Colombia is largely free of political violence today—is the setting of the chapter by Javier Arellano-Yanguas. His rich, conceptually sophisticated analysis of Catholic pastoral accompaniment of local communities confronting extractive industries makes a notable contribution to the contemporary study of social conflict. Arellano-Yanguas carefully distinguishes accompaniment from other possible ways in which the Church might respond to such local conflict (avoidance, mediation, and leadership) and analyzes the various means by which clergy "listen" to local communities. He suggests that the "existence of a spirituality of accompaniment filters the ideological element of liberation theology and generates a distinctive type of Church involvement that respects the leadership of local communities"—a hypothesis worthy of research in other settings. So, too, is his provocative conclusion that in his examined conflicts, the "real incorporation of environmental and human rights discourses with a religious framework was driven by pastoral practices at the grassroots level."

Complementing the chapters by Pachico and Arellano-Yanguas, Winifred Tate offers deeply informed insights into a repertoire of Catholic pastoral responses to different forms and phases of violence in a frontier region of Colombia. Her thoughtful, nuanced analysis considers responses ranging from accompaniment of communities to dialogues with armed actors to "prophetic" advocacy before officials to various forms of "compassionate witness" to suffering. Tracking developments over some three decades, she demonstrates the enduring legacy of pastoral ministries based on "native son" clergy that respond to the needs and possibilities of different periods, including empowering women and documenting historical memory ("in anticipation of a future time when public accounting might be possible"). In all, Tate offers a revealing example of a contemporary Catholic approach to social ministry, with a "pastoral obligation to minister to all," intra-Church linkages, and relationships with national and international agencies. Robert Brenneman documents high levels of violence in Central America today and the strength of both Catholic and Evangelical religion. Contrasting present with past violence, he argues that the social legitimacy of the churches gave them a certain power to delegitimize violent actors in the past, such as repressive governments or guerrilla revolutionaries, but that that instrument is less effective against today's criminal mafias and youth gangs, which do not seek the "blessing" of religious legitimation. He compares the pastoral strategies of Catholic and Pentecostal churches, providing particular insight into evangelical "gang rescue" ministries that aim to demonstrate the redemptive power of God's love by converting those who have rejected (and been rejected by) society.

Andrew Johnson presents an eloquent complementary analysis of contemporary Pentecostal prison ministries in Rio de Janeiro, addressed to a similarly marginalized, ostracized social group. He explains the range of specifically religious values and practices motivating them and examines the ways in which these churches and their pastoral ministries fill needs unmet by state institutions. Although initially critical of their purely spiritual focus on individual rather than social/structural solutions to the problems of this population, Johnson comes to appreciate their belief that just being present, regularly, in dangerous prison spaces is an important form of witness that can offer some protection. It constitutes, he argues, a "politics of presence" that challenges Brazilian authorities and society. Amelia Frank-Vitale's chapter compares and contrasts three local-level shelters—two Catholic and one secular—that provide refuge, services, and advocacy for Central American migrants facing violence in contemporary Mexico. She describes two ways in which the priests heading the Catholic shelters have built some protection (*blindaje*) into their pastoral strategies, one drawing on the support of his local community and the other on regional and international resources. She demonstrates persuasively that despite different views of liberation theology, the two priests have been led by pastoral practice to a shared embrace of human rights in their ministries. The last study on contemporary violence is a rich chapter by Kimberly Theidon on Evangelical churches working with demobilized combatants in a violent region of Colombia. She underlines the distinctive religious emphases of pastoral strategies for peacebuilding—

human dignity and reconciliation rather than revenge—in contrast to those of government and international agencies, which largely ignore the importance of human moral agency. Theidon offers a fascinating brief analysis of how Evangelical churches can offer an alternative sense of masculine identity to men whose lives have been defined by violence suffered or committed. She contrasts the racial composition of the Catholic and Evangelical churches in this region, as well as their pastoral approaches. But her description of how the martyrdom of a local Pentecostal pastor inspires faith suggests parallels with Catholic experience in other places examined in this volume and perhaps important commonalities inherent in religious commitment in the ministries of both traditions when they are rooted in the lives of the poor.

The book concludes with a brief afterword.

Notes

1. Based at the Center for Latin American and Latino Studies at American University and supported by the Henry R. Luce Initiative on Religion and International Affairs.

2. "Real existing democracies" is a slightly ironic term that is meant to characterize the electoral systems of governments present everywhere in Latin America in 2014 (except Cuba), with their multiple (and in some cases quite substantial) deficiencies. Purely descriptive rather than analytical, it alludes to the "real existing socialisms" in the USSR and Eastern Europe during the Cold War, which fell as far from the ideal of socialism as "real existing democracies" do from ideal democracy.

3. Recent general studies of the human rights movement acknowledge the importance of the Latin American churches, but analysis is still incipient on how and why they rallied behind the cause and on their distinctively religious contributions (Kelly, this vol.; Wilde 2013). Lowden's (1996) study of "moral resistance" in Chile is an impressive pioneering effort that should stimulate greater attention to this dimension of human rights history.

4. Based also on the author's personal correspondence with Phillip Berryman.

5. Levine and Wilde (1977) distinguished "political" and "pastoral" Church involvement in Colombia during the 1970s *but without reference to human rights*, which had not yet become an organized cause there. For the subsequent development of the Colombian human rights movement, see Tate 2007. As Kelly argues in his chapter in this volume, religious rejection of torture in Brazil antedated the "human rights" framing and alliances that later gave significant new grounding to such concerns.

References

Berryman, Phillip. 1984. *The Religious Roots of Rebellion: Christians in Central America's Revolutions.* Maryknoll, NY: Orbis Books.

Brenneman, Robert. 2011. *Homies and Hermanos: God and Gangs in Central America.* New York: Oxford University Press.

Burdick, John. 1993. *Looking for God in Brazil: The Progressive Catholic Church in Urban Brazil's Religious Arena.* Berkeley: University of California Press.

———. 2004. *Legacies of Liberation: The Progressive Catholic Church in Brazil at the Start of a New Millennium.* London: Ashgate.

Chesnut, R. Andrew. 1997. *Born Again in Brazil: The Pentecostal Boom and the Pathogens of Poverty.* New Brunswick, NJ: Rutgers University Press.

———. 2003. *Competitive Spirits: Latin America's New Religious Economy.* New York: Oxford University Press.

Cleary, Edward L. 2007. *Mobilizing for Human Rights in Latin America.* Bloomfield, CT: Kumarian Press.

———. 2011. *The Rise of Charismatic Catholicism in Latin America.* Gainesville: University Press of Florida.

Cleary, Edward L., and Timothy J. Steigenga, eds. 2004. *Resurgent Voices in Latin America: Indigenous Peoples, Political Mobilization, and Religious Change.* New Brunswick, NJ: Rutgers University Press.

Cleary, Edward L., and Hannah Stewart-Gambino, eds. 1992. *Conflict and Competition: The Latin American Church in a Changing Environment.* Lanham, MD: Rowman and Littlefield.

Dodson, Michael, and Laura O'Shaughnessey. 1990. *Nicaragua's Other Revolution: Religious Faith and Political Struggle.* Chapel Hill: University of North Carolina Press.

Drogus, Carol Ann, and Hannah Stewart-Gambino. 2005. *Activist Faith: Popular Women Activists and Their Movements in Democratic Brazil and Chile.* University Park: Pennsylvania State University Press.

Fleet, Michael, and Brian H. Smith. 1997. *The Catholic Church and Democracy in Chile and Peru.* Notre Dame, IN: University of Notre Dame Press.

Freston, Paul, ed. 2008. *Evangelical Christianity and Democracy in Latin America.* New York: Oxford University Press.

Garrard-Burnett, Virginia. 1998. *Protestantism in Guatemala: Living in the New Jerusalem.* Austin: University of Texas Press.

———. 2010. *Terror in the Land of the Holy Spirit: Guatemala under General Efraín Ríos Montt, 1982–1983.* New York: Oxford University Press.

Garrard-Burnett, Virginia, and Paul Freston, eds. Forthcoming. *The Cambridge History of Religions in Latin America.* New York: Cambridge University Press.

Green, James. 2010. *We Cannot Remain Silent: Opposition to the Brazilian Military Dictatorship in the United States.* Durham, NC: Duke University Press.

Hagopian, Frances, ed. 2009. *Religious Pluralism, Democracy, and the Catholic Church in Latin America.* Notre Dame, IN: University of Notre Dame Press.

Iriye, Akira, Petra G. Goedde, and William I. Hitchcock, eds. 2012. *The Human Rights Revolution: An International History.* New York: Oxford University Press.

Ishay, Micheline R. 2004. *The History of Human Rights: From Ancient Times to the Globalization Era.* Berkeley: University of California Press.

Keck, Margaret E., and Kathryn Sikkink. 1998. *Activists beyond Borders: Advocacy Networks in International Politics.* Ithaca, NY: Cornell University Press.

Levine, Daniel H. 1981. *Religion and Politics in Latin America: The Catholic Church in Venezuela and Colombia.* Princeton, NJ: Princeton University Press.

————. 1992. *Popular Voices in Latin American Catholicism.* Princeton, NJ: Princeton University Press.

————. 2012. *Politics, Religion, and Society in Latin America.* Boulder, CO: Lynne Rienner.

————, ed. 1980. *Churches and Politics in Latin America.* Beverly Hills, CA: Sage.

————, ed. 1986. *Religion and Political Conflict in Latin America.* Chapel Hill: University of North Carolina Press.

Levine, Daniel H., and Alexander Wilde. 1977. "The Catholic Church, 'Politics,' and Violence: The Colombian Case." *Review of Politics* 39, no. 2 (April): 220–49.

Lowden, Pamela. 1996. *Moral Opposition to Authoritarian Rule in Chile, 1973–90.* New York: St. Martin's Press.

MacLean, Iain S. 2006. *Reconciliation, Nations and Churches in Latin America.* London: Ashgate.

Mainwaring, Scott. 1986. *The Catholic Church and Politics in Brazil, 1916–1985.* Stanford, CA: Stanford University Press.

Mainwaring, Scott, and Alexander Wilde, eds. 1989. *The Progressive Church in Latin America.* Notre Dame, IN: University of Notre Dame Press.

Mallimaci, Fortunato, and Marta Villa. 2007. *Las comunidades eclesiales de base y el mundo de los pobres en la Argentina: Tensiones por el control del poder en el catolicismo.* Buenos Aires: CIEL/PIETTE/CONICET.

Méndez, Juan E., and Marjory Wentworth. 2011. *Taking a Stand: The Evolution of Human Rights.* New York: Palgrave Macmillan.

Mignone, Emilio. 1988. *Witness to the Truth: The Complicity of Church and Dictatorship in Argentina.* Maryknoll, NY: Orbis Books.

Moyn, Samuel. 2010. *The Last Utopia: Human Rights in History.* Cambridge, MA: Harvard University Press.

Neier, Aryeh. 2012. *The International Human Rights Movement: A History.* Princeton, NJ: Princeton University Press.

O'Donnell, Guillermo A. 2004. "Why the Rule of Law Matters." *Journal of Democracy* 15, no. 4 (October): 32–46.

O'Neill, Kevin Lewis. 2010. *City of God: Christian Citizenship in Postwar Guatemala.* Berkeley: University of California Press.

Schmitter, Philippe. 2009. "Defects and Deficits in the Quality of Neo-Democracy." In *Democratic Deficits: Addressing Challenges to Sustainability and Consolidation around the World,* edited by Gary Bland and Cynthia J. Arnson, 19–35. Washington, DC: Woodrow Wilson International Center for Scholars.

Serbin, Kenneth. 2000. *Secret Dialogues: Church-State Relations, Torture, and Social Justice in Authoritarian Brazil.* Pittsburgh, PA: University of Pittsburgh Press.

Smilde, David. 2007. *Reason to Believe: Cultural Agency in Latin American Evangelicalism.* Berkeley: University of California Press.

Smith, Brian H. 1982. *The Church and Politics in Chile: Challenges to Modern Catholicism.* Princeton, NJ: Princeton University Press.

Steigenga, Timothy J. 2001. *The Politics of the Spirit: The Political Implications of Pentecostalized Religion in Costa Rica and Guatemala.* Lanham, MD: Lexington Books.

Steigenga, Timothy J., and Edward L. Cleary, eds. 2007. *Conversion of a Continent: Contemporary Religious Change in Latin America.* New Brunswick, NJ: Rutgers University Press.

Stites Mor, Jessica, ed. 2013. *Human Rights and Transnational Solidarity in Cold War Latin America.* Madison: University of Wisconsin Press.

Stoll, David. 1991. *Is Latin America Turning Protestant? The Politics of Evangelical Growth.* Berkeley: University of California Press.

Tate, Winifred. 2007. *Counting the Dead: The Culture and Politics of Human Rights Activism in Colombia.* Berkeley: University of California Press.

Tovar, Cecilia, ed. 2006. *Ser Iglesia en tiempos de violencia.* Lima: Instituto Bartolomé de las Casas, Centro de Estudios y Publicaciones.

Verbitsky, Horacio. 2005. *El silencio: De Paulo VI a Bergoglio: Las relaciones secretas de la Iglesia con la ESMA.* Buenos Aires: Editorial Sudamericana.

———. 2006. *Doble juego: La Argentina católica y militar.* Buenos Aires: Editorial Sudamericana.

———. 2007. *Cristo vence: De Roca a Perón.* Buenos Aires: Editorial Sudamericana.

———. 2008. *La violencia evangélica. Tomo II: De Leonardi al Cordobazo (1955–1969)*. Buenos Aires: Editorial Sudamericana.

———. 2009. *Vigilia de armas. Tomo III: Del Cordobazo de 1969 al 23 de marzo de 1976*. Buenos Aires: Editorial Sudamericana.

Vidal, Hernán. 2005. *Las capellanías castrenses durante la dictadura: Hurgando en la ética militar chilena*. Santiago: Mosquito Comunicaciones.

Wilde, Alexander. 2013. "Human Rights in Two Latin American Democracies." In *Sustaining Human Rights in the Twenty-First Century: Strategies from Latin America*, edited by Katherine Hite and Mark Ungar, 35–71. Baltimore, MD: Woodrow Wilson Center Press, Johns Hopkins University Press.

Wolseth, Jon. 2011. *Jesus and the Gang: Youth Violence and Christianity in Urban Honduras*. Tucson: University of Arizona Press.

CHAPTER 1

THE EVOLUTION OF THE THEORY AND PRACTICE OF RIGHTS IN LATIN AMERICAN CATHOLICISM

DANIEL H. LEVINE

The theory and the practice of rights gained prominence in Latin American Catholicism as a surge of violence from the 1960s to the mid-1980s brought the concept home to Church leaders, activists, and rank-and-file believers across the region. The working theory of rights that emerged drew on papal documents, episcopal proclamations, and theological reflection. Ideas about rights were energized and given form in response to pressure from those suffering the impact of war and violence and by contact with national and transnational human rights movements. Practice and ideas affected one another in a continuing process. The theory and practice of rights is never exclusively legal, religious, or secular: it is all of these, and it is deeply shaped at all stages by the dynamic of practice. It is essential at the outset to acknowledge that practice (and ideas) stems as much from groups and individuals on the ground as from institutional leaders. Together they place issues of rights on the public agenda and tie this agenda into national and transnational networks publicizing and pursuing rights.[1]

Ideas about rights have deep roots in natural law tradition and in the legal and institutional history of Latin America. The recent history of Latin America added something new, a massive practice of rights, impelled by countless local, regional, national, and transnational groups. The institutional Church in all its forms (bishops, clergy, vicariates, religious orders) played a central role in this effort, along with a host of religiously linked and inspired groups and individuals. Together they documented abuse and aided victims, families, and survivors with moral and material resources, ranging from medical assistance to legal representation to help getting out of the country (MacLean 2006). A central fact of this process is that working definitions of rights expanded from classic civil and political rights centered on defense against torture, official impunity, and aid to victims to more holistic definitions that brought together a range of social, economic, cultural, and personal rights (to health, work, land, assembly, movement, education, etc.) in a coherent whole.

The theory and practice of rights has been and remains a deeply contested terrain in Latin American Catholicism. There are complexities and overlaps, but broadly speaking, it is possible to identify two positions, whose relative strength has shifted over time as changes in leadership and staffing of core institutions have varied and as alternative centers of thought and action have emerged within the umbrella of the Church.[2] The first relies on traditional alliances and associations of religion with order and control, and in this light sees demands for rights as evidence of the decay and subversion of that order, something to be resisted. Rights are subordinate to order and to the defense of the institutional Church, which is contingent on alliances with established power. This view predominated in the Latin American Church before the Second Vatican Council. It was exemplified by the words and actions of the Argentine Catholic hierarchy during the last military dictatorship, 1976–83. The second position grounds commitment to rights in beliefs about natural law and the belief that all have rights as children of God. This strain has historical precedents in the Latin American Church (Cleary 2007, 2009) but gained new prominence in the aftermath of the Council. Liberation theology has also had a significant impact on this position, above all, as a result of its characteristic insistence on justice and on accompaniment (*acompañamiento*), the idea that authentic faith requires believers (and the

Church) to share the experience of the poor and powerless, to side with and empower victims, and to build the kingdom of God starting now.

Rights defined in this way fit within the "option for the poor," but there are tensions and ambiguities of several kinds. A core aspect of any preferential option for the poor that goes beyond simple charity is sharing the conditions of the poor, being present among them, with all the risks that this can entail. This very presence can be seen by those in power as subversive to order. It has been the occasion of much abuse, with kidnapping, arrest, torture, and murder of catechists and pastoral agents who make their commitment to be present in poor neighborhoods (Catoggio 2008; Del Carril 2011; Mignone 1988; Morello 2012; Ranly 2003; Tovar 2006). This commitment stemmed from a deliberate effort to follow the pastoral guidelines outlined by the bishops at Medellín and Puebla, which made the struggle against institutionalized violence central to the Church's option for the poor, and in this way made the Church seem like an ally to those struggling to cope with inequality and violence.[3]

Ambiguities arise from the fact that many of those who made a preferential option for the poor central to their lives drew on elements of liberation theology that came slowly to the theory and practice of rights as a core concern, because they saw insistence on rights as a bourgeois, "individualist" issue, subordinate to class struggle and collective action for structural change. This initial reluctance notwithstanding, ideas about rights gained prominence with this group of Church people and activists as the violence claimed victims among clergy, catechists, and ordinary believers. Those advancing this position often came into conflict not only with abusive states but also with violent insurgent groups, as in Peru, where Shining Path guerrillas saw Church activists as competitors (Tovar 2006; Ranly 2003). The reconciliation of a commitment to human rights with the preferential option for the poor also gained strength from gradual accommodation to democracy as something good in itself, an accommodation spurred by the horrific experiences of the 1970s and 1980s that pushed and pulled much of Latin America's left to a position that welcomed democracy and worked within its structures and rules (Levine 2012).

Any discussion of the place of rights in the recent experience of Latin American Catholicism has to begin by acknowledging the impact that violence and civil wars have had on the Church. There was direct physical violence (burning churches; killing or injuring priests, sisters, catechists, and laypeople) that created martyrs, impelled moves to institutional self-defense, and spurred a sense of identification with victims. Religious personnel and Church institutions (like radio stations or educational organizations) have been prime targets of violence in El Salvador, Guatemala, Chile, Brazil, Paraguay, and Peru. This direct experience of terror led many in the churches to see themselves as victims, to identify with victims, and to ally themselves with victims in defense of the right to life and the right to be free from abuse and torture (Levine 2010, 2012; Noone 1995). As targets and victims of violence, religious institutions, groups, and individuals caught up in the violence tried to make sense of what was happening, and at the same time to bear witness to the violence, searching for responses that would defend and preserve the lives of loved ones and of the community as a whole. In Brazil, Chile, Peru, and El Salvador, church leaders and church-sponsored organizations became prime protagonists of movements for human rights. This was often undertaken through ecumenical coalitions.

As part of this volatile mix of violence and religious transformations, important changes took place in the theology and ideological repertoire of the Church. Issues of justice, rights, participation, and liberation were articulated in Church documents, and there was a sustained effort to give these issues a primary place in the agenda of Church institutions and affiliated groups and movements. Beginning with the documents of Medellín (1968) and Puebla (1979), specified further in the theology of liberation and carried to the public sphere in numerous pastoral letters and in the programs and commitments of groups and social movements, elements in the Catholic Church broke long-standing alliances with political and social power and put themselves on the side of those seeking change (Gutiérrez 2004; Levine 1992, 2012; Smith 1991). They articulated a view in which suffering is not the result of sin or a sign of the coming of the Millennium but rather is to be understood as the result of an unjust social order and a repressive government. Believers identify these as structures of social sin, and this legitimizes resistance and enjoins working actively with others in defense of life. From this position, elements in the churches put themselves on the side of social and political change and resisted authoritarian rule.

Religion and Rights: Theory and Practice

This has not been a simple or easy process. The theory and practice of rights is contested terrain in the Church, with ongoing struggles to control the public agenda of the churches and to determine how Church resources should be used.[4] The continuing contest over rights underscores the point that religion (and churches) is not well understood as monolithic or unidimensional. Multiple tendencies coexist, often uneasily, and draw on variations in the legal and theological traditions of any faith. Analysis that centers attention exclusively on the institutional Church and its leaders or on formal Church documents may therefore miss much of the action. Leaders and documents are important: they control resources and can legitimate or disavow initiatives. But they are not all there is to the process, nor do they act alone.[5] They must be seen in a context of ideas and initiatives arising from civil society, *including civil society within the Church itself* (Levine 2009; Romero 2009).

The idea of a civil society in the Church may surprise those who remain wedded to an exclusively hierarchical understanding of the Catholic Church, in which power, authority, and knowledge cascade from the top. In this view, the pope knows more than the cardinals, the cardinals more than the bishops, the bishops more than the priests, the priests more than the nuns, the nuns more than laypeople, and so on. But this is not the only model available for the Church. Not all authority (even in the Catholic Church) is authoritarian in concept or exercise.[6] Recovering older traditions, core documents of the Second Vatican Council stressed that the Church is more than its legally defined institutions and offices: it is the Pilgrim People of God making its way through history. Ordinary believers are also, and primarily, "the Church" and have insights and beliefs of independent value. As an empirical matter, the Catholic Church combines centralization with diversity and decentralization. Multiple groups and voices enjoy considerable autonomy, despite pressures from prelates or Vatican officials. Relevant groups include religious congregations of men and women, educational institutions (including universities), journals, publishing houses, and organizations and coalitions of laypeople. Many of the policies and public positions of Popes St. John Paul II and Benedict XVI, and their repeated stress on unity and discipline, can be understood as an effort to rein in this diversity and control these voices. Simply put, these efforts did not succeed.[7]

These notable pluralities and complexities mean that conventional references to "church and state" no longer provide an adequate frame of analysis, if they ever did. There are too many actors with a stake in the process, not only churches as organizations, but also groups whose affiliation to the institutional churches is much looser than traditional models suggest (Levine 2012). How Church leaders respond in practice to Church-affiliated or religiously inspired groups is central to the evolving practice of rights. The possibilities range from rejection and marginalization (Argentina) to broad sponsorship and protection (Brazil, Chile), with many points in between. To complicate things further, there are often strong divisions within the Church hierarchy and between bishops and religious orders.

The legal and theological traditions of any great religion are in any case never static: a continuous process of argument, renovation, and rediscovery is at work, making older ideas relevant in new and changing circumstances (Appleby 2000). In the particular case of rights in Latin America, leaders and activists have drawn freely on recent papal encyclicals (*Pacem in Terris, Mater et Magistra, Evangelii Nuntiandi*), on the documents of Vatican II, on the conclusions of regional meetings of Catholic bishops at Medellín and Puebla, on the pastoral letters of individual bishops and national episcopal conferences, and, as noted above, on elements of liberation theology that provide a basis for rights as well as the outlines of a program for action (Levine 2006a, 2006b, 2009, 2010, 2012).[8]

In his recent history of the human rights movement, Neier (2012, 27) states that a concept of human rights requires a commitment to three principles: "that rights are natural and therefore inherent in all human beings and not only in those who derive them from their relation to a particular entity or political regime; that all are equal in their entitlement to rights; and that rights are universal and therefore applicable everywhere." Wolterstorff (2012, 43) points out that the idea of natural human rights is grounded in a view of natural law that was taken for granted by the Church fathers, and includes not only what we might call civil rights but also rights to land, to health, to a decent and dignified life. Rights thus have sociality built into them and make sense in the context of communities. Claims to rights are founded in the worth of the rights holder, which rests, in natural law, on the belief that humans are created in God's image: "all human beings bear the *imago dei*, not just certain kinds of human beings, all of them" (Wolterstorff 2012, 55). This general view is amplified by St. Paul, who declares flatly that there is no partiality in God; fellowship is offered to all.[9]

This character of rights, inherent in individuals, expressed in social relations but not dependent on the particular rules of communities or political systems, inalienable and universal, expandable beyond civil and political rights to all areas of life, is critical to the meaning of rights as the concept and practice evolved in the recent experience of the churches in Latin America. The prominence of rights in the recent theory and practice of the Catholic Church in Latin America raises an obvious question. Through much of human history, most people have been told that they have no rights. So how do they become aware that rights exist, and convinced of the fact that they have rights? What makes them think that it is possible to claim and exercise these rights—that there are allies and available pathways? How do the churches get to be seen as reliable allies in this effort? The question is about ideas and more specifically about how an understanding of faith is linked to a commitment to rights. The relation of ideas is important, but of course ideas never exist in a vacuum. We also need to ask who articulates these ideas, who carries them to audiences, who makes the ideas work in practice, and how the ideas get embedded in community norms.

For ideas about rights to acquire a meaningful social presence, to become embedded in laws and institutional practices, a few things have to happen. Concepts of rights need to be created and given legitimacy in the churches and other institutions. In addition, someone—perhaps the same person who articulates the concept—must spread the message, packaging it in an accessible form and bringing it to an audience. Those who hear the message also need to have a sense that what the words articulate is not only good but also possible. This requires trust in the agents who bring the message and also benefits from a sense that one is not alone. The experience of group solidarity is critical in turning individual claims of rights into something with ordered social meaning.

Some examples may help to drive the point home. With support from the World Council of Churches, the Brazilian Catholic Bishops Conference printed two million copies of the Universal Declaration of Human Rights to be distributed to congregations throughout the country.[10] On the grassroots level, working with peasants and with the landless movement, the Pastoral Land Commission of Brazil's Catholic Church has worked long and hard to inform peasants of their rights. When the earliest peasant delegations went to discuss land claims with government officials, they were asked to demonstrate that they had rights. At a loss for words, they left, crestfallen. Given this experience, teams from the Pastoral Land Commission developed booklets and flyers detailing precisely how rights to land were specified in legislation. These pamphlets were widely diffused and were the subject of much discussion in peasant meetings. They gave legal specification to the broader belief that God made the land for all, not just for a few landowners. This conviction, enhanced by group solidarity, reinforced the capacity of peasants to make and sustain claims in the future. The Pastoral Land Commission strengthens this capacity by deploying teams of lawyers and extensive networks of pastoral agents dedicated to work with land claimants from the outset of their struggles (Carter 2003, 2010; French 2007; Rodríguez 2009). Examples could be multiplied indefinitely. The point is that the experience of rights is multidimensional, putting the creation of new words and symbols together with agents who can package and deliver them to people and social innovations that provide a framework for sustained collective action.[11]

In her analysis of moral opposition to authoritarian rule in Chile, Lowden (1996, 13) writes, "The term human rights is contemporary idiom for natural rights, and as such, is intimately related to the concepts of natural law shared by Western secular and religious institutions alike. For Christianity, natural law is God's law; one of its pillars is that people are made in the image of God. Therefore, violation of human rights and dignity is also an attack on God." Writing about the experience of Mayan groups in southern Mexico, Kovic (2005, 101) extends this insight, noting that the view of human rights in liberation theology differs significantly from that of Western European legal codes: "The protection of human rights follows from the liberating mission of Jesus Christ and extends beyond individual conceptions of rights. Liberation theologians cite

John 10:10 in which Jesus states 'I came so that all may have life and may have it abundantly' in describing why God is a God of life. Following from the idea of a preferential option for the poor comes the idea of the 'rights of the poor,' specifically concerned with basic human needs or economic and social rights."

Elsewhere, I consider this process in terms of the creation of a practical vocabulary of rights in Latin American Catholicism. It is *practical* because in addition to naming and justifying rights, this vocabulary points to instances in which rights arise and can be defended and encourages, legitimates, and facilitates the creation of new forms of organization and association (Levine 2006a, 2012). Working definitions of rights expand in response to practice, which may take them far beyond what leaders of Church institutions, or even theologians, expect. It is impossible to know what comes first—the idea or the commitment. The bottom line is that the precedent to commitment is rooted in earlier exposure to these ideas, but particular events spur their transformation into action. The question is not one of faith *or* action, ideas *or* practice. These evolve and change together in a dynamic that is amply documented in recent Latin American experience (Aguilar 2003; Brysk 1994; J. Burdick 2004; M. Burdick 1995; Carter 2003; Del Carrill 2011; Drogus and Stewart-Gambino 2005; Fitzpatrick-Behrens 2012; French 2007; Kovic 2005; Levine 2012; Lowden 1996; MacLean 2006; Rodríguez 2009; Youngers 2003).

The dynamic noted here—concepts of rights grounded in natural law, belief that authentic faith requires action, and commitment to share the conditions of the poor and the vulnerable—laid the groundwork for an epistemological shift, a change in the standpoint from which Church people view events. A choice is made to view and evaluate events from the standpoint of those on the margins of power, to identify with, serve, and be with the powerless. Sharing the life of the poor and powerless and joining them in their struggles give flesh and bone to concepts like preferential option for the poor. It can and has meant sharing their fate as well (Noone 1995). Pfeil (2006) cites the case of El Salvador's Archbishop Óscar Romero, who famously pointed to sin as the death of Salvadorans, early and needless death caused by structures of sin including poverty, ill health, and violence.[12] Once he adopted this perspective, Pfeil writes, "the central moral and pastoral task shifted from identifying concrete sinful acts to comprehending the ethical significance of institutionalized violence that led inexorably to the death of human beings. The language of social sin allowed him to blame and denounce not only particular offences against life but also the social structures that resulted from and prepared the ground for the sins revealed in the crucified bodies of his people" (175).

I have already pointed to the impact of liberation theology on the theory and practice of rights, but the issue is sufficiently important to warrant further comment. Central to liberation theology is the idea that God is the God of life, the friend of life, and that human history and sacred history are joined. Life is not merely existence over a span of years: life means fulfilling human potential and removing the obstacles that poverty, disease, violence, and lack throw up in the way of achieving a fully realized life for individuals, families, and communities. Because there is only one history, being true to God's plan is a task for this life, and building the kingdom of God is something that properly begins here and now ("The Kingdom of God is not coming with signs to be observed, nor will they say, 'Lo, here it is.'. . . For behold, the kingdom of God is in the midst of you," Luke 17:20–21).

The theologian Gustavo Gutiérrez refers to poverty as "early death"—a condition that leads to limited, truncated, and often painful lives. In the final analysis, Gutiérrez (1996, 57) writes, the "decision to side with the poor is a decision 'for the God of life, for the friend of life,' as it says in the Book of Wisdom [11:25]. Our daily experience of violence and unjust death will not permit us to engage in evasions or abstract reflections on the resurrection of Jesus without which our faith would be in vain, as Paul says."[13] He draws an explicit connection between commitment to the God of Life, commitment to the poor, and concern for human rights.

> In the final analysis, poverty means death: the physical death of many as well as cultural death from the disregard in which many others live. A few decades ago, our perception of this situation led to preoccupation with the theme of life as a gift from the God of our faith. The assassination of Christians, victims of their testimony to the Gospel, made this concern all the more urgent. Reflection on

this experience of persecution and martyrdom has given strength and breadth to a theology of life that helps us see that the option for the poor is, at root, an option for life. (Gutiérrez 1996, 56)

A vision of God as the God of Life and insistence that there is only one history acquire practical focus through the analysis and understanding of poverty not as a natural condition but rather as the product of specific social and historical circumstances. The conceptualization of poverty that undergirds liberation theology is simultaneously material and concrete, spiritual and a matter of commitment. Gutiérrez (1996, 7–8) writes: "We live in a continent that is both Christian and overwhelmingly poor. The presence of this massive and inhumane poverty drove us to reflect on the biblical meaning of poverty. Toward the middle of the 1960s, three understandings of the term *poverty* were formulated among theologians: (a) *real* (often called 'material') poverty, as a scandalous state, not desired by God; (b) *spiritual* poverty, in the sense of a childlike spirituality one of whose expressions is indifference to the goods of this world; and (c) poverty as *commitment*, solidarity with the poor, and protest against poverty."

The power of this formulation lies in how it combines an understanding of social conditions with a commitment to action and roots both in a biblical vision of the God of life. The actions enjoined are very specific: solidarity, accompaniment, and working with the poor and powerless to empower them as they strive for change. This stated preference for the materially poor is often criticized as too exclusive, partial, or excessively politicized.[14] But those working in a liberationist perspective insist that their stance is deeply biblical, an essential element of any authentic faith. Gutiérrez states the matter plainly:

The root motive for commitment with the poor and oppressed does not come from the social analysis we use, nor from our human compassion, or even from the direct experience we may have of poverty. All of these are valid reasons that doubtless play an important role, but for Christians this commitment is based fundamentally in the God of life. It is a theocentric and prophetic choice rooted in God's freely given love and demanded by it. In other words, the poor are preferred not because they are morally or religiously better than others but because God is God, He for whom "the last shall be first." This assertion clashes with our narrow understanding of justice, but it is precisely this preference for the poor that reminds us that God's ways are not our own. (2004, 571)

Gutiérrez acknowledges that many have questioned whether the Church may be losing its religious identity through such deep involvement in politics. Others, he notes, have gone further: "From positions of power they have openly violated the human rights defended in Church documents and struck blows against those Christians who gave voice to their solidarity with the poor and oppressed." Echoing Archbishop Romero, he continues: "A correct insertion into the world of the poor does not distort the mission of the Church. The truth is that this is where the Church finds her fullest identity as a sign of the Kingdom of God to which we are all called and in which the poor and insignificant have a privileged place. The Church does not lose its identity in solidarity with the poor, it strengthens it" (2004, 592).

Expanding the Reach of Rights

The preceding discussion points to the evolving bases for an expanded, or what we might term a holistic view of rights in Latin American Catholicism. A holistic view considers economic, social, legal, and political rights as necessarily and properly connected, and as nurturing one another. This holistic view gains moral and practical force from a religiously rooted vocabulary that legitimizes organization and action in defense of these rights as an expression of authentic faith. Commitment to the God of life and demands for solidarity and accompaniment point the Church beyond acting *for* the poor to accompanying them and putting institutions and resources at their disposal. They also broaden the range of issues beyond narrowly legal defense of rights to embrace a definition of rights that includes education, land, work, health, and freedom of movement, among others. Given these understandings, a transition from legal issues to support of movements by landless peasants, urban squatter settlement dwellers, political prisoners, the unemployed, and similar groups is straightforward. In Peru and El Salvador, grassroots ecumenical coalitions worked to defend rights, while in Brazil, Peru, and Chile the Catholic Church with support from others and access to important transnational networks put resources at the service of the defense of human rights and of the victims of repression (Brysk 2004; J. Burdick 2004; Carter 2010; R. Chapman 2012; Fitzpatrick-Behrens 2011; Kovic 2005; Sikkink 1993, 2011; Wechsler 1990; Youngers 2003).

To put the matter this way is not to disparage the importance of legal rights, and of the defense of classic civil rights. They are, of course, essential to the ability to exercise any rights at all, and central to the effort to defend the lives of victims of official abuse and to help their families. The defense of classic human rights (opposition to torture and abuse, protection of the integrity of the body, promotion of rights of speech, press, and assembly) is often associated with the effort to promote rights in other areas, including rights of the powerless to have access to institutions and to be able to articulate their needs in an effective way. Legal issues are important in their own right, and also for the role that has been played in so many cases by individual lawyers, legal associations, and councils of jurists. The case of Argentina's Emilio Mignone is exemplary (Del Carril 2011; Mignone 1988, 1991). Mignone was a prominent Catholic layman, a lawyer and political figure with conservative political antecedents. His daughter, Mónica, was abducted by "security forces" shortly after the military coup of 1976 and disappeared, never to be found. Her crime was her commitment to the preferential option for the poor, which led her (like many young Argentines who also were kidnapped, tortured, and disappeared) to work in poor neighborhoods, an effort seen as deeply subversive by the military authorities (Catoggio 2006, 2008; Mallimaci 2009; Mallimaci, Cucchetti, and Donatello 2006; Morello 2012). His son Augusto also disappeared later that year. Finding no help through the typical channels (friends or contacts in church or government), Mignone turned to legal and institutional action.[15] He joined the Permanent Assembly for Human Rights and later (1979) was a founder of the Center for Legal and Social Studies (Centro de Estudios Legales y Sociales, CELS) which became a key group in the effort to document abuse and make national and transnational connections for the human rights community.

Mignone's own analysis of his evolving position is worth citing. He insisted that his views had always been consistent, inspired by the Gospels and their injunction to love one another and to respect and value life, without distinctions, political or otherwise. In a letter to another daughter, Isabel, he wrote, "Your view that I have moved from a conservative to a progressive Catholicism is incorrect. I have neither been one or the other. . . . [The truth is that] I was ahead of the times, with positions later adopted by the Second Vatican Council. Now I simply advance others that may someday be adopted by a Universal Council of the twenty-first century which, when it happens, might well be in Jerusalem, not Rome." In earlier letters cited by his biographer, he roots his beliefs in the sacred value of life: "This is not a matter of one historical period or another. It is neither ancient nor modern. It is eternal. If it is violated, everything falls apart, and that is the source of all misfortunes. If the principle that killing is legitimate or not according to the person or the ideology of the victim is accepted, this opens a terrible breach and unleashes a series of troubles, of horrible injustices, because a value that is sacred, not human, has been broken. This doctrine may not be easy to follow in practice, but it is the only true one" (quoted in Del Carril 2011, 354, 356).

In publications, organizational work, and tireless activism on a national and transnational scale, Mignone laid bare the collaboration of the Argentine hierarchy with the military and the complicity of many Church leaders with the crimes of the regime (Mignone 1988, 1991). His actions strengthened national and transnational ties for all rights groups in Argentina, including but not limited to those of religious inspiration. Mignone's efforts were joined by those of many human rights groups in Argentina, including family-based movements of survivors and relatives of the detained and disappeared, religious and nonviolent groups like Service for Peace and Justice (Servicio Paz y Justicia, SERPAJ), whose director Adolfo Pérez Esquivel won the Nobel Peace Prize in 1980, Jewish and ecumenical groups, and of course the well-known example of the Madres (Mothers) de la Plaza de Mayo (later also Grandmothers of the Plaza de Mayo) (Brysk 1994).

The experience of SERPAJ and the Madres speaks both to religious inspiration and to the work of transnational contacts. SERPAJ arose as part of a Quaker outreach through the Fellowship of Reconciliation

(FOR) seeking to promote nonviolent groups and methods (Pagnucco and McCarthy 1992). The Madres had early support from SERPAJ, and both worked out of religious principles in the face of hostility from the Church itself. Brysk (1994, 42) writes of the Madres and related groups that "they turned to protest because their families and communities had been shattered, their neighbors were silent, and their own government denied their existence. Their public demonstration of personal anguish and quixotic principled challenge to the ruthless exercise of state power barely registered in their own society, but it was sustained and amplified in the international arena." The commitment of the Madres, like that of SERPAJ or of individuals like Emilio Mignone, was rooted in an understanding of Christian principles, an understanding that was rejected by the leadership of Argentina's Catholic hierarchy. A text on the early efforts of the Madres to search for missing children and grandchildren (often born to political prisoners who were killed after giving birth) makes clear the reception they found in the official Church: "We also had recourse to the Catholic Church and to the Ecclesiastical Hierarchy from the first days of our tragedy. We found closed doors, offensive and sometimes cruel words: 'they are in the hands of people who have paid 5 million for the babies, so they are in good hands, do not be concerned.' 'We cannot do anything, go away.' 'Pray, you are lacking in faith.' . . . We never recovered a child through the mediation of the Church" (quoted in Brysk 1994, 205).

Although the close association of the hierarchy with the military makes Argentina something of an extreme case, like many extremes it illuminates the possibilities. The point to make here is not one of ideological connection: the views of the Argentine hierarchy were matched by commitments of churches and individuals elsewhere to promote and defend rights. Notable cases at the national level include the efforts of the Vicaría de la Solidaridad (Vicariate of Solidarity) in Chile, Tutela Legal (Legal Assistance) in El Salvador, the Comisión Episcopal de Acción Social (CEAS) in Peru, and numerous church organizations in cases as distinct as Brazil and Paraguay. If we get down to the local level the instances multiply accordingly (French 2007; Kovic 2005; Tate 2007; Youngers 2003). The point to make is that whenever one scratches the surface of a particular national history, what seem like discrete events that

begin at a particular point in time turn out to have long and multiple antecedents. There is a prehistory, something like an invisible transition to
activism, and there is also a posthistory, manifest in the effort to put issues of rights and accountability permanently on the agenda of legislation
and institutions and to create a constituency that will keep them there.
This invisible transition to a practice of rights has also been a transition
of ideas. I have cited the impact of the Second Vatican Council, of bishops' meetings like Medellín or Puebla, and of liberation theology, all of
which can be located with some precision in time. But of course none of
these events simply appeared fully formed out of the blue. In each case
there were earlier initiatives and precedents that created what in retrospect
we can see as a constituency for these ideas, ready to accept them, work
with them, and turn them into regular kinds of practice, even in situations of long odds and great danger (Levine 2012).

A case in point is the more or less simultaneous surge of human rights
groups across Peru in the aftermath of official repression of the general
strike of the late 1970s. Following protests against police violence that
spurred the end of military rule, and efforts by CEAS to coordinate and
promote these, the theory and practice of rights as something integral to
the mission of the churches crystallized in the context of the long and
bloody war with Shining Path that occupied the country through the
1980s and into the early 1990s. During the war churches and Church
people were commonly caught between the armies of the state and the
forces of the Shining Path. The army suspected them of subversion, while
the Shining Path feared them as competitors (CEAS 1990; Youngers
2003). There is a broadly comparable evolution of ideas, organizations,
and commitments in cases as distinct as Chile, Argentina, Brazil, Guatemala, Mexico, El Salvador, and Colombia (Del Carril 2011; Garrard-
Burnett 2010; Kovic 2005; Neier 2012; Ranly 2003; Tate 2007; Theidon
2004; Tovar 2006; Whitfield 1994).

The preceding considerations suggest that what is at issue here is not
a matter of religious *or* political *or* social motivation: it is all of these at
once, and arises out of the dynamic of practice. In the case of Mayan organizations in Chiapas detailed by Kovic (2005), the easy mixing of different areas of rights is striking. Kovic reproduces several lists compiled
by participants in workshops promoted by Pueblo Creyente, a rights

organization sponsored by the Diocese of Chiapas. The rights enumerated by participants combine theology with politics, ordinary life with "big issues." Asked why they have rights, participants in one workshop responded, "Because we are human beings. Because we are made in God's image. Because we are free people capable of living and thinking. Because we are sons and daughters of God. Because God our Father sent his son to teach us to struggle. Because Jesus taught us to say the truth and taught us to defend our human rights. God formed and made us so all could eat. Because God formed the world and made all free so that the great (or powerful) don't take advantage of the small" (quoted in Kovic 2005, 108). Two further examples include the right to "live, be equal, be free, work, be paid a just salary, enjoy the fruits of our work, be doctors or professionals, eat, talk, think, sleep or rest, have dignity, education, a home, marry freely and have the children that we want, have a car and go up in a plane; go to other countries; advise others, live in the country or the city; enjoy protection of the law, justice, organize in our homes, travel in the street, and work for the betterment of our family" (quoted in Kovic 2005, 108). Moreover: "We have the right to own land, request land, grow fruit trees, have cattle, form collectives, have sports facilities, roads, electricity, potable water, health clinics, schools, buy goods cheaply, receive a just price for our harvest, cooperate in the community, organize ourselves, participate in solving problems in the municipality, elect our authorities, hold demonstrations, get rid of our municipal president if he doesn't work, have a political opinion and occupy political positions" (quoted in Kovic 2005, 108).

The Diocese of Chiapas facilitated these workshops, creating conditions for bringing people together by providing transportation, a place to stay, food to eat, and working materials. But the diocese did not create these ideas out of nothing. The efforts promoted in Chiapas drew strength from a host of local initiatives in a region shot through with activism of various kinds, including the Zapatista movement. Here as elsewhere, sponsorship by the institutional Church also provides valued legitimation, lending the moral authority of the Church to the practice of rights.

The preceding discussion is relevant to the general issue of the link between theory and practice of rights in the churches and the expansion of the rights movement generally. Latin American experience affirms that what was at work in the emergence of rights as a prime issue and area of practice for the Church in the period between the mid-1960s and the late 1980s was an alliance or meeting of the minds between individuals and communities with urgent needs, groups of religious inspiration, and, sometimes, elements in the institutional Church. This alliance was sometimes accidental, turning on a local event, the commitment undertaken by an individual priest or group of clergy, or the example of someone like Camilo Torres who inspired many in Colombia and throughout Latin America (Tate 2007; Levine 2011). This alliance also commonly arose from the deliberate effort of Church groups, pastoral agents, and inspired laypeople to accompany the poor and in this way find an outlet for their sense of mission. Many cases, particularly those linked directly to human rights at the outset, arose when those in urgent need learned (perhaps through direct contact, perhaps through word of mouth or reading flyers) that Church agents could be trusted and could provide concrete help. All these efforts point to the fact that when it comes to the practice of rights, and how that grows and is institutionalized, a wide range of groups in civil society (including religious groups) play a central role in articulating rights, making and sustaining transnational contacts, placing rights on the agenda of public institutions and actors, and keeping the issues alive through regular mobilization and public pressure.[16]

From Theory to Practice and Back Again: Triggering Events

How do incipient and general ideas about rights and their defense get turned into systematic and sustained practice? How are strategies identified and developed, resources and staff collected? How do individual acts and particular cases come to form part of a self-conscious movement? In all the cases I have examined, a triggering event or events of some kind provided the spark that converted new ideas about rights into sustained action. These events can turn long-standing pressures or general issues into specific, sustainable reactions. Such events can include local or regional reactions to war or state repression, individual searches for missing family members, community efforts to shield themselves from violence, and the like. From these beginnings, and often through trial and error and growing connections across local, regional, national, and transnational levels, those involved with the cause of rights acquire the language of transnational human rights organizations, which means in effect learning how to manage statistics, or as Tate (2007) puts it, "counting the dead" in ways that will resonate with the larger rights community.

A parallel kind of learning involves the expansion of concepts of rights from initial and urgent focus on the defense of life and resistance to torture to embrace a broader range of social, economic, and cultural issues. It is not easy to disentangle ideas from practice here, but what seems to happen is that the meeting of minds noted earlier leads to a series of coalitions between religiously inspired or linked individuals or groups, often brokered by the institutional Church and its leaders, that leads to initiatives on specific issues that then consolidate and expand. The churches provide critical resources, both material and moral. Where such resources and legitimacy are denied or withdrawn, the religious impulse may remain but is likely to migrate to other channels. As a practical matter, many nonreligious rights movements are staffed by former clergy.

I mentioned earlier that the invisible transition to rights is commonly sparked by a triggering event: a land invasion (as in the case of the Brazilian peasant group noted above), a military coup (Chile), simultaneous reactions to official abuse in different parts of Peru, or in Chiapas a combination of local incidents with new ideas and resources coming from the bishop and clergy of the diocese, opposed in this case by the papal nuncio. What churches can do very well in cases like this is to link isolated incidents and communities with one another, to provide a sense of solidarity, a sense that one is not alone. This provides legitimation to local activists, along with access to broader networks and the resources, connections, and publicity they can provide. The epistemological shift in the churches to which I referred earlier creates greater openness to issues of rights, puts Church people in places where they are likely to come face-to-face with pressing cases, and spurs initiatives to go beyond helping victims to working to prevent or at least contain abuses. There is an identification with the victim, but more is at issue. The epistemological shift is linked to what Tate (2007) calls a "paradigm of transformative witness." The idea of transformative witness has several dimensions that are worth considering separately. It sheds light on how the experience of action in pursuit or defense of rights transforms those taking the action, moving them beyond their initial positions. Which comes first, ideas or experience? Does violence lead to identification with victims, or is it theological change that leads to identification with victims that invites state violence? As an empirical matter it is difficult to tell: they evolve and change together; they are part of a common process.[17] Further, witness and testimony of this kind, testimony through action, is seen as a good in itself. In legal parlance a witness states the truth of what he or she has seen; religious understandings of witness go further. One witnesses to the truth of values by living in accordance with them, and one gives testimony to their worth by advancing them in practice. This kind of understanding lies at the core of religious efforts to promote rights. Rights are due to all as children of God, because all are made in the image of God. And because we do not live alone, rights are mediated through communities, through solidarity and collective action to promote and defend them. The very act of participation in the promotion and defense of rights transforms the actor because it strengthens values by living them out (cf. Stokes 1995).

Rights, Reconciliation, and the Postviolence Period

In Latin America, as in South Africa or Eastern Europe, religiously inspired groups (occasionally but not always joined by leaders of the institutional churches) that arose to articulate and defend rights have also played a part in brokering an end to dictatorship, mediating truces, negotiating conclusion to civil wars, and in preparing for and legitimating truth and reconciliation commissions. Care is needed when speaking about a "postviolence" role, for example, in arrangements for reconciliation.[18] Although civil wars and industrial-scale repressive political violence have largely passed from the scene, this does not mean that there is no violence. Violence of all kinds remains, and the churches (and their working concepts of rights) have played a varied role in addressing them. Some churches have also, but more haltingly, taken a rights-based position on flare-ups of violence around land conflicts (on Brazil and Chile, see Carter 2003; French 2007; Rodríguez 2009); police abuse in the cities; drugs and gangs; and housing issues, particularly in the cities; as well as the violence associated with illegal migration (see Martínez 2013; Frank-Vitale, this vol.).

Many but not all institutional churches played an important role in supporting, staffing, and legitimating truth commissions and efforts at reconciliation, including reparations; concrete aid to victims, families, and survivors; and recovery of memory (A. Chapman 2001; Wilde 2013). Prominent cases include Chile, Guatemala, and Peru but not of course Argentina, where the truth commission and its report were contested, when not wholly ignored, by the hierarchy. Those opposed to a supporting role for the Church often argue that such efforts simply stir up the past, and some—like the Argentine Catholic bishops—call for a "balanced" history, one that legitimizes the role of military and police institutions in combating subversion (Mallimaci 2005). But on the whole, religious language and organizations have been deployed in support of these efforts.

In a commentary on the report of the Peruvian Truth and Reconciliation Commission, Gutiérrez notes that ignoring the past means refusing to face a present that has deep roots in that very past, and thus making a repetition all the more likely. He does not use the language of restorative justice made famous by Archbishop Tutu and the South African Truth and Reconciliation Commission but insists that pardon (a totally free act taken from a perspective of faith) be distinguished clearly from a just sanction for crimes committed. Citing the biblical injunction "Blessed are those who weep those who feel compassion, those who feel as their own the sufferings of others [Matt. 5:4]," he continues:

There is a gesture that the prophet Isaiah presents us with in beautiful and moving terms: "The Lord will wipe away the tears from all faces and remove the condemnation of the people from the earth. Blessed, happy are those who act in this way." In the words of Luke, we can say, "Woe to them who present themselves before the God of justice and mercy with dry eyes. Because they did not know how to share their time, their concern and their feelings with those whose dignity as human beings, as daughters and sons of God was trampled upon, those who have suffered forgotten and in silence." . . . The Bible calls this "consolation." But let us be precise. This consolation has the sense not only of welcoming and listening, but also, and above all, of liberating from all that creates an inhuman situation. Will we let this opportunity pass? The opportunity for reconciliation. We cannot allow truth to remain hidden under ground, in one of these unmarked graves that hold so many dead. (Gutiérrez 2004, 464–65)

Much of this action is of the kind that legitimates action or denounces abuses, although there are also instances of the provision of legal and economic assistance (French 2007; Hayner 2002). One often hears that "words are cheap," and it may be fair to ask what impact words, in this case the transformation of a language of rights, can have in the long run. Do not actions count more than words? The preceding discussion underscores how closely related words are to actions. The transformations in religion in Latin America outlined here, and the creation of a new moral vocabulary of rights has had tangible consequences and long-lasting impact in the region. Human rights are now firmly on the agenda of all major institutions. Networks of local groups of all kinds (including those dedicated to human rights) now exist, often with extensive transnational connections. This is not to say that abuses no longer exist. But there is now an organized and vocal constituency that monitors and denounces them (Sikkink 1993, 2011; Brysk 2005; Cleary 2007; Friedman and Hochstetler 2002; Perruzzotti and Smulovitz 2006). The link of religious change to expanded understandings of rights expressed in language is also manifest in collective social action through a broad network of social movements—a civil society—that in most cases simply did not exist twenty years ago. Despite the many difficulties such movements have encountered, and the often exaggerated expectations and hopes placed in them, their presence does change the social and political landscape, providing new venues for action and sources of new leadership that are only now beginning to make themselves felt.

THE THEORY and practice of rights have deep roots in religion. Their particular expression in Latin American Catholicism draws on these roots and enriches and extends them into new fields of action because of the conjunction of two elements: the preferential option for the poor that led many religious activists to be present among poor populations, sharing their lives and conditions; and the violence exercised by fearful regimes who saw this kind of commitment as subversive of social order and a betrayal of the Church's authentic mission. The practice of rights has been deeply shaped by the violent environment Latin Americans have experienced in the past fifty years.

A striking aspect of the story of rights in Latin American Catholicism is the strong role played by civil society, including what I have called civil society within the churches. Groups and individuals within the Church, along with others outside its organizational structures but of clear religious inspiration, interacted with Church leaders as part of their efforts to articulate and defend human rights and extend concrete help to survivors and families. Experiences like this are often framed as a kind of *history from below*, in which practice and pressures from outside the formal boundaries of the institution play an autonomous and determining role. There is much truth in this view, but it is important to temper attention to the role of pressures from below with acknowledgment of the continuing power Church leaders have to advance or curtail initiatives, to encourage or delegitimize them, to open or cut off access to resources and networks. As a practical matter, the surge of commitments by the institutional Church to the articulation and defense of broad concepts of rights from the mid-1960s to the late 1980s in Latin America was associated with a particular generation of prelates, most of whom have now passed from the scene. In Latin America, as elsewhere in the Catholic world, their replacements are more conservative and much concerned with repairing relations with the state while reinforcing Church authority for the struggle with surging Pentecostal Protestantism. The sheer plurality of available networks and levels of action now in play throughout Latin America limits the power of Church leaders to curtail work for human rights, but it does not eliminate it completely.

In all cases, there is a visible process by which local and regional groups make contacts and form alliances, often, as in Peru, Chile, or Brazil, brokered by Church agencies (Lowden 1996; Drogus and Stewart-Gambino 2005; Carter 2003, 2010; Tate 2007; Youngers 2003). Where key Church hierarchs were indifferent or actively opposed to advancing human rights as an issue, the burden of action and coordination fell on groups in civil society, or on autonomous elements within the churches. This is the case with the Catholic Church in Argentina, in Peru now with Cardinal Cipriani, and in Colombia where organization is more scattered and the Centro de Investigación y Educación Popular (CINEP), a Jesuit organization, has taken a leading role in documentation and public education on rights.[19]

This is a dynamic and continuing process, so any conclusion can be at best interim. Issues of rights remain prominent in struggles to recover and define memory, in laws, and in the agendas of church groups, social movements, and public institutions. But, as noted, in theory and practice rights are contested terrain in the Church and in any case have long passed from center stage in the public agenda of most church groups. Times have changed, transitions to civilian rule and democracy make rights seem like yesterday's issues, and the generation of prelates put in place by the previous two popes has other priorities, most notably, reinforcing Church structures and discipline for the competition with Pentecostal Protestantism. The obvious question is whether the commitment to human rights that was so prominent in the public position of the churches in recent years is likely to continue. If so, in what form, with what emphasis, which allies?

The answer is not clear. Much depends on the ability of groups in civil society and of a civil society in the churches (situated in universities, research centers, religious orders and publications, media, and other groups) to keep human rights on the public agenda. One hopeful sign is that a review of the evidence makes it clear that the story of human rights is one of multiple and simultaneous innovation and pressure. There is no single center, no unique point of origin from which ideas and practices about rights diffuse. To say that there is no single center is not to affirm that there are no influences or interactions, local-regional-national-transnational. Initiatives continue to pop up independently, drawing on common ideas and nurtured by evolving links within and between countries and groups. These links are reinforced in practice as the international human rights community has grown and extended its outreach (Neier 2012; Méndez 2011). It is also clear that lots of local and regional groups are aware of something called the Universal Declaration of Human Rights, and if they don't know it at first, they soon come in contact with something known as international humanitarian law and with the norms about reporting that are common in transnational rights groups (Glendon 2001; Tate 2007; Youngers 2003).

All this is well documented and supplements but not does not eliminate the role played by religious ideas and by religiously inspired and linked individuals and groups at all levels. Complete understanding of the trajectory of rights as theory and practice requires us to make a prominent place for civil society and, within that, for religion (churches, groups, and individuals).[20] Beginning in the 1970s, organizations centered on rights and linked in some way with religion were set up throughout Latin America. These arose sometimes within the institutional churches (CEAS in Peru, Vicaría de la Solidaridad in Chile, Comissão Pastoral da Terra in Brazil, Tutela Legal in El Salvador, CINEP in Colombia, Pueblo Creyente in Chiapas), sometimes as a result of international outreach (as with the role of the Quaker outreach FOR in the creation of SERPAJ in Argentina). They have also been inspired by a search for survivors and family members (as with the Madres of the Plaza de Mayo) or by a mix of religious inspiration with legal training and connections, as was the case with Emilio Mignone and CELS in Argentina, the Institute for Legal Defense (IDL) in Peru, or the many regional human rights commissions that emerged in Peru in the late 1970s and 1980s (Youngers 2003).

Elements of the institutional Church provided critical support, staffing, legitimation, and protection to the emerging human rights movement, but of course they did not do so alone. In Latin America, as in other cases where religion played a prominent role in the articulation and active promotion of rights (South Africa, Eastern Europe before the fall of communism, the U.S. Civil Rights Movement), the churches were part of a broad alliance. They provided moral and material resources, moving beyond sympathy or simply help for victims to active engagement, to staffing of organizations and commissions (Levine 2012; Toft, Philpott, and Shah 2011).

The preceding considerations provide us with a few elements for reflection. To begin with, it is clear that the theory and practice of human rights in the churches is marked by a commitment to action rooted in an understanding of faith. This commitment is undertaken by churches as institutions. But actions by the institutional Church or its leaders do not exhaust the possibilities. Such actions are everywhere accompanied by commitments undertaken by individuals and groups linked to the churches and inspired by a vision of faith who may act independently of Church leaders and sometimes in opposition to them. Commitments drive the practice; practice refines the ideas and strategies and reinforces the commitments, often in the face of great danger.[21] The pervasive and intense violence that so much of Latin America experienced in recent decades rooted the theory and practice of rights in what I have termed classic human and civil rights, but practice quickly expanded the definitions to embrace rights beyond the legal and civil: the right to land, to education, to health, to freedom of movement, to a decent burial, to work, to organize.

This intense and repeated dialectic of ideas and practice suggests a few points to bear in mind when thinking about the possible futures for the theory and practice of rights. Although the legal grounding of rights is essential, in practice rights involve more than laws and regulations. Further, the practice of rights, the way they are pursued and the particulars of context, leadership, and opposition, has a profound impact on how the theory and practice of rights evolves. Finally, the cases mentioned here affirm the importance of links across levels, contacts, and a flow of resources and information that bind local events to national and transnational networks.

Religion in all its forms and manifestations (institutional churches, ideas, ecumenical coalitions, clergy, catechists, groups and individuals with some religious inspiration or connection) has been involved with rights in Latin America both as a source of legitimation and as a source of infrastructure and resources to facilitate identification, claiming, promotion, and defense of rights. The multiplicity of forms and organizational vehicles reaffirms the point that religion and churches are not well understood as undifferentiated wholes. It is misleading to speak about "the Church" and rights, as if this were a simple relation, to be discovered by reading "official documents" or speaking to authorized spokesmen. At issue in the relation of religion to rights is a host of interactions and contestation within and between churches and religious organizations, all loosely tied together by common bonds of identity as Christians. Because religions are complex internally, it is no surprise that these are contested matters. Commitments to rights may rise and fall within the churches and the religious community more broadly. What the institutional Church gives (resources, legitimacy, connections) it can also take away, and it has, but because the institutional Church does not exhaust the possibilities of religious expression, because religious life multiplies beyond the formal boundaries of Church organizational charts, the commitment to rights remains lively and widespread with roots solid enough to survive and to continue inspiring and sustaining activism.

Notes

I am grateful to Alexander Wilde for his detailed comments and for his willingness to engage in extended correspondence on this chapter.

1. Although I focus here on the Catholic Church, it is important to recognize the plurality of churches and groups involved with rights. Individual churches (Lutherans in El Salvador, Chile, or Brazil; Pentecostal alliances in Peru), ecumenical alliances, and multiple actors within any given church ("official" groups including commissions and vicariates, organizations sponsored by church leaders, and of groups of religious inspiration acting independently of church authorities) have all played a role, often working with local, regional, and national human rights commissions, associations of attorneys, and groups set up by survivors and families. Many also collaborated with transnational actors who played a prominent role in publicizing cases and providing resources and protection, where possible, to those working on the ground.

2. That this remains an ongoing struggle is manifest in the sudden (September 2013) closure by Church leaders of El Salvador's Tutela Legal. This organization, established by Msgr. Rivera y Damas in 1982, has long played a central role in the struggle to document, defend, and promote human rights and to press for accountability for crimes and abuses of power.

3. In this vein, the report of Peru's Commission on Truth and Reconciliation states, "In general, wherever the church had renovated itself on the lines of the second Vatican Council and the Episcopal Conferences of Medellín and Puebla, there was much more resistance to the appeals of subversive groups, because [the churches] developed a social presence that linked them to the population and responded to their needs with a discourse of change and a demand for

justice while rejecting violence. In contrast, where the church had not taken into account the changes pushed by the Council, subversion encountered much more fertile ground in which to root itself" (Comisión de la Verdad y Reconciliación, Peru, 2004, III:415–16; my translation). This commitment weakened notably in subsequent decades, as a new generation of bishops came to dominate the country's hierarchy. Many of these new prelates are members of the highly conservative Opus Dei (as of 2011, two archbishops, including one cardinal and eleven bishops). Once in office they went about dismantling many of the pastoral structures so visible in earlier decades. To cite the Peruvian commission once again, "The majority of bishops, priests, and sisters and many laypeople constituted a moral force and a source of hope. Nonetheless, we note that in some places ecclesiastical authorities maintained a deplorable silence about the violations of human rights committed by security forces" (III:379; my translation).

4. See, e.g., Faggioli 2012 on the ongoing contest within the Catholic Church over the meaning of the Second Vatican Council.

5. Such a focus (Hagopian 2009) runs the risk of exaggerating the extent to which Church-affiliated groups operate in some direct way as the hierarchy's "eyes and ears on the ground."

6. Elsewhere I have written extensively on these themes of authority in church and society; see Levine, 1978, and, most recently, 2014.

7. For a lively account of the failure of the policies of Benedict XVI, see Thavis 2014.

8. A parallel process is visible in the Protestant community as the Lausanne Covenant and subsequent declarations, along with the active role played by the World Council of Churches, helped raise the profile and the legitimacy of rights issues for Protestant and Evangelical churches (Freston 2001, 2008; Lumsdaine 2008; Borer 1998; Levine 2012; López 1998). There is also a striking awareness in many groups of the existence of the Universal Declaration of Human Rights (see Glendon 2001).

9. Wolterstorff (2012) notes that claims to rights are rooted in the worth of the rights bearer, which comes from being a child of God. In contrast to the idea that rights emerge exclusively out of ideas about possessive individualism (MacPherson 1962), Wolterstorff stresses that rights have claims to sociality built into them.

10. See Harper 2009; Kelly, this vol. The edition incorporated biblical citations to support each article. It was also printed in Spanish and English and circulated widely in the Americas and Europe.

11. The process recalls Harris's (1999, 2003) description of how religious faith and membership work on politics in the African American community of

the United States. The churches, he notes, provide micro and macro resources: micro resources include a sense of legitimacy and personal efficacy which gains effectiveness through the tangible macro resources that collective organization can provide—a place to meet and material support for action.

12. In his speech, "The Political Dimensions of the Faith from the Perspective of the Option for the Poor," delivered at the University of Louvain, Belgium, on February 2, 1980, Romero (1985, 183) wrote, "I insist again on the existence in our country of structures of sin. They are sin because they produce the deaths of Salvadorans—the swift death brought by repression or the long, drawn out, but no less real death from structural oppression."

13. Unless noted otherwise, this and subsequent translations are my own.

14. There are parallels to the debates in many countries about the recovery of historical memory, particularly the memory of dictatorship, between those who want justice for perpetrators of state violence and those who assert the need for a "balanced" approach.

15. Mignone's experience was a common one. Méndez (2011, 51) writes, "Even if religious leaders were sympathetic—and some were—they had little or no influence over the military government. Those priests and bishops who did maintain good relationships with the government generally tried to dissuade the families of the disappeared to stop looking and resign themselves to their fate."

16. In contrast, Moyn (2010) disparages the impact of both religion and civil society in articulating rights, making and sustaining transnational contacts, and keeping rights on the public agenda.

17. To the academic, this will smack of an "endogeneity" problem, a situation in which in effect the supposed cause may affect the result but the result also causes the cause. So ideas cause actions, which cause violence and which have a rebound effect on ideas, and so on. This makes it difficult, if not impossible, to sort out cause and effect. In my view, this is a problem only if we insist on linear explanations of causality. But reality is not like that: these are dialectical experiences that evolve and change over time. People try things out, their experience affects the ideas with which they started, they try again, and so on. Is this a case of ideas causing action or actions leading to a search for justifying ideas? Are these isolated local cases with specific causes, or are there connections to other levels of action? As we have seen, the answer to all these questions is yes.

18. In the intimate details of local life, reconciliation with perpetrators of violence requires a long and difficult process of again living as neighbors with onetime murderers, regardless of their professions of repentance. Theidon (2004, 190–208) uncovers what she calls a "chronology of compassion" in a series of acts that work to remove "the moral stain" from those responsible for the violence. Reconciliation cannot be understood only through the lens of national elites and

institutional concepts of justice. Theidon details the lack of fit between popular notions of justice, pardon, and reconciliation in Peru and the vision of reconciliation advanced by transitional governments and state-sponsored systems of justice (258). "Reconciliation," she writes, "is an ongoing process that seeks to replace antagonistic memories with memories of earlier social ties, to replace the history of innocents caught 'between two fires' with a history that allows for understanding who Sendero really was, and why" (257).

19. See www.cinep.org.co for a list of programs and publications.

20. This is a central weakness of Moyn (2010), whose account of the history of human rights disparages most influences from civil society and religion, even though what he actually cites shows a strong influence from these sources. He also says almost nothing about Latin America, where both the human rights movement and the role of religion have been notable, and what he says is not accurate or substantiated.

21. This suggests the inadequacy of analysts who explain the political choices of the Catholic Church in Latin America (or of comparable groups elsewhere) in terms of short-term calculation of benefits, a simple reaction to competition—more competition, more advanced positions (e.g., Gill 1998). Religious leaders, activists, and movements have varied greatly in their responses to competition and political conflict. In cases like South Africa, East Germany, the American South, and Indonesia, some doubled down on risky bets while others continued policies of passive accommodation. What makes a difference in these cases is the power of legitimating ideas as they find social expression in a pluralism that continues to bubble up and empower resistance despite efforts to tighten repression and control.

References

Aguilar, Mario I. 2003. "Cardinal Raúl Silva Henríquez, the Catholic Church, and the Pinochet Regime, 1973–1980: Public Responses to a National Security State." *Catholic Historical Review* 89, no. 4: 712–31.

Appleby, Scott R. 2000. *The Ambivalence of the Sacred: Religion, Violence, and Reconciliation*. Lanham, MD: Rowman and Littlefield.

Borer, Tristan. 1998. *Challenging the State: Churches as Political Actors in South Africa, 1980–1994*. Notre Dame, IN: University of Notre Dame Press.

Brysk, Alison. 1994. *The Politics of Human Rights in Argentina: Protest, Change, and Democratization*. Stanford, CA: Stanford University Press.

———. 2004. "From Civil Society to Collective Action: The Politics of Religion in Ecuador." In *Resurgent Voices in Latin America: Indigenous Peoples, Political*

Mobilization, and Religious Change, edited by Edward L. Cleary and Timothy Steigenga, 25–40. New Brunswick, NJ: Rutgers University Press.

———. 2005. *Human Rights and Private Wrongs: Constructing Global Civil Society*. New York: Routledge.

Burdick, John. 2004. *Legacies of Liberation: The Progressive Catholic Church in Brazil at the Start of a New Millennium*. London: Ashgate.

———. 2010. "Religion and Society in Contemporary Latin America." *Latin American Politics and Society* 52, no. 2 (Summer): 167–76.

Burdick, Michael. 1995. *For God and the Fatherland: Religion and Politics in Argentina*. Albany: State University of New York Press.

Carter, Miguel. 2003. "The Origins of Brazil's Landless Rural Workers' Movement (MST): The Natalino Episode in Rio Grande do Sul (1981–84), a Case of Ideal Interest Mobilization." Working Paper Series CBS 43–2003. Oxford: University of Oxford Centre for Brazilian Studies.

———. 2010. "The Landless Worker's Movement and Democracy in Brazil." *Latin American Research Review* (Special Issue): 186–217.

Catoggio, María Soledad. 2006. "Vigilancia, censura, gobierno y castigo en el caso de la llamada 'Biblia latinoamericana': Una perspectiva foucaultiana." *E-L@tina: Revista Electronica de Estudios Latinoamericanistas* 4, no. 14 (January–March): 3–24.

———. 2008. "Movimiento de sacerdotes para el tercer mundo y servicios de inteligencia: 1969–1970." *Sociedad y Religión* 17, no. 30–31: 171–89.

Chapman, Audrey. 2001. "Truth Commissions as Instruments of Forgiveness and Reconciliation." In *Forgiveness and Reconciliation: Religion, Public Policy, and Conflict Transformation*, edited by Raymond G. Helmick and Rodney L. Petersen, 257–77. West Conshohocken, PA: Templeton Foundation Press.

Chapman, Richard. 2012. "Still Looking for Liberation? Lutherans in El Salvador and Nicaragua." *Journal of Latin American Studies* 44, no. 1 (February): 39–70.

Cleary, Edward L. 2007. *Mobilizing for Human Rights in Latin America*. Bloomfield, CT: Kumarian Press.

———. 2009. *How Latin America Saved the Soul of the Catholic Church*. Mahwah, NJ: Paulist Press.

Comisión de la Verdad y Reconciliación, Peru. 2004. *Hatun Willakuy: Versión abreviada del Informe Final de la Comisión de la Verdad y Reconcilación*. Lima.

Comisión Episcopal de Acción Social (CEAS). 1990. *La Iglesia católica en el campo peruano en la década del 80: Elementos para una evaluación*. Lima.

Del Carril, Mario. 2011. *La vida de Emilio Mignone: Justicia, catolicismo y derechos humanos*. Buenos Aires: Grupo Editorial Planeta.

Drogus, Carol Ann, and Hannah Stewart-Gambino. 2005. *Activist Faith: Popular Women Activists and Their Movements in Democratic Brazil and Chile*. University Park: Pennsylvania State University Press.

Faggioli, Massimo. 2012. *Vatican II: The Battle for Meaning*. New York: Paulist Press.

Fitzpatrick-Behrens, Susan. 2012. *The Maryknoll Catholic Mission in Peru, 1943–1989: Transnational Faith and Transformation*. Notre Dame, IN: University of Notre Dame Press.

French, Jan Hoffman. 2007. "A Tale of Two Priests and Two Struggles: Liberation Theology from Dictatorship to Democracy in the Brazilian Northeast." *The Americas* 63, no. 3 (January): 409–43.

Freston, Paul. 2001. *Evangelicals and Politics in Asia, Africa, and Latin America*. New York: Cambridge University Press.

———, ed. 2008. *Evangelical Christianity and Democracy in Latin America*. New York: Oxford University Press.

Friedman, Elisabeth Jay, and Kathryn Hochstetler. 2002. "Assessing the Third Transition in Latin American Democratization: Representational Regimes and Civil Society in Brazil and Argentina." *Comparative Politics* 35, no. 1 (October): 21–42.

Garrard-Burnett, Virginia. 2010. *Terror in the Land of the Holy Spirit: Guatemala under General Efraín Ríos Montt, 1982–1983*. New York: Oxford University Press.

Gill, Anthony. 1998. *Rendering unto Caesar: The Catholic Church and the State in Latin America*. Chicago: University of Chicago Press.

Glendon, Mary Ann. 2001. *A World Made New: Eleanor Roosevelt and the Universal Declaration of Human Rights*. New York: Random House.

Gutiérrez, Gustavo. 1996. *¿Dónde dormirán los pobres?* Lima: Instituto Bartolomé de las Casas, Centro de Estudios y Publicaciones.

———. 2004. *Gustavo Gutiérrez: Textos esenciales: Acordarse de los pobres*. Lima: Fondo Editorial del Congreso del Perú.

Hagopian, Frances, ed. 2009. *Religious Pluralism, Democracy, and the Catholic Church in Latin America*. Notre Dame, IN: University of Notre Dame Press.

Harper, Charles R. 2009. *O Acompanhamento: Ecumenical Action for Human Rights in Latin America, 1970–1990*. Geneva: WCC Publications.

Harris, Fredrick C. 1999. *Something Within: Religion in African-American Political Activism*. New York: Oxford University Press.

———. 2003. "Ties That Bind and Flourish: Religion as Social Capital in African American Politics and Society." In *Religion as Social Captial: Producing the Common Good*, edited by Corwin E. Smidt, 121–37. Waco, TX: Baylor University Press.

Hayner, Priscilla B. 2002. *Unspeakable Truths: Facing the Challenge of Truth Commissions*. New York: Routledge.

Kovic, Christine Marie. 2005. *Mayan Voices for Human Rights: Displaced Catholics in Highland Chiapas*. Austin: University of Texas Press.

Levine, Daniel H. 1978. "Authority in Church and Society: Latin American Models." *Comparative Studies in Society and History* 20, no. 4 (October 1978): 517–44.

———. 1981. *Religion and Politics in Latin America: The Catholic Church in Venezuela and Colombia*. Princeton, NJ: Princeton University Press.

———. 1992. *Popular Voices in Latin American Catholicism*. Princeton, NJ: Princeton University Press.

———. 2006a. "Pluralidad, pluralismo y la creación de un vocabulario de derechos." *América Latina Hoy* 41 (December): 17–34.

———. 2006b. "Religión y política en América Latina: La nueva cara pública de la religion." *Sociedad y Religión* 18, no. 26–27: 7–29.

———. 2009. "The Future of Christianity in Latin America." *Journal of Latin American Studies* 41, no. 1 (February): 121–45.

———. 2010. "Reflections on the Mutual Impact of Violence and Religious Change in Latin America." *Latin American Politics and Society* 52, no. 3: 131–50.

———. 2011. "Camilo Torres: Fe, política y violencia." *Sociedad y Religión* 21, no. 34–35: 59–91.

———. 2012. *Politics, Religion, and Society in Latin America*. Boulder, CO: Lynne Rienner.

———. 2014. "Is There a 'Francis Effect' in Latin America?" *Americas Quarterly* (October): 26–31.

López, Darío. 1998. *Los evangélicos y los derechos humanos: La experiencia del Concilio Nacional Evangélico del Perú*. Lima: Ediciones Puma.

Lowden, Patricia. 1996. *Moral Opposition to Authoritarian Rule in Chile, 1973–90*. New York: St. Martin's Press.

Lumsdaine, David H. 2008. *Evangelical Christianity and Democracy in Asia*. Oxford: Oxford University Press.

MacLean, Iain S. 2006. *Reconciliation, Nations and Churches in Latin America*. London: Ashgate.

MacPherson, C. B. 1962. *The Political Theory of Possessive Individualism: Hobbes to Locke*. London: Oxford University Press.

Mallimaci, Fortunato. 2005. "Catolicismo y política en el gobierno de Kirchner." *América Latina Hoy* 41 (December): 56–76.

———. 2009. "Catolización y militarización, catolicismos y militarismos: La violencia y lo sagrado en la Argentina del terrorismo de estado." Paper presented at the symposium Katolische Kirche und Gewalt im 20 Jahrhundert, Wesfalishche Wilhelms-Universitat Munster, Germany, May 19–21.

Mallimaci, Fortunato, Humberto Cucchetti, and Luis Donatello. 2006. "Caminos sinuosos: Nacionalismo y catolicismo en la Argentina contemporánea." In *El altar y el trono: Ensayos sobre el catolicismo político iberoamericano,* edited by Franscisco Colom and Ángel Rivero, 155–90. Bogotá: Anthropos.

Martínez, Oscar. 2013. *The Beast: Riding the Rails and Dodging Narcos on the Migrant Trail.* Translated by Daniela María Ugaz and John Washington. London: Verso.

Méndez, Juan E. 2011. *Taking a Stand: The Evolution of Human Rights.* New York: Palgrave Macmillan.

Mignone, Emilio F. 1988. *Witness to the Truth: The Complicity of Church and Dictatorship in Argentina, 1976–1983.* Translated by Phillip Berryman. Maryknoll, NY: Orbis Books.

———. 1991. *Derechos humanos y sociedad: El caso argentino.* Buenos Aires: Centro de Estudios Legales y Sociales.

Morello, Gustavo. 2012. "Secularización y derechos humanos: Actores católicos entre la dictadura argentina (1976) y la administración Carter (1977–1979)." *Latin American Research Review* 47, no. 3: 62–82.

Moyn, Samuel. 2010. *The Last Utopia: Human Rights in History.* Cambridge, MA: Harvard University Press.

Neier, Aryeh. 2012. *The International Human Rights Movement: A History.* Princeton, NJ: Princeton University Press.

Noone, Judith M. 1995. *The Same Fate as the Poor.* Maryknoll, NY: Orbis Books.

Pagnucco, Ronald, and John D. McCarthy. 1992. "Advocating Non Violent Direct Action in Latin America: The Antecedents and Emergence of SERPAJ." In *Religion and Politics in Comparative Perspective: Revival of Religious Fundamentalism in East and West,* edited by Bronislaw Misztal and Anson Shupe, 120–50. Westport, CT: Praeger.

Perruzzotti, Enrique, and Catalina Smulovitz, eds. 2006. *Enforcing the Rule of Law: Social Accountability in the New Latin American Democracies.* Pittsburgh, PA: University of Pittsburgh Press.

Pfeil, Margaret R. 2006. "Social Sin, Social Reconciliation." In *Reconciliation, Nations and Churches in Latin America,* edited by Iain S. MacLean, 171–89. London: Ashgate.

Ranly, Ernesto. 2003. *Los religiosos en tiempos de violencia en el Perú: Crónica y teoría de la no-violencia.* Lima: Confederación de Religiosos del Perú.

Rodríguez, Patricia M. 2009. "With or without the People: The Catholic Church and Land-Related Conflicts in Brazil and Chile." In *Religious Pluralism, Democracy, and the Catholic Church in Latin America,* edited by Frances Hagopian, 185–224. Notre Dame, IN: University of Notre Dame Press.

Romero, Catalina. 2009. "Religion and Public Spaces: Catholicism and Civil Society in Peru." In *Religious Pluralism, Democracy, and the Catholic Church in Latin America*, edited by Frances Hagopian, 365–401. Notre Dame, IN: University of Notre Dame Press.

Romero, Óscar A. 1985. *Voice of the Voiceless: The Four Pastoral Letters and Other Statements*. Translated by Michael J. Walsh. Maryknoll, NY: Orbis Books.

Sikkink, Kathryn A. 1993. "Human Rights, Principled Issue Networks, and Sovereignty in Latin America." *International Organization* 47, no. 3: 411–41.

———. 2011. *The Justice Cascade: How Human Rights Prosecutions Are Changing World Politics*. New York: W. W. Norton.

Smith, Christian. 1991. *The Emergence of Liberation Theology: Radical Religion and Social Movement Theory*. Chicago: University of Chicago Press.

Stokes, Susan C. 1995. *Cultures in Conflict: Social Movements and the State in Peru*. Berkeley: University of California Press.

Tate, Winifred. 2007. *Counting the Dead: The Culture and Politics of Human Rights Activism in Colombia*. Berkeley: University of California Press.

Thavis, John. 2014. *The Vatican Diaries*. New York. Penguin.

Theidon, Kimberly. 2004. *Entre prójimos: El conflicto armado interno y la política de la reconciliación en el Perú*. Lima: Instituto de Estudios Peruanos.

Toft, Monica Duffy, Daniel Philpott, and Timothy Samuel Shah. 2011. *God's Century: Resurgent Religion and Global Politics*. New York: W. W. Norton.

Tovar, Cecilia, ed. 2006. *Ser iglesia en tiempos de violencia*. Lima: Instituto Bartolomé de las Casas, Centro de Estudios y Publicaciones.

Weschler, Lawrence. 1990. *A Miracle, a Universe: Settling Accounts with Torturers*. New York: Pantheon Books.

Whitfield, Teresa. 1994. *Paying the Price: Ignacio Ellacuría and the Murdered Jesuits of El Salvador*. Philadelphia, PA: Temple University Press.

Wilde, Alexander. 2013. "A Season of Memory: Human Rights in Chile's Long Transition." In *The Politics of Memory in Chile: From Pinochet to Bachelet*, edited by Cath Collins, Katherine Hite, and Alfredo Joignant, 31–60. Boulder, CO: Lynne Rienner.

Wolterstorff, Nicholas P. 2012. "Christianity and Human Rights." In *Religion and Human Rights: An Introduction*, edited by John Witte Jr. and M. Christian Green, 42–55. New York: Oxford University Press.

Youngers, Coletta. 2003. *Violencia política y sociedad civil en el Perú: Historia de la Coordinadora Nacional de Derechos Humanos*. Lima: Instituto de Estudios Peruanos.

CHAPTER 2

VIOLENCE AND EVERYDAY EXPERIENCE IN EARLY TWENTY-FIRST-CENTURY LATIN AMERICA

ROBERT ALBRO

It was a dubious distinction in 2012 when Juárez, Mexico, lost its status as the world's most violent city to another Latin American competitor, Honduras's San Pedro Sula, a city with a homicide rate of 173 per 100,000. In the words of one mortician, "The devil himself lives in San Pedro."[1] In fact, all but one of the twenty most dangerous cities on earth are found in Latin America. Despite the turn from authoritarian to democratic forms of governance throughout the region beginning in the 1980s, the homicide rate has increased by 50 percent since that time (Imbusch, Misse, and Carrión 2011), and the total number of homicides in the region has risen each year between 2000 and 2012 (OAS 2012, 17). Over a decade ago, Frühling and Tulchin (2003) had already noted that homicide rates across Latin America rose consistently during the previous twenty-five years, regardless of whether a given country began with a low or high murder rate. This ongoing and increasingly violent state of affairs is now described as Latin America's worst "epidemic,"[2] with more people dying violently than from HIV.

If the average number of deaths per 100,000 people in Latin America is 25.6, making it the most violent region globally, in Honduras it rises to a stunning 92 per 100,000 (OAS 2012, 18). Equally shocking has been the extent of the human toll during Mexico's hard-on-crime war on drug cartels, begun in 2007: at least 60,000 Mexican lives, with little impact on reducing drug trafficking.[3] Other worsening trends include rampant domestic violence. No fewer than 53 percent of women in Bolivia report having been victims at some point in their lives (Bott et al. 2012, xvi). The region has the second highest number of female deaths due to violence and the highest rate of children killed in the world (OAS 2012, 52). Other expressions of violence include alarmingly high numbers of assaults and rampant property crime, which has more than tripled in many parts of the region in the past twenty years (Bergman 2006); regular police violence against nonaffluent populations, typically with an indifferent judicial response (Brinks 2008); an upward trend in the frequency of kidnapping across much of the region, with almost 106,000 in Mexico in 2012 alone (OAS 2012, 74); and the need to coin a new word—*femicide*—to categorize the violation, torture, and killing of young women as part of a rising trend in sexual violence.[4] Among all the world's regions, Latin Americans are now the least likely to feel safe in their communities,[5] and for the first time in decades surveys find that Latin Americans list crime ahead of unemployment as their primary concern (IACHR 2009, ix).

Statistics alone do not tell the full story. The vast majority of violence remains unreported, and contemporary crime figures do not convey how populations are burdened by the numerous ways violence regularly affects peoples' lives, including legacies of dictatorship across the region. This chapter, therefore, aims to illuminate the meanings of violence as an integral part of everyday life in Latin America today.[6]

The present discussion does not aspire to offer an exhaustive description of the scope of violence in the region, to identify all the forms violence takes in the region today, or to classify these as part of some overarching or comparative framework. Instead this chapter selectively describes and compares expressions of violence to illustrate how varieties of violence shape everyday expressions of collective social, cultural, and political life. This includes tracing how some expressions of everyday violence influence the context and meaning of "rights-based" claims and, in so doing, complicate religious responses to today's violence that might draw from traditions of human rights advocacy under authoritarian rule.

This chapter begins with a consideration of legacies of the recent period of dictatorships in Latin America and then considers the postauthoritarian and increasingly nonstate violence of today. Throughout, it is concerned with the relationship between expressions of violence and systematic state or popular responses to them. It also considers some lingering effects of the inconclusive response to the terror of the authoritarian period on public understandings of violence today. The chapter concludes with an analysis of how memories of violence give rise to new solidarities and experiences of belonging.

Political Violence: Perpetrators and Victims

Although pervasive violence is not new in Latin America (see Franco 2013; Grandin and Joseph 2010), the authoritarian period from the 1960s to the 1980s and the responses of states and civil society to violence significantly frame both the "reckoning" with legacies of past violence and efforts to make sense of high levels of continuing violence experienced under subsequent democratic regimes (see Atencio 2014; Lewis 2005; Nelson 2009; Stern 2010).[7] Kidnappings, detentions, disappearances, clandestine prisons, torture, and murders were all practices associated with military regimes in Argentina, Chile, Brazil, and several Central American countries during this period.[8] These forms of violence also proliferated amid the protracted civil conflicts that wracked Central America, Colombia, and Peru during this era (see, e.g., Burt 2007) and that in the case of Colombia continues to do so.

Although violence took many forms then as now, the violence of the recent past is often primarily depicted as varieties of "political violence," that is, violence employed by the state or, less frequently, by opposition groups in order to defend or destroy specific regimes (see, e.g., Fowler and Lambert 2006; Robben 2005; Schirmer 1998). If details vary, such is the case with Marcia Esparza's (2011, 2) summation of this period as a "shared history of state-organized violence." Violent actions by or against states have also been the historical focus for human rights–based and religious responses to the violence, including support for institutional mechanisms of transitional justice intended to move societies beyond the collective experience of violence. Their efforts assume the ability to publicly and categorically distinguish perpetrators from victims of political violence—even if the specific circumstances of violence varied, culpability remains contested, and the vast majority of individual identities remain unknown (the many "numbers without names," to paraphrase Jacobo Timerman [2002]). Conflict and violence in Latin America today may have a political dimension, as we were reminded by street demonstrations in Venezuela and Brazil in 2013 and 2014, but it is an error to see them in terms of past contests over the machinery of state power (e.g., Grandin and Joseph 2010). As I suggest in this chapter, historical presuppositions about the primacy of the political can be misleading in considering current, often apolitical and nonstate, violence and unhelpful for developing constructive responses to it, including religious responses.[9]

Religious advocacy on behalf of the victims of political violence in the past, particularly the efforts rooted in liberation theology, also prioritized the state and assumed that victimhood could be clearly identified. As Garrard-Burnett points out in this volume, the focus of the Catholic Church in the 1980s on cases of "institutional violence" and "revolutionary priests" in Central America took for granted that such violence was an expression of contention over control of the state, where the effort was understood to directly influence the state's repressive machinery and to mediate between the state and society. Similarly, in her discussion of Argentina's Truth Commission in this volume, Catoggio notes the then-prevailing "theory of two demons," that is, a narrative of violence as perpetrated either by the military or by the guerrilla but largely ignoring civilian actors. This theory was, in turn, reflected in accounts of the Church as either complicit with or persecuted by state violence (see chapters by Morello, Queiroz, and Wilde, this vol.).

Today the state may still be an important actor in social conflicts, as with extractive conflicts in Peru (Arellano, this vol.) or the conflict with the FARC guerrillas in Colombia (Tate, this vol.), and they tend to elicit a pastoral response of accompaniment or mediation comparable to that of the era of political violence. I would also suggest that, as with the "option for the poor" in the past, pastoral interventions of this sort today are often understood in terms of well-defined groups or categories of people, for example, "prisoners" (Johnson, this vol.) or "migrants" (Frank-Vitale, this vol.). In contrast, in his discussion of gang violence in Central America, Brenneman (this vol.) points to the challenges churches face in developing responses to nonstate violence where actors do not seek institutional legitimacy. Religious responses to violence, in other words, may depend on conceiving well-defined categories of victims as collective subjects. But in the context of today's largely nonstate violence, people's relationships to acts of violence are various and defining the victims has become harder.[10]

Democratic Transitions and Truth Commissions

Transitions to democracy in Latin America have often incorporated public processes meant to address the violence of the preceding era, frequently taking the form of official truth commissions.[11] The commissions' data collection methods have included gathering records from human rights organizations (many closely linked to the Catholic Church), public hearings, exhumations of mass graves, and interviews of victims, survivors, witnesses, and perpetrators of human rights violations. They have aimed to publicize atrocities and to give voice to the victims of violence, especially state violence, with the goal of restoring their human dignity. Public testimony has been central to the intended impact of truth commissions on political transitions. The 1984 report of Argentina's National Commission on the Disappeared (ANCD 1986), for example, presented more than 9,000 individual cases. The 1991 report of the Chilean National Commission on Truth and Reconciliation drew on over 19,000 cases of human rights abuses assembled by the Catholic Church's Vicariate of Solidarity from testimonies of victims and family members (Stern 2010). Guatemala's Commission for Historical Clarification's 1999 report is based on over 8,000 testimonies of survivors (Sanford 2003). And the 2003 report from Peru's Truth and Reconciliation Commission included over 17,000 testimonies and fourteen public hearings, along with evidence from hundreds of archives (Laplante and Theidon 2007).

The use of testimony in truth commission reports establishes a particular relationship to historical memory. It strategically foregrounds the first-person authority of the direct experiences of people engaged in common struggles, as a "community of the witness" (Gugelberger 1996, 9), in order to expose the facts of often government-sponsored injustice (Beverley 2004; Yúdice 1991). Church responses to political violence, then and now, have made use of testimonial strategies as well. Tate's description (this vol.) of pastoral accompaniment of communities caught in the Colombian state's struggle with the FARC, as "compassionate witness to community suffering," is a case in point. The Catholic Church has played a notable role in efforts to define the legacies of state-based violence in Latin America by means of the public institutionalization of historical memory through the work of truth commissions (see chapters by Wilde and Queiroz, this vol.).

Characterized by often graphic accounts of specific acts of violence by identified types of perpetrators, such *testimonio* has also been understood as "an account of the defense of human rights" (Fernández Benítez 2010, 50). It is one important tool for human rights and religious advocates to publicly and dramatically expose rights violations. Truth commission testimonies are conceived as a way to uncover previously hidden (mostly political) violence, to make them part of the public record, and to link the facts of violations to popular rights claims. In this way they are intended to rehabilitate otherwise nameless victims of violence as rights-bearing subjects. The naming of names and the sheer volume of recorded words from thousands of testimonies offering graphic descriptions of countless horrific details of violence compose the heart of each report. And they are meant to demystify the mechanisms of violence and the varieties of victimhood perpetrated by the state and/or its enemies.

As Payne (2008) has argued for Argentina, Brazil, and Chile and as Oglesby (2007) has suggested for Guatemala, the work of truth commissions is often described as airing grievances while catalyzing contentious public debate to encourage movement toward a more deliberative approach to governance. In Ogelsby's (2007, 79) words, in this way the public process of truth gathering is presented as an "exposé of brutality," an open and public record of exactly what happened, and a past contrasting with the evident "triumph of democracy," which is represented by the successful management of a truth and reconciliation process. Similarly, Fernández Benítez (2010, 51) characterizes the *testimonio* as aiming to promote the transition to "societies founded upon solid democratic pillars and which avoid a repetition of the violence, pain, and horror" depicted in truth commission reports.

However, some scholars have criticized truth commissions as vehicles for dealing with the past, noting that political identities are attenuated by the litanies of names, numbers, and testimonies that constitute their reports. In her analysis of Guatemala's 1999 report, Oglesby (2007, 80) finds a narrowly circumscribed account of historical memory that asserts the facts of mass victimhood but as "individualized dehistoricized injury," in ways that ignore the particular social, cultural, class, or gendered identities of victims. Others have pointed out the limitations of truth commissions in confronting the legacies of past violence and the conflict that has continued after transition over divergent memories of the authoritarian period. As Stern (2010) explores in depth for Chile, the "contentious memory" of the Pinochet years has operated selectively and corrosively among different social sectors and political actors—including former parties to and victims of the regime's violence—in ways that highlight social impasses and lead to regular friction. He argues that these unresolved tensions between truth, justice, and memory have, over time, only gradually begun to coalesce into a new national script of "shared tragedy" (5). In such cases victims and perpetrators continue to argue over the identity of victims and the extent of their complicity in past repressive acts. Referring mainly to the recent period of state violence in Latin America's Southern Cone, Jelin (2003) emphasizes the difficulty of official attempts to achieve closure and suture past wounds. Efforts to come to terms with past violence, she argues, are contested and remain openended, often as lightning rods of further conflict. In Latin America such violence continues to bleed into the present.

As instruments of democratic transition, truth commissions in Latin America were also intended to rehabilitate the legitimacy of the state as an "arbiter of legal dispute and protector of individual rights" (Grandin 2005, 47). They have been viewed as vehicles for reconstituting the state as the basis for the rule of law through the identification and defense of rights. However, clearly, democratic regimes of rights have not eliminated pervasive violence in Latin America. In part this is because, particularly in situations of absent, weak, or corrupt state institutions, popular conceptions of rights now also connect them to the illicit and the illegal as potential sources of violence.

Political Violence and Making Victims Visible

In ways comparable to the goals of official truth and reconciliation efforts, popular responses to the political violence of the authoritarian era were also frequently focused on exposing state terror by drawing public attention to the victims of its violence. State repression of popular opposition to dictatorships in Argentina, Chile, and Guatemala, for example, included the notorious strategy of "disappearing" thousands of people whom the regimes deemed a threat (e.g., Timerman 2002; Robben 2005). Most of the disappeared were killed, but many left no trace, and demands for accountability from groups of survivors and relatives evolved into influential movements in various places.

Among the best known were the Madres de la Plaza de Mayo in Argentina, a small group of mothers who began public protests in the late 1970s on behalf of an estimated 15,000 to 30,000 people who were disappeared during the country's Dirty War of state terror between 1976 and 1983. In their now four-decade-old effort to hold the military regime accountable for its crimes, the Madres have been at the center of a performative and theatrical protest movement and spectacle that Robben (2005, 301) describes as "the exteriorization of personal pain" to make visible the invisible who were disappeared. Their weekly and collective rituals of protest in Buenos Aires's central square, together with commemorative activism such as petitions and frequent temporary exhibits of pictures, names, and murals of the disappeared, are parts of a theatrical politics of memory designed to draw public attention to the clandestine acts of state violence, the criminal extent of the state's actions against its own population, and the still unaccounted for victims of that period of political violence (see Bosco 2004; Werth 2010).[12]

It is no accident that the Madres became a cause célèbre as the subjects of an elaborate and international human rights network and eventual campaign focused on calling Argentina's government to account (see Guzman 2002). In this case, given the clear assignation of blame to a specific regime as the deliberate agent of violence, and the accompanying sharp and stable distinction between the identities of both "victimizer" and "victim" (see Keck and Sikkink 1998, 27), the Madres were a good fit as protagonists of an international human rights campaign. The violence characterizing the Dirty War, and responses to it, composed clear fault lines of a repressive state and state-enacted disappearances, silences, and violations of human rights, on one side, and a public performance of protest, on the other, in order to reclaim a voice and to make visible the states' atrocities.

As with Argentina's Madres, popular responses to state violence have sought to identify the extent of its otherwise anonymous victims and to bring the facts of this violence into public view.[13] The Madres' ongoing public performance of collective memory has been one attention-getting strategy among others, including museum projects, street theater, promotion of historic sites, and public art. Although the fates of many remain unknown, the character and sources of violence in Argentina during that period are well established. If Argentina experienced a "collective trauma" (Robben 2005, 277) that continues to haunt its present, the public debates and private nightmares all take for granted the same frame of reference of state terror and popular responses to it. With violence today, however, the situation often appears to be the inverse, where there are too frequent and macabre spectacles of violence in plain sight but where the best responses have proven elusive.

From Testimony to *Desconfianza*

If intended as transitional projects designed to engineer democratic legitimacy, truth commissions also connect their vivid testimonial content to potential postconflict solidarities. Though in clear tension with the narrower version of historical memory designed to serve the political needs of regime transition, the relationships of political solidarity—the so-called community of the witness—enacted through the testimonial voice also directly depend on bearing personal witness to tragedy. As

Gilmore (2003) suggests of Rigoberta Menchú's testimony about war-torn Guatemala,[14] the solidarity generated by its telling, among victims and with the reader, is not with any particular indigenous or rural prole-tariat, gendered or leftist political identity so much as established by the vivid and prolonged descriptions of carnage: the multiple imprison-ments, torture, and assassination of her father or the lengthy and grue-some itemization of each step in the kidnapping, torture, rape, and murder of her mother.

While describing her mother's extended torture and death, Menchú (1983, 199) notes, "We have to keep this grief as a testimony." If her tes-timony posits a collective "we," it does so, in Gilmore's (2003, 708) words, by adopting this still unrepaired "traumatic wound" as its political subject. In other words, the promise of accountability and justice for pre-viously second-class citizens and victims of the violence of counterinsur-gency in nominally democratic Guatemala is at the same time, as Victor Turner (1968) elsewhere put it, membership in a "cult of affliction." See-ing how the terms of participation in everyday social life in Latin America have come to encompass different experiences and understandings of violence—and where the collective experience of violence is at the same time integral to different postconflict conceptions of rights, membership, and solidarity—is critical to understanding better how violence has changed from the past to the present.

Writing almost twenty years after Menchú, the genocide survivor Victor Montejo (1999) offered a different, updated account of the testi-monial voice in Guatemala, one much less sure about who speaks and why. Throughout Menchú's celebrated testimony, it is clear who the vic-tims and the perpetrators are in ways consistent with the human rights–based approach previously described. In Montejo's case, this clarity has been replaced by creeping ambiguity. Montejo understands his work as a contribution to Mayan cultural survival, but he also describes his own double identity as both Mayan and non-Mayan and offers the testimony of Chilin Hultaxh, a former soldier and up-close witness to the army's counterinsurgency operations but also a person whose identity is open for debate. If Hultaxh's is a self-described "story of great pain" (Montejo 1999, 83), it is an ambivalent one. Hultaxh evidently worked as a mem-ber of a military intelligence unit and was present at interrogations, tortures, and murders. While describing these often terrible incidents, and testifying to his fear, the authority of his experience is not simply as a victim but also as a participant, the extent of which is never entirely apparent.

If Hultaxh was a victim of the army's deep institutional racism, he also participated in its counterinsurgency operations. If he was later denounced by a fellow community member, he was also asked to work as an informer for his former comrades. Hultaxh's narrative is about constant surveillance, the collapse of mutual trust, and the ways talking can quickly become informing. It is apparent that Hultaxh is wounded. It is less clear what he did and did not do while in the army or afterward. The shift in the location of voice between Menchú and Montejo is commensurate with the lingering implications of this inconclusive conflict and an increasingly blurred line between victim and perpetrator. In Montejo's account (as in Theidon's chapter in this volume), perpetrators are also victims and still very much at large.

Criticizing the victim-centered focus of official truth and reconciliation efforts, Theidon (2012) similarly pushes beyond conventional arguments about the social processes and trauma of postconflict reconstruction in Ayacucho, the onetime heartland of the Shining Path guerrillas in Peru. The setting for extreme fratricidal violence, where perpetrators were frequently also close relatives, friends, or neighbors of victims, Ayacucho, according to Theidon, is a still fractured landscape populated by former enemies and survivors—army veterans, civilian sympathizers, widows, and orphans—now living side-by-side and all too aware of the potential dangers posed by their immediate neighbors. In Theidon's words, they are "intimate enemies." The people of this landscape maintain an uneasy truce through pacts of silence and conciliation. But they also suffer from ongoing physical afflictions, madness, and fright-induced soul loss, expressed through *llakis*, songs concerned with memory and private loss and pain but also collective suffering.

Nelson (2009) describes postconflict Guatemalan society as one of continuous "reckoning" with this legacy, paralyzed by people's many complicities in the country's war-related horrors, both as victims and as perpetrators. People view the state as at once a source of persecution and succor, of suffering and potential benefits. Nelson is clear that, since few escaped some sort of collaboration in the violence, Guatemala's current predicament is that of pervasive *desconfianza*—a loss of trust and bad faith in social relations with others and with the state.

Given the ongoing lack of transparency, trust, or accountability, Nelson identifies a two-faced character in people's identities, entailing the regular use of concealment, secrecy, and masquerade. As she puts it, in the postwar climate, Guatemalans are prone to tell stories involving doubleness, deception, and duplicity (*engaño*),[15] stories in which the faces of perpetrator and victim are not easily distinguished. As the discussions of Montejo, Theidon, and Nelson foreground, efforts to identify the sources and perpetrators of violence in Guatemala or Peru have become much less straightforward in the postconflict era. These efforts also fail to address the experience of violent legacies, where that sort of clear disambiguation does not reflect the daily business of living with these legacies.

Interpreting Nonstate Violence Today

In recent years the perceived sources of pervasive regional violence are many and varied and the explanations at least as diverse. They include structural inequalities, lack of opportunities and social mobility, the absence of government institutions or the existence of underdeveloped ones, the impacts of U.S. policies, the drug war, proliferating gangs, legacies of past violence, poverty, the negative effects of neoliberalism, the segregation of urban spaces, a still incomplete transition to democracy, lingering authoritarian institutions and behaviors, and new criminal economies— or some combination of these (see, inter alia, Adams 2012; Arias and Goldstein 2010; Bowden 2011; Cruz 2011; Imbusch, Misse, and Carrión 2011; Johnson et al. 2013; Pearce 2010).

For present purposes I do not propose to sort through these competing explanations. As Bergman (2006, 223) observed in an earlier review of the scholarship on crime and insecurity in Latin American democracies, little of a definitive sort can be said about causality in efforts to explain the region's high crime rates. This is still largely the case, as Bowden (2011) has suggested in his arresting recent discussion of the futility of trying to make comprehensive sense of the horrors of "murder city" (Juárez, Mexico). Instead, I want to draw attention to some of the ways this growing array of often conflicting interpretations about the sources and reasons for persistent violence in Latin America has itself become an evident challenge, as governments and civil society actors struggle to make sense of, combat, and reduce crime and violence.

As considered above, political violence and its legacies have contributed directly to a set of current social and cultural conditions in Latin America: hard to repair fracturing and fragmentation of the body politic, festering distrust of government and of others in postconflict societies, increased ambiguity in distinguishing victimizer from victim, and the confounding of previously well-defined or traditional social locations. These contextual factors contribute directly to continuing violence in the region. In this section, I compare two cases of nonpolitical violence characteristic of Latin America in recent years, femicide and lynching or near-lynching, as a way to highlight how these contextual factors are destabilizing definitive understandings of today's types of violence. Both femicide and lynching challenge existing frameworks for making sense of violence. And a prevailing lack of consensus about culpability, the identities of victims, and the meaning of these acts has, in turn, complicated potential responses to them.

Gender-based violence and instances of femicide—particularly in Mexico, Honduras, Bolivia, and El Salvador—are on the rise.[16] Perhaps the most notorious case of femicide in Latin America to date is the sexual serial killing in and around the border city of Juárez. Between 1993 and 2005 there were a total of 150 cases of femicide in Juárez, and as of 2011 the total number of kidnapped, raped, and disappeared or murdered women in this city had risen to more than 900 (Tabuenca Córdoba 2011, 115). The Juárez case shows how contradictory public representations of women, as agents and subjects of violence, both silence victims' voices and undermine the possibilities for a constructive and collective response to the problem of femicide (see Tabuenca Córdoba 2011).[17]

The Juárez case illustrates several conjoined problems. The vast majority of victims have been low-income factory workers, that is, young single women working in factories outside the home, often as primary family wage earners. In response to the femicide in Juárez, both the media and politicians have often described victims as working-class "women of dubious reputation" engaged in "looseness/mischief" (Tabuenca Córdoba 2011, 116, 124). The autonomy that these women exercised invited the label of prostitute, and Juárez residents described them as leading a "double life": "chaste factory work by day and sinful bar-hopping by night" (Nathan 1999, 26). The victims of femicide in Juárez have been the subject of a misogynist public discourse that too often appears to blame the victims, as "names with no meaning" (Tabuenca Córdoba 2011, 133), who have received little protection from the state and have been denied basic constitutional rights.

As reference to these women's "double life" suggests, the violence of femicide is hard to disentangle from women's rapidly changing identities in Mexican society. They are victims, in other words, of evolving tensions between the private space of the home and the autonomy of new economic roles, the traditional cultural expectations for womanhood and accusations of sexual degeneracy, still patriarchal family hierarchies and the transgressive freedoms of factory work. Church responses to femicide in Juárez have been mixed. Especially initially, the victims were presented as "fallen women" who deserved their fate. As the femicide epidemic unfolded in Juárez, the Catholic Church maintained a steadfast silence (see Maher 2013), in large part because of its ambivalence about the increasing contradictions surrounding women's traditional and changing roles. This is in contrast to the eventual responses of a variety of churches in communities where this tragedy continues to unfold: they have become local centers of activism in efforts to raise public awareness.[18]

Present debate about acts of lynching across the region is also a case in point of the current instability of meaning surrounding many acts of violence. As recently analyzed by Goldstein, frequent lynchings and attempted lynchings along Bolivia's urban periphery have been variously understood by participants and observers as an urban expression of indigenous customary law and communal justice; an illustration of the agency of the mob and irrationality of the crowd; an indication of local lack of confidence in a corrupt judicial system; a collective expression of rage and frustration by a community where state law does not operate; a practice intended to bring about security; or a form of collective organization, demonstration of unity, and warning to potential delinquents. One challenge in coming to terms with lynching events, at least in Bolivia, is that these accounts are not mutually exclusive.

As Goldstein (2012, 148) is at pains to emphasize, the meaning of any given lynching event is unstable, often contradictory, and characterized by public ambivalence, uncertainty, disagreement, and regular debate. At present there exists little consensus—among observers, participants, or public opinion—on the import of lynching events along Latin America's urban frontiers. Religious responses to lynching in Bolivia reflect this debate, and pastoral interventions are notably absent along the urban periphery, though the Bolivian Episcopal Conference is on record calling the perceived savagery of such forms of community justice "anti-Christian" (185). As with the case of femicide, part of the problem is that the identities of community members taking part in lynching are, in some respects, suspect. They are at once indigenous, poor, desperate, and responding on their own to chronic problems of property theft and a lack of effective municipal policing. Yet they are not simply victims but also, controversially, vigilantes in their own right.

The duplicitous stories of *engaño* of Guatemala's reckoning with its postwar present, the side-by-side intimacy of enemies in post–Shining Path Peru, the "double life" attributed to the women of Juárez, and the ambivalent victimhood and vigilantism of lynching in Bolivia are all part of a current landscape in Latin America where the social locations of violence are debated, and criminality and violent actors relate in uncertain ways to legality and the victims of violence. Casting about for how to describe this troubling circumstance, scholars of violence in Latin America have turned to Primo Levi's concept of the gray zone, his effort to describe the nature of his experience in a concentration camp (see Adams 2012; Auyero 2007; Bourgois 2001). The "gray zone" is characterized by the breakdown of a division between the "we" of victimhood and the "they" of persecutor, where both victim and oppressor are "in the same trap" (Levi 1989, 24), where all survivors share a violent bond of complicity and collaboration with their torturers and persecutors and victims alike suffer the almost total erasure of identity.

Writing about political violence in Argentina, Auyero (2007) describes the gray zone as those spaces where the meanings and practices of political culture blur the lines between state coercion and popular collective action. For our purposes, in contrast to the political violence of the past, many expressions of violence across postconflict Latin America today—particularly nonstate violence—resist any easy set of distinctions about causes, perpetrators, and victims. This categorical unease is a major part of the difficulty of mounting any organized collective response to such violence at present.

Violent Legacies and Absent States

Despite expectations to the contrary (see Keane 2004; Payne 2008), the turn to democratic governance has not meant an end to pervasive violence in Latin America, as we have seen. As Holston (2008, 271) noted for Brazil, "Precisely as democracy has taken root, new kinds of violence, injustice, corruption and impunity have increased dramatically."[19] Scholars have sought to describe the continuous facts of violence in the aftermath of democratic consolidation throughout the region, referring to Latin America's "disjunctive democracies" (Holston 2006), "violent democracies" (Arias and Goldstein 2010), "perverse democracies" (Pearce 2010), or "uncivil democracies" (Imbusch, Misse, and Carrión 2011). Other commentators have identified the "extreme cruelty" accompanying approaches to governance in the region (see Franco 2013), characterized by the "everyday incivilities" (Holston 2008, 275) and the myriad dimensions of insecurity that inform what Rotker and Goldman (2002, 12)—referring to the deterioration of security in Latin America's violence-wracked cities—has called "the citizenship of fear."[20] Too often, state conduct is itself violent when institutions of governance are ineffectual or wholly absent, contributing to the routine insecurities of everyday life.

A recent Inter-American Commission on Human Rights report (IACHR 2009, 11) on citizen security noted the "illegal and arbitrary use of force" by many Latin American governments, which effectively undermines public confidence in the rule of law. The sources and circumstances of illegality are important to note; they include the continued operation of agencies, institutions, relationships, and behaviors from the preceding authoritarian periods or protracted conflicts as part of nominally democratic governments. Their incorporation, as integral to the contemporary experience of democratic states and as part of the failure of ongoing institution building (particularly institutions of state security), is a regular source for the reproduction of criminal violence.

Cruz (2010, 2) notes, for example, that when polled over 60 percent of the populations in Guatemala, Venezuela, Bolivia, and Argentina assumed that police are routinely involved in criminal activities. Yashar (2013, 432) has recently highlighted the frequent mediation of the relationship between states and citizens in Latin America by the operation of informal and illicit institutions. This mediation includes such violent actors as gangs and criminal organizations that function through mechanisms of patronage and clientage in ways that muddle any clear distinctions between criminal police as state representatives, on the one hand, and criminals with direct access to the resources and authority of the state, on the other.

Cruz (2011) notes the continued role of "violent entrepreneurs" in government in Central America, carried over from the civil wars of the 1980s. He describes these as typically private, informal, and armed civilian collaborators who mutate into roles in criminal organizations while using state institutions as a front. In a similar analysis, Arias (2006) explores the localized dimensions of contemporary "criminal governance" by drug traffickers along Brazil's urban periphery. He details the varieties of informal relationships and incentives—like trading votes for order and support—between government officials, civic leaders, and traffickers, who run virtual parastate fiefdoms with police protection (see also Goldstein 2003).

Drug gangs finance community festivities and provide order, loans, infrastructure, and basic services to local residents, who in turn support the gangs. Criminals are able to appropriate state power through their connections to state officials. Arias (2006) describes criminal governance of this sort as a form of localized sovereignty that undermines human security and democratic guarantees. Such an analysis shows how violence has remained an instrument of political rule. Newly democratizing states have not made clean breaks with the past, and state actors may remain key perpetrators despite the formal end of authoritarian rule. Such a context, in which it is difficult to distinguish criminals from the police, helps us understand better the ways, and the extent to which, violence is a fundamental basis for everyday interactions with the state in Latin America.

Organized criminal violence is, likewise, evidence for the continuing incompleteness of the state (see Koonings and Kruijt 2004). Government voids and state failures to provide basic services effectively and reliably are a big part of the story of why life continues to be a struggle for so many in Latin America (see Johnson, this vol.). In such cases violence proliferates in what O'Donnell (2004) has called "brown areas," that is, specific zones within a nation-state characterized by the lack of public institutions or by their dysfunction, where state-sanctioned rights are often irrelevant. Institutional weaknesses are a large part of this problem. Cuervo Restrepo's (2003) characterization of Colombia's malfunctioning criminal justice system, including persistent impunity, clientelism, the lack of judicial autonomy, judicial corruption, a long backlog of cases, erratic enforcement of judgments, and a fear to prosecute, is typical in this regard.

An alarming account of violence replacing the absent state is Scheper-Hughes's (1993) harrowing analysis of the routinization of death in Brazil's favelas. In a context of chronic scarcity and government neglect, amid the generalized collapse of social support and community and the "emptied out" lives of favela dwellers, Scheper-Hughes chronicles the fatalism of favela mothers toward high infant mortality and the routine deaths of their babies. Favela mothers express little or no emotional attachment to these infants and understand them as dispensable, nameless beings whose deaths are of no real account and go unmourned. Scheper-Hughes equated the violence of this state of affairs with the near-total erasure of the personhood of these dead infants.[21]

Another expression of the problem of the absent state is the diminution and segregation of public spaces, as those who can afford to do so now retreat behind what Caldeira (1996), referring to São Paulo, has called "fortified enclaves": typically gated communities, privately owned, and protected by an increasingly privatized security apparatus.[22] As of 2008, Brazil had a total of 2,904 registered private security services, with personnel that outnumbered the police (OAS 2012, 140). As with the parastate spaces controlled by criminal militias, or the marginal urban barrios where lynchings are one expression of community self-help strategies, or the recent emergence of self-defense groups in Mexico to combat criminal gangs,[23] or fortified urban enclaves in Brazil, "security," not "rights," is the idiom of response to the perceived dangers generated by the inadequacy of state services.

Violence and Negative Solidarity

In addition to the problem of the absent state, Latin America today exhibits several forms of social membership, sources of solidarity, and cultural belonging that are also significantly constructed through everyday conceptions of violence and corruption. Elsewhere I have called this "negative solidarity" (Albro 2010, 191–93), referring to processes of identity formation among provincial Bolivian political operatives, culturally grounded in shared experiences of struggle, stigma, privation, displacement, estrangement, and violence. The violent legacies and experiences composing different negative solidarities are a dimension of the everyday in Latin America that we should not neglect, since they underscore the extent to which violence remains a problematically constitutive source of social solidarity and cultural belonging.[24]

If, as Anderson (1991) has classically explained, cultural belonging in the nation is conventionally understood to derive from the imagined community of participation in the symbols and rituals of national identity, negative solidarities are underwritten instead by shared histories and experiences of tragedy and violence. Examples already discussed include the testimonial "community of the witness," the script of "shared tragedy" in post-Pinochet Chile, and the "citizenship of fear" of urban insecurity. Latin American churches have likewise served as avenues for such alternative solidarities. For some Central American gang members, religious conversion and participation in Evangelical churches have become an exit strategy, where one set of identity markers, symbols, rituals, and community is traded for another, those of the church (see Brenneman 2011 and this vol.). Burdick (1990, 154), in turn, has described how working-class women, faced with daily domestic conflict aggravated by the suspension of traditional institutions of social control during Brazil's most recent authoritarian period, sought out Pentecostal churches to build new social solidarity "through the experience of suffering." Theidon (this vol.) similarly describes efforts of social repair among Evangelical former combatants in Colombia as rituals of rupture and acts of "redemption and reconciliation" intended to leave their former identities behind.

Green (1999) describes a comparable scenario of the embrace of Evangelical churches by widows who are victims and survivors of Guatemala's civil war. Amid the collapse of the traditional gender division of labor caused by the removal of men from their communities, these women have become more economically vulnerable. In a context of an inconclusive end to political conflict and ongoing militarization of daily interactions, and where community civil patrols continue to denounce family, friends, and other community members to the local military, community relations themselves have become an expression of struggle and potential source of violence. Relationships among family members continue to be marred by distrust, fear, and terror. Green (1999, 120) describes how many of these widows suffer from *susto* (fright), a kind of illness with non-specific symptoms. However, their participation in Evangelical churches offers an opportunity to form relationships through their shared malady in rituals of healing that build sociality, where personal memory and pain become a regenerative basis of new forms of community.

Present-day Mexico offers a different example of negative solidarity at the level of the nation-state. Lomnitz (2005) sees Mexican national identity as intimately connected to the variegated depreciations of life, which he identifies as a dominant feature of Mexico's public sphere at present, depreciations that also directly inform the upsurge of violence with which Mexicans are currently grappling. Lomnitz elaborates the many connections in Mexico between death, the state, and the popular imagination, in the process extending what García Canclini and Rosas Mantecón (1996) described as "democratic forms of degradation," such as widespread pollution, corruption, and urban violence. Lomnitz understands such depreciations as a direct source of a process of national identification through common problems and forms of decay instead of, say, the positive rituals and symbols of nationhood identified by Anderson or shared rights-based membership in the body politic.

For Lomnitz, the ongoing deterioration of social conditions in Mexico—the violence, insecurity, fear, impunity, daily urban risks, and collapsed buying power currently experienced by ordinary people—is expressed through current popular enthusiasms for "fatalism" as a reified national trait used to rationalize law-breaking behavior and public celebrations of death. In a comparable analysis, Fowler (2006, 1) similarly identifies Mexican national identity with a historical "vicious circle of unresolved tragedies," which finds its sources in repeated acts of bad faith on the part of the Mexican state. The "fatalism" Lomnitz describes as an aspect of the popular imagination is a growing part of what it means to be "Mexican." And as these several cases of negative solidarity suggest, violence, corruption, and the illicit underwrite social relations and cultural belonging in ways hard to displace from people's lives.

Violence and the Future of Rights

Latin America's transition to democracy has been accompanied in recent decades by an intense period of constitutional change across the region, beginning with Brazil in 1988 and Colombia in 1991 and ending with Bolivia in 2009 (see Negretto 2012). This most recent round of constitutional reforms has sought to expand the availability of rights beyond individual civil and political rights to incorporate a broad array of new collective political, economic, and cultural rights (see Van Cott 2008), with the goals of decolonizing and enfranchising diverse historically marginalized subnational groups and identities.

Beginning in the authoritarian period, religious responses to violence also embraced a new moral vocabulary of rights through adoption of the "natural law tradition" and new Church-lawyer collaborations in the effort to fight state oppression. In this way, religious advocates in the cause of human rights utilized the language of law while helping to nurture "the expanding reach of rights" (see chapters by Levine, Kelly, Wilde, and Queiroz, this vol.). But these rights-based approaches were responses to the circumstances of state violence of that era and not the mostly nonstate violence of today. As this chapter has shown, it is often harder categorically to identify "victims" as rights-bearing subjects today, and the concept of rights is itself challenged by the actual experience of everyday life.

If classically the benefits of nation-states are understood to include the extension of protection, services, rights, and membership (see Marshall 1963), the pervasive contemporary facts of violence highlighted here are to some extent undermining the exercise of rights. Throughout the hemisphere the specific rights of political membership have been actively "contested" of late (see Yashar 2005), as indigenous peoples, women, LGBT groups, and even the middle class have at different moments mobilized to question rights regimes or to claim additional rights. Constitutional change and the expansion of rights have occurred alongside popular expressions of disillusionment and groundswells of protest over the lack of tangible benefits for ordinary people. Repeated large-scale street protests in Brazil in 2013 and 2014 are just the most recent in a succession of sometimes violent popular mobilizations articulating dissatisfaction with how public resources are claimed, used, and redistributed (see Saad-Filho 2013).

In Latin America today there remain too many situations where the rule of law does not operate effectively, a circumstance that contributes to the perception of rights as provisional and unevenly applied. Legal regimes in Brazil, for example, maintain close relationships to illegality. Holston (2008, 137) has explored the "unstable and perverse relation between [the] illegal and legal" and the several ways that "illegality produces legality and rights" (145) along the urban peripheries of São Paulo, as different actors seek to solidify initially murky claims of ownership to land or property. He describes a scenario in which distinctions between the legal and the illegal are not sharp and the law is a "means of manipulation, complication, stratagem, and violence" (203), to establish and enforce legal claims in order to capture resources. Here the illicit and illegal are part and parcel of efforts to produce and to claim rights in ways similar to what I described above for social and cultural relations.

Historically human rights have been a primary tool in many efforts to hold the agents of violence accountable in Latin America (see Keck and Sikkink 1998; Brysk 2013). And yet one of the pernicious effects of the consistently violent terms of everyday life across the region has been the increasingly negative perception of rights, for example, among victims of petty crime and police neglect along the region's growing urban periphery. There, criminals are often perceived by would-be lynchers to have rights at the expense of the community and of justice (Goldstein 2012). In this scenario rights are perceived to be part of the problem.

Governments contribute to the popular perception that the distribution of rights in Latin America is at best "differentiated" (see Holston 2008) when they decline to police some forms of violence—as has been the case with femicide—or fail to act on behalf of victims. This is also true of government scapegoating or use of hard-line *mano dura* policies in the authoritarian mode to "defend" the state against perceived internal enemies (see Adams 2012); El Salvador's ineffective policy between 2003 and 2009 of the largely indiscriminate incarceration of gang members in its war on gangs is one among many contemporary examples. Current forms of violence transgress old categories and, together with a more ambivalent reception of rights, raise the question of whether a rights-based approach will be an effective tool in the future, as it has been in the past, for secular and religious efforts to confront violence.

Notes

1. Quoted in Sibylla Brodzinsky, "Inside San Pedro Sula—the Most Violent City in the World," *Guardian*, May 15, 2013.

2. Rory Carroll, "Rampant Violence Is Latin America's 'Worst Epidemic,'" *Guardian*, October 8, 2008.

3. Jo Tuckman, "Mexico's Drug Wars: Mystery Surrounds How Many Are Dying, and Who," *Guardian*, December 8, 2011.

4. See Aaron Shulman, "The Rise of Femicide," *New Republic*, December 29, 2010.

5. Hasan Tuluy, "Latin America: Violence Threatens a Decade of Progress," available at http://blogs.worldbank.org/latinamerica/latin-america-violence -threatens-a-decade-of-progress.

6. What I have described here is just a sample of the range and breadth of the kinds of violence across the region, which also includes some stranger horrors, such as persistent rumors of foreign organ donor trafficking (Samper 2002) and the rising trend of acid attacks on women in Colombia—otherwise almost unheard of outside conservative Muslim and Hindu parts of the world (Guerrero 2013).

7. The term *reckoning* has been used by various authors to describe the response to state violence and ongoing efforts by societies to come to terms with that violence, including for Guatemala (Nelson 2009), Chile (Stern 2010), and Brazil (Atencio 2014).

8. If this contrast is frequently drawn, exceptions during this period, such as Colombia and Mexico, should also be recognized (see Wright 2007).

9. An example of this tendency is the recent volume edited by Johnson, Salvatore, and Spierenburg (2013) on murder in Latin America. Despite rising murder rates across the hemisphere and despite the fact that much of this increase represents varieties of nonstate violence, their volume focuses on cases of state-supported murder.

10. It is not just that, for example, in the case of "femicide" today, most states do not specifically define such a crime in their criminal codes. It is also that many such victims are not always treated as victims at all, either by law enforcement, or the media, or the court of public opinion.

11. Beginning with Bolivia in 1982, there has been a total of thirteen official truth commissions in Latin America, with Brazil's the most recent, created in

2011. This does not include many additional and similar commissions and reports organized and produced by nongovernmental human rights organizations or by church groups.

12. Pastoral responses have also been comparable to efforts like those of Argentina's Madres. As Tate (this vol.) details, grassroots religious interventions in the now fifty-year conflict between Colombia's government and the FARC have focused on acts of "public commemoration," including street theater and the creation of a Memory Museum.

13. This said, it is notable that, while the Madres often publicly expressed their cause in religious terms—drawing connections between their own plight and that of the Virgin Mary—and while the Madres sought the support of the Catholic Church in Argentina, the Church hierarchy made it clear that it did not agree with their public protest and did not support them (see Guzman 2002).

14. As is well known, Stoll (1999) questioned factual details of Menchú's widely read testimony of Guatemala's counterinsurgency war, based on his ethnographic work in the Ixil Triangle, also the setting for Menchú's account. Here I am not concerned with the relative accuracy of Menchú's narrative so much as with the possibilities and limits of her testimonial approach as a way to publicize state violence.

15. Stories of *engaño* also figure in Theidon's (2012) account of postwar legacies of violence in Ayacucho, Peru, often as part of people's explanations of how they came to participate in Shining Path.

16. See Sara Miller Llana and Sibylla Brodzinsky, "Violence against Women in Latin America: Is it Getting Worse?," *Christian Science Monitor*, November 20, 2012.

17. It also illustrates the vulnerability of women to violence, given their continued "legacy of dependent citizenship" (Haney 2012, 238) in many parts of Latin America.

18. Damien Cave, "Angels Rushing in Where Others Fear to Tread," *New York Times*, November 9, 2011.

19. Given the pervasiveness of violence and its stubborn ubiquity in the region, and despite three and four decades of democratic governance in many instances, the problematic, uneven, and still violent unfolding of "actually existing democracy" (see Fraser 1990) across Latin America has provoked a reevaluation of the ways violence and democratic governance coexist and, in some cases, might also be mutually entailed.

20. Space does not permit more development of this theme, but the ubiquity of violence in Latin America is also frequently connected to the absence or underdevelopment of citizenship, described as a case of democracy "without citizenship" (Howard, Hume, and Oslender 2007, 719) or characterized by "dangerous spaces of citizenship" (Holston 2008, 275).

21. Scheper-Hughes's (1993) discussion of the fatalistic worldview of mothers in Brazil's favelas vis-à-vis the frequent deaths of their infants illustrates what Herzfeld (1992) has aptly called the "social production of indifference."

22. Arias and Goldstein (2010) suggested that the violence characteristic of the urban peripheries of fast-growing Latin American cities, as well as the privatization of public space, is a direct result of the neoliberal retreat of the state that accompanied democratization in the region. Brenneman (this vol.), meanwhile, refers to the emergence of "free-market violence" in Central America.

23. See Patricio Asfura-Heim and Ralph H. Espach, "The Rise of Mexico's Self-Defense Forces," *Foreign Affairs*, July–August 2013.

24. Here I engage with Richard Rorty's (1989) exploration of democratic promise as an exercise in solidarity building opposed to cruelty, where solidarity building is understood as a process that widens public and political frames of belonging and so minimizes conflict as a result of social or cultural differences. In contrast to Rorty, I focus on the ways and extent to which a public culture of democracy—as the potentially enabling social context and cultural content for a democratic politics across the region—can also problematically generate a lack of solidarity or conceptions of negative solidarity that themselves originate in experiences of violence.

References

Adams, Tani Marilena. 2012. *Chronic Violence and Its Reproduction: Perverse Trends in Social Relationships, Citizenship, and Democracy in Latin America*. Washington, DC: Woodrow Wilson International Center for Scholars.

Albro, Robert. 2010. *Roosters at Midnight: Indigenous Signs and Stigma in Local Bolivian Politics*. Santa Fe, NM: School for Advanced Research Press.

Anderson, Benedict. 1991. *Imagined Communities: Reflections on the Origin and Spread of Nationalism*. London: Verso.

Argentine National Commission on the Disappeared (ANCD). 1986. *Nunca Más: The Report of the Argentine National Commission on the Disappeared*. New York: Farrar, Straus and Giroux.

Arias, Enrique Desmond. 2006. "The Dynamics of Criminal Governance: Networks and Social Order in Rio de Janeiro." *Journal of Latin American Studies* 38, no. 2 (May): 293–325.

Arias, Enrique Desmond, and Daniel M. Goldstein, eds. 2010. *Violent Democracies in Latin America*. Durham, NC: Duke University Press.

Atencio, Rebecca J. 2014. *Memory's Turn: Reckoning with Dictatorship in Brazil*. Madison: University of Wisconsin Press.

Auyero, Javier. 2007. *Routine Politics and Violence in Argentina: The Gray Zone of State Power*. Cambridge: Cambridge University Press.

Bergman, Marcelo. 2006. "Crime and Citizen Security in Latin America: The Challenges for New Scholarship." *Latin American Research Review* 41, no. 2 (June): 213–27.

Beverley, John. 2004. *Testimonio: On the Politics of Truth*. Minneapolis: University of Minnesota Press.

Bosco, Fernando J. 2004. "Human Rights Politics and Scaled Performances of Memory: Conflicts among the Madres de Plaza de Mayo in Argentina." *Social & Cultural Geography* 5, no. 3 (September): 381–402.

Bott, Sarah, Alessandra Guedes, Mary Goodwin, and Jennifer Adams Mendoza. 2012. *Violence against Women in Latin America and the Caribbean: A Comparative Analysis of Population-Based Data from 12 Countries*. Washington, DC: Pan American Health Organization.

Bourgois, Philippe. 2001. "The Power of Violence in War and Peace: Post–Cold War Lessons from El Salvador." *Ethnography* 2, no. 1 (March): 5–34.

Bowden, Charles. 2011. *Murder City: Ciudad Juárez and the Global Economy's New Killing Fields*. New York: Nation Books.

Brenneman, Robert. 2011. *Homies and Hermanos: God and Gangs in Central America*. New York: Oxford University Press.

Brinks, Daniel M. 2008. *The Judicial Response to Police Killings in Latin America: Inequality and the Rule of Law*. New York: Cambridge University Press.

Brysk, Alison, ed. 2013. *The Politics of the Globalization of Law: Getting from Rights to Justice*. New York: Routledge.

Burdick, John. 1990. "Gossip and Secrecy: Women's Articulation of Domestic Conflict in Three Religions of Urban Brazil." *Sociology of Religion* 51, no. 2: 153–70.

Burt, Jo-Marie. 2007. *Political Violence and the Authoritarian State in Peru*. New York: Palgrave Macmillan.

Caldeira, Teresa P. R. 1996. "Fortified Enclaves: The New Urban Segregation." *Public Culture* 8, no. 2: 303–28.

Cruz, José Miguel. 2010. "Police Misconduct and Democracy in Latin America." *Americas Barometer Insights* 33, no. 2.

———. 2011. "Criminal Violence and Democratization in Central America: The Survival of the Violent State." *Latin American Politics and Society* 53, no. 4 (Winter): 1–33.

Cuervo Restrepo, Jorge Iván. 2003. "La reforma del estado y el ajuste estructural en América Latina: El caso de Colombia." *Revista Opera* 3: 67–110.

Esparza, Marcia, Henry R. Huttenbach, and Daniel Feierstein, eds. 2011. *State Violence and Genocide in Latin America: The Cold War Years*. New York: Routledge.

Fernández Benítez, Hans M. 2010. "'The moment of testimonio is over': Problemas teóricos y perspectivas de los estudios testimoniales." *Íkala, Revista de Lenguaje y Cultura* 15, no. 24: 47–71.

Fowler, Will. 2006. "The Children of the *Chingada*." In *Political Violence and the Construction of National Identity*, edited by Will Fowler and Peter Lambert, 1–18. New York: Palgrave Macmillan.

Fowler, Will, and Peter Lambert, eds. 2006. *Political Violence and the Construction of National Identity in Latin America*. New York: Palgrave Macmillan.

Franco, Jean. 2013. *Cruel Modernity.* Durham, NC: Duke University Press.

Fraser, Nancy. 1990. "Rethinking the Public Sphere: A Contribution to the Critique of Actually Existing Democracy." *Social Text*, no. 25–26: 56–80.

Frühling, H. Hugo, and Joseph Tulchin, eds. 2003. *Crime and Violence in Latin America: Security, Democracy, and the State.* Washington, DC: Woodrow Wilson International Center for Scholars.

García Canclini, Néstor, and Ana Rosas Mantecón. 1996. "Las multiples ciudades de los viajeros." In *La ciudad de los viajeros: Travesías e imaginarios urbanos: México, 1940–2000*, edited by Néstor García Canclini, Alejandro Castellanos, and Ana Rosas Mantecón, 61–106. Mexico, DF: Editorial Grijalbo.

Gilmore, Leigh. 2003. "Jurisdictions: I, Rigoberta Menchú, the Kiss, and Scandalous Self-Representation in the Age of Memoir and Trauma." *Signs: Journal of Women in Culture and Society* 28, no. 2 (Winter): 695–718.

Godoy, Angelina Snodgrass. 2006. *Popular Injustice: Violence, Community, and Law in Latin America.* Stanford, CA: Stanford University Press.

Goldstein, Daniel M. 2012. *Outlawed: Between Security and Rights in a Bolivian City.* Durham, NC: Duke University Press.

Goldstein, Donna M. 2003. *Laughter out of Place: Race, Class, Violence, and Sexuality in a Rio Shantytown.* Berkeley: University of California Press.

Grandin, Greg. 2005. "The Instruction of Great Catastrophe: Truth Commissions, National History, and State Formation in Argentina, Chile, and Guatemala." *American Historical Review* 110, no. 1 (February): 46–67.

Grandin, Greg, and Gilbert M. Joseph, eds. 2010. *Century of Revolution: Insurgent and Counterinsurgent Violence during Latin America's Long Cold War.* Durham, NC: Duke University Press.

Green, Linda. 1999. *Fear as a Way of Life: Mayan Widows in Rural Guatemala.* New York: Columbia University Press.

Guerrero, Lisa. 2013. "Burns Due to Acid Assault in Bogotá, Colombia." *Burns* 39, no. 5 (August): 1018–23.

Gugelberger, Georg M. 1996. *The Real Thing: Testimonial Discourse and Latin America.* Durham, NC: Duke University Press.

Guzman Buovard, Marguerite. 2002. *Revolutionizing Motherhood: The Mothers of the Plaza de Mayo*. New York: Rowman and Littlefield.

Haney, Charlotte. 2012. "Imperiled Femininity: The Dismembering of Citizenship in Northern Mexico." *Journal of Latin American and Caribbean Anthropology* 17, no. 2 (July): 238–56.

Herzfeld, Michael. 1992. *The Social Production of Indifference*. Chicago: University of Chicago Press.

Holston, James. 2006. "Citizenship in Disjunctive Democracies." In *Citizenship in Latin America*, edited by Joseph S. Tulchin and Meg Ruthenberg, 75–94. Boulder, CO: Lynne Rienner.

———. 2008. *Insurgent Citizenship: Disjunctions of Democracy and Modernity in Brazil*. Princeton, NJ: Princeton University Press.

Howard, David, Mo Hume, and Ulrich Oslender. 2007. "Violence, Fear, and Development in Latin America: A Critical Overview." *Development in Practice* 17, no. 6 (November): 713–24.

Imbusch, Peter, Michael Misse, and Fernando Carrión. 2011. "Violence Research in Latin America and the Caribbean: A Literature Review." *International Journal of Conflict and Violence* 5, no. 1: 87–154.

Inter-American Commission on Human Rights (IACHR). 2009. *Report on Citizen Security and Human Rights*. Washington, DC. Available at www.oas .org/en/iachr/docs/pdf/CitizenSec.pdf.

Jelin, Elizabeth. 2003. *State Repression and the Labors of Memory*. Minneapolis: University of Minnesota Press.

Johnson, Eric A., Ricardo Salvatore, and Pieter Spierenburg, eds. 2013. *Murder and Violence in Modern Latin America*. London: Wiley-Blackwell.

Keane, John. 2004. *Violence and Democracy*. New York: Cambridge University Press.

Keck, Margaret E., and Kathryn Sikkink. 1998. *Activists beyond Borders: Advocacy Networks in International Politics*. Ithaca, NY: Cornell University Press.

Koonings, Kees, and Dirk Kruijt, eds. 2004. *Armed Actors: Organised Violence and State Failure in Latin America*. New York: Zed Books.

Laplante, Lisa J., and Kimberly Theidon. 2007. "Truth with Consequences: Justice and Reparations in Post-Truth Commission Peru." *Human Rights Quarterly* 29, no. 1 (February): 228–50.

Levi, Primo. 1989. *The Drowned and the Saved*. New York: Vintage International.

Lewis, Paul H. 2005. *Authoritarian Regimes in Latin America: Dictators, Despots, and Tyrants*. New York: Rowman and Littlefield.

Lomnitz, Claudio. 2005. *Death and the Idea of Mexico*. New York: Zone Books.

Maher, Monica A. 2013. "Spiritualities of Social Engagement: Women Resisting Violence in Mexico and Honduras." In *Religion and Politics in America's*

Borderlands, edited by Sarah Azaransky and Orlando Espín, 119–42. Lanham, MD: Lexington Books.

Marshall, Thomas Humphrey. 1963. "Citizenship and Social Class." In *Class, Citizenship, and Social Development: Essays by T. H. Marshall*, edited by T. H. Marshall, 71–134. Garden City, NY: Doubleday.

Menchú, Rigoberta. 1983. *I, Rigoberta Menchú: An Indian Woman in Guatemala.* London: Verso Books.

Montejo, Victor. 1999. *Voices from Exile: Violence and Survival in Modern Maya History.* Norman: University of Oklahoma Press.

Nathan, Debbie. 1999. "Work, Sex and Danger in Ciudad Juárez." *NACLA Report on the Americas* 33 (December): 24–30.

Negretto, Gabriel L. 2012. "Replacing and Amending Constitutions: The Logic of Constitutional Change in Latin America." *Law & Society Review* 46, no. 4 (December): 749–79.

Nelson, Diane M. 2009. *Reckoning: The Ends of War in Guatemala.* Durham, NC: Duke University Press.

O'Donnell, Guillermo A. 2004. "Why the Rule of Law Matters." *Journal of Democracy* 15, no. 4 (October): 32–46.

Oglesby, Elizabeth. 2007. "Educating Citizens in Postwar Guatemala: Historical Memory, Genocide, and the Culture of Peace." *Radical History Review* 97: 77–98.

Organzation of American States (OAS). 2012. *Report on Citizen Security in the Americas.* Washington, DC: OAS Hemispheric Security Observatory. Available at www.oas.org/dsp/alertamerica/Report/Alertamerica2012.pdf.

Payne, Leigh. 2008. *Unsettling Accounts: Neither Truth nor Reconciliation in Confessions of State Violence.* Durham, NC: Duke University Press.

Pearce, Jenny. 2010. "Perverse State Formation and Securitized Democracy in Latin America." *Democratization* 17, no. 2: 286–306.

Robben, Antonius C. G. M. 2005. *Political Violence and Trauma in Argentina.* Philadelphia: University of Pennsylvania Press.

Rorty, Richard. 1989. *Contingency, Irony, and Solidarity.* New York: Cambridge University Press.

Rotker, Susan, and Katherine Goldman, eds. 2002. *Citizens of Fear: Urban Violence in Latin America.* New Brunswick, NJ: Rutgers University Press.

Saad-Filho, Alfredo. 2013. "Mass Protests under 'Left Neoliberalism': Brazil, June–July 2013." *Critical Sociology* 39, no. 5 (September): 657–69.

Samper, David. 2002. "Cannibalizing Kids: Rumor and Resistance in Latin America." *Journal of Folklore Research* 39, no. 1 (January–April): 1–32.

Sanford, Victoria. 2003. *Buried Secrets: Truth and Human Rights in Guatemala.* New York: Palgrave Macmillan.

Scheper-Hughes, Nancy. 1993. *Death without Weeping: The Violence of Everyday Life in Brazil.* Berkeley: University of California Press.

Schirmer, Jennifer G. 1998. *The Guatemalan Military Project: A Violence Called Democracy.* Philadelphia: University of Pennsylvania Press.

Starn, Orin. 1999. *Nightwatch: The Politics of Protest in the Andes.* Durham, NC: Duke University Press.

Stern, Steve J. 2010. *Reckoning with Pinochet: The Memory Question in Democratic Chile, 1989–2006.* Durham, NC: Duke University Press.

Stoll, David. 1999. *Rigoberta Menchu and the Story of All Poor Guatemalans.* Boulder, CO: Westview Press.

Tabuenca Córdoba, María Socorro. 2011. "Ciudad Juárez, Femicide, and the State." In *Meanings of Violence in Contemporary Latin America*, edited by Gabriela Polit Dueñas and María Helena Rueda, 115–47. New York: Palgrave Macmillan.

Theidon, Kimberly. 2012. *Intimate Enemies: Violence and Reconciliation in Peru.* Philadelphia: University of Pennsylvania Press.

Timerman, Jacobo. 2002. *Prisoner without a Name, Cell without a Number.* Madison: University of Wisconsin Press.

Turner, Victor Witter. 1968. *The Drums of Affliction: A Study of Religious Processes among the Ndembu of Zambia.* London: International African Institute in association with Hutchinson University Library for Africa, 1968.

Van Cott, Donna Lee. 2008. *Radical Democracy in the Andes.* New York: Cambridge University Press.

Werth, Brenda. 2010. *Theatre, Performance, and Memory Politics in Argentina.* London: Palgrave Macmillan.

Wright, Thomas C. 2007. *State Terrorism in Latin America: Chile, Argentina, and International Rights.* Lanham, MD: Rowman and Littlefield.

Yashar, Deborah J. 2005. *Contesting Citizenship in Latin America: The Rise of Indigenous Movements and the Postliberal Challenge.* New York: Cambridge University Press.

———. 2013. "Institutions and Citizenship: Reflections on the Illicit." In *Shifting Frontiers of Citizenship: The Latin American Experience*, edited by Mario Sznajder, Luis Roniger, and Carlos Forment, 431–58. Leiden: Brill.

Yúdice, George. 1991. "Testimonio and Postmodernism." *Latin American Perspectives* 18, no. 3 (Summer): 15–31.

PART I

RETHINKING RELIGIOUS
CONTRIBUTIONS TO HUMAN RIGHTS

CHAPTER 3

HUMAN RIGHTS AND CHRISTIAN RESPONSIBILITY

Transnational Christian Activism, Human Rights, and State Violence in Brazil and Chile in the 1970s

PATRICK WILLIAM KELLY

"September 11, 1973,"—the date of the Chilean coup that overthrew the elected Socialist president, Salvador Allende—"opened the eyes of many Christians in Chile," said Helmut Frenz in 1976 while on a speaking tour of the United States. A German Lutheran who immigrated to Chile in the 1960s, Frenz crossed denominational lines to help establish the Comité Pro-Paz, the first domestic human rights organization in Chile. Three years after the coup and roughly a year after his own expulsion from Chile for challenging the abuses of the military dictatorship, Frenz reflected on the relationship between Christian theology and the recent rise of human rights concerns in a speech reprinted in the U.S. weekly, *Christianity and Crisis*. Noting "that the Bible makes no mention of human rights" and that the Universal Declaration of Human Rights of 1948 "lie[s] completely beyond the horizon of the Bible," he nonetheless declared that "divine rights constitute human rights." After the coup, Frenz recalled, "it became clear to us . . . that defending human rights and a commitment to human dignity were . . . [integral to] preaching the Gospel."[1]

Frenz's words conveyed an expansive Christian embrace of human rights as an organizing principle for both theology and praxis in the 1970s. Why did Christians, in ever increasing numbers, call for a coupling of human rights and Christian responsibility?[2] This chapter contends that violence in Brazil and Chile in the 1970s provoked a local, regional, and transnational embrace of human rights ideology by Christian activists around the world.

Only in the past ten years has the field of human rights coalesced as a new lens through which historians see and think about the past. What makes this lens useful is that human rights is perhaps our most salient contemporary moral universalism. A group of scholars, led by the intellectual historian Samuel Moyn, sees the 1970s as the breakthrough epoch in human rights history.[3] It was only in that decade, Moyn argues, that the idea of human rights captured the activist imagination in any profound or sustainable way. And it was only on the ruins of previous utopias—Marxism and revolutionary nationalism, to name two of the most significant—that human rights emerged as a viable alternative. Empirical evidence for the argument comes from the steady proliferation in membership of nongovernmental organizations (NGOs) such as Amnesty International, the efforts of dissidents in Eastern Europe and congressional and state actors in the United States and Europe, and the activism of political exiles and others engaged in transnational solidarity during the decade.[4] In short, it was only in the 1970s that human rights became credible as a widespread transnational, at times global, program for social action.

The most startling omission in recent works on the 1970s, however, is the almost total lack of attention to the role of religious actors, both in Latin America and farther afield. Rather than simply the object of human rights activism, religious activists from Latin America and abroad were among the primary agents in the construction of novel forms of transnational activism.[5] If and when they do appear, it is as a mere afterthought to more commonly told stories that emphasize the role of U.S. congressional actors, President Jimmy Carter, or NGOs like Amnesty International. The absence is striking: minimized or inadequately analyzed, the contributions of Christian activists were, in fact, historic. This chapter argues that they spearheaded the turn to human rights and knit together different activist groups in powerful transnational human rights coalitions. Indeed, one would be hard pressed to find actors in the early 1970s as transnational as the Catholic Church and the World Council of Churches, whose reach extended across the globe and penetrated down to local levels in particular places such as the Southern Cone of Latin America (Casanova 1997; Hervieu-Léger 1997; Aranda 2004).

In reviving discussion of religion as a primary component of both international politics and international history,[6] this chapter seeks to analyze the role of transnational religious activists in galvanizing human rights activism, especially in the 1970s. It provides an on-the-ground examination of what Margaret Keck and Kathryn Sikkink (1998) described as transnational advocacy networks, where local and international actors find common cause in campaigns such as those in defense of human rights.[7] However, Keck and Sikkink's revolutionary approach to international relations theory has not always found a receptive audience in the discipline of history, which has tended to focus on local explanations, especially when it discusses religion and rights activism in the Southern Cone in the 1970s (for a recent example, see Bruey 2013). While not dismissive of the local or national (see Wilde, this vol.), this chapter focuses especially on the efforts of transnational religious activists and the direct partnership formed between local and transnational groups, which have not been properly historicized. It places emphasis on the role of Protestant organizations, especially the World Council of Churches, whose source material is both richer and more accessible than that of Roman Catholic groups and whose efforts have yet to be discussed in any depth.

At the same time, this chapter sheds light on the relationship between ideas and action on behalf of human rights. Scholars have generally assumed that action for human rights flows naturally from human rights ideas. But what if the true causality is one where human rights ideas are often shaped and forged as a result of action? Christians expressed rhetorical concern for human rights as part of Christian social thought in various texts and pronouncements throughout the twentieth century. But the linkage of human rights with Christianity fundamentally changed in the 1970s when Christians began to act in a moment of total crisis on behalf of victims of violence in the Southern Cone. In striving to save lives and end suffering in Brazil and Chile, Christians developed a praxis of human rights that had never existed before.

The first section of this chapter traces Christian rights discourse before the 1970s. While Christians spoke of "human rights" before that decade, I argue that scholars should resist relying on explanations that stress the deep roots of Christian human rights. The second section focuses on transnational religious activism related to increasing state violence in Brazil after 1968. Beyond tracing the important efforts of activists in the United States and Brazil, I aim to historicize the contributions of the World Council of Churches (WCC),[8] whose trailblazing efforts in the defense of human rights are reduced, when they are mentioned at all, to its support for the *Tortura: Nunca mais* report in Brazil (Weschler 1990).[9] The third section addresses transnational activism after the Chilean coup of 1973. There, a similar set of trailblazing religious activists, both internally with the ecumenical Chilean Comité Pro-Paz and transnationally through the WCC, formed alliances to protest the Pinochet Junta's use of torture and other repressive acts. Taken together, these three sections point to the 1970s as the exceptional moment for the Christian turn to human rights. It was precisely in response to the violence in the Southern Cone that human rights became a framework for oppositional activism.

Rhetoric without Praxis: Christian Human Rights before the 1970s

What are the origins of concern over human rights in Christian theology and praxis? A sort of rhetorical archaeology would find Christians employing the words *human rights* before the 1970s. Catholics developed some of the first articulations of human rights ideas in the twentieth century. But before human rights could be seen as part of a Christian's primary "responsibility," Catholicism would have to reconcile itself with political liberalism. Catholics long viewed Enlightenment rights with suspicion, for they were centered "in the freedom and autonomy of the individual person, which Catholicism strongly opposed," as Charles Curran (2002, 215) elucidates. But by the mid-1930s, under the direction of Pope Pius XI, this suspicion paled before the specter of the totalitarian state, and it was at this moment—precisely in response to the escalating totalitarian power of the state vis-à-vis the individual—that the Catholic

Church embraced individual rights such as freedom and equality (Moyn 2011, 91; 2015; Curran 2005, 225).

One can find scattered references to human rights starting in the 1930s. In 1938, for instance, Pope Pius XI stated, "Christian teaching alone gives full meaning to the demands of human rights and liberty because it alone gives worth and dignity to human personality" (quoted in Curran 2005, 225).[10] That articulation resonated for some American Catholics on the campus of Notre Dame who created the Committee of Catholics for Human Rights in 1939. In the 1940s, the concept was influenced by the notion of personalism—a school of thought that stressed the dignity of the human person—advocated by figures such as Jacques Maritain and Emmanuel Mounier.[11]

Christian thought more generally most certainly played a significant role in the drafting of the United Nations' Universal Declaration of Human Rights (UDHR) in 1948. Three leading figures who shaped the UDHR—John Humphrey, Charles Malik, and Eleanor Roosevelt—subscribed to some variant of Christian social thought (Moyn 2010, 50, 65). But human rights failed to capture the global imagination in the 1940s.[12] Notably, it inspired no international or transnational human rights movement. While the UN Charter mentioned the concept, that document mainly enshrined national sovereignty.[13] The UDHR, for all the impressive work of its drafting committee, was little more than a glorified set of enumerated rights that lacked enforcement power.[14] While the postwar moment saw religious groups enter transnational alliances in the 1940s—the World Council of Churches originated in 1948—it was not due to any generative force of human rights. The fundamental point is that the 1940s in human rights history, while important, did less than we may think to pave the road on which 1970s activists traveled.

Still, one could argue that the Christian vision of human rights as transcendent and universal, a protection of the individual and a critique of the excesses of the state, was one of the few visions that survived the deep freeze of the Cold War to link the 1948 UDHR with the unexpected ascendance of human rights in the 1970s.[15] Pope John XXIII's deployment of "human rights" in *Pacem in Terris* in 1963 has led many scholars to signal the Second Vatican Council as the essential tipping point in the Christian embrace of human rights.[16] In some senses, they are partly right: Vatican II documents such as *Pacem in Terris* and *Lumen Gentium* showed Christian theologians flirting with notions of human rights. But as Jo Renee Formicola (1988, 86) has argued, Vatican II "gave no specific guidelines by which the Church should proceed in the future to make human rights a reality." Moreover, the early 1960s references to human rights in *Pacem in Terris* are scant compared to their richer theological elaboration in John Paul II's 1979 address to the United Nations, to take only one example.[17] To elevate those early references to human rights, then, is to miss their relative marginality in the 1960s and obscure the moment of their true flowering in the 1970s.

In Latin America, the 1968 Consejo Episcopal Latinoamericano (CELAM) in Medellín produced a concluding document that nodded to human rights in passing.[18] In 1970, several Christian activists from the Americas assembled in New York City for a meeting on the topic "Human Rights and the Liberation of Man in the Americas" under the auspices of a Catholic Inter-American Cooperation Program (Colonnese 1970). These early incidents formed important historical precedents for the rise of human rights activism in South America, of course, and must also be recognized for their role in familiarizing certain actors with a nascent language of human rights. They also reveal how concern over rights violations brought together Catholics and Protestants in ecumenical alliances almost unheard of before this time.

That said, the key point is that the conflation of the 1960s with the 1970s confuses early signs of theological thinking in the former with a full-throated theological and activist embrace in the latter. It is more telling to consider when human rights became a primary prism through which Christians imagined the contours of their activism. The 1970s were a critical turning point in that transformation. Christians did allude to "human rights" before the 1970s, but the idea competed with so many other ways to envision the limits and potentials of Christian praxis that it is misleading to assign too much importance to those earlier invocations. Let me be clear: documents written to flesh out Christian social thought and day-to-day social activism to save lives are markedly different. To speak of human rights as either a set of claims concretized in the UDHR or appended to Christian theological works is a far cry from the urgent activism in the 1970s that picked up the human rights banner in a period of emergency and, for many, despair and political defeat. Earlier usages are relevant to our understanding of human rights activism, but a fuller and truer perspective requires more properly locating the historical moment that activism both went transnational and crossed the religious divide to build coalitions with secular nongovernmental actors in response to escalating violence in South America.

Brazil and the Politics of Torture

Escalating violence in Brazil in the late 1960s drew the attention of a diverse array of actors throughout the Western world. The Brazilian military came to power in 1964, but the passage of Ato Institucional No. 5 (Institutional Act No. 5, or AI-5) in late 1968 marked a notable increase in government repression. AI-5 represented the victory of the so-called *linha dura*—the hardliners in the Brazilian military—who sought to eviscerate democratic rights. The act derogated basic due process rights, closed Congress and ended political parties, increased state censorship, and also saw the Junta increase its use of arbitrary arrests and torture.[19] This turn to greater repression produced a response among activists outside of Brazil, many of whom began to denounce torture in Brazil, although not within a broader "human rights" critique. As I develop more fully elsewhere, the contemporary link between torture and human rights had not yet been made in the early 1970s, in part because the idea of human rights itself was not yet the primary umbrella category under which all rights denunciations fell (see Kelly 2015).

Outside organizations began to take notice of the increase in state violence in Brazil. Amnesty International, for one, prodded by Brazilian exiles like Annina de Carvalho, a refugee in Paris, started to investigate the case of Brazil. Soon thereafter, in 1972, Amnesty released its massive "Report on Allegations of Torture in Brazil."[20] Amnesty's efforts concerning Brazil, which built on its first global Campaign against Torture (1972–74), dovetailed with transnational religious activists who saw the state practice of torture as a kind of epidemic that was spreading throughout the world. As harsh military dictatorships in Uruguay (1973), Chile (1973), and Argentina (1976) followed Brazil, Amnesty mounted a poignant publicity campaign about rising violence in the Southern Cone, which in turn prompted many outsiders to get involved in human rights advocacy. For example, Jeri Laber, one of the founders of Helsinki Watch (the forerunner to Human Rights Watch), notes in her memoir that it was Rose Styron's late 1973 article on torture in the *New Republic* that spurred her initial interest in human rights.[21] By the end of the decade, if not sooner, torture had become the chief human rights abuse in the global human rights imagination.[22]

Activists in the United States were on the front lines of an embryonic transnational movement.[23] These activists—men such as Tom Quigley of the United States Catholic Conference (USCC), Rev. William Wipfler of the National Council of Churches (NCC), Methodist minister Brady Tyson at American University, and Ralph Della Cava at Columbia— worked in tandem with Brazilian exiles such as Márcio Moreira Alves and Marcus Arruda. They first formed the American Committee for Information on Brazil (ACIB) in February 1970 in New York City to denounce the Brazilian Junta's use of torture. Relying on testimony from Brazilian exiles, ACIB released a report, "Terror in Brazil," in April 1970. "We cannot remain silent to the flagrant denial of human rights and dignity coming to us from Brazil," the dossier stated. Signed by some thirty-four different groups, the document was a harbinger of human rights investigative reports to come. It was rather informal and amateurish—a testament to the still incipient human rights activism in this moment—when compared to the more robust human rights reports by NGOs later in the decade.[24] Building on the work of the ACIB, both the National Council of Churches and the World Council of Churches issued press releases that called for the Brazilian Junta to stop its use of torture and other violent acts.[25]

Inside Brazil, antidictatorship campaigns were led principally by Brazilian bishops through the Conferência Nacional dos Bispos do Brasil (CNBB). As Kenneth Serbin (2000) has documented, Brazilian bishops engaged in a series of "secret dialogues" with Junta members over the military's use of torture. The bishops called for it to end, while the military sought official Catholic support for the regime instead of future public rebukes. These "dialogues" were indeed one way in which the bishops attempted to influence the regime. While not to be dismissed, it is more important to note how their tactics changed from closed-door negotiations to the more confrontational, public, and manifestly transnational nature of Christian activism that developed throughout the 1970s. In 1973 the CNBB significantly changed its approach to human rights, most notably in its decision to adopt the Universal Declaration of Human Rights—a kind of "rediscovery" of the 1948 text, building on Pope John XXIII's reference to it in *Pacem in Terris*—and to popularize it in churches throughout Brazil. Working via the newly established Ecumenical Coordination Service (CESE),[26] religious activists, with help from the WCC, printed some two million copies of the UDHR to be dispersed to congregations throughout the country (Harper 2006, 9). CESE also inserted passages from scripture and theological treatises to supplement each of the UDHR's thirty articles. For example, article 3 reads, "Everyone has the right to life, liberty and security of person." A citation from Exodus 20:13, "You shall not murder," follows. In reinterpreting the UDHR as another embodiment of sacred biblical text, Brazilian bishops were fleshing out their own vision of human rights that the global Catholic Church had initially started to articulate in the 1960s after Vatican II. They gave religious legitimation to universal concepts in light of their experience confronting national realities. "The evident affinity," the CESE booklet read, "between the Declaration, Church thought and the Word of God will serve as a stimulus for this publication to be studied in all related communities of the Church." As they gradually assimilated the language into their daily vocabulary, bishops imposed theological readings on secular documents like the UDHR, adding new layers to the human rights conceptions that emerged in the 1970s. The CESE publication, printed in Portuguese, Spanish, and English, circulated among religious organizations in Latin America, North America, and Europe throughout the decade (Harper 2006, 9).[27] It was the document that most patently represented the connective tissue between Catholic theology and human rights activism that had begun to form in the early 1970s.

Building on their work through CESE, Dom Hélder Câmara, archbishop of Recife and Olinda, and Cardinal Paulo Evaristo Arns, archbishop of São Paulo, played the largest role in fomenting transnational human rights activism. Dom Hélder, especially, traveled throughout Europe and North America—speaking to French Roman Catholic clergy and with Rev. Ralph Abernathy of the Southern Christian Leadership Council, the religiously based U.S. civil rights organization—lambasting the Brazilian Junta for its use of torture. He became, in many senses, a leader and champion of the global Catholic left and the Global South more generally. In retaliation for his larger-than-life persona and out-spoken defiance, the Junta barred him from public speeches and allowed him only one scheduled sermon a week. They called him a Communist—nothing more than "Fidel Castro in a cassock." On one level, Câmara spoke out against torture because he "could no longer remain silent," echoing words used by the ACIB. "The tortures are a calamity. They must stop," he declared. Implicitly challenging Brazilian sovereignty, Câmara added, "If the Government is certain of the nonexistence of political pris-oners and torture, there is no shame in opening Brazilian prisons to a visit from the International Red Cross."[28]

Beyond his criticism of torture, Dom Hélder articulated a more ex-pansive notion of human rights, including land reform, slum clearance, and improved conditions for the poor, further ostracizing himself in the eyes of the Brazilian dictatorship. Building on the currents that co-alesced at CELAM in 1968, Dom Hélder referred often in sermons to the sentiments of Pope Paul VI's 1967 encyclical, *Populorum Progressio*, which combined theories of development and rights.[29] For these inspir-ing efforts, Archbishop Câmara was nominated for the Nobel Peace Prize in 1970.

Some scholars too quickly conflate the changes in the Latin American Church in the 1960s with those of the 1970s, sweeping both decades into the same human rights story. It is true that this broader Catholic concep-tion of human rights, at least in part, reflected the evolution of compo-nents of the Latin American clergy in the 1960s after Vatican II toward a more direct engagement with the region's disenfranchised and marginal-ized; many were also shaped by the growing sway of liberation theology in calling attention to the plight of the poor. Such a capacious under-standing of human rights at times conflicted with Amnesty International's narrower focus on political and civil rights.

For his part, Archbishop Arns also clearly took advantage of the growing proliferation of transnational networks to promote the cause of human rights in Brazil. In July 1972, for example, he telephoned the

French section of Amnesty International to relay news that thirty-six Brazilian prisoners were starting their thirty-fourth day of a hunger strike, an effort to protest the "most decrepit and diseased, infected dungeons" in which prisoners were held. When Amnesty asked Arns for advice on how to respond, he replied, "They need only to eat . . . we have to act, we must all intervene, we must save the lives of the thirty-six prisoners." But when Amnesty probed further, Arns correctly expressed doubt that Brazilian officers, given their stalwart defense of the doctrine of state sovereignty, would allow any international organizations to enter the country.[30] Amnesty fired off a dispatch to national sections on behalf of the thirty-six prisoners, urging them to write letters on the prisoners' behalf.[31] Nine days later, the hunger strike ended and the prisoners were taken to a hospital to recuperate.[32]

At the same time, Brazilian Church efforts were aided by the World Council of Churches, a global ecumenical body based in Geneva that also grew concerned over torture in Brazil in the early 1970s. Given its long-time geographic proximity to the UN Commission on Human Rights, also housed in Geneva, the WCC sought to pressure the Brazilian dictatorship through mechanisms available at the UN, where the WCC, like many NGOs, had consultative status. In its "United Appeal to the Brazilian Government," signed by the World Federation of Trade Unions and the International Commission of Jurists (ICJ), the WCC denounced the "systematic violation of human rights by the Brazilian authorities."[33] Reflecting the transnational flow of information about rights abuses, the "United Appeal" made reference to declarations by the CNBB that protested the lack of due process rights and the military's rampant use of torture. The human rights language in the appeal was also the diplomatic language necessary to take action, and it was presented as evidence at the UN's Commission on Human Rights. However, the ICJ did not always fluently speak the language of human rights in the early 1970s. For example, while it signed the WCC appeal, the ICJ's own report on "political repression and tortures," released in July 1970 after an in loco study in Brazil, did not use the words *human rights*.[34] This provides further evidence that moral appeals were still in an embryonic state in the early 1970s. It was only after the Chilean coup of 1973, as the next section explains, that social activists, including Christians, began turning to the language of human rights in more significant numbers.

Chile, the Comité Pro-Paz, and the World Council of Churches

Far more than events in Brazil, the Chilean coup of September 11, 1973, reconfigured the moral geography for many in the Western world.[35] To Tom Quigley, a staff member at the U.S. Catholic Conference, human rights were "the air we breathed at the time." And the Chilean coup was "the event that catalyzed everything else."[36] In the coup's aftermath, hundreds of NGOs and solidarity organizations formed, many of which forthrightly employed a newfound language of human rights. In the United States, the most prominent example was the Washington Office on Latin America (WOLA), founded by an ecumenical alliance of activists including Quigley and Wipfler and headed by the Methodist minister Joseph Eldridge, a former missionary in Chile. WOLA established one of the first human rights lobbying presences on Capitol Hill in early 1974, bringing together religious and leftist activists in an unprecedented and apolitical defense of human rights.[37] Transnational religious activists not only worked with these new solidarity and human rights organizations, but also in tandem with international groups like the WCC as well as groups in Chile itself to shine a spotlight on widespread violations of human rights there.

In the days after the coup, domestic and international organizations initially focused on the humanitarian crisis: the fifteen thousand or so stranded South American exiles, an additional ten thousand Chilean refugees. The vast majority of exiles were leftists, from Bolivia, Uruguay, Argentina, and especially Brazil, who had come to Santiago to take part in Allende's leftist experiment in democratic socialism. The military Junta saw them as a potential threat. Fearful of what it considered to be international subversion from Marxist "terrorists," the Junta went to great lengths to arrest and detain a disproportionate number of foreigners. Leaflets dropped over Santiago encouraged Chileans to help round up all foreigners who were allegedly aiming to help "Marxist extremists . . . assassinate members of the Armed Forces and the Police."[38]

While the International Red Cross was the first international organization allowed access to the refugees, representatives from the United Nations High Commissioner for Refugees (UNHCR) and the International

Committee for Migration were soon admitted, though not without some resistance from Chilean military officials. However, the Red Cross and the UNCHR were limited in their ability to act: the former for its long-standing stance of neutrality and unwillingness to involve itself in domestic political issues; the latter, given that its mandate was only to help refugees, which by definition in international law excluded Chileans because they had not crossed a national border.

Most Chilean Church leaders reacted cautiously, but some more progressive religious leaders stepped into the void that trapped Chilean refugees. A coalition of seven Catholic, Protestant, and Jewish congregations formed the Comité Nacional de Ayuda a los Refugiados (CONAR) to coordinate with international bodies.[39] At roughly the same time, officials in the various churches recognized the need to establish an organization with a more expansive vision to deal with the escalating crisis in a country without the rule of law. "It [was] clear to us," Bishop Frenz (2006, 127) later reflected, "[that] the task had become grander and more complicated than ever in our country," as the Church was effectively the only civil society organization permitted by the military government. With money from the World Council of Churches, they created the Comité para la Cooperación para la Paz (Committee for the Cooperation for Peace, colloquially known as the Comité Pro-Paz) less than a month after the coup, on October 6, 1973. The Lutheran Frenz and the Catholic bishop Fernando Ariztía were chosen as co-presidents of the ecumenical organization, and the whole operation was sanctioned by the formidable archbishop of Santiago, Cardinal Raúl Silva Henríquez (Harper 2006, 31–34). In what follows, I discuss the efforts of the World Council of Churches to combat violence in Chile, which has received little scholarly attention. My analysis leaves aside the important Catholic role that has already been discussed in excellent detail in works by Pamela Lowden (1996) and Brian Smith (1982).

The growth of human rights organizations in Chile, as in Brazil, received financial and logistical support from transnational activist organizations like the World Council of Churches. The WCC, as we have seen in Brazil, had a concern for human rights before the Chilean coup. It had held an inter-American conference in San Juan, Puerto Rico, in February 1973, whose final report, *Derechos humanos y las iglesias en América Latina,* "urg[ed] the churches and the Council to create ecumenical instruments for the implementation of human rights" (quoted in Harper 2006, 30). This farsighted call would be answered by activists in Chile after the coup when the WCC, in conjunction with a remarkable array of nongovernmental and intergovernmental organizations, responded to savage repression by the Junta.

Charles Harper, who eventually led the WCC's human rights office on Latin America, called the coup an "earthquake that woke up the sensibility and the conscience of peoples and nations in the world."[40] Within a week, the WCC's general secretary, Philip Potter, sent an appeal to the Junta expressing his concern over the chaotic situation unfolding in Chile; he sent a similar appeal a few days later to the UN Security Council and to ambassadors from countries throughout the world.[41] In the months immediately following the coup, Harper and others established the Chile Emergency Desk "as a direct response" to coordinate with international and intergovernmental organizations on the ground in Chile, to spread information about escalating violence, and eventually to funnel massive amounts of financial support to the Comité Pro-Paz.[42] In addition to direct funding, the WCC often pooled donations from organizations and countries throughout the Western world that responded to its pleas.[43] In Chile the "earthquake" took the form of an unfolding refugee emergency, with which the WCC assisted from the beginning. Shortly after the coup, it sent two relief teams to Chile and the neighboring countries of Argentina and Peru to coordinate with intergovernmental relief groups at the United Nations and other NGOs.[44] By April 1974, slightly more than six months after the coup, the WCC and other international organizations had resettled more than ten thousand Chileans and foreigners in countries throughout the world, principally in France, Sweden, the German Federal Republic, and the German Democratic Republic. (This does not include another ten thousand who fled through unofficial channels.)[45] As the WCC explained in a press statement, the refugee operation led to the creation of parallel ecumenical committees in countries throughout Latin America to assist with the refugee flow. Both the number of refugees aided and the degree of international cooperation were rather astounding.[46]

The focus on resettling refugees reflected the fact that much human rights activism at the WCC and elsewhere after the Chilean coup was ad hoc and temporary. While the outpouring of international support should be recognized, the mechanics of the operation revealed a few drawbacks in the international conceptual framework of the refugee. The WCC's insistent focus on the refugee, for instance, struck Harper as ill conceived. He soon realized the limits of the UN's category "stateless and politically inert refugee." In a private letter in early 1974, Harper expressed concern that the WCC failed to offer "refugees any alternative." Indeed, "by encouraging them into the UNHCR-type 'pipeline,'" refugees found themselves in "'new homes' where they are integrated, taught a new language, stamped, and told to forget their past!" Unwittingly, the WCC and the broader international community had, in some senses, facilitated the Junta's efforts to rid itself of political enemies.[47]

The initial involvement in the refugee emergency developed into a sustained effort on the part of the WCC to develop a more systematic response to the human rights catastrophe. The coup set in motion a process whereby the WCC imagined new transnational limits and potentials to its social activism. Memos discussed how to think about its activism by "developing new contacts, amplifying existing ones, thinking of new ways and means to respond . . . to emerging needs and crises, drawing conclusions and advising."[48] In other words, the coup produced "a new form of church response," not least because the churches were the only institutions able to act and protest in Chile itself. For its part, the WCC returned to the Universal Declaration of Human Rights as the foundational document with which—in line with a general rediscovery of the UDHR among other activist groups—it could protest the Junta's action, in Brazil, Chile, or elsewhere. The WCC cataloged the rights abused by the Junta and compared it to the UDHR; one memo claimed the Junta had violated articles 1–3, 5–15, 18–21, 23, 25, 26, 28, and 30—all from a document with only thirty articles.[49] The WCC also developed ongoing ties with groups like Amnesty International's Germany and Luxembourg sections, which often looked to it for financial assistance and to coordinate activities.[50]

As mentioned earlier, the coup encouraged the WCC to foment ecumenical action that previously would have been unfathomable.[51] To take only one obvious example, the WCC encouraged a long-standing coordination with Rev. William Wipfler at the National Council of Churches in the United States through meetings and correspondence about how best to shed light on the human rights emergency in the Southern Cone. Such connections demonstrate how activists who began with antitorture movements in Brazil progressed to subsequent involvement in Chile and other rights emergencies in Latin America.[52]

Perhaps most important, domestic religious leaders in Chile often looked to Geneva to coordinate activities with the World Council of Churches and other international organizations. Only three months after the coup, Bishop Frenz's schedule showed that Geneva was the place to be: in one day, he engaged in shuttle diplomacy with the Intergovernmental Committee for European Migration (ICEM), the UNCHR, and the World Council of Churches.[53] At the meeting with the WCC, Frenz laid out the situation in fairly clear terms: the Comité Pro-Paz needed "just money, money, really."[54] Similarly, José Zalaquett, head of the Comité Pro-Paz's legal department, visited the WCC and the ICJ in late May 1974 to discuss the internal situation in Chile.[55] Zalaquett stressed that the WCC and similar groups should "expose the sham and the myth" of the Junta's "economic justice" program to the world.[56] Frenz's and Zalaquett's visits reveal the centrality of the WCC to the Comité Pro-Paz in serving as the international institutional hub that linked disparate groups together. Of course, the WCC also was the chief means of financial support for the Comité. Hundreds of thousands of dollars were funneled on an annual basis to the Comité Pro-Paz, reaching US$1 million annually by the time the Vicaría de la Solidaridad took over the institutional apparatus of the Comité in January 1976. This amounted to between 50 and 60 percent of the Vicaría's entire budget.[57]

A series of evaluation memos in 1974 and 1975 attest to the change in the nature of the WCC's work after the Chilean coup. In one, Charles Harper described an unprecedented human rights emergency. "The flight, imprisonment, harassment, censorship, torture of people is not isolated any longer," Harper wrote, for "it is a mass, and massive problem[;] . . . an ever greater number of persons are persecuted, made refugees, prisoners, tortured, for their political views." He contended that this new reality was tied to the "increasing militarization of Latin American society."[58] In the atmosphere of what it perceived as unprecedented violence, the WCC saw the churches as "one of the only institutions . . . [that] are potentially free to respond." As such, they needed to work with international bodies to the extent possible, as well as foment local networks with groups on the ground, like the Comité in Chile.

THE BRAZILIAN and Chilean cases altered how Christian activists envisioned the horizon of social activism in the name of human rights. At the Fifth Assembly of the World Council of Churches, in Nairobi in December 1975, delegates clearly expressed their objection to the "systematic increase of human rights violations on that continent [Latin America]" and urged governments "respectfully but energetically . . . [to] comply with the provisions of the Universal Declaration of Human Rights."[59] The linkage between Christian thought and praxis and human rights persisted in the decades after the 1970s, especially as human rights became an important popular language of moral justice around the world. Moreover, in the aftermath of events in Brazil and Chile, both the Protestant and Catholic Churches, in Latin America and elsewhere, became primary brokers in the struggles over truth, justice, and memory (Harper 1996; Philpott 2006). Yet in the Catholic world since the election of Pope John Paul II, the vision of human rights as promoted by the Catholic Church has been restricted if compared to the previously more capacious and influential understandings of Catholic praxis, notably liberation theology. Since his election in 2013, Pope Francis has attempted to reverse this conservative course—although the extent to which he will be successful remains to be seen.

Religious actors in Latin America and globally were more important in the advent of transnational human rights activism in the 1970s than is reflected in the extant historical literature. This chapter has aimed to recover those Christian voices by showing how violence in Brazil and Chile helped to spur a linkage between Christianity and human rights. If Christians had some familiarity with the language of human rights, words occasionally alluded to in some Christian social thought before the 1970s, this chapter proposes that state repression in the Southern Cone encouraged the development of a unique praxis of human rights among different Christian groups.

The chapter is one piece of a much bigger historiographical focus on the growth of transnational activism in the decades since the 1970s. Historians are just beginning to draw attention to and write nuanced histories of transnational activism. The timing is ripe, for it is at the analytical level of the transnational that I believe our understanding of the contours of present and future violence in Latin America would benefit. As relayed throughout this chapter, domestic groups in Brazil and Chile relied both financially and in more existential ways on the intervention of, and their own participation in, transnational networks of religious and secular actors. At the same time, transnational actors relied on their courage and hard work on the ground. The local and the transnational formed a symbiotic relationship. Transnational activism is not a panacea for all of society's ills: it functions best when it engages the right configuration of external actors that empower domestic ones. As we look for solutions to present and future problems in Latin America, we should keep in mind the possibilities of transnational activism, whether in the language of human rights or not.

The best history approximates a vision of the past as it really was rather than as we imagined it to be. The next generation of human rights historians, of both religious and secular actors, should remember that the historian's duty is not to celebrate and construct creation myths but to analyze and grasp a moment, concept, event, or phenomenon in time— as a function of a series of possibilities that were neither inevitable nor desirable. Discussions of the history of human rights activism exhibit some tendencies to glorify in the past what we hold dear in the present. As one particular form of social activism and one particular form of political language that found some success in the past forty years, human rights activism is a fruitful subject for careful historical analysis. Only through that process can we assess how best to articulate contemporary issues of violence in Latin America with a vocabulary of human rights— or with a different language, if deemed appropriate.

Notes

1. Helmut Frenz's speech was reprinted as "Human Rights: A Christian Viewpoint," *Christianity and Crisis* 36, no. 11 (June 21, 1976): 150–51.
2. Human Rights and Christian Responsibility was the name of a steering committee established by the World Council of Churches' Commission of the Churches on International Affairs (CCIA). See "Report of Programme Unit II:

Justice and Service," August 11–18, 1974, folder 429.02.01, Archives of the World Council of Churches, Geneva, Switzerland (hereafter WCC Archives).

3. See Moyn 2010; Eckel 2015; and P. Kelly 2013a, 2013b, 2014a. On challenges to Moyn's new emphasis on the 1970s in human rights history, see Pendas 2012; Weitz 2013; and Bradley 2011. Almost all works skirt the formative role played by transnational Christian activists in the explosion of human rights activism in the 1970s.

4. On the 1970s, in addition to Moyn, Eckel, and Kelly, cited in note 3 above, see Mazower 2012, 317–31. As it happens, not all scholars listed here would signal the 1970s as the critical turning point in human rights history. See Snyder 2011; Beckerman 2010; Nathans forthcoming; and Keys 2014. For analyses of Carter's human rights foreign policies, see Schmitz and Walker 2004; Schmidli 2011; Skiba 2013; and Simpson 2009.

5. A few exceptions can be found, although these works are not generally in dialogue with human rights history. See Green 2010; and Stites Mor 2013. Scholars outside the discipline of history, notably, political science, have crafted some of the only extant outlines of the work of transnational religious activists. See, e.g., Sikkink 2004; and Cleary 1997, especially chapters 6 and 7.

6. See, e.g., Shah, Stepan, and Duffy Toft 2012, especially the chapter by Witte and Green.

7. See also Sikkink 1996; Cleary 1997; and Smith 1995.

8. There are no comprehensive histories of the World Council of Churches beyond congratulatory self-reflection, and few of the broader ecumenical movement. See Rouse and Neill 1954, especially chapter 16 on the origins of the WCC by its general secretary, Willem Adolf Visser't Hooft; see also Briggs, Oduyoye, and Tsetsēs 2004; FitzGerald 2004; World Council of Churches 1988; and Moyn 2011, 68.

9. See also folders 429.07.01, 429.07.02, WCC Archives.

10. See also Hehir 1996, 101–2. Hehir gives more weight to Pius XII, who had three major contributions in his view: "the inclusion of political-civil rights, the limits on the role of the state, and the international dimensions of human rights."

11. For more on Maritain, see Moyn 2011. Maritain examined the idea of human rights in relation to Catholic traditions in *The Natural Law and Human Rights* (1942).

12. On the conditions of possibility for human rights in the 1940s, see Bradley 2009.

13. For recent attention to the Jewish contribution to international human rights in the UN Charter, see Loeffler 2013.

14. Much of the existing history of human rights has far overplayed the extent to which the Universal Declaration of Human Rights was a breakthrough in human rights history (see Glendon 2002). For a critique of that approach, see Moyn 2010, especially the chapter "Death from Birth."

15. Beyond Christian invocations, human rights talk persisted especially in Europe, where conservatives emphasized political and civil rights in the construction of the European Convention on Human Rights. On this, see Duranti 2012; on the role of human rights in the United Nations and in the context of decolonization debates, see Burke 2010. For her part, Teretta (2010) emphasizes the role of anticolonial human rights organizations. Her analysis fails to recognize the marginality of these actors within a broader global picture.

16. Typical of the tendency to elevate the Second Vatican Council as the critical moment in the Catholic turn to human rights is Crahan 1996, 262–65; Hollenbach 1979; and Hehir 1996.

17. Note the escalation of human rights discourse in John Paul II's address to the United Nations (1979) and encyclical *Centesiumus Annus* (1991). *Pacem in Terris* (1963), a 16,000-word encyclical, mentions "human rights" but only four times, and not until the sixty-first paragraph. John Paul II's 1979 address at the United Nations, only 6,800 words, invokes "human rights" twenty-one times.

18. See the "documentos finales" at www.ensayistas.org/critica/liberacion/medellin/.

19. See Skidmore 1990; Moreira 1985; Figueiredo 2009; and Green 2010; see also Gaspari 2002a, 2002b, 2004.

20. Amnesty International, "Report on Allegations of Torture in Brazil," AMR 19—Executive Director Files, Americas-Brazil, 1967–70, 1972 folder, Amnesty International of the USA Records, Center for Human Rights Documentation and Research, Columbia University, New York (henceforth AI-USA); Tracy Ulltveit-Moe, written correspondence with author, April 18, 2012; interview with author, June 29, 2012. Tracy Ulltveit-Moe was the Brazilian researcher at Amnesty at the time.

21. For Rose Styron's article, see "Torture," *New Republic*, December 8, 1973.

22. For initial efforts to historicize concern over torture, see T. Kelly 2011, 2012; and Keys 2012.

23. The work of these groups is taken up in far more detail in Green 2010, especially chapter 5.

24. See, more generally, Tom Quigley's statement before the subcommittee, 195–207; Quigley, interview with author, November 19, 2010; Quigley, correspondence with author, May 26, 2010; A. D. Horne, "34 Groups Score Torture in Brazil," *Washington Post*, April 19, 1970, A4.

25. See, e.g., Letter to Archbishop Hélder Pessoa Câmara on João Francisco de Sousa by Rev. Frederick McGuire, April 6, 1973, http://old.usccb.org/sdwp/international/1973-04-06-ltr-brazil-imprisonment-joao-desousa.pdf.

26. CESE was created on June 13, 1973, in Salvador, Bahia. It is composed of an ecumenical mix of Brazilian Christian organizations, including the CNBB, Igreja Episcopal do Brasil, Igreja Evangélica Pentecostal "O Brasil para Cristo," Igreja Metodista, and Missão Presbiteriana do Brasil Central, and has the support of the World Council of Churches. See Declaração Universal dos Direitos Humanos (Edições Paulinas, São Paulo, [1973] 1978), folder 429.09.01—Church statements and theological reflections (1974–90), WCC Archive.

27. It was reprinted in 1978 on the thirtieth anniversary of the UDHR and distributed in Chile by the Vicaría de la Solidaridad, in Argentina by the Movimiento Ecuménico por los Derechos Humanos, in Paraguay by the publication *Acción*, and throughout the continent by the Latin American Council of Churches (CLAI). See various copies of the document in WCC Archives, folders 429.09.01 and 429.09.02.

28. Quoted in Joseph A. Page, "The Little Priest Who Stands Up to Brazil's Generals," *New York Times Magazine*, May 23, 1971, 26–27.

29. Dom Hélder urged "human promotion that will shape the masses into a people. We must educate people for development. To do this it is necessary to make people conscious of the conditions which oppress them, so that they can help themselves. But this requires democracy and free institutions, like the trade unions. And the Government is afraid of this." Yet when pressed for details on how he would enact such a world, Dom Hélder demurred: "I am not a technician." See Joseph A. Page, "The Little Priest Who Stands Up to Brazil's Generals," 26; and Joseph A. Page, "Church in Latin America May Clash With Rightist Governments," *New York Times,* July 10, 1972, 10.

30. "Appeal from the Archbishop of São Paulo on behalf of 36 dying prisoners," February 16, 1972, AMR 19—Executive Director Files, Americas-Brazil, 1971 folder, AI-USA.

31. AI memo to All National Sections, marked Urgent, from Tracy Ulltveit-Moe, July 12, 1972, AMR 19, 1972 folder, AI-USA.

32. "Church Appeal to Amnesty Ends Brazil Hunger Strike," *Catholic Herald* (UK), July 21, 1972.

33. "Document submitted to the United Nations Human Rights Commission on the Situation in Brazil which reveals a Consistent Pattern of Violations of Human Rights," March 23, 1971, folder 429.07.02—Brazil, WCC Archives; "Jurists Describe Brazil Torture," *Washington Post*, July 23, 1970, A16.

34. Commisão Internacional de Juristas, "Relatório sobre a repressão policial e torturas infligidas à oposição e prisioneiros políticos no Brasil," July 22, 1970, folder 429.07.02—Brazil, WCC Archives.

35. See Kelly 2013a.

36. Quigley, correspondence with author, May 26, 2010.

37. See the Washington Office on Latin America Records, Duke University, Rare Books, Manuscript, and Special Collections Library, Archive for Human Rights. On WOLA, the best source is Youngers 2006. See also Sikkink 2004, 50, 67–68; Schoultz 1981; and Cleary 1997.

38. International Secretariat (IS) memo, "Subject: Refugees in Chile," November 1973, AMR-22, Executive Director Files, Americas-Chile, AI-USA.

39. The seven denominations were Catholic, Lutheran, Baptist, Methodist, Methodist Pentecostal, and Greek Orthodox churches, and Jewish community. On the events more generally, see Stern 2006.

40. World Council of Churches, "Former WCC official Harper receives Chilean award," March 5, 2010, copy in WCC Archives.

41. "WCC General Secretary Urges Chilean Junta to Respect Refugee Rights," September 14, [1973], and "Dr. Potter Urges UN Security Council Protect Exiles in Chile," September 17, [1973], both in folder 429.01.04, WCC Archives.

42. "The Human Rights Resources Office for Latin America (HRROLA) and the Chile Emergency Desk, 1973–1990," box 429.01—HRROLA, WCC Archives; see folder 429.02.02—MINUTES OF HRROLA, Staff Advisory Group (1974–96); see also Harper 2006, 35–36.

43. See, e.g., "WCC Appeals for Help for Refugees in Chile," October 16, [1973], and "New Appeal regarding the situation in Chile for $1,200,000," January 31, 1974, both in folder 429.01.04, WCC Archives.

44. "Report of the WCC Emergency Task Force on the Chilean Situation," August 7–9, 1974, folder 429.02.01, WCC Archives; see also folder 429.01.05.

45. See "Statistical Data Annex," April 4, 1974, folder 429.02.01, WCC Archives.

46. Notably, Peru, Argentina, Costa Rica, Honduras, Ecuador, and Panama. "Last Foreign Refugees to Leave Chile Next Week," January 31, 1974, folder 429.01.04, WCC Archives.

47. Charles Harper to Graeme Jackson, "Our conversations about the work of the WCC with Latin America re: human rights and refugees," February 1, 1974, box 429.01, WCC Archives.

48. "Excerpt from minutes of the Chile Task Force June 10, 1974, on creation of the Human Rights Resource Office on Latin America as the successors of the Chile Emergency Desk," box 429.01—Human Rights Resources Office for Latin America (General) (HRROLA), WCC Archives.

49. "Chile: the internal structure of police and judicial repression," April 6, 1974, folder 429.02.02, WCC Archives.

50. Chile Emergency Desk to Task Force Members Memo, November 27, 1973, folder 429.02.02, mentioned linkages; see also Gerson Meyer to TF members Memo, January 7, 1974, same folder.

51. WCC, "Progress Report, Chile Task Force," June 22, 1974, box 429.01—Human Rights Resources Office for Latin America (General) (HR-ROLA); "Report of the WCC Emergency Task Force on the Chilean Situation," August 7–9, 1974, WCC Archives.

52. Minutes of the Staff Advisory Group, meeting, February 4, 1975, folder 429.02.02; Latin America Desk to Chile Task Force Memo, November 13, 1973, folder 429.02.02—MINUTES OF HRROLA, Staff Advisory Group (1974–96); see correspondence between Wipfler and the WCC, folder 429.02.03, WCC Archives.

53. Charles Harper to Chile Task Force members, December 17, 1973, folder 429.02.02, WCC Archives. The ICEM was renamed Intergovernmental Committee for Migration in 1980 and International Organization for Migration in 1989.

54. Task Force Meeting with Bishop Frenz, December 17, 1973, folder 429.02.02, WCC Archives.

55. Charles Harper to Chile Task Force and interested friends, June 6, 1974, folder 429.02.02, WCC Archives.

56. Charles Harper to Chile Task Force and interested friends, June 6, 1974, folder 429.02.02, WCC Archives.

57. "Minutes, Human Rights Resources Office for Latin America," February 24, 1976, folder 429.02.02—MINUTES OF HRROLA, Staff Advisory Group (1974–96), WCC Archives. This amount steadily rose throughout the 1970s, reaching over US$1.3 million in 1978. See Confidential Budget Memo, December 20, 1978, folder 429.02.02, WCC Archives.

58. Charles Harper, "Human Rights and Christian Response in Latin America," June 11, 1975, folder 429.01.04, WCC Archives.

59. "Human Rights in Latin America," Resolution of WCC at Fifth Assembly, Nairobi, December 1975 (177 of 1,553), folder 429.02.02, WCC Archives; see also Paton 1976.

References

American Committee for Information on Brazil (ACIB). 1970. "Terror in Brazil: A Dossier." New York: ACIB.

Aranda, Gilberto C. 2004. *Vicaría de la Solidaridad: Una experiencia sin fronteras.* Santiago: CESOC.

Beckerman, Gal. 2010. *When They Come for Us, We'll Be Gone: The Epic Struggle to Save Soviet Jewry*. Boston: Houghton Mifflin Harcourt.

Bradley, Mark Philip. 2009. "The Ambiguities of Sovereignty: The United States and the Global Human Rights Cases of the 1940s and 1950s." In *The State of Sovereignty: Territories, Laws, Populations*, edited by Douglas Howland and Luise White, 124–47. Bloomington: Indiana University Press.

———. 2011. "Writing Human Rights History." *Il Mestiere di Storico* 3, no. 2: 13–30.

Briggs, John, Mercy Amba Oduyoye, and Georges Tsetsēs, eds. 2004. *A History of the Ecumenical Movement*, vol. 3, *1968–2000*. Geneva: WCC Publications.

Bruey, Alison. 2013. "Transnational Concepts, Local Contexts: Solidarity at the Grassroots in Pinochet's Chile." In *Human Rights and Transnational Solidarity in Cold War Latin America*, edited by Jessica Stites Mor, 120–42. Madison: University of Wisconsin Press.

Burke, Roland. 2010. *Decolonization and the Evolution of International Human Rights*. Philadelphia: University of Pennsylvania Press.

Casanova, José. 1997. "Globalizing Catholicism and the Return to a 'Universal' Church." In *Transnational Religion and Fading States*, edited by Susann Hoeber Rudolph and James Piscatori, 121–43. Boulder, CO: Westview Press.

Cleary, Edward L. 1997. *The Struggle for Human Rights in Latin America*. Westport, CT: Greenwood Press.

Colonnese, Louis M., ed. 1970. *Human Rights and the Liberation of Man in the Americas*. Notre Dame, IN: University of Notre Dame Press.

Crahan, Margaret E. 1996. "Catholicism and Human Rights in Latin America." In *Religious Diversity and Human Rights*, edited by Irene Bloom, J. Paul Martin, and Wayne L. Proudfoot, 262–77. New York: Columbia University Press.

Curran, Charles E. 2002. *Catholic Social Teaching: 1891–Present: A Historical, Theological, and Ethical Analysis*. Washington, DC: Georgetown University Press.

———. 2005. *The Moral Theology of Pope John Paul II*. Washington, DC: Georgetown University Press.

Duranti, Marco. 2012. "Curbing Labour's Totalitarian Temptation: European Human Rights Law and British Postwar Politics." *Humanity: An International Journal of Human Rights, Humanitarianism, and Development* 3, no. 3 (Winter): 361–83.

Eckel, Jan. 2015. *Die Ambivalenz des Guten: Menschenrechte in der internationalen Politik seit den 1940ern*. Göttingen: Vandenhoeck und Ruprecht.

Eckel, Jan, and Samuel Moyn, eds. 2013. *The Breakthrough: Human Rights in the 1970s*. Philadelphia: University of Pennsylvania Press.

Figueiredo, Lucas. 2009. *Olho por olho: Os livros secretos da ditadura*. Rio de Janeiro: Editora Record.

FitzGerald, Thomas E. 2004. *The Ecumenical Movement: An Introductory History*. Westport, CT: Praeger.

Formicola, Jo Renee. 1988. *The Catholic Church and Human Rights: Its Role in the Formulation of U.S. Policy, 1945–1980*. New York: Garland.

Frenz, Helmut. 2006. *Mi vida chilena: Solidaridad con los oprimidos*. Santiago: LOM.

Gaspari, Elio. 2002a. *A ditadura envergonhada*. São Paulo: Companhia das Letras.

———. 2002b. *A ditadura escancarada*. São Paulo: Companhia das Letras.

———. 2004. *A ditadura encurralada*. São Paulo: Companhia das Letras.

Glendon, Mary Ann. 2002. *A World Made New: Eleanor Roosevelt and the Universal Declaration of Human Rights*. New York: Random House.

Green, James. 2010. *We Cannot Remain Silent: Opposition to the Brazilian Military Dictatorship in the United States*. Durham, NC: Duke University Press.

Harper, Charles R. 2006. *O Acompanhamento: Ecumenical Action for Human Rights in Latin America, 1970–1990*. Geneva: WCC Publications.

———, ed. 1996. *Impunity: An Ethical Perspective: Six Case Studies from Latin America*. Geneva: WCC Publications.

Hehir, Bryan. 1996. "Religious Activism for Human Rights: A Christian Case Study." In *Religious Human Rights in Global Perspective*, edited by John Witte Jr. and Johan D. van der Vyver, 97–120. The Hague: Martinus Nijhoff.

Hervieu-Léger, Danièle. 1997. "Faces of Catholic Transnationalism: In and beyond France." In *Transnational Religion and Fading States*, edited by Susann Hoeber Rudolph and James Piscatori, 104–18. Boulder, CO: Westview Press.

Hollenbach, David. 1979. *Claims in Conflict: Retrieving and Reviewing the Catholic Human Rights Tradition*. New York: Paulist Press.

Keck, Margaret, and Kathryn Sikkink. 1998. *Activists beyond Borders: Advocacy Networks in International Politics*. Ithaca, NY: Cornell University Press.

Kelly, Patrick William. 2013a. "The 1973 Chilean Coup and the Origins of Transnational Human Rights Activism." *Journal of Global History* 8, no. 1 (March): 165–86.

———. 2013b. "'Magic Words': The Advent of Transnational Human Rights Activism in Latin America's Southern Cone in the Long 1970s." In *The Breakthrough: Human Rights in the 1970s*, edited by Jan Eckel and Samuel Moyn, 88–106. Philadelphia: University of Pennsylvania Press.

———. 2014. "On the Poverty and Possibility of Human Rights in Latin American History." *Humanity: An International Journal of Human Rights, Humanitarianism, and Development* 5, no. 3 (Winter): 435–51.

———. 2015. "Sovereignty and Salvation: Transnational Human Rights Activism in the Americas in the Long 1970s." PhD dissertation, University of Chicago.

Kelly, Tobias. 2011. "What We Talk about When We Talk about Torture." *Humanity: An International Journal of Human Rights, Humanitarianism, and Development* 2, no. 2 (Summer): 327–43.

———. 2012. *This Side of Silence: Human Rights, Torture, and the Recognition of Cruelty.* Philadelphia: University of Pennsylvania Press.

Keys, Barbara. 2012. "Anti-Torture Politics: Amnesty International, the Greek Junta, and the Origins of the Human Rights 'Boom' in the United States." In *The Human Rights Revolution: An International History*, edited by Akira Iriye, Petra Goedde, and William I. Hitchcock, 201–22. New York: Oxford University Press.

———. 2014. *Reclaiming American Virtue: The Human Rights Revolution of the 1970s.* Cambridge, MA: Harvard University Press.

Laber, Jeri. 2002. *The Courage of Strangers: Coming of Age with the Human Rights Movement.* New York: Public Affairs.

Loeffler, James. 2013. "'The Conscience of America': Human Rights, Jewish Politics, and American Foreign Policy at the 1945 United Nations San Francisco Conference." *Journal of American History* 100, no. 2 (September): 401–28.

Lowden, Pamela. 1996. *Moral Opposition to Authoritarian Rule in Chile, 1973–90.* Oxford: St. Anthony Press.

Maritain, Jacques. 1942. *The Natural Law and Human Rights.* Windsor: Christian Culture Press.

Mazower, Mark. 2012. *Governing the World: The History of an Idea.* New York: Penguin Press.

Moreira, Maria Helena. 1985. *State and Opposition in Military Brazil.* Austin: University of Texas Press.

Moyn, Samuel. 2010. *The Last Utopia: Human Rights in History.* Cambridge, MA: Harvard University Press.

———. 2011. "Personalism, Community, and the Origins of Human Rights." In *Human Rights in the Twentieth Century*, edited by Stefan-Ludwig Hoffmann, 85–106. New York: Cambridge University Press.

———. 2012. "Substance, Scale, and Salience: The Recent Historiography of Human Rights." *Annual Review of Law and Social Science* 8: 123–40.

———. 2015. *Christian Human Rights.* Philadelphia: University of Pennsylvania Press.

Nathans, Benjamin. Forthcoming. *A Curious Kind of Liberty: Soviet Dissidents, Human Rights, and the Soviet Union after Stalin*. Princeton, NJ: Princeton University Press.

Paton, David M., ed. 1976. *Breaking Barriers, Nairobi 1975: The Official Report of the Fifth Assembly of the World Council of Churches, Nairobi, 23 November–10 December, 1975*. Grand Rapids, MI: Eerdmans.

Pendas, Devin O. 2012. "Toward a New Politics? On the Recent Historiography of Human Rights." *Contemporary European History* 21, no. 1 (February): 95–111.

Philpott, Daniel. 2006. *The Politics of Past Evil: Religion, Reconciliation, and the Dilemmas of Transitional Justice*. Notre Dame, IN: University of Notre Dame Press.

Rouse, Ruth, and Stephen Charles Neill, eds. 1954. *A History of the Ecumenical Movement, 1517–1948*. London: SPCK.

Schmidli, William Michael. 2011. "Institutionalizing Human Rights in U.S. Foreign Policy: U.S.-Argentine Relations, 1976–1980." *Diplomatic History* 35, no. 2 (April): 351–77.

Schmitz, David F., and Vanessa Walker. 2004. "Jimmy Carter and the Foreign Policy of Human Rights." *Diplomatic History* 28, no. 1 (January): 113–43.

Schoultz, Lars. 1981. *Human Rights and United States Policy toward Latin America*. Princeton, NJ: Princeton University Press.

Serbin, Kenneth. 2000. *Secret Dialogues: Church-State Relations, Torture, and Social Justice in Authoritarian Brazil*. Pittsburgh, PA: University of Pittsburgh Press.

Shah, Timothy Samuel, Alfred Stepan, and Monica Duffy Toft, eds. 2012. *Rethinking Religion and World Affairs*. New York: Oxford University Press.

Sikkink, Kathryn. 1996. "The Emergence, Evolution, and Effectiveness of the Latin American Human Rights Network." In *Constructing Democracy: Human Rights, Citizenship, and Society in Latin America*, edited by Elizabeth Jelin and Eric Hershberg, 59–84. Boulder, CO: Westview Press.

———. 2004. *Mixed Signals: U.S. Human Rights Policy and Latin America*. Ithaca, NY: Cornell University Press.

Simpson, Brad. 2009. "Denying the 'First Right': The United States, Indonesia, and the Ranking of Human Rights by the Carter Administration, 1976–1980." *International History Review* 31, no. 4 (December): 798–826.

Skiba, Lynsay. 2013. "Shifting Sites of Argentine Advocacy and the Shape of 1970s Human Rights Debates." In *The Breakthrough: Human Rights in the 1970s*, edited by Jan Eckel and Samuel Moyn, 107–24. Philadelphia: University of Pennsylvania Press.

Skidmore, Thomas E. 1990. *The Politics of Military Rule in Brazil, 1964–1985.* New York: Oxford University Press.

Smith, Brian. 1982. *The Church and Politics in Chile: Challenges to Modern Catholicism.* Princeton, NJ: Princeton University Press.

Smith, Jackie. 1995. "Transnational Political Process and the Human Rights Movement." In *Research in Social Movements, Conflicts, and Change,* edited by Michael N. Dobkowski, Isidor Wallimann, and Christo Stojanov, 185–219. Greenwich, CT: JAI Press.

Snyder, Sarah. 2011. *Human Rights Activism and the End of the Cold War: A Transnational History.* New York: Cambridge University Press.

Stern, Steve J. 2006. *Battling for Hearts and Minds: Memory Struggles in Pinochet's Chile, 1973–1988.* Durham, NC: Duke University Press.

Stites Mor, Jessica, ed. 2013. *Human Rights and Transnational Solidarity in Cold War Latin America.* Madison: University of Wisconsin Press.

Teretta, Meredith. 2010. "'We Had Been Fooled into Thinking That the UN Watches over the Entire World': Human Rights, UN Trust Territories, and Africa's Decolonization." *Human Rights Quarterly* 34, no. 2 (May): 329–60.

Weitz, Eric D. 2013. "Samuel Moyn and the New History of Human Rights." *European Journal of Political Theory* 12, no. 1 (January): 84–93.

Weschler, Lawrence. 1990. *A Miracle, a Universe: Settling Accounts with Torturers.* New York: Pantheon Books.

World Council of Churches (WCC). 1988. *And So Set Up Signs . . . : The World Council of Churches' First 40 Years.* Geneva: WCC Publications.

Youngers, Coletta. 2006. *Thirty Years of Advocacy for Human Rights, Democracy, and Social Justice.* Washington, DC: Washington Office on Latin America.

CHAPTER 4

CHURCH RESPONSES TO POLITICAL VIOLENCE IN CENTRAL AMERICA

From Liberation Theology to Human Rights

VIRGINIA GARRARD-BURNETT

In the late 1970s, broadsides circulated on the streets of San Salvador reading, "Haga patria: mate a un cura" (Build the country: kill a priest) (Sobrino 2007, 4). In little more than a decade, the Catholic Church in Central America and elsewhere in Latin America was transforming itself from a conservative institution allied with the rich and powerful to a "Church of the poor," some of whose clergy became champions of the struggle for social justice. This position, along with the critical thinking behind it, became known as liberation theology. It combined the fundamental teachings of Christ and the new dictates of the magisterium of the Church with political analysis drawn from dependency theory and even strands of Marxism. Liberation theology sought to carve out a new mandate for Latin American Catholicism: a radical embrace of social justice for the poor. Just how far this new formulation of the Catholic "social question," which had traditionally focused on Christian charity and social order, would advance was not altogether clear in the beginning. In Central America from the 1960s into the 1980s, however, a minority of

Catholic clergy came to the conclusion that the prevailing and extreme social and political repression, the deep roots of what came to be called "structural sin," and the ruling oligarchies' unwillingness to entertain even the most modest suggestions for social reform led, ineluctably, to the embrace of violent, armed revolution.

But violence and Christianity did not rest easily together, nor did the forces in power allow them to. By the mid-1980s, Church people associated with liberation theology helped lay the groundwork for a new struggle for social justice framed around human rights—the idea that there is a moral rule of law and of rights above that of the nation-state, a concept that, in its modern form, was sui generis to that era.[1] In the pages that follow, I trace the path to "Christian" violence and then to reconciliation based on fundamental demands for human rights during the so-called Central American crisis.

Finding the Preferential Option for the Poor

In 1968, the Latin America Council of Bishops (CELAM) convened its Second General Conference in Medellín, Colombia, to consider the specific application of Vatican II to the region. The conference was also propelled by movements for reform within the Latin American Church that had anticipated the Vatican's new direction (Levine 1986). In particular, the convening bishops articulated the Church's "preferential option for the poor" and called for biblically based *concientización* (consciousness-raising) to help the poor take control of their lives in the temporal world. This was the heart of the approach that took its name—"liberation theology." Although Pope Paul VI opened the conference with words of caution ("not in hate, not in violence"), the bishops called for the Church to "denounce the fact that Latin America sees itself caught between these two options [capitalism and communism] and remains dependent on one or other of the centers of power which control its economy" (CELAM 1968). It would not be long before some clergy began to read these words through the lens of militancy.

Liberation theology had a galvanizing effect throughout Latin America, bringing thousands of the faithful to an informed understanding of its beliefs and to social action for the first time. It is hard to overstate the significance of the strong position taken at the Medellín conference, not only for the Catholic Church, but also for ordinary Catholics all over Latin America. Penny Lernoux, a journalist for the *National Catholic Reporter* whose book, *Cry of the People* (1980), first introduced these ideas to a wide American audience, succinctly summed this up. "Medellín was one of the major political events of the century," she wrote. "It shattered the centuries' old alliance of Church, military, and rich elites" (37).

This was especially true for Central America, where in three countries—El Salvador, Nicaragua, and Guatemala—armed leftist movements, many of them influenced and supported by revolutionary Cuba, were forming to overthrow repressive and retrograde governments. The movements varied considerably in their ideologies and alliances, but virtually all of them sought to bring about a more equal distribution of resources, especially land, that had long been in the hands of tiny elites and foreign interests. Two powerful forces, liberating Catholicism and popular armed movements, came together, linked not by ideology or even, generally speaking, methodology (although many liberationists did not disdain Marxist analysis) but by common understanding of the roots of injustice and inequality. Where Marxist guerrillas might blame dependency, exploitation, and capitalism, liberationist Catholics decried "structural sin" and "institutionalized violence" (see CELAM 1979). Yet a common concern with the welfare of the poor, ideology notwithstanding, would eventually make radical Catholics and Marxist guerrillas very strange bedfellows in Central America. Ultimately, however, it would be the issue of violence—by, for, and against the poor and the liberationist clergy themselves—that would push the revolutionary Church from advocating radical change to urging peace and reconciliation.

Applying the Principles of Medellín

With the sea changes of Vatican II and Medellín, Catholic clergy in Latin America found themselves suddenly cast in a new paradigm of social justice that departed dramatically from traditional Catholic social thought.

Earlier formulations had been built largely on customary ideas of charity, noblesse oblige, or, in the early twentieth century, the welfare of "corporate" groups such as workers and youth that organizations such as Catholic Action promoted. The call for a preferential option for the poor turned traditional Catholic social thought, based on patriarchal and Thomistic models, on its head, by emphasizing the majority of Catholics in Latin America who were poor and by calling on clergy to join the poor and share their struggles. From rectories that were luxurious by the standards of the surrounding communities, clergy moved into barrios and remote rural communities to live among the poor. Many priests (unsuccessfully) encouraged their parishioners to call them by their first names to emphasize that rather than authorities and direct intercessors with God they were spiritual "animators"—a term often used in Christian base communities (CEBs)—and *compañeros* in the struggle for social justice.

This transition was not always an easy one for parishioners or clergy; the emphasis of Vatican II on rationality and worldliness often unsettled those whose faith centered on the saints, popular devotions, and sacred images that the Church seemed now to disdain. As the religious studies scholar Robert Orsi (2005, 56) writes, "[People were surprised] when all of sudden the altar was turned around, new movements were required in church, they could eat meat on Fridays. One day the saints disappeared, the rosaries stopped, the novenas ended, just like that." Even priests who were coming of age at the time of Vatican II had been trained in Tridentine seminaries. *Lumen gentium*, Vatican II's encyclical challenge to take the "Church to the world," gave a whole new meaning to what constituted evangelization and parish work.

Nor did the institutional Church at large or diocesan bishops offer clear instructions as to how these changes should be construed. To the contrary, one of the paradoxes of the 1968 Medellín conference is that while the "radical," liberationist members of CELAM managed to push forward a highly progressive agenda for the Latin American clergy, less liberal and even very conservative bishops, a vocal minority at Medellín, managed to block many of the conference's mandates. In El Salvador, for example, where liberation theology produced some of its greatest theologians and also its most noted martyrs, the hierarchy was divided from the start, resulting in a decidedly mixed pastoral message. El Salvador's archbishop, Luis Chávez y González, a strong anticommunist, was deeply affected by the new direction proposed by Vatican II. The bishops instructed their clergy that they could, and indeed should, "accompany"—that is, support but not lead—the people in their struggle, but they were not to take a political stance (Montgomery 1982, 101).

In Nicaragua, Archbishop Miguel Obando y Bravo, primate of the three large metropolitan dioceses that would become revolutionary hotbeds in the coming years, was another ambivalent figure. Although he opposed the Somoza family dynasty, he adjured radical solutions, including the experiments practiced by his own priests in Nicaragua. However, Obando's gesture of selling the Mercedes Benz that Somoza had bestowed on him and giving the money to the poor clearly signaled that the institutional Nicaraguan Church wished to distance itself from the dictatorship (Dodson and Nuzzi O'Shaughnessy 1990, 120). Guatemala's archbishop, Mario Casariego, by contrast, the most conservative of the Central American archbishops, vociferously opposed Medellín's progressive liberationist documents and refused to sign them.

Despite such ambivalence, in June 1970 the Central American bishops met in Antigua, Guatemala, to acknowledge their obedience to the doctrines of Medellín and to draw a blueprint of how its conclusions could best be implemented. The bishops stated their desire to convey the gospel in such a way as to "better serve the salvation of the Central American man, especially the poor and humble," and denounced "repressive measures and obstacles" that stood in the way of development. However, they also strongly affirmed that only development (that is to say, not violence or revolution) could bring about "authentic liberation" (quoted in R. Cardenal 1985, 143–44).

The gap between ecclesiastical discourse and praxis, between the episcopacy and the "lower" clergy, overshadowed the promises of Medellín from the beginning. Thus it fell to the local clergy to figure out how best to put the new mandates of liberation theology into motion. Two religious orders—the U.S.-based Maryknolls and the Jesuits, who had long records of independent action in Latin America—took the lead in this effort, although many other clergy, both secular and those from orders such as the Franciscans, Dominicans, and Salesians, also became integrally involved in the process.

Putting the Option for the Poor into Practice

Because many if not the majority of clergy in Central America were originally from outside the region, their notions of what constituted "social justice" for the poor varied. American clergy working in Central America were likely to conceptualize social justice along *desarrollista* lines, more or less paralleling the aid-and-development model favored by U.S. government entities such as the Alliance for Progress and USAID. This approach was designed to deter the advance of communism with social betterment for the poor through access to education, land reform, increased agricultural productivity, and industrialization. This decidedly middle-of-the road alternative to Marxist revolution was stridently nonviolent in its approach and envisioned the rise of an educated, middle-class citizenry that favored a Catholic and, quite likely, pro-U.S. outlook.

The number of articles written by Catholic clergy in the late 1960s and 1970s on such unlikely topics as the use of fertilizer and land use, as well as on education—a traditional Catholic concern—underscore the popularity of this approach. They also align these sorts of "liberationist" clergy with centrist Christian Democratic leaders such as José Napoleón Duarte, a moderate political figure and friend of the United States who served as president of El Salvador in the early 1980s.[2] Yet even this centrist, nonviolent, and nonrevolutionary line was enough to bring such "liberationist" priests to the hostile attention of the violently anticommunist governments in the countries in which they served. As we shall see, some paid the ultimate price for even a moderate position in favor of the poor and the marginalized.

Nicaragua proved the exception to this rule. Under the long and rapacious rule of the Somoza dynasty, Nicaragua struggled under the burden of some of the lowest social indicators of any country in the Western Hemisphere outside of Haiti. Life expectancy in Nicaragua in 1970, for example, was only fifty-three years; only 49 percent of the population was literate. Nicaragua's "superlatives" were equally dubious: it suffered the highest murder rate, the highest accident rate, and the highest alcoholism rate in Central America (Booth 1982, 85).

Here local circumstances were so dire that Catholic clergy undertook progressive social action early, as they began to reinterpret the gospel from a see-judge-act perspective (a methodology for action pioneered by the Belgian priest Joseph Cardijn, founder of the Young Christian Workers movement) that anticipated the praxis of liberation theology. One of the first such theological experiments in living took place on the island of Solentiname, a poor community located in the middle of Lake Nicaragua, which Ernesto Cardenal, a Catholic priest, established in 1966. In 1976, Cardenal produced a highly influential book on this exercise in practical theology that was based on edited tapes of participatory discussions of the gospel in the community. First published in Spanish and eventually in multiple languages, *The Gospel in Solentiname* soon became a road map for community liberationist hermeneutics throughout Latin America.

The Solentiname experiment was only one of several new Catholic initiatives for social justice that inexorably propelled the Church away from its support of the Somoza regime. Among the most important of these was the Jesuit-founded Comité Evangélico de Promoción Agraria (CEPA), a program to train peasant leaders, and the Delegados de la Palabra, a new type of lay group that allowed nonordained people to perform certain sacramental functions and, by extension, to become community leaders (Dodson and Nuzzi O'Shaughnessy 1990, 124–25). As these popular Catholic organizations spread throughout rural Nicaragua and in the slums of Managua, their members contributed directly to the Sandinistas' growing insurrection against the Somoza regime in the late 1970s. Christian catechists (members of CEBs) became active participants in Sandinista cadres, taking up arms against the Somocista National Guard (see Berryman 1984, 51–89).

While Nicaragua led the vanguard of progressive CEB formation in Central America, similar faith communities quickly emerged elsewhere. Writing in the early 1980s about El Salvador, Tommie Sue Montgomery (1982, 99) noted, "It can be argued that these communities are the most revolutionary development in the Latin American church because, for the first time in history, the masses of the people are participating in and taking responsibility for important aspects of their own lives and for each other; they were no longer merely observers at a ritual conducted for their benefit by a resident or visiting priest." She added that this form of participation, however, "has had some social consequences." As indeed it had.

Although liberationist priests themselves did not take up arms against the Somoza regime, many actively supported its overthrow and the role that Christians—not only Catholics but also, as we shall see later, some Protestants—were playing in the insurrection. When the Sandinistas defeated Somoza and came to power in July 1979, no less than four Catholic clergy assumed high positions in the new administration.[3] It was in part the prominence of these clergy in the Sandinista government that caused Pope John Paul II's censure of the leftist regime during his controversial visit to Nicaragua in 1983.

At first, the Sandinistas, then a fairly conventional Marxist group, disdained religion for raising false consciousness and were dubious of Christians' participation as combatants in a struggle for the violent overthrow of the government (Dodson and Nuzzi O'Shaughnessy 1990, 128). Yet the enthusiasm of young catechists and priests, inspired by their faith if not always by Marxist ideology to fight against a repressive regime, eventually convinced the guerrillas to take them in as comrades in arms.

Fernando Cardenal, the brother of Ernesto and a Jesuit priest, came to openly embrace the Sandinista cause and fully understood that doing so meant engaging in violent acts. Unlike some former revolutionary clergy elsewhere in Central America, Cardenal remains unambivalent about his role in the armed uprising, noting with uncharacteristic pride that he was able to "help idealistic young people overthrow a brutal dictatorship."[4] When the Sandinistas first invited him to join their movement, Cardenal recalls asking himself, "What would God do in this case?" Remembering the parable of the Good Samaritan, he accepted the Sandinistas' offer and was given the nom de guerre Marcos, after the Gospel writer. Of this moment, Cardenal (2008, 88) writes, "I had never read a book by Carlos Marx, I had never read a book by Lenin, but I had read the Gospel and I had read the Latin American reality. My motivation to become a militant was profoundly religious, inspired by the word of Jesus and sealed by what had happened at Medellín. This was the motivation: *profunda, clarísima, clarísima, clarísima.*" "Thus," he adds, "did this Nicaraguan priest become a militant of the Frente Sandinista de la Liberación Nacional, putting myself and all I had [*ponerme yo y todo lo mío*] at the service of the revolution of our people."

Taking the Revolutionary Road

Nicaragua was not the only place where some Catholic clergy took the challenge of the preferential option for the poor to its logical extreme, taking up arms with Marxist-oriented popular movements attempting to overthrow repressive governments. In so doing, they were following the model of one of the first "revolutionary priests," Camilo Torres, who had—after officially, though not morally, renouncing his clerical vows—joined the Ejército de Liberación Nacional (ELN) in Colombia and then died in combat in 1966—two years prior, it bears noting, to the Medellín conference.

A sociologist and academic by training, Torres had tried in his professional writing to reconcile Christianity and Marxism. His reading of Colombia's social problems through the lenses of his academic discipline and of the gospel pushed him first toward socialism and then armed revolution. Eventually, Torres became famous for declaring, "If Jesus were alive today, He would be a *guerrillero*," as well as for the manner of his death (Sánchez Lopera 2006). Writing clandestinely from the field in 1965 to a group of fellow clergy in Latin America, Torres (1969) grappled directly with the issue of the role of armed violence in pursuit of social justice—declaring that the guiding principle of Catholicism is "love thy neighbor" but that this principle could only be fully realized if the "minority"—the rich and powerful—were willing to give up their privilege in favor of the poor and oppressed. "The revolution can be peaceful," he wrote, "[only] if the minority do not resist violently," a condition that Torres understood correctly to be improbable (11).

Torres was among the first Catholic priests of the era to choose the path of armed resistance to the entrenched powers that liberation theology identified as structural sin, and many interpreted his death as a martyrdom. It served as an inspiration to those clergy in Central America who saw in the repressive power structures of El Salvador, Guatemala, and Nicaragua conditions that demanded they consider throwing their lot in with armed guerrillas, usually inspired and often trained by Cuba, whose stated goals of equality and justice for the poor were framed in a different ideology but otherwise largely seemed to mirror their own. In late 1967, three Maryknoll clergy—the brothers Thomas and Arthur Melville and a nun, Sister Marian Peter—were expelled by the Guatemalan government for being in contact, with the intent to join, the Cuban-supported Fuerzas Armadas Rebeldes (FAR) guerrillas (Berryman 1995, 15). The *New York Times* and State Department documents at the time averred that the clergy's connections with the armed movement were still preliminary.[5] In 1968, however, Sister Marian, by then laicized from Maryknoll and using her baptismal name Marjorie, spoke directly of the need for armed revolution and her commitment to it. "I must prove by my acts that a sincere Christian must look for unity with all revolutionaries and stay ready to give her life for her friends," she declared. "I am not enthusiastic about the idea and the thought of having to carry a weapon. But if I think again on indigenous families carrying their burdens, moving on toward the hot [coastal] lands, horribly paid, and treated worse than beasts, then I feel ready to defend them and to fight" (Peter 1969, 81).

This process was not easy, and the majority of social justice–oriented Catholic clergy could not reject Christ's calls for peaceability by embracing acts of violence by themselves or their parishioners. Nevertheless, documents circulated privately among clergy advocating "liberating violence in exceptional cases when no other alternative existed to the 'institutionalized violence' of an unjust socio-economic system that left the poor permanently disenfranchised and disgraced" (Iriarte 1985, 99–101). Blase Bonpane (1985), a Maryknoll priest who became part of the popular movement in the Guatemalan highlands in the mid-1960s, explained his understanding of the role of the militant priest. "The presence of a priest within a rebel group will undoubtedly encourage many who are yet unsure to join forces," he wrote. "The presence of a priest can bring moderation, however, to the violence that is the unfortunate tool of revolution. It can also give qualities of forgiveness and not vengeance to the new order, once established" (79). Juan Luis Segundo, an influential Jesuit theologian in Uruguay, however, cautioned against this kind of equivocation. "No one can enter into the revolutionary process," he warned his brethren, "without forming some idea for himself of the goal of the process and the proper means to be used to achieve it" (Segundo, quoted in Jackson, 2003, 112).

Yet the road from the altar to revolution was not always direct, as evinced by the case of Father Rutilio Grande, a Salvadoran Jesuit priest whose training and orientation were entirely upended by the new liberationist thought and theology. Ordained in 1959 and close to prominent members of the Church hierarchy, Grande's career trajectory was initially conventional and institutional: early in his ministry, he served as prefect of discipline and professor of pastoral theology in the diocesan seminary. In the mid-1970s, however, Grande left his position as director of Social Action at the Jesuit seminary in San Salvador to follow his seminarians into parish work among the poor in and around the *municipio* of Aguilares. Aguilares was a poverty-stricken village located in a region where several militant groups—later united in 1980 under the Frente Farabundo Martí para la Liberación Nacional (FMLN)—were organizing among the poor against the Salvadoran government and the elite coffee barons—the so-called 14 Families—who controlled the country.

In 1975, the disputed shooting of a prominent landholder from Aguilares fed a growing sense among the landholding class that the Church was fostering the armed revolutionary movement (R. Cardenal 1985, 536–37). Government repression against the popular organizations in the region was swift and severe, and many of Grande's parishioners were killed or disappeared. On October 4, 1975, hostile attention turned to Padre Grande himself. On the feast day of St. Francis of Assisi, he said Mass for a wealthy landholding family and used the opportunity to preach against the mistreatment and exploitation of workers in the name of the humble saint. This message greatly inspired the workers in attendance but infuriated the landowners. A conservative eyewitness later denounced the sermon as "the moment when the Jesuit mask fell away and out jumped a person full of prejudices, slander and rancor, spewing out political social communist discourse and injecting discord in the minds of the humble workers and all those present toward the *patrones* and the constitutional authorities of the nation" (R. Cardenal 1985, 469).

Grande was not expressly political, nor was he a member of one of the popular organizations; his view was that overtly political organizations and armed entities in particular should not be identified with the Church. However, the implications of organizing communities for "self-evangelization" and reflection in CEBs and urging his people to emerge from their "*conciencia mágica*" and fatalism to strive for a better, more just life were political (R. Cardenal 1985, 235–36). In 1977, the government attempted to seal off the area to prevent further guerrilla recruitment. Father Grande offered a fiery sermon (later dubbed the Apopa Sermon, for the village where he preached it) against this measure that ultimately cost him his life. "I'm very aware that very soon the Bible and the Gospel won't be allowed to cross our borders," he preached. "I think that if Jesus himself were across the border in Chalatenango, they wouldn't let him in. . . . They would accuse the man . . . of being a rabble-rouser, a foreign Jew, one who confused the people with exotic and foreign ideas, ideas against democracy—that is, against the wealthy minority, the clan of Cain! Brothers and sisters, without any doubt, they would crucify him again. And God forbid that I be one of the crucifiers!"[6] Shortly thereafter, Grande uttered some of his most famous words, "It's a dangerous thing to be a Christian in this world," which proved a prophetic statement. The priest and two parishioners—a teenage boy and an elderly man—were machine-gunned to death by Salvadoran security forces on March 12, 1977 (Montgomery 1982, 109).

Many clergy struggled with the issue of armed violence in the name of social justice, and it is important to note that the vast majority of them did not take up arms. While it was one thing to support the armed movement from a moral or even strategic perspective, it was another entirely to actually become a combatant and thus violate one of the most fundamental teachings of the faith—thou shall not kill—in the name of social justice for the poor. There were gradations of support for the guerrillas— *simpatizante* (sympathizer), *colaborador* (someone who knowingly gave assistance, such as providing food or delivering a package), to outright *miembro* (member), someone who placed himself under the discipline of the organization, to do whatever was required. Of course, any level of participation demanded commitment and secrecy, since the ardently anti-communist governments in power did not recognize these distinctions.

Among liberationist clergy who came to support the guerrilla movements, most fell into the lower categories of support. For many, the question of revolutionary violence was simply an unbreachable barrier to full revolutionary participation. "El deber de todo cristiano es ser revolucionario [The duty of every Christian is to be revolutionary]," Torres had once written (quoted in Levine 2011, 60). Even so, not all—probably not even most—radical clergy could share Torres's clarity or conviction when it came to the matter of revolutionary violence.

The writings of a Spanish Jesuit, Fernando Hoyos Rodríguez, who worked in Guatemala during the 1970s, offer a window on the tension between Christian "duty" and revolutionary violence that confronted liberationist priests. The 1954 coup and years of military government, with strong U.S. support, had resulted in fierce cycles of popular protest and harsh counterinsurgency throughout the late 1960s, until the Guatemalan military virtually crushed the guerrilla movement. By the mid-1970s, however, new popular movements such as the Comité de Unidad Campesina (CUC), established by young leaders who had become politicized in part through their participation in organizations like Catholic Action and CRATER, a Catholic student group, had begun to move their struggle to the Maya highlands. The formation of the Guatemalan "new left" had its parallel in El Salvador, where the popular movement took off after the fraudulent presidential elections of 1972, and Nicaragua, where multiple popular movements were then coalescing under the Sandinistas, who in 1979 would overthrow the dictatorship of Anastasio Somoza. In this rapidly changing political context, the mantra of Catholic Action, "see-judge-act," took on a new immediacy.

Shortly before his ordination to the priesthood in early 1974, the young Hoyos—who died in 1983 at age thirty-nine during a firefight with Guatemalan soldiers—wrote to his friends and family about his eagerness to embrace the opportunity to work among the poor, who in his words "are persecuted, who cry, who hunger and thirst for justice." "In my priesthood, I want to fight in a special way to take part in the building of a new society, different from the current one" he explained. "I am becoming a priest to 'carry the good news of the Gospel to all men, to announce to those who are held captive, to give light to the blind, and to free the oppressed' (Luke 4:18)."[7]

Over the next few years, Hoyos's experiences of the grievous poverty, racism, inequality, and ruthless violence afflicting the indigenous poor in rural Guatemala radicalized him. One turning point seems to have been when the Church's work among victims of a catastrophic earthquake in February 1976 provoked Guatemala's vice president to observe that "the Church [wa]s an instrument of communism" (Hoyos de Asig 1997, 75). In 1980, after much consideration and reflection, Hoyos joined the Ejército Guerrillero de los Pobres (EGP) as a combatant.

He detailed the process that led to this decision in letters to his family and to his fellow "Zone 5 Jesuits"—a group of like-minded clergy who had developed a radical perspective from living and working among the poor in a blighted section of Guatemala City. At first, Hoyos equivocated about his priestly status. "For me," he wrote, "this does not signify my leaving the Company of Jesus; however, I am open to the future and it could be that within a few months I may not think so." "But if it is incompatible for me to continue feeling like a Jesuit," he added, "I will never stop being a Christian, and I think that even if I were to stop believing in God, he would never stop believing in me. . . . The Christian principles that have always guided me will continue to guide me wherever I go, and God, present in the people, will be my compass, *hasta la victoria siempre*" (quoted in Hoyos de Asig 1997, 96–97).

The issue of revolutionary violence soon forced Hoyos to change his mind about his priestly vocation. Writing to his family in November 1980, he explained, "My tasks in the EGP are more political than military. However, I am convinced of the necessity of weapons in Central America. The only way to shine light is to use arms against those who quench life. To not use arms is to be complicit in the thousands of assassinations that take place not only with weapons but through [the] hunger, sickness, and malnutrition suffered by the majority of our population." Shortly thereafter, he bid farewell to his Jesuit brothers with these words: "Mi camino va por otro rumbo [I must follow a different path]" (quoted in Hoyos de Asig 1997, 97–98).

The history of Central America in the late 1970s and early 1980s reads like a martyrology, replete with dozens of killed and assassinated clergy and many hundreds more Catholic (and to a lesser extent, Protestant) politically active laypeople who died, mainly at the hands of national security forces in El Salvador and Guatemala, for their real or perceived associations with the armed Left. The numbers from this period are chilling: in El Salvador, nine priests, nuns, and lay sisters killed; in Guatemala, twenty-seven clergy killed, all by security forces or the military, between the mid-1970s and mid-1980s; and several hundred lay activists killed in both countries. The most violent decade of El Salvador's civil war is bracketed by the murders of Catholic church people. In March 1980, El Salvador's metropolitan archbishop, Óscar Arnulfo Romero, was assassinated before his altar by a gunman linked to right-wing death squads. Later that year, four American churchwomen were raped and murdered by national guardsmen (Brett and Brett 1988). In 1989, the Salvadoran military ordered the execution-style killing of six prominent Jesuit clergy (along with their housekeeper and her daughter) for their intellectual associations with the FMLN. Even after the violence in Central America had subsided, outspoken clergy were in danger. Bishop Juan Gerardi was murdered in Guatemala immediately after the publication of the Catholic Church's searing truth commission report, "Informe REMHI," in 1997 (Goldman 2007).

Although most of the violence that affected Christian activists was directed at Catholics during this period, ecumenical Protestants who identified with the poor were also targeted. Military leaders in both El Salvador and Guatemala shared a perception that *evangélicos* (as all Protestants are commonly termed in Central America) were "apolitical" or even pro-government, a belief underscored by General Efraín Ríos Montt's conflation of evangelical theology and war against the guerrillas in Guatemala. His draconian "beans and bullets" campaign killed many thousands of Guatemalans in 1982 and 1983 (Garrard-Burnett 2010).

While many Central Americans fled to evangelical religion as a refuge from the military persecution, some Protestants, in particular, Lutherans and Presbyterians, found common cause with Catholics on issues of social justice during this period (Chapman 2012; Garrard-Burnett 1998). Yet even for conservative Evangelicals, church affiliation did not necessarily guarantee safety from government violence. Such was the case in one of the most notorious events in El Salvador's civil war, the massacre of more than eight hundred civilians at El Mozote in December 1981. More than half the residents of the town were *evangélicos* who, in the words of a reporting officer for the U.S. Embassy, "unwisely chose to stay behind" (Danner 1993, 19, 112, 119). In a fatal miscalculation, they believed they would be safe from government reprisals because of their religious affiliation.

Archbishop Óscar Arnulfo Romero: Moderate Martyr

Archbishop Romero, perhaps the best known victim of the attacks on progressive clergy in Central America, has become both a martyr of the faith and an icon of liberation theology, so much so that the process for his canonization for sainthood—usually fast-tracked for martyrs of the Church—was stalled until quite recently in the Vatican, where conservatives attempted to "domesticate and privatize" his image (Vásquez and Peterson 2009). A little more than a month after assuming office, Pope Francis, the first Latin American pope, officially "unblocked" Romero's path to canonization. In February 2015 Francis named Romero a "martyr for the faith," a significant measure that positioned Romero's assassination as a direct result of his faith, not his politics, and further strengthened his case for sainthood.[8]

Beyond the image, Romero's ministry and martyrdom are instructive. Unlike the militant clergy described above, Romero at the time of his appointment as archbishop in February 1977 was seen by all sides as a moderate, not necessarily a compliment in the highly polarized El Salvador of the late 1970s. Some worried he would exacerbate divisions among the clergy (Whitfield 1994, 103). Rich and powerful Salvadorans first distrusted and then reviled him for what turned out to be his strong support of the Church of the poor. The radical left mistrusted him for his failure to endorse the armed revolution. His commitment to the poor, fueled in part by his reflections following the death of his friend Rutilio Grande, among others, was matched by his profound belief in the power of nonviolence.

As violence in El Salvador rose dramatically in the late 1970s, Romero became increasingly outspoken. Although his words and gestures were not, strictly speaking, partisan, El Salvador's murderous right wing, the authors of the most pernicious violence of those days, correctly understood his denunciations as directed at them. During the nation's descent into a nightmare of violence and chaos, Romero issued a series of four pastoral letters between 1977 and 1980. To today's reader, the sermons are remarkable for their consistency, their passion for social justice and against inequality, but also for their air of calm restraint. The third letter is especially salient. Issued in August 1978 and titled, "The Church and Popular Political Organizations," it spoke directly to the question of violence, and revolutionary violence in particular: "The Christian is peaceful. . . . [He is] not simply a pacifist, for he can fight, but prefers peace to war" (Romero 1985, 109). This same pastoral letter exhorted Salvadoran

Catholics—that is to say, virtually all Salvadorans at that time—to adopt a position of nonviolence. Like a "voice crying in the desert," he said, we must continually say "no to violence, yes to peace" (106). The letter outlined the evils of "institutional violence" and repression but emphasized nonviolence as a response. "The Gospel's advice to turn the other cheek to an unjust aggressor, far from being passivity and cowardice," he wrote, "is evidence of great moral strength that can leave an aggressor morally defeated and humiliated. 'The Christian can fight, but prefers peace to war'" (107–8). With such arguments, Romero anticipated what would become a significant pivot in the radical wing of the Church, from support for armed revolution to a demand for human rights. Although the bishop did not himself use the term *human rights*, his discourse was deeply grounded in a basic demand for respect for justice and the fundamental dignity of every human being.

Romero was fully aware that his words echoed not only the teachings of Jesus but also those of Gandhi and Martin Luther King Jr.; he was equally mindful that all three came to a violent end. In early March 1980, he told a Guatemalan reporter, "I have often been threatened with death. If they kill me, I shall arise in the Salvadoran people. If the threats are fulfilled, from this moment I offer my blood to God for the redemption and resurrection of El Salvador. Let my blood be a seed of freedom and the sign that hope will soon be reality" (quoted in Dear 2001, 146).

Romero's voice of reason did indeed speak too loudly for the authorities. As violence escalated at the turn of the decade, so did the bishop's demands for it to end. His words, directed in particular toward the leaders of death squads, hit their mark. On March 23, he issued his most blistering indictment against violence in a weekly radio address, speaking directly to members of the armed forces and the paramilitaries:

I would like to make an appeal in a special way to the men of the army, to the police, to those in the barracks. Brothers, you are part of our own people. You kill your own *campesino* brothers and sisters. And before an order to kill that a man may give, the law of God must prevail that says: Thou shalt not kill! No soldier is obliged to obey an order against the law of God. No one has to fulfill an immoral law. It is time to recover your consciences and to obey your consciences rather than the orders of sin. The church, defender of the rights of God, of the law of God, of human dignity, the dignity of the person, cannot remain silent before such abomination. We want the government to take seriously that reforms are worth nothing when they come about stained with so much blood. In the name of God, and in the name of this suffering people whose laments rise to heaven each day more tumultuously, I beg you, I ask you, I order you in the name of God: Stop the repression! (Quoted in Brockman 1989, 241–42)

The next day, March 24, 1980, Archbishop Romero was shot to death while saying Mass, joining other great champions of nonviolence in martyrdom. Among Romero's last words were these: "[May we] give our body and our blood to suffering and pain—like Christ, not for self, but to bring about justice and peace to our people" (Romero 1990, 306). At his funeral, security forces attempted to disperse the crowd with tear gas and rifle shots. Between thirty and fifty people died in the resulting chaos. Although at the time, many—including his killers—saw Archbishop Romero as a martyr of liberation theology, in fact, his death both marked and hastened the Church's redefinition of its option for the poor in favor of human rights, not revolution. Indeed, it is Archbishop Romero's martyrdom that inspired a new commitment to nonviolence within the Latin American Catholic Church. Although the Church would continue to provide many other martyrs in the coming decade, Romero's death in many ways marks the beginning of the end of the Church's ties to radical militancy.

Religious Actors in the Central America Peace Process

In the 1980s, the "popular" Church's commitment to liberation theology in its most radical form—overt or covert support for the popular movements and sometimes an endorsement of armed revolutionary violence—thus began to wane. The election in 1979 of Pope John Paul II, a theological conservative, signaled the Vatican's growing displeasure with liberation theology. In 1979, CELAM met again, but this time the bishops excoriated the liberationist turn. In his opening address, Pope John

Paul II declared, "We are going to proclaim once again the truth of faith about Jesus Christ," a challenge rendered much more concretely in Puebla's final documents, which called for the Church's traditional Christology to be made new again. In a direct reproach to liberation theology, the CELAM documents insisted that it is the Church's "duty to proclaim clearly the mystery of the Incarnation, leaving no room for doubt or equivocation. . . . [It] cannot distort, factionize, or ideologize the person of Jesus Christ by turning him into a politician, a leader, a revolutionary, or a simple prophet" (Opening Address by Pope John Paul II and Document #178, quoted in Sobrino 1987, 7).

The deep divisions within the Nicaraguan Catholic Church between "popular" (pro-Sandinista) Catholics and an increasingly wary institutional Church contributed to radical liberation theology's decline, or at least its sharp reorientation. This was clearly evident in the pope's 1983 visit to Central America, where, among other incidents, he famously castigated Ernesto Cardenal on the tarmac at the Managua airport and where Sandinista cadres attempted to shout him down while he was saying Mass in the Plaza de la Revolución. Yet this kind of confrontation seemed almost inevitable given the pope's stated purpose for making the trip to a region of the world at that time in the midst of war: to provide a pastoral presence to suffering Catholics, to press for peace, and, significantly, to "secure the identity of the Church in light of the teachings of the Second Vatican Council *and the CELAM meeting in Puebla*" (L'Osservatore Romano 1983, 66; my emphasis). With this, the doors of the institutional Church slammed shut on liberation theology. But the mobilized faith of many Catholics on the ground, both clergy and laity, simply and slowly began to channel their energies in a new direction, from revolution to human rights.

Indeed, the deaths of Romero, scores of priests, and hundreds of lay Catholics in Central America led many surviving activist clergy and laypeople to reassess the moral cost of putting so many lives on the line. This was more than simply a matter of strategy. The Christian injunction to "love thy neighbor" had never fit easily alongside the ideology and exigencies of class struggle.

But it was the issue of violence—both the philosophical considerations associated with its use and, critically, the state-sponsored violence against Catholic lay and clerical leaders—that compelled theologians and

Catholic activists to move in a new direction. It is important to underscore that in Central America prior to the era of "crisis," poverty and all its pathogens were rampant, but institutional violence, whether emanating from revolutionaries or, more commonly, the state, was relatively rare, and violence against the Church and especially its clergy, who had traditionally held a hallowed space in society, was rarer still. The armed struggles and counterinsurgency movements of the 1970s and 1980s turned this equation on its head, and gruesome, wholesale "industrial-scale violence" against individuals and communities became commonplace, leaving few untouched.

The magnitude of this violence against the Church—both its people and the institution—is hard to fathom and was profoundly instrumental. In El Salvador, for example, between January 5, 1980, and February 27, 1981, in addition to the assassination of Archbishop Romero in March and the four American churchwomen in December, there were some three hundred attacks on the Church, including thirty-nine assassinations, nineteen bombings, forty-three shootings at church buildings, and thirty robberies of church properties (Mich 1998, 255). While the original focus of liberation theology had been poverty, it was the Central American governments' brutal repression of the poor, including those who had become political activists through work in their parishes, that shifted the popular Church's quest for social justice toward a new imperative, human rights, by the most basic, corporal definition: the right to stay alive, freedom from torture and violence, and the fundamental right to personhood.

By the mid-1980s, human rights had become the rallying point for moral action, thus moving the option for the poor from revolution to, eventually, reconciliation (which demands all sides come to grips with their own culpability in order to begin a process that may end in mutual forgiveness or at least trust) and peace. Like the militant impulses that grew out of Medellín, the fight for human rights, too, could lead to "prophetic," sometimes dangerous, religious work. But as a concept, it fit easily with traditional Catholic moral theology. It also appealed as a moral cause to the many Catholics who had been driven away from social action by the violence (either by or against practitioners) that they believed was an implicit part of revolutionary liberation theology.

Toward Dialogue and Human Rights

After Archbishop Romero's assassination, the Salvadoran popular Church adopted a position known as *acompañamiento* (accompaniment), which called on liberationist Catholics and their leaders to "accompany" the poor in their struggle but not necessarily to lead in the vanguard of that struggle.[9] Ignacio Ellacuría, a priest and philosopher and rector of the Universidad Centroamericana "José Simeón Cañas" (UCA), advocated for dialogue between combative parties in El Salvador. This suggestion was so ahead of its time that the Secret Anti-Communist Army (ESA) denounced it in 1983 as "treason to the fatherland." Ellacuría never wavered from his commitment to the process, however, pressing all sides, including the U.S. government, to work as a force for good.

In the forefront of forging new approaches that framed the option for the poor, more in terms of the effects of violence than of poverty was the Spanish Jesuit Ignacio Martín-Baró. Martín-Baró had long taught at San Salvador's UCA and witnessed the nation's atrocities firsthand. He sought new, nonviolent ways to advance social justice that broke away from the political model of liberation. He developed an innovative approach he called "liberation psychology" that tried to change the sociopolitical structure by psychotherapeutic methods rather than through intractable politics or revolutionary violence. Martín-Baró was among those in the vanguard of vernacular theologians and activists who were beginning to construct a new pastoral method that framed responses to violence and, by extension, human rights as the forefront of lived theology. This approach attempted to understand the psychology of the people in impoverished communities and address in a practical way the oppressive sociopolitical structures under which they lived.

A noted social psychologist as well as a priest, Martín-Baró's work (see 1983, 1989) was gaining momentum in both liberationist and professional psychoanalytic circles at the time of his murder by Salvadoran security forces on November 9, 1989—he was one of the six Jesuit martyrs—and remains influential among psychotherapists today. In his posthumously published work, *Poder, ideología y violencia*, Martín-Baró argued that violence had become so embedded in Salvadoran society that it was no longer mundanely *political* per se, but, thanks to the nation's particular history and its people's long-conditioned psychological expectations, had become a formative element of the Salvadoran social system. At the time of his death, Martín-Baró was attempting to build an epistemological argument by which to explain El Salvador's violence in terms of human behavior and the ways in which societal violence becomes "acceptable" when supported by an ideology that, due to social conditioning, seems to direct, support, legitimate, justify, and ascribe meaning to it (Martín-Baró 2003). That four of Ellacuría's and Martín-Baró's Jesuit colleagues were assassinated because of their ideas by Salvadoran security forces in their campus residence at the UCA on November 16, 1989, only, perhaps, underscores the credibility of Martín-Baró's hypotheses.

As theological innovators on the ground began to redirect the current of liberation theology toward human rights and denunciations of violence, the institutional Church continued to distance itself. At the next CELAM meeting, held in Santo Domingo in 1992, for example, the convocation's Final Document—a highly mediated text subject to much scrutiny, redaction, and interlineation—made no mention at all of any of the Central American martyrs. Jon Sobrino—another Salvadoran Jesuit theologian—called this silence "absolutely incomprehensible, highly suspicious, and above all, terribly impoverishing" (Sobrino, quoted in Mich 1998, 255). Such a significant omission clearly signaled that the institutional Church was still not ready to position itself as a champion against violence and human rights abuses, even when its own clergy and laity had already put their own lives on the line in the name of their faith.

Yet the failure to do so reflected two pragmatic considerations within the Vatican. The first was political, as John Paul II's "New Evangelization" moved sharply away from the reforms of Vatican II. But even more fundamentally, the idea of human rights—the protection of the "unencumbered individual" in the modern sense—is something that grows out of a modern, secular liberal worldview. In the words of a contemporary American Jesuit writer, "For a Catholic tradition to embrace a liberal human rights ethic would be subversive of its insights into the importance of the community and the common good." Yet these lofty considerations meant little to Central American clergy and "ordinary" Catholics whose lives and communities had been swept by waves of violence and for whom "human rights" was focused not so much on political empowerment but on the literal embodiment of dignity and human survival (Hollenbach, in Douglass and Hollenbach 2002, 130).

Much of the discussion above has focused on questions of religion and violence in Guatemala and El Salvador. But it is important to remember that Nicaragua was at the vortex of this crisis, especially from the point of view of the United States, which actively sought the overthrow of the leftist Sandinista regime through aid, training, and military support to anti-Sandinista Contra rebels. There were some religious dimensions to this showdown (vividly illustrated by the pope's 1983 pastoral visit to Central America). The pope subsequently demanded that any priests holding public office—a direct reference to Nicaragua's Sandinista priests—withdraw from priestly "faculties." Relations between the Sandinistas and the institutional Church already had begun to fray by the early 1980s, and Archbishop Obando, once a reluctant supporter of the Sandinista revolution, became its enemy.[10] However, outright violence against church people in Nicaragua, though not unheard of, was rare in the 1980s, very much unlike the situation in neighboring Guatemala and El Salvador (Brown 1993, 11).

Nevertheless, progressive Catholics (now known as the "popular Church," as opposed to the institutional one headed by Obando) and ecumenical Protestants alike continued to express solidarity with the Sandinistas. Unlike in Guatemala, Protestants in Nicaragua—with the important exception of Moravians and others on the Miskito Coast who resisted the Sandinistas for ethnic and political reasons—did not fall into the easy division of "radical Catholics" and "conservative *evangélicos*" (Belli 1985). After Nicaragua's devastating earthquake of December 1972, Nicaraguan *evangélicos* had formed a nationwide relief organization, the Comité Evangélico Pro-Ayuda al Desarrollo (CEPAD) to help with earthquake relief. Within a short time, this organization took on a political dimension that drew it closer to the Sandinistas by the mid-1970s (Booth 1982, 137). Nicaraguan Protestants worked alongside Catholic Sandinistas during the insurrection, and the idealism of the Sandinista revolution in its early days appealed to many ecumenical Protestants outside of Nicaragua whose theology fell in line with modern Catholic notions of social justice and structural sin.

Two of the most prominent progressive Protestant U.S. theologians, William Sloane Coffin, a former civil rights activist and senior pastor of New York's Riverside Church, and Robert McAfee Brown, a professor at Union Theological Seminary who had served as a Protestant observer at the Second Vatican Council, were deeply affected by the work of the Church in Nicaragua and also by its "Calvary" in El Salvador and Guatemala. Brown's work, *Unexpected News: Reading the Bible with Third World Eyes* (1984), in particular, distilled and to some extent domesticated the liberationist movement for an American readership by explaining and contextualizing the ongoing struggles in the developing world and the role the Bible played in building people's hopes and expectations for a better life. The work of Coffin (2008) and Brown encouraged the solidarity movement among Christians in the United States, especially progressive Evangelicals who found in their writings and sermons theological justification for their opposition to Ronald Reagan's foreign policy in Central America.

The Solidarity Movement in the United States

When Reagan became president of the United States in 1981 and elevated the Central American struggles to the level of Cold War competition, with threats of potential U.S. intervention, church people, mainly because of their experience and contacts in the region, joined the vanguard of an emerging solidarity movement with Central America in the United States. In November 1981, the U.S. Catholic bishops questioned Reagan's framing of the crisis in the East-West paradigm. Over the next few years, literally hundreds of small organizations began to crop up around the country—the 1985 Directory of Central American Organizations lists 850 different groups—working in solidarity with the people of Central America. Many of these groups had religious roots and were often ecumenical; they pushed for changes in U.S. policy on the region, basing their concerns on human rights and advocating for peace.[11] Other prominent organizations had what might be called a "religious sensibility" regarding human rights and peace initiatives in the region. A good example would be the Washington Office on Latin America (WOLA), whose founders, ongoing board membership, and initial funding came from the progressive ecumenical community.

Some, most notably Witness for Peace and the Sanctuary Movement—a group that harbored and aided Central Americans who had made their way to the United States seeking refugee status—worked directly with religious groups and were among the most vocal advocates for peace in Central America as well as fierce opponents of U.S. policy in the region (Berryman 1995, 227; Tomsho 1987). It was through such emerging solidarity networks that the "accompaniment" of Central America's poor became less a journey toward revolution than one directed to peace and human rights. And thus it was that Protestants as well as Catholics came to play active roles in the initiatives that finally brought peace to Central America in the 1990s.

U.S. Clergy and the Congress during the Central American Crisis

American clergy—Catholic priests in particular, but also religious brothers and sisters—played significant behind-the-scenes roles in opposition to the U.S. policy of support for the Salvadoran government and the Nicaraguan Contras under Presidents Reagan and George H. W. Bush. Two factors made their advocacy unusually effective, especially among U.S. policy makers and Catholic legislators. One was the widespread recognition of their long experience in Central America; the other was the perception, correct or not, that church people—nuns in particular—claimed a moral high ground. In all, their efforts illustrate what Keck and Sikkink (1998, 232) call the "boomerang effect," wherein certain groups are able to forge transnational linkages to advance or protect human rights in ways that transcend national boundaries, not only because Catholics, and many Christians in general, often share a sense of universality, but also because so many members of these groups had a grassroots presence in the communities where rights were under threat.

For example, Peggy Healy, a Maryknoll sister who had worked in Nicaragua, became a critical liaison in relaying information to Congress and WOLA and to ordinary citizens in talks to church and other community groups throughout the northeastern United States. Through family connections, Healy came to know the powerful Democratic Speaker of the House Thomas "Tip" O'Neill. Thanks to her credible testimony, O'Neill became a vigorous opponent of Reagan's support for the Contras against the Sandinista government. When Reagan made his infamous reference to the Contras as the "moral equivalent of the Founding Fathers," O'Neill challenged the president's reliance on CIA intelligence. "My information is much more accurate than that," O'Neill retorted. "I get mine from nuns" (quoted in Byrnes 2011, 100).

American clergy also had an impact on U.S. aid to El Salvador, particularly after the barbarous murder of six Jesuits and their housekeeper and her daughter in November 1989. The Jesuits, who had already suffered losses throughout Latin America, were galvanized to push for a complete investigation of the killings and for an end to U.S. support of the Salvadoran military, basing their arguments on demands for justice and human rights. Many congressional Democrats were already opposed to Reagan's policy in El Salvador, but with pressure from Jesuit college presidents and the order's provincials, that opposition became acute (Byrnes 2011, 56).

Religious Actors in the Peace Accords

The "Central American crisis" was actually three separate struggles in which the U.S. supported one side: the governments in both El Salvador and Guatemala in armed conflicts with leftist guerrillas and the effort to destabilize the revolutionary government of Nicaragua through the antigovernment Contras. The United States and other key actors defined these national conflicts as regional and interrelated, but various peace initiatives based on that understanding all failed. Finally, Costa Rica, a famously pacifist nation without an army, which felt threatened by the rising hostilities and the wave of arms and foreign military aid flooding into the region, offered to mediate. Its president, Óscar Arias, who had impeccable credentials as a moderate and an impartial mediator, convened intensive peace talks, the first round held in 1986 in the small Guatemalan city of Esquipulas, which was, coincidentally or not, an important religious pilgrimage site for Central Americans.

Subsequent meetings led to the Esquipulas II Accord in August 1987. Although the fighting did not end then, the even-handedness and equity of the Accord paved the way for the signing of peace agreements in El Salvador and Guatemala in 1992 and 1996, respectively. The Accords called for (1) the implementation of measures to promote national reconciliation; (2) an end to hostilities; (3) democratization and free elections; (4) the termination of all assistance to irregular forces; (5) negotiations on arms control; and (6) assistance to refugees (Murillo Zamora 2006). While Esquipulas II and the two peace agreements are correctly viewed as triumphs of diplomatic skill and negotiation—Arias won the 1987 Nobel Peace Prize for his role—it was, in fact, largely church people, working as impartial and trusted brokers, who moved the processes to a successful conclusion. They were able to play this role because many of them had the close contact with conditions on the ground that gained them the trust and confidence of both sides and also because their sense of the proper church role had shifted from social justice activism to active pursuit of reconciliation and peace.

This outlook was sorely needed. At Esquipulas, mutual mistrust and unwillingness by some of the parties to negotiate seriously led to stalemate. According to Luis Guillermo Solís Rivera, who served as a key adviser to Arias during the talks and who in 2014 was elected Costa Rica's president, it was not until religious observers of the process, both Catholic and Protestant, took action that the talks restarted. The Vatican's secretary of state, Agostino Casaroli, one of John Paul II's most trusted advisers and an unusually deft diplomat, played a central mediating role in helping to break down the walls that prevented dialogue. U.S. clergy were also key. "I can assure you that seeking and getting the support of religious institutions was of utmost importance in Congress," Solís Rivera recalled, "particularly given the violence experienced by many US missionaries in El Salvador and Guatemala."[12] Rev. Joseph Eldridge, for example, a Methodist minister and former director of WOLA, was instrumental in getting several U.S. religious organizations involved in Washington lobbying for the Arias Plan, which WOLA vigorously supported. Prominent among these were the Jesuit community, clergy at the University of Notre Dame and the Lutheran Church, which had become especially active in El Salvador after the death of Romero. It was the leader of El Salvador's small but vigorous Lutheran Church, Bishop Medardo Gómez, who largely assumed Romero's moral mantle and voice and later attended the peace talks (Jahnel 2009). His efforts complemented those of the Catholic Tutela Legal, established in 1978 to investigate and disseminate information about the war's atrocities, which was one of the first formal Church organizations in Central America to conceptualize "liberation" in terms of human rights.

Church people played equally instrumental roles in the subsequent peace talks in both El Salvador and Guatemala, and not always in ways that one might expect. On the signing of the Peace Accords in Guatemala on December 29, 1996, Rolando Morán (the nom de guerre of Ricardo Rolando Ramírez), *comandante* of the Unidad Revolucionaria Nacional Guatemalteca (URNG), spoke of the role of Guatemala's archbishop Rudolfo Quezada Toruño, acting not only in his capacity as bishop but also through his membership in the National Reconciliation Committee (CNR) required by the Esquipulas Accords. According to Morán, Quezada had approached the guerrillas with the offer to mediate between them and the Guatemalan government. This process started in 1991 and resulted in the Accords five years later; Quezada's gesture, Morán said, "opened the political conditions and established a national consciousness that made peace possible" (quoted in Reyes 1997, 139–40). Quezada's aggressive leadership in the CNR—hotly opposed by Guatemala's oligarchy but respected by the military—eventually pulled all parties into what they called the "Grand Dialogue" in 1989. By framing social justice not in terms of liberation but of human rights, the Central American churches were beginning to provide the higher authority and the mediation function that the historian Samuel Moyn sees as helping to shape our modern concept of human rights.[13]

Behind the scenes, other religious actors were also at work. One was Paul Wee, an American Lutheran, who then served as assistant general secretary for international affairs and human rights for the World Lutheran Federation (WLF). Wee had visited Guatemala in the mid-1980s and seen the terrible devastation of the war for himself. At one point, he contacted major actors on all sides—the army, government, the Vatican, the URNG, other church people—and with WLF funds sent them plane tickets to Oslo, for fresh negotiations. To the surprise of Wee and the other planners, everyone showed up (Jeffrey 1998, 15–16). The conference did not start well, but the WLF had organized dinner and drinks for all the delegates at the end of the long workdays. "In the very private moments after dinner they would talk about their youth and childhood and hopes for Guatemala," Wee remembered. "We discovered during those nights some common interests" (quoted in Jeffrey 1998, 16). One URNG representative later recalled, "We finally remembered over that Lutheran liquor that we had all grown up together, that we had known one another since infancy. And we found that we could talk to each other again."[14] Soon after, the thick dam of hostility and mistrust broke. The Oslo talks—started, mediated, and massaged by Catholic and Lutheran religious intermediaries and also by ecumenical representatives from Presbyterian and Episcopal churches—produced a peace process that ended the bloodiest and longest war in Central America.

DESPITE THE Catholic Church's shift away from liberation theology, we can still see its ideas and influence, for example, in the landless Movimento sem Terra in Brazil or in Mexico's *albergues* for immigrants. But the liberation theology that swept Central America between the mid-1960s and the 1980s was very much a product of its era, framed by both the idealism and the hard binaries of the Cold War. That time is now long past; we have seen how even within the most politically committed sectors of the Church, the struggle for social justice shifted from calls for "liberation" to demands for respect for human rights, a position that, in Moyn's words, was "built on the ruins of prior dreams."[15]

Liberation theology obviously did not die with Archbishop Romero. But historical circumstances and a confluence of hostile forces—an oppositional Pope John Paul II and curia, the incursions of the Reagan administration, a radicalized faithful mowed down by their own governments, and a rising disillusionment on the Left with the promises of revolution—forced liberation theology to divert its powerful currents into new directions during the 1980s. But for progressive laity, priests, and even bishops, the cause of human rights, which bundles common and familiar (progressive) Christian concerns for personal welfare, peaceability, and nonviolence into a (theoretically) nonideological package, became the new venue for the movement for social justice. The institutional

Church under Popes John Paul II and Benedict never fully embraced the cause of human rights as I have discussed it here, and, in fact, appropriated much of that language for other moral battles, especially against abortion—an emphasis that shows signs of change under an Argentine pope. But the idea that Christianity should stand in the vanguard of those who champion the dignity and safety of every human being remains a closely held value of many who work among the poor and repressed in Latin America today, where in some locations quotidian violence is as bad or even worse than it was during the armed conflicts. Father Alejandro Solalinde, who defies cartels, gangs, and even Mexico's ruling party, the PRI, to provide shelter to Central American immigrants traveling at great peril through Mexico, or Bishop Fabio Colindres, who negotiated a truce between warring gangs in El Salvador, are just two examples of this value.

Even now, the hard questions raised by revolutionary Christianity in the 1960s—whether supreme injustice can justify violence, whether the greater good is best served when one willingly follows Jesus's call to "lay down his life for his friends," whether the duty of the true Christian is to seek out peace and reconciliation even at high cost—still cry out for our attention. The original goal of liberation theology was to bring about a "new Church in a new society," rooted in ordinary people and seeking an egalitarian society organized around the needs of all (Berryman n.d., 5). That prophetic vision did not unfold, either for society or for the Church itself. Yet the arc of liberation history from revolution to human rights was an entirely logical one. The idea that every person—every child of God—is entitled to certain basic inalienable rights—such as the right to live in peace and without abuse—simply because she or he is a human being is in some ways every bit as revolutionary and as transformative as a preferential option for the poor. That too is liberation.

Notes

I am grateful to Alex Wilde for his careful comments on this chapter and especially to Phil Berryman, whose insights, experience, and critique were enormously helpful.

1. Samuel Moyn, "Human Rights in History: Human Rights Emerged Not in the 1940s but the 1970s, and on the Ruins of Prior Dreams," *The Nation*, August 30, 2010, 2.

2. See, e.g., Falla 1972. Ricardo Falla was part of a group in Guatemala City that eventually became known as one of the Zone 5 Jesuits, a group of clergy led largely by the direction and inspiration of the Spanish priest Fernando Hoyos, who had adopted a radical praxis by the late 1970s. For more on Hoyos, see Hoyos de Asig 1997.

3. See Zwerling and Martin 1985. The priests in the Sandinista government included Edgard Parrales, Nicaraguan ambassador to the Organization of American States; Ernesto Cardenal, minister of culture; Fernando Cardenal, director of the National Literacy Crusade; and Miguel D'Escoto, foreign minister.

4. Fernando Cardenal, personal conversation, February 5, 2009.

5. George Dugan, "Maryknoll Suspends 2 Priests as Guatemala Guerrilla Aides," *New York Times*, January 19, 1968, 15.

6. "Telling the Stories That Matter: Rutilio Grande," www.ttstm.com/2010/03/march-13-rutilio-grande-martyr-priest.html.

7. See "Carta del EGP a la Familia de Fernando Hoyos, October 1982," in Hoyos de Asig 1997, 206. It is interesting to note that this letter states that Hoyos was killed in combat in July 1982. However, Spanish and Guatemalan newspapers did not publish news of his death until March 1983—coinciding with Pope John Paul II's visit to Guatemala during his trip to Central America. See "El ex-jesuita español Fernando Hoyos murió como guerrillero guatemalteco," *El País*, March 4, 1983.

8. John L. Allen, "Francis 'Unblocks' Romero's Beatification, Official Says," *National Catholic Reporter*, April 22, 2013, http://ncronline.org/blogs/ncr-today/francis-unblocks-romero-beatification-official-says; Thomas Reese, "Oscar Romero, Martyr to the Faith," National Catholic Reporter, February 3, 2015, http://ncronline.org/blogs/faith-and-justice/oscar-romero-martyr-faith.

9. As the continued violence against church people during that period plainly shows, however, this position is not one that all radicalized Catholics chose to adopt, nor did it necessarily provide them with any political or social protection. Church people would continue to die, most of them "ordinary" laymen and local church leaders whose names few people now remember.

10. Conor Cruise O'Brien, "God and Man in Nicaragua," *Atlantic Monthly*, August 1986, 132.

11. A few organizations, such as the neoconservative Catholic Michael Novak's Institute for Religion and Democracy, took a pro-U.S. government position but also focused much of their effort on Central America–related issues. See Novak 2013.

12. Luis Guillermo Solís Rivera, former *jefe de gabinete* of the Ministerio de Relaciones Exteriores y Culto, personal communication, November 6, 2012. Solís was elected president of Costa Rica in 2014.

13. Moyn, "Human Rights in History."

14. EGP negotiator, anonymous by request, personal communication, April 2002.

15. Moyn, "Human Rights in History."

References

Belli, Humberto. 1985. *Breaking Faith: The Sandinista Revolution and Its Impact on Freedom and Christian Faith in Nicaragua*. Westchester, IL: Crossway Books.

Berryman, Phillip. 1984. *The Religious Roots of Rebellion: Christians in Central America's Revolutions*. Maryknoll, NY: Orbis Books.

———. 1986. "El Salvador: From Evangelization to Insurrection." In *Religion and Political Conflict in Latin America*, edited by Daniel H. Levine, 58–78. Chapel Hill: University of North Carolina Press.

———. 1995. *Stubborn Hope: Religion, Politics, and Revolution in Central America*. Maryknoll, NY: Orbis Books.

———. n.d. "Liberation Theology: What Happened to the Dream?" Unpublished paper.

Bonpane, Blase. 1985. *Guerrillas of Peace: Liberation Theology and the Central American Revolution*. Boston: South End Press.

Booth, John A. 1982. *The End and the Beginning: The Nicaraguan Revolution*. Boulder, CO: Westview Press.

Brett, Donna Whitson, and Edward T. Brett. 1988. *Murdered in Central America: The Stories of Eleven U.S. Missionaries*. Maryknoll, NY: Orbis Books.

Brockman, James R. 1989. *Romero: A Life*. Maryknoll, NY: Orbis Books.

Brown, Robert McAfee. 1984. *Unexpected News: Reading the Bible with Third World Eyes*. Philadelphia, PA: Westminster Press.

———. 1993. *Liberation Theology: An Introductory Guide*. Louisville, KY: Westminster John Knox Press.

Byrnes, Timothy A. 2011. *Reverse Mission: Transnational Religious Communities and the Making of US Foreign Policy*. Washington, DC: George Washington University Press.

Cardenal, Fernando. 2008. *Sacerdote en la revolución: Memorias*. Vol. 1. Managua: Anamá Editoriales.

Cardenal, Rodolfo. 1985. *Historia de una esperanza: Vida de Rutilio Grande*. San Salvador: UCA Editores.

Chapman, Richard. 2012. "Still Looking for Liberation? Lutherans in El Salvador and Nicaragua." *Journal of Latin American Studies* 44, no. 1 (February): 39–70.

Coffin, William Sloane. 2008. *The Collected Sermons of William Sloane Coffin: The Riverside Years.* Louisville, KY: Westminster John Knox Press.

Concilio Vaticano. 1965. *Concilio Vaticano II: Documentos completos.* Guatemala: Ediciones San Pablo.

Consejo Episcopal Latinoamericano (CELAM). 1968. "Justice." Segunda Conferencia General del Episcopado Latinoamericano, September 6. Available at http://personal.stthomas.edu/gwschlabach/docs/medellin.htm#justice.

———. 1979. *The Church in the Present-Day Transformation of Latin America in the Light of the Council: II. Conclusions.* Washington, DC: Secretariat for Latin America, National Conference of Catholic Bishops.

Danner, Mark. 1993. *The Massacre at El Mozote: A Parable of the Cold War.* New York: Vintage Books.

Dear, John. 2001. *Lazarus, Come Forth! How Jesus Confronts the Culture of Death and Invites Us into the New Life of Peace.* Maryknoll, NY: Orbis Books.

Dodson, Michael, and Laura Nuzzi O'Shaughnessy. 1990. *Nicaragua's Other Revolution: Religious Faith and Political Struggle.* Chapel Hill: University of North Carolina Press.

Douglass, R. Bruce, and David Hollenbach, eds. 2002. *Catholicism and Liberalism: Contributions to American Public Policy.* New York: Cambridge University Press.

Falla, Ricardo. 1972. "Hacia la revolución verde: Adopción y dependencia del fertilizante químico en un municipio del Quiché, Guatemala." *Estudios Sociales* 6 (1972): 16–51.

Garrard-Burnett, Virginia. 1998. *Protestantism in Guatemala.* Austin, TX: University of Texas Press.

———. 2010. *Terror in the Land of the Holy Spirit: Guatemala under Gen. Efraín Ríos Montt, 1982–1983.* New York: Oxford University Press.

Goldman, Francisco. 2007. *The Art of Political Murder: Who Killed the Bishop?* London: Atlantic.

Gutiérrez, Gustavo. 1968. "Towards a Theology of Liberation." In *Liberation Theology: A Documentary History*, translated and edited by Alfred T. Hennelly, 62–76. Maryknoll, NY: Orbis Books.

Hollenbach, David. 2002. "A Communitarian Reconstruction of Human Rights: Contributions in Catholic Tradition." In *Catholicism and Liberalism: Contributions to American Public Policy*, edited by R. Bruce Douglass and David Hollenbach, 127–50. New York: Cambridge University Press.

Hoyos de Asig, María del Pilar. 1997. *Fernando Hoyos ¿dónde estás?* Guatemala: Fondo de Cultura Editorial.

Iriarte, Gregorio. 1985. *La realidad latinoamericana: Respuestas cristianas.* Buenos Aires: Ediciones Paulinas.

Jackson, Timothy Patrick. 2003. *The Priority of Love: Christian Charity and Social Justice*. Princeton, NJ: Princeton University Press.

Jahnel, Christoph. 2009. *The Lutheran Church in El Salvador: Becoming a Church in the Context of an American Mission, Denominational Pluralism, Social Anomie, and Political Repression*. Translated by Erika Gautschi. San Salvador: Servicio Educativo Cristiano.

Jeffrey, Paul. 1998. *Recovering Memory: Guatemalan Churches and the Challenges of Peacemaking*. Uppsala: Life and Peace Institute.

Keck, Margaret E., and Kathryn Sikkink. 1998. *Activists without Borders*. Ithaca, NY: Cornell University Press.

Lernoux, Penny. 1980. *Cry of the People: United States Involvement in the Rise of Fascism, Torture, and Murder and the Persecution of the Catholic Church in Latin America*. Garden City, NY: Doubleday.

Levine, Daniel H. 2011. "Camilo Torres: Fe, política y violencia." *Sociedad y Religión* 21, no. 34–35: 59–91.

———, ed. 1986. *Religion and Political Conflict in Latin America*. Chapel Hill: University of North Carolina Press.

Martín-Baró, Ignacio. 1983. *Acción e ideología: Psicología social desde Centroamérica*. San Salvador: UCA Editores.

———. 1989. *Sistema, grupo y poder: Psicología social desde Centroamérica*. San Salvador: UCA Editores.

———. 2003. *Poder, ideología y violencia*. Madrid: Editorial Trotta.

Mich, Marvin L. Krier. 1998. *Catholic Social Teaching and Movements*. Mystic, CT: Twenty-Third Publications.

Montgomery, Tommie Sue. 1982. *Revolution in El Salvador: Origins and Evolution*. Boulder, CO: Westview Press.

Moyn, Samuel. 2010. *The Last Utopia: Human Rights in History*. Cambridge, MA: Harvard University Press.

Murillo Zamora, Carlos. 2006. *Paz en Centroamérica de Nassau a Esquipulas*. San José: Fundación Arias para la Paz y el Progreso Humano, Editorial de la Universidad de Costa Rica.

Novak, Michael. 2013. *Writing from Left to Right: My Journey from Liberal to Conservative*. New York: Image.

Orsi, Robert A. 2005. *Between Heaven and Earth: The Religious Worlds People Make and the Scholars Who Study Them*. Princeton, NJ: Princeton University Press.

L'Osservatore Romano. 1983. "En Roma el Papa evoca su ministerio pastoral en los países centroamericanos." *L'Osservatore Romano: Viaje apostólico de Juan Pablo II a Costa Rica, Nicaragua, Panamá, El Salvador, Guatemala, Honduras, Belice y Haiti*, edición especial, número extraordinario, May.

Peter, Marian. 1969. "Cristianismo y guerrilla." In *Cristianismo y revolución*, 79–82. Bogotá: Ediciones E.S.E.

Reyes, Ursula. 1997. *De las palabras a las obras: El desenlace de las negociaciones y el fin del enfrentamiento armado, 1996. Crónica de la paz*. Guatemala: Presidencia de la República, Coordinación de la Crónica Presidencial.

Romero, Óscar A. 1985. *Voice of the Voiceless: The Four Pastoral Letters and Other Statements*. Translated by Michael J. Walsh. Maryknoll, NY: Orbis Books.

———. 1990. "Archbishop Oscar Romero, Last Homily, March 24, 1980." In *Liberation Theology: A Documentary History*, translated and edited by Alfred T. Hennelly, 304–6. Maryknoll, NY: Orbis Books.

Sánchez Lopera, Alejandro. 2006. "Ciencia, revolución y creencia en la experiencia de Camilo Torres ¿una Colombia secular?" *Nómadas* 25 (October): 241–58.

Segundo, Juan. 1982. *The Liberation of Theology*. Translated by John Drury. Maryknoll, NY: Orbis Books.

Shepherd, Frederick M., ed. 2009. *Christianity and Human Rights: Christians and the Global Struggle for Justice*. Lanham, MD: Lexington Books.

Sobrino, Jon. 1987. *Jesus in Latin America*. Maryknoll, NY: Orbis Books.

———. 2007. "Carta a Ignacio Ellacuría. El Padre Arrupe: Un empujón de humanización." Centro de Estudios Ellacuría Fundazioa. Available at www.centroellacuria.org/imgx/analisis/carta_a_ignacio_ellacuria.pdf.

Tomsho, Robert. 1987. *The American Sanctuary Movement*. Austin: Texas Monthly Press.

Torres, Camilo. 1969. "Mensaje a los Cristianos." In *Cristianismo y revolución*, 11–13. Bogotá: Ediciones E.S.E.

Vásquez, Manuel A., and Anna L. Peterson. 2009. "Óscar Romero and the Politics of Sainthood." *Postscripts: Journal of Sacred Texts and Contemporary Worlds* 5, no. 3: 265–91.

Wheaton, Philip. 1971. "From Medellín to Militancy: The Church in Ferment." In *Conscientization for Liberation*, edited by Louis M. Colonnese, 281–302. Washington, DC: Division for Latin America, United States Catholic Conference.

Whitfield, Teresa. 1994. *Paying the Price: Ignacio Ellacuría and the Murdered Jesuits of El Salvador*. Philadelphia, PA: Temple University Press.

Zwerling, Philip, and Connie Martin. 1985. *Nicaragua: A New Kind of Revolution*. Westport, CT: Lawrence Hill.

CHAPTER 5

THE INSTITUTIONAL CHURCH
AND PASTORAL MINISTRY

Unity and Conflict in the Defense of
Human Rights in Chile

ALEXANDER WILDE

In 2011, Chilean national television broadcast *Los archivos del Cardenal*, a gripping twelve-part fictionalized series set during the Pinochet dictatorship (1973–90). It was a docudrama, its creators concerned, as filmmakers generally are, to tell a good story. It had the look and feel of the times—the clothes, the haircuts, the cars, the old buildings of Santiago's center, and the then-recent suburbs. Its characters spoke the language of the times, and its story lines conveyed their human dramas—quotidian concerns shaped and heightened by fear, violence, and the denial of fundamental human rights. To its great credit the series illuminated not only how human rights were violated but also how they were defended. As the series title suggests, at the center of that story were the archives of the Catholic Vicaría de la Solidaridad (Vicariate of Solidarity), created and protected by Cardinal Archbishop Raúl Silva Henríquez.

The places of Cardinal Silva and the Vicaría in the history of the Church's defense of human rights are secure and deserved.[1] But looking back today, decades after the events, we can begin to see processes and dynamics that were less apparent at the time or perceived differently than they appear in longer historical perspective. This is particularly so if we reconsider what is meant by "the Church," which the familiar narrative almost always understands as the ecclesiastical institution, with its bishops and priests, religious orders, and faithful flock led by Cardinal Silva into battle with General Augusto Pinochet. It is true that that battle cannot be understood without analyzing the Church's institutional dimension, reminiscent of historical struggles between church and state, but it is a partial perspective. It neglects the significance of the internal conflicts among Catholics over what "the Church" should be—conflicts that preceded the 1973 military coup and continued throughout the dictatorship. It also fails to analyze how defending "human rights" posed problems for the Church, arising from how this novel cause related to different visions of its pastoral mission and political role. The Church's defense of human rights did not appear full-blown after the coup, in a flash of theological insight. It was defined over time by practices and processes that evolved in response to changing perceptions of violence and politics.

That process may have been providential, but it was not inevitable, nor is it fully understood even today. In contrast to countries such as Argentina, in which military interventions were common, the Pinochet dictatorship posed unprecedented challenges to older Chilean traditions. It was a sharp, harsh, and prolonged caesura in more than a century of national history. The cause of human rights was similarly unprecedented, and the path the Church followed to embrace it was strewn with perceptions, events, and choices for which the past provided limited guidance. The bishops made important institutional choices, which conditioned their responses in critical ways, but the Church was also carried along by the internal dynamic within it.

Seeing this long historical experience with fresh eyes, "historicizing" it (see Kelly, this vol.) by looking beyond the premises and perspectives of the time, is a large undertaking, one this chapter can only begin. It is important to attempt because it can help us think more deeply about why and how religion may embrace human rights as a response to violence, and about the circumstances in both the external context and the religious sphere that may facilitate, or limit, its impact. This chapter focuses on the internal life of "the Church" during this period. It analyzes the varied ways that Chilean Catholics took action to defend other Chileans in the name of their "human rights" and examines how this cause produced conflicts within the Church over theology, praxis, and politics. In some of these conflicts—such as the tensions between the bishops and other levels of the Church throughout the seventeen years of the dictatorship—historical perspective helps us discern better how pastoral practice moved the institutional Church over time. Some developments—such as the religious legitimation of active nonviolence—stand out more in retrospect than they did in the turbulence of ongoing events.

The following section of this chapter discusses the institutional Church, particularly its leadership, and its embrace of the idea of human rights. It challenges a certain teleological tendency in the literature by considering obstacles to this historical process as well as factors that favored it. The third section examines the character of pastoral ministry, which I believe was crucial in forging a robust religious defense of human rights. It identifies a long-term dynamic in intra-Church conflicts that was overlaid by the experience of violence and in important ways shifted earlier perceptions. The fourth section analyzes the new context of the 1980s and the "varieties of violence" that accompanied the mass protests and reappearance of opposition politics. It finds a conflicted but ultimately fruitful interaction between leaders of the institutional Church and its pastoral base that reestablished human rights as a source of internal unity and political influence. The conclusion considers how religious contributions to the human rights movement during the dictatorship have affected the Church's role since the transition to democracy. It identifies an important moral legacy that shaped how Chile has dealt with its past but has been limited in other respects by a more traditionally institutional conception of its mission, one that would have to change if it were to play a larger, more vital part in a democratic context.

The Embrace of Human Rights: Ideas, Action, and the Institutional Church

Viewed among its sister churches in the 1960s through the 1980s, the Chilean Catholic Church appears striking for its unity in the defense of human rights. That unity is usually judged in institutional terms, by the success of the hierarchy in speaking with a common voice. But looking back now we can also perceive a different kind of unity in the degree to which the ecclesiastical institution moved toward what the Second Vatican Council called the "People of God." Neither of these two forms of unity was fully achieved; there were internal conflicts throughout this period—particularly between the bishops and the "civil society of the Church" (see Levine, this vol.) that grew up under the peculiar conditions of the dictatorship. However, the defense of human rights opened new common ground because Church authorities were in close touch with different levels in the Catholic community, down to the grassroots. They attended to diverse voices and concrete actions among the faithful, which were tested against the demands of Christian belief in a specific but shifting context. The outcome was greater unity in both senses than other national Churches at the time and also—significantly—than during its own history before 1973.

Historically, the Chilean Church had both a strong sense of its identity as a national institution and a socially progressive tradition in theology and pastoral ministry. After the division of church and state in 1925, it developed active programs of Catholic Action meant to enlist lay Catholics, with clerical advisers, to promote social change. It also possessed large cultural influence, particularly among Chilean elites, through its educational system. Although the institutional Church consciously attempted to separate itself from partisan politics, it enjoyed considerable indirect political influence, particularly in the Christian Democratic Party. During the Christian Democratic government of Eduardo Frei-Montalva (1964–70), it experienced growing tensions over the political and social elements of its institutional trajectory.

During the half dozen years preceding the military coup, the Church was in fact rent by profound divisions. It was affected by the growing polarization of Chilean politics engendered by the faltering reforms of the Frei government and Salvador Allende's increasingly beleaguered Popular Unity coalition (1970–73). But although Catholics reflected political divisions, they also clashed over religious values and, more specifically, over different visions of what "the Church" should be in Chilean society. These conflicting "ecclesiologies" spanned a spectrum from pre-Conciliar

Catholics (notably among conservative laypeople) to priests, nuns, and lay leaders (particularly in grassroots ministries) stirred by liberation theology and hope for a "popular Church." A majority of the hierarchy and many clergy and lay Catholics occupied a centrist position, theologically as well as politically. They accepted an ecclesiology of support for social but not political action by a Church with firm obedience to ecclesiastical authorities (Smith 1982, 1986; Cavanaugh 1998).

Before 1973, conflicts in the Church led to breakaway movements of the religious left such as the Iglesia Joven (Young Church) and Christians for Socialism and to Christian-inspired political groups such as the Movimiento de Acción Popular Unitario (MAPU) and the Izquierda Cristiana (Christian Left). Catholics on the right associated with the politically militant Patria y Libertad (Homeland and Freedom) and the religiously pre-Conciliar Tradición, Familia y Patria (Tradition, Family, and Homeland). For their part, the bishops were determined to preserve Church unity by avoiding what they saw as political entanglements, particularly on the religious left. After a running battle with the Christians for Socialism, they rejected what they judged the group's theological errors in a long formal document completed in August 1973 but only made public in October, following the military coup.

The military dictatorship established a radically changed context, but the Church as institution and community only adjusted to it, in different rhythms, over time. Many moderate and conservative Catholics supported the overthrow of the Allende government, and most of the hierarchy welcomed it as an end to what it perceived as growing chaos and violence. Some bishops publicly supported the new regime. Emilio Tagle, archbishop of Valparaíso from 1961 to 1983, was particularly outspoken, but this group also included Juan Francisco Fresno, archbishop of La Serena (1971–83), who later succeeded Silva Henríquez as archbishop of Santiago. It was only over time that the hierarchy, and the faithful, found a new basis for unity within the Church in the mission to defend human rights.

Before 1973 "human rights" were present in the discourse of Chilean Catholics, but it was only under military rule that they became a compelling cause. On this point, the Jesuit *Mensaje*, a monthly of broad intellectual influence in Chile since 1951, is a telling source. In the decade before the dictatorship, the subject of human rights is present both in theological and philosophical essays and in articles on the growing violation of human rights elsewhere. The essays reflect the epochal influence of the Second Vatican Council and the working out of its implications for the Church in Latin America following the 1968 meeting of the Latin American bishops in Medellín, Colombia.[2] *Mensaje* takes up human rights within a broader debate about liberation theology and its manifestations in Chile: in the Iglesia Joven, Christians for Socialism, and small Christian-inspired political movements such as MAPU and the Christian Left. Before 1973 *Mensaje* also addressed with increasing frequency the subject of the violation of human rights in regional neighbors such as Brazil, Uruguay, Paraguay, and Colombia. Together these two lenses—one focused on theology, the other on violence elsewhere in Latin America—suggest a great deal about the limited place of "human rights" in the Chilean Church before the massive repression unleashed by the military after it seized power.[3]

Within the first weeks after that event, together with other religious communities and international agencies, the Church mobilized to protect thousands of foreigners drawn to Chile during Allende's Popular Unity government who had suddenly become political refugees. These efforts quickly evolved to include Chileans persecuted by the dictatorship, leading to formation of the ecumenical Pro-Peace Committee. When Pinochet threatened the Committee for this work directly, Cardinal Silva created a new entity, the Vicaría, to carry it forward under the ecclesiastical protection of the Santiago Archdiocese, with Msgr. Cristián Precht as its first vicar. An innovation institutionally (see chapters by Arellano, Pachico, and Tate, this vol.), the Vicaría was to prove a bastion in the larger movement for human rights in Chile and beyond (Lowden 1996; Aranda 2004).

Silva had participated in the Second Vatican Council and as a cardinal participated in the election of Pope Paul VI (1963–78), who would prove a friend and ally on human rights. Silva was also a member of the Salesian order, which had a pastoral orientation to the young and the poor (Silva Henríquez and Cavallo 1991). His personal commitments to social change were reinforced by strong currents in the Chilean Church supporting a social mission and pastoral ministries at the grassroots.[4] The hierarchy at the time of the coup included other bishops (including many named by Paul VI) who also embraced the progressive currents coming out of the Council (Smith 1982). New ideas and the practices for implementing them—the Church as the People of God, the "preferential option for the poor," and pastoral "accompaniment," the whole reorientation of how the Church should relate to history and the world—resonated with their national ecclesial tradition. Cardinal Silva and many bishops, then, had a certain predisposition to embracing the new cause of human rights when it appeared after the 1973 coup.

Nevertheless, as we have seen, the hierarchy was initially divided in its stance toward the dictatorship. It also faced ideological opposition from conservative, pre-Conciliar Catholic supporters of the new regime, starting with a junta that justified itself in the name of "Christian civilization." After the coup, the regime's leading intellectual, Jaime Guzmán Errázuriz, attempted to legitimate it with distinctly pre-Conciliar Catholic concepts (see Smith 1982, 303). Guzmán spoke for an important older strain of Church tradition, for which the idea of human rights was associated with secular, liberal, and anticlerical views (see Levine, this vol.). The bishops, however, came to perceive the actions of the dictatorship as manifestations of the "National Security Doctrine," a Cold War ideology propagated by the U.S. and other militaries that denied basic human dignity and defined those with dissenting (especially Marxist) political views as "enemies." Since they increasingly interpreted the regime in ideological terms, they were drawn to defending their own alternative vision of society, framed by post-Conciliar Catholic theology, in which the idea of human rights—including the (secular) UN Universal Declaration of Human Rights of 1948—was one thread. Pope Paul VI was strongly supportive—and actively followed developments in Chile before and after the coup.[5]

More surprising to us today, perhaps, the hierarchy also faced initial ideological opposition to the idea of human rights from the Catholic left, those most associated with liberation theology. Although their voices are muted in the subsequent literature celebrating Church defense of human rights, they vividly convey the religious divisions that persisted even after the coup over what the Church should be and how it should respond to violence and the dictatorship. They were critical of "human rights" as a weak substitute for "liberation." They acknowledged humanitarian assistance to suffering individuals, carried out in the spirit of the Good Samaritan, but contrasted it with the "Liberating Church" and "Prophetic Church" that understood the class character of the dictatorship and were willing to confront it forcefully as illegitimate on religious grounds rather than merely denounce its violations of human rights (*La Iglesia chilena* 1975; Hinkelammert 1977; Fernández 1996; Cavanaugh 1998). These "liberationists" are important because they articulated grassroots perspectives within the Church and remained engaged with ecclesiastical authorities throughout the dictatorship (in a dynamic over pastoral practice analyzed below). Their critique also helps us understand better the legacy of the Church's defense of human rights during this period after Chile's return to democratic rule (considered in the conclusion).

Over time the idea of human rights, however, did become a source of unity in the Chilean Church. One important reason was the simultaneous emergence of the international human rights movement, for which Chile was an important focus. Neither the bishops nor their liberationist critics initially grasped the potential significance of this novel development. The movement's strongly legal orientation made the actions of the dictatorship "legible" to the Church itself and the world as "state violence," carried out by institutions and agents of the state against its citizens (Tate 2007).[6] Amnesty International was a major influence, and its emphasis on individual "prisoners of conscience" of diverse political beliefs struck a resonant chord in Chile. More broadly, the idea of human rights expressed the bishops' vision of the Church as an institution vital to Chilean nationality. It seemed to open a new path forward from the violent clash of political ideologies before the coup—one based on truths about the human individual too undeniable to be lost in struggles between competing visions over how societies may advance. Even so, it took time for the Chilean Church to incorporate the idea of human rights into its theology (Aldunate, Castillo, and Silva 1983).[7]

Beyond theology and ideas, the Church's defense of human rights was defined by action. The most important institutional decision was taken directly by Cardinal Silva Henríquez in 1976: the creation of the Vicariate of Solidarity in response to Pinochet's pressure to disband the Pro-Peace Committee. The Vicaría reflected both legal and experiential perspectives in the Church's understanding of human rights. Legal defense quickly became fundamental to its work (see Queiroz, this vol.). The Vicaría carefully assembled evidence from the testimony of victims and their families. These individual case files were then presented as complaints (*recursos de amparo*, a form of habeas corpus) before the courts, initially in military trials and then before normal civilian tribunals (a contrast to the human rights movement in Argentina). Although the courts seldom offered legal protections, this method provided a credible basis for aggregated analyses of types of violations and gradually of the different state agents responsible for them. As such, it served an important political purpose, initially outside Chile: it established systematic patterns built up from individual cases that were documented according to international human rights standards and norms. The Vicaría represented a commitment by the Chilean Church to the rule of law, which took on new weight in the political debates of the 1980s, and its legal approach had a powerful and enduring influence well beyond its borders (Lowden 1996; Aranda 2004; Hau 2006; Tate 2007).

Another side of the work of the Vicaría reflected the Church's understanding of what human rights must entail: extensive humanitarian assistance at the grassroots in poor communities. This included soup kitchens for the poor in the slums of Santiago and other cities, health clinics, workshops and job placement to address widespread unemployment, and psychological counseling to victims and their families.[8] These efforts helped address pressing material needs—but they also kept alive some sense of hope and community against a government that ruled through fear and division. This was a form of pastoral ministry in hard, dark times but also work for human rights in the broad sense, social and economic rights as well as political and civil rights, encompassing the whole human person (see Levine, this vol.)—even if in this period protecting the most fundamental rights to life and physical integrity and securing basic civil and political rights were the primary objectives.

Beyond creating the Vicaría, Church authorities took another key decision that receives only passing notice in most studies but proved to have major consequences for the defense of human rights: they gave space and shelter to family members, overwhelmingly women, who were seeking—and increasingly advocating on behalf of—loved ones.

"Decision" may give an air of misleading concreteness to what was, as so often in the early days after the coup, ad hoc and improvised. But this practice developed during the Pro-Peace Committee in 1974–75 and was in effect ratified and extended after creation of the Vicaría in 1976, providing these women with quarters directly adjacent to Santiago's Cathedral in the Plaza de Armas (Vidal 1996; Precht 1998; Lowden 1996). The first of these relatives' groups—the Agrupación de Familiares de los Detenidos-Desaparecido (AFDD), for those who disappeared while in detention—was joined over time by others formed under this protection of the institutional Church. They effectively became part of the larger Church in this period, like the grassroots Christian base communities (CEBs). This popular Church took initiatives that often discomforted institutional authorities but ultimately contributed to a new dynamic between the base and the leadership. More specifically, the Agrupaciones and CEBs pioneered forms of active nonviolence that deepened and gave practical expression to the Church's support for peace and human rights, and they remained influential actors after democratic transition on issues of transitional justice and historical memory.

Pastoral Ministry: The Origins of Active Nonviolence

The pastoral presence of the Chilean Church at the grassroots of society—especially the marginal *poblaciones* (slums) of the poor in Santiago and other cities—was vital to its defense of human rights. As noted, it had a history of active social pastoral ministry framed by a dedication to "accompany" the poor. In the chaotic conditions following the 1973 coup, Chileans in search of missing friends and family went to police stations, detention centers, government offices—and church vicarages. They quickly found that only the Church offered real understanding of and help for their plight. Priests, nuns, and lay workers witnessed firsthand the human tragedy unfolding under military rule. As did bishops.[9] During the dictatorship their experience ministering to the suffering taught the Church what was at stake in defending human rights.

It also moved human rights to the center of the Church's pastoral ministry, as the concrete expression of the most fundamental of Christian values concerning life and human dignity. And it brought the issues raised by this active, creative pastoral presence—a "pastoral de fronteras," as Cristián Precht (1998, 28–29) put it—into the heart of the Church.[10] In this defense of human rights on the ground, we may discern two elements of faith that framed action. One was shared across Christian traditions: a profound concern for the human individual as the reflection of God. The other was a particularly Catholic belief (post–Vatican II) that Christian communities should have an active relationship with other progressive forces in the larger society.

The first carried the Chilean Catholic Church beyond the collective thinking and political ideologies that had dominated the period before the coup. The pastoral strategies of accompaniment that had brought priests and nuns closer to the lives of the poor gave them a direct, immediate experience under the dictatorship with the human beings who suffered and could recover their capacity to act and live. This moved them closer to the individualist perspective of the movement for human rights as it developed in this period, particularly the work of Amnesty International (Wilde 2013a). It also affected the perceptions of those on the political left. Viviana Díaz, whose Communist father was among the disappeared, described these grassroots experiences as spaces in which "we came to know the Church and they came to know us, too" (quoted in Fernández 1996, 174).[11] Mario Garcés, who had belonged to Christians for Socialism, later explained that the "practical humanitarian assistance" of the Church had helped leftists see the institution differently and rethink their "somewhat dogmatic traditional discourse" (quoted in Fernández 1996, 173–74).

The second frame—the active commitment of the Christian community to make common cause with others to change society, whether or not they were Catholics or even professed Christians—expresses a kind of Christian humanism that goes beyond liberal individualism or religious ecumenism, which had been historically concerned with finding theological and doctrinal common ground. It is a faith rooted in the need to respond through action to concrete realities facing a particular society at a moment in its history. Liberationist thought is clearly evident here, but it was through taking action—through praxis—that this faith evolved toward values of tolerance, respect, solidarity, and agency. This grass-roots work of the Chilean Church may have begun with compassion and charity for "victims," but those carrying out these ministries came to believe that their fundamental mission was to empower, to provide "support for poor people to organize themselves, so that they themselves [could] defend their rights" (quoted in Fernández 1996, 181). The role of the Church in these trying times was to accompany individuals and their communities in ways that allowed them to become active subjects in forging new lives.

This grassroots pastoral accompaniment was the source of new tactics of symbolic nonviolent resistance that began in the late 1970s. Nonviolence was built into the cause of human rights as a principle[12]—with due reference to Gandhi, Martin Luther King Jr., and the Brazilian prelate Dom Hélder Câmara (see Queiroz, this vol.)—and active nonviolence had been discussed among bishops as a conscious method as early as 1977 (Vicaría de la Solidaridad 1978b). Theology was buttressed in Chile particularly by the protest methods of Agrupaciones beginning in the same period: demanding to know the whereabouts of "disappeared" family members (¿Dónde están?), they participated in marches, processions, and sit-ins in front of the presidential palace; chained themselves to fences outside prominent buildings; and engaged in hunger strikes. The political and theological implications of their acts were debated. What right, asked conservatives and many institutional Catholics, did they have to commit the Church to such radical postures? But these actions from within Catholicism's "civil society" gradually moved ecclesiastical authorities and unquestionably brought greater awareness to the broad public of their problem—and that of Chile as a nation.

The first of these actions to spark national debate about human rights was a nine-day hunger strike by family members of the disappeared at the Santiago headquarters of the UN Economic Commission for Latin America (ECLA) in June 1977. This was followed in 1978 by the "long" hunger strike, seventeen days, from May 22 to June 7, which developed this tactic further. Initiated by the AFDD, the strike from the beginning had support from priests, nuns, deacons, lay workers, and Christian communities, some one hundred people in all. Actions in solidarity spread to multiple sites across Santiago, the country, and internationally. Archbishop Silva eventually intervened to broker an agreement with the government, which promised to investigate disappearances. When the regime repeatedly failed to do so, the Church grew convinced that strong declarations must be accompanied by militant nonviolent action (Vidal 1996, 107–10; Hoyl Cruz 2003, 350–63; Fernández 1996, 189).

The long hunger strike of 1978 reveals a great deal about the pastoral roots of active nonviolence as a political tactic. One of its leading figures was Fr. José Aldunate, S.J., who was associated with Chile's grassroots Church but also loyal to the institution. He defended the willingness of the strikers (including himself) to risk their own lives through dramatic action:

> I think that the people who believe we did wrong have not really suffered deeply for a loved one, a child, a husband or young father. . . . It is very different to speak from outside and to be involved inside the problem. I have wanted to act "from inside," that is from within the love that the strikers lived, discerning the moral and spiritual authenticity of their attitude. . . . The fact that this experience has been lived by people who are not Christian, many of them Marxists, is not an argument against its spiritual validity. It only demonstrates that the Holy Spirit works freely also outside the institutional Church and knows how to communicate its love to men of good faith and to direct their steps on the roads of salvation. (Quoted in Vicaría de la Solaridad 1978a [unpaginated])

The religious terms of his defense represent a new application of liberationist thinking and practice—of "accompaniment," for example—to the cause of human rights (see Garrard-Burnett, this vol.). Aldunate also noted that the hunger strike was "certainly a form of active nonviolence, almost [wholly] new in the country, that apparently took many sectors by surprise, *perhaps particularly the parties of the left*, that were unaccustomed to such methods. . . . [I]t demonstrated the efficacy of an approach that is, above all, an appeal to [our] consciences" (Vicaría de la Solaridad 1978a; my emphasis). During the 1980s, which saw a new dynamic of violence in Chile, active nonviolence was to become for the Church a morally preferable and potentially more effective form of resistance.[13]

The Church and Varieties of Violence: The New Dynamic of the 1980s

During the 1970s, as we have seen, the faithful at the grassroots took initiatives that in effect challenged leaders at the top to defend and legitimate certain actions in the name of human rights. In the 1980s, this process continued but in a changed context that challenged both the bishops and the civil society of the Church to reconsider violence and how they should respond to it. We can observe a kind of ongoing debate over the varieties of violence. In one way it was a theological debate, if we understand "theology" to include praxis as well as ideas. Both the leadership and the base defended their positions in theological terms. It was also a political debate about the role of violence in ending the dictatorship. In still another way it was a debate about how the Church should understand and defend "human rights"—a cause that had become by the 1980s a powerful social movement and touchstone for political opposition. This decade, then, opened a new period, distinct from the Church's initial embrace of human rights, when those within it rethought how best to defend those rights in the context of ending the dictatorship.

By the 1980s violence had been a public issue in Chile for nearly two decades. From the late 1960s to the early 1970s, there had been a growing climate of violence in public life. Threats of force from both the political left and right—with emblematic acts of violence amplified by political rhetoric—proved a mere harbinger of the violent repression unleashed by the military after it seized power.[14] After the coup, Pinochet and his secret police (the DINA) hunted down the leadership and cadres of the Socialist and Communist parties and the Movement of the Revolutionary Left (MIR), a radical guerrilla group already active during Allende's government, and then turned to centrist political forces, such as the Christian Democrats. Within a few years the earlier left-right dynamic of violence was replaced by violence wielded exclusively by the state.

It took some time for Church leaders to understand this change and act on it. Where the regime—unrestrained by any institutional accountability and increasingly isolated from society—pursued Marxists and other political forces as "enemies" of Chile, bishops sought "reconciliation" between Chileans of opposing political views. The hierarchy had a long-standing commitment to peaceful, nonviolent change, reinforced by papal authority,[15] but its public exhortations had little discernible effect amid the polarization before the coup or, indeed, for some time after. Their words had a certain abstract quality, divorced from the real dynamics of Chile's unfolding history. In 1974 Cardinal Silva repeated a much-quoted formulation that he had originally articulated during the last year of Allende's government: "Violence only engenders violence, and that is not the path to making a more just and better society. We have said to our people [and] to our authorities . . . that human rights are sacred, that no one can violate them. . . . We have not been heard" (quoted in Hinkelammert 1977, 128). It took the active defense of human rights that developed in the 1970s, as analyzed in the above, to begin to give some purchase to "peace" and "nonviolence." But in the 1980s the Church's role—and its impact—changed in important ways.

In 1980 the dictatorship attempted to consolidate its legitimacy with a new constitution, which fostered the reemergence of more open party politics. The deep economic depression of 1982 led to a wave of mass protests (eleven of national scope between May 1983 and October 1984; De la Maza and Garcés 1985) and stimulated public democratic opposition under the leadership of party politicians. But the rebirth of party and popular politics was accompanied by a counterpoint of renewed political violence. Over time the protests became more violent and were met by waves of repression by the regime. MIR guerrillas with military experience in Central America infiltrated back into the country. The Communist Party (despite its long history of electoral politics) adopted armed resistance among "all means of struggle" against the dictatorship, giving birth to the Frente Patriótico Manuel Rodríguez. The armed left carried out bank robberies and political assassinations, narrowly failing to kill Pinochet himself in 1986. It brought in some fifty tons of weapons from Cuba (discovered by military intelligence) to support an armed uprising. The regime responded with massive sweeps through the *poblaciones*, systematic torture of detainees, and a series of highly public atrocities, such as the grisly execution of three opposition figures, including a beloved longtime figure of the Vicaría, José Manuel Parada, a Communist. What had been solely state violence became a new dialectic of political violence between the regime and the opposition confronting it.

The Frente and kindred militant groups employed violence initially against property (bombings, bank robberies, attacks on electrical towers) as a form of "armed propaganda" to supplement traditional forms of grassroots resistance in the slums (e.g., bonfires, street barricades). This effort to assert leadership within ongoing popular social protests, however, evolved over time, and its strictly military dimension assumed greater importance for these groups, for the regime in its repressive tactics, and for the emerging political debate about how to end the dictatorship (De la Maza and Garcés 1985, 17–72, 84). Although it is difficult to say with confidence how violence was perceived by those most affected—the *pobladores* (slum dwellers)—there is some evidence that they regarded militant resistance as legitimate if exercised in "self-defense" against state repression (see, e.g., Oxhorn 1995, 228–30). The broader effect it had on opposition political leaders was far more visible.

In this context the institutional Church adopted a newly significant role in mediating political conflict. With Cardinal Silva's retirement in 1983, Juan Francisco Fresno became archbishop of Santiago. Publicly known for his sympathy for the military coup, a conservative by temperament, Fresno was chosen by the Vatican to maintain Church unity in a period of growing confrontation. But what would unite the Church by this point was no longer what it had been in 1973 (when the hierarchy strongly criticized the Christians for Socialism) or even 1978 (when it organized an international conference in Santiago on human rights). Amid continuing popular protests and repression by the regime, Fresno was quickly challenged by the deteriorating relations between the institutional Church and the regime.

In January 1984 the alleged assassins of the military intendant of Santiago took refuge in the papal nunciature, which jealously defended the right of asylum. In February the Church was accused of having organized a massive hostile demonstration against General Pinochet in Chile's southernmost city, Punta Arenas. In August Archbishop Fresno accepted a proposal from the Vicaría to support a public Jornada por la Vida (March for Life), which represented a rebuke to rising violence and, implicitly, the dictatorship. In September a police bullet killed the French priest André Jarlan during a sweep of the *poblaciones*. In October a bomb placed by a military intelligence officer destroyed a parish church in Punta

Arenas. In November Santiago's city government prohibited a socially oriented religious celebration in a Christian community; the regime barred the reentry of the then-vicar of solidarity, Fr. Ignacio Gutiérrez, who had met with political exiles in Rome, and banned publication of a declaration by Archbishop Fresno about abuses he had witnessed in a slum.

Fresno's role as mediator entailed gaining the trust of the different sides involved in conflict (see Pachico, this vol.). After a failed attempt to help broker discussions between officials of the dictatorship and the democratic opposition in 1983, the events of 1984 gradually pushed him toward the latter. In 1985 he gave the Church's blessing to the National Accord for Transition to Full Democracy, an agreement endorsed by a broad coalition spanning the political center and "renovated" left that rejected violence as part of a larger democratic consensus (and excluded the Communist Party and a wing of the Socialist Party).[16] This positioned the institutional Church firmly on one side of the debate within the political opposition, in favor of a nonviolent path out of the dictatorship against those who worked to overthrow it. In the event Pinochet dug in, and the National Accord did not produce a democratic transition in the short run. But it did lay the groundwork for the later Concertación coalition that triumphed in the plebiscite of 1988, won the national elections of 1989, and took power in 1990.

The shift of the institutional Church toward a mediating role clearly drew on its older national traditions and was encouraged by the Vatican, but it also aroused criticism in its pastoral base in the *poblaciones*, where militant elements saw it as a way of legitimating the dictatorship. There were similar reactions there to the idea of nonviolence, which the hierarchy had embraced as critical morally and vital politically to ending the dictatorship and restoring democracy.[17] The hierarchy responded by repeatedly underlining its stand against state violence but also condemning the new political violence. *Mensaje* editorialized in October 1983, "We reject the terrorism and vandalism promoted by extremist or antisocial groups. But we are very conscious that they are not the principal actors in the enormous violence recently unleashed in our country" (no. 323, 542). In January 1984 *Mensaje* castigated the "war mentality" leading Chile to confrontation as "doubly fatal, not only for the pain and death it causes but [also] because it does not lead us toward democracy. As we do not accept torture, neither do we accept terrorism. The [recent] attacks that have claimed various victims among the police seem to us as reprehensible as the sinister terrorism with which the CNI [state military intelligence] pretend to safeguard public order" (no. 325, 6).

Despite the apparent clarity of this distinction, implementing it in practice was not determined by ecclesiastical authorities alone but shaped by the dynamic between them and the Church's own "civil society." One important dimension of this interaction involved religiously based active nonviolence, which developed further the tactics and methods used in the 1970s. The other was a pattern of actions taken at lower levels, in a context changed from the previous decade, which challenged Church authorities to respond. These two dimensions of this religious dynamic, I believe, led the institutional Church to close ranks around its defense of human rights as a commitment fundamental to Church unity in the 1980s.

In these years Christians increasingly took initiatives that pitted active nonviolence against the practices of a violent state. The most famous of these was the Sebastián Acevedo Movement against Torture, which grew out of a Christian base community founded in the 1970s. In 1983 it took its name to honor a worker whose children had been arrested by the military intelligence service and who, after being denied access to them, immolated himself in protest before the cathedral in Concepción. With Father Aldunate as its spokesman, this small, informal group carried out brief, evanescent symbolic actions targeting physical sites associated with the regime's most notorious practices. In an age before social media and the Internet, their demonstrations materialized as if from nowhere and, at first, dispersed just as quickly. When the police learned to react to this new tactic, demonstrators allowed themselves to be arrested in the time-honored practice of nonviolent resistance. They did not exclude those associated with armed groups but did demand—at a time when the large protests were often marked by violence—that demonstrators were resolutely nonviolent in their actions, avoiding even aggressive or insulting language. Although the Sebastián Acevedo and kindred groups never represented more than a small minority within the protest movement of the time, Chilean media coverage gave them a significant impact on public opinion—and in the Church (Vidal 2002; De la Maza and Garcés 1985, 84).

Ecclesiastical authorities were also affected by the political sympathies of a significant proportion of priests, nuns, and lay workers at the grassroots (De la Maza and Garcés 1985, esp. 111–13; Lowden 1996; Drogus and Stewart-Gambino 2005). Like Amnesty International, the Vicaría chose not to give legal defense to those who took up arms.[18] But Chilean Christians included not a few priests, male and female religious, and pastoral agents who were sympathetic to militants of the MIR and the Frente. They engaged in hunger strikes, held Masses for those killed in regime protests, and publicly condemned state repression. They also often protected armed rebels—hiding fugitives, seeking medical attention for the wounded, aiding them to obtain political asylum—in the face of a government that offered no legal or institutional guarantees against arbitrary and violent treatment. When such acts led to public confrontations with the dictatorship, Church officials in practice defended these initiatives as acts of mercy—in effect, extending the protection of the institution to those labeled "terrorists" by the regime.[19]

Perhaps the most famous of such incidents during these years began in April 1986 with the assault by the Frente on a bakery in which a policeman was killed. A wounded *frentista* had made his way to the Vicaría, where he was attended by two staff members, referred to a clinic, and later arrested and imprisoned. For more than two years the military prosecutor assigned to the case sought the Vicaría's medical files on the case with Javert-like tenacity. His opponent was the formidable vicar general, Bishop Sergio Valech,[20] a political conservative who came to describe himself as a *momio renovado* ("a reactionary whose consciousness had been raised") according to a longtime Vicaría staff member (quoted in Fernández 1996, n. 155, 226). He was also a resolute defender of the Church's institutional authority and resisted every effort to make him surrender Vicaría files, adding that he was willing to accept all consequences, including arrest and imprisonment. Through this long-running drama he received unstinting public support from the hierarchy ("the Bishop Vicar of Solidarity has chosen to obey his conscience before obeying men. What else could a Bishop do?") as well as from church authorities around the world, foreign governments, and a wide range of Chilean organizations. In the end, the prosecutor did not obtain the files. As Bishop Valech noted at the time, "We received a huge . . . amount of support, which also served to make the whole country more aware of our work. . . . [The] whole affair was quite Providential, and I am someone who believes in Providence."[21]

In short, we may observe in the 1980s an internal interaction between the ecclesiastical leadership of the Church and its pastoral base that played an important role in moving the institution into clear opposition to the dictatorship. An active pastoral presence among the popular sectors meant that Christians were part of their politicization during these years, forming a community that "found its space inside ecclesial dynamics, gaining certain degrees of autonomy" (De la Maza and Garcés 1985, 112–13). Human rights also remained a foundation for unity, among the bishops and the popular Church alike. The Church rethought its earlier defense of human rights in response to the reappearance of armed resistance to a dictatorship ready to employ violence to protect its rule. Its leaders explicitly endorsed nonviolence in action as well as principle. They took pains to explain their new position in religious terms: human rights and nonviolence were two manifestations of its common commitment to a fundamental "right to life." As Monsignor Precht (1998, 34) put it, the Church wanted "to defend zealously the right to life from whomever might threaten it and to reject the paths of violence as ways to resolve social conflicts." This formulation, which might merely have expressed a pious hope, took on concrete meaning and had real consequences in the context of the 1980s.

The Church was accused of intervening in politics (while also being urged to do so by the opposition) through the last years of the dictatorship (Correa and Viera-Gallo 1986; Dooner 1989). Institutionally, it clearly supported democratic transition, for political reasons but also for its religious commitment to human rights. It became convinced that without democracy, fundamental human rights would always be violated by the state—that this form of violence was inherent in authoritarian rule and antithetical to human rights. This stance was criticized by both the right and the left—the regime and its supporters calling it de facto complicity with violent opposition, the left condemning its failure to endorse "all means of resistance" to an illegitimate regime. Elements in the Church's base communities retained a longing for more confrontational, "prophetic" leadership, and tensions remained within the Church during the 1980s (Drogus and Stewart-Gambino 2005), but there was more support there than often acknowledged.[22] In a longer view what stands out are the Church's unity around the defense of human rights and the fruit-ful internal dynamic between its institutional leadership and its own in-ternal civil society. Together they made possible the Church's distinctive contributions to the cause of human rights and the historical processes that produced a transition to elected government in 1990.

REEXAMINING HOW the Chilean Catholic Church took up the cause of human rights illuminates the range of factors within the religious sphere that gave it a singular unity of purpose. The Church had been divided by the ambitious (and exclusionary) political programs that polarized Chile from the late 1960s to 1973. In the new context established by the dicta-torship, when violence was identified with state repression, a process of internal healing began through a pastoral ministry built on human rights under the courageous and astute leadership of Cardinal Silva. In the 1980s a host of changes introduced new dynamics: a new semiauthoritar-ian constitution, a deep economic depression, massive street protests, the emergence of a democratic opposition, and the reappearance of political violence. Church leadership was fruitfully challenged from within and renewed its commitment to human rights—now linked to the restoration of democratic institutions—and explicitly supported nonviolence.

The Church gave a distinctive imprint to the human rights cause in Chile. The larger movement that grew up was composed of many dif-ferent organizations and went much beyond the Church itself (see Orel-lana and Hutchison 1991), but looking back on this history today, one is struck by how the Church's actions gave the whole movement a religious character. The most visible action was its public witness and presence from the beginning to the end of the dictatorship, from the level of na-tional institutions to that of local communities throughout the country. The protected spaces of human rights were often churches,[23] and it was often religious ceremonies that opened the streets to the cause. Masses, funerals, vigils, and processions were relatively protected public events. They marked the early years of the movement, when the regime prohib-ited "political" demonstrations, but they continued throughout the pro-tests of the 1980s as an expressive leitmotiv.[24] As De la Maza and Garcés (1985, 113) note, "The Church of the slums became a place in which many sectors met and re-emerged, contributing both to popular organization and the construction of a new Christian identity marked by an effort to bring faith together with life, with politics [and] with a popularly based project of liberation." Both its active presence at the grassroots and the public stance of the institution made the cause of human rights a moral cause that partially overcame continuing partisan political divisions.

Another way to understand how religion inflected the defense of human rights in Chile is at the personal level, through the human experience of the work in Church-linked organizations such as the Agrupaciones. From the central staff of the Vicaría down to local communities, face-to-face relationships among Christians and other Chileans, many with allegiance to Marxist parties, grounded religious teaching about tolerance in lived experience. These relationships built trust based on human solidarities rather than political ideologies, which had been the source of so much conflict. Tensions and partisan loyalties remained, but during the dictatorship human rights became a common ground that allowed people with diverse political beliefs to work together. The Church's insistence on respect for all Chileans, regardless of their political beliefs, proved to be a major factor influencing the country's return to democratic rule.

The concept of human rights defended by the Church in Chile was based on certain elementary human values—most fundamentally, the rights to life and physical integrity—built on a bedrock commitment to the rule of law. During the dictatorship the Church hierarchy also frequently spoke about social and economic rights, and the humanitarian side of the Vicaría's work at the grassroots gave such rights concrete expression. Since the restoration of democracy, the hierarchy has continued to speak out in broad terms about these rights, consistent with Catholic theology and Vatican guidelines. But the Church has not been a significant voice in contemporary public debates on human rights (with one important and revealing exception, discussed below), whether on Chile's glaring economic and educational inequalities or its recurrent conflicts over the rights of its native peoples. The hierarchy's emphasis on doctrinal orthodoxy (regarding, for example, marriage and sexual issues), the influence of conservative elite Catholics (such as Opus Dei), and the management of damaging internal scandals (concerning money and sex) have all reinforced a disposition to steer clear of protests with political overtones. But context also explains in part why the Church has been largely content to restrict itself to a subsidiary role on economic and social issues: the very conditions of a normal electoral democracy in which they have been represented by secular political forces since 1990.

That said, it is worth reflecting more deeply on the historical legacy left by the Church's active defense of human rights in the past. In his chapter in this volume, Daniel H. Levine eloquently describes the religious bases for a more "capacious" understanding of human rights, encompassing the whole human person in his or her social, economic, and cultural dimensions. The Chilean hierarchy has continued to proclaim this broader conception within the more conservative ecclesial orientation promoted by Popes John Paul II (1978–2005)[25] and Benedict XVI (2005–13), but that orientation—which not only entails appointments of bishops but also affects the whole life of the institutional Church—has unquestionably contributed to limiting its public role. It has returned to a more traditional ecclesiology, with authority conceived as founded in consecrated stewardship of timeless truths and exercised hierarchically over clergy and the faithful alike. In this perspective its experience during the dictatorship was exceptional—a time when the Church institution and its internal civil society converged in important respects and authority was understood more in terms of sensitivity and responsiveness to its pastoral bases. There is abundant evidence even before the democratic transition in 1990 that ecclesiastical leaders in Chile and the Vatican wished to draw the institution back toward a more traditional concept of internal authority—and to a more restricted role of the Church in society.

Despite this trend, however, the Church's historical defense of human rights left an important mark on Chile after 1990—the exception noted above. Chile's long transition to a fuller democracy, less encumbered by the institutions and habits of prolonged authoritarian rule, has been characterized by moral questions that became public issues, above all, concerning the violation of fundamental human rights during the dictatorship (Wilde 2013b). During the two past decades, the Church has contributed significantly to broader efforts to address the consequences of Pinochet's regime for the victims and for Chile as a nation (see Queiroz, this vol.). It has played a visible role in validating Chile's two truth commissions

(1990–91 and 2003–4, chaired by Bishop Valech) and supporting public policies to restore the human dignity to victims through a range of material and symbolic reparations. The archival records of the Vicaría, and many of its former staff members, have been indispensable to the hundreds of human rights prosecutions in Chile's "post-transitional" justice of the past decade (Collins 2013). And as suggested at the beginning of this chapter, the Church has given major support to Chile's engagement with historical memory of the dictatorship, which it has seen as a process fundamental to binding up the wounds of the past. More broadly, I believe, the experience of those who took part in religiously linked organizations has been felt in countless secular institutions since the return to democracy, even if that influence is not easily documented. All of this represents a kind of extension of its defense of human rights during the dictatorship, when an active pastoral ministry at the grassroots so shaped the role of the institutional Church.

Nevertheless, the Chilean Church's legacy has clearly not carried into a broader human rights agenda. Socially committed Catholics tend to blame its return to a more traditional ecclesiology and its effects on the inner life of the Church. They see the Church's sexual and financial scandals and reflexive institutional responses to cover them up—in Chile and so many other places in our contemporary world—as the product of its own authoritarian character. How, they ask, can the Church effectively defend human rights in society when it does not practice them within its own institution? Another critique, more rooted in perspectives of the secular political left, locates the limitations of its legacy in the restricted ways the Chilean Church actually defended human rights during the dictatorship (e.g., Albanesi 2013; Sabrovsky 2013). Echoing liberationist views after the coup, these critics blame that defense as narrowly individualistic, lacking in a realistic appreciation of structural factors of power. In their view, "human rights," as they were defined in practice in the 1970s and 1980s, have proven all too compatible with "neoliberal" capitalist economies and "democracies" that are incapable of tackling fundamental inequalities (see Albro, this vol.).

Both these lines of critique are important and deserve debate, but this chapter presents an interpretation that begins to address the concerns they raise—and some insights, I believe, that illuminate other dimensions of human rights as a religious response to violence. One is that the institutional character of the Church can reinforce its larger social influence—if its authorities are committed to a social pastoral mission of accompaniment and can accept some degree of internal conflict as the path to deeper institutional unity. The context of systematic, repressive state violence has passed, but "solidarity," "social justice," and "human rights" all remain relevant to conflict in contemporary Chile. And the Church can have far greater impact if theological and institutional proclamations of such values draw from its shared experience with "the poor"—those who suffer and are marginalized by the large processes of social and economic change (a finding echoed in the chapters by Arellano, Tate, and Frank-Vitale, among others, in this volume).

Another insight that derives from the Church's experience under Pinochet, I believe, is that its message must relate to the lives of individual human beings. It was not wrong to recoil from the divisiveness of mutually exclusionary political ideologies and proclaim the need for "reconciliation," but it took an active, firm defense of fundamental human rights to make that message real to Chileans who might or might not have shared its theology and doctrinal teaching. It took that defense to bring the Church closer to the individuals and communities whose energies were required to build the way to a durable transition to democracy. And it will require their efforts in Chile today to find a way forward out of conventional politics toward a deeper democracy. In a more open context it is actually much freer to address how structures of power affect human lives and in the spirit of the Second Vatican Council to join its forces to "all men of good will" for progressive change. Support from Rome was an aspect of the institutional Church that was important to its active defense of human rights during the dictatorship, and with the accession of Pope Francis (2013–), it may find greater sympathy from that quarter. Francis's grassroots pastoral orientation and personal experience of the effects of violence on the Latin American Church make him a very different pope from his immediate predecessors. Although it is too early to predict his impact, he does reawaken hope that the moral legacy of the Chilean Church in its defense of human rights may help give it a more vital role in addressing the conflicts of contemporary democracy.

Notes

1. In Santiago's Museum of Memory and Human Rights (inaugurated in 2010), this narrative predominates in the long second-floor gallery devoted to the movement that defended human rights in Chile. The exhibit inside the ground-floor museum entrance frames Chile's historical experience within the greater movement to defend human rights worldwide. This notably affirms the universality of human rights beyond polemics about its particular political history and resists the siren calls of Chile's nationalistic exceptionalism. On broader issues here, see Stern and Straus 2014.

2. More distantly, the Chilean Church was in important ways attuned to theological developments in France in the aftermath of World War II. Jacques Maritain was a particular influence, with his distinction of "planes" to legitimate greater Christian involvement in ("secular") society. At a time when the Allies in World War II began to justify their cause as a defense of "human rights," Maritain (1942) examined the idea in relation to Catholic traditions. Cavanaugh (1998) provides a theological critique of the distinction between planes and its application in Chile.

3. Beginning in the late 1960s, *Mensaje* also published a stream of articles warning against the consequences of growing violence in Chile, in rhetoric and action.

4. These socially progressive elements within the clergy, inspired by Bishop Manuel Larraín and Fr. Alberto Hurtado, S.J. (d. 1951; canonized as a saint 2005), were very strong by the 1960s. They were disappointed when the Vatican passed over Larraín to appoint Silva Henríquez archbishop of Santiago in 1961.

5. In 1981 the Vicaría published a collection of his statements on the subject under the title *Pablo VI y los derechos humanos*. In November 1973 Cardinal Silva had already traveled to Rome to seek his counsel on how to respond to the shocking conditions that followed the military takeover. At this early point in the dictatorship, Silva convinced the pope not to issue an already prepared public condemnation of human rights abuses in Chile—an example of the recurring question of whether the Church should assume the role of "prophet" or "mediator" in Chile (see chapters by Arellano and Tate, this vol.). Brian Smith's 1975 survey of attitudes in the Chilean Church found that almost half of the priests and nearly three-fifths of the nuns and laity preferred more prophetic leadership at that point (see Smith 1982, 304). But the Church's increasingly conscious, committed defense of human rights came to serve as the foundation for its forthright condemnation of the regime's violence.

6. Although a person's human rights can be violated by state inaction (to provide basic security, for example), in the formative period, it was the direct

actions of the state and its agents that tended to define human rights violations in practice. Then, and perhaps since, it was extrajudicial execution, torture, "disappearance," and kidnapping—violations against life and physical integrity by state agents—that particularly moved activists and eventually public opinion.

7. This long book on the Chilean Church and human rights, which appeared in 1983, explicitly addresses its "doctrine" and not "practice" (1). It is telling that at this late date the place of human rights in Catholic theology still required extensive justification.

8. This latter mission was also central to the predominantly mainline Protestant Fundación de Ayuda Social de las Iglesias Cristianas (FASIC), which was founded after dissolution of the ecumenical Pro-Peace Committee. Its work is documented by Garcés and Nicholls 2005.

9. Let us consider one pastoral experience that must stand for the uncounted others that led the Church to embrace the defense of human rights. On September 26, 1973, the bishop of Talca, Carlos González Cruchaga, received a phone call at 6:00 p.m. from the new military governor of the region, who had just received an order to execute the previous governor, Germán Castro Rojas. Castro, a Socialist, had fled after the coup toward Argentina and was captured in a shoot-out in which a policeman was killed. At 8:00 p.m. Bishop González, the only visitor permitted, saw Castro in his cell. He requested that the prisoner's handcuffs be removed, so that he could write his wife and children a farewell. He then sat with him and they talked during the following hours. He gradually came to understand, he later recalled, "what it meant to a man condemned to death to have someone to talk to." The bishop took his confession and gave him forgiveness and Extreme Unction. At midnight Castro was executed by firing squad in the Talca Regiment. He died, as Bishop González wrote later, with "faith in God and formation as a Christian" and also "convinced of his socialist ideals. . . . [I] still remember vividly all the details of that afternoon and night. . . . It is possibly the event that had the greatest impact on me during all the years of the Military Government" (González Cruchaga 1998, 98–100).

10. That this was "*una pastoral de fronteras*" was recognized by thoughtful observers at the time. See, e.g., the memoirs of Gazmuri and Martínez (2000, 181). The phrase evokes care in an unsettled region and calls to mind the vivid metaphor of Pope Francis of the Church "as a field hospital after battle" (see Antonio Spadaro, "A Big Heart Open to God," *America*, September 30, 2013). In this volume, see chapters by Arellano and Tate.

11. All translations from Spanish are my own.

12. See Appleby's (2000) insightful broader discussion of religious nonviolence.

13. Father Aldunate defended the "right of rebellion" against tyranny in principle (i.e., Catholic "just war") but rejected its application to Chile on the

grounds that the evils of violence outweighed the potential benefits and that armed resistance had no chance of overturning the dictatorship (see Vidal 2002).

14. The "state violence" after the coup was far greater than the "political violence" that preceded it. Political violence in Chile before 1973 also differed in kind from the mixture of political and state violence experienced in contexts of armed conflict, such as those in Central America, Colombia, Peru, and Argentina.

15. See, e.g., "Voz de los Obispos," *Mensaje* 220 (1973): 287–89.

16. This political line closely paralleled that of the Christian Democratic Party and its leftist allies most shaped by Christian thinking—notably the MAPU. It is beyond the scope of this chapter to examine the relationships between Jesuits, individual bishops, and the Christian Democrats (many of them with long-standing ties to the Church dating to their education in Church institutions). But see the volumes by MAPU leaders: Gazmuri and Martínez 2000; Correa and Viera-Gallo 1986.

17. This echoed the postcoup liberationist critique of nonviolence, discussed earlier in this chapter, which saw it as a recycling of Christian Democratic opposition to Allende and the Popular Unity. See *La Iglesia chilena*, 46.

18. It was dissatisfaction precisely with this religiously based policy that led to the founding of the left-linked secular human rights organization CODEPU in 1980. CODEPU defended all "political prisoners," including those who espoused or practiced violence, based on their legitimate right to due process of law. The Vicaría instead defended "prisoners of conscience," that is, those persecuted for their ideas, adopting the characterization employed by Amnesty International. Its policy paralleled that of the broad national network of Peruvian human rights organizations, the Coordinadora Nacional de los Derechos Humanos (see Coletta Youngers 2003).

19. Several early examples of this dynamic occurred in 1975. Jaime Guzmán, the regime's right Catholic intellectual, publicly attacked Cardinal Silva for offering Church protection to several MIR leaders. Silva threatened to excommunicate him, and Guzmán backed down (see Smith 1982, 303). Another such episode is described by Cassidy (1977).

20. Valech was designated vicar of solidarity in June 1987 by Cardinal Fresno, having exercised de facto authority through the previous year during the serious illness of the then-vicar, Santiago Tapia.

21. Lowden (1996, 113–15, 120–25) recounts the story with characteristic insight, brio, and telling detail. The first quotation is from "Miremos el futuro del país," Permanent Committee of the Episcopal Conference, March 3, 1989: *Documentos 1988–1991*, 38, cited by Lowden, 123. The second quotation is from an interview with Bishop Valech by Lowden, April 10, 1992, cited by

Lowden, 125. Valech would later serve as chair of Chile's second truth commission (2003–4) on political imprisonment and torture.

22. Existing studies recognize the vitality of the grassroots Church in Chile during the dictatorship but tend to stress its conflict with the hierarchy rather than the ways in which Church leadership responded to and ratified initiatives taken there. See, e.g., Smith 1982; Drogus and Stewart-Gambino 2005; and Schneider 1995. Although Drogus and Stewart-Gambino emphasize the base's anger at what was taken as the Church's abandonment of their cause, they also provide considerable evidence of disaffection there with militant leftist politics. See also De la Maza and Garcés 1985; Bruey 2013.

23. In his study of community-level organizations during the mass protests of the 1980s, Oxhorn finds that more than half met in churches (1995, table A-3, 338–40).

24. Hernán Vidal's works (1995, 1996) are particularly insightful on this dimension.

25. It is worth noting, however, that specifically in the case of Chile, John Paul II endorsed the Chilean Church's support for democratization to end the dictatorship, which he judged "not only possible, but also necessary as part of the pastoral mission of the Church" (quoted in Lowden 1996, 116, from *La Época* [Santiago], April 1, 1987).

References

Albanesi, Annalisa. 2013. "Derechos Humanos y Justicia Social: Repensando el papel de la Iglesia Católica chilena respecto al régimen militar desde la historia global (1973–1980)." Paper delivered at the Latin American Studies Association, Washington, DC.

Aldunate, José, S.J., Fernando Castillo, and Joaquín Silva. 1983. *Los derechos humanos y la Iglesia chilena.* Santiago: ECO Educación y Comunicaciones.

Appleby, Scott R. 2000. *The Ambivalence of the Sacred: Religion, Violence, and Reconciliation.* Lanham, MD: Rowman and Littlefield.

Aranda, Gilberto C. 2004. *Vicaría de la Solidaridad: Una experiencia sin fronteras.* Santiago: Ediciones Chile y América–CESOC.

Bruey, Alison J. 2013. "Transnational Concepts, Local Contexts: Solidarity at the Grassroots in Pinochet's Chile." In *Human Rights and Transnational Solidarity in Cold War Latin America,* edited by Jessica Stites Mor, 120–42. Madison: University of Wisconsin Press.

Cassidy, Sheila. 1977. *Audacity to Believe.* London: William Collins and Son.

Cavanaugh, William T. 1998. *Torture and Eucharist: Theology, Politics, and the Body of Christ.* Oxford: Blackwell.

Collins, Cath. 2013. "The Politics of Prosecutions." In *The Politics of Memory in Chile: From Pinochet to Bachelet,* edited by Cath Collins, Katherine Hite, and Alfredo Joignant, 61–89. Boulder, CO: Lynne Rienner.

Collins, Cath, Katherine Hite, and Alfredo Joignant, eds. 2013. *The Politics of Memory in Chile: From Pinochet to Bachelet.* Boulder, CO: Lynne Rienner. In Spanish: *Las políticas de la memoria en Chile: Desde Pinochet a Bachelet.* Santiago: Ediciones Diego Portales.

Correa, Enrique, and José Antonio Viera-Gallo. 1986. *Iglesia y dictadura.* Santiago: Ediciones Chile y América–CESOC.

De la Maza, Gonzalo, and Mario Garcés. 1985. *La explosión de las mayorías: Protesta nacional, 1983–1984.* Santiago: ECO–Educación y Comunicaciones.

Dinges, John. 2004. *The Condor Years: How Pinochet and His Allies Brought Terrorism to Three Continents.* New York: New Press.

Dooner, Patricio. 1989. *Iglesia, reconciliación y democracia: Lo que los dirigentes políticos esperan de la Iglesia.* Santiago: Andante.

Drogus, Carol, and Hannah Stewart-Gambino. 2005. *Activist Faith: Grassroots Women in Democratic Brazil and Chile.* University Park: Pennsylvania State University Press.

Fernández Fernández, David. 1996. *La "Iglesia" que resistió a Pinochet.* Madrid: IEPALA.

Fleet, Michael, and Brian H. Smith. 1997. *The Catholic Church and Democracy in Chile and Peru.* Notre Dame, IN: University of Notre Dame Press.

Garcés, Mario, and Nancy Nicholls. 2005. *Para una historia de los DD.HH. en Chile.* Santiago: LOM.

Gazmuri, Jaime, and Jesús Manuel Martínez. 2000. *El sol y la bruma: Jaime Gazmuri.* Santiago: Ediciones B Chile.

González Cruchaga, Carlos. 1998. *Con verdad se construye la reconciliación: Chile, 1970–1988.* Talca: Maranatha.

Hagopian, Frances, ed. 2009. *Religious Pluralism, Democracy, and the Catholic Church in Latin America.* Notre Dame, IN: University of Notre Dame Press.

Hau, Boris. 2006. "La fuerza de la vida: La defensa de los derechos humanos del Departamento Jurídico del Comité Pro-Paz y de la Vicaría de la Solidaridad." Thesis, Universidad Alberto Hurtado.

Hinkelammert, Franz J. 1977. *Ideología de sometimiento: La Iglesia Católica chilena frente al golpe, 1973–1974.* San José, Costa Rica: Editorial Universitaria Centroamericana.

Hoyl Cruz, Ana María. 2003. *Por la vida.* Santiago: Ediciones ChileAmérica.

La Iglesia chilena y la junta military de Chile (Documentos). 1975. Buenos Aires: Tierra Nueva.

Levine, Daniel H., ed. 1986. *Religion and Political Conflict in Latin America.* Chapel Hill: University of North Carolina Press.

Lowden, Pamela. 1996. *Moral Opposition to Authoritarian Rule in Chile, 1973–90.* New York: St. Martin's Press.

Maritain, Jacques. 1942. *Natural Law and Human Rights.* Windsor, OH: Christian Culture Press, Assumption College.

Orellana, Patricio, and Elizabeth Quay Hutchison. 1991. *El movimiento de derechos humanos en Chile, 1973–1990.* Santiago: Centro de Estudios Latinoamericanos Simón Bolívar.

Oxhorn, Philip D. 1995. *Organizing Civil Society: The Popular Sectors and the Struggle for Democracy in Chile.* University Park: Pennsylvania State University Press.

Precht, Cristián. 1998. *En la huella del Buen Samaritano: Breve historia de la Vicaría de la Solidaridad.* Santiago: Editorial Tiberíades.

Rojas, Sandra. 1991. *Vicaría de la Solidaridad: Historia de su trabajo social.* Santiago: Ediciones Paulinas.

Sabrovsky, Eduardo. 2013. Address delivered at the Conference, "Cátedra de la Memoria 2013: 40 Años del Golpe." Santiago, September 6.

Schneider, Cathy Lisa. 1995. *Shantytown Protest in Pinochet's Chile.* Philadelphia, PA: Temple University Press.

Silva Henríquez, Raúl, and Ascanio Cavallo. 1991. *Memorias.* 3 vols. Santiago: Ediciones Copygraph.

Smith, Brian H. 1982. *The Church and Politics in Chile: Challenges to Modern Catholicism.* Princeton, NJ: Princeton University Press.

———. 1986. "Chile: Deepening the Allegiance of Working-Class Sectors in the Church in the 1970s." In *Religion and Political Conflict in Latin America,* edited by Daniel H. Levine, 156–86. Chapel Hill: University of North Carolina Press.

Stern, Steve J., and Scott Straus, eds. 2014. *The Human Rights Paradox: Universality and Its Discontents.* Madison: University of Wisconsin Press.

Tate, Winifred. 2007. *Counting the Dead: The Culture and Politics of Human Rights Activism in Colombia.* Berkeley: University of California Press.

Vicaría de la Solidaridad. 1978a. *La huelga de hambre por los detenidos-desaparecidos: Alcances morales.* Santiago.

———. 1978b. *La no violencia evangélica, fuerza de liberación.* Santiago.

Vidal, Hernán. 1995. *Frente Patriótico Manuel Rodríguez: El tabú del conflicto armado en Chile.* Santiago: Mosquito Editores.

———. 1996. *Dar la vida por la vida: Agrupación Chilena de Familiares de Detenidos Desaparecidos.* Santiago: Mosquito Editores.

———. 2002. *El Movimiento contra la Tortura Sebastián Acevedo.* Santiago: Mosquito Editores.

Wilde, Alexander. 2013a. "Human Rights in Two Latin American Democracies." In *Sustaining Human Rights in the Twenty-First Century: Strategies from Latin America*, edited by Katherine Hite and Mark Ungar, 35–71. Baltimore, MD: Woodrow Wilson Center Press, Johns Hopkins University Press.

———. 2013b. "A Season of Memory: Human Rights in Chile's Long Transition." In *The Politics of Memory in Chile: From Pinochet to Bachelet*, edited by Cath Collins, Katherine Hite, and Alfredo Joignant, 31–60. Boulder, CO: Lynne Rienner.

Yáñez Rojas, Eugenio. 1989. *La Iglesia chilena y el goberno militar: Itinerario de una difícil relación (1973–1988)*. Santiago: Editorial Andante.

Youngers, Coletta. 2003. *Violencia política y sociedad civil en el Perú: Historia de la Coordinadora Nacional de Derechos Humanos*. Lima: Instituto de Estudios Peruanos.

CHAPTER 6

VIOLENT TIMES

*Catholicism and Dictatorship
in Argentina in the 1970s*

MARÍA SOLEDAD CATOGGIO

Argentina's return to democracy in December 1983 was built on the promise of closing the book on political violence in the country. To that end, the state put in motion two strategies, both unprecedented in the region. The first was a legal approach, which took shape through trials of both military junta members and guerrilla leaders. The second sought to reconstruct the truth about the nation's traumatic past. It was captured in *Nunca más* (Never Again), a report prepared by the National Commission on the Disappearance of Persons (CONADEP 1984). The first strategy quickly ran into difficulties with the Full Stop Law (1986) and the Law of Due Obedience (1987) (see Crenzel 2008). Both strategies unfolded in a context in which a "theory of the two demons" was taking shape. Placing responsibility equally on the military authorities and guerrilla organizations, this theory cast a mantel of innocence over civilian leaders in political parties, unions, and corporations who were part of the repressive web of the military regime. In this context, public debate about the role played by the Catholic Church in Argentina during the dictatorship

191

was secondary. However, unresolved tensions within the very heart of the Catholic world erupted in force in each of the strategies put forward by the democratic government.

Political institutions, especially state institutions, sought to label the transition a "national reconciliation." This term had already been used in the 1981 Church document *Iglesia y comunidad nacional* (Church and National Community). Actors from across the political and religious spectrum battled to apply their own definitions in order to expand, restrict, or reject the demands of justice (Bonnin 2012). These tensions erupted with virulence in the courts, where the victims and the victimizers turned to theological definitions as the basis for their arguments. At the same time, CONADEP was including testimonies that incriminated priests such as Cristián von Wernich while also distinguishing "religious victims" as a particular category within the group of victims of state terrorism. Finally, Emilio Mignone, a devout lifelong Catholic turned national and international human rights icon, made his disenchantment with the Church public in his book *Iglesia y dictadura*, where he laid out the thesis of the two churches: one complicit, the other persecuted.

Although this thesis may have reassured those who maintained a Catholic identity and were trying to preserve the institution's reputation, it simplifies sociological and historical reality. This chapter presents a fresh analysis of the long, complex, conflicted relationship of the Catholic Church to politics, violence, and the state, with particular emphasis on how Peronism shaped religious perceptions and actions in the period leading to the military dictatorship of 1976–83. Drawing on a range of important recent scholarship, it traces the deep internal religious divisions that undermined corporate solidarity in the institutional Church and contributed to an understanding of how it was possible for victims and perpetrators to live together within it. Very few bishops spoke out against violations of human rights, but as analyzed in this chapter, Catholic officials and laypeople did intervene in a variety of ways on behalf of "religious victims" during the dictatorship. The national perspective of this chapter complements studies of regional and local realities (see Morello, this vol.) and presents a contrasting case to the Chilean Church under Pinochet (see Wilde, this vol.).

Encounter with Peronism: The Rending of Catholicism

The Second Vatican Council, which shaped a Catholic identity for more than a generation, seemed to be a radical break with the past. In reality, it grew out of a process within the Church whose origins date to the end of the nineteenth century. In the 1891 papal encyclical *Rerum Novarum* we see the formulation of a social action program that encouraged Catholics to take the reins of politics. In Argentina, Catholicism after Vatican II brought together several national traditions, from the Catholic workers' circles of Fr. Federico Grote in 1892 to the various specialized branches of Catholic Action. In the mid-1940s, many believed that Peronism was an incarnation of the Church's social teaching in the encyclical.

In his speeches during the campaign, then-Colonel Perón claimed for himself elements of Catholic social teaching and appropriated material and symbolic elements of vernacular Catholicism (Cuchetti 2005). Broad segments of Catholics were attracted by this appeal. In this context, Peronism facilitated the confluence of a "true cacophony of ideologies, cultures, and types, to which Perón tried to bring order by playing, within the vast sheet music of the Catholic national myth, now the 'popular' and 'democratic' strain, now the soothing note of moderation, now the tune of militaristic order turning its face toward nationalism" (Zanatta 1999, 430).

In effect, Catholics from different social milieux converged around this "movement with a Christian inspiration," bringing with them diverse backgrounds in political socialization and demands that were not always reconcilable. Under the National Liberation Alliance, prominent figures in nationalist circles, like Fr. Leonardo Castellani, were nominated as candidates for Congress and supported Perón's presidential bid. Also coming from these circles, such figures as Jordán Bruno Genta and Julio Meinvielle understood that voting for Perón's labor agenda was a strategy that would break the isolation that surrounded nationalism, identified as it was with an authoritarianism incongruent with the new context of democracy (Zanatta 1999, 429). A significant group from the ranks of Catholic Action, including Emilio Mignone, joined the workers' party (Mallimaci 2001, 226). Specifically, those who had been socialized through the experiences of the Catholic Workers' Youth and Catholic labor unions would see in Peron's *justicialismo*—which blended elements of different political ideologies—a promise for expanding their demands of social justice and at the same time an effective counter to communism within union ranks. Following in this anticommunist—and antiliberal— vein, many Catholic intellectuals who had studied the *Cursos de cultura católica*,[1] along with noteworthy contributors to the journal *Criterio*, would support the labor agenda (Mallimaci 2001, 227). Finally, without leaving their positions in the Church, members of the clergy like Hernán Benítez had a prominent place in directing Peronist public imagery.

The romance between Peronism and the Church would last a full five years before the 1950s brought an institutional confrontation. Major events in this process included the breaking off of relations with the papal nuncio, trials of military chaplains accused of conspiracy against the government, the legalization of divorce, the reinstitution of the *la ley de profilaxis social* (lit., "the law of social cleansing"), equal standing for le-gitimate and illegitimate children, and the suppression of the decree on religious instruction. The greatest illustration of the divide was, without a doubt, the "Christ Conquers" insignia carried by the navy planes that bombed the Plaza de Mayo in June 1955, a prelude to the coup that would overthrow Perón several months later.

In spite of all this, the linkages endured. For some analysts, the origi-nality of Peronism lay in its creating a unique conception of the religious through the empowerment of workers, the civil-religious cult of his wife, Eva, and the construction of a lineage in which he cast himself as the con-tinuation of a "primitive Christianity" (Caimari 1995; Cuchetti 2005). This had the dual effect of generating a challenge to ecclesiastical au-thority while simultaneously maintaining an identity-based appeal to seg-ments of the Catholic population.

In this sense, the trauma produced by the encounter—and collision— between Perón and the Church broke up the corporate solidarity of an institution that, until then, had been managed in a strongly hierarchical manner (in contrast to the Chilean Church; see Wilde, this vol.). In re-sponse to this phenomenon, there were Peronist Catholics, like Justicial-ist deputy Antonio Cafiero, who solved the dilemma by breaking with Perón, and there were Catholic Peronists, like Fr. Hernán Benítez, who deepened their loyalty to Perón at the cost of confrontation with their own church institutions.

However, for major segments of Catholicism in Argentina, the institutional rift between Catholicism and Peronism signaled an irreconcilable break. They condemned Perón's appropriation of the sacred. Appealing to their old alliance with the military to overthrow a "heretical" movement, they enthusiastically welcomed the 1955 coup that was announced in Christ's name.

The result was that Peronism, which had been born from the old alliance between the Catholic religion and the military, was also excluded from political participation, from which it was proscribed for eighteen years. This double expulsion of Peronism had the effect of legitimizing an alternative path to state power: revolution.

The 1960s: Corporate Solidarity in Crisis

The renewal brought about by Vatican II reopened the unhealed wounds of the Peronist experience within the heart of Argentine Catholicism. On one side, the more theologically intransigent camp rejected the Council's changes out of hand as a capitulation in the face of modernity. On the other side, a certain European-style theological modernism, represented by the then-editor of *Criterio*, Jorge María Mejía, who had covered the Council, focused on how its decisions should be *implemented* in Argentina. Finally, a generation of young Catholics, ideologically and politically close to Peronism, who clamored for the *reformulation* of the Council's reforms in specifically Latin American and Argentine terms, came together around emerging leaders such as Lucio Gera and Enrique Angelelli (see Gera and Rodríguez Melgarejo 1970).

Within the first group were those who closed ranks around the medieval philosophy of St. Thomas Aquinas, the "Thomist tower" built by Bishop Octavio Derisi at the Catholic University of Argentina. Without openly criticizing the Council, they assailed the "new theology" expounded there in the journal *Estudios Teológicos y Filosóficos*. Others like Julio Meinvielle and Leonardo Castellani, elder statesmen of nationalist Catholicism from the 1930s and 1940s, returned to the public eye with their openly anti–Vatican II criticisms, which were published in the journals *Verbo* and *Cabildo*. In addition, there were men who would become key figures during the dictatorship, like Bishop Adolfo Tortolo, who gained notoriety by voting against all of the Council's modernizations (see Mallimaci 1993).

At the same time, clergy and laity favoring Council positions were divided between those who limited their support to applying its decisions (such as the contributors to *Criterio*) and those who demanded a reformulation better tailored to conditions within the country and who were identified with a greater sense of social responsibility (Soneira 1989). These positions developed along separate lines over time. Eduardo Pironio and Antonio Quarracino ascended to the cardinalship,[2] whereas Bishops Alberto Devoto and Enrique Angelelli, especially the latter, came to embody alternative models of legitimate authority. They helped bring together those who, appealing once again to the model of "primitive Christianity," made up what was known as *tercermundismo*.[3] The time of Vatican II created an effervescent atmosphere of social creativity that allowed for significant levels of conflict within the Church. It also generated discussion of topics previously unthinkable, such as a "Christian-Marxist dialogue."

The Dispute over "Legitimate Violence": Armed Struggle, the Violence of the Oppressed, and Just War

Resorting to violence as a method for changing the order, or for ordering the changes, occurs throughout twentieth-century Argentine history.[4] The succession of military coups reflects, at the same time as it reinforces, a widespread lack of confidence in bourgeois forms of democratic politics across many segments of civil society. The triumph of the Cuban Revolution and the process of decolonization in the Third World gave political violence renewed legitimacy as a pathway to social transformation. The lesson drawn was that a revolutionary vanguard could create focal points of insurrection (foco theory) that would accelerate the conditions for revolution. In other words, the revolutionary struggle would generate consciousness *on its own*, without the need to wait until objective conditions signaled the time for revolution.

Against this background, significant groups of Catholics were encouraged by the declarations of the Second Conference of Latin American Bishops (II CELAM), which met in 1968 in Medellín, Colombia. Echoing the 1967 encyclical *Populorum Progressio*, the conference restated Catholic doctrine on legitimate defense against tyranny.[5] In this context, Latin America, which was defined as a "continent of violence"—a structural violence of injustice—became an appropriate stage on which another form of violence, "the violence of the oppressed"— temporary and redeemable—could emerge.[6] A wide range of Catholics read the document as a call for Christians to awaken the consciousness of the oppressed. There then occurred a process of politicizing the old "social issue" that had mobilized Catholics in Argentina since the turn of the century, that of integrating into the fabric of the nation those who had been marginalized by the then-fashionable liberal political and economic model. Under the slogan "an option for the poor" they changed the way in which poverty was explained and the role that was assigned to the poor in the Church, society, and politics (Levine 1996, 91, 94). From this perspective, the poor were viewed as subjects, not objects, of social and political transformation, endowed with their own unique capital: a privileged perception of reality arising from their very condition of material poverty (Catoggio 2013b, 249).

For Catholics of the time, the "option for the poor" comprised a wide range of possibilities. In practice, several models of social transformation existed together, each of them emphasizing a particular sphere of action (the factory, the university, the slum, the community, the rural cooperative) and focusing on a particular revolutionary subject (workers, the youth, the indigenous, the poor). There were a few at the extreme who, following the example of the Colombian priest Camilo Torres, thought armed struggle necessary for change. The insurrection route, however, was a part of the "legitimate popular violence" that was encouraged by significant elements within the clergy (Donatello 2010; Bonnin 2013). Because of their role in educating young people, some members of the clergy had an influence on young Catholics who took the path of armed struggle.

A new element is taking shape within this panorama of misery and injustice: the fact that an exploited people is rapidly become conscious of itself, sensing and ascertaining the real possibilities of its

liberation. For many, this liberation is impossible without a fundamental change in the socio-economic structures of our continent.
There are not a few who believe that all routes toward achieving this
change by purely pacific means have been exhausted. Due to the
power of repression that the privileged minorities use to stand in the
way of this process of liberation, many see no solution other than
the use of force by the people. Many devout Christians, who sin-
cerely reflect on their lives in the light of the gospel, are also coming
to this conclusion.[7]

Within this framework, we find priests recognizing political martyrs
like Ché Guevara and leaders of militant organizations invoking Camilo
Torres as a revolutionary icon. While both men were clearly defined by
combat and were therefore indisputably associated with armed struggle,
the category "martyr" as applied to others left room for ambivalence
with respect to participation (or lack of participation) in militant organizations. The figure of the martyr, a symbol with a tradition in Christianity
going back to imperial Rome, could be seen as providing meaning to the
ultimate and inescapable results of political violence. This figure stood at
the center of two simultaneous and complementary processes. First, it
permitted the "secularization" of major religious figures by putting emphasis on the *political* dimension of their actions. Second, it incorporated
important individuals from nonreligious arenas into (Catholic) religious
imagery (see Catoggio 2011).

This dispute was one facet of a social and political climate in which
violence became an unavoidable topic in dealing with the challenges of
the period. As a counter to the martyr, the idea of "clerical subversion"
had the effect of desacralizing the religious world of Catholicism by planting suspicion of "infiltration" in the institution, as in the following argument from a military perspective.

The Movement of Priests for the Third World is an organization of
priests in the Argentine Republic that has as its goal the installa-
tion of a socialist-Marxist government, using, as its means, Marxist
dialectic with all that this entails: class struggle, brainwashing, violence, and revolution. . . .
    Such that they commit a substantial double error:

a.   Claiming that the fundamental goal of the church is to directly solve socioeconomic material problems; and

b.   That they do so through an immoral system, long ago rejected, the implementation of which would cause greater evils than those that it claims to cure.

According to the *tercermundista* priests, the mission of the Church would consist of this double error, and where the hierarchy does not support them, they actually found a parallel church.[8]

In fact, the messianic attitude adopted by the army and security forces during the dictatorship has its roots in an enduring symbiosis between the armed forces, the Catholic faith, and the citizenry that lent continuity to the various Argentine dictatorships. In the wake of the coups, the Catholic Church strengthened its bureaucratic structure, expanded the number of dioceses, achieved (in large measure) its demands, and exercised its veto power in the field of public policy. At the same time, military leaders built up the legitimacy of their exercise of power by association with religious authorities, who represented broad swaths of Argentine society (see Mallimaci 1992). This slow building of a "community of interest" between church and military—a process not without its conflicts—led in the long term to the crystallization of a modus operandi based on the exchange of legitimacies and cooperation in colonizing the state apparatus. It made room for a certain confluence between the military and ecclesial spheres as well. On the one hand, the presence of clergy and laity like the above-mentioned Julio Meinvielle and Jordán Bruno Genta, who had been providing training to the military since the early 1930s, stamped the armed forces with an ideological outlook. On the other hand, the military life adopted by chaplains within the armed forces thoroughly permeated the points they emphasized in their doctrinal statements (see Ruderer 2010).

This ecclesiastical-military alliance, which accorded the two groups the status of guarantors of the nation, was woven during the course of the twentieth century. It led to novel statements when, with the coming of the dictatorship of the 1970s and 1980s, the mind-set of a "nation at war" was created (see Vezzetti 2002). In fact, under these circumstances, the theological-political justification of the "struggle against subversion" was built firmly on the idea of just war. This formulation, supported by authoritative citations from St. Augustine, St. Thomas Aquinas, and Francisco de Vitoria, referred to a Christian idea that the limited use of violence is allowed, under certain predetermined conditions and as a last resort, to restore peace and order (see Ruderer 2010).

In 1976, Bishop Adolfo Tortolo, who since 1970 had been simultaneously president of the conference of bishops and vicar general of the armed forces, invoked Aquinas to justify the military vicariate's task: "One must not forget that legitimate defense is 'legitimate.' It must also be taken into account that the subversive delinquent is generally suffused with an ideology that still speaks to him when he is detained: 'I will return to killing.' Those who defend their homeland in the name of their country fulfill their duty in war. And the matter of war is studied by St. Thomas Aquinas, in his chapter on virtue and love, as an act of love" (*Bulletin of the Military Vicariate*, no. 52 [December 1976], quoted in Ruderer 2010, 5).

At the same time, for Gen. Jorge Rafael Videla, who oversaw most of the military's operations, "a terrorist is not only someone with a pistol or a bomb, it is also someone who spreads ideas that are contrary to Western, Christian civilization" (quoted in Robin 2005, 430). This religious framework for military repression cast those who implemented it as an "elect" who would relentlessly pursue their convictions.

Legitimation of Repressive Violence in the 1970s Military Dictatorship

The alliance with the de facto regime found its expression in the role played by the Catholic leadership, and by other social and political leaders, in legitimizing the exercise of military power on a political-religious basis (Quiroga 1994, 70–71). This was not unique to the period of authoritarian rule that began in 1976. It had been carried out by such leaders, to a greater or lesser degree, since the century's first military-civil-religious coup in 1930. What made the post-1976 period different was the high level of involvement by certain segments of the clergy in legitimizing the so-called struggle against subversion and in actually taking part in violent repression.

Vital to this effort was the military vicariate, created in 1957, which offered hybrid career paths in both the military and the Church. With the passage of time, this organization, with its nationwide jurisdiction, would gain autonomy from the Church and authority within the military. This occurred to such an extent that members of the military clergy came to distinguish themselves by holding military rank together with their positions as ministers of the Church. This created an abundance of jurisdictional conflicts during the dictatorship and brought to the surface the tension of an unresolved power struggle within the Church hierarchy.[9] Around 1976 there were 214 Argentine military chaplains, more than in any other country in Latin America (see Ruderer 2010).

As noted above, some chaplains became active in training military troops in the tactics of "counterrevolutionary war" at the Escuela Superior de Guerra and other military educational institutions.[10] Others performed religious services in honor of those "fallen in the struggle against subversion" or said field Masses in places where military operations were ongoing (Obregón 2005, 91). This kind of legitimation was part of a long-established tradition of Catholicization within the armed forces (see Mallimaci 1992).

The most salient case of an ordained priest's deep involvement in the "struggle against subversion" is that of Cristián von Wernich, a police chaplain, who was sentenced in 2007 for crimes against humanity. Von Wernich, however, is only the tip of a much deeper iceberg. Other priests—even bishops—were known to have undertaken similar activities in secret detention centers (see Badenes and Miguel 2007, 8). According to a number of reports, they participated in torture and/or in military and security operations.[11] The symbiosis between sectors of the Catholic Church and the world of the military allowed for the former's denunciation of their own colleagues among the clergy.[12]

The positions taken within the Catholic Church on the subject of violence worsened its already frayed sense of corporate solidarity. The bishops accepted the military intervention in its own sphere to reestablish the ecclesiastical relationships of authority and obedience, which had been called into question by the debate over how to treat the Vatican II reforms. Also the clergy appealed to the military to resolve ideological and internal conflicts with other priests (see Catoggio 2013a). In this context, the combination of institutional discipline, denunciation, and state repression produced a set of victims among the clergy. These victims shared specific characteristics not generally found across the overall set of victims of Argentine state repression.

Clerical Strategies in the Face of Violent State Repression

Clerical victims of state repression tended to be priests between the ages of thirty and forty. Members of this group were special objects of detention and murder, distinct from most of the disappeared among the victims of state terrorism. Of the 113 cases that make up this group, we find 51 detentions, 36 disappearances, 17 murders, and 9 instances of bombings and/or forced entry. Their inherent visibility as Church officials, augmented by the public notoriety gained by many during the 1960s and 1970s, provides an explanation for why these actors predominated among those detained at the behest of the National Executive (Poder Ejecutivo Nacional). Disappearances were most frequent among clerics who followed unusual career paths, such as those whose backgrounds were filled with periods spent abroad or moved from the religious to the secular sphere or from the hierarchy to a local parish, or vice versa. This intra-Church mobility, which also meant geographic mobility, tended to dilute their institutional rootedness, thereby accentuating their anonymity. This made it easier to strip them of the holiness of their office and equate them with so many other civilians who were accused of being "subversive." Although detention was used frequently against secular clergy, disappearances were directed primarily against those who were members of religious orders. Murder, by contrast, occurred among both groups and created a sense of terror in both (see Catoggio 2013c).

Among clerical victims and their supporters, the repression led to various defense strategies: recourse to Church authorities, overtures to the papal nuncio, diplomatic pressure through embassies (usually in cases where the victim was of foreign origin), appeals to ties of family or friendship with the military, requests to the military vicariate for mediation, appeals to the courts, spreading news about incidents through the press, requesting help from domestic and international human rights organizations, and, finally, exile. All of these strategies were used throughout the dictatorship, with mixed results.

In the face of state repression against members of the clergy, *informing the bishop* was among the first measures to which people turned. Indeed, given the vertical and hierarchical character of Argentine Catholicism, such notification was a habitual and immediate recourse, regardless of the bishop's ideological position. In these situations, personal interventions by the bishops generally consisted of letters and interviews with officials in the military government and, in the case of detentions, visits to the prisons. The literature on this matter has emphasized the "private" nature of this type of intervention (see Mignone 1986, 77, 146–47; Soneira 1986, 58) and pointed out that such "secret" negotiations did nothing to create the conditions for a movement opposing the military regime. There was no official open accusation of human rights violations by the Church, even though the violations were well known to the bishops.[13] There were, nevertheless, cases in which individual appeals to the bishops brought the full weight of Church institutions to bear successfully to free clergy members from the clutches of repression. Even those bishops known for public denunciation in the early 1970s shifted their strategy, adopting private channels in proportion to the worsening of repression among their own ranks. But there were also instances of public accusations from bishops, made in their personal capacity as individual citizens, which bore no fruit (Catoggio 2013a).

Far from offering a guarantee of safe conduct, recourse to the bishop led to a variety of outcomes. Among the cases that were successful, we can note those of Juan José Czerepack, Aníbal Coerezza, and Omar Dinelli. They were detained by the dictatorship and freed in large part thanks to the individual efforts of their respective bishops: Jorge Keremer, Antonio Aguirre, and Manuel Marengo.[14] In other cases, the inquiries or efforts put forward by the bishops were unsuccessful. One can think, for example, of the role of Cardinal Eduardo Pironio in the case of the disappearance of Fr. Pablo Gazarri. Likewise, Miguel Hesayne, bishop of Viedma, officially joined the families of those who were disappeared from Iglesia Santa Cruz in their letter of petition to the military government. Among the missing were the French nuns Alice Domon and Léonie Duquet. Both Gazarri and Domon are missing to this day; Duquet's remains were recovered from the sea and identified in 2005.

As a second strategy, many Catholic victims of state repression *approached the papal nunciature*, seeing it as the primary and direct link to the international community. Nuncio Pío Laghi's stature as an expert in managing foreign relations made him a hinge between the military authorities and the international community. Many in Argentina turned to him: the military for legitimacy in the "struggle against subversion," American diplomats for evaluation of the state of human rights violations in the country, the victims of state repression themselves (or their families) for safety in their personal lives. How Laghi responded to the different requests made to him led to mixed interpretations of his performance in office.

Declassified documents from the U.S. Department of State offer a good example of the ambivalent way in which Laghi was portrayed at the beginning of the dictatorship with respect to the "question of human rights." In a 1976 memorandum recounting a conversation between Laghi, Deputy Assistant Secretary of State Charles W. Bray, and the political adviser Wayne S. Smith, Laghi is quoted as follows: "The Nuncio then commented that [the] Church's greatest concern is implicit in the first two reservations mentioned: human rights. That there are serious excesses and violations there can be no doubt. *The Church cannot but be concerned and the government must realize it. What attitude can the latter expect the Church to take when its priests disappear, or are picked up and tortured, or even killed.*"[15]

About three months later, in a memorandum describing a conversation at the nunciature between Laghi, U.S. Ambassador Robert Hill, and the American diplomats Patricia Derian, Fernando Rondon, and Robert S. Steven, the portrayal of Laghi differs substantially.

When asked if he considered that the Church and Catholics were persecuted in Argentina, he showed surprise and quick denial. He said that individuals among the 5,500 priests and 11,000 nuns had been arrested or abused, but rejected the suggestion that the Church as such was under attack. At the moment there were 12 priests in detention, 7 of whom were non-Argentine. . . . The Nuncio stated that about 7 of the total 12 priests had admitted their involvement in or association with subversion.[16]

While repression of Catholics is seen as evidence of the "excesses" of the so-called struggle against subversion, the nuncio rejects out of hand the notion that there exists "persecution" of Catholicism as such. Critics believe Laghi even justified harsh measures against priests on the grounds that they were suspected of being involved with armed opposition groups; his defenders emphasize his good intentions and positive role.[17]

Embassies were another obvious nexus with the international community. They were especially sought out in cases of repression against foreign clerics and members of religious orders. In such cases, the convergence of pressure and influence exerted by bishops, superiors in the religious orders, and the nuncio accompanied the diplomatic approach to the military government. The results indicate that foreign citizenship carried more weight than their status as clerics. Even so, the effectiveness of the diplomatic approach in negotiating the mazes of the state's repressive apparatus was mixed.

The cases of the American priest James Weeks and the Irish priest Patrick Rice are representative of successful interventions. The procedures were analogous in both cases. With Rice, the Irish ambassador, M. Wilfred Lennon, contacted military authorities immediately. Thanks to the embassy's initiative, the case received press attention. This resulted in Argentina's foreign affairs minister being asked about Rice's whereabouts during a United Nations meeting in New York. In the short term, the embassy's pressure brought about a substantial improvement in Rice's status, from being "disappeared" to being "detained." In the long term, it achieved his release (testimony of Patrick Rice, quoted in ICRC 2002, 74–75). His case also demonstrated the convergence of pressures and influence from ecclesiastical sources: bishops, superiors of the religious order, and the papal nuncio.[18]

In Weeks's case, as in Rice's, his foreign citizenship carried more weight than his status as a cleric. Because of his American citizenship, Weeks, who was detained along with five seminarians, was released days before his Latin American counterparts. The time gap was even greater between Rice and Fátima Cabrera, who had to serve years in detention as a political prisoner before being released.[19]

However, diplomacy often failed as a strategy to confront repression against Catholic foreign clergy. The French nuns are not the only example. The Uruguayan priest Mauricio Silva, who belonged to the religious congregation Fraternity of the Gospel, is another. His disappearance is an example of how strong the international network of repression was in the Southern Cone. Foreign citizenship actually made him vulnerable, compared to native Argentines. Transnational networks of Catholics pushed accusations about Silva's case in the United States beginning in 1978. Efforts by brothers of his congregation who had gone into exile were joined with the actions of human rights organizations linked to church movements in Uruguay, such as the Mothers of Disappeared Uruguayans in Argentina and Servicio Paz y Justicia (SERPAJ).[20] Declassified correspondence from the U.S. State Department shows how ineffective the diplomatic approach was in Silva's case. The American ambassador to Uruguay informed the State Department that the Uruguayan government refused to give answers about the cases of Uruguayans who were disappeared in Argentina.[21]

Use of preexisting links to members of the armed forces, the *military approach*, was another strategy for seeking influence in cases of repression. Family relationships between military and ecclesiastical institutions and the historical community of interests between the armed forces and the Catholic Church forged links of a modus vivendi between the two institutions. It was assumed that access to such links would be useful to address what were at that time considered mere "excesses" of the repression experienced within Catholicism. But this strategy achieved only limited results.

The case of two Jesuit priests, Orlando Yorio and Francisco Jalics, who were kidnapped together with a group of their catechism students, stands out for the high number of blood ties and/or political relationships with the military. Among the catechumens, Mónica Quinteiros, a former member of the Daughters of Mercy, was the daughter of Capt. Oscar Quinteiros of the Argentine navy; Silvia Guiar was the niece of a former marine, Francisco Manrique; César Lugones was a distant relative of Gen. Suárez Mason. Father Yorio himself was the son of a retired army officer; María Ester Lorusso was the sister of an army doctor, Capt. Carlos Lorusso. Catechumens Mónica Mignone and María Marta Vázquez, were, respectively, daughters of Emilio Mignone, a former official in the earlier military government of Gen. Juan Carlos Onganía, and José María Vázquez, a diplomat and minister in the military government then in power. Another of the catechumens, Horacio Pérez Weiss, had in-laws in the army's intelligence headquarters, among them Hernán Fagnini Fuentes.

These ties were called on immediately after the kidnapping. As a result, as Emilio Mignone argued in his testimony at the Trial of the Juntas, they managed to have their demands heard very quickly by the highest-ranking members of the governing military junta, including Adm. Emilio Eduardo Massera and Gen. Rafael Videla.[22] However, other than Silvia Guiar, who was quickly released, those who were kidnapped received no immediate advantage from close family links to the military.

The release of Fathers Jalics and Yorio months later, however, suggests a hypothesis: the military approach was successful only to the extent that it managed to exploit tensions within the machinery of repression itself. A former Jesuit priest explained:

> What saved them was an overlap in jurisdictions between the armed forces. . . . [T]hat area belonged to the army, and it was actually the navy that took them. . . . Orlando [Yorio] said it seemed odd to him that when they took them in the cars, they said, "to port, lieutenant," or "to starboard." . . . And one of the girls they took was a niece of Manrique (head of the Federalist Party), who was a former naval officer. . . . And he stirred up a commotion among them, and then the army didn't have a record of any operation . . . [and] then they kicked the ball back to the navy, who had them at ESMA.[23] . . . And as a result of this conflict, the navy finally had to take them out of there. They . . . found no evidence against them, of course[,] . . . [and then] the navy rented a house . . . specially for them, and took them there . . . out of sight, but the commotion that had been raised in Buenos Aires over their disappearance was too great. . . . This is the story I received from Jalics and Yorio.[24]

The strategy of appealing to the *civilian courts* in cases of repression against clergy was little used. Even when organizations like the Center for Social and Legal Studies (CELS), founded by prominent Catholic figures such as Mignone and Augusto Conte McDonald, devoted themselves specifically to offering legal aid to the families of disappeared clergy, most did not seek a writ of habeas corpus.[25] In general, this was because they first exhausted the path of direct appeal to the military authorities as described above. For those who had traditionally viewed the armed forces as one of the pillars of social order and Argentine identity, it seemed senseless to petition the courts. Only exceptionally, in cases of prolonged disappearances, were petitions for habeas corpus sought, part of a repertoire of efforts undertaken, most of them fruitless.

The strategy of bringing accusations to *international human rights organizations* was not decisive in the short run for rescuing individual clergy members. Nevertheless, it was an approach frequently adopted. The travels of members of religious orders and their contacts abroad gave them an advantage when trying to mobilize international networks and human rights organizations. The range of organizations sought out was wide: Amnesty International, the International Committee of the Red Cross, the United Nations Commission on Human Rights, the United Nations High Commissioner for Refugees, the Ecumenical Human Rights Defense Service (Paris), the World Council of Churches, the International Movement of Catholic Jurists (part of Pax Romana), and Pax Christi International are among the groups most often cited in our testimonies.[26] Once direct petitions and inquiries to the Church and military authorities had been exhausted, making accusations to international organizations served as a way to try to keep cases alive and spark an alert among the international community.

The case of Fr. Patrick Rice, a member of the Fraternity of the Gospel, is an example. Once he was released and sent into exile, Rice agreed to a press conference in London to testify about his experiences. The event was organized by Amnesty International and scheduled for December 7, 1976. Five months later, Rice brought his accusations to the Inter-American Commission on Human Rights (IAHCR). The IACHR's resolution, issued on November 18, 1978, was meant to shed light on his treatment and judge those responsible for it. While this strategy made victims subject to judicial action—and served an important purpose in broader international human rights campaigns—it was less effective in "rescuing" specific victims in the short term. And direct contacts with or appeals to national and international human rights groups sometimes had negative results. A case in point is Alice Domon, the French nun who was a member of the Ecumenical Movement for Human Rights and was associated with the founding members of the Madres de la Plaza de Mayo. She disappeared in 1977.

In the short term, clerical victims were extremely cautious about going to *the press*, including the international press, out of concern for those still in the state's grasp. For instance, extracts from declassified State Department documents make this clear in the case of James Weeks.

> Weeks does not wish to talk to the press. The five seminarians who were arrested with him are still being held in Cordoba and he fears that any statement on his part might prejudice their case and even heighten danger to their safety. The only information Embassy is making available to press here is that Weeks is in good health, has been released, and will be departing Argentina shortly.[27]

Contrary to common belief, a significant number of cases of clerical victims were covered in the Argentine press during the military regime, but the stories were generally brief and vague as to whether the government was responsible. (At times, in fact, these stories seemed part of a regime strategy to distance itself from the events reported.) Given the high level of censorship and the complicity of the press on the national stage, victims' advocates tended not to see the media as a means to protect them. Nevertheless, in time the news reports became useful for documenting, and even analyzing, the regime's repressive practices and the strategies of resistance and survival that developed in response to them. Finally, the press reports provided testimonies and documents for the trials that unfolded after the return to democracy (which also occurred in Chile; see Wilde, this vol.). As an example, the report of Rice's disappearance was key to proving that he was actually being held—a fact that military officials denied in court—and it later supported the accusations he made to the IAHCR.[28]

Finally, within the repertoire of available strategies, *exile* was sometimes a preemptive measure taken by individuals or members of groups threatened by the regime. However, exile was also forced in cases of "release and expulsion" following a period of detention. For the clergy especially, preemptive exile was a readily available option for those who saw themselves or were seen by their superiors as being in danger, especially since the transnational network of the Catholic Church offered the possibility of transfer to other positions. Several anecdotes illustrate how this worked.

> We went to pick him up at the hiding place, another padre and I took him to the police station, where the staff . . . were going to take his passport back. . . . I went to pick it up, made an idiotic face (which wasn't very hard), and they gave it to me. . . . I had assurances that [Junta member Admiral] Massera had said he would have his protection, his help to leave the country. We brought him, took him to the nunciature, he bathed, dressed smartly [laughs], and we took him in the nuncio's car, from there to Ezeiza Airport, with the nuncio's secretary, and we stayed there until we saw the airplane leave.[29]

> I was the last of the survivors. . . . In the end, I had nowhere to live . . . until . . . a nun, a very good friend, took me to her convent, took me to the nunciature, and I left . . . through the nunciature.[30]

The nunciature, then, could be crucial and effective in arranging preemptive exile, helping clergy targeted by the regime to leave under its auspices before they could be detained. However, priests often rejected this option because it would mean using privileges that called into question their commitment to the "world of the poor."

Finally, alongside this repertoire of strategies available to threatened clergy, a range of ad hoc actions were employed to manage the sense of danger day to day. They buried books, rotated the places where they slept, varied the routes they took, put together alarms and warning devices, made themselves homemade weapons—preventive measures that were indispensable for continuing with daily life while still being on alert.

What emerges from this overview is that all the most commonly used strategies to protect clergy members against repression assumed that Church authorities, the nuncio, military officers, and diplomats could directly influence the state's repressive machinery. Lack of confidence in the judicial system, consistent with the lack of faith in democratic institutions that had developed throughout the twentieth century, explains the appeal in a time of crisis of a modus operandi long practiced by the Catholic clergy: direct negotiations between the religious and military powers. That Catholic victims were members of a social elite facilitated immediate access to other elite circles. But despite access, these attempts often failed to rescue victims. The other options available, the courts, the press, national and international human rights organizations, and even exile, were in most cases quite ineffective in the short term. In the long run, though, they helped create the context for constructing alternative versions of the dictatorship's history and for pressing claims for justice that would eventually be heard when the rule of law had been restored.

DEFINED BY their history, different groups of Catholics in Argentina in the 1960s and 1970s understood (and at some level accepted) political violence as necessary to both revolutionary change and military order. This understanding underlay a theological-political conflict within the Church during those years over the legitimation of violence—whether armed struggle, the just violence of the oppressed, or just war. The positions taken did not split the Church in two but did open fissures within the Catholic world, revealing how the political battles of prior decades had eroded the Church's corporate solidarity and spawned a diversity of political-ideological paths within it.

Tensions deepened as state repression increased, especially under the military dictatorship. Within the Church, denunciations by peers combined with the mechanisms of institutional discipline and state repression to produce tragic results. Under these conditions, it is an important but often-neglected fact that clergy who were suspected of subversion and thus in danger and who had previously faced off against their bishops over changes following Vatican II almost automatically turned to the hierarchy for assistance. This central fact and other findings analyzed in this chapter challenge the dominant historical narrative of a simple division between an institutional Church complicit with the dictatorship and the clergy it persecuted. It should make us rethink the role of the Church as an institution in the extreme conditions of this period.

Finally, the cycle of repression started by the dictatorship also shifted the terms of the debate. Questions about the morality of political violence were relegated to secondary status in light of the urgent need to deal with the sufferings of the victims of violent state repression. In response, the first Argentine human rights organizations were born as defensive strategies, to deal with the plight of the victims and their friends and relatives. These organizations were created and nurtured by figures and resources from the Catholic world. Laypersons like Emilio Mignone, for example, who had previously had no qualms about working in a military government, made the cause of human rights their own and became leading opponents of the dictatorship. In this way, the broader religious community contributed to building a humanitarian appeal that was crucial in indicting the military regime and initiating the democratic transition.

Notes

1. Designed by Tomás Casares in the 1930s, this course of Thomistic studies was eventually adopted by the Catholic University of Argentina.

2. Quarracino became known for his later condemnation of fellow clergy who embraced the "Marxist solution."

3. Literally, "Third Worldism," commonly associated with the Movement of Priests for the Third World (MSTM), which arose in 1967 out of the *Manifiesto de 18 Obispos del Tercer Mundo*. In practice, *tercermundismo* served as a broader source of identity that encompassed a variety of nonconformist attitudes within Catholicism in Argentina (see Martín 1992).

4. This section may usefully be compared to Wilde's analysis in this volume of the legitimacy of political institutions and violence in the Chilean Church.

5. For a specific study on the making of the *Final Documents of Medellín*, see Bonnin 2013.

6. "Letter of the Movement of Priests for the Third World to Pope Paul VI and the bishops meeting in Medellín," June 1968, quoted in García Conde and González 2000, 158–63.

7. Ibid., 163.

8. Naval Operations Command, Puerto General Belgrano Naval Base, *¿Qué es el Movimiento de Sacerdotes para el Tercer Mundo?*, 1970, 30. Document in the Archives of the Programa Cultura, Sociedad y Religión, Bahía Blanca, CEIL-CONICET.

9. Emblematic of this tension was the confrontation between Bishop Jaime de Nevares and Military Pro-Vicar Victorio Bonamín in 1971. The conflict grew out of a labor dispute over better working conditions for workers at Hidronor who were building a hydroelectric dam at El Chocón. The strike ended with the

firing and arrest of several workers, including Pascual Rodríguez, a workers' priest who had pastoral care over that area. In the face of these actions, Bishop de Nevares refused to bless a chapel that the company had built in the dam's vicinity or to officiate in any Mass at that location. The dispute moved from the work site into the church when Bishop Bonamín agreed to bless the chapel.

10. Antonio López Crespo, "2-Ámbito Religioso," 1984, 10. Internal document of the Ecumenical Movement for Human Rights (MEDH).

11. The most eloquent source is a study prepared by Antonio López Crespo, a lawyer for the CONDEP and member of the Ecumenical Movement for Human Rights, which named specific church personnel, sites, and forms of involvement. It was originally intended to be part of *Nunca más* but was eliminated during political negotiations over that report. Personal communication from Arturo Blatezky, a member of the board of the Ecumenical Movement.

12. López Crespo, "2-Ámbito Religioso," 4–5.

13. As has been shown previously by Mignone, the bishops' public documents—taken together—did occasionally mention abductions, disappearances, killings, and mistreatment of detainees during the last military dictatorship. However, such interventions only presented the bare details as reported by family and friends of the victims rather than as facts proven by the bishops themselves. They fell short of openly blaming the military regime and instead purposely left ambiguous the identities of those responsible (Mignone 1986, 44–46, 53–61).

14. Bishop Marengo is also recognized for intervening, together with Bishops Vicente Zazpe and Jorge Casaretto, in the cases of the priests Raúl Troncoso and Elías Musse, both of whom spent long periods in detention on the orders of the dictatorship. Troncoso was held between March 19, 1976, and September 16, 1981. Musse was detained on August 4, 1976, and freed after seven years. On Marengo's efforts at Unit No. 9 in La Plata, see Gasparini 2008.

15. Argentina Project, U.S. Department of State, "Conversation with Papal Nuncio," December 10, 1976; my emphasis. Available at http://foia.state.gov/searchapp/DOCUMENTS/Argentina/0000A232.pdf.

16. Argentina Project, U.S. Department of State, "Papal Nunciatura, Buenos Aires," March 29, 1977. Available at http://foia.state.gov/searchapp/DOCUMENTS/Argentina/0000A0D9.pdf.

17. Cf. Verbitsky 2006, 50, and Passarelli and Elenberg 1999, 109–11. Laghi's actions in this period remain controversial.

18. Argentina Project, U.S. Department of State, "Irish Priest Patrick Rice detained under state of siege," November 3, 1976. Available at http://foia.state.gov/searchapp/DOCUMENTS/Argentina/0000A132.pdf.

19. Fátima Cabrera was a catechist in the Buenos Aires suburb of Villa de Retiro during the 1970s. On October 12, 1976, she was kidnapped together with

Father Rice. She was disappeared for ten days and then remained a political prisoner until January 1978. Between 1984 and 1987 she lived in Venezuela. During this period, Rice left the priesthood, he and Cabrera married, and they had three children. Both took part in the founding of FEDEFAM, Latin American Federation of Associations of Relatives of Detenidos-Desaparecidos (those disappeared after detention).

20. See Argentina Project, U.S. Department of State, "Disappearance of Father Maurice Silva," July 19, 1978; "Serpaj Uruguay, n° 5, junio-julio 1982"; "Uruguayans missing in Argentina," November 19, 1982. Available at http://foia.state.gov/searchapp/DOCUMENTS/Argentina/0000A915.pdf; http://foia.state.gov/searchapp/DOCUMENTS/Argentina/0000AFBD.pdf; and http://foia.state.gov/searchapp/DOCUMENTS/1-FY2013/O-2011-03444ER1/DOC_0C17642321/C17642321.pdf, respectively.

21. Argentina Project, U.S. Department of State, "Memorandum of conversation. Embassy Commentary on 'Desaparecidos' List," June 8, 1979. Available at http://foia.state.gov/searchapp/DOCUMENTS/Argentina/0000A9C9.pdf.

22. Videla was de facto president of Argentina from 1976 to 1981.

23. The Escuela de Mecánica de la Armada (Fleet Mechanics' School), an infamous detention center in Buenos Aires in which thousands perished during the dictatorship.

24. Interview with a former Jesuit priest, 2009. It is interesting that the military vicariate, which acted as an intermediary between the military and numerous families of the detained and disappeared, did not play the same role for victims from among the clergy. On the one hand, the identification of military chaplains as chiefly members the military and the fact that they sided with the armed forces in the Church-military conflicts that began at the end of the 1960s had clearly established their autonomy. On the other hand, the Catholic clergy's generally close relationships with the military contributed to their status as social elites and facilitated direct links between victims of repression and the military, links that offered information and exercised some influence on behalf of the victims' families. These links removed the need for a mediator, such as a military chaplain.

25. It could also be the case that some of the individuals in the cases studied followed this course of action without considering it a significant effort and thus did not bring it up in their life stories or include it in their memoirs.

26. See Catoggio 2010.

27. Argentina Project, U.S. Department of State, "Father Weeks to depart Argentina," August 18, 1976. Available at http://foia.state.gov/searchapp/DOCUMENTS/Argentina/0000A055.pdf.

28. See *La Nación*, October 14, 1976.

29. Interview with a former Jesuit priest, 2009.

30. Interview with a priest from the Little Brothers of the Gospel, 2006.

References

Badanes, Daniel, and Lucas Miguel. 2007. "Cristian Von Wernich condenado a reclusión perpetua." *Puentes* 7, no. 22 (December): 5–17.

Bonnin, Juan Eduardo. 2012. *Génesis política del discurso religioso: Iglesia y comunidad nacional entre la dictadura y la democracia en Argentina*. Buenos Aires: Eudeba.

———. 2013. *Discurso político y discurso religioso en América Latina: Leyendo los borradores de Medellín*. Buenos Aires: Santiago Arcos.

Caimari, Lila. 1995. *Perón y la Iglesia católica: Religión, estado y sociedad en la Argentina, 1943–1955*. Buenos Aires: Ariel Historia.

Catoggio, María Soledad. 2010. "Contestatarios, mártires y herederos: Sociabilidades político-religiosas y ascesis altruista del catolicismo argentino en la dictadura y la pos-dictadura." PhD dissertation, Universidad de Buenos Aires.

———. 2011. "Mártires y sobrevivientes: Figuras de la violencia política en los años sesenta y setenta." *Lucha Armada en la Argentina* (Yearbook): 100–109.

———. 2013a. "Argentine Catholicism during the Last Military Dictatorship: Unresolved Tensions and Tragic Outcomes." *Journal of Latin American Cultural Studies: Travesia* 22, no. 2: 139–54.

———. 2013b. "Católicos en el 'mundo de los pobres': Imaginarios y sentidos frente a la situación represiva durante la última dictadura militar argentina, 1976–1983." In *Cristianismos en América Latina: Tiempo presente, historias y memorias*, edited by Elizabeth Judd and Fortunato Mallimaci, 247–67. Buenos Aires: CLACSO.

———. 2013c. "Represión estatal entre las filas del catolicismo argentino durante la última dictadura militar: Una mirada del conjunto y de los perfiles de las víctimas." *Journal of Iberian and Latin American Research* 19, no. 1: 118–32.

Comisión Nacional sobre la Desaparición de Personas (CONADEP). 1984. *Nunca más: Informe de la Comisión Nacional sobre la Desaparición de Personas*. Buenos Aires: Eudeba.

Crenzel, Emilio. 2008. *La historia política del "Nunca más": La memoria de las desapariciones en la Argentina*. Buenos Aires: Siglo XXI.

Cucchetti, Humberto. 2005. *Religión y política en Argentina y en Mendoza (1943–1955): Lo religioso en el primer peronismo*. Buenos Aires: CEIL-PIETTE CONICET.

Donatello, Luis Miguel. 2010. *Los católicos y la lucha armada: Montoneros, 1966–1976*. Buenos Aires: Manantial.

García Conde, Luis, and Lidia González. 2000. *Monseñor Jerónimo Podestá: La revolución en la Iglesia*. Buenos Aires: Instituto Histórico de la Ciudad de Buenos Aires.

Gasparini, Osvaldo. 2008. *Días de prisión: Memorias de Caseros, Sierra Chica, La Plata U9*. Buenos Aires: Dunken.

Gera, Lucio, and Gabriel Rodríguez Melgarejo. 1970. "Apuntes para una interpretación de la Iglesia Argentina." *Cristianismo y Revolución* 25: 61–79.

International Committee of the Red Cross (ICRC). 2002. *Moyens de prévenir les disparitions et de traiter les cas de personnes portées disparues*. Geneva.

Levine, Daniel H. 1996. *Voces populares en el catolicismo latinoamericano*. Lima: Instituto Bartolomé de las Casas, Centro de Estudios y Publicaciones.

Mallimaci, Fortunato. 1992. "El catolicismo argentino desde el liberalismo integral a la hegemonía militar." In *500 años de cristianismo en Argentina*, edited by M. Cristina Liboreiro, 197–365. Buenos Aires: Centro Nueva Tierra-CEHILA.

———. 1993. "La continua crítica a la modernidad: El análisis de los 'Vota' de los Obispos argentinos al Concilio Vaticano II." *Sociedad y Religión* 10–11: 62–83.

———. 2001. "Los diversos catolicismos en los orígenes de la experiencia peronista." In *Religión e imaginario social*, edited by Fortunato Mallimaci and Roberto Di Stefano, 215–32. Buenos Aires: Manantial.

Martín, José Pablo. 1992. *Movimiento de Sacerdotes para el Tercer Mundo: Un debate argentino*. Buenos Aires: Guadalupe.

Mignone, Emilio F. 1986. *Iglesia y dictadura: El papel de la Iglesia a la luz de sus relaciones con el régimen militar*. Buenos Aires: Ediciones del Pensamiento Nacional.

Obregón, Martín. 2005. *Entre la cruz y la espada: La Iglesia católica durante los primeros años del "Proceso."* Buenos Aires: Universidad Nacional de Quilmes.

Passarelli, Bruno, and Fernando Elenberg. 1999. *Il cardinale e i desaparecidos: L'opera del nunzio apostolico Pio Laghi in Argentina*. Rome: EDI.

Quiroga, Hugo. 1994. *El tiempo del "Proceso": Conflictos y coincidencias entre políticos y militares, 1976–1983*. Rosario: Fundación Ross.

Rice, Patricio, and Luis Torres, eds. 2008. *En medio de la tempestad: Los Hermanitos del Evangelio en la Argentina (1959–1977)*. Buenos Aires: Doble Clic.

Robin, Marie Monique. 2005. *Escuadrones de la muerte: La escuela francesa*. Buenos Aires: Editorial Sudamericana.

Ruderer, Stephan. 2010. "Entre religión y política: El vicariato castrense en las últimas dictaduras de Chile y Argentina." Paper presented at the 2010 Latin American Studies Association Congress, Toronto, October 6–9.

Soneira, Abelardo. 1986. "La Iglesia católica argentina a 20 años del Concilio." *Revista del CIAS* 350: 49–61.

———. 1989. *Las estrategías institucionales de la Iglesia católica (1880–1976).* 2 vols. Buenos Aires: Centro Editor de América Latina.

Verbitsky, Horacio. 2006. *Doble juego: La Argentina católica y militar.* Buenos Aires: Editorial Sudamericana.

Vezzetti, Hugo. 2002. *Pasado y presente: Guerra, dictadura y sociedad en la Argentina.* Buenos Aires: Siglo XXI.

Zanatta, Loris. 1999. *Perón y el mito de la Nación Católica.* Buenos Aires: Editorial Sudamericana.

CHAPTER 7

TRANSFORMATIONS IN CATHOLICISM UNDER POLITICAL VIOLENCE

Córdoba, Argentina, 1960–1980

GUSTAVO MORELLO, S.J.

During the last decades of the twentieth century in Latin America many religious actors were caught up in violent situations as victims of terror, or champions in the defense of human rights, or, in some cases, as supporters of torturers. While some Catholics had a prominent role defending victims, challenging power, and informing the world about what was going on, others supported state terror or at least did not oppose it as expected. Argentina's Church was not an exception to this pattern of contradictory stances toward state terrorism.

The first accounts of those years in Argentina highlighted the Church's collaboration with the military government (Mignone 1986; Dri 1987). After forty years, many studies still do, though some acknowledge isolated exceptions (Verbitsky 2006, 2010; Mallimaci 2008). These works see a conservative and ultramontane theology as the reason for Church acquiescence to the repressive state. The usual perception of the Argentine Church is that the majority of bishops were aligned with the military government and therefore supported state terrorism. In this chapter, I challenge those assumptions, exploring the multiplicity of Catholic responses to violence in the specific context of the province of Córdoba.

The goal is to comprehend how different sectors within Argentine Catholicism understood and responded to various forms of political violence. Religious actors are part of society. In Argentina this meant they were embedded in a social process that accepted violence as a legitimate tool of political action (Gordillo 2009). I want to examine the following questions: How did Argentine political violence affect local Catholics? Did they use religious ideas to make sense of political violence? Levine (2003, 2012) suggests we should pay attention to the "longer cycles" of social history that surround the time period we are trying to understand. In Argentina the last wave of political violence involving religion started in the 1960s. For this reason, I make references to Argentina's last two dictatorships: the so-called Revolución Argentina (1966–73) and Proceso de Reorganización Nacional (1976–83).

Argentine Catholics' positions with regard to political violence were shaped by the political context as well as the transformation of religious identity. In the 1960s, global Catholicism was reexamining its identity through the Second Vatican Council, in subsequent meetings like the Second Conference of Latin American Bishops in Medellín in 1968, and in documents such as *Populorum Progressio* and the "Manifesto of 18 Bishops of the Third World." I adopt what Levine (2012) calls a phenomenological perspective in focusing on the changes in the Catholic senses of mission and identity and in the needs and desires of the faithful in a very specific moment of history.

I begin with an overview of the Argentine political context so that we can understand the transformations that took place in Argentine Catholicism. In a context of social acceptance of political violence, those transformations provoked a new relation with the people, with the state, and with the Church's own authority. I then explore the ways in which different Catholic actors coped with state terror in order to understand better the choices they made regarding political violence.

Political Context and Changes in Catholic Identity

A military regime headed by Gen. Pedro Aramburu overthrew Juan Perón's government in 1955 and banned Peronism, charging that the populist leader was imposing a Nazi regime.[1] It is true that Peronism was bullying the political opposition. However, the proscription of the Peronist party vitiated Argentine democracy, since the majority of the constituency (62 percent according to the vice presidential election in 1954) could not vote for the party of their choice. When the civil governments elected between 1958 and 1964 allowed Peronist candidates to run for some minor offices in interior provinces, the military blocked them. Finally, in June 1966, the army decided to end its tutelage and Gen. Juan Onganía assumed the presidency of a government called Revolución Argentina. In 1964, just two years earlier, Onganía had argued in a speech at the U.S. West Point Military Academy that Latin America was fighting a world war against communism. In this battle, he said, national borders were no longer geographic but ideological. The frontier was inside the country, in any place where national identity was challenged, and any challenge was a Marxist deviance. When Onganía seized power, this army perspective became the guide to state action, and political violence was adopted as the way to stop communist infiltration. He saw religious legitimation as key to establishing a national security state to defend Western and Christian civilization. And the Church was willing to provide it.

In pursuit of Church support, Onganía appointed many Catholics to his cabinet and signed a new concordat with the Vatican. The Argentine Church had always considered itself the soul of the nation, a pillar of the country (Di Stefano and Zanatta 2000). It was a "church" in the Weberian sense (Casanova 1994): a religious community that identified itself with the political community of a given territory. For most of the Argentine bishops, who advocated for Catholic values in every aspect of private and public life (Mallimaci 1992a), Onganía seemed the one who would put the "New Christendom" ideal into practice: a regime where the state was the "secular arm" of the Catholic Church.

The problem was that things had changed significantly in Rome. The Second Vatican Council sought dialogue with mainstream Catholicism around the world, and therefore the supporters of the New Christendom model lost Rome's blessing. Argentine bishops had ignored the Council, expecting it would be a mere confirmation of the Neo-Christendom project (Mallimaci 1992b). But the Catholic Church that emerged from the Council was not what they expected. Encouraged by the Vatican's sponsorship of the transformation of Catholic identity, many religious actors engaged in a dialogue with social and political sectors about the role of Catholicism in society.

Córdoba's Catholicism is a clear example. By 1964, Bishop Ramón Castellano had still said nothing about the Council that had started two years earlier. A group of some thirty priests (including the auxiliary bishop and the rector of the seminary, who later would become leaders of the Catholic renewal in Córdoba) decided to address the problem by themselves. With the help of laypersons from Catholic associations, they orchestrated a public debate on the discussions in the Council. In April 1964, *Córdoba*, a left-wing newspaper, interviewed Frs. Erio Vaudagna, Nelson Dellaferrera, and Orestes Gaido, three members of the group, and carried their statements about the new trends in the Catholic Church for three days. Then the rest of the group sent a letter of support, and soon philosophers, writers, and politicians commented on the priests' interviews in the pages of the newspaper (Morello 2005). Bishop Castellano was overwhelmed by the situation. Vatican Nuncio Msgr. Umberto Mozzoni went to Córdoba and made a Solomonic decision. The three priests were removed from their positions in the diocese, and six months later the bishop resigned.

The new bishop, Raúl Primatesta, called the priests back and put them in charge of a new parish, Christ the Worker, which opened in September 1965, to minister to students and youth in Córdoba. In this parish, as in many others around the city, a large number of groups gathered to discuss and debate the new trends in Catholicism. Clergy stimulated thinking about the social situation and encouraged engagement with the poor. Inspired by post-Council theology, religious actors encouraged young people to commit themselves to the struggle against poverty and injustice through work in rural areas and slums. Because of the impact of such experiences, most Christian groups agreed it was necessary to change the system in order to "construct a better world" (Terán 2006, 21). Values and structures that caused the exploitation of the poor were questioned. For these Christians, it was clear that misery contradicted the gospel's message. Injustice, not Marxism, was the enemy of Catholicism (Morello 2003). They wanted to create a society where the "new man" could develop and debated which political ideas were most appropriate for achieving structural transformation in Argentina. Similar groups arose throughout the country.

The groups gathered to discuss Vatican II documents and to read the "signs of the times" (*Gaudium et Spes* 1965, §9), one of the main invitations of the Council. Many Catholic activists saw such a "sign" in the revolutionary wave of national independence and socialist movements in Africa and Latin America. In August 1967, eighteen "Third World" bishops signed a letter saying that socialism was a system aligned with the gospel's concern for justice (*Gaudium et Spes* 1965, §14). It had a huge impact on Argentina's Catholics. Almost 10 percent of the clergy subscribed to the letter and formed an association known as the Movement of Priests for the Third World (MSTM). The first meeting of the MSTM was held in Córdoba in 1968. Most of the priests who had opposed Castellano signed up. *Tercermundismo* became a way of describing Catholics committed to social activism (Lacombe 2010). They were nourished by readings from the Medellín conference, texts from Teilhard de Chardin and Emmanuel Mounier, and even literature from Cuba. "I remember as if it were today when the OLAS [Organización Latinoamericana de Solidaridad, a federation of revolutionary groups based in Cuba] message arrived," said a former member of the Montoneros—a revolutionary group with significant numbers of Catholics—"and the violence, we felt as Christians, the urgency to turn to arms to defend an exploited people."[2] The "sign of the times" seemed to be the oppressed peoples of the world claiming their liberation.

The simultaneous transformations of Catholicism and the Argentine political system went in opposite directions, and many religious actors were caught at the crossroads. While Catholicism was opening to a dialogue and new forms of mission, the political system was closing ways of participation and narrowing Argentine identity. For Onganía's regime, to be a real Argentine was to be an anticommunist Catholic. Political participation was banned, and unions, students associations, and political parties were suspended. One of the few open spaces for social involvement was the Catholic Church and its religious associations. In this context of political violence, Argentine Catholics revisited their identity and their mission in the secular world. For many, being Catholic meant to be engaged with the poor, to be in dialogue with the world, and to seek justice. These transformations of Catholicism, in that context of social acceptance of political violence, ended up creating a new relation with the people, a new relation with the state, and a new relation with Church authority.

A New Relation with the People

The changes in the Church encouraged more horizontal pastoral work as many religious thought they should be involved with the world they were going to serve. This new sense of mission put local Catholics in contact with the poor. Usually, the clergy and the laypeople of Catholic Action in Córdoba were middle class, with some level of college education.[3] Through their mission in slums and rural areas they became aware of the poverty of the people. In Europe the "sign of the times" was secularization, and the main concern was life after death. In Latin America the problem was poverty, and the main concern was life *before* death. The sign of a Latin American Catholic was commitment to be with the people.

Two main trends appeared as Catholicism sought to establish a new relation with the people. The distinction between the two helps explain the state's persecution against Catholics a few years later. One trend, which I call *committed Catholicism*, was formed when laypersons, nuns, bishops, and priests moved into poor areas to live with the people. In 1966 Córdoba's seminary allowed its students to move out to parishes located in working-class neighborhoods.[4] Those seminarians embodied a Catholicism that identifies itself with the marginalized of the world. And they reinterpreted their faith from that location, with God's people, outside the clerical walls, as a struggle for social and political rights with the poor of Latin America (Morello 2012). In 1971 the Congregation of our Lady of La Salette chose to build its seminary in a workers' neighborhood. The "commitment was made in accord with the Gospel. . . . [I]n order that [our seminarians] would come to love the poor, we lived . . . in slums . . . and worked there. . . . Our charism is to be with those who are marginalized in the Church and the world," said the former rector of the seminary.[5] This commitment meant living austerely, doing manual labor, and looking for pastoral alternatives in keeping with that lifestyle. "We lived a rather austere life because we chose it," a seminarian explained.[6] Driven by "Evangelical inspiration" which could have been labeled romantic or naive, they intended "to reach to the limits, to live the evangelical radicalism of a simple life."[7] (I come back to the story of the seminarians of the Congregation of Our Lady of La Salette later.) For these Catholics the new relation with the people was mainly a religious concern, and their goal was the transformation of the Church. They wanted to bring the institution closer to the people and transform it into a tool for improving people's lives. Most of these religious actors used their privileged social positions as priests and nuns to ask for health centers, roads, schools, and the like.[8]

For other Catholics, closeness to the people meant something else. Inspired by their faith, they also committed to the people, but their concern was political. For these *revolutionary Catholics*, the goal was not only the transformation of the Church, but of the whole political system that was exploiting the poor. Ignacio Vélez explained, "By that time we went to Buenos Aires and Fr. Carlos Mugica [took us to the slum]. He suggested that we should live there to share the suffering and deprivation of our brothers, that was the path to transformation into 'new men,' in imitation of Christ. We refused. We had already taken the path of political engagement and criticized the idea of *asistencialismo* [mere charity] because it maintained the exploitation that our brothers and sisters were suffering. It was just a palliative for the social drama."[9] Revolutionary Catholics identified the situation as social sin, and, realizing that political participation was forbidden, they concluded that revolution was the only way to change it.

Some parishioners of Christ the Worker took this path from "committed" to "revolutionary" Catholicism. While keeping their social linkages, they set revolutionary, not religious goals (Donatello 2003). After a political gathering in November 1966, they founded the Córdoba chapter of Cristianismo y Revolución (CyR),[10] the name of both a national social network and a magazine (Morello 2003). In CyR, they found a link with similar organizations across the country and also a vehicle for their political concerns. CyR was based on two ideals: that of the Colombian priest Camilo Torres ("the duty of every Christian is to be a revolutionary") and that of the Argentine-born guerrilla Ché Guevara ("the duty of every revolutionary is to make the revolution"). CyR countered Catholic legitimation of Onganía's government by legitimating revolution as a response to unbearable and unjust structures (1: 3–5) and a means to change unjust systems (Supplement 6–7: 2–3). The new Catholic mission implied fighting for liberation (25, 80) with violence, allowed by the Catholic tradition of "just war" (10: 13–14). Therefore, revolution was a Christian duty (1: 14–20). Catholic faithful should engage with revolutionary war as a step forward in identification with Jesus. For revolutionary Catholics, the question became not if a Catholic could be a revolutionary but rather if there was any other way of being truly Catholic. CyR's social network ended up forming the Comando Camilo Torres, a small revolutionary organization that split, with one group founding the Montoneros, the biggest guerrilla army in Argentina's contemporary history (Morello 2003).

A New Relation with Church Authorities

We tend to think that progressive or left-wing Catholics were the challengers of Church authority in the second half of the twentieth century. The sanctions against liberation theology (1984, 1986) and the censorship of some theologians (e.g., Leonardo Boff, in 1985 and 1992; Jon Sobrino, in 2007) reinforces that view. However, it is important to note that despite being sanctioned or expelled, committed Catholics never wanted to leave the Church. The more serious challenge to Catholic authority came from the right. One of the most prominent rebels was Marcel Lefebvre, the French bishop who openly and repeatedly challenged Rome's authority. He broke with the papacy on July 1, 1988, creating the only schismatic division in Catholicism in the twentieth century. The dispute was about ecclesiology. Lefebvre and his followers complained that the "new" Church had supported bishops' collegiality instead of strengthening the primacy of the papacy. But this reflected a deeper disagreement: they rejected any compromise with the modern world. I refer to them here as *antisecular Catholics*.

In Córdoba, these Catholics were convinced that Communists had infiltrated the Church because of the weakness of the hierarchy and that the Second Vatican Council was proof. Dialogue with the secular world was "treason to the Western traditions" and "corruption of the sacred," said the philosopher Alberto Caturelli (2001), a representative of this trend in the city. Another follower was Dr. José Carlos Caballero, Onganía's governor of Córdoba. Caballero was part of the Catholic City (Cité Catholique), an organization started in France in 1959 that based its support for an anti-Communist war on religious ideas. It was founded by the French theologian Jean Ousset, a follower of Charles Maurras (founder of Action Française, a nationalistic and anti-Communist group in early twentieth-century France). They were staunchly anti-Communist, opposed cultural secularization, and postulated a Catholic society. Catholic City considered Bishop Primatesta, who was appointed during the Council, a "crypto-Communist" whom they scornfully nicknamed "Testarossa" ("Redhead," a play on the bishop's Italian family name). They blamed him for the seminarians' closeness to the poor, the presence of MSTM priests in Córdoba, and "modern" pastoral approaches, like the Christ the Worker parish.

This antisecular trend, at the national level, gathered around Msgr. Adolfo Tortolo, bishop of the city of Paraná. In 1970, his fellow bishops (most of them pre-Conciliar appointments) elected Tortolo head of the Argentine Bishops' Conference (CEA). From that position he discouraged Vatican II reforms in Argentina. To transform the Argentine Church along the lines of the Council reforms, Pope Paul VI appointed more open-minded bishops whenever possible. Some of them had problems with military authorities, for example, Jaime De Nevares (in Neuquén, in 1969–70), Eduardo Pironio (in Mar del Plata, in 1974–75, before going into exile in Rome), Carlos Ponce de León (in San Nicolás, from 1975 until he was killed in 1977), and Enrique Angelelli (during his tenure as bishop of La Rioja, from 1968 to 1976, when he was killed). The antisecularists accused the committed Catholics of following the Church of John XXIII and Paul VI (Baronetto 1996).[11] When these conflicts went public, Bishop Tortolo, rather than support his fellow bishops (who were, after all, being accused of following the pope!), openly sided with the military (San Sebastián 1997).[12] In this regard, the difference from the Chilean Church is remarkable (see Wilde, this vol.).

In 1975, Tortolo was appointed military bishop. When Gen. Jorge Videla seized power in March 1976, antisecular Catholics were delighted. Finally they were running the Church and the country. They saw a chance to fight against Communism in society and within Catholicism. They openly opposed the changes encouraged from Rome. For them, any change in Catholic identity was a change in national identity. They made no distinction between a revolutionary fighter and a socially committed catechist; both were false Catholics. More than that, they were infiltrators trying to destroy the Church and the Fatherland.

A New Relation with the State

After the journey toward national independence in most of Latin America early in the nineteenth century, in the majority of Latin American countries movements arose seeking separation of church and state. The Catholic Church rejected any attempt to come to terms with "liberal democracies." The modern state that threatened to seize Church properties and take over the Church's social functions was an enemy, and the nineteenth century saw a full-time battle against secular culture, scientific ideas, and liberal politics. This position changed only after Vatican II. The state was no longer defined as an arm of the Church doing earthly work but as an autonomous institution. The role of the Church then was that of mediator between state and society. This is the position of what I call *institutional Catholics.*

If antisecular Catholics thought the state should be a tool in the Church's hands to fight Communism, for institutional Catholics the state was a separate institution, with its own aims. The rationale for the Church's mediating role was that the nation cannot function by itself and needs the tutelage of the Church. At that time, there was no perception of a public sphere independent of both church and state. The social responsibility of the Church, therefore, was to mediate between state and society for the common good. Therefore, bishops, priests, and laypersons tried to keep the Church outside political disputes and maintain a fluid relationship with the authorities. Institutional Catholics disliked the idea of the state as the "secular arm" of the church, which was what the antisecular Catholics desired. Institutional Catholics wanted to preserve the Church's autonomy.

Bishop Raúl Primatesta represented this trend. During his first years in Córdoba he made his point of view clear, saying that he would support any state's authority and that judging its legitimacy was not a bishop's job.[13] He stood for the neutrality of the Church in public matters.[14] On January 1, 1976, he called for a "truce" in the "fratricidal war," the fight between the guerrillas and the military.[15] Most of Argentina's bishops agreed with his position and, not surprisingly, appointed him head of the CEA in May 1976, replacing Tortolo. Primatesta would not criticize the government, but neither did he support it unconditionally (Obregón 2005).

Catholicism and Political Violence

Political violence had worsened in Argentina by 1970. In June 1970, the Montoneros carried out their first public act, kidnapping and killing former president Gen. Pedro Aramburu, who had banned Peronism in the 1950s. Gen. Roberto Levingston replaced Onganía in June 1970, and Gen. Alejandro Lanusse followed him in March 1971. A few months later, other guerrilla groups made public statements and committed acts of violence. With the military regime unable to continue to outlaw political discussion, General Lanusse called for elections in 1973, putting an end to the Revolución Argentina government. Peronists won the election, and Héctor Cámpora assumed the presidency on May 25, 1973. But political violence continued. On June 20, 1973, Peronist unions and Montoneros clashed violently in an airport crowd at Eseiza awaiting Perón's return from exile. Once in the country, Perón discouraged the Montoneros. Cámpora called for a new election, this time without proscriptions, in an attempt to curb the violence.

Juan Perón (with his third wife, María Estela Martínez, as vice president) won the election with 62 percent of the votes on September 23. Two days later, FAR guerrillas (soon to merge with the Montoneros) killed José Rucci, a Peronist union leader. Perón's government allowed paramilitary gangs (e.g., the Argentine Anticommunist Alliance, or Triple A) to attack its enemies. At the head of Triple A was José López Rega, Peron's minister of welfare. From then on, paramilitary groups began operations against everything considered left-wing infiltration. The democratically elected and legitimate Peronist government had begun to foster state terrorism. In May 1974, the Triple A killed Fr. Carlos Mugica, the main public figure of the MSTM. When Juan Perón died on July 1, 1974, political violence increased again. The struggle between government-sponsored gangs and left-wing guerrillas caused more than 1,700 casualties in two years (Morello 2011).

With political violence palpable in Córdoba and other parts of the country, many people, and most of the Catholic bishops, hoped the military would end the chaos. A coup in March 1976 put Gen. Jorge Videla at the head of a military government's self-designated Proceso de Reorganización Nacional (PRN), which promised to pacify the country. But the killing worsened. By the end of the PRN in 1983, an estimated 30,000 Argentines had been disappeared. The number of certain killings was close to 13,000, with 112 Catholic leaders (nuns, committed laypeople, priests, and bishops) among them.

Committed Catholics as Torture Victims

The ideas behind state-sponsored violence were embodied in a system of concentration camps and in the military's claim that it was waging an "intelligence war." Interrogation sessions in this war were the final battlefield, and "interrogation" was the euphemism for torture, the apex of political violence. Who the enemies were, and why the military persecuted them, was grotesquely revealed in the torture chambers (Calveiro 2006; Marchak 1999; Osiel 2001; Graziano 1992). There, the different reactions and responses to political violence within Argentine Catholicism confronted one another as religious ideas permeated torture sessions. Committed, institutional, and antisecular Catholics responded in different ways to this specific form of political violence.

I analyzed one of the many cases of state terror in which victims and perpetrators identified themselves as Catholics and were recognized as such by the others. On August 3, 1976, a group of La Salette missionaries living in a workers' neighborhood were kidnapped. That evening, a gang from Córdoba's State Police broke into a house and took the rector, James Weeks, as well as José Luis Destéfani, Daniel García Carranza, Alfredo Velarde, Alejandro Dausá, and Humberto Pantoja, all of whom were seminarians of the Congregation of Missionaries of Our Lady of La Salette, also known as Salettinians. Joan McCarthy, an American who had been a nun and then worked as a lay missionary in the north of Argentina, was a guest in the house but was not kidnapped. During the raid some ten members of the gang wrecked the house, defaced a picture of Father Mugica by writing "kaput" on it, and desecrated the chapel by drawing a swastika and dressing up in vestments.[16] They beat the Salettinian missionaries, tied them up, and threatened to kill them, broke everything in the house looking for weapons, and finally plundered it. At the police station, the prisoners were blindfolded, interrogated, and beaten repeatedly. After three days they were sent to the Encausados jail, where conditions included isolation and lack of hygiene, food, and clothing. For further interrogation, the missionaries were taken to La Perla, an army garrison ten kilometers west of Córdoba city that was the largest center for torture in Argentina outside Buenos Aires.

For many victims of state terror, religious faith played an important role in their survival (CONADEP 1984), helping to preserve their humanity. This faith, says Calveiro (2006, 107), was a universe the torturer could not reach, a horizon of hope. Many prisoners made small crucifixes with whatever was available to them (CONADEP Delegación Córdoba 1984, 65), and one of the seminarians carved a small rosary in a piece of wood that he had found in his cell. For the prisoners, a religious perspective seemed to give meaning to their suffering (Tello 2012).

The military seemed aware of this. While ordinary prisoners in Argentina received religious attention, political prisoners could not even attend Mass, a way of cutting them off from the source of their commitment. Weeks came up with a strategy to have a daily Mass and preserve their Catholic identity: "Every day at 5, let's say, we're going to celebrate the Mass. Every day they gave us a big piece of bread, and 'I have water . . . so let's do the miracle.'"[17] "If Christ turns that water into wine . . . I will celebrate the Mass. . . . [I]n my cell I will consecrate the bread and in your cells you will take communion."[18] Since they did not have access to a Bible, the prisoners proposed some excerpts they recalled from the Gospel: "Today we are going to reflect on the Beatitudes or another reading from the Gospels."[19] It was a way of affirming the identity of the group, of saying, "We are Catholics, victimized because we live a new way of being Catholic," that of commitment to the poor.

In the torture centers, the prisoners encountered antisecular Catholics who criticized the life of poverty they had chosen. They demanded to know, according to one person I interviewed, "why we lived in that dump, when we should live in houses that resemble the military structure, big houses, respectful houses."[20] "They told me, 'It is worse to work with the poor because when you do so, the poor feel encouraged, they join together and that's dangerous.'"[21] Alfredo Velarde remembers the torturers saying, "All those who work with poor people are against the state, because the poor must know nothing."[22] Another man said, "[The soldiers held that] the real poor were the rich people, and that I should devote myself to them because they needed salvation."[23] A torturer told the seminarians that the rich were rich and the poor were poor because it was God's will, and it was subversive to change that (Geuna 1998, 39). "We evidently did not fit in their definition of what a Catholic should be," Weeks told the U.S. Congress in a September 1976 hearing.[24]

Antisecular Catholics despised the prisoners as false Catholics. Alejandro Dausá reported, "All their opinions were contemptuous. [For them] we cannot exist, and we should not exist. . . . Then they dehumanized us and did what they wanted [to us]."[25]

Antisecular Catholics as Perpetrators

The clandestine repression system revealed the state's intention to impose a model of Catholicism. The army had a military intelligence unit in charge of watching its political enemies, including the Catholic Church (Geuna 1998, 14). The military saw itself as interpreter and guardian of a hypothetical authentic Catholicism.[26] For antisecular Catholics, any change in the Church's identity was the result of Communist infiltration. Gen. Luciano Menéndez, military chief in Córdoba, was reported by several sources to be particularly concerned about books that affected "the Christian lifestyle" (Meschiati 1984, 41).

General Menéndez established a special team trained in theology and informed about "who was who" in the Catholic realm.[27] During interrogation sessions, torturers at La Perla tried to corroborate their hypothesis that the Church had been infiltrated. Even Pope Paul VI, who was elected during the Vatican Council, was a dubious figure in their eyes. Both military and civilian torturers at La Perla subscribed to Lefebvre's branch of Catholicism and considered the pope a heretic (Meschiati 1984, 40). Menéndez said that the Medellín bishops' document "encouraged responding to violence with violence."[28] He equated the document to Marx's *Manifesto*, Communism embodied in Catholicism. Primatesta was considered a "Red bishop," even a "Red pig."[29] While Menéndez criticized Córdoba's bishop in harsh terms (Meschiati 1984, 71), Capt. Jorge Acosta and Capt. Ernesto Barreiro (in charge of La Perla) wanted him dead (Geuna 1998, 39). The torturers Carlos González and Ricardo Lujan, along with Luis Manzanelli, boasted of having participated in the killing of Bishop Angelelli, Primatesta's former auxiliary bishop (CONADEP Delegación Córdoba 1994, 69). They also put Msgr. Eladio Bordagaray, Primatesta's secretary, under surveillance. Intelligence personnel recorded his student masses, as reported by Primatesta at the Bishops Assembly in September 1976.

Roberto Mañay, nicknamed "the Priest," was in charge of "interrogation sessions." He was a civilian working for the army. His goal was to obtain information about "Third World priests" and about the beliefs of detainees (Geuna 1998). "During one interrogation, Mañay called one of the hostages . . . and said, 'Tell him what you think of Bordagaray.' . . . [Mañay] was a sinister guy."[30] Victims reported he could handle religious discussions very well. One man reported, "He was a first-class philosopher and theologian. . . . You could have a one-on-one discussion with him about any matter related to philosophy and theology."[31] Since committed and revolutionary Catholics were both *tercermundistas*, antiseculars saw no differences between them: all were Communists, and all deserved the same fate. Anything that questioned antisecular Catholicism was seen as Communist, even contraception. Sometimes Mañay interrupted an interrogation so that other detainees, usually women brought into the torture chamber to type the Salettinians' statements, were compelled to comment on their sexual experiences and on the contraceptive methods they had used. Mañay's point was that those birth control methods proved the Marxist character of the organizations they belonged to.[32] Any compromise with the world, from working for social justice to taking a birth control pill, was Marxism. Mañay was a soldier fighting against the secularization process.

Another participant in torture sessions was Lt. Carlos González, whose nickname was "Monsignor." He was a member of the Catholic organization Cursillos de Cristianidad (Short Retreats on Christianity), a very popular group in those years. Dausá said, "In one of the interrogations he remained silent and then at the end the guy got closer to me and told me, 'There are many people praying for you.'"[33] González talked about religious matters and publicly professed his faith. He considered himself a restorer of the natural order who was taking part in a holy war (Meschiati 1984, 40). His mentality was that of an inquisitor, a soldier in a war to purify the kingdom of God (Contepomi 1984, 40). He accused the prisoners of being the Antichrist. "I am not a torturer, I am an inquisitor," he insisted (Graziano 1992, 31). The religiosity of González may have put certain limits on him: nobody saw him torturing anyone directly (he did not apply electricity to the prisoners or waterboard them, though he was present at the "interrogations"). "He had a positive attitude, and he showed more respect than the rest of the officers. Because of him some were released" (Meschiati 1984, 80). In other situations, he let the prisoners pray before their executions (Geuna 1998, 27).

Mañay and González participated in the torture of the seminarians but within limits, perhaps because they were afraid that it would result in some kind of religious punishment by Church authorities for them.[34] This "religious fear" may have contributed to saving the seminarians from being killed (Geuna 1998; Meschiati 1984).[35]

The rationale of the antisecular Catholics in the Argentine military is further explained in documents produced during the La Salette kidnapping. While the *saletenses* were in prison, their religious superior, Fr. Rolando Nadeau, went to meetings and talked to as many people as he could, attempting to free them. He briefed Bishop Primatesta about his efforts and the information he received. He reported a meeting in which Gen. Antonio Vaquero told him the suspicions were that Weeks was training the seminarians as "subversives," proof of which was Weeks's travels to Bolivia; that the parish house was used as a hideout; that they received too many visits; that they had a sandbag to practice karate, a proof of guerrilla training; and that Weeks was against the rich.[36] Meanwhile, Gen. Luciano Menéndez, head of the army in Córdoba, explained officially that the proof of the prisoners' deviance was in the twenty-two books and the vinyl disc confiscated. For the general, these were "not the usual theological or mystical readings leading to the formation of future priests."[37] His report charged that Weeks "was an apologist for Third World ideas and had a pastoral bias," that his involvement with the poor was "on the pretext of leading a life of poverty," and that he "advised the seminarians not to wear a Roman collar."[38]

For these antisecular Catholics, the seminarians, led by Weeks, were carrying out Marxist indoctrination disguised as religious ministry. They saw them as "Communist infiltrators, followers of a Third World theological trend, which was anthropocentric and atheist, earthly because they work for liberation on earth and the coming of the Kingdom of God on earth, and of the new ecclesiology which does not differentiate between the Church and the world."[39]

Institutional Catholics and Torture

While antisecular Catholics attacked those they did not consider true Catholics, institutional Catholics failed to stand by the victims publicly, and that is the most important criticism committed Catholics leveled against them. An important group of victims of state terror were persecuted *because* of their Catholicism. When the *saletenses* were persecuted, institutional Catholics did not come to their defense. Daniel García Carranza reported, "The Church did not consider itself persecuted! They felt that we were all a bunch of 'weird people'" rather than representatives of the Church.[40]

This is consistent with the response the papal nuncio Pio Laghi gave Patricia Derian, a State Department official, when she visited Argentina. "When asked if he considered that the Church and Catholics were persecuted in Argentina, he showed surprise and quick denial. He said that individuals . . . had been arrested or abused, but rejected the suggestion that the Church as such was under attack. . . . [A]side from these cases and isolated episodes such as those involving . . . Father Weeks, it could not be said that the Church was subject to special persecution by the government."[41] However, Laghi made private inquiries on behalf of the more than five thousand disappeared (Passarelli and Elenberg 2000; see also Catoggio, this vol.).

The new relation with the state that the "institutional" Church adopted in Argentina after Vatican II—independent of the state, so that it could mediate between it and society, but also working with state authorities for the welfare of the people—clashed with the views of antisecular Catholics, who saw the state as the "secular arm" of the Church. Institutional Catholics believed that the bishops' responsibilities included supporting state authorities, for the common good should inhibit them from protesting openly, even when reliable sources told them about torture. According to Robert Hill, U.S. ambassador in Argentina, "The Church is well informed as to what is going on. . . . [T]he nuncio said, 'Enough military officers have come to us to tell us that they cannot sleep at night because of the acts of torture during the day so that we have a very clear idea as to how deeply involved the military is in violation of human rights.'"[42] But the "mandate" to not break with the state was stronger than the violations of human rights, which they thought were episodic. They understood them as "abuses" but not as "state terrorism." They believed that a supportive relationship with the state would allow them to intercede in particular cases.

Laghi told Derian that most bishops "remained moderate, and placed themselves above the political struggle."[43] The Argentine Church fostered the idea of neutrality in earthly conflicts, so as to be able to mediate among her "children." The bishops tried to cool the rage of committed Catholics by helping behind the scenes and attending particular cases and individual requests. They also tried to calm the government by not siding with the human rights claims. Institutional Catholics wanted to remain neutral in order to be able to mediate. The fight was among "brothers," so the Church should not take a side. This position, which was criticized by committed Catholics, also made the antisecular regard institutional Catholics as unreliable.

WHAT EXPLAINS such wide divisions within Argentine Catholicism on the issue of state terror? An answer can be found in the various positions among Catholics on the transformation of their religion that began to be felt in the 1960s. Beliefs about the various kinds of relationships that should exist with the people, with the state, and with the authority of the Church itself help to explain the political position that various groups of Catholics took on political violence in Argentina from 1960 to 1980.

Context matters. Argentina, unlike Chile, had a tradition of military coups and rulers. General Perón, perhaps the most important political figure in Argentina in the twentieth century, is an example of that tradition. The social achievements of his rule were significant and long-lasting, although they cannot obscure the fact that the opposition was persecuted during his tenure. The last wave of state terrorism in Argentina started in that way, with police harassment of political opponents during his second government, which had come to power with the votes of 62 percent of the electorate. It was under this democratic government that the Triple A (created by Perón's minister José López Rega) initiated a wave of political repression. Its emblematic murder of Fr. Carlos Mugica in 1974 occurred while Perón was still alive.

How the unity of the Church was conceived is another point of difference with the Chilean case. The perception of the Catholic hierarchy in Argentina was that the Church was divided, and the CEA official documents in those years regularly called for unity (Marchak 1999; Obregón 2005). The bishops feared the direction committed Catholics were giving pastoral and liturgical renewal but were mainly concerned about the political involvement of the antisecular Catholics. It was the latter who were challenging the authority of Rome, aligning with the claims of Bishop Marcel Lefebvre, who had broken with the Vatican. When the institutional Catholics claimed "neutrality" and "responsibility for the common good" in internal political discussions, their interlocutors were the antisecular Catholics, not the committed ones. As we saw, institutional Catholics preferred separation from the state but struggled to keep good relations with the authorities. This resulted in some private protests of state repression but no open criticism. Breaking with the military regime would have implied breaking with the antisecular Catholics too.

To some extent the criticism of committed Catholics' criticism was that there was no sense keeping good relations with state authorities if the Church was not going to use them. However, the main concern of committed Catholics was deeper: Why didn't institutional Catholics use their special access to the authorities to intercede for the victims? The answer committed Catholics received was difficult to accept: institutional Catholics did not act because they did not recognize that some victims were persecuted because they were Catholics. The heart of the matter is that institutional Catholics did not consider them true Catholics. Committed

Catholics following Church teachings believed their place was with the poor. And when many of them suffered the full weight of state repression for that belief, institutional Catholics not only failed to support them but also doubted the authenticity of their faith.

In this chapter, I offer a sociological explanation for the division within Argentine Catholicism on the issue of state terror. There were antisecular Catholics, who collaborated with a state that used violence to fight Communism. There were institutional Catholics, who preferred separation from the political sphere but kept good relations with the regime, avoiding public criticism of the authorities while interceding privately in some particular cases. Finally, there were committed Catholics, who wanted to be closer to the people and stayed with them during state repression.

The first accounts of the Argentine Church during the dictatorship (Mignone 1986; Dri 1987) set the tone for subsequent scholarship (Mallimaci 2008; Verbitsky 2006) and were written by committed Catholics. They were the ones who suffered state repression and Church rejection most deeply. However, their analysis is more moral than sociological. And to some extent, they raise a different question than I have here, a theological one that I am not able to answer: who was a true Catholic, and who acted as such? Official acknowledgment of committed Catholics as real Catholics is still a debate in the Argentine Church. Were they victimized because of their faith or their secular political choices? Are they martyrs? Should they or should they not be canonized like the Spanish or Polish victims under Socialist and Communist regimes?

Notes

1. For a more detailed account of the Peronist years, see Catoggio, this vol.
2. Interview with Ignacio Vélez, April 2001.
3. Interview with Quico Emma Rins, August 2007.
4. Interview with Víctor Acha, October 2009.
5. Interview with James Weeks, July 2008.
6. Interview with Daniel García Carranza, November 2007.
7. Interview with Alejandro Dausá, August 2009.
8. Interview with Bitín Baronetto, May 2009.

9. Interview with Ignacio Vélez, April 2001.

10. All references to the periodical *Cristianismo y Revolución* cite issue and page numbers.

11. According to one source (who asked not to be named) interviewed by the author, July 2010. Paul VI thought Tortolo was "Lefebvrist." In fact, Tortolo is the only CEA president who was never made a cardinal.

12. See also Bonamín's personal journal, "Diario: Agenda con anotaciones personales de los años 1975 y 1976; más los meses de enero y febrero de 1978." In the author's possession.

13. See Raúl Primatesta, "El arzobispo frente a la realidad," *Aquí y Ahora* 2, no. 10 (1970): 17–18.

14. See Raúl Primatesta, "Exclusivo: Reportaje al Cardenal Primatesta." *Aquí y Ahora* 5, no. 49 (1973): 22–24.

15. See Raúl Primatesta, "Mensaje en la jornada de la paz: El camino de los hombres y la búsqueda de las verdaderas armas de la paz en la Argentina," unpublished manuscript, January 1, 1976, 14.

16. Interview with Joan McCarthy, February 2008.

17. Interview with James Weeks, July 2008.

18. Remembered by Alfredo Velarde, May 2008 interview.

19. Interview with James Weeks, July 2008.

20. Interview with Daniel García Carranza, November 2007.

21. Interview with Alejandro Dausá, August 2009.

22. Interview with Alfredo Velarde, May 2008.

23. Alejandro Dausá, "No Exit," unpublished manuscript.

24. Hearings before the Subcommittee on International Organizations of the Committee on International Relations, House of Representatives, 94th Cong., 2nd sess., September 28–29, 1976, 1–67.

25. Interview with Alejandro Dausá, August 2009.

26. Dausá, "No Exit."

27. Luciano Menéndez, "Report," 2, in Archivo Provincial de la Memoria, Provincia de Córdoba, Caja Arzobispado (hereafter cited as APM).

28. Ibid., 10.

29. Interview with Daniel García Carranza, November 2007.

30. Interview with Alejandro Dausá, July 2007.

31. Interview with Daniel García Carranza, November 2007.

32. Ibid.

33. Interview with Alejandro Dausá, August 2009.

34. Interview with Daniel García Carranza, November 2007.

35. See Contepomi 1984.

36. Nadeau, "Letter," August 18, 4, APM.

37. Luciano Menéndez, "Report," 5, APM.

38. Ibid., 8.

39. Ibid., 10.

40. Interview with Daniel García Carranza, November 2007.

41. "Memorandum of conversation, March 29, 1977," declassified State Department document, available at www.desclasificados.com.ar/.

42. "Telegram, September 17, 1976," declassified State Department document, available at www.desclasificados.com.ar/.

43. "Memorandum of conversation, March 29, 1977."

References

Baronetto, Luis Miguel. 1996. *Vida y martirio de Mons. Angelelli: Obispo de la Iglesia católica*. Córdoba: Ediciones Tiempo Latinoamericano.

Calveiro, Pilar. 2006. *Poder y desaparición: Los campos de concentración en Argentina*. Buenos Aires: Colihue.

Casanova, José. 1994. *Public Religions in the Modern World*. Chicago: University of Chicago Press.

Caturelli, Alberto. 2001. *Historia de la filosofía en la Argentina, 1600–2000*. Buenos Aires: Ciudad Argentina–Universidad del Salvador.

CONADEP. 1984. *Nunca más: Informe de la Comisión Nacional sobre la Desaparición de Personas*. Buenos Aires: Eudeba.

———. Delegación Córdoba. 1984. *Informe: Familiares de desaparecidos detenidos por cuestiones políticas*. Córdoba.

Contepomi, Gustavo. 1984. *Testimonio sobreviviente de La Perla*. Córdoba: El Cid.

Di Stefano, Roberto, and Loris Zanatta. 2000. *Historia de la Iglesia argentina: Desde la Conquista hasta fines del siglo XX*. Buenos Aires: Grijalbo-Mondadori.

Donatello, Luis Miguel. 2003. "Religión y política: Las redes sociales del catolicismo post-conciliar y los Montoneros, 1966–1973." *Estudios Sociales* 24: 89–112.

Dri, Rubén R. 1987. *Teología y dominación*. Buenos Aires: Roblanco.

Gaudium et Spes. 1965. Available at www.vatican.va/archive/hist_councils/ii_vatican_council/documents/vat-ii_cons_19651207_gaudium-et-spes_en.html.

Geuna, G. 1998. "Declaración ante el Cónsul Español en Ginebra." Unpublished manuscript.

Gordillo, Mónica B. 2009. "El Cordobazo, a cuarenta años . . . " In *Reseñas de enseñanza de la historia*, 261–71. Córdoba: Asociación de Profesores de Enseñanza de la Historia en Universidades Nacionales.

Graziano, Frank. 1992. *Divine Violence: Spectacle, Psychosexuality and Radical Christianity in the Argentine "Dirty War."* Boulder, CO: Westview Press.

Lacombe, Eliana. 2010. "La palabra empeñada: Análisis del boletín *Enlace*, publicación del Movimiento de Sacerdotes para el Tercer Mundo (1968–1973)." Paper presented at the Tercer Simposio Internacional sobre Religiosidad, Cultura y Poder, organized by GERE, Instituto de Historia Argentina y Americana "Dr. Emilio Ravignani," University of Buenos Aires, Buenos Aires, August 25–27, 2010.

Levine, Daniel H. 2003. "Theoretical and Methodological Reflections about the Study of Religion and Politics in Latin America." In *Religion, Culture, and Society: The Case of Cuba*, edited by Margaret E. Crahan, 3–16. Washington, DC: Woodrow Wilson International Center for Scholars.

———. 2012. *Politics, Religion, and Society in Latin America*. Boulder, CO: Lynne Rienner.

Mallimaci, Fortunato. 1992a. "El catolicismo argentino desde el liberalismo integral a la hegemonía militar." In *500 años de cristianismo en Argentina*, edited by M. Cristina Liboreiro, 197–365. Buenos Aires: Centro Nueva Tierra–CEHILA.

———. 1992b. "The 'vota' of the bishops of Argentina." In *Christianity and Churches on the Eve of Vatican II*, 97–120. Bologna: Istituto per le Scienze Religiose.

———, ed. 2008. *Modernidad, religión y memoria*. Buenos Aires: Colihue.

Marchak, Patricia. 1999. *God's Assassins: State Terrorism in Argentina in the 1970s*. Montreal: McGill-Queens University Press.

Meschiati, Teresa. 1984. "Testimonio de Teresa Celia Meschiati sobre el campo de concentración 'La Perla,' Córdoba-Argentina." Legajo CONADEP, no. 4279. Buenos Aires: CONADEP.

Mignone, Emilio F. 1986. "Iglesia y dictadura: La experiencia Argentina." *Nueva Sociedad* 82 (March–April): 121–28.

Morello, Gustavo. 2003. *Cristianismo y revolución: Los orígenes de la guerrilla argentina*. Córdoba: Editorial de la Universidad Católica de Córdoba.

———. 2005. "La libertad de opinión en la Iglesia de Córdoba." In *A 40 años del Concilio*, edited by Carlos Schickendantz, 231–98. Córdoba: Editorial de la Universidad Católica de Córdoba.

———. 2011. "El terrorismo de Estado y la redefinición de lo secular en Argentina." *Jahrbuch für Geschichte Lateinamerikas/Anuario de Historia de América Latina* 48: 285–310.

———. 2012. "Catholicism(s), State Terrorism and Secularization in Argentina." *Bulletin of Latin American Research* 31, no. 3 (July): 366–80.

Obregón, Martín. 2005. *Entre la cruz y la espada: La Iglesia católica durante los primeros años del "proceso."* Buenos Aires: Universidad Nacional de Quilmes.

Osiel, Mark. 2001. *Mass Atrocity, Ordinary Evil, and Hannah Arendt: Criminal Consciousness in Argentina's Dirty War.* New Haven, CT: Yale University Press.

Passarelli, Bruno, and Fernando Elenberg. 2000. *Il Cardinale e i desaparecidos: L'opera del nunzio apostolico Pio Laghi in Argentina.* Rome: EDI.

San Sebastián, Juan. 1997. *Don Jaime de Nevares: Del Barrio Norte a la Patagonia.* Buenos Aires: Ediciones Don Bosco Argentina.

Tello, Mariana. 2012. "(Sobre)VIDAS: Objetos, memorias e identidades en la transmisión de experiencias concentracionarias." *Revista del Museo de Antropología* 5: 141–48.

Terán, Óscar. 2006. "La década del 70: La violencia de las ideas." *Lucha Armada* 2, no. 5: 20–28.

Verbitsky, Horacio. 2006. *Doble juego: La Argentina católica y militar.* Buenos Aires: Editorial Sudamericana.

———. 2010. *La mano izquierda de Dios. Tomo IV, La última dictadura (1976–1983).* Buenos Aires: Editorial Sudamericana.

CHAPTER 8

RELIGION MEETS
LEGAL STRATEGY

Catholic Clerics, Lawyers, and the
Defense of Human Rights in Brazil

RAFAEL MAFEI RABELO QUEIROZ

This chapter analyzes the joint struggle by members of the Catholic Church and lawyers against various forms of violence, especially torture and the assassination of political opponents, carried out by the military dictatorship that controlled Brazil from 1964 to 1985. This story is told here mostly from the point of view of the lawyers who defended political prisoners during the military regime,[1] drawing on thirty-six interviews conducted in 2011–12 about various dimensions of that work, including their collaboration with other institutions of organized civil society such as the Catholic Church.[2] That collaboration was effective in sparing many individuals from torture and death and was ultimately decisive in building opposition to the military regime.

After first examining an obvious hypothesis to interpret the historical facts under analysis, I offer a brief political history of Brazil to illuminate the context in which Church members and lawyers were working at the time. I then suggest what seem to be the particular motivations that led members of each group, and eventually their institutions (the Conferência Nacional dos Bispos do Brasil [CNBB] and the National Bar Association), to take a more forceful role in opposition to the military government. Following that, I analyze the factors that I believe were decisive in bringing key segments of the Catholic Church together with lawyers in their opposition to the government. Last, I attempt to trace the effects of their collaborative efforts on institutions since redemocratization, such as present-day penal laws and the National Truth Commission that is currently seeking to assign responsibilities for the human rights violations that took place during the 1964–85 dictatorship.

The History of a Common Effort: A Hypothesis

In 1985 the Archdiocese of São Paulo published the results of the most comprehensive research at that time on the various forms of abuse— murder, torture, sexual violence, and so on—perpetrated by state agents between 1964 and 1979. The researchers aimed to systematically identify acts of violence, as well as the perpetrators and victims of abuse, to foster collective memory of those events and, in the words of the report's opening chapter, "contribute to the formation of a national conscience that will never allow the repetition of the facts herein described" (Arquidiocese de São Paulo 1985a, xix). The title of the full six-volume report and its shorter published version clearly state that intention: *Brasil: Nunca mais* (Brazil: Never Again).[3]

Though published by a religious organization headed by a prominent Catholic prelate, Cardinal Paulo Evaristo Arns, closely aided by a Presbyterian minister, Jaime Wright, *Brasil: Nunca mais* (*BNM*) is nothing short of a book on contemporary Brazilian legal and political history, intertwined with technical interpretations of military criminal procedure. The book argues its conclusions as a lawyer would argue before jurors. With the exception of sporadic moral claims for the value of truth, sometimes supported by biblical quotes—"Then you will know the truth, and the truth will set you free" (John 8:32)—and invocations of human dignity, the book proceeds in straightforward legal language, connecting evidence gathered from witnesses and documents, describing the actions of specific persons, and assigning liability for the violation of norms, standards, and legal procedures.

Why did the Archdiocese of São Paulo produce a book on legal history and criminal procedure? Why did it choose to take the *legal* point of view, when others were available? Most other analogous inventories of human rights violations in Latin America up to that time were based on oral history methods, as Weschler (1990) reminds us. An answer emerges from a review of the names and professions of those responsible for carrying out the *BNM* project: most were lawyers recruited by the Justice and Peace Commission of São Paulo's archdiocese. In addition to interviewing surviving victims of physical violence and family members of deceased prisoners, they read, summarized, and copied 707 criminal lawsuits based on the various national security laws of the period, extracting from them all available evidence of human rights violations. Because, as Jaime Wright noted, the military dictatorship in Brazil had a technocratic mentality, allegations of torture, for example, made when a defendant denied a previous confession, ended up in the records of criminal trials filed in the archives of the Superior Military Tribunal in Brasília (Weschler 1990, 25). The Amnesty Law of 1979 gave lawyers a legitimate reason to review these files: all political dissidents were filing for amnesty, and evidence from those old trials was needed to process their appeals. A dozen lawyers took the risk of bringing three copy machines into a rented room in Brasília and made copies of every possible official record of violence and torture contained in the archives that had been assigned to them. They secretly worked on the material for the next six years, until the final report was made public in 1985. This accounts for *BNM*'s most striking feature: the violence it describes but also the sources it relies on—official records of the military regime itself (Weschler 1990, 17). Lawyers are, of course, most comfortable in this terrain. Drawing conclusions based on bureaucratic paperwork is a large part of what a trained legal professional does.

Following the Second Vatican Council (1962–65) and the Latin American Bishops' Conference held in Medellín, Colombia (1968), the National Conference of Brazilian Bishops (CNBB) instituted the Brazilian Justice and Peace Commission (JPC), whose first working meeting took place in January 1969. In 1972, Arns, already archbishop of São

Paulo, requested and obtained papal license to create a justice and peace commission for his archdiocese, to be directly coordinated by him, assisted by a ten-member board.

Five of the founding members of São Paulo's JPC were legal professionals, four lawyers and one public prosecutor (Sydow and Ferri 1999, 120–21). Two of the lawyers were well-known professors at the University of São Paulo (USP), the most famous and most traditional law school in the country: Dalmo Dallari, professor of public law and political philosophy, and Fábio Konder Comparato, at the time professor of commercial and corporate law and later professor of legal philosophy. From the regime's early days, Dallari and Comparato were among the most prominent USP law professors to speak out against human rights violations. Two other commission members were full-time lawyers intensely involved in defending political prisoners: Mario Simas and José Carlos Dias. The prosecutor was Hélio Bicudo, known for energetic prosecutions against corrupt and violent members of the police.[4]

BNM, published by São Paulo's archdiocese, took a legal approach because legal professionals dominated the Justice and Peace Commission that prepared it. If we ask why such prominent jurists were recruited by the Catholic Church and what this tells us about the defense of human rights in the context of the criminal justice system, an obvious hypothesis suggests itself: the Church and lawyers had shared beliefs about the importance of the human rights of prisoners and joined forces to protect them during the military regime. There are some problems with this hypothesis, however.

First, it ignores the fact that many lawyers and clerics were at first openly favorable to the military regime and highly dismissive of political and human rights violations.[5] Jurists were some of the most brilliant minds among the regime's intelligentsia: Francisco Campos, who provided the first theoretical justification of the coup in the preamble of the Institutional Act of April 9, 1964 (Gaspari 2002a, 123–24);[6] Alfredo Buzaid and Antonio da Gama e Silva, professors and deans at the USP Law School, who ran the national Secretariat of Justice during the regime's darkest years; Carlos Silva and Hely Lopes Meirelles, virtually the founders of contemporary Brazilian administrative law, who were two of the most dedicated collaborators with the dictatorship in their areas of expertise.

Second, as our 2011–12 interviews with political lawyers revealed, although some defenders of political prisoners had strong Catholic ties, many did not, and some appear to have been opposed to religion. Most of these lawyers seem to have been motivated to fight to preserve constitutional government—in favor of democracy and the rule of law. Others appear to have taken up "political" cases rather by chance: "a friend's friend needed a lawyer, and I was available." None of the interviewees cited unconditional appreciation for the value of human life as determining their initial commitment to political lawyering, though with time it increasingly gained importance in their scale of values.[7]

Third and finally, the preliminary hypothesis overlooks the way membership in a social group—members of the Church or the legal profession here—implies a distinct set of values that motivates members' actions. The actions may coincide, but the motivations may be different.

The data collected, mostly through interviews and historical research in primary and secondary sources, suggest another interpretation: namely, that the motivations of certain lawyers and certain members of the Church for engaging in the struggle against the violation of citizens' rights were in the beginning quite different, but their common enemy made them political allies, and out of their ongoing work together grew shared normative beliefs about human dignity and about how the instrumentality of law must serve justice. This connection is relevant, I think, for grasping how a human rights movement arose in Brazil, and it also helps us understand the particular character of human rights activism in Brazil today—one that unites legal strategy, civil society articulation, and strong normative claims for the recognition of unconditional and universal rights.[8] I develop this argument in greater detail below.

Patriarchal Politics

Understanding the sequence of events that led to joint institutional efforts by the Catholic Church and lawyers in defense of human rights and democracy requires a brief look at the political and social history of Brazil. Using Max Weber's (1964, 180–84) famous typology, many scholars of Brazilian politics point out the "traditional" rather than "legal-rational" basis of Brazilian society. Despite the formal existence of a liberal, demo-cratic, and bureaucratically organized government since the early nine-teenth century, power relations, especially in agrarian regions—where most of the population lived until well into the twentieth century—remained personalistic, reflecting what Sérgio Buarque de Hollanda called "the colonial family."[9] The juxtaposition of liberal political institutions and an archaic, agrarian social structure led to a patriarchal model of state power (see Leal 1997, chap. 1).

Patriarchalism produces an administrative structure controlled by a traditional leader whose legitimate authority rests on immemorial val-ues. In such a structure, the distribution of power, though oriented by these social values, is largely at the ruler's will, unlike what happens in the bureaucratic, rule-following, and efficiency-oriented political structure Weber believed characterized a modern political society. Family, friends, and political allies in general are the preferential recruits for filling posi-tions in the state's power structure. This private disposition of the structure of political power leads to what Weber (1964, 185) calls patrimonialism, a political system marked by personal subjection and obedience to political leaders who, ignoring statutes and formal procedures, freely dispose of public offices and institutions as part of their assets (Freund 2010, 174). In this context, personal proximity to such political leaders can be very useful for achieving one's political goals and an adversarial relation can, in contrast, bring increased difficulties. Or, as bluntly expressed by Victor Nunes Leal (1997, chap. 1), "Those with close ties to political leaders rely on all sorts of favors, both legal and illegal, for their causes, while those who confront them are forced to struggle even for their most basic rights."

Thus where patriarchal politics are present—as was certainly the case in early and mid-twentieth-century Brazil—members of any institution or social group with a political agenda must advance claims and propos-als by cultivating close relations with and providing support to the po-litical elite. This was true both for the Church and the Bar well before and into the military regime initiated by the 1964 coup.

Though Brazil became a secular republic in 1891, Church-state rela-tionships remained highly collaborative. In the years immediately before the 1964 coup, the CNBB and the civil government were "intimate," ac-cording to an ecclesiastical historian (Castro 1978, 53). Ideology was not always a determining factor in this political arena: the deposed president João Goulart, the army's number one adversary, was personally close to highly placed figures in the Church, and he openly used this proximity to try to increase his political support in the days before the coup.[10] The coup against him, however, was defended by sectors of middle- and upper-class civilians based on traditional values of "God and Family," and the CNBB publicly welcomed this military intervention in Brazil's political life in 1964 (Alves 1978, 229).

Because of this "generous relationship" (Alves 1978) with the ruling political elite, the Church enjoyed many benefits. One anecdotal example: the 1955 International Eucharistic Congress held in Rio de Janeiro had its venue personally guaranteed by President Getulio Vargas when a dispute over the site arose between the Catholic Church and the Museum of Modern Art (Castro 1978, 54).[11] At this time, Dom Hélder Câmara, secretary of the CNBB (who would later turn against the military regime and find himself called "Fidel Castro in a cassock" by São Paulo's governor, Roberto de Abreu Sodré; see Gaspari 2002b, 295), had the private numbers of the five previous presidents of Brazil in his personal telephone book (Castro 1978, 54). Intimacy with political power was a valuable and frequently employed asset.

Like the Catholic Church, the National Bar celebrated Goulart's overthrow by the army. Povina Cavalcanti, the Bar's president, issued an official statement calling the coup a defensive move to preserve the rule of law against "communist-unionist evils" in the country.[12] The legal rationale for Goulart's overthrow was his alleged violation of Article 66, VII, of the 1946 Constitution, according to which the president needed the permission of Congress to leave the country. Goulart was accused of having fled to Uruguay, when it was in fact known he was flying to his family's rural property in São Borja, in the state of Rio Grande do Sul (Gaspari 2002a, 111). In other words, the National Bar justified the military's intervention based on a juridical premise known to be false.

In addition to professional advantages for the lawyers (the Bar in Brazil is highly protectionist and lobbies governments for protective legislation), good Bar-government relationships ensured that elite lawyers had favored access to restricted spheres of political power. When in 1965 the Second Institutional Act (AI-2) increased the number of Supreme Court justices from eleven to sixteen, allowing greater influence of the executive over the judiciary, the National Bar, instead of condemning the move, was pleased because one of the five new justices, José Eduardo do Prado Kelly, had been its recent president. Kelly is still the only Bar president ever named to Brazil's Supreme Court. He had also been president of the National Democratic Union (UDN), the civilian political arm of the military regime after the 1964 coup. Having a former Bar president in the inner circles of political power of course meant possible political advantages, but it also implied that legal and humanitarian violations might be overlooked. Breaking up such relationships and moving into political opposition could invite difficulties, especially in a dictatorship. Unlike many individual lawyers who opposed the regime since its first illegalities became known, that choice did not come naturally to the Bar.

These traditional relations between state, Bar, and Catholic Church would start to shift as lawyers and clerics themselves became victims of the regime and religious humanitarianism came in contact with the professional skills of certain lawyers. A struggle for human rights armed with legal rationality began to take shape.

The Shift in the Church

Unlike what happened with lawyers, whose shift of position regarding the military regime began with individuals and moved to their professional institution, the Bar, the Church's change of position contains elements of actions from individuals and small groups, such as the Dominicans in São Paulo, but also clear orientation from the Vatican and from official ecclesiastical forums.

Factions of "progressive," "traditionalist," and "moderate" clerics existed in Brazil well before the 1960s. As Serbin (2006, 158) points out, economic, political, and even demographic changes since the mid-1940s forced the Church to reposition itself within the modern Brazil then in the making, growing richer and more urban and pluralistic. The cleavage between progressives and traditionalists started then and spiked in the 1960s, when these local factors met other influences, such as the growing fear of communism, the sexual revolution, and the counterculture. While the conservative wing tended to prevail initially, the progressives eventually made their influence felt in the higher ranks, aided by influences from the Second Vatican Council (1962–65) and its impact in Latin America, particularly in the Second Conference of Latin American Bishops (II CELAM) in Medellín, Colombia, in 1968. By then, the Cold War political context in the region was already marked by a wave of military interventions. In the few years between the convening of Vatican II and Medellín, military presidents or juntas came to power through coups in Argentina (1962), the Dominican Republic (1963), Ecuador, Guatemala, and Honduras (1963), Brazil and Bolivia (1964), Argentina (1966), and Panama and Peru (1968). Issues of social inequalities, poverty, and oppression in its various forms—and, naturally, human dignity and human rights—became inescapably major political questions. In Brazil, the conservative wing of the Church, which dominated the hierarchy in the mid-1960s, sided with the coup and allied with the military against the communist threat. This group included Dom Eugenio Sales (Rio de Janeiro), Dom Agnelo Rossi (São Paulo), and Dom Vicente Scherer (Porto Alegre).

In Medellín, the spirit of political unrest was very much present, and a large part of the discussion was framed by participants who argued that the Church's proper role was to promote "liberating education" (Sydow and Ferri 1999, 87). For liberation theologians, who wanted a Church oriented to the poor and oppressed, human dignity was seen as directly connected to social and moral autonomy, which is the core of the most important thread in Western philosophy of human rights, the Kantian tradition. Education was conceived as a means of emancipation, not a process of rote learning. Though a minority in CELAM, this group would have remarkable influence on the continent, especially in Brazil, in the following years. They valued evangelization by means of learning the problems especially of the poor and of direct organized social work aiming at the improvement of social justice and life in general. This line of work had been practiced since the 1940s by Dom Hélder Câmara in the state of Pernambuco, in northeastern Brazil. Câmara would turn out to be one of the leading figures in the progressive Church hierarchy in the 1960s and 1970s, along with São Paulo's Dom Paulo Evaristo Arns, Volta Redonda's Dom Waldyr Calheiros, and Araguaia's Dom Pedro Casaldáliga, among others. The views defended by the progressive clergy provided the bridge that connected left-wing politics and religion. In the words of

Frei Betto (1982, 61), one of the Dominican priests who served four years in prison for subversive activities:

> Wherever there is justice, freedom, and love, there rest the seeds of the Kingdom of God. . . . Faith reveals, before the words of God, the ideological discourse of dominators. Jesus takes the identity of the oppressed, and through them He wants to be loved and served. . . . Serving the cause of the liberation of the poor is, therefore, serving Christ himself. A part of the Church made herself historically distant from this proposition of the Gospels. . . . Christianity became the religious spirit of liberalism. . . . But God has never abandoned His people. The Second Vatican Council and the Episcopal Conference of Medellín announced a new Church, reconverted toward her true historical origins.[13]

In 1968, most Brazilian bishops were still fierce anti-Communists, but the ideas coming out of Medellín had considerable acceptance among the lower clergy. Since the 1960s, they had been broadly supportive of President Goulart's "populist, proto-socialist reforms" (Weschler 1990, 30). It is easy to understand how some of them came to have serious problems with the military authorities after the coup.

What was at first a cordial and convenient relationship between the Church and the government turned into a crisis when members of the clergy with ties to left-wing political leaders became victims of torture and abuse. The prelates responded by defending the Church and its freedom of action, as well as its members, against the military government's systematic use of torture in police interrogations. The beginning of violence against Church members was decisive for a shift of position within the hierarchy: moderates and even traditionalists took a more decisive stand in favor of the Church and against the military regime, within which the so-called hardliners (*linha dura*) were given greater latitude. From then on, as Della Cava points out, the Church settled for its own "institutional integrity against the assaults of an increasingly illegal government" (Della Cava 1978, 236). Progressive clerics ascended in the hierarchy and traditionalists lost sway, exemplified dramatically by Arns replacing Rossi as archbishop of São Paulo. In less than ten years, the hierarchy went from welcoming the regime as an anti-Communist protector to systematically reporting torture, violence, and murder and institutionally promoting a culture of human rights in Brazil. This phenomenon is worth describing in more detail.

The first conflicts occurred when the political police moved against the Catholic Youth Union (JUC) and other Catholic institutions with close ties to universities. The Church response at the time was low-key. JUC members were students, and in the 1960s students almost routinely got in trouble with the authorities. The hierarchy—still then predominantly traditionalist—perceived police action not as a move against the Church, but against students and student organizations. Certain clerics were also subjected to physical and moral violence from the earliest days of the coup. Fr. Antonio Lage was one of them, and, according to his testimony published in the *Brasil: Nunca mais* extended report (Arquidiocese de São Paulo 1985b, 983), approximately thirty priests were subjected to physical and moral abuse on the eve of the military government. Those were, according to him, the priests whose line of work consisted in "assisting the humble ones" (985). Father Lage came from Diamantina, in the state of Minas Gerais, where conflicts between traditionalists and progressives became acute (Serbin 2006, 190). These cases, however, were not sufficient to draw an institutional response from the Church against torture at that moment.

While progressive clergy never gave up their struggle, the hierarchy of the Church would change its position in the years to come, as time made it clear that torture and violence had become a permanent strategy of the government for dealing with political adversaries, including a growing number of clerics. Several dramatic cases of violence against Church members in October 1969 proved to be decisive in the institution's shift. The first was the murder of twenty-nine-year-old Fr. Antonio Henrique Pereira da Silva Neto, D. Hélder Câmara's close assistant, whose brutalized corpse was found on March 27, 1969 (Castro 1978, 79). He would be the first of seven clerics murdered by the military regime (Serbin 2006, 187). The second case was that of Sister Maurina Borges da Silveira, who ran a foster home in Ribeirão Preto, in the state of São Paulo. She was arrested on suspicion that she was a member of the Armed Front for National Liberation (FALN), a guerrilla group that fought against the military dictatorship. An FALN member who also belonged to the Catholic Youth Union had stored suspicious materials in the foster home. Sister Maurina was arrested, immediately tortured, and afterward imprisoned in the northern area of the city of São Paulo, at the Presídio Tiradentes, where most political prisoners were sent.

At the time of her arrest, the auxiliary archbishop for that area of São Paulo was D. Paulo Evaristo Arns, who would become a major critic of torture and human rights violations. Arns met Sister Maurina while she was held in Presídio Tiradentes. Soon after, he made the first of many public accusations of torture against the military regime (Sydow and Ferri 1999, 92). Sister Maurina would be sent into exile a few months later. She was one of the political prisoners exchanged for Nobuo Okuchi, the Japanese consul who was kidnapped by the People's Revolutionary Vanguard (VPR), another guerrilla group. She would live the remaining years of her life in Mexico, never ceasing to proclaim her innocence. The morning before her release, Arns, in another politically significant action, celebrated Mass for her in prison. The archbishop of Ribeirão Preto, D. Felício Vasconcellos, excommunicated two police chiefs he held responsible for the violence against Sister Maurina (Sydow and Ferri 1999, 92).

This case is seen as the first explicit attempt by the political police to publicly draw a direct connection between the Catholic Church and Communism. Media coverage at the time conveys that purported linkage. A 1969 article in *Folha de São Paulo*, one of the two major São Paulo newspapers, reported, "Madre Maurina was connected to several terrorists and [the foster home she ran] served as the clandestine meeting point for the group."[14] These were the opening events of what would soon be called a church-state crisis in Brazil.

Shortly after, in November 1969, a couple of young Dominican friars were arrested in a massive operation that ended with the death in a São Paulo police ambush of the former Communist congressman Carlos Marighella, leader of the National Liberation Alliance (ALN), a left-wing guerrilla group based in São Paulo. Marighella had been declared "public enemy number one" by the military regime at the time of his death. Eventually, two other friars were arrested. The four Dominicans had helped house and transport wanted members of the ALN, who would most likely have been tortured if arrested. All the friars but Frei Betto, whose uncle was an army general, were brutally tortured. One of them, Frei Tito, developed severe post-traumatic neurosis and hanged himself years later while exiled in Paris.[15]

D. Agnelo Rossi, archbishop of São Paulo at the time, received the reports of torture but ignored them (Sydow and Ferri 1999, 93). Cardinal Vicente Scherer of Porto Alegre, where Frei Betto had been arrested, went on radio and legitimized what he called "serious accusations against [the priest]," saying "he would be surprised if he were able to refute all the evidence gathered against him" (quoted in Betto 1982, 133). To preserve good relations between the Church and the government, Rossi and Scherer chose to see the arrest and torture of the four Dominicans, not as a blow against the Church, but rather against subversive students who happened to be clerics. Arns, on the other hand, frequently visited the Dominicans in prison and used his authority as archbishop to highlight their case. He worked closely with a few lawyers, including Mario Simas, who eventually defended the Dominicans in military court.

Arns's most explicit and public condemnation of torture against Church members came in 1971, when he denounced the torture of Fr. Giulio Vicini and his assistant, Yara Spadini. Unlike Sister Maurina and the Dominican friars, Vicini's and Spadini's torture was limited to beating and electrical shocks to the ankles. Arns, however, reacted by publishing an open letter condemning their treatment and had it affixed to the doors of every church in São Paulo. He held the state governor, the army commander, and the chief of the political police responsible. The archbishop's letter was a bombshell. The mainstream press immediately published it, as did foreign news outlets.[16] Two weeks later, the National Conference of Brazilian Bishops issued a public demand that authorities respect human rights.[17]

The blooming church-state crisis was a major concern for the government of a profoundly Catholic country like Brazil. The regime responded by creating the Bipartite Commission, whose membership was made up of representatives of the government and the Church. On the military side, the leading negotiator was Gen. Antonio Carlos Muricy; on the Church's side, Dom Eugênio Sales (Rio de Janeiro's archbishop), Dom Ivo Lorscheider (CNBB's general secretary), and Dom Aloisio Lorscheider (Fortazela's archbishop), along with Professor Candido Mendes de Almeida. The meetings were attended by several other army officials and members of the Church hierarchy.[18]

Though nothing very concrete ever resulted from it, the Bipartite Commission was important in that it recognized the Church as an institution that the government had to handle differently. Unlike Congress and political parties, it could not be shut down; unlike judges, professors, and public employees, the clergy could not be suspended or dismissed on charges of political subversion. And, of course, the Catholic Church was the institutional representative of a priceless symbolic asset in Brazil's cultural stew: Roman Catholicism, adopted by the vast majority of Brazilians. As early as 1969, a CIA special report on Brazil had correctly pointed out that the Church was the only social institution still capable of standing up to the regime: "We believe that the Church is the only institution that could begin to marshal serious resistance against the government" (CIA, 1969, 9). The Bipartite Commission shows that the government, too, recognized that risk. Nevertheless, the commission's meetings—over twenty—never reached productive results. According to Gaspari (2003, 385), this was due to the single topic of torture, which "poisoned the Bipartite meetings whenever a Bishop came up with soundly proven accusations," which were invariably ignored by the army's participating generals. This failure affected the high ranks of both institutions and led to deteriorating church-state political relations.[19]

D. Paulo Arns is only one—though possibly the most relevant—example of what Ralph Della Cava meant when he told Lawrence Weschler (1990, 29) that "the Brazilian episcopate, in the last three decades [ca. 1960–90], has emerged as the most innovative, from the pastoral point of view, most complex, in terms of its organization, and most progressive, in the theological point of view, in the world." Arns appeared on the "bad bishops lists" kept by Gen. Ernesto Geisel (r. 1974–78), who became president after torture and assassinations had peaked under General Medici (r. 1970–74) and was determined to mend church-state relations (Gaspari 2003, 375). "Bad bishops"—those who used their social and moral status to condemn repression, torture, and assassination by the state—also included Waldyr Calheiros, then bishop of Volta Redonda, an industrial city in the north of Rio de Janeiro state;[20] Hélder Câmara, then archbishop of Olinda / Recife and former CNBB secretary; and even

Pope Paul VI. All of them influenced the Brazilian Church's change in perspective.

Calheiros spoke out in favor of the regime's victims in northern Rio de Janeiro, mostly unionized workers, and denounced the brutal murder of four young soldiers at the army's barracks in the city of Barra Mansa, near Volta Redonda (Serbin 2000, 186–94; Gaspari 2002, 322). Câmara began his career in the 1940s in northeastern Brazil, a region of shocking poverty and famine. A constant critic of Brazil's economic inequality, he worked closely with peasants and their political leaders, who were considered Communists by the military government. When violence and torture claimed victims around him—his assistant, Father Henrique, was murdered, and several civil collaborators were imprisoned by the political police (Castro 1978, 83)—Calheiros became the opposition's principal voice of protest in the international arena. His role in making the torture and human rights violations in Brazil known worldwide eventually garnered him four nominations for the Nobel Peace Prize (a record unequaled by any other Brazilian). For the regime, he and Arns were the most dangerous prelates in the church-state conflict. Secretary of Justice Alfredo Buzaid coordinated an international campaign against Câmara's Nobel nomination (Gaspari 2002b, 297). São Paulo's governor Abreu Sodré prepared a dossier against the so-called Red Bishop and gave it to Arns's predecessor, Agnelo Rossi, as he was leaving for a post in Vatican City.[21] Rossi, as always, temporized and was praised for that by Buzaid.[22]

Eventually the hierarchy took on the combative style of Calheiros, Arns, and Câmara. More conservative prelates such as Rossi, who claimed to act silently while pulling strings in the background, lost public standing. Rossi was accused of being too mild in condemning human rights violations. His departure from São Paulo to head the College of Cardinals in Rome, the highest Church post ever held by a Brazilian, was seen by many as a decision to pull him off the front lines for poor performance (Sydow and Ferri 1999, 100). Pope Paul VI was acquainted with the progressive wing of the Brazilian Church through his personal friendship with D. Hélder Câmara, whom he admired (Gaspari 2002, 246). It seemed no accident that he replaced Rossi with Arns, who by 1970 was known as the leading public enemy of torture and ill treatment of prisoners in São Paulo.

The Shift in the Legal Community

To understand how the legal community came to the public defense of human rights, it is important to note that Rio de Janeiro retained considerable power and influence even after Brasília replaced it as the nation's capital in 1960. In terms of military politics, it was still the most important center in the country. Many public institutions did not move to Brasília until years later; the Superior Military Tribunal (STM), for example, functioned in Rio until 1974. In contrast to other parts of the country, Rio had a recent history of political trials: the Tribunal for National Security had tried many rivals of former president Getulio Vargas not long before 1964. After the military seized power, Rio was the only place where there were lawyers experienced in handling cases for those charged with political crimes—as well as the only place where convictions in any of the fifteen military *auditorias* spread around Brazil could be appealed.

Heraclito Sobral Pinto, one of the most important defense lawyers for political prisoners after 1964, was at the time of the coup the personal lawyer of the governor of Guanabara, Carlos Lacerda. In contrast, José Carlos Dias, probably the lawyer most active in the defense of political prisoners in São Paulo state, had received his bachelor's diploma only a few weeks before the coup.[23] Their two professional trajectories illustrate the striking difference between political lawyers in Rio de Janeiro and elsewhere.

Individual lawyers who defended political prisoners from the beginning of the regime began their involvement as lawyers usually do: their help was sought by people in trouble with the law, among whom political opponents of the government were a growing segment after 1964. There were many reasons why those lawyers, and not others, wound up defending political prisoners.

Some, especially in Rio de Janeiro, were elite criminal lawyers with previous professional experience and a reputation for defending political prisoners gained in the by-then-extinct Tribunal of National Security.[24] Some were younger lawyers with a strong commitment to the rule of law who chose to assist more experienced lawyers defending political prisoners. One lawyer, for example, transferred her graduation from another state to the city of Rio de Janeiro just for the chance to work with Sobral Pinto, the most prestigious of the political lawyers.[25] In São Paulo, some young lawyers began defending victims of political persecution very early in the military government and made quick names for themselves while more experienced *paulista* lawyers ignored the issue.[26] Eventually these pioneering lawyers gained prestige and attracted the next generation to "political lawyering."

There were lawyers with previous connections to groups ideologically opposed to the military regime, such as political parties, unions, artists, students, and sectors of the Church. Some had represented unions and union leaders; some were previous leaders of left-oriented student associations. Here we see the most direct link between a leftist political ideology and the decision to defend political prisoners.

Finally, there were lawyers who took up this task on purely professional grounds: it was a promising field, one that few lawyers were willing to explore, that could pay off in the long term in different ways, especially politically. The years since have shown that they were quite correct in this perception.

Although different trajectories can be inferred from the interviews, in reality the same human rights lawyer may have had several different motivations or circumstances that drew him or her into the work. The categories reflect the many motivations and values that led different lawyers to make defending political prisoners part of their professional lives.[27] At the same time, they show why it is incorrect to assume that it was shared ideological values that brought clergy and human rights lawyers to work together. In fact, a common ideology did not exist even among the lawyers themselves.

What these groups of lawyers did have in common, apparently, was a growing perception of belonging to a social group—criminal lawyers defending political prisoners—that was itself increasingly victimized by the regime. As repression grew, the work of these lawyers became more and more difficult. Eventually they started to suffer abuses and violence not because of their politics but because of their professional practice. Or, more precisely, because the police deduced a political orientation that made them as subversive as their clients. Countless times they heard questions like, "Who pays your legal fees, Moscow or China?," in police precincts.[28] Harassed in their profession, these lawyers eventually gained the support of the Bar and worked strategically with other people and institutions that swelled the ranks of the opposition.

The Bar's position in the first years of the regime was open support for the coup. The forced retirements of public employees and expulsions failed to elicit even a formal note of protest from the institution. Individual defense lawyers in these years had to struggle to gain access to and interview their clients, to gain access to formal accusations, and to carry out myriad other professional responsibilities. These men and women who sought to defend not only their clients but also their professional freedom as lawyers worked on their own. In the words of one of the interviewees, "The Bar, in 1964, took the wrong direction. . . . But from 1968 on, it became clear that the Bar stood up against the regime."[29]

What had changed? State repression reached lawyers and social groups close to them. For lawyers, this became flagrant when repression came at the cost of limiting habeas corpus and other legal tools. As one of the interviewees explained, "The Bar took this position against the military dictatorship also because they were defending our livelihood. I mean, in the dictatorship, they took away our habeas corpus. That's like taking the scalpel away from the surgeon."[30] Another interviewee, who would later hold important positions at the Bar in São Paulo and in the state government after redemocratization, saw things in a similar light: "In the beginning, the Bar was timid, even supportive of the so-called revolution. But when violence victimized many lawyers' freedom, the Bar took a turn for the better."[31]

Violence against lawyers went well beyond making their jobs harder. Several of the interviewees reported having suffered various forms of physical and psychological abuse, such as beatings and electrical shocks in police precincts and long-term arrests or short-term kidnappings.[32] Other lawyers had their offices searched and their professional telephones tapped,[33] in clear violation of their professional rights even by the repressive legal standards of the period.

It was not only lawyers who were victimized by the military regime's illegalities but also others they knew professionally and socially. It is significant that into the 1960s, law schools also offered the best humanities courses in Brazil. There were few schools of journalism, arts, or social sciences at the time. The writers, poets, and journalists persecuted by the military government were frequently bachelors of law, although not practicing law as a profession. They and lawyers were often college friends who belonged to the same social circles and shared common views of the world and of politics.[34] This helps explain why the organizations of lawyers saw things differently when artists and journalists got in trouble with the authorities, as opposed to, say, industrial workers, union leaders, and philosophy students.

By the beginning of the 1970s, it had become clear to both the Church and lawyers' organizations—at least to those members most vocal in their opposition to the government—that they were on the list of the regime's political enemies and would be treated as such. It made perfect sense for them to start working together.

Joining Hands

At a time when people were dragged out of prison to be executed by the so-called Death Squad or were tortured out of their sanity in police stations where upper-middle-class neighbors could hear their screams, survival and avoidance of torture were primary goals—and help from any institution that could offer it was readily accepted. In addition to Church members and lawyers, such groups as the Brazilian Press Association (ABI), unions, foreign academics, and international human rights organizations (Amnesty International had a key role, according to many interviewees) played a role in the struggle. Various legal and political strategies were used. Here I examine those that help explain the praxis that ended up uniting lawyers and the Catholic Church.[35]

The first point of connection was of course the most obvious: priests and nuns accused of subversive actions were prosecuted based on national security laws, foreign clerics were subject to expulsion procedures, and Church leaders needed lawyers to defend them. They turned to lawyers they respected for their professionalism who were also practicing Catholics. These lawyers either took the cases or passed them on to other trustworthy lawyers whom, religious or not, they trusted to be committed to the defense of human rights and civil liberties.

Therefore, the group of political lawyers included not only those who defended political prisoners in the military *auditorias* but also those who, practicing in other areas of law, provided indirect support by referring those in need to colleagues active in political cases. For example, Fabio Konder Comparato—one of the best known corporate and banking lawyers of the time and a respected commercial law professor at USP—arranged for the defense of the tortured Dominican friars. At his request, Mario Simas—a respected political lawyer, founding member of the Justice and Peace Commission in São Paulo, and, like Comparato, a practicing Catholic—took the case and obtained impressive results in favor of the four young priests.[36]

The lawyers learned from these connections that at least certain segments within the Church—elements that might influence the ecclesiastical institution as a whole—were potential allies in the struggle against the dictatorship and its violence. Modesto da Silveira, possibly the most active political lawyer in the country during the 1960s and 1970s, said, "The National Conference of Brazilian Bishops started to feel that the Catholics of the New Church, which preached humanism, were being victimized. So CNBB had to take a stand, and eventually it did."[37]

Silveira was referring specifically to the military regime's defamation campaign against D. Hélder Câmara. Câmara's conflict with military authorities took place between 1969 and 1970. It is seen by Gaspari as the point where the Church chose the protection of its hierarchy over the political conveniences of an alliance with the government, breaking the traditional patriarchal bond.[38] Silveira's account shows that lawyers perceived CNBB's shift of position and that this helped them see the Church hierarchy as a potential ally. By the end of the 1960s, according to many interviewees, the Church and some of its important institutions (CNBB, archdioceses) had reached a similar conclusion: they could use the help of lawyers and the Bar. From this point on, the lawyer-Church alliance was no longer just a contingent bond between practicing Catholic lawyers and persecuted individual church members. It became, instead, a locus of collective action by two social groups.

In this alliance, lawyers, of course, did the legal work, while the Church carried out a broader political role, both nationally and internationally, and took the lead in raising financial resources. The Church's central political work, according to most lawyers interviewed, was making the systematic practice of torture widely known, in Brazil and abroad. This role was crucial in shifting public opinion to the opposition. As many of the regime's victims became known—among them students, doctors, dentists, lawyers, journalists—the public found it easy to identify with them.[39] The archbishops of São Paulo and Recife, Arns and Câmara, were crucial in this work.

Câmara, as mentioned earlier, was the most outspoken Brazilian prelate in the international arena about human rights violations. He focused world attention on the military regime's systematic use of torture to investigate and punish its opponents. In the spring of 1970, Câmara spoke bluntly at the Palais des Sports, in Paris: "Torture is a crime that should be abolished. Those guilty of treason to the people of Brazil are not those who speak out against it, but the ones who persist in employing torture. I ask you to tell the world that torture takes place in Brazil. I ask you this because I deeply love my country, and torture dishonors Brazil" (quoted in Gaspari 2002b, 291–92).

The Europeans took Câmara's accusations seriously. A few days after the speech, the weekly magazine *Paris Match* published a four-page article titled, "Yes, in my country we torture."[40] José Lourenço de Lima, professor of classics at the Federal University of Pernambuco—Câmara's home state—was in Europe on a scholarship at the time. He returned to Brazil a few days after these events, complaining that, at that point, the country was known in Europe for nothing other than soccer (Pelé and the national team had just won the 1970 World Cup in Mexico) and torture.[41] The Brazilian government was infuriated by Câmara's actions and accused him of being an antipatriotic Communist.

It was less than a year later that Archbishop Arns in São Paulo posted his open letter, his first public condemnation of torture, concerning the case of Fr. Giulio Vicini and his assistant. Arns's legal references are relevant to our analysis here:

> On January 30, 1971, some newspapers reported the arrests of Father Giulio Vicini . . . and Yara Spaldini . . . under the headlines "Two Subversives Arrested in a Favela" and "Subversive Priest Arrested." . . . As the Archbishop of São Paulo, I have the duty and the

right to inform that 1) Neither Rev. Father Giulio Vicini nor Mrs. Yara Spaldini should be considered subversive before their trial by a lawful tribunal, with full right of defense. . . . 3) Unfortunately, Rev. Father Giulio and Mrs. Yara were tortured, despicably, at the Political Police Headquarters [DEOPS] of our city, as I and the Episcopal Vicar of Southern São Paulo personally verified.[42]

Arns went on to ask for a forensic examination of Vicini and Spaldini in order to address questions about their physical integrity during custody—another clearly "legal move." As this letter illustrates, by the early 1970s the Church had begun to employ legal strategies in its broader quest for the human rights of political prisoners. It is, of course, no accident that throughout the Vicini incident Arns was assisted by a lawyer, Mario Simas. Having tried to visit the torture rooms in DEOPS by himself without success, Arns sought Simas's aid. He also informed the governor of São Paulo, Abreu Sodré, that he would take action in response to the torture of Father Vicini and Mrs. Spaldini. The letter on church doors soon followed.

Father Vicini's case was not the first in which Arns used legal language as a political tool. After becoming archbishop, he continued to visit political prisoners, often unannounced. Getting access to the cells was not always easy. To hide mistreatment, or simply to make communication with political prisoners more difficult, clerics were barred from entering prisons and police precincts. But because the Constitution of 1967 ensured religious freedom and the 1957 Lei de Execução Penal, which at the time regulated prisons in Brazil, provided for religious education, Arns was able to gain access based on prisoners' right to religious liberty and education. On these occasions, he explicitly mixed his religious and moral authority with the laws and the Constitution. Dressed in liturgical garb, he would present a copy of the 1967 Constitution to anyone denying him access and announce, "I am the archbishop of São Paulo and, if my entry is denied, you will suffer a lawsuit based on our Constitution. You must let me in."[43]

Arns relied on the collaboration of lawyers—the founding members of São Paulo's Justice and Peace Commission among them—and under his leadership the Church in São Paulo repeatedly used the language of law in the struggle for human rights. A good example is the manifesto issued at the 1972 conference of the states' archbishops in the small city of Brodósqui, in northwestern São Paulo state. Known as the "Brodósqui Document" and signed by all the states' bishops, it could well be incorporated into a textbook on human rights, criminal law, or criminal procedure.

> Once again, we feel impelled to bring to the consideration of those responsible for public security . . . acts known nationally and internationally, which violently harm physical integrity, psychological integrity, and human dignity in its moral and religious values. . . . It is illicit to carry out arrests in the manner in which they have been happening among us: with no proper identification of the accountable authority or the agents that execute it; with no communication to the lawful judge within legal deadlines. . . . The laws that rule us, which originate in the 1964 Revolution itself, clearly state that "no one shall be arrested other than in flagrant commission of a crime, or by written order of a lawful authority" (1969 Constitution, art. 153, 1). It is illegal to utilize, in the interrogations of suspected individuals, in order to obtain confessions, any methods of physical, psychological, or moral torture, especially when they lead to mutilations, loss of health, and even death, as has been happening. All of [these practices are] in flagrant contradiction to our Constitution, which explicitly orders that "all authorities should be mindful of the integrity of detainees and prisoners" (art. 153, 14). It is illegal to deprive accused persons of their right to defend themselves, or to threaten them, or to prejudge the accused before due trial, or to delay indeterminately the lawsuit against them, when our Carta Magna determines that "the law will guarantee all accused persons the right to fully defend themselves, with all the appeals thereby entailed" (art. 153, 15). . . . We regret the suspension of habeas corpus. We put ourselves on the side of those who demand the return of this guarantee. (Quoted in Sydow and Ferri 1999, 124–25)[44]

Because of censorship, the Brodósqui Document never appeared in the press, but its language reveals how closely legal professionals and the

Church were working in São Paulo. By 1972 the Church had clearly realized the benefits of appeals to legality, especially against a regime that sought to legitimize itself as based on law.

For their part, lawyers were keenly aware that the Church was a valuable asset for making politically sensitive information public. Going after an archbishop was harder than going after a lawyer, particularly after the Ninth General Assembly of Brazilian Bishops in 1970 condemned torture and demanded respect for the basic human right of lawful defense against criminal accusations.[45] At the same time the national hierarchy expressed its clear support for prelates like Arns, Câmara, and Waldyr Calheiros, who were on the front lines of the struggle.

One important episode in 1975 illustrates how the Church's communications role facilitated the work of lawyers. Vladimir Herzog, a Yugoslavian journalist of Jewish origin, died in a torture session at the DOI-CODI headquarters in São Paulo in October 1975.[46] Herzog, at the time director of journalism at a São Paulo television station, had voluntarily turned himself in for interrogation the night before.[47] São Paulo's public security secretary, Col. Erasmo Dias, claimed Herzog had committed suicide in his cell by hanging himself with a belt tied to the bars of the cell's window. This was clearly unlikely, since the belt was suspended about four feet above the ground. The photograph of Herzog's hanging body is one of the most infamous images of the Brazilian military dictatorship.[48] Herzog was the eighth person who, according to official statements of the military government, killed himself by hanging from less than body height (Gaspari 2004, 177).[49]

After Herzog's death, José Carlos Dias, one of the lawyers assisting his widow, Clarice Herzog, interviewed Rodolfo Konder in a simulated judicial inquiry. Konder—a fellow journalist and also a torture victim— was a prisoner in the cell next to Herzog's the night of his death. Konder's testimony made clear that Herzog had been killed in a torture session that went too far. He testified in a conference room at Dias's law firm before a group that included lawyers (Dias and his colleagues Arnaldo Malheiros Filho, José Roberto Leal de Carvalho, and Maria Luiza Flores da Cunha Bierrenbach), a public prosecutor (Hélio Bicudo), the president of the Brazilian Press Association (Prudente de Moraes Neto), and a priest, Olivio Caetano Zolim, who was personally named by Arns.[50]

According to Dias, Konder's testimony had both judicial and political impact. It permitted Clarice Herzog to sue the state of São Paulo for civil damages, and as a document circulated internationally it deeply embarrassed Brazilian authorities that had insistently denied torture and human rights violations. Much of the international impact was possible due to the Church's well-established transnational networks.[51]

In the 1970s, collaboration between the Church and lawyers intensified as Catholic institutions began to provide financial support for the defense of clients it sent to lawyers. Two São Paulo lawyers stated that several of their clients came to them through the recommendations of priests, though, they insisted, they rarely made any money on those cases.[52] A Rio de Janeiro lawyer reported that there, too, "many cases came to law firms sent by the Church."[53]

In northeastern Brazil, Church financial support for lawyers was particularly significant. One lawyer from the state of Ceará said he received payments from the archbishop of Maranhão state.[54] Pedro Eurico de Barros e Silva, a lawyer from Pernambuco, was hired full-time by the Church to work on human rights cases. "At a certain point in time," he said, "I had up to 102 lawsuits that referred to agrarian conflicts. They involved thousands of people. I was also the lawyer for many political prisoners, as well as social organizations that worked for agrarian reform."[55]

Church support differed in kind according to the region. In São Paulo and Rio, where wealth was concentrated, political support was more important than financial support. Political lawyers could afford some pro bono cases. In northeastern Brazil, historically the poorest area of the country, Church funding for defense lawyers was particularly important. But São Paulo also benefited from the Church's fund-raising efforts: the *Brazil: Nunca mais* project, possibly the most important initiative on the right to truth, was backed institutionally and financially by the World Council of Churches (WCC) (see also Kelly, this vol.). Archbishop Arns was in personal contact with the WCC's general secretary, Philip Potter, an enthusiastic supporter of the project from the beginning (Weschler 1990, 24).

In sum, lawyers and the Church—especially key prelates, liberation theologians, those inspired by Vatican II and Medellín, and defenders of a "Church of the poor"—worked side by side, using both political and legal tools, creating a political discourse based on ideals such as the universal respect for human dignity, the importance of compliance with the law, and respect for established legal institutions. This was the very amalgam of the human rights movements that gained importance in Brazil from the 1970s on.

Toward the Present

Any complete history of recent human rights movements in Brazil must consider, at least in part, their origins in the joint efforts of sectors of the Church and certain lawyers, to address the rights of prisoners, rights to land and means of subsistence, and the right to truth. The current opposition of religious institutions to parts of the current Brazilian human rights agenda (such as gay marriage and the right to abortion) should not obscure the historical record—or its enduring contributions to the human rights movement. From the 1960s through the 1980s, clerics and jurists working together combined a particular normative discourse to universalize all rights intrinsic to human beings with a particular strategy to use the legal system for the protection and implementation of those rights. I conclude with several examples of contemporary achievements in human rights that were, in my opinion, significant consequences of the approach they forged together.

Beginning toward the end of the military dictatorship and continuing into redemocratization, Brazil significantly reformed its penal legislation.[56] These reforms included a new Criminal Code in January 1984 and, in July 1984, passage of an entirely new law, the Lei de Execuções Penais, to regulate prison rules and conditions for provisional detainees and convicted persons.[57]

During the period of Brazil's redemocratization, the Church's relative importance as a political actor naturally diminished: other civil society actors had emerged, and society as a whole was more liberal and pluralist in its mores than three decades earlier. With those changes in mind, one cannot help wondering why the 1984 law was literally much more "religious" than its predecessor of 1957. In the earlier statute, religious education appeared very marginally, in a single passage. In the 1985 statute, however, the word *religious* appears nine times, twice as often as *education*.

What the Lei de Execução Penal does, directly, is fully guarantee religious assistance to prisoners. Indirectly, it guarantees that religious institutions have a legal right to permanent access to all penal facilities in Brazil. This was, as we have seen, one of the struggles of Arns and other clerics during the military regime. And, as with Arns in the past, religious institutions remain to this day important actors in publicizing human rights violations in penal facilities, especially through the Penitentiary Pastoral (Pastoral Carcerária) created by the CNBB in 1986.

The penal field, including prisons, is in fact one in which Church and jurists still work together. The Church has even become co-responsible for the administration of several corrections facilities in Brazil. This role derives from the pioneer experiences of the Associação de Proteção e Assistência aos Codenados (APACs) in the 1970s, the cornerstone of which resides in Mario Ottoboni's volunteer work among detainees, which he called "an apostolate in favor of prisoners" (Camargo 1984, 36). Ottoboni's idea was to mitigate the segregation between prisoners and the community by bringing lay volunteers into prisons for activities such as workshops and courses. This idea was presented to a judge of Ottoboni's acquaintance, Silvio Marques Neto, who, like Ottoboni, attended social Catholic meetings in the city of São José dos Campos. Marques Neto, who supervised all penal facilities in the region, immediately embraced the idea and institutionalized the APACs in 1975. By then formal civil associations run by devoted laymen like Ottoboni and São Paulo's Pastoral Carcerária, the APACs had extraordinary results in reintegrating prisoners socially, which drew the attention of the national Ministry of Justice. By 1978 there were more than thirty APACs in Brazil, and today existing APACs are still seen as role models in the Brazilian penal system. The same collaboration occurs in securing provisional prisoners' voting rights, developing adequate penal facilities for women, and banning of intrusive strip-searches of women visiting detained persons.[58] In some of these projects, the Pastoral Carcerária works alongside human rights nongovernmental organizations (NGOs), bar associations (at the state and national levels), and other organizations of legal professionals such as the Associação Juízes para a Democracia.[59]

Another very important longer-term consequence of Church-lawyer collaboration for human rights is the National Truth Commission (NTC), which was created in 2011 by statute (Federal Law 12,528/2011) and implemented in 2012, when President Dilma Rouseff appointed its members by decree.

In 2010, the Brazilian Supreme Court upheld the legality of the military government's 1979 self-amnesty protecting state agents responsible for murders, torture, and other human rights violations. With that decision, the NTC emerged as the best alternative for those seeking an official institutional response to those acts of violence. The NTC was empowered to determine the facts about human rights violations during the military regime, and its investigations formed the basis of the public report on violations and, by name, the officials responsible for them, which was released in December 2014 (Comissão Nacional da Verdade 2014).

One might question the point of finding the truth if no legal consequences derive from it, since Brazil's Supreme Court upheld the amnesty for torturers and murderers. The answer lies in the arguments in *Brasil: Nunca mais*, which have resonated ever since its release in 1985: the official recognition that truth has an inherent value and that Brazil's legal system has a fundamental duty to ensure that basic human values, including truth, are facilitated rather than hindered—as important theologians[60] and contemporary natural law jurists have argued.[61]

Seen from this perspective, the NTC is far more than a "mere" truth seeker with no punitive powers: it can promote the historical and moral responsibility that was not obviated by the military self-amnesty of 1979.[62] It can foster the rights to memory and truth and, at last, promote national reconciliation, as the statute that created it says it should.

The NTC represents the institutionalization not only of the value *Brasil: Nunca mais* sought to preserve—truth—but also of the method by which it establishes that truth: rational investigation based on empirical evidence (documents, testimonies, etc.) carried out by a legally constituted body, all familiar steps in the criminal law system. It is no accident that the individual who conceived the idea of photocopying criminal lawsuits to preserve historical evidence was not a historian but a lawyer. And it is no coincidence that jurists were prominent among the original members of the NTC, many of them with close connections to the Church and the prelates and Catholic institutions that struggled to defend human dignity during the dictatorship.[63]

Finally, the field of labor law has been another important sector of collaboration between Church and legal professionals. In this issue, the relevant social work of Pastoral Operária and Pastoral da Terra carry on an even older tradition, of which D. Hélder Câmara's earlier work in the 1940s is an example: the struggle against the everlasting poverty of large groups of the Brazilian population, for which the country's overall economic improvements seldom result in better life conditions. This has been the drama of Brazil's economic modernization since President Vargas. Both *pastorais* are a major voice advocating better living conditions for poor workers in the countryside and in the city, and often collaborate with political organizations of legal professionals (such as the Associação Nacional de Magistrados Trabalhistas, a national association of labor law judges) and various NGOs. A recent example is the notable effort of the Pastoral da Terra in denouncing slavelike working conditions in Brazil.

In these examples we see concrete consequences of the ideals and strategies that the two partners learned from each other. They mirror the advocacy strategy of many human rights groups in Brazil, which seeks to promote justice for the oppressed and mobilizes legal tools in that cause.

Notes

I thank Alex Wilde and Patrick Breslin for their thorough revision of an earlier version of this text. A version of this work was presented at the Faculty Workshop of the University of São Paulo's Law School, when I received various relevant suggestions, many of which were incorporated into the final text.

1. For the sake of brevity, I will sometimes refer to the lawyers that defended political prisoners as "political lawyers." The term should be taken in this narrow sense.

2. These interviews were conducted for a different research project, coordinated by me and Paula Bartolini Spieler, from the Rio de Janeiro Law School of Fundação Getulio Vargas (FGV Direito Rio). The project was funded by a consortium of FGV and the Amnesty Commission of Brazil's Ministry of Justice (Comissão de Anistia do Ministério da Justiça), through an initiative called Marcas da Memória. The thirty-six complete interviews will be published in a book titled *Advocacia Arte: A luta de advogadas e advogados contra a ditadura militar de 1964–1985* (Curitiba: Ed. Juruá). The conclusions presented here are my own, as are mistakes they might contain.

3. The University of Texas Press in 1998 published an English-language edition of *Brazil: Nunca mais* under the title *Torture in Brazil: A Shocking Report of the Pervasive Use of Torture by Military Governments, 1964–1979*, translated by Jaime Wright.

4. The history of Bicudo's fight as a prosecutor against assassinations and organized crime in the police at the time is told in detail in his book (2002).

5. Almost every human rights lawyer interviewed claimed that fellow lawyers often deprecated their work. Some claim to have been hindered in their work by other lawyers, especially in São Paulo. The National Bar Association was supportive of the coup in 1964 and only slowly shifted its position, mostly because of violations of lawyers' rights. Raids on law firms, telephone monitoring, and detention of lawyers were reported by all interviewees throughout the country. The National Bar Association only became actively engaged with the cause of restoring democracy under the presidency of Raimundo Faoro (1977–79).

6. Institutional Acts, legal instruments of the military dictatorship in Brazil, were pieces of legislation with constitutional power directly decreed by the president and not subject to review by Parliament. For a contemporary interpretation of the legal characteristics of institutional acts, see Silva 1969.

7. The interviews overwhelmingly show that it became clear to the interviewees that human integrity and dignity were the most important things they were fighting to defend in each case they took.

8. Editor's note: The international movement for human rights that emerged in the 1970s bore a strong legal orientation. Among other Latin American countries, this was particularly notable in Chile. See, e.g., Collins 2010; and Wilde, this vol.

9. "Representing the only segment where the authority principle is undisputed, the colonial family provided the most normal image of power, respectability, obedience, and social cohesion among individuals" (Holanda 1985, 85). For a contemporary view, cf. "Brasil, 1870–1914: A força da tradição," in Carvalho 1998, 107–29.

10. Seeking to preserve power against the rising opposition, Goulart deceived Archbishops Câmara (Recife) and Carmelo (Aparecida) by publishing a picture of a private meeting with them. He had promised the picture, taken a day before its publication by all major papers in Rio de Janeiro, would not be made public and would go directly to his personal files. For a narrative of the episode, see Castro 1978, 58.

11. President Vargas died in August 1954. Though the International Eucharistic Congress only took place in 1955, the political negotiations that settled its venue were completed before Vargas's death. Vargas, an anticlerical positivist

during his youth in Porto Alegre, made strategic alliances with the Catholic Church during his many years as president (Neto 2013, 202).

12. Ordem dos Advogados do Brasil, "O Estado de exceção." Available at www.oab.org.br/historiaoab/estado_excecao.htm.

13. Frei Betto's most relevant "subversive activity" was helping politically persecuted persons flee the country into Uruguay and Argentina. He was at the time a student at the Jesuit seminary in the city of São Leopoldo, in the state of Rio Grande do Sul. To be a wanted member of a "terrorist organization," as the parapolitical oppositionist groups (i.e., those who struggled for political causes outside the formal political arena) were known at the time, meant sure imprisonment, probable torture, and possible death.

14. "Desbaratado grupo terrorista que planejava levante armado," *Folha de São Paulo*, November 14, 1969, 6.

15. The story of the Dominicans and their relationship to Carlos Marighella is wonderfully told in Betto 1982.

16. "Arquidiocese emite nota sobre prisões," *Folha de São Paulo*, February 6, 1971, 4. For foreign news outlets, see Sydow and Ferri 1999, 116.

17. "Os bispos emitem comunicado após encerramento da assembléia da CNBB," *Folha de São Paulo*, February 18, 1971, 4.

18. This group, known as the Bipartite Commission (Comissão Bipartite), brought together members of the military regime's political elite, including the army, the navy, the air force, and intelligence units, with members of the Church hierarchy. Gaspari (2002b, 309) notes, "It lasted until 1974 and got together at least 23 times." The meetings invariably ended in verbal abuse hurled by one party against the other. See also Serbin 2000.

19. A thorough documentation of news, documents, and reports regarding church-state relations during the military years in Brazil is available in the six-volume work, *As relações Igreja-Estado no Brasil* (1986), put together by Centro Pastoral Vergueiro (currently Centro de Documentação e Pesquisa Vergueiro), founded in 1973 by Dominican priests. Dominicans were in constant conflict with the government throughout the regime. The order came close to being banned from the country.

20. On D. Waldyr Calheiros, see his autobiographical testimony in Costa, Pandolfi, and Serbin 2001.

21. "Abre Sodré leva a D. Agnelo o dossiê contra D. Hélder Câmara," *Folha de São Paulo*, October 24, 1970, 1.

22. "Buzaid satisfeito com mensagem de D. Agnelo," *Folha de São Paulo*, October 22, 1970, 4.

23. Interview by Rafael Mafei Rabelo Queiroz, Paula Bartolini Spieler, and André Javier Payar with José Carlos Dias, São Paulo, May 23, 2012. The presence

of experienced lawyers, some with political connections, explains, I think, why lawyers in Rio were not subject to physical torture like some in São Paulo were— though many of Rio's elite lawyers were harassed, spied on, arrested, and even kidnapped.

24. The Tribunal de Segurança Nacional (TSN) was created in 1936 (Law 244) by President Getulio Vargas as a special court with jurisdiction over military crimes, including political subversion. TSN was Vargas's most direct response to an attempted Communist uprising in 1935. It tried hundreds of his political opponents until 1945, when it ceased to exist.

25. Interview by Rafael Mafei Rabelo Queiroz and Paula Bartolini Spieler with Eny Raimundo Moreira, Rio de Janeiro, August 16, 2012.

26. On defense of victims, interview by Rafael Mafei Rabelo Queiroz, Paula Bartolini Spieler, and André Javier Payar with José Carlos Dias, São Paulo, May 23, 2012; on those who ignored the issue, interview by Rafael Mafei Rabelo Queiroz and André Javier Payar with Belisário dos Santos Júnior, São Paulo, June 26, 2012.

27. This conflict helps explain some internal skirmishes between lawyers of political prisoners ("I can't believe you interviewed that guy. He was in it just for the money, not for the principle").

28. Interview by Rafael Mafei Rabelo Queiroz, Paula Bartolini Spieler, André Javier Payar, and Alynne Nayara Ferreira Nunes with Idibal Almeida Pivetta, São Paulo, March 23, 2012.

29. Interview by Rafael Mafei Rabelo Queiroz and Paula Bartolini Spieler with Nélio Roberto Seidl Machado, Rio de Janeiro, July 16, 2012.

30. Article 10 of Institutional Act No. 5 (December 13, 1968) prohibited the issuing of habeas corpus writs in favor of those accused or convicted of political crimes and crimes against national security, among others. Interview by Rafael Mafei Rabelo Queiroz, Paula Bartolini Spieler, and André Javier Payar with Mario Simas, São Paulo, May 14, 2012.

31. Interview by Rafael Mafei Rabelo Queiroz, Paula Bartolini Spieler, and André Javier Payar with José Carlos Dias, São Paulo, May 23, 2012.

32. For the beating, interview with Idibal Pivetta, São Paulo, March 23, 2012; for the electrical shocks, interview with Maria Luiza Bierrenbach, São Paulo, June 26, 2012; for the arrests, interviews with Idibal Pivetta, São Paulo, March 23, 2012, and Eny Moreira, Rio de Janeiro, August 16, 2012; for the kidnapping, interviews with Antonio Modesto da Silveira, Rio de Janeiro, July 17, 2012, and Eny Moreira, Rio de Janeiro, August 16, 2012. José Carlos Dias, a founding member of São Paulo's Justice and Peace Commission, reported both short-term detentions and office searches (interview, São Paulo, March 23, 2012).

33. For the office search, interview with Alcyone Barreto, Rio de Janeiro, July 11, 2012; for the tapped telephones, interview with Idibal Pivetta, São Paulo, March 23, 2013.

34. I am here borrowing, though for a different historical period, the hypothesis of the role of law schools in the ideological formation of Brazilian elites examined most relevantly by Carvalho (2003, chap. 4).

35. I thank Alex Wilde for the clarifying remark on praxis as an appropriate description of the Church-lawyer collaboration in this context.

36. Simas himself, in his interview, revealed—according to him, for the first time—that he took the case after Comparato's request. See Simas 1986, 79–145. For a narrative of Simas's work from the point of view of one of the accused priests, see Betto 1982, 167–75. Simas was meticulous in analyzing police evidence and photographs published by the media on Marighella's death. Though the four friars were convicted by São Paulo's military *auditoria*, Simas appealed the conviction and succeeded in cutting their prison sentences in half. By the time the appeal was tried, they had already served enough time to comply with their reviewed sentence and were immediately set free.

37. Interview by Rafael Mafei Rabelo Queiroz and Paula Bartolini Spieler with Antonio Modesto da Silveira, Rio de Janeiro, July 17, 2012.

38. "The Church's hierarchy, which in 1964 had removed [D. Hélder Câmara] from the National Conference of Brazilian Bishops, came together in his defense [against accusations that he was a Communist]" (Gaspari 2002b, 295).

39. After 1985, state violence resumed its standard practice in Brazil, victimizing history's usual suspects in our society—the marginalized, the black community, the poor. With this shift, the middle class to a large extent withdrew support for human rights. Cf. Lopes 1987.

40. "Oui, dans mon pays on torture," *Paris Match*, June 6, 1970.

41. "Atitude condenável e antipatriótica," *Folha de São Paulo*, July 30, 1970.

42. The document's full text is printed in Sydow and Ferri 1999, 114–15.

43. Arns's biographers recount this attempt to visit prisoners at Christmas 1967, at the headquarters of São Paulo's political police (DEOPS). The guard admitted Arns. See Sydow and Ferri 1999, 108–9.

44. Carta Magna is how jurists—and only jurists, i.e., those with formal legal training—refer to the Constitution in Brazil.

45. "Pastoral de Brasília é aprovada por 159 a 21," *Jornal do Brasil*, May 28, 1970, 12.

46. DOI-CODI (Destacamento de Operações e Informações–Centro de Operações de Defesa Interna) was the army investigation division created especially for political repression. It relied principally on threats and torture to obtain confessions and information against political opponents of the Brazilian military dictatorship.

47. Police investigators came to TV Cultura looking for Herzog and another journalist whom they suspected were involved with the Brazilian Communist Party, which was illegal at the time.

48. For a recent reprint of the image, see "Fotógrafo do caso Herzog reconstituirá cena do crime," *Folha de São Paulo*, May 27, 2013.

49. Gaspari also states that in two of these eight cases, the victims were sitting down at the time of their "hanging." When Herzog died, the official statistics accounted for thirty-eight suicides of political prisoners while in custody, eighteen of them (including Herzog) by hanging, according to the authorities.

50. Part of Konder's account of Herzog's murder is in the fifth volume of the complete version of *Brasil: Nunca mais* (Arquidiocese de São Paulo 1985, 5: 359). For Arns's designation of Father Zolim, interview by Rafael Mafei Rabelo Queiroz, Paula Bartolini Spieler, and André Javier Payar with José Carlos Dias, São Paulo, May 23, 2012.

51. Interview by Rafael Mafei Rabelo Queiroz, Paula Bartolini Spieler, and André Javier Payar with José Carlos Dias, São Paulo, May 23, 2012.

52. Interview by Rafael Mafei Rabelo Queiroz and André Javier Payar with Belisário dos Santos Júnior, São Paulo, June 26, 2012; and interview by André Javier Payar with Luiz Olavo Baptista, São Paulo, August 16, 2012.

53. Interview by Paula Bartolini Spieler with Manuel Jesus Soares, Rio de Janeiro, August 16, 2012.

54. Interview by André Javier Payar with António de Pádua Barroso, Fortaleza, September 13, 2012.

55. Interview by André Javier Payar with Pedro Eurico de Barros e Silva, Recife, September 14, 2012.

56. After proclaiming amnesty for itself for its crimes in 1979, the military government began a slow process of political change that culminated with handing government back to civilians in 1985. A new constitution—Brazil's seventh since its independence in 1824—came into effect in October 1988. During the years immediately prior to the return to civilian government, the regime faced intense political pressure and large popular demonstrations for redemocratization.

57. Federal Law 7,210 (July 11, 1984).

58. Several recent reports confirm the Pastoral Carcerária's permanent and present work in favor of detainees. Examples are the 2010 report, *Relatório sobre tortura: Uma experiência de monitoramento dos locais de detenção para a prevenção da tortura*, an institutional publication of Pastoral Carcerária itself; the 2012 report on provisional detainees in the city of São Paulo, published in collaboration with the human rights NGO Instituto Terra, Trabalho e Cidadania (ITTC); and the 2007 report on the condition of incarcerated women in Brazil.

59. The aforementioned report on incarcerated women resulted from a joint collaboration of the Pastoral Carcerária, the National Bar Association, the national Associação Juízes para a Democracia, and ITCC.

60. On normative elements intrinsic to law, see Thomas Aquinas, *Summa Theologica*, Ia IIae, Q.90, esp. A.2.

61. For John Finnis (1980, 59–79), "knowledge," which includes truth, is one of the paramount values toward which any legal system should orient itself.

62. On the NTC as an institutional alternative to ordinary criminal liability for human rights violations during the military dictatorship, see Neves 2012.

63. Claudio Fontelles, a retired federal prosecutor, is a man of known Catholic convictions with relevant institutional participation in the Church to this day. He recently relinquished his seat on the NTC, the reasons for which are unclear. The prevailing interpretation is that he and other members of the NTC disagreed on the strategy of the Commission's work. Another Commission member, José Carlos Dias, has been prominent in this chapter: he was one of the most active lawyers of political prisoners in São Paulo and a trusted ally of D. Paulo Arns, a founding member of the state's Justice and Peace Commission by Arns's personal invitation.

References

Alves, Márcio Moreira. 1978. *A igreja e a política no Brasil.* Lisbon: Sá da Costa.

Arquidiocese de São Paulo. 1985a. *Brasil: Nunca mais.* Petrópolis: Vozes.

———. 1985b. *Projeto "Brasil: Nunca mais,"* tomo 5, vol. 1 (*A tortura*). São Paulo.

Betto, Frei. 1982. *Batismo de sangue: Os dominicanos e a morte de Carlos Marighella.* Rio de Janeiro: Civilizaçao Brasileira.

Bicudo, Hélio. 2002. *Meu depoimento sobre o esquadrão da morte.* São Paulo: Martins Fontes.

Camargo, Maria Soares de. 1984. *Terapia penal e sociedade.* Campinas: Papirus.

Carvalho, José Murilo de. 1998. *Pontos e bordados: Escritos de história e política.* Belo Horizonte: Editora UFMG.

———. 2003. *A construção da ordem: A elite imperial.* Rio de Janeiro: Civilização Brasileira.

Castro, Marcos de. 1978. *Dom Hélder, o bispo da esperança.* Rio de Janeiro: Graal.

Central Intelligence Agency (CIA). 1969. "Special National Intelligence Estimate 93–69." www.foia.cia.gov/sites/default/files/document_conversions/89801/DOC_0000753959.pdf.

Centro Pastoral Vergueiro (Fernando Prandini, Victor Petrucci, and Frei Romeu Dale). 1986. *As relações Igreja-Estado no Brasil.* São Paulo: Loyola.

Collins, Cath. 2010. *Post-Transitional Justice: Human Rights Trials in Chile and El Salvador.* University Park: Pennsylvania State University Press.

Comissão Nacional da Verdade. 2014. *Relatório.* 3 vols. Brasília-DF.

Costa, Celia Maria Leite, Dulce Chaves Pandolfi, and Kenneth Serbin. 2001. *O bispo de Volta Redonda: Memórias de Dom Waldyr Calheiros*. Rio de Janeiro: FGV.

Della Cava, Ralph. 1978. "Política a curto prazo e religião a longo prazo: Uma visão da Igreja católica no Brasil (em abril de 1978)." In *Encontros com a Civilização Brasileira*, vol. 1, 242–57. Rio de Janeiro: Civilização Brasileira.

———. 1988. "A Igreja e a abertura, 1974–1985." In *Democratizando o Brasil*, edited by Alfred Stepan, 231–73. Rio de Janeiro: Paz e Terra.

Finnis, John. 1980. *Natural Law and Natural Rights*. New York: Oxford University Press.

Freund, Julien. 2010. *Sociología de Max Weber*. Rio de Janeiro: Forense-Universitária.

Gaspari, Elio. 2002a. *A ditadura envergonhada*. São Paulo: Companhia das Letras.

———. 2002b. *A ditadura escancarada*. São Paulo: Companhia das Letras.

———. 2003. *A ditadura derrotada*. São Paulo: Companhia das Letras.

———. 2004. *A ditadura encurralada*. São Paulo: Companhia das Letras.

Holanda, Sérgio Buarque de. 1985. *Raízes do Brasil*. São Paulo: Companhia das Letras.

Instituto Terra, Trabalho e Cidadania (ITTC) and Pastoral Carerária (CNBB). 2012. *Tecer justiça: Presas e presos provisórios na cidade de São Paulo*. ITTC: São Paulo.

Krischke, Paulo José. 1979. *A Igreja e as crises políticas no Brasil*. Petrópolis: Vozes.

Leal, Victor Nunes. 1997. *Coronelismo, enxada e voto: O município e o regime representativo no Brasil*. Rio de Janeiro: Nova Fronteira.

Lopes, José Reinaldo de Lima. 1987. "Direitos humanos no Brasil: Compreensão teórica de sua história recente." *Revista de Informação Legislativa* 24, no. 95: 5–22.

Neto, Lira. 2013. *Getúlio: 1930–1945. Do governo provisório à ditadura do Estado Novo*. São Paulo: Companhia das Letras.

Neves, Raphael. 2012. "Uma comissão da verdade no Brasil? Desafios e perspectivas para integrar direitos humanos e democracia." *Lua Nova* 86: 155–86.

Pastoral Carcerária (CNBB). 2010. *Relatório sobre tortura: Uma experiência de monitoramento dos locais de detenção para a prevenção da tortura*. São Paulo.

Serbin, Kenneth. 2000. *Secret Dialogues: Church-State Relations, Torture, and Social Justice in Authoritarian Brazil*. Pittsburgh, PA: University of Pittsburgh Press.

———. 2006. *Padres, celibato e conflito social: Uma história da Igreja católica no Brasil*. São Paulo: Companhia das Letras.

Silva, Carlos Medeiros. 1969. "Atos institucionais e atos complementares." *Revista de Direito Administrativo* 282, no. 95.

Simas, Mario. 1986. *Gritos de justiça: Brasil, 1963–1979.* São Paulo: Editora FTD.

Spieler, Paula, and Rafael Mafei Rabelo Queiroz. 2013. *Advocacia em tempos difíceis: Brasil, ditadura militar, 1964.* Curitiba: Juruá.

Sydow, Evanize, and Marilda Ferri. 1999. *Dom Paulo Evaristo Arns: Um homem amado e perseguido.* Petrópolis: Vozes.

Weber, Max. 1964. *Economía y sociedad.* Mexico, DF: Fondo de Cultura Económica.

Weschler, Lawrence. 1990. *Um milagre, um universo: O acerto de contas com os torturadores.* São Paulo: Companhia das Letras.

PART II

CONTEMPORARY MINISTRIES
RESPONDING TO VIOLENCE

CHAPTER 9

BUILDING PEACE AND DIGNITY

Jesuit Engagement in Colombia's Magdalena Medio

ELYSSA PACHICO

The Jesuits and the Catholic Church

The Pope does not, of course, intend to condemn every possible form of social conflict. The Church is well aware that in the course of history conflicts of interest between different social groups inevitably arise, and that in the face of such conflicts Christians must often take a position, honestly and decisively.
—Pope John Paul II, "The Hundredth Year," 1991

Fr. Luis Raúl Cruz apologized for dating massacres by their proximity to religious holidays. Between Palm Sunday and Tuesday of Easter 2001, he remembers twelve people disappeared. They included a mother and father who sent their teenage daughters to stay with relatives outside the city because the paramilitary troops of the Central Bolívar Bloc had no qualms about using girls as "weapons of war," he said. On Trinity Sunday, he remembered one of the worst displacements: by 6:00 a.m. people were already loading up their cars and stuffing garbage bags full of clothing. "That was a difficult exodus," he said, and he has many others from which to choose. During the first nine months of 2001, nearly 1,300 people left Barrancabermeja, a city with a name that even sounds like an omen of violence—the "barrancas bermejas," or red river embankments. During that same period, over 7,000 people arrived in the city, trying to escape the paramilitaries' scorched earth tactics in the countryside (Observatorio del Programa Presidencial de Derechos Humanos y Derecho Internacional Humanitario 2001, 12).

Father Luis is the Jesuit head of Barrancabermeja's Church of the Sacred Heart, one of three Jesuit parishes in the river port city. Barranca is dominated by an oil refinery, the largest in Colombia, with sixty-meter stacks spewing black smoke that can be seen from miles away in the surrounding swamplands. About three quarters of Colombia's fuel is produced here. The city's official symbol is an iguana, as is that of the national oil company, Ecopetrol, a business as essential to Barranca's economy and its identity as General Motors once was to Detroit. The city's main highway has a statue of iron iguanas crouching on branches; the animals were once a common sight in the straggly trees along the river but are now rarely seen. The city's other prominent symbol is the "Petroleum Christ," a twenty-six-meter statue of a resurrected Jesus in the middle of a polluted swamp.

Ticking through his list of Holy Days that coincided with people dying, Father Luis made it clear that it would have been all too easy to throw up his hands in the face of Barranca's violence. The city was once a bastion of a leftist guerrilla group, the National Liberation Army (ELN), which openly ruled entire neighborhoods, hosting political rallies and collecting war taxes from households. When a right-wing paramilitary group, the Central Bolívar Bloc, began its advance into the city in 1998, it warned there would be "enough blood to paint the walls" (Banco de Datos de Derechos Humanos y Violencia Política 2001, 357).

But Father Luis insisted on putting himself in the middle of the fighting, sometimes literally. He remembered pulling wounded fighters off the street after a gun battle in a park, putting army and guerrilla conscripts alike, none of them past their early twenties, into the back of a van. Before slamming the door shut, he told them, "Now you can keep on fighting each other with your teeth." That part of the story now makes him laugh. He left the injured army troops in the hospital and the injured ELN fighters in safe houses where they could recover without fear of being shot in their hospital beds by paramilitaries. He had never seen the local army commander so angry as when he learned what he had done. But as Father Luis says, "It was a question of doing the right thing."

But he was also running a serious risk. The paramilitaries had killed Jesuits before—such as Fr. Sergio Restrepo, gunned down in a dusty Caribbean town in 1989, and Mario Calderón, a former priest killed with his partner in their Bogotá apartment in 1997. Guerrilla groups also were known to execute priests; any religious figure deemed too politically partisan, who spoke out too forcefully against either the *paras* or the guerrillas, risked being killed.

Father Luis's belief that the most Christian way of "serving one's neighbor" was to become personally involved in Colombia's struggle is emblematic of the hands-on approach the Jesuits have assumed toward the violence in Barrancabermeja and the surrounding region—an area of thirty thousand square kilometers and twenty-nine municipalities, known as the Magdalena Medio, or Middle Magdalena.

This is one of Colombia's strategic heartlands, both in terms of the oil economy and the civil conflict. Not only did the ELN first emerge here, but the paramilitaries of the United Self-Defense Forces of Colombia (AUC) later made a home in the area. For centuries before, the Magdalena Medio was a blank space on official maps. Barrancabermeja only appeared as a tiny dot in 1851, just a trading post for steamboats and canoes on the river (Molano 2010, 25). The government never really had jurisdiction over the vast space, which was instead populated by Liberal refugees of Colombia's civil wars, socialist ideologues attracted by Barrancabermeja's vibrant labor movements and coca pickers looking to spend their earnings on prostitutes and beer.

The Jesuits have long been the face of the Colombian Church in this region of swamplands, gold, oil, and revolution. They founded their first haciendas in the area in 1774, ministering to a population that included runaway slave communities and Yariguí Indians. When the Magdalena Medio's first prefecture was established in 1928, it was staffed entirely by the Society of Jesus. Over the next six decades, Jesuits headed the ecclesiastical structures of the region, even though such top-level appointments remain relatively unusual for Jesuits in Colombia. Jesuit priests practiced an early form of *acompañamiento* in the Magdalena Medio—accompanying the poor in their struggles. They marched with landless peasants, mingled with dockworkers, took part in labor union struggles, and generally tried to take a proactive approach in the region. By subscribing so early to this brand of Christianity, the Jesuits put themselves in the dead center of the broader conflict that afflicted Colombia's Catholic Church—one of the most conservative in Latin America—in the twentieth century.

The Colombian Church was historically linked with the Conservative Party and hostile to its Liberal rival. With conflict and violence growing between the two traditional parties after 1930, the hierarchy was increasingly divided over whether the Church should assert greater independence from politics. During this same period the Jesuits began new forms of a social mission in a changing society, as in the Magdalena Medio. By the 1960s more radical religious responses appeared. The most famous was that of the sociology professor and priest Camilo Torres, who grew deeply frustrated with the Church's position and opted to resign and join the ELN guerrillas in 1965. His decision caused a national scandal, and some of his writings—including his assertion that "the duty of every Christian is to be a revolutionary"—became slogans for the progressive left across the continent. He became a face of liberation theology, even though he predated the movement's spread by several years. Camilo's legacy was assured when he died in his first battle in 1966. The ELN made the guerrilla priest an official martyr and named their military front in the Magdalena Medio after him.

Other priests followed in Torres's footsteps and joined the ELN, including three Spaniards: Manual Pérez (who would eventually rise to become the ELN commander-in-chief before dying of hepatitis B in 1998), Domingo Laín (shot in 1973, earning the honor of having another military front named after him), and José Antonio Jiménez (believed killed by a snakebite during a long march). While they were the exception rather than the rule, the guerrilla priests confirmed for many in Colombia, as Robin Kirk (2003) writes in her study of Colombian violence, that liberation theology contained "deadly" ideas. Simply talking about poverty and justice in a way that appeared influenced by liberation theology was proof enough that the speaker was a Marxist—and therefore, by association, a guerrilla sympathizer. The Church grew chary of public positions with political overtones, especially leftist political overtones.

This created serious dilemmas for those in the Church who wanted to address Colombia's violence. The Church had assistance programs like Pastoral Social, which focused on short-term relief for the poor: food and clothing drives, hot meals, health education workshops, and so on. But for those keen on confronting the structural problems underlying Colombia's conflict, the question was how to bring about revolutionary change without advocating—or being seen as advocating—armed insurrection, especially since so many movements for social and political change in Colombia had been quickly and violently repressed.

The Jesuits have long been the more progressive wing of Colombia's Church, willing to ask hard questions about social realities and the policies they see responsible for the country's decades of civil violence. They have traditionally been active in higher education and intellectual life, positions enabling them to think critically and to question the Church's role in society. Jesuits have also provided basic services for Colombia's most marginalized communities in areas where the state was otherwise absent: health clinics, night schools, and meal centers. Their presence in slums on the fringes of cities like Barrancabermeja did much to boost their credibility among the poor and working class and formed part of the Society's central ethos: instead of avoiding areas with the greatest conflict or poverty, the Jesuits actively sought them out.

The creation of a research institute, the Center for Research and Popular Education (CINEP), was an important Jesuit initiative to complement its other programs and support nonviolent social change as an alternative to armed revolution.[1] Since its founding in 1972, CINEP has established itself as a leading think tank on the character, causes, and consequences of conflict. It has also been investigated by the state intelligence agency and accused of being "subversive." In 1997 five gunmen invaded the apartment of two CINEP staff members—including former Jesuit Mario Calderón—and killed them. The forces opposed to radical change were powerful in many places in Latin America during these decades, but in Colombia the threats were particularly deadly. The Jesuits wanted to address the root causes of Colombia's violence, but for some, even asking these questions revealed the poisonous influence of the guerrillas and warranted a violent response. "If I give food to a hungry person, then I'm being charitable," Barranca's Father Luis said, paraphrasing Brazil's Hélder Câmara. "But if I ask why this person is hungry in the first place, then I'm a Communist."

The Jesuits confronted these dilemmas directly in the Magdalena Medio—one of Colombia's poorest, most violent areas, the strategic heartland of the conflict, where Camilo Torres had died years before and where Father Luis still spends his mornings talking with displaced refugees in his parish sitting room. Under the leadership of Fr. Francisco De Roux, the Jesuits forged a program intended to solve the root problems behind the region's violence.[2] The focus was twofold: building peace from the ground up and encouraging the emergence of an economy that lifted up the very poorest. The resulting initiative—the Development and Peace Program of the Magdalena Medio (the PDPMM, henceforth referred to as the PDP)—was a faith-driven program that insisted on living religious faith through engagement with the world. What the PDP actually does is akin to community organizing: sometimes directly funding civic groups, other times providing training or linking local organizations and economic co-ops with similar collectives to create broader coalitions. Its visibility and scope make it unique among the Jesuits' range of social activism. At its core, the PDP is an expression of the Jesuits' fundamental belief that the appropriate response to Colombia's violence is to address the structural problems behind the conflict in order to bring about gradual and long-term change. Turning that belief into action presented strategic challenges. More radical Jesuits were uncomfortable with the project's economic goals, embedded as they were in a capitalist development framework. Meanwhile, its peace-building goals had to confront the hard realities of an ongoing conflict, where the combatants and the rules of engagement were changing constantly and where the state was unable to establish control.

They confronted these dilemmas by ensuring that the project's overarching vision was spiritual, drawing heavily on the idea that Christians should engage actively with the world. This meant that despite the many difficulties on the ground, the theological base for the project remained sound: values that emphasized peace and human dignity were the motor that kept the program moving forward despite tough and shifting challenges. That the Jesuits embraced and communicated this spiritual dimension within the PDP was crucial to building its integrity. This chapter attempts to illuminate this dimension of the Jesuits' effort while also examining their achievements on the ground.

After presenting an overview of the Magdalena Medio's history of violence and the conditions that made possible a project like the PDP, I examine how this immensely ambitious program was set up and the dilemmas the Jesuits faced in doing so. I then consider the PDP's impact, its economic projects and peace building from the ground up. In the final section I assess how these projects embodied spiritual values and how this shaped their impact in less tangible ways.

Conflict in the Magdalena Medio

The government's violence . . . taught the peasants many lessons.
It taught them that their real enemy is the oligarchy.
—Camilo Torres, 1965

The Magdalena Medio is Colombia's crossroads, offering access to the country's interior and north to the Caribbean coast (fig. 9.1). It also has some of the country's most fertile land, supporting African palm plantations and stretches of coca and marijuana fields. These characteristics help explain why the area has long been strategically important for armed groups. In many ways, the Magdalena Medio is a microcosm of the issues driving the Colombian conflict: the lack of state presence, land conflict, unequal distribution of wealth and poverty. All have fed the growth of insurgencies and paramilitary groups, making violence endemic.

The region became a central hub for oil production during the 1920s and has remained an enclave economy ever since. Although few profits trickled down to local residents, the oil industry has allowed the development of an active working class, adept at organizing strikes and protests, alongside peasant struggles for land reform. This history of community organizing, among both the proletariat and the peasantry, would later provide the base on which Jesuit-backed projects such as the PDP were built.

Figure 9.1. Map of Magdalena Medio, Colombia

Courtesy of Jorge Saldarriaga.

The oil boom transformed Barrancabermeja. Squatters' neighborhoods appeared at the city's fringes, typically named after the date when the first house was built: 20 de Enero, Nueve de Abril, Primero de Mayo. "Almost everyone was illiterate," said the union leader Ramón Rangel. "The way you got hired was by sticking out your hand, and if it was callused enough, you got the job." Political leftists accompanied the influx of male job seekers. These included members of the Communist Party, which became heavily involved in helping the squatters lobby for basic government services. Local priests such as Fr. Floresmiro López, who was close to the Jesuits, and the Jesuit priest Ignacio Rosero also played a role in these campaigns, which built their credibility with the local population.[3]

The area developed a well-deserved reputation for radicalism: some of the activists involved in peasant movements, members of the Liberal Party and the Labor Union of Petroleum Industry Workers (Unión Sindical Obrera de la Industria del Petróleo [USO]) would later help establish the ELN guerrillas in the San Lucas Mountains of Bolívar in 1964, taking up arms alongside rebels trained in Communist Cuba (Hataya 2009, 29). The guerrilla Revolutionary Armed Forces of Colombia (FARC) also established an early presence, forming its Fourth Front from peasant self-defense groups in 1965, just a year after the FARC itself was founded.

The Magdalena Medio is also known as the cradle of paramilitarism, after local landowners, cattle ranchers, and drug traffickers began organizing a self-defense force in the early 1980s to battle guerrilla kidnappings and extortion. In 1998 one paramilitary faction, the Central Bolívar Bloc, set its sights on Barrancabermeja, announcing its arrival by massacring thirty-two people in working-class neighborhoods dominated by the ELN. It was just the beginning of the region's bloodiest era. According to a 2005 PDP presentation, between 1996 and 2004, the height of paramilitary activity in the Magdalena Medio, some 1,730 civilians died and more than 83,000 were displaced.[4]

When the first demobilizations of the AUC began in 2004, they did little to permanently dismantle the paramilitary factions responsible for much of the violence in the Magdalena Medio. Remnants of the Central Bolívar Bloc, now calling themselves the Black Eagles (Águilas Negras), concentrated in southern Bolívar, while former members of the Self-Defense Forces of the Magdalena Medio, the "Botalones," maintained their center of operations in Puerto Boyacá, with some presence in Barrancabermeja. Control of the city today is divided between several of these new-generation "criminal bands" (*bandas criminales*, or BACRIM). Homicides dropped in the city after the groups came to an agreement in 2010.

The Peace and Development Program

If "development is the new name for peace," war and military preparations are the major enemy of integral development of peoples. . . . On the contrary, in a different world, ruled by concern for the common good of all humanity, or by concern for the "spiritual and human development of all" instead of by the quest for individual profit, peace would be possible.

—Pope John Paul II, "On Social Concern," 1987

Fr. Francisco De Roux's first experience in the Magdalena Medio came at the end of the 1970s, when he happened to be in Barrancabermeja at the same time that the Communist Party was organizing mass street protests demanding potable water. The protests were fierce, with demonstrators prying out rails from the train tracks and building barricades in the streets. The priest returned again in 1985 to attend the funeral of a former ELN guerrilla turned mayoral candidate (Molano 2010, 66–67). De Roux knew the city's contradictions from direct experience: populist politics openly expressed in the streets while the most active community organizers were threatened or killed.

Thanks to their long history of activism in the region, the Jesuits were trusted by the labor unions. "The rectory was like a second home. We never saw any difference between us and them," said Ramón Rangel. While the Jesuits had a warm relationship with the USO, the Barrancabermeja Diocese built bridges to the state oil firm, Ecopetrol. When Jaime Prieto, an outspoken priest who had studied sociology in Rome, was appointed bishop of the diocese in 1993, he quickly established a close relationship with Ecopetrol's vice president, Alberto Merlano. Merlano wanted to set up a program to study the root causes of violence in the

Magdalena Medio. As the journalist Alfredo Molano (2010, 68) wrote in a CINEP-commissioned study on the PDP, "The relationship between Merlano and Prieto—to which Francisco De Roux would be added—was a fortunate one at a crucial moment for the region." In 1995 the three spearheaded a study (with backing from the USO) aimed at analyzing the social problems of the Magdalena Medio. With De Roux at the helm, a team surveyed thousands of local residents, asking what people thought were the reasons for so many homicides in the region, and why a region so rich in resources had so many people in poverty. The findings of the survey team, the PDP, recommended the creation of a social organization dedicated to building peace from the ground up. In 1998 the PDP became an officially registered nonprofit organization and set about trying to promote sustainable development and peace.

The PDP has nothing if not scope and ambition. Deputy Director Santiago Camargo calls it "utopia in practice"—a project that ultimately aims to demonstrate that "another model of peace and development is possible, that structural changes are feasible" (Barreto Henriques 2007, 9). As Molano (2010, 86) wrote in his study, "Its priority is that development be human, integral, inclusive, sustainable, and tangible, while peace, going down this road, is built slowly. The central idea is to 'steal' people from the war via productive, organizational, and social projects that transform the conditions in which people live."

That the Jesuits were able to set up the project and attract major international investment was arguably a success in itself. The World Bank, the European Union (EU), USAID, and the Japanese embassy have all contributed millions of dollars through grants and loans, allowing the PDP to fund some six hundred projects since 1995. The World Bank provided a US$7 million loan between 1998 and 2000 and a US$5 million loan between 2001 and 2003 (Hataya 2009, 34–35). Ecopetrol, UN agencies, and several European NGOs also provided funding (Barreto Henriques 2007, 5).

The most heavily funded of the PDP's projects was the Peace Laboratory, which received €42 million from the EU between 2002 and 2010. It pursued the same goals as the PDP, building peace and sustainable development for the poor from the ground up. Some of the initial subprojects are still ongoing today, including the "humanitarian spaces" (discussed later).

The PDP directly funds economic projects: cacao and African palm co-ops, fruit farms, and fisheries. It has also acted as a mediator, sitting at the table when local peasants' associations clashed with national palm oil companies and supplying legal advisers to a peasant community displaced from its land. As the current director, Ubencel Duque, said, one of the basic aims of the program has been just to get people talking: "We want people to absorb that idea, that dialogue is a way they can keep themselves from getting displaced, a way to propose projects, a way of living. We want this to be the region where everybody talks."

From the very beginning, PDP was built around the idea that getting communities to actively participate in and talk about their own development is a viable alternative to armed conflict. According to Molano (2010, 70), this participatory methodology was inspired in part by the Colombian sociologist (and Protestant layman) Orlando Fals Borda. Fals was, with Camilo Torres, a founder of Latin America's first sociology department, at Bogota's National University. As Molano (2010, 70) noted, the two had different visions and the PDP was distinct from both: "Camilo believed that the main tool of political movements was weapons. In contrast, Fals argued that the founding of a political party should be based on research and participatory political action. The PDP differs from the solution proposed by Camilo, as it rejects weapons and all forms of violence; but it deviates from Fals's thesis because it doesn't have the goal of forming a political party."

The PDP's ultimate ambition is to fight for the peasantry using World Bank loans and peace workshops instead of AK-47s. As the Jesuit historian Fernán González put it in an interview, "The PDP is interested in concrete projects. . . . It is interested in what works, not following an ideology. The focus is on the practical."

De Roux, an economist by training, encouraged this pragmatic approach, although it earned the ire of the radical left, both inside the Society of Jesus and from outside observers (Loingsigh 2010). While some Jesuits see the PDP as a pragmatic rather than a spiritual project, Father González insisted that Jesuits "do not separate spirituality from worldly action: we are, as St. Ignatius of Loyola said, 'in action contemplative.'" This seems a key expression of the Jesuits' founding values: turning faith into action. According to González, "The PDP didn't create a theology and put it into practice. . . . It theorized about itself, on the basis of what it practiced." This forms the core of the PDP's theological approach: an emphasis on pastoral theology that stems from practice.

Still, the PDP faced challenges. Community organizers associated with the initiative were threatened and sometimes killed. There was also the question of resistance from the Church itself. The PDP had stalwart support from Jaime Prieto, one of Colombia's most outspoken bishops, who frequently made headlines with his statements. He publicly decried paramilitary-state collusion in Barrancabermeja and declared that he would negotiate with the AUC leader Carlos Castaño himself if it would bring about a decrease in violence. González noted that Prieto made "plenty of enemies" with such statements. Tensions culminated in the early 2000s, when the hierarchy tried to transfer Prieto out of Barrancabermeja to another city, Duque said. "They tried to make it seem as though it were an issue of security, but it wasn't," he explained. "He was making powerful interests uncomfortable. He was one of the few bishops speaking out at the time." Prieto was transferred to a border city, Cúcuta, in 2008, and died two years later.

These apparent tensions between Prieto and the hierarchy were emblematic of a larger trend across Colombia, in which clergy in the provinces were frequently more proactive about confronting Colombia's violence than urban-based Church leaders. "The Church hierarchy was never homogenous," said González. "The bishops in the peripheral zones usually are much more open-minded than the bishops from the large capital cities."

The PDP served as a kind of "bridge" between the Society of Jesus and the fierier local bishops, González said, despite the undeniable tensions between the Church and the Jesuits in the past. These tensions culminated in 1981, when the government accused CINEP of being infiltrated by Communists, and few in the hierarchy challenged the allegations. Tensions also arose from how differently the Church and the Society of Jesus interpreted the purpose of service. According to González, "Bishops were focused on doing short-term social work. But the Jesuits wanted to look at the structural problems. They didn't want to give paternalistic charity." From the Jesuit perspective, "occasional philanthropy just doesn't work."

Despite this history, by and large the institutional Church has backed the PDP, seeing it as a program that brings positive results not just for the Magdalena Medio but for the Church as well. "The Church sees [the PDP] as a committed project—it accepts it, loves it, watches over it. It is critical at times but it's a criticism to allow the program to improve," said CINEP director Luis Guillermo Guerrero. "The Church doesn't just accept the PDP, they admire it." One of the clearest indications of Church support is the replication of one of PDP's emblematic programs, the Peace Laboratory, in nineteen locations across the country. Many of these are headed by clergy (Jesuit and non-Jesuit) and typically focus on issues related to peace and development, geared to the specific problems in any given region. One based in the unofficial capital of Colombia's Eastern Plains, Villavicencio, focuses on land reform issues, while another in the lower Magdalena Medio promotes economic projects meant to benefit fishermen, the main economic livelihood in the area. The nineteen programs form part of a broader coalition of community organizations that work to promote peace in Colombia, known as Redprodepaz (Pro-Peace Network), whose strategic director is the former bishop of Magangué, a close ally of De Roux and Prieto. According to González, "For the bishops in conflict zones, the PDP was like a flag that they knew they had to take up"—leading to the creation of similar programs in different regions.

Building Peace

Peace is not merely the absence of war. Nor can it be reduced solely to the maintenance of a balance of power between enemies. Nor is it brought about by dictatorship. Instead, it is rightly and appropriately called "an enterprise of justice" (Is. 32:7).
—Vatican II, "The Church in the Modern World," 1965

Castulo Bermúdez, a gray-haired farmer seemingly immune to the clouds of swamp mosquitoes that buzz outside his house, does not have much to say about the Jesuits. During the four years he was displaced from his shabby wooden hut and his three-hectare farm, he wandered along the Caribbean coast and only bothered to attend Evangelical churches. In

2009, he returned home, finding the house covered in weeds, and set about replanting his fields. At the moment, he is in talks with a PDP agronomist about what kind of fertilizer mixture he should use for his plantains. Bermúdez once formed part of a group of activist farmers who came together in 2005, under the wing of the PDP, and declared their territory—known as the Opón marshlands—officially neutral in the conflict. The Opón, some twenty-five kilometers outside of Barrancabermeja, is home to about 250 families, who have seen their share of warfare. Between 1986 and 2000, the area experienced four major displacements, instigated by the FARC's 24th Front and the paramilitary Self-Defense Forces of the Magdalena Medio. At various times, Bermúdez was forced to hand over his river boat to the paramilitaries and allow the FARC to take his plantain, yucca, and corn. Once the guerrillas took a ring he had bought in Cúcuta, which was the farthest he had ever ventured from home. Because many swamp-dwelling families were too frightened to travel into Barrancabermeja to stock up on basic goods, prices shot up.

In 2005, the Opón community council, Junta de Acción Comunal (JAC), declared the Opón a "humanitarian space" (*espacio humanitario*), one of thirteen such areas the PDP would eventually support. In a PDP news bulletin announcing the initiative, the campesinos described what led them to declare themselves neutral: "We don't work with the guerrillas, we don't fish for them, we don't plant yucca, corn, or plantain in hand with the ELN or the FARC. The farmer always gets stuck in the middle of the conflict because if someone passes by and tells you to sell them a chicken or a soup, someone else will point the finger at you, and that's the problem."[5]

The declaration was more than just symbolic. Those who lived in humanitarian spaces like the Opón suddenly found themselves plugged into an organizational network. The PDP's Observatory of Integral Peace used its conflict database to track each and every killing, kidnapping, and other disruption in the Opón, incidents that would otherwise have been ignored. PDP community organizers were sent to the zone to help residents come together and decide on a set of common goals, dubbed the Opón Development Plan.[6] They agreed to lobby the municipal government for improvements in the Opón schoolhouse (including air conditioning), and to campaign for electricity to be installed in the districts without it.

They would study the possibility of starting up a joint sugarcane planta-
tion and push the provincial government to invest 500 million pesos
(about US$280,000) to improve and build new houses.

Bermúdez was not there to see how the Development Plan played
out. In late 2005, a group of paramilitaries showed up at his house at 4:30
a.m. and threatened to decapitate him with a chainsaw. He left the Opón
marshes and did not come back for another four years. "The PDP had
good intentions, but we're Colombians," he says. "And Colombians like
to do what's bad."

First initiated as projects of the PDP's Peace Laboratory, the humanitarian spaces were meant to be islands of civil resistance, to encourage the
civilian population to report paramilitary and guerrilla threats, as well as
crimes committed by the state. Even after the Peace Laboratory project
formally ended in 2010, the thirteen humanitarian spaces remained.[7] As
described in a 2007 paper by the Colombian conflict analysis think tank
CERAC, "These are places where people said "no more" to war. . . . They
chose not to join the armed groups, nor to be displaced. They took a third
way—the way of civil disobedience and civil resistance" (Barreto Henriques 2007, 23).

Humanitarian spaces like the Opón are supposed to represent peace
building in action. This emphasis fits the PDP's overall theological approach, which draws on Christian ideals of tolerance and pacifism. As
Deputy Director Santiago Camargo put it, the program's peace goals are
part of a "utopian vision" meant to show that another way of achieving
peace in Colombia is possible: instead of waiting for the state to bring
about an end to the conflict, citizens at a regional level can take matters
into their own hands. This emphasis on citizen action embodies one of
the program's fundamental Christian values: namely, the idea that God
wants his people to be the subjects of history, not its victims, and that he
realizes his purposes through them.

This particular theological approach helped the PDP have an impact
on the Magdalena Medio in several ways. It expressed the program's overall goal of encouraging the empowerment of citizens to bring about peace
and social change. This could be seen in the humanitarian spaces, which
essentially became "safe spaces" where residents could lobby for change
and practice civil resistance, assuming a proactive rather than a defensive
position toward Colombia's civil conflict. In the Opón, residents in hu-

manitarian spaces became involved in lobbying for certain rights, from the provision of basic services (electricity, schooling) to the building of new facilities.

The PDP's theological approach also fed into its commitment to promote negotiations between citizens and armed groups in the Magdalena Medio. Such negotiations were seen as another way the region's residents could become proactive and empowered in their own peace-building process. The PDP did not keep an official count of how many negotiations took place but says they helped avoid assassinations and displacement that would have otherwise occurred. As noted by the PDP's most recent assessment report, "It can be said that throughout the process [of the humanitarian spaces], there were many 'peace negotiations' with the guerrillas, the paramilitaries, and the security forces that, depending on the circumstances, could take aggressive actions against the local population. In the majority of cases, these negotiations had no protagonist, nor did local or national media know about them. Nevertheless, aggressions were avoided, many lives at risk were defended, and many displacements were avoided" (PNUD 2008, 44).

One of the most notable of these citizen-led negotiations took place in a humanitarian space in Bolívar Province in the village of Micoahumado. According to the PDP, the town entered into negotiations in December 2002 after the ELN and the AUC virtually blockaded it: they planted land mines, blocked roads, cut water services, and stopped all food and medicine from entering the village. Sometime after New Year's Day 2003, Micoahumado residents successfully lobbied the ELN to remove the mines from their territory. Such successes were emblematic of one of the ultimate aims of the humanitarian spaces, said Duque: to "empower the community to monitor the conflict themselves."

To summarize, theologically the PDP emphasized a proactive approach to peace building, which helped bring about a certain degree of positive change in the Magdalena Medio. Still, there were limits to what the PDP managed to accomplish. According to Duque, "There have been regional achievements, but the fundamental problem of the conflict is still there. The national problems are still there."

Indeed, the spaces did little to reverse the broader trends of the conflict in the Magdalena Medio. During the years in which the humanitarian spaces were active—2002 to the present—they failed to significantly reduce displacement rates in their respective municipalities. Bermudez's forced abandonment of his home in the Opón was just one of many cases in which the symbolic power of the humanitarian spaces was not enough to protect those who lived in the territory.

It is a different story for homicide rates. Based on the data made available by Colombia's forensic institute, homicide rates in the municipalities that hosted humanitarian spaces did in fact drop over time. The decrease is particularly evident in Barrancabermeja, which registered a rate of 243 killings per 100,000 people in 2000, two years before the PDP's Peace Laboratory began implementing the humanitarian spaces. Barrancabermeja's murder rate steadily decreased over the decade, registering 34 murders per 100,000 inhabitants in 2011, on par with Colombia's national average.

However, it is difficult to quantify how much of the reduction in violence was because of programs like the PDP and how much of it has to do with broader forces. Even if murders were going down, the number of disappearances was going up, according to the head of the PDP's conflict observatory. The other question is whether violence decreased because the paramilitaries cleared the way for the military to enter the territory, meaning that the relative peace that now exists in the Magdalena Medio was actually the result of the AUC's campaign of terror.

The PDP's spiritual dimension arguably helped in its attempts to influence the Magdalena Medio in another way: its very strong association with the Church gave the program some degree of political shielding. While the armed groups in Colombia's conflict have proved willing to target Church workers in the past, the killings have provoked widespread condemnation. Armed groups who target the Church risk damaging their political image. As a result, the Church enjoys some protection and immunity in Colombia's conflict. The PDP's support from international organizations like the EU is also believed to have "served as a kind of a political shield. . . . It has, to some extent, offered some protection to [the PDP's] activities and organizations" (Barreto Henriques 2007, 35).

But this "political shield" only went so far. By the PDP's count, thirty-nine community organizers linked to the PDP have been killed since 1995 (twenty-three were directly involved in PDP-supported initiatives; seventeen were indirectly linked). One victim, Alma Rosa Jaramillo (killed in June 2001 in Morales, Bolívar), was dismembered and could only be identified by birthmarks on her body, a reminder of the savagery that the AUC was willing to use against those they identified as "subversives." Some killings were a reminder that the status and trust that the Jesuits had built up in the Magdalena Medio were not enough to protect the PDP's associates from the armed groups.

Of course, it was never really within the PDP's capacity to change the wider dynamics of the conflict. Peace building is fundamentally difficult to measure in quantitative terms, so it is hard to say how much violence and displacement was avoided in the Magdalena Medio thanks to the PDP's work. What does seem clear is that the PDP allowed many communities to become empowered and openly denounce the violence they were living through and to participate in collective actions even when they were living under siege.

Economic Impact

> Individual initiative alone and the mere free play of competition could never assure successful development. One must avoid the risk of increasing still more the wealth of the rich and the dominion of the strong, whilst leaving the poor in their misery and adding to the servitude of the oppressed.
> —Pope Paul VI, "On the Development of Peoples," 1967

The Merquemos Juntos office is in a two-story building constructed with donations the PDP procured from the French Catholic Church and the Japanese embassy. The co-op's founder, a sixty-eight-year-old matriarch, had recently been diagnosed with diabetes, and the day-to-day running of the organization was left to the treasurer, Lucía García, a perky woman with freckled cheeks. Tapping on a glass display case, she pointed out plastic bags of locally produced yogurt—raspberry and passion fruit flavor—that the Merquemos Juntos store was now selling, part of a new PDP project supporting local dairy farmers. "We want the things that people eat to have been made here," she explained. Her words echo Father González's description of the PDP's mission when it comes to economic projects: "The idea is that what gets produced in the region stays in the region."

Merquemos Juntos had come a long way from its beginnings in the early 1990s, when a group of women who attended the same church in a working-class Barrancabermeja neighborhood decided to start pooling their money to buy groceries in bulk. They took turns waking up at three o'clock in the morning and heading to the Plaza Torcoroma market, where they bought bags of rice and soup bones straight from the suppliers. Members of the co-op paid 200 pesos a week, and those with refrigerators agreed to store food for those without.

The group first came into contact with the PDP through their neighborhood church. In one of their first meetings, when they were talking about what the co-op needed to grow, a PDP employee told them, "What you women already have is balls." Their neighborhood was ELN territory, where Lidia said it was common to see nine-year-old boys manning roadblocks. The Merquemos Juntos co-op would be robbed four times by the ELN over the years, for refusing to pay extortion fees. On one occasion the guerrillas drilled a hole through the roof and made off with a month's worth of food supplies and an armload of cash.

"For us, the PDP has been like the hand that pulls you up and teaches you how to walk," Lidia said. The PDP gave the organization 20 million pesos (about US$11,000) in 1998, the first of several donations extending over the next fourteen years that helped Merquemos Juntos grow steadily. It is now a multipronged project: a grocery co-op, a microfinance company, a school supply store, and a restaurant that sells inexpensive meals for displaced families. From eleven women in 1992, it now includes thirty-three families. By Lidia's estimates, they have supported some 160 businesses with their microloans and given loans to approximately 1,100 people. The loans helped families pave the dirt floors of their houses and start up local businesses like photocopying and printing shops.

Merquemos Juntos is one of hundreds of economic projects supported and helped to expand significantly by the PDP. They ranged from urban initiatives like Merquemos Juntos to farming co-ops in the countryside. PDP support did not always consist of direct donations to specific projects. It helped farming co-ops get their papers and land titles in order, offered accounting and administration workshops, and deployed agronomists to help farmers take soil samples and teach more efficient production techniques.

Rather than count the number of projects that have become self-sustaining, the PDP focuses on measuring their overall economic impact in the region.[8] In their most recent impact assessment, released in 2008, it estimated that its productive projects brought some $US19.3 million to the Magdalena Medio's economy that year and created 13,582 jobs. PDP's 1995 diagnostic survey of the Magdalena Medio provides some perspective: it estimated the total worth of the peasant economy in the region at $US142 million (PNUD 2008, 140). PDP also keeps an updated account of the amount of land that because of its productive projects ends up being used by small (less than twenty hectares) farms. As of 2010, this included 6,050 hectares of African palm, 5,720 of cacao, 495 of fruit, and 1,629 of forest. The focus on supporting small farms (*fincas campesinas*) is meant to slowly but steadily transform the Magdalena Medio's economy from one of coca bushes and vast palm oil plantations to one in which small-scale growers and local entrepreneurs stand a better chance of making a good living. Given the degree of unequal land distribution in the region, the PDP sees supporting small farmers as crucial. A study conducted in 1999 in select municipalities, showed that 54 percent of the productive land was in the hands of less than 5 percent of all registered landowners—farms that were on average larger than two hundred hectares (PNUD 2008, 141).

Promoting sustainable development was a top priority of the PDP from the very beginning. The recommendations of the program's first survey, released in May 1996, called for development that supported local economic structures. Camargo said this focus has caused some debate: "In some ways the Church looks at the PDP as something funny—it's not the Church's job to get involved in farming projects."

But the Jesuits' interest in using economic projects to fight poverty did not emerge from a vacuum. PDP's founder, Father De Roux, studied at the London School of Economics and was long interested in what the Jesuits could do in terms of sustainable development. He saw Jesuit theologians like Bernard Lonergan—and the Society's history of running *reducciones* (self-sustaining, sometimes even profitable, agricultural microeconomies in southern South America during the seventeenth and eighteenth centuries)—as examples of the Jesuits' long history of involvement with economic projects. The Jesuits oversaw similar initiatives in Colombia's Eastern Plains during the colonial era. In De Roux's view, such historical examples put the Jesuits' economic work in the twentieth century in perspective. During the 1980s, in conjunction with CINEP, De Roux had sought to build up urban co-ops and microfinance projects in Bogotá. This work would later form a preamble for the sustainable development projects run under the PDP.

The focus on achieving sustainable development feeds into the PDP's larger theological approach: achieving a more just economic system as a way of rebuilding the dignity of an entire region. This concept of dignity—owed to every human life—is strongly rooted in Christian theology and is frequently cited as a core PDP aim. Of the nine core values identified by PDP, respect for dignity is second, just after the organization's oft-repeated slogan "*Primero la vida*" (First, life) (PNUD 2008, 38). When discussing the primary objective of the PDP, Father De Roux (1999, 18) has cited the attainment of "the dignified life" above all else. For him, dignity is such a nondebatable, inherent human value that it practically exists apart from concepts like development.

> The equal dignity of all human beings is given as an absolute value for each person, always. Dignity does not depend on society, and it is not granted by the state, nor any national or global institution, religious or secular. Dignity may be had simply by being human, and it cannot be violated by any institution. . . . The dignity of people does not increase because of a country's economic growth, nor because of studies that people do, nor because they are residents of [a country that is] an international power, nor is it lessened by being a resident of a poor country. Dignity cannot be developed. What can be developed are the conditions for every person to protect and freely express their own dignity. (Quoted in PNUD 2008, 209)

As the above passage shows, much of PDP analysis directly parallels modern conceptions of human rights. But the PDP resists defining itself as solely a human rights organization. And De Roux remains emphatic that the program's core goals are intrinsically linked to rebuilding the region's dignity.

But even as the PDP maintains that it can use economic projects to rebuild the dignity of the Magdalena Medio, it embraces the neoliberal ideas that some argue are responsible for perpetuating poverty in the first place. "The PDP represents a break away from the idea that capitalism is something perverse," said González. In that sense, he added, the PDP does not fall in line with the more radical interpretations of liberation theology, which see the free market as inherently problematic. If the PDP truly embraced liberation theology, "then we wouldn't have accepted money from the World Bank and Ecopetrol." Even as one of the core ideas of liberation theology—its attention to the "preferential option for the poor"—holds obvious sway in the PDP, nothing in the organization's philosophy demands that capitalism be dismantled completely. González said this approach caused significant internal debates among the Jesuits, particularly between the Society's more radical wing and those who were more centrist.[9]

The PDP's economic projects had microlevel impact, creating dozens of projects that otherwise would not have existed, and allowing preexisting projects like Merquemos Juntos to expand significantly. These projects aimed to transform the Magdalena Medio's economy into one more supportive of the urban and rural poor. But there was also a spiritual bent: to rebuild the dignity of the region via more sustainable development. As De Roux wrote, the choice is between a concept of development as "a sustainable expansion of the possibilities of human dignity in a territory, or understanding development as the use of a territory to expand the profits of large-scale national and international companies" (quoted in PNUD 2008, 210).

By emphasizing its spiritual bent, the PDP transcended being just another NGO promoting economic projects. The goal was not merely to create a certain number of campesino-friendly farming initiatives; rather, it was to allow the region to reclaim dignity. By identifying the rebuilding of dignity as one of its core values, the PDP found a way to sidestep political objections to the program. This meant it could accept money from the World Bank, because its core principles technically had nothing to do with promoting and acting on a left-leaning agenda. This fed into the PDP's fundamentally practical approach—its focus on doing what works rather than adhering to a particular political ideology. Hence the Jesuits could criticize the downsides of globalization and the actions of large-scale national and multinational companies but at the same time do what needed to be done in order to ensure that the PDP would work. Making the focus the building of the region's dignity through economic development arguably allowed the PDP to work within capitalism even as some factions of the Jesuits remained very critical of it. In some ways, the Jesuits' spiritual approach allowed them to transcend the political.

Conclusion

> For unless the Christian message of love and justice shows its effectiveness through action in the cause of justice in the world, it will only with difficulty gain credibility with the people of our times.
>
> —Synod of Bishops, "Justice in the World," 1971

If the Jesuits had not already built decades of trust in the Magdalena Medio, it would have been difficult for the PDP to earn the status and credibility that it currently enjoys. In many ways, no one else but the Jesuits could have initiated a program like the PDP in the region: they already had a relationship with many community organizations there, and various popular movements already existed and were active before the PDP was founded in 1995. This special relationship between the Jesuits and the Magdalena Medio led CINEP director Luis Guillermo Guerrero to describe the PDP's creation as "a perfect example of a social movement happening from the inside out, not the outside in."

In some ways the very survival of the PDP was a success in itself. The Magdalena Medio is one of Colombia's most complex conflict zones. The region has long served as the stage for bloody confrontations, from the civil war of the midcentury to the current low-intensity conflict. It is a region where violence has always been a favored tool for bringing about political and social change. Residents in the Magdalena Medio have had to resort to violence in order to fight for their basic rights, while armed groups have used violence in order to keep themselves in power. The PDP is an attempt to create an alternative to the use of violence, in order to confront more effectively the root causes of the region's social problems.

The project never defined "success" as having a specific quantitative impact on the Colombian conflict; the focus was on planting the seeds that would bring about long-term change in the region. While homicides have dropped in the region, this cannot be solely attributed to the PDP's work, for there are too many other forces at play that could have contributed to this decrease. Arguably, the real merit of the PDP was its theological approach—affirming the importance of peace, tolerance, and dignity. Such an approach helped the PDP have a positive impact on the Magdalena Medio because, to a certain extent, it allowed the project to transcend the conflict. The PDP was able to call attention to these core values in a region consumed by violence; in that sense, it can be said to have fulfilled its mission.

The PDP boosted the status and the influence of the Jesuits in Colombia. The program and its former director Father De Roux have won numerous international peace prizes (recently, De Roux received the Chirac Foundation Prize, the most prestigious award in France, for conflict prevention). The Jesuit analysis institute CINEP, meanwhile, remains hugely influential and continues to release investigative reports on the conflict. One of CINEP's head researchers, Fr. Javier Giraldo, remains one of the most outspoken critics of collusion between the Colombian state and the paramilitaries.

Another sign of the PDP's impact is that one of its signature projects, the Peace Laboratory, has been replicated widely across Colombia, from the Eastern Plains to the Caribbean coast. There are currently nineteen Peace Laboratories, many of them headed by clergy. They work similarly to the PDP, supporting economic projects alongside community organizing initiatives. According to the PDP subdirector, Colombian government institutions like the Ministry of Agriculture have also approached the PDP, asking about its experience in running small-scale economic projects and expressing interest in expanding such programs.

Evidence cited in this study suggests that the Jesuit response in the Magdalena Medio—as represented by the creation of the Peace and Development Program—has by and large been positively received on the ground and is having some positive impact. Within the Society, few seemed to think that the program represented a radical break from the Jesuits' past response to problems of poverty and violence. The Jesuits argue that, fundamentally, their aim is to try to address the deep-rooted causes of the Colombian conflict rather than provide short-term aid. But the findings from this study also highlight the limits to what the Church can reasonably expect to achieve. It is no substitute for the state when it comes to consolidating development and peace.

But the fact that the PDP has brought some limited gains to the Magdalena Medio has important implications for how the Church—both inside and outside Colombia—should respond to violence. Even while Christian ideals were central to the formulation of the PDP's main goals, the program is, at its core, concerned with practical action. It is a mixture of nonprofit, community organization and Church initiative, but it is more interested in what works rather than adherence to a specific political or religious ideology. For policy makers and other faith-based groups looking for effective responses to contemporary violence in Latin America, the work of the Jesuits in Colombia's Magdalena Medio should prove a useful case study.

Notes

1. It was originally called the Center for Social Research and Action (CIAS).

2. De Roux, a priest with a PhD in economics, was CINEP's director from 1987 to 1994. Personal contact with the region in his formative years seems to have informed his shaping of the Magdalena Medio project.

3. López was the quintessential social activist priest, heavily involved in leftist political activism throughout his career, even founding the Camilo Torres School in Barrancabermeja in the 1970s. In an anecdote illustrative of the Jesuits' hands-on approach in the region, Rangel remembers Rosero "physically putting himself in the middle" of violent protesters and the police in order to prevent angry demonstrations from escalating.

4. Observatorio de Paz Integral, "La población civil y el conflicto armado en el Magdalena Medio, 1996–2004," 2005 presentation. Available at www.opi .org.co/pdfs/Informe_Poblacion_conflicto_MM_1996_2004.pdf.

5. Observatorio de Paz Integral, "Boletín especial: Informe de Coyuntura: Ciénaga del Opón," 2005. Copy in author's possession.

6. See Programa Desarrollo y Paz del Magdalena Medio, *Plan de desarrollo e intervención para el Corregimiento de Ciénaga del Opón*, n.d. Available at www .etpbarranca.org/cienagadelopon/Archivos/PlanDeDesarrollo.pdf.

7. The PDP remains directly involved with seven of these humanitarian spaces, although it no longer has personnel in the other six, part of a series of program cutbacks.

8. Not all projects were designed to become self-sustaining over time; some were only intended to achieve certain results within a six-month timeframe.

9. As to which side of the debate ended up winning, according to González, "Most of those who really believed in radical interpretations of liberal theology ended up leaving [the Society]."

References

Banco de Datos de Derechos Humanos y Violencia Política. 2001. *Deuda con la humanidad, paramilitarismo de Estado en Colombia, 1988–2003*. Bogotá: Centro de Investigación y Educación Popular.

Barreto Henriques, Miguel. 2007. "Peace Laboratory of Magdalena Medio: 'A Peace Laboratory'?" Centro de Recursos para el Análisis de Conflictos, Bogotá.

De Roux, Francisco José. 1999. "El Magdalena Medio en el centro del conflicto y de la esperanza." *Controversia* 174: 14–37.

Hataya, Noriko. 2009. "Community-Based Local Development and the Peace Initiative of the PDPMM in Colombia: Resource Mobilization under Extreme Conditions." In *Protest and Social Movements in the Developing World*, edited by Shinichi Shigetomi and Kumiko Makino, 19–50. Northampton, MA: Edward Elgar.

Isacson, Adam. 2001. "'The New Masters of Barranca': A Report from CIP's Trip to Barrancabermeja, Colombia, March 6–8." Center for International Policy, Washington, DC. Available at www.ciponline.org/images/uploads/publications/0401barr.pdf.

Kirk, Robin. 2003. *More Terrible than Death: Massacres, Drugs, and America's War in Colombia*. New York: Public Affairs.

Loingsigh, Gearóid. 2010. "In the Midst of Deceit: The Magdalena Medio and the World Bank." *Cepa* 2, no. 11. Accessed at www.pasc.ca/fr/node/2993.

Molano, Alfredo. 2010. *En medio del Magdalena Medio*. Bogotá: Centro de Investigación y Educación Popular.

Observatorio del Programa Presidencial de Derechos Humanos y Derecho Internacional Humanitario. 2001. *Panorama actual de Barrancabermeja*. Bogotá: Vicepresidencia de la República de Colombia.

Programa de la Naciones Unidas para el Desarrollo (PNUD). 2008. *Rutas y vivencias de nuestra gente: Sistematizacion de experiencias en los procesos de los pobladores y pobladoras del Magdalena Medio*. Bogotá: Pro-Offset Editorial.

CHAPTER 10

FROM PREACHING TO LISTENING

Extractive Industries, Communities, and the Church in Rural Peru

JAVIER ARELLANO-YANGUAS

This chapter examines the involvement of sectors of the Catholic Church in some of the recent emblematic conflicts in Peru over the expansion of extractive industries.[1] The multiplication of such conflicts is currently significant in Peruvian politics, and political actors, ranging from government ministers to corporate managers, have openly accused the Church of instigating them.[2] This chapter also seeks to understand the transformation of the institutional presence of the Church in such settings. For most observers, the Church's recent role in extraction-related conflicts matches neither what they anticipated nor the Church's actions in other historical moments. Below, I attempt to account for that change.

I start by differentiating four types of Church involvement in these conflicts: avoidance, mediation, leadership, and accompaniment. Next I describe the variety of Church responses to relatively similar situations, and also the importance of "accompaniment" as a new form of presence in which the clergy gives prominence to local communities' criteria and supports them. The third section presents two emblematic conflicts in the north of Peru and what scholarly literature says about Church

involvement in this type of popular mobilization. It concludes that neither pure ideological approaches nor strategic calculus satisfactorily explains the Church's role in those conflicts. The final three sections use
data collected from actors directly involved in the conflicts to explain
what has shaped the distinctive role of the Church as "accompanying"
local populations in their struggles.

My analysis shows a nuanced interplay between religious and political processes in which the Church's previous involvement in local networks is the most influential factor, reinforced by a spirituality that
recognizes the primacy of the initiatives of local communities. "Social interpreters," local leaders who have close ties with bishops, priests, and
nuns, are found to be crucial to shaping the Church's understanding of
social processes and its subsequent involvement in them. They explain the
local context and the people's vision in ways that official representatives
of the Church can understand. Finally, the Church does not adopt a
purely passive approach. The incorporation of environmental and human
rights discourses into a religious framework provides legitimacy for
popular mobilizations and amplifies the social space of the Church at the
local level.

I draw on two different phases of field research. Between 2007 and
2009, I interviewed the protagonists of social conflicts in five Peruvian
mining regions (Ancash, Cajamarca, Cusco, Moquegua, and Pasco). I also
spoke with parish priests in those areas, because they are a good source of
local information. In the second phase, 2010–12, I focused on the involvement of the Church in two key conflicts: Majaz and Bagua. The
inquiry benefited from my participation in a workshop on what led to the
terrible clash in Bagua and its aftermath that was held in Santa María
de Nieva (territory of the Awajun people) in November 2010 and included pastoral agents and indigenous leaders. In 2012 I interviewed key
religious figures who played a direct role in the two conflicts analyzed.[3]
My analysis focuses primarily on the presence and behavior of local
groups, organizations, and people who are publicly and officially recognized as part of the Catholic Church. These local manifestations of the
Church may include the diocesan bishop, parishes, local clergy, religious
congregations, catechists, and other pastoral agents and local Catholic
nongovernmental organizations (NGOs). They act at the local level

and are in close contact with local communities. At some points during the analysis, I differentiate them from the centralized ecclesial institutions and from the behavior of some prominent figures in the Catholic hierarchy in the country. Finally, "accompaniment" emerges in the analysis as the key concept; it is a new and distinctive form of church involvement in social struggles. In the interviews and in their speeches in meetings and workshops, the priests and nuns used the word to denote a pastoral strategy in which the Church gives prominence to grassroots groups: they are not only the target of the Church mission but also the main actors in that mission. This concept is deeply rooted in Christian spirituality, and the interviews suggest it can be traced to two sources: liberation theology, mainly its argument for God's predilection for the poor; and Ignatian spirituality.[4] The Spiritual Exercises of St. Ignatius of Loyola assume a God acting permanently in the world and in history. St. Ignatius wrote that directors of the Exercises must not transmit their ideas, but rather help participants discover the presence of God in their own lives.[5] This approach was neglected for most of the nineteenth and twentieth centuries, when the Spiritual Exercises were preached in endless sermons and the participants were forced to listen. Following the reforms of Vatican II, there was a strong movement toward the recovery of the original interpretation of the Spiritual Exercises. In that context, spiritual accompaniment replaced spiritual direction to highlight the centrality of the personal experience.

Types of Church Involvement in Conflicts Opposing Extraction

This analysis focuses on the participation of the Church in conflicts that either oppose the expansion of extractive industries or aim to radically modify the conditions of extraction to preserve rural livelihoods and local control over key assets such as water and land (Bebbington and Bury 2009). There are other types of conflicts related to extractive industries, but these are the most politically relevant. With a state eager to promote investment in the extractive sector, these conflicts have the potential to challenge government policies and disrupt official plans (Arellano-Yanguas 2011, 2012).

Four types of Church involvement can be distinguished. Table 10.1 presents them as a function of the combination of two variables: (a) the Church's attitude toward the conflicts and (b) the main leaders determining the local strategy. Of course, the boundary between types is fuzzy, in at least three ways. First, in some conflicts different groups within the local Church assume diverse attitudes. Second, frequently the approach of the Church does not conform to one pure type. For example, the Church can combine mediation with accompaniment or even with leadership. And third, the Church position can change over time to adapt to the circumstances of conflicts. For example, it can pass from being a mediator to a defender of local demands against companies. Despite these limitations, the typology is an analytical tool that helps identify distinctive features of the diversity of Church attitudes toward conflicts.

In the first two types, avoidance and mediation, the local Church tries not to be dragged into the conflict. The tendency to avoid involvement frequently reflects a conservative political stance that correlates with a local Church weakly connected to the mobilized population. The official discourse is that the Church should not be involved in politics, an attitude widely understood as implicit support of the government's plans and of corporate interests. This approach is very rare at the local level; however, it has some high-ranking representatives in Peru, such as the archbishop of Lima, Cardinal Juan Luis Cipriani, and other bishops who use the antipolitics argument to discredit active support for popular demands among other Church members.

Table 10.1. Types of Church Involvement in Conflicts Opposing Extractive Industries

			Main Actors Defining Local Strategy	
			Church	Local groups
Church Attitude toward the Conflict		Detached from the conflict	*Avoidance*	*Mediation*
		Active support of local demands	*Leadership*	*Accompaniment*

The role of mediator between opponents to extraction on one side and the government and companies on the other is more common at the local level. In these cases, Church leaders do not actively support the mobilizations, usually as a result of the combination of two factors: ideological differences with the leaders of the mobilization and lack of local consensus on whether investment in mining or hydrocarbons can benefit the local economy. However, unlike the first type, the Church remains connected to the local population, is sensitive to its demands, and frequently takes on the mediator role in response to its requests. Mediation by the Church is usually a last resort, occurring when the conflict is stalemated. Assumption of the mediator role tends to reinforce the Church's public legitimacy and usually does not demand that it discard its neutral stance. Such mediation can help alleviate the most violent expressions of conflict but rarely solves the problems at their roots. The Church took this role in the disputes over the expansion of the open pit in Cerro de Pasco (Pasco) by Volcan Mining Company.[6] More recently, in the case of Conga (Cajamarca), the government appointed a bishop and a well-known priest from outside Cajamarca as mediators,[7] and the local bishop approved their participation.[8]

In the remaining two types of involvement, the Church supports local opposition to the expansion of extractive industries but in significantly different ways. It can assume a leadership role in the conflict, the work of Marco Arana in Cajamarca being the most salient example. Arana, a former diocesan priest and environmental activist, has monitored the activities of the Yanacocha gold and copper mining company for more than a decade and has been highly influential in coordinating local opposition to its behavior.[9] For many years, his work inspired both diocesan priests and religious congregations, such as the Franciscans and the Carmelite Sisters, to take a public stance against Yanacocha's plans for expansion, including active opposition to the controversial Conga project.[10] Despite Arana's prominence, the Church does not often take on this leading role.

In most conflicts over extraction, the Church assumes the more subordinate role of accompanying the local struggle. The crucial point here is the novelty of this approach. The prevalence of accompaniment reveals a deep transformation in the presence of the Church in rural settings. It

moves from preaching to listening, from following a predetermined blueprint to discovering new dimensions of its mission. The next sections
present some cases of these types of involvement and analyze the internal
processes shaping the Church's attitude. They also shed light on the nov-
elties emerging in the relationship between religions and contentious political processes in contemporary Latin America.

Emblematic Conflicts in the North and Academic Explanations of Church Involvement in Popular Mobilizations

Two conflicts in neighboring areas in the north of Peru—Majaz and
Bagua—stand out in recent Peruvian history. Majaz is a wholly owned
subsidiary of the British company Monterrico Metals PLC. Monterrico's
main asset is the Rio Blanco Project, located in Henry's Hill in the mountains of Piura, close to the department of Cajamarca and the border with
Ecuador.[11] The project site is in territory belonging to the peasant communities of Segunda y Cajas and Yanta. The company planned to construct an open pit copper mine that would be among the twenty biggest
mines in the world[12] and a bridgehead for the establishment of a mining
district exploiting other important mineral deposits nearby. The location
of this project in an important watershed, its influence on a number of
districts in two different departments, its proximity to the Tabaconas-
Namballe Natural National Sanctuary, and its potential to open the region to new mining investments made the proposal highly contentious
from its inception (Bebbington 2007).

The first skirmishes broke out in 2003 during the exploration stage.
The immediately previous experience of successful popular opposition
to a gold mine in the neighboring town of Tambogrande facilitated the
formation of environmental defense groups, the Frentes de Defensa del
Medio Ambiente (Defense Fronts of the Environment) in the provinces
of Ayabaca and Huancabamba. Initially the *rondas campesinas*,[13] members of environmental organizations, mayors, and councilors, made up
those fronts. Different views about the real possibilities for peaceful co-
existence between mining and agriculture were at the core of the conflict.
In 2004 hostilities escalated. Police forces stopped a popular march to the
projected mine site, killing a peasant. Twenty-three leaders were arrested.
Supporters and opponents of the project engaged in heated, sometimes

violent, confrontations. The *rondas campesinas* actively confronted company workers, while police, in collusion with the company, harassed local leaders of the opposition.

In this contentious environment, the bishops of Piura, Jaén, and Chulucanas sided with the peasant communities and called for the suspension of mining activities in their dioceses because of feared negative environmental and social impacts (Revesz 2009, 49–60). As had occurred in Tambogrande, the Church's support of the antimining mobilization added to its legitimacy (Troeltsch 1931, 331–43). The institutional reputation of the Catholic Church helped win the sympathy of a wider segment of the regional and national population. At the same time, Church support opened opportunities for coordination with several national and international organizations, reinforcing the technical ability and negotiation leverage of the opponents (Bebbington et al. 2008; Paredes 2008).

Obviously, the mining companies and the government disliked the Church's position. The acting vicar of Jaén and director of Radio Marañón, Fr. Francisco Muguiro, S.J., was the target of corporate criticism. A national TV channel and a regional newspaper accused him of associating with terrorist groups. Since then, the conflict between the company and the communities has continued, and the company's plans for exploiting the mineral deposit are blocked. Throughout the process, personnel of the vicariate of Jaén,[14] officially entrusted to the Jesuits, and some of their organizations (e.g., the Pastoral Office for the Environment, Radio Marañón) have supported the communities in their demands and court cases.[15]

The tragic clash in Bagua on June 5, 2009, epitomizes the second conflict. The riot police's attempt to end a roadblock set up by Awajun and Wampis indigenous people led to a toll of twenty-four policemen and ten civilians dead and more than 150 injured. The introduction of a series of laws facilitating investment in extractive activities in the Amazon (oil, gas, mining, and logging) triggered the conflict. The new legislation eased the market for land purchases, eroding indigenous people's power to control their own territory and ignoring commitments to international treaties on the protection of indigenous people.

The Awajun and Wampis territory is within the domain of the vicariate of Jaén, the same ecclesial jurisdiction as some of the communities that could be affected by Majaz. However, the presence of the Catholic

Church in these territories is quite different. The Church has historically exercised a profound influence in the communities around Majaz, whereas its presence among the Awajun and Wampis goes back only seventy years and is weaker.[16] Nevertheless, the Church has had an important influence on the indigenous population through the education system, the formation of local leaders, and the support of indigenous organizations (see below).

In the aftermath of June 5, observers and some members of a special commission[17] reviewing the events named the local Church among those responsible for the conflict. The official report on the clash compares the local Church's supposed confrontational approach with its behavior in other regions of the country (Comisión Especial de Investigación 2009, 82). These charges are contradicted by interviews with different people in the region who said the Church did not have a direct influence on the conflict's outbreak.[18] Later, during the roadblock, the vicariate provided the protesters with food and water on humanitarian grounds. Moreover, the bishop mediated between the protesters and the army to achieve a peaceful and orderly withdrawal. Only after the clash did the Church assume a higher profile, giving shelter to hundreds of Awajun and Wampis people, taking care of those wounded during the clash, providing legal assistance to those slated for prosecution, and speaking out against the criminalization of the indigenous organizations by authorities. This involvement in favor of the indigenous population reinforced the vicariate's public image as supportive of local communities mobilizing against corporate plans.

Given the diverse positions of the Peruvian Catholic Church in social conflicts across the country,[19] it is instructive to examine the reasons and mechanisms that determined the participation of the local Church in these two conflicts. Previous academic studies have highlighted three factors to explain the commitment of sectors of the Catholic Church to the cause of marginalized groups. First, some authors stress either the agency of bishops (Levine and Mainwaring 1989), priests, sisters, and lay workers (Adriance 1991) or of progressive theologians and Catholic intellectuals (Peña 1994). They agree that individuals make a difference in the stance the Church takes at the local level. The second approach emphasizes the role of ideas, specifically, those of liberation theology and the evolution of Catholic doctrine after the Second Vatican Council (Holden and Jacobson 2009). This approach analyzes how the emergence of a progressive interpretation of Catholic doctrine has led the Church to defend the poor and their interests. Third, some scholars highlight the importance of the Church's strategic behavior (Trejo 2009). According to them, the Church's support of popular movements in rural settings is a retention strategy to cope with the growing competition of Protestantism.

The first two types of explanation underscore the influence of factors internal to the Church, while the third emphasizes the context in which the Church operates. Taken separately, none of the factors satisfactorily explain the different types and degrees of Church involvement. On the one hand, the focus on the agency of key persons and their adherence to progressive interpretations of Catholic doctrine tends to assume a top-down approach that downplays the agency of the local population and its interpretation of the context. Paradoxically, some advocates of the role played by the progressive wing of the Church (Holden and Jacobson 2007, 2009) and corporate defenders coincide on this point, because both attribute to the clergy and other conventional religious figures responsibility for mobilizing the people. Advocates of the progressive Church position see clergy as empowering the poor; corporate defenders see manipulation of the local population in the clergy's actions. On the other hand, the explanation that the Church's behavior is purely strategic fails to account for the obvious plurality of the Catholic Church within a given country and the diversity of its actions in similar contexts (Romero 2009). My own analysis of the local Church's participation in these two conflicts reveals that internal factors and context interact in a quite distinctive way.

Institutional Embeddedness or Personal Prominence

The analysis of Church involvement in social conflicts has frequently focused on the role of bishops, priests, and nuns. This approach tends to overstate the importance of personal leadership and to simplify local politics. The need of governments, corporations, and mass media to make local processes readable explains this biased perspective (Scott 1998). In looking at conflicts, they search for clearly recognizable actors to whom they can attribute responsibility. Religious figures are the most visible to external observers who have a prejudiced view of local people's ability to act independently. The dynamics surrounding the conflict in Majaz contradict this perspective.

Since the early stages of the Majaz conflict, Fr. Francisco Muguiro has been a central figure. Corporate managers and some of the national media blamed him for local resistance to the operation. Moreover, the proliferation of new mining projects in the same region and the local refusal to provide the social license to operate exacerbated corporate animosity against Muguiro.[20] Some companies were so convinced of Muguiro's power that they asked him to approve their operations and to mediate their interactions with the peasant communities. Muguiro consistently answered that he had neither the power nor the will to determine what the communities should do. According to Muguiro, the role of the vicariate was limited to accompanying the local peasant communities in their decisions and responding to their demands. Was he posturing to hide his real power and shun responsibility? This does not seem to be the case. The sequence of events leading to the involvement of the Church confirms the subordinate role the vicariate played in the development of the conflict.

In 2003 the Church did not participate in the Frentes de Defensa del Medio Ambiente against the presence of Monterrico Metals in the communities of Segunda y Cajas and Yanta. The *rondas campesinas*, environmental organizations, and a group of municipal authorities were the main actors of the front. Only in 2004, after the first serious clash with the police and the prosecution of local leaders, did the Church become involved. What prompted this involvement? In the context of strong popular Catholicism, the outbreak of a violent conflict demands the attention of the Church, which usually mediates to reduce the tension. However, to explain the subsequent open support by the Church for local demands, it is also necessary to consider the close connection between the catechist movement and the *rondas campesinas* in the region. The physical impossibility of the missionaries individually serving all rural communities and the shortage of native clergy led to the promotion of catechists as intermediaries between the missionaries and the communities.[21] For more than forty years, the vicariate of Jaén trained thousands of catechists. They became not only pastoral agents but also true social leaders in their communities. In the early 1980s, the *rondas campesinas* spread from their birthplace of Chota to other communities in Cajamarca and the neighboring department of Piura (fig. 10.1). With this expansion, the *rondas* took root in several settlements in the provinces of Jaén and San Ignacio, both within the territory of the vicariate of Jaén and close to the Majaz project. They also proliferated in other provinces of Cajamarca, including Celendín, where the Conga project is based. In those places, catechists were frequently elected leaders of the newly formed *rondas*. Some of the catechists believed that "the rondas carried out the Christian ideal in a melding of religion and politics" (Starn 1999, 92).

The fusion of religious and social ideals generated strong ties among the communities and the vicariate's different organizations, such as Radio Marañón, the Pastoral Office for the Environment, and Caritas.[22] This relationship was cemented in the 1980s and 1990s when the collapse of the Peruvian state forced peasant communities to resort to the Church for health services, technical training, information, or microcredit. The catechists exercised their role as intermediaries very effectively, strengthening both the position of the communities and the reach of the Church in the countryside. In turn, they gained legitimacy.

In the early 2000s, when mining companies rushed into the Andean region searching for mineral deposits to exploit, the peasant communities in Cajamarca and Piura, seeking to protect their own livelihoods, opposed their presence more than communities had in other regions. In Majaz, as was the case more recently in Conga, the peasants thought mining was incompatible with their agriculture. Moreover, the negative experience in peasant communities around the nearby Yanacocha mine led them to distrust official promises about the potential benefits of mining. These concerns were more than enough to catalyze local resistance. The peasants did not need the Church to rally in defense of their livelihoods. The *rondas* were key actors in the opposition, because they already had the supracommunity organizational structures needed to mobilize. However, once the conflict broke out, the communities asked for the support of the Church.

The involvement of the Church had two different but equally important meanings. From an internal perspective, given the pervasiveness of religiosity in the rural mind-set, Church backing unified the communities'

Figure 10.1. Map of Piura and Cajamarca, Peru

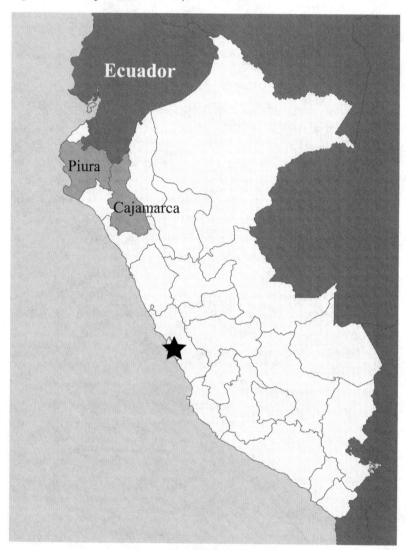

Courtesy of Center for Latin American and Latino Studies.

resistance to companies and official policies. And the presence of the Church legitimized the communities' stance in the eyes of the public, regionally and nationally. Moreover, the Church linked the local struggle to national and transnational activist networks (Theije 2006) and sometimes provided the legal defense and material infrastructure necessary to sustain the mobilization over time.

The Church's positive response to the communities' demands was rooted in a historically close relationship. The role of the catechists within the communities, including their active participation in the *rondas*, was key for the Church in determining its stance. The Church and its organizations were compelled to side with the communities, because the local pastoral agents were already deeply connected with their daily struggles.

The involvement of the Church in Bagua reinforces these patterns. The Church has less direct influence on local dynamics among the Awajun and Wampis people, because only a small proportion are Catholic. In fact, the penetration of Christian missions in the Awajun-Wampis territory is very recent. After several attempts from the seventeenth through nineteenth centuries to establish the Catholic Church failed, Protestant missionaries succeeded in creating a permanent base among the Awajun in 1925. This led to the arrival in 1947 of the Summer Institute of Linguistics (SIL), a North American missionary and bilingual education organization. It was not until 1949 that the Jesuits established the first Catholic mission in Awajun territory (Guallart 1990). In 1950 the Peruvian government divided responsibility for the management of the education and health systems in this indigenous territory between the SIL and the Catholic Church's vicariate of Jaén.[23] Both organizations competed to provide services and gain the loyalty of the different family clans. In a few years, they became the most powerful organizations in the area.

The situation changed dramatically in the 1970s when several events coincided to transform the power relationship between the Awajun-Wampis people and Church organizations. First, the revolutionary government of Velasco Alvarado took on the management of public services, a decision that undermined the power of both the vicariate and the SIL. Second, the increasing concentration of the population around the schools, the incursion of oil companies for exploration, and the arrival of settlers from other parts of the country catalyzed the creation of the first indigenous organization of the region, the Awajun-Wampis Council (CAH), in 1977.[24] Third, younger Jesuits and nuns, influenced by Vatican II reforms, wanted to get rid of institutional structures and promote more horizontal relationships with indigenous peoples and their culture. But their plans did not take into consideration the contextual changes. The newly formed indigenous organization needed to assert its authority against the established powers, and the Church was the obvious target. The CAH increasingly alienated the Church, weakening its influence. In the 1980s, its profile was very low in the region. In that context, the Jesuits decided to work on their traditional ministry: the education of youth. In the only boarding school that remained under their control after the Velasco Alvarado period, they indigenized the pedagogy and the daily organization of the school, cultivated supportive relationships with the communities around them, and introduced the students to the basics of political analysis. In parallel, Fr. Carlos Diharce, another Jesuit, initiated a new educational experience with a group of young Awajun. They went to live together, as a community, in a remote area of the rainforest. The experiment aimed to foster an understanding of the Christian gospel in the context of Awajun religious tradition. The Jesuit was initiated into the world of indigenous religious beliefs and practices, including the ritual consumption of different plants, while the young Awajun people carried out the Spiritual Exercises of St. Ignatius.

Both the school and the spiritual experiment had unexpected results that influenced the dynamics of Awajun-Wampis society and the involvement of the Church in indigenous struggles. Over the years, the Jesuit school educated hundreds of youngsters who went back to their communities to become *apus* (leaders). Most of them were not Catholics and did not convert to Catholicism but established a friendly rapport with the priests and vice versa. By the end of the 1990s, these *apus* and the Jesuits formed a dense network that helped to reverse the previous isolation of the Church. Among the students who participated in the community experience was Santiago Manuin, one of the most notable Awajun-Wampis leaders of the past few decades. From 1991 to 1994, as president of the CAH, Manuin built collaborative relationships with the vicariate and unified the Awajun-Wampis communities to deter the invasion of indigenous territories by the Tupac Amaru Movement (MRTA), the Shining

Path, and the drug cartels. After completing his term, Manuin worked for a Jesuit NGO to achieve official recognition of Awajun-Wampis ancestral territory. In 2003 he took a course on human rights and founded Bikut, an association of Awajun-Wampis leaders for the training of younger leaders. When in 2007 the indigenous population started to mobilize against the policies of Alan García's government and the intrusion into their territories of mining and oil companies (ODECOFROC 2009), Manuin was appointed president of the Defense Front; he was likewise appointed president in 2009 during the roadblocks in Bagua. During the June 5 clash, he was wounded by a bullet in the abdomen while attempting to negotiate with the police the withdrawal of the protesters.[25]

Manuin's involvement and the participation of many other indigenous people who were well known to the priests and nuns determined the position of the Church during the mobilization of 2008 and 2009. Initially, the Church maintained a discreet but supportive role. It was clear that the indigenous organizations seized the opportunity, defined the objectives, and managed all practical arrangements. In May 2009, after weeks of roadblocks, deterioration in health conditions, and dwindling food supplies, the vicariate started to provide food and medical care to the protesters. Sister Mari Carmen Gómez, of the Servants of St. Joseph congregation, decided to stay with the crowd and Radio Marañón broadcast the events, amplifying the reach of the mobilization.[26] As happened in Majaz, the Church moved toward involvement in the conflict not because it organized the mobilization but because its previous involvement bound it to accompany the people.

To this point, the communities have been discussed as relatively unified entities with common goals and opinions. Obviously, that image is distorted. Communities engaged in conflicts over extractive industries frequently face traumatic internal divisions as well as tensions with neighboring settlements that have divergent interests. Often, extractive companies encourage such divisions to weaken opposition. In such situations, how does the Church decide whom to support? I have already mentioned the importance of the catechists, pastoral agents, and alumni. However, their position is not always unanimous. In such cases the vision of "social interpreters" is crucial. Those "interpreters" are recognized local leaders who, beyond their official role as catechists or local authorities, enjoy privileged access to priests and nuns by virtue of friendship or personal links. Most of the priests and nuns do not live permanently in the rural or indigenous communities, and even when they do, they lack the background to fully understand the nuances of local social interactions. Therefore, they rely on people they trust to read the local reality. Through social interpreters, priests and nuns know whom they should follow.[27] Manuin is a clear example of a social interpreter. He has a close relationship with the Jesuits, knows the Church quite well, and has the ability to translate the indigenous mentality into "Western" categories and vice versa. In addition to informal interactions, Manuin is regularly invited to internal meetings of the vicariate to help the Church understand the social and political indigenous context. Of course, Manuin is not the only social interpreter of the Awajun-Wampis reality, but he is an important one.

These examples make clear that accompaniment as a definition of the Church position in conflicts between communities and extractive industries is highly complex, with factors such as personality, shared experiences, and the navigation of cultural differences playing important roles. However, two important questions remain about the distinctive stance of the Church in these conflicts. The first relates to the religious logic behind this loyalty: why does the Church bind itself to following the vision of these communities? The second concerns the religious discourses and practices that the Church uses to support the mobilizations and to justify that support: how does the Church incorporate environmental and human rights concerns into its doctrine?

The Spirituality of Grassroots Agency

Numerous studies conclude that the adherence of priests and other pastoral agents to liberation theology influences the local Church's position on social and political issues (Holden and Jacobson 2009; Norget 1997) and that there is a causal link from ideology to social engagement. Without denying this link, I argue that the interaction between theology and practice is more complex and is mediated by spirituality. Here I understand spirituality as religious doctrines incarnated into personal ideas and beliefs about the relationship between the divine and the immanent world and the consequent values and behavior inspired by these ideas and beliefs. Thus the same doctrine might lead to different spiritualities depending on such factors as personal experiences, context, or belonging to different types of congregations.

Differentiating two dimensions within liberation theology helps to explain the distinctive behaviors of the Church in Majaz and Bagua. The first relates to the content of Jesus's teachings, understood in terms of liberation from unjust economic, political, or social conditions. The second relates to the vision of the poor as the main actors in the historical process, not merely passive beneficiaries of liberation (Gutiérrez 1971). The weight given to each dimension generates different types of spirituality and, therefore, different types of Church involvement in social issues. In theory, both dimensions are complementary; however, they frequently clash in real life. Those who focus on the content of liberation highlight the importance of social and political analysis and design of good strategies. This approach reinforces the priests' position vis-à-vis the communities. It correlates with a prophetic spirituality in which pastoral agents feel the responsibility to lead the people and speak for those without a voice. On the contrary, those who focus on the primacy of the poor's agency refuse to take on leading roles. They develop a spirituality centered on accompanying the people in their own processes and assume a subsidiary role.

Of course, there are infinite intermediate positions between these two extreme characterizations of spiritualities derived from liberation theology. This dual differentiation helps to explain why the Church opted to follow the people and refused to set the agenda in Majaz and Bagua. It also reveals a more nuanced relationship between adherence to liberation theology and different approaches to social involvement. The vicariate of Jaén's participation in Majaz and Bagua illustrates these points.

The vicariate's reputation as an advocate for the rights of indigenous and peasant communities began in the early 1990s. The bishop at the time, José María Izuzquiza, a Spanish Jesuit, was not a progressive cleric. In fact, in the previous decade he had confronted a group of young Jesuits responsible for training seminarians in the vicariate because he thought them too sympathetic to liberation theology. Nevertheless, Izuzquiza himself was very close to the peasant communities. For decades he had been responsible for training catechists and had traveled extensively on horseback from village to village to visit them. He knew the suffering of the peasants firsthand and decided that the Church should work to promote development as part of its mission. None of this was particularly liberationist. Rather, Izuzquiza held a conventional modernization approach. A nuclear physicist by training, he described himself as a practical man who did not like ideology and politics. Paradoxically, in 1992 he gained national fame by openly confronting the corrupt government of Alberto Fujimori.

During that same year, INCAFOR, a lumber company linked to some members of the government, began indiscriminate logging in the province of San Ignacio. Some peasants decided to defend the forest. The government reacted violently and arrested eleven of them, labeling them terrorists. Among them were members of the *rondas* and catechists. Izuzquiza involved himself in their defense. In the process, he underwent a personal conversion toward a more liberationist perspective of his religious mission. He decided that the vicariate should help the communities defend their human rights and the environment, and he created Church organizations to accompany the communities in their demands. He thus became a public figure and a thorn in the side of the government. From the perspective of his personal trajectory, his closeness to the grassroots led him to change his view of his religious mission.

Subsequent bishops continued to support the communities in their interactions with government and business. Muguiro arrived at the vicariate in the early 2000s, bringing rich experience in social involvement as director of Diaconía, the human rights office of the dioceses of Piura. He quickly established a strong rapport with the communities by supporting their initiatives. Muguiro has said he does not agree in every case with the communities' positions on mining exploitation. He has his own ideas about specific situations and tries to share his thoughts with local leaders. However, the communities make their own decisions, and Muguiro contends that the Church should accompany them in their struggles.[28]

The same kind of spirituality, which emphasizes the agency of local communities, can be found in the accounts of members of the religious congregations that were close to the communities in the Bagua conflict.

Mari Carmen Gómez, the nun who stayed with the Awajun and Wampis people during the roadblock, said that, beyond the content of their demands, she wanted to accompany the indigenous people in those difficult times. She was definitely not a political activist.[29] The indigenous leaders openly thanked the Church for its support. However, they repudiated allegations of manipulation by the Church or other external actors and emphasized that they were not puppets.[30]

This brief look at the internal processes of the Church suggests that religious logic cannot be reduced to ideological projections. The existence of a spirituality of accompaniment filters the ideological dimension of liberation theology and generates a distinctive type of Church involvement that respects the leadership of local communities.

Incorporating Environmental and Rights Discourses into a Religious Framework

Accepting the role of accompaniment in its relationship with the communities, however, does not imply a passive Church that merely responds to external demands. Even if the Church assumes a subordinate role, it needs to articulate its support in a way that helps the communities meet the government and the powerful companies on more equal grounds. Usually the Church can offer two kinds of support. The first kind has to do with tangible factors, such as physical infrastructure and other material resources, organizational capabilities, and access to national and international networks. The second kind has to do with constructing discourses and symbols that mobilize people and make popular demands more legitimate. I contend that the incorporation of references to the environment and human rights into explicit religious discourses and Catholic rituals has been the Church's biggest contribution to the legitimacy of these movements.

In the early 1990s, the vicariate of Jaén set up an office for the defense of human rights. The internal war of the 1980s had devastated the Peruvian countryside, so the vicariate focused on the rights of peasants and indigenous peoples. The conflict with INCAFOR reinforced Izuzquiza's determination to establish the office. Simultaneously, the environment became a key issue on the international developmental agenda as the Rio Summit in 1992 signaled the emergence of a post–Cold War order less concerned with the conventional right-left cleavage. The readiness of international donors and NGOs to support an environmental agenda prompted the vicariate to implement development projects with an environmental focus.

Initially, the commitment to human rights and the environment was seen as external to the Church—something the Church did but not essential to its mission. During the 1990s, growing Church involvement in these issues raised the question of how to incorporate them into its doctrinal corpus. Social activism and reformulation of religious discourse became mutually reinforcing processes in a dialectic process of integration. The more pastoral agents worked on these topics, the more they discovered the religious meaning of their work.[31]

The emphasis on God as the God of life, a central concept of liberation theology, catalyzed the formation of a religious discourse on rights and the environment (Levine 2006, 131). On the one hand, it emphasized the importance of human well-being and agency. In the early 1990s, at an assembly in the vicariate of Jaén, advocates of the Church's involvement in social issues borrowed a sentence from St. Irenaeus, bishop of Lyon in the second century: "the glory of God is man fully alive." This statement highlights the religious content of human plenitude, including spiritual and material well-being, and also the respect for human rights and dignity. On the other hand, the more general reference to life extends the religious meaning to all living beings and the environment. Accordingly, nature is important not only because it serves the people, but because of God's presence within it.[32]

In the 1980s Jürgen Moltmann (1985), one of the most influential theologians of the twentieth century, theorized on the interweaving of God, the environment, and people. Leonardo Boff (1996) and other liberationist authors echoed those discussions in the Latin American context. But these reflections had little practical influence.[33] The real incorporation of environmental and human rights discourses within a religious framework was driven by pastoral practices at the grassroots level.

On the one hand, priests and other Church agents quickly realized that presenting God as the creator and champion of the environment was strongly embraced among peasants and indigenous populations, because it reconnected religion with the defense of their livelihood and their traditional spirituality that recognized the presence of God in hills, streams, and lakes. On the other hand, the human rights framework allowed the Church to link its doctrine on inalienable human dignity with a secular discourse that was widely accepted. Thus the Church could offer peasants and indigenous people a powerful discourse to confront abuses and social injustice without having to resort to more ideological analyses. Since the early 1990s, the vicariate has systematically included the defense of the environment and human rights in the syllabus for the formation of catechists and *etsejim* (indigenous catechists), highlighting how these issues affect the daily life of the people. Moreover, the Church expressed these concerns in radio programs, mainly through Radio Marañón, and publications designed to reach the Awajun-Wampis population.[34]

The incorporation of environmental and human rights discourses into the core of religious doctrine was a complex process. A significant part of the contribution came from the grassroots. In the words of a nun living among the Awajun, "We [nuns, priests, and *etsejim*] started to formulate our mission and our own personal experience of faith incorporating these new categories."[35] This bottom-up movement was well received by some bishops. The biblical roots of the environmental discourse and, in comparison to conventional liberation theology, its apparently milder ideological approach, led the hierarchy to accept it. In a few years, the Church officially sanctioned the incorporation of this hybrid discourse into the core of religious doctrine. The inclusion of a section devoted to the environment in the final document of the Fifth General Conference of Latin American Bishops epitomized this recognition (CELAM 2007, 470–75).

Bishop Pedro Barreto played a key role in achieving this official endorsement. Barreto was bishop in the vicariate of Jaén for a little more than a year, until September 2004, when he was appointed bishop of Huancayo. His public condemnation of the environmental damage in the mining town of La Oroya upset the mining corporations but also brought him wide social recognition. In 2005 he addressed the Synod of Bishops on the Eucharist held in Rome. In his speech, Barreto analyzed the formula of the Offertory: "Blessed are you, Lord God of all creation, for through your goodness we have received the bread we offer you: fruit of the earth and work of human hands, it will become for us the bread of life." He discussed how the earth, the people, and God appear closely interconnected in the Eucharist. Accordingly, any damage inflicted to the earth or to humans would go directly against God.[36] Barreto's presentation was well received; in the following years he was promoted to important positions in the Church.[37] This recognition provided a more legitimate standpoint from which those working on human rights and environmental issues within the Church could oppose corporate interests and resist pressure from conservative sectors.

The combination of discourses is also reflected in religious rituals that the Church and the communities use as strategies in their fight against extractive activities. Since the 2004 Majaz clash, on the last weekend in October the communities in the area have organized a Mass on one of the hills where the companies have mining rights or where unlicensed miners have started to exploit mineral deposits. These pilgrimages of thousands of people reinforce the fusion between religion and defense of the environment, consecrating those spaces. Moreover, the popular presence in those contentious territories has a dissuasive effect on the companies and the unlicensed miners, making them acknowledge the vigilant presence of the communities.

IN THE CONTEXT of community struggles against the incursion of extractive industries in their territories, accompaniment has become the dominant form of involvement of the Peruvian Catholic Church. It signals a new form of presence in which the Church gives prominence to local communities and subordinates its actions to their decision making. The Church participates in the conflict, not because local clergy organized the mobilization, but because they take the side of the people with whom they share daily experiences.

This type of involvement depends on three factors. The first is the degree to which the Church is (and has been) present in the local communities. The history of the presence of the Church in the cases studied reveals a dialectic interaction between the Church and the local populations; locals frequently have the ability to shape Church understanding of reality and, consequently, its actions. The second factor is the existence of social interpreters—local leaders close to the Church—who help

Church authorities understand the social reality, thus influencing their decision making regarding the Church's public stance. The third factor is the development of a spirituality that assumes and promotes the agency of the poor, an explicit religious logic that incorporates discourses and rituals. Over the past two decades, the Church, especially the local Church in rural settings, has incorporated environmental and human rights discourses into the Catholic doctrinal corpus in a complex process influenced by both the presence of the Church at the grassroots level and the intervention of key religious figures. This has contributed to raising local consciousness about the consequences of extraction and to building local capacities for mobilization. In parallel, the Church's official recognition of these discourses has legitimated the participation of the local Church (priests, nuns, and Catholic groups) in these antiextraction conflicts. Understanding the interplay of these factors is crucial for a better understanding of the interaction between religion and politics in contemporary Latin America.

Notes

1. In June 2013 the Ombudsman's Office reported that 55 percent of the 223 social conflicts counted in the country were related to mining (105 cases) and hydrocarbon exploitation (18 cases).

2. See "Mining in Peru: Dashed Expectations," *Economist*, June 23, 2012, 53; personal interview with senior manager of an important mining corporation, Lima, November 6, 2007; and Radio Programas Perú, "Pastor a Cabrejos: Contribuyeron a generar mayor conflicto en Bagua," Lima, August 7, 2009.

3. Some of the conflicts are ongoing and can involve legal responsibilities. This analysis maintains the anonymity of sources to protect the interviewees. Accordingly, the text discloses only the real identities of those actors who have expressed their opinions in public.

4. Most of the interviewees who "accompanied" communities in the conflicts analyzed belong to religious congregations inspired by Ignatian spirituality (Society of Jesus, Missionary Society of the Sacred Heart, Servants of St. Joseph, and Medical Mission Sisters).

5. See Spiritual Exercises of Saint Ignatius, nos. 15–17.

6. Interview with JCC, Pasco, April 25, 2008.

7. The conflict of Conga (Cajamarca) broke out in 2011. Conga should be considered the continuation of the protracted problematic relationship between

the Yanacocha Company and the surrounding communities. In the context of declining production in its initial operation, Yanacocha proposed an investment of more than US$4.8 billion for the construction of an open pit gold and copper mine. Peasant communities downstream from the operation and a segment of the wider population opposed the project on the grounds that it would destroy the source of multiple streams that the people rely on for their livelihood and drinking water. The conflict escalated at various times in 2011 and 2012. Violent clashes resulted in the deaths of some peasants. See Edgar Jara and Luciana Zavaleta, "Monseñor Cabrejos y el padre Garatea facilitarán el diálogo en Cajamarca," *La República*, July 7, 2012, 5.

8. Interview with MCH, Lima, November 26, 2012.

9. Marco Arana left the priesthood in 2010 to enter party politics.

10. Interview with MCH, Lima, November 26, 2012.

11. In April 2007 the Zijin Consortium, a partnership of three Chinese companies, bought 79.9 percent of Monterrico Metals.

12. Data from www.monterrico.com/s/RioBlanco.asp?ReportID=144255 (accessed January 2013).

13. The *rondas campesinas* are traditional rural organizations that were set up to prevent cattle rustling. Later they started to play an important role in settling disputes among villagers and providing security for the population. Since the 1980s, these *rondas* emerged as the main organizational structures in the countryside in some regions of Peru. In some parts of the country they played a crucial role in the fight against the Shining Path.

14. Within the Catholic Church, a vicariate is an ecclesial jurisdiction whose management has been entrusted by the Vatican to a religious congregation.

15. Revesz (2009) and Bebbington (2007) present rigorous accounts of this conflict.

16. Only around 20 percent of the Awajun and Wampis people declare themselves Catholic (INEI 2010).

17. This was an official commission: the government appointed the members of the commission, and in some cases the appointments were based on previous agreements with indigenous organizations.

18. Interviews with participants in a workshop held in Santa María de Nieva, November 16, 2010; MCG, Lima, October 31, 2010; AMC, Lima, November 23, 2012; and MC, Lima, November 26, 2012.

19. See typology in the previous section. Romero (2009) also gives an informant account of the plurality within the Peruvian Catholic Church.

20. The companies had to get explicit permission from the local communities to proceed with their activities (World Bank 2004, 21, 50). Failure to procure this social license to operate led to serious loss of reputation thanks to the action

of global networks that connected local disputes to international forums (Bebbington et al. 2007).

21. Cleary (2004, 46–48) documents the crucial social role played by catechists in Peru.

22. Caritas is the Church department in charge of channeling social and developmental support.

23. At the time named vicariate of San Francisco Javier del Marañón.

24. The CAH was also one of the first indigenous organizations in the country and became one of the most influential at both the national and international levels (Greene 2006).

25. Santiago Manuin survived. He still is persecuted for his involvement in the events of Bagua. Despite that stressful situation and his diminished health, Manuin was elected regional councilor in the 2010 regional elections.

26. Interview with MCG, Lima, October 31, 2010.

27. Interview with MC, Lima, November 26, 2012.

28. Interview with PM, Bilbao, November 20, 2012.

29. Interview with MCG, Lima, October 31, 2010.

30. Workshop in Santa María de Nieva, November 2010.

31. Interview with BW, Lima, November 28, 2012.

32. Interviews with MC, Lima, November 26, 2012; and BW, Lima, November 26, 2012.

33. The condemnation of Leonardo Boff's writings by the Vatican was significant in determining this lack of influence.

34. *Jempe*, a quarterly magazine, is the most influential. An issue of *Jempe* on the 2008 mobilization is available at www.caaap.org.pe/archivos/JEMPE%2035.pdf.

35. Interview with MR, Santa María de Nieva, November 12, 2010.

36. Interview with MPB, Lima, November 26, 2012.

37. Barreto was appointed vice president of the Peruvian Bishops Conference, president of the Office for Justice and Solidarity of the Latin American Episcopal Council, and member of the Pontifical Council for Justice and Peace.

References

Adriance, Madeleine. 1991. "Agents of Change: The Roles of Priests, Sisters, and Lay Workers in the Grassroots Catholic Church in Brazil." *Journal for the Scientific Study of Religion* 30, no. 3 (September): 292–305.

Arellano-Yanguas, Javier. 2011. "Aggravating the Resource Curse: Decentralisation, Mining and Conflict in Peru." *Journal of Development Studies* 47, no. 4: 617–38.

————. 2012. "Mining and Conflict in Peru: Sowing the Minerals, Reaping a Hail of Stones." In *Social Conflict, Economic Development and Extractive Industry: Evidence from South America*, edited by Anthony Bebbington, 89–111. New York: Routledge.

Bebbington, Anthony. 2007. *Mining and Development in Peru*. London: Peru Support Group.

Bebbington, Anthony J., and Jeffrey T. Bury. 2009. "Institutional Challenges for Mining and Sustainability in Peru." *Proceedings of the National Academy of Sciences* 106, no. 41: 17296–301.

Bebbington, Anthony, Jeffrey Bury, Denise Humphreys-Bebbington, Jeannet Lingan, Juan Pablo Muñoz, and Martin Scurrah. 2007. "Movimientos sociales, lazos transnacionales y desarrollo territorial rural en zonas de influencia minera: Cajamarca-Perú y Cotacachi-Ecuador." In *Minería, movimientos sociales y respuestas campesinas: Una ecología política de transformaciones territoriales*, edited by Anthony Bebbington, 163–230. Lima: Instituto de Estudios Peruanos.

Bebbington, Anthony, Denise Humphreys-Bebbington, Jeffrey Bury, Jeannet Lingan, Juan Pablo Muñoz, and Martin Scurrah. 2008. "Mining and Social Movements: Struggles over Livelihood and Rural Territorial Development in the Andes." *World Development* 36, no. 12: 2888–905.

Boff, Leonardo. 1996. *Ecología: Grito de la tierra, grito de los pobres*. Madrid: Trotta.

Cleary, Edward. L. 2004. "New Voice in Religion and Politics in Bolivia and Peru." In *Resurgent Voices in Latin America: Indigenous Peoples, Political Mobilization, and Religious Change*, edited by Edward L. Cleary and Timothy J. Steigenga, 43–64. New Brunswick, NJ: Rutgers University Press.

Comisión Especial de Investigación. 2009. "Informe final de la Comisión Especial para investigar y analizar los sucesos de Bagua." Lima.

Consejo Episcopal Latinoamericano (CELAM). 2007. *V Conferencia General del Episcopado Lationamericano y del Caribe: Documento conclusivo*. Aparecida, May 13–31. Available at www.celam.org/conferencias/Documento_Conclusivo_Aparecida.pdf.

Defensoría del Pueblo. 2013. "Reporte de conflictos sociales." Lima.

Greene, Shane. 2006. "Getting over the Andes: The Geo-Eco-Politics of Indigenous Movements in Peru's Twenty-First-Century Inca Empire." *Journal of Latin American Studies* 38, no. 2 (May): 327–54.

Guallart, José María. 1990. *Entre pongo y cordillera: Historia de la etnia Aguaruna-Huambisa*. Lima: Centro Amazónico de Antropología y Aplicación Práctica.

Gutiérrez, Gustavo. 1971. *Teología de la liberación: Perspectivas*. Lima: Centro de Estudios y Publicaciones.

Holden, William N., and R. Daniel Jacobson. 2007. "Ecclesial Opposition to Mining on Mindanao: Neoliberalism Encounters the Church of the Poor in the Land of Promise." *Worldviews* 11: 155–202.

———. 2009. "Ecclesial Opposition to Nonferrous Mining in Guatemala: Neoliberalism Meets the Church of the Poor in a Shattered Society." *Canadian Geographer* 53, no. 2 (Summer): 145–64.

Instituto Nacional de Estadística e Informática (INEI). 2010. *Análisis etnosociodemográfico de las comunidades nativas de la Amazonía, 1993 y 2007.* Lima.

Levine, Daniel H. 2006. "Religious Transformations and the Language of Rights in Latin America." *Taiwan Journal of Democracy* 2, no. 2 (December): 117–41.

Levine, Daniel H., and Scott Mainwaring. 1989. "Religion and Popular Protest in Latin America: Contrasting Experiences." In *Power and Popular Protest: Latin American Social Movements*, edited by Susan Eckstein, 203–40. Berkeley: University of California Press.

Moltmann, Jürgen. 1985. *God in Creation: An Ecological Doctrine of Creation.* London: SCM Press.

Norget, Kristin. 1997. "The Politics of Liberation: The Popular Church, Indigenous Theology, and Grassroots Mobilization in Oaxaca, Mexico." *Latin American Perspectives* 24, no. 5 (September): 96–127.

Organización de Desarrollo de las Comunidades Fronterizas del Cenepa (ODECOFROC). 2009. *Perú, crónica de un engaño: Los intentos de enajenación del territorio fronterizo Awajun en la Cordillera del Cóndor a favor de la minería.* Lima: IWGIA.

Paredes, Maritza. 2008. "El caso de Tambogrande." In *Defendiendo derechos y promoviendo cambios: El Estado, las empresas extractivas y las comunidades locales en el Perú*, edited by Martin Scurrah, 269–300. Lima: Instituto de Estudios Peruanos.

Peña, Milagros. 1994. "Liberation Theology in Peru: An Analysis of the Role of Intellectuals in Social Movements." *Journal for the Scientific Study of Religion* 33, no. 1 (March): 34–45.

Revesz, Bruno. 2009. "Disputas por la legalidad, los derechos de propiedad y el futuro agrícola o minero de la sierra de Piura: El caso Majaz." In *Minería y conflicto social*, edited by José de Echave, Alejandro Diez, Ludwig Huber, Bruno Revesz, Xavier Ricard Lanata, and Martín Tanaka, 17–44. Lima: Instituto de Estudios Peruanos.

Romero, Catalina. 2009. "Religion and Public Spaces: Catholicism and Civil Society in Peru." In *Religious Pluralism, Democracy, and the Catholic Church in Latin America*, edited by Frances Hagopian, 365–401. Notre Dame, IN: University of Notre Dame Press.

Scott, James C. 1998. *Seeing Like a State: How Certain Schemes to Improve the Human Condition Have Failed*. New Haven, CT: Yale University Press.

Starn, Ornin. 1999. *Nightwatch: The Politics of Protest in the Andes*. Durham, NC: Duke Universtiy Press.

Theije, Marijo de. 2006. "Local Protest and Transnational Catholicism in Brazil." *Focaal* 2006, no. 47 (Summer): 77–89.

Trejo, Guillermo. 2009. "Religious Competition and Ethnic Mobilization in Latin America: Why the Catholic Church Promotes Indigenous Movements in Mexico." *American Political Science Review* 103, no. 3 (August): 323–42.

Troeltsch, Ernst. 1931. *The Social Teaching of the Christian Churches*. Vol. 1. Louisville, KY: Westminster/John Knox Press.

World Bank. 2004. "Striking a Better Balance—The World Bank Group and Extractive Industries: The Final Report of the Extractive Industries Review." Washington, DC. Available at http://bankwatch.org/sites/default/files/WBGroup_manag_responses_final_ eng_1.pdf.

CHAPTER 11

VIOLENCE AND PASTORAL CARE IN PUTUMAYO, COLOMBIA

WINIFRED TATE

[During the violence] we had to take a stand. We had to decide to accompany the community, to be a witness. . . . We had to collect the dead because no one else would do it. . . . When the guerrillas or the AUC took people, we had to go to them, we had to carry out pastoral dialogues. Sometimes we got them to release people, not always, but sometimes.

—Putumayo parish priest

The southern Colombian state of Putumayo, a region of frontier colonization along the Ecuadoran border, has been the scene of entrenched violence and illegal drug production for more than three decades (fig. 11.1). During its domination by the country's largest and oldest guerrilla group, the Revolutionary Armed Forces of Colombia (FARC), peasant farmers in the area came to supply more than 50 percent of the coca used in the world cocaine trade. Beginning in the late 1990s, violence spiked as right-wing paramilitary groups steadily gained control of small towns. At the same time, the United States orchestrated a major military counternarcotics intervention in the region, funding training and equipment for army battalions as well as aerial fumigation with chemical herbicides. Through these distinct phases of the conflict, local priests developed various forms of pastoral care in order to both comply with their sacramental duties and respond to the violence besieging the communities in which they worked.[1] Priests in Putumayo organized workshops, set up peasant and women's organizations, and trained local leaders. They met with guerrilla leaders to advocate on behalf of communities. As violence escalated in the region, priests registered abuses and killings, collected commemorative objects, interceded with paramilitary commanders, and assisted families with the retrieval of the dead. Throughout, they worked with transnational groups to secure resources.

This chapter examines Catholic pastoral care as a series of practices that have emerged in dialogue with secular projects for development, popular education, and human rights. In the case of Putumayo, the cohort of priests I discuss were influenced by liberation theology but did not make theological study their focus, nor did they adopt the organizational forms associated with it, such as Christian base communities.[2] Rather, they identified with the broader reform movement within the Church. "We were children of Vatican II," one priest told me. "We identified with the communities. . . . I never understood how the Church could stay limited to just four walls. We had a different vision. All the people here are the living Christ, and we had to bring them down from the cross. We understood the pain of the people." This vision inspired priests to accompany communities, by their physical presence as well as through efforts to channel institutional concern and resources to them (see Roberts 2012; Lamberty 2012). For many activists in both the United States and Colombia involved in such efforts, accompaniment emerges from deeply religious roots.[3] In this case, the political capital and legitimacy of priests, as well as their higher levels of education, national and transnational connections, and in some cases semigovernmental status, allowed them to play a particularly powerful role in rural southern Colombia.

The priests' legitimacy allowed them to represent community concerns to a range of authorities, central state officials as well as command-

Figure 11.1. Map of Putumayo, Colombia

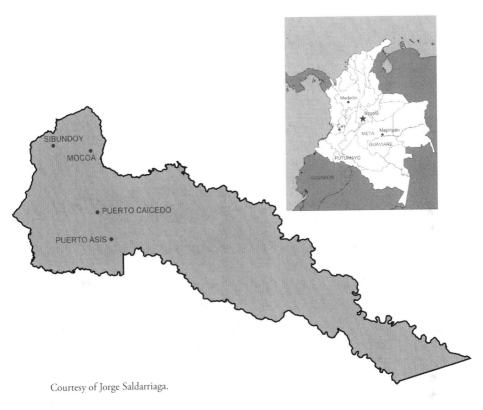

Courtesy of Jorge Saldarriaga.

ers of illegal armed groups. Priests enjoyed political legitimacy because of the minimal state infrastructure in this remote frontier region, often making them the only educated men attached to (legal) national networks who regularly visited. However, the increasing conflict made priests less able to intercede with armed commanders and play a mediating role. As the guerrillas' control of the region was contested by paramilitary forces, their abuses escalated, and they became less receptive to priests' concerns. The nature of the armed groups also played a role in the decreasing ability of priests to advocate with local commanders. Paramilitary forces employed dramatically higher levels of brutality, operated with an overtly authoritarian vision, and arrived from distant communities, making them fundamentally less susceptible to pressure from priests and others advocating for improved treatment of the population.

The role of priests as legitimate political interlocutors with transnational publics became critical as the region became the center of U.S. intervention through Plan Colombia, which channeled hundreds of millions of dollars to the security forces in Putumayo.[4] Many U.S. activists as well as officials viewed Putumayans with suspicion and fear because of their presumed criminality and widespread participation in illegal coca farming.[5] At the same time, many U.S. solidarity networks that had developed during the 1980s peace movement in Central America, including faith-based groups, became interested in the region.[6] Priests were thus particularly well positioned to connect to transnational political resources in the form of training, programs, funding, and solidarity efforts.

The priests profiled here were frustrated by their inevitable inadequacies in the face of the overwhelming violence and intense suffering of the communities in southern Colombia. But their efforts challenge us to conceive a counterfactual history, to imagine the devastating consequences if they had not acted even in the minimal ways they could. The impact of these efforts emerges over time, resurrected after intense persecution and substantial shifts in conflict dynamics. The creative strategies emerging from their attempts to confront the challenges facing the region—economic decline with the shifting coca crop, the massive influx of extractive industries, ongoing violence from armed groups—continue to inspire.

Father Alcides Jiménez: Organizing Putumayo

As a frontier region, Putumayo has been simultaneously remote and marginal and deeply implicated in national and transnational projects. The region is lowland jungle with a small population of indigenous groups and poor *colonos* (settlers) that was made into a department in 1991. It lacks an entrenched political and economic elite on the scale of those in urban areas or regions with longer histories of settlement. Local political culture reflects an ethos of colonization, exploration, and creation. Waves of colonization were spurred in part by the area's designation by the central government as *tierras baldías*, or empty, ownerless lands that were free for settlers who needed only a machete and a tolerance for backbreaking rural labor. The region played a central role as one of the escape valves for escalating land pressure, in the context of Colombia's extreme land inequality and repeated waves of violence to dispossess small farmers from their holdings (Reyes Posada and Duica Amaya 2009). Historically Putumayo has been deeply enmeshed in transnational economic and political processes, including Catholic missionary efforts, quinine, fur, rubber and oil exploitation, and coca paste for the illegal international drug market.[7] Beginning in the 1970s, the wild profits of dramatically expanded coca cultivation brought thousands of small farmers into the region, where they settled into newly created villages and began organizing to secure state services such as roads, schools, and health centers (Torres Bustamante 2011).

The Catholic Church has played a disproportionately powerful role in Putumayo. In a frontier region with minimal state presence, the Church was positioned to fully exploit the special powers granted to it by the 1886 Constitution. From 1896 until the early 1970s, the Capuchin order was authorized to provide education, build infrastructure, evangelize, and colonize what is now known as Caquetá, Putumayo, and Amazonas. In 1951 the area was upgraded to a new ecclesiastical administrative level, and the three regions were separated, with the Putumayo Apostolic Vicariate operating out of Sibundoy. During this period, the Catholic welfare program, Social Action, significantly expanded its programs, as it did throughout the country.[8] By the 1970s the first generation of local boys was educated and consecrated as priests, self-described "native sons" who were assigned to parishes and given significant latitude for local initiatives by the bishop, Arcadio Bernal Supelano. These priests worked to connect Putumayo farmers in remote hamlets to national and transnational networks promoting popular education, sustainable development, and human rights.

The work of Fr. Alcides Jiménez, a parish priest in the region from 1977 until his assassination in 1998, exemplified this process. His pastoral care emphasized the transformative power of collective participation, using the resources of the Church to encourage personal and collective transformation, as well as challenging existing social, economic, and political relationships. He prioritized development of individuals' leadership qualities, of women, of sustainable economic development programs, and of community autonomy in the face of armed groups' efforts to establish their authority. As a "native son" diocesan priest in a local parish, his pastoral power and ecclesiastical leadership and authority were not based on his hierarchical position within the Church but on his personal charisma and ability to marshal national and transnational resources and relationships for his people. He was able to simultaneously challenge some of the Church's traditional tenets and mobilize Church resources to support his projects and his transformative vision. One community leader fondly recalled that his nickname was "'the Bishop,' because he was the one who really knew what was going on; he organized everything." Bernal Supelano, the actual bishop at the time, was described in interviews with Father Jiménez's colleagues as someone who "let [us] act." He developed the first comprehensive pastoral plan to facilitate projects across the region.

Father Jiménez was the anchor of a cohort of priests, almost all born in the region, who were profoundly influenced by his vision of community development and pastoral leadership. In his writings, he traced his interest in community development and sustainable agriculture to both his study of Vatican II and growing up on a small farm without electricity and with few public services. His early career was spent in the neighboring Cauca region, home to Colombia's most organized indigenous communities and many local peasant initiatives. Jiménez brought his experience working with alternative farming and indigenous efforts to recover traditional Amazonian plants in Putumayo. Based in Puerto Caicedo from 1983 until his death in 1998, he played a central role in the department by generating multiple local organizations and training programs.

Father Jiménez's vision included women working as partners with their husbands and as beneficiaries of rural development programs. He created special leadership and training courses for local women. Through his rural development program Mujeres, Caminos y Futuro (Women, Roads, and Future) he promoted a view of women as leading voices against coca cultivation, able to convince their husbands to plant food and cash crops to improve their families' situation. This led to small loan funds and cooperatives for women, generating possibilities for economic independence. His mother played a central role in inspiring his respect for and advocacy with women. Another critical influence in this area was a lay Catholic missionary family from Austria that lived and worked in the parish in 1984–85. Many local residents recalled the workshops on human sexuality, gender equality, and other social issues the couple offered, their living example as parents of small children who shared domestic tasks equally, and Father Jiménez's ongoing commitment to family planning for rural women.

In 1987 women active in the parish founded ASMUM, the Municipal Women's Association. Representatives of the group traveled to national and international conferences on feminism and development. Three members participated in the Beijing Women's Conference in 1995. Upon their return, they shared their experiences of networking with women activists from around the world in local workshops. In 1996 ASMUM representatives also participated in the national feminist meetings in Bogotá that resulted in the founding of one of the country's most important women's collectives, the nationwide pacifist, antimilitarist alliance, la Ruta Pacífica de Mujeres (the Women's Path to Peace), known simply as la Ruta. La Ruta organizes marches, workshops, and training for women around the country.[9] It has a central office in Medellín and regional branches, including a small storefront in Puerto Caicedo. Many Putumayo members of the organization trace their awakening to Father Jiménez's training initiatives.

At the same time, Father Jiménez was promoting sustainable agricultural development. With minimal funding, mostly from Catholic-affiliated European development NGOs, he offered workshops on a range of topics that included water filtration systems, basic health and first aid, malaria management and prevention, land and climate management, alternative medicine, and small-scale projects for Amazonian products. The training led to the establishment of wide networks of health and rural development promoters throughout the department. Parish leaders also established a community radio network with locally produced news as well as distance learning programs. It continues to broadcast to this day.

In addition to their development work, priests in the region began to work with a small but important group of national and transnational human rights groups. The Bogotá-based Jesuit Center for Research and Popular Education (CINEP) sent a staff member to the region in the early 1990s to organize, together with a local priest, the region's first human rights group. It was forced to disband in 1991 following the first wave of narco-paramilitary violence, but the staff member, Nancy Sánchez, remained in the region, working on community outreach with the public health agency. She maintained her ties to the national human rights community, particularly with MINGA, a Bogotá-based group founded in 1992 that combined legal services with grassroots activism in conflict regions.

Pastoral Dialogues with the Guerrillas

From the 1970s to the early 1990s, the FARC was the major political power in the region. Its 32nd Front settled in Putumayo in the early 1980s when the FARC was still a marginal group with minimal national presence. The remote region was logistically important because of the shared border with Ecuador and Peru. In Putumayo the FARC encountered little state resistance, no public services, and a ready base of social support in the growing population of *colonos*, many of whom had experienced guerrilla leadership in other rural areas. Described by local residents as "the law," FARC leaders came to control much of the social and economic life of the region, maintaining a strong militia presence in hamlets and town centers and regularly patrolling rural areas. They used their military power to mediate disputes and enforce local contracts, as well as to organize community improvement projects. As one priest told me, "People depended a lot on them. There would be lines of people taking their problems to the commander—infidelity, conflict in the communities. The guerrillas took on the role of the state. They were the judges."

During the years of FARC domination, local priests viewed guerrillas both as part of their broad religious community—to be accorded the rights and obligations of ministry and pastoral care—and as military authorities with whom they engaged in delicate mediation and advocacy efforts on behalf of their parishioners. Many rural priests knew that their parishioners had family connections to the FARC. Priests carried out what they called "pastoral dialogues" with the guerrillas, which included traveling to their camps to conduct Mass and baptisms and meetings with commanders and troops. Such missions could generate problems with the state security forces; priests who traveled into guerrilla areas refused to allow photos of themselves to be taken. "You have to go baptize children, that is part of the job," one priest told me, describing a baptism party with a band from Ecuador that was organized by the commander. "The bishop gave a short sermon and left without eating anything. He told them, 'Don't ask my priests to do this because it is dangerous for them.' But as a religious sacrament, the Church has to do it."

"In general we had good relations with the guerrillas," one priest recalled, speaking of the time when the FARC was the uncontested power in the region. "There weren't as many human rights violations as there were later, because the territory wasn't under dispute." Communication between priests and FARC commanders required judicious use of diplomacy. The commanders controlled travel in the region, maintaining riverine checkpoints and intelligence networks. "We weren't interested in fighting with them," one priest said. "It was impossible to get into the communities if we confronted them." Into the 1990s the bishop met with FARC commanders to discuss the Church's pastoral plan, in part to guarantee safe passage for priests in rural areas. "I had to say Mass with the guerrillas there, with their uniforms and their guns," one priest recalled. "It wasn't anything admirable, but we had to celebrate the Mass. We had to be careful. It was not that easy; you had to depend on the commander."

At the same time, priests attempted to confront the guerrillas when they abused the community. "We took advantage of the fact that when the priest arrived for the Mass, everyone had to go and listen to him," one priest said, and so moral instruction was provided through the sermon. Another priest described saying Mass for teachers killed by the FARC. In other cases, priests intervened when their parishioners were detained or accused by the FARC of crimes or infractions. The diocese maintained a fund to provide support for people fleeing the region. In some cases, rural priests were forced from the area if local commanders viewed them as threats. One priest told me of being accused at gunpoint by a commander of "trying to create leaders against the guerrillas, against their principles of communism," because of the Church's community education program. In a meeting with the commander, he was further accused of failing to report to a requested meeting and failing to follow FARC "orders and orientation." After armed FARC soldiers questioned his right to say Mass in a rural hamlet, and amid continuing rumors of a possible guerrilla attack, the priest was reassigned.

During the 1980s and 1990s, the FARC used increased revenue from taxing the drug trade to fund a dramatic expansion, almost doubling the number of its troops and increasing its military capabilities. The FARC conducted itself more like a standing army than a guerrilla force, beginning with the 1996 attack on Las Delicias military base in Putumayo. In this and later attacks the FARC captured hundreds of police and soldiers and held them as hostages. They began increasing the *gramaje*—tax per gram of coca paste produced—and mobilizing peasant farmers to oppose U.S.-funded fumigation campaigns. FARC militias based in small towns became more abusive and violent toward the local population.

The beginning of U.S.-sponsored operations further destabilized the region. As the United States began to fund aerial spraying of chemical herbicides—ostensibly to kill coca plants but also destroying legal cash and food crops as well as jungle growth—in the neighboring state of Guaviare, peasant farmers began to organize protests. In 1996 the *cocalero* peasant marches paralyzed the region for several months, as peasant coca farmers occupied small town plazas and blocked major roads. They demanded an end to fumigation and an increase in state services. Many U.S. and Colombia policy makers claimed the marches were simply motivated by pressure from the FARC. In fact, however, the peasant leadership was attempting to claim citizenship rights while negotiating space for relatively autonomous community organizing in the face of extreme pressures from guerrillas and state security forces (Ramírez 2011). They wanted more state presence in their region, along with the full range of state services, benefits, and opportunities for participation in the political process. Putumayo priests mediated a settlement of these protests with an agreement known as the Orito Accords, in which the state promised to dramatically increase public services in the region.[10] Following the march, many of the leaders were killed or forced to flee.

The shifting dynamics of the conflict spurred local priests to play new roles, including confronting guerrilla commanders over escalating abuses and encouraging peasant autonomy and leadership. While peasant leaders attempted to mobilize for increased state recognition and services, the FARC was committed to limiting local autonomy and co-opting collective organizing. It called for a boycott of the 1997 elections, threatening and even killing candidates for local office. Family members of threatened politicians in Putumayo asked the bishop for help, and in response he traveled downriver to speak to the commander of the FARC's Bloque Sur, Joaquín Gómez. "It was hard for us, talking about all the people who were killed," a priest who accompanied him recalled. "The FARC said they had to kill people because they had no jails, only settling of accounts [*ajusticiamientos*]." Guerrilla commanders gave them the names of intended targets, putting priests in the position of communicating the threats to them. At the same time, the bishop attempted to explain the role of the Church in the region.

Meanwhile, new actors in the conflict were arriving in the region. Paramilitary groups were growing in strength throughout the country. Their first incursions into Putumayo came in the late 1990s, with threats and selective assassinations. In 1997 paramilitary leaders from northern Colombia, including the charismatic spokesman Carlos Castaño, announced the creation of the National Self-Defense Forces of Colombia (AUC), which claimed to be a new national command structure representing regional groups. One year later, the AUC announced a military offensive into new regions of the country. Putumayo was among the regions targeted. Newly created "mobile squads" carried out these operations, which included numerous massacres of civilians. Throughout the country, the AUC coordinated with, and received logistical support from, local military commanders. Paramilitary excursions into the south began with a July 1997 massacre in the Meta region. From July 15 to July 20, 1997, some two hundred gunmen from the AUC took control of Mapiripán and killed at least forty people and threw their dismembered bodies in a river. After the massacre, AUC chief Carlos Castaño promised "many more Mapiripáns" (Human Rights Watch 1998, 119). The paramilitary forces that arrived in Putumayo in 1997 were part of the AUC's expansion strategy. They established permanent bases in small towns and carried out massacres and killings.[11]

Coexistence with Coca Culture

Illegal coca cultivation and refining was clearly the central economic engine of the region, financing a range of secondary businesses, including restaurants, retail stores, and transportation services.[12] Coca farming in Putumayo at the time paid better than any of the other options, such as corn, beans, or yucca. But the harvesters and farmers, while relatively prosperous compared to those growing subsistence food crops, lived a life that was a far cry from the glamorous extravagance of urban traffickers in Medellín and Cali. Many residents used small coca plots to supplement their income from legal food crops or from salaried positions. As was common in other kinds of agricultural production, the middlemen who brought rural products to their urban consumers made most of the profits; in this case that would be the *traquetos*, or local traffickers, who bought coca paste from the farmers in the municipal centers and sold it for further processing.[13]

In oral history interviews, residents expressed ambivalence to the coca economy, reflecting with wonder on the opportunities and material rewards offered but wary of the many associated dangers. They described how the coca trade transformed the remote rural area into a vibrant economy, bringing riches, new people, and movement. But they also recalled the violence, conflict, and mistrust it generated. Their criticism of *la cultura de la coca*, or coca culture, was directed less at the coca-farming peasants than at those who grew rich as *traquetos*, known for their flashy fashion, young girlfriends, conspicuous consumption—and violence.

For the Church, coca production presented a complex challenge. The vast majority of parishioners in Putumayo's rural areas participated in the trade as farmers and agricultural workers, but the crop is entirely illegal in Colombia (unlike Peru and Bolivia, which allow small farmers to grow limited amounts for indigenous use). The priests I interviewed recognized the ritual use of coca by indigenous groups as legitimate but lamented the violence and corruption associated with the international drug trade. According to one priest, "The Church rejects drug trafficking, but we distinguish between coca and cocaine. . . . We give classes and workshops, with the participation of international organizations . . . and the National Bishops' Conference, about the serious consequences of the narco economy." "The problem wasn't so much that people didn't know that it was damaging but that it was economically viable," he continued. "It was possible to grow almost anywhere, and if you didn't, you didn't make any money." The priests defined coca growing not as a "criminal problem but as a social problem." Through their sustainable development programs, Father Jiménez and his colleagues offered one of the only organized alternatives to coca cultivation in the region. At the same time, they were aware that donations sustaining their churches came from coca. "We knew that coca was selling for a good price when the donations went up," one priest told me with a smile.

During interviews, I also heard of the many ways coca culture directly affected individual priests. The prevalence of illegal activity made priests vulnerable to charges of corruption. One priest told me of his fear that the local military would plant coca paste on him at a roadblock and then use that evidence to discredit his accusations of military-paramilitary collusion. In another case, a community leader told of a priest who had saved many lives by helping shelter residents who were threatened. Fearing for his life during the escalating violence, he would say Mass "with a pistol stuck in the back of his pants," according to one member of his parish. Eventually, the community leader told me, Bogotá-based NGOs helped him flee to Canada with his married girlfriend. "He came back once," she continued, "in a private plane he contracted from Bogotá. People said, 'What is this guy into that he came in a private plane?' People were saying he must have been drug trafficking in Canada."

Fr. Carlos Palacios is perhaps the most infamous example of a local priest seduced by the coca culture. A native Putumayan who dabbled in coca farming as a youth, he and his brother joined the priesthood and worked with Father Jiménez during his early years in the Puerto Caicedo parish. Palacios left the priesthood to marry his longtime companion shortly before the birth of their first child and began a career in politics. His legitimacy as a community-focused religious leader was a central factor in his successful campaign for governor. Late in his term, he was removed from office and investigated for corruption. He was sentenced to three years in prison, most of which he has served under house arrest in Mocoa, capital of the department of Putumayo. During a 2010 interview, he freely wandered the streets near his family compound in downtown Mocoa. When we went to a nearby store to buy bread and cheese, he was frequently stopped on the street and greeted with calls of, "Hey, Father Carlos!" He told me proudly that he was still identified with his role as priest and planned to work as a counselor in a Catholic school once he had served his prison term.

Escalating Violence and Increasing Paramilitary Domination

As paramilitary forces steadily gained control over urban centers, FARC commanders became increasingly paranoid and draconian, heightening the danger for priests who challenged their abuses. Deeply concerned about infiltration and betrayal, the guerrillas viewed any attempts to establish autonomous organizations with great suspicion. But as guerrilla abuses and drug trade violence increased, Father Jiménez, using a curriculum from Bogotá-based Codecal, an NGO devoted to participatory rural education, began a yearlong series of workshops with six other priests and approximately thirty-five community and peasant leaders to create a local Catholic peace network (Red de Formadores de Paz). National Catholic institutions, including the Bogotá-based Jesuit group CINEP, were promoting active neutrality whereby communities resisted the presence of any armed actors (including state security forces) on their territory. Father Jiménez participated in workshops in which activists working with Colombia's most famous peace community, San José de Apartadó, founded in 1997, described their strategies and experiences (Alther 2006). When the guerrilla commanders in Putumayo attempted to pressure communities to come out for another large-scale protest march in 1997, Father Jiménez urged community leaders to resist. Following his counsel, many peasants refused to participate, arguing that the previous marches had led to increased violence and poverty without any gain for the communities involved.

On September 11, 1998, Father Jiménez was killed by the FARC while saying Mass celebrating the end of Peace Week; the attack was widely viewed as retaliation for encouraging autonomous community organizing. One participant in the workshops he organized recalled his work promoting such independent groups as "more dangerous than being a human rights defender [who were also widely targeted]. In this rural area, [he was] giving workshops that people shouldn't go into the war, that they shouldn't use arms. . . . The FARC was mad because they thought that he was taking people away from them, that he was too critical of them. And he was very much against coca."

The Height of the Violence

Between 1998 and 2005, Putumayo became an intense conflict zone, with guerrillas controlling the rural areas and paramilitary groups working with the security forces from the urban centers. In addition to their use of violence, paramilitary commanders regulated public space, individual comportment, and interpersonal relationships. They ordered communities to clean their streets and display specific decorations. Commanders intervened in local disputes, regulating domestic violence and punishing thieves. They held frequent large public meetings in the plazas to inform residents of their rules. I heard stories from many local residents about how commanders charged local businesses "taxes" (which some called extortion), as well as percentages of all government contracts. Any travel within the region required advance permission. Rural people, accused of sympathizing with guerrillas, were no longer able to travel to markets in town, and townsfolk were prevented from going to their farmland. Women from urban centers who worked in church, government, and community outreach programs told me they could not travel to meet with their rural counterparts. One lay Catholic agricultural extension agent said, "If the community committee [*junta de acción communal*] was going to go out, they had to get permission . . . because they [the paramilitaries] became like the state."

Pastoral practices shifted in response to the changing dynamics of the violence. Workshops and sustained rural development initiatives were largely abandoned as too dangerous, particularly as catechists, health promoters, and agricultural extension agents were targeted by paramilitaries (and to a lesser extent, guerrillas). Some chose to focus on daily accompaniment, being present in communities during intense violence, serving as compassionate witnesses to community suffering, and registering abuses. Pastoral Social provided material and religious support for communities and confronted and publicly denounced abusive armed actors, including official security forces working with paramilitary groups in the area. Fr. Eduardo Ordóñez, head of Pastoral Social from 2000 to 2005, described its work as focused on three areas: documenting and in some cases denouncing abuses; providing temporary emergency aid, including food and rent subsidies, for displaced families; and helping families with burial paperwork, transportation, and rites. They also developed connections with new international allies, who provided human rights training and accompaniment. "I learned about the issue of human rights not from the Church," one priest told me, "but from human rights organizations I worked with."

In many cases, priests negotiated directly with paramilitary commanders for the return of bodies, an experience that highlighted the differences between paramilitary and guerrilla commanders. Paramilitaries were largely from distant communities, not embedded in local kinship networks; employed much more brutal methods; and were largely impervious to priests' claims to authority. "The commanders wouldn't always agree to speak with us," Father Ordóñez told me. "[They wouldn't return the bodies because] it was a way to demonstrate that the person that they killed was a delinquent, was an enemy, and that they could do what they liked with him. . . . [They] were the most difficult to speak with, more bitter, rougher, harder. They made us a little more terrified. . . . Some were more docile and nicer, but that was more in the guerrillas. Because in some ways, the guerrilla saw that the Church did many things for the rural areas. The paramilitaries didn't care about that."

Fr. Campo Elías de la Cruz, who had served as a novice under Father Jiménez and was the most outspoken of this cohort, developed what he called a "prophetic voice," explicitly linking his religious vocation with what he viewed as a moral duty to denounce paramilitary violence in the region. Even as he recognized that ministering to the security forces remained part of his sacramental duties, he was aware of their role in the violence. "I knew that my work as a priest was to be there for everyone, for the soldiers too," he told me. "I knew that there were things going on that weren't right. On that short stretch of road between [the military base of] Santa Ana and Puerto Asís, so many bodies appearing there and it was such a short piece of road, right there near the base. I would talk about these things in the Mass, and the colonel didn't like it. . . . I knew that the security forces weren't doing the right thing, and I would say it."[14]

As part of his "prophetic" denunciation he accompanied a peasant march to Bogotá. In a meeting with then-president Ernesto Samper, he and march leaders described the state's support of paramilitary forces. Many of the leaders were killed on their return to Putumayo. Father de la Cruz made similar reports during local meetings convened by state officials to discuss the escalating violence. He also worked closely with the regional human rights ombudsman, Germán Martínez, to document cases and assist victims, including families seeking refuge in churches.

During this period, the United States began sending millions of dollars for training and equipping elite Colombian army counternarcotics battalions, aerial fumigation with chemical herbicides, and alternative crop projects for Putumayo farmers. As a result, U.S.-based human rights and solidarity organizations began to focus on the region as well. Local priests were a critical linchpin in these transnational alliances because they were viewed as legitimate sources of analysis and insight into conditions there. Priests met with visiting researchers and activists and traveled to the United States on speaking tours sponsored by Catholic Relief Services, solidarity committees, and Witness for Peace. The first U.S. NGO delegation to the region in 2000 included representatives of the Washington Office on Latin America (WOLA), the U.S. Committee for Refugees, and Colombian-based human rights groups. The Center for International Policy, Amnesty International, and Human Rights Watch reported on the situation as well. Witness for Peace brought delegations of Americans and wrote grassroots policy reports documenting the impact of U.S. policy.[15]

In at least one case, international solidarity efforts played a decisive role in limiting paramilitary activity. Members of a large Witness for Peace delegation traveled to the town of Sibundoy, where paramilitaries worked closely with local police and military officers. "People were panicked," Father de la Cruz recalled, following the appearance of graffiti threatening local residents. "You could see [the paramilitaries] bringing in weapons." The priests convened a meeting with civilian and military officials, warning them they were responsible for the security of the local population and filing a report on the threat with government officials in Sibundoy and, with the assistance of MINGA, in Bogotá. A delegation from the town met with Colombia's vice president to register its complaints. At the same time, Witness for Peace delegates participated in a

Mass denouncing the atrocities and the role of the state. Following the resulting publicity, police and military officials who had been working with the paramilitary forces were transferred. "The Church played an important role, with Witness for Peace," Father de la Cruz told me. "[The Witness for Peace representatives] spoke strongly during the Mass, and this helped make visible what was going on. . . . The police thought that no one was going to notice."

This success was impossible to replicate in other areas of Putumayo. The area near Sibundoy had a longer history of settlement, meaning there was more social trust and cohesion, which facilitated collective action, and there was less involvement in the drug trade, meaning fewer resources were at stake. In other parts of the department, limited resources, widespread criminal violence, and the lack of robust civil society organizations prevented transnational NGOs from providing long-term accompaniment. Priests there were unable to advocate as effectively with paramilitary commanders who arrived from distant regions, were allied with security forces, and were uninterested in respecting existing community authority structures. Father de la Cruz described one failed intervention when paramilitaries detained Church catechists participating in a human rights course.

> We [three priests] went to the human rights course. Many leaders were coming. Two were taken by the paramilitaries. The mother came to us, saying, "Father, they have taken my sons." So we said . . . we are going to . . . see if they will let them free. . . . We had to go walking down this rutted street, and we saw their weapons. We saw that the [prisoners] were crying. There were many armed men around, all dressed as civilians. One of the men said, "You don't have any business here, get out." Nelson said, "We are priests." The man said, "You didn't understand me, get out." Alfonso said, "Those men are church leaders," and we got out of the car. The men who were tied up were crying; they couldn't speak, but they were crying, and that was their way of asking us for help. There were a lot of people waiting in line to talk to the commander. One of them was shepherding the line, telling people when it was their turn. The mother

was crying, she got on her knees, crying for her sons. The man pushed her with his foot, so she went backwards a little.

"We know who the guerrillas are," the commander said. "We investigate them." I said, "You have committed serious mistakes." I was so afraid. But I said, "They are catechists, *animadores*, from the church." The man looked at me, a terrible look. He took his radio and gave the order for them to kill them [*ejecutarlos*]. It only took fifteen minutes. They killed them, untied them, and threw them in a ditch. I told Father Nelson, "We need to ring the bells at the church." [The paramilitaries] were right there, at the side of the church, they heard . . . everything we said. At the Mass I talked a bit harshly, about the value of life.

We called the bishop. We told him, "The Church is sleeping. How can you let this happen, that they are in their cars and motorcycles right outside the church, they are living next to the church and the Church does nothing?"

The army detained us when we were going back, and searched us. We argued with them, a harsh discussion with them. In the middle of the night, the army came in to get the paramilitaries, but no one was there. They had everything well coordinated; they organized things together. They got them out of the church, they moved them somewhere else.

There were many cases of such encounters. Trying to get people out, teachers, peasants. I had to send in reports, how many people we got out.

As the violence worsened, Church authorities began taking more conservative positions in an effort to safeguard their personnel. Father de la Cruz recalled a message from the National Bishops' Conference to "be prudent, that the Church shouldn't get involved in 'that kind of stuff.' They thought we should celebrate the Mass but nothing else, not get involved." By the early 2000s, the danger for outspoken priests was growing. Witness for Peace facilitated contacts with a church in Minneapolis, and Father de la Cruz spent eighteen months there before returning to Colombia but not to Putumayo. Other priests were sent to Chile or other parishes to escape the mounting pressure.

Witness to Violence in Putumayo

Local priests felt silenced by political violence and by the lack of support from the Church hierarchy. In later interviews, several discussed bitterly what they described as abandonment by the Church leadership in Putumayo and nationally. For example, the network of lay missionaries (*promotores*) established by Father Jiménez lost the bishop's support; the house where one group lived was given to a new group of charismatic *promotores* and the network dismantled. For many priests in the remote hamlets occupied by paramilitary forces that were enforcing vicious and arbitrary rules on local inhabitants, efforts to denounce specific cases seemed futile. In a June 2005 interview, a priest in La Dorada told me, "I am very disillusioned. . . . So many people came to visit, so many reports filed with NGOs, ACNUR [Spanish for UNHCR], the UN, and nothing changes, nothing happens. I thought something would change, but no."

Accordingly, many priests developed a vision of pastoral care that avoided confrontation or public complaint, drawing on the long Catholic tradition emphasizing the importance of compassionate witnessing of suffering. Some of them did occasional low-profile work with national and transnational NGOs and multilateral organizations present in the region to safeguard local residents where possible. These entities included CINEP, the Quaker American Friends Service Committee (Servicios Andinos), the UN High Commissioner for Refugees (UNHCR), and the International Red Cross. For many living in small towns occupied by paramilitary forces, serving as a witness to the violence in anticipation of a future time when public accounting might be possible was part of their pastoral mission. For example, during a 2001 interview, the priest who replaced Father Jiménez admitted that work with community organizations had been largely halted. At the same time, he pulled out a handwritten ledger that he was afraid to have seen even by local residents in which he recorded all the deaths in the region. While unable to provide Catholic funeral rites such as Mass or in many cases even burial, he was able to accompany the dead through prayer, the secret ledger, and communication with the family members if he knew them. A La Dorada priest interviewed in 2005 also maintained a list of the dead. During the course of our interview, he read some of the names for me and told me any details he knew, such as age, profession, or local family members. He also expressed his frustration with this limited system: "Of course many deaths are not reported. Or they are just rumors. People say, 'The chickens are eating one over there.'"

Fr. Nelson Cruz's Memory Museum (Museo de la Memoria) was another example of silent witnessing in Putumayo. As the parish priest in El Placer, he was asked by Pastoral Social to prepare a document about the situation for distribution to interested journalists, NGOs, and human rights organizations. He refused, arguing that a written account would endanger both him and local residents. Instead, he proposed using space in the church buildings to house a collection of objects related to the violence that could be observed and photographed by interested visitors. Pastoral Social accepted his proposal; the museum collection grew from donations by local residents and objects collected during Father Cruz's pastoral trips to rural hamlets. All were labeled with the date and place they were found. They included grenades and other weapons fragments, uniforms and armbands from the armed groups, even items of daily use such as cooking utensils with bullet holes. The Museo served as a public acknowledgment of the toll of the conflict, even if it could not be articulated in the form of a complaint, and a demonstration that the Church accompanied residents during this time of violence. A reduced collection of objects remains displayed on a wall facing an interior courtyard inside the parish compound, and residents are currently discussing efforts to install the entire collection in a local memory house (*casa de la memoria*). Reflecting on his experience, Father de la Cruz mused, "Each one has its way of working. Nelson was very smart, he had to remain silent. If he hadn't, he would not have been able to stay accompanying his people."

Father Jiménez's Legacy in Contemporary Putumayo

Many of the projects begun by Father Jiménez lay dormant in the years immediately after his death, as paramilitary violence peaked between 1999 and 2003. But his legacy is felt in the local civil society and religious organizations that have emerged in the past decade after talks led to demobilization of the paramilitaries. That opened up some space for organizing and dramatically reduced the levels of daily violence, although the conflict in Putumayo continues. The demobilization occurred after talks between the AUC leadership and government representatives, mediated by senior Catholic officials; by 2007 more than 31,000 paramilitary troops had passed through the process. In Putumayo, on March 1, 2006, 504 members of the regional paramilitary bloc went through the official demobilization process.[16] While reconstituted paramilitary forces remain active, the brutality by paramilitary groups occupying small towns has abated. The FARC continues to employ deadly landmines, forced recruitment, and intimidation, but the number of combat operations has greatly declined and the nightly 6:00 p.m. curfew has been lifted. Female community activists who for several years could not leave the urban centers have begun traveling to rural regions once more.

The Putumayo Women's Alliance (la Alianza de Mujeres del Putumayo) is one of the most prominent groups that emerged in part from Father Jiménez's decades of work. Female teachers and community leaders, many of whom had participated in his work, came together to support women who had survived the violence in the region. At their first retreat, in November 2003, they adopted three themes to guide their work: human rights and armed conflict, women's history and political participation, and social and economic development. With funding from a range of national and international allies, the Alliance holds workshops, forums, and meetings throughout the department and attempts to connect specific, women-initiated community development projects to those funders. The Alliance also supports women under threat by using contacts with national and international NGOs.

With the support of the Catholic Church, the Alliance has focused on public commemoration—permanent memorials and marches—in an effort to claim not only the right to grieve but also public spaces for themselves as political actors. The "Wall of Truth" is one such effort. Each of the 170 bricks on an exterior wall of the Catholic cathedral in Mocoa's central plaza contains the name, occupation, and date of death of a woman killed violently in the department. There is no mention of the perpetrators and circumstances of death. The panel of bricks is set within a pastoral scene of blue sky, rolling hills, and regional flowers, the name of the Alliance in large letters across the top, the slogan "Not a single one more!" along the bottom. The wall has become a point of pride and public encounter for the women of the Alliance, who gather there to sing, light candles, and reflect during workshops and meetings. They have built another wall in the neighboring town of Villagarzón, and additional walls are being planned.

A new Catholic youth group in Puerto Caicedo, inspired by la Ruta and the legacy of Father Jiménez, has also staged periodic public events. Using *teatro efímero* (ephemeral theater), which they learned from Fundación Rayuela (Hopscotch), a Bogotá-based youth theater project, its members work with groups of twenty to thirty youths to collectively diagnose and analyze social problems in the area. They then script, design, and produce street theater productions based on those issues. Rayuela says this process involves human rights education and creates empathy and community through the public commemoration of specific forms of violence in order to contest the multiple forms of authoritarianism at work in these communities. Following their initial training workshops, the Puerto Caicedo *teatro efímero* group now participates in collective actions as well as street theater productions. One example of their work is "The Colombian Situation," performed on September 9, 2009, for the annual commemoration of the life and work of Father Jiménez on the anniversary of his assassination. The work, performed in Puerto Caicedo's central plaza, consisted of three "living photographs," short scenes enacted within a large constructed frame. In the first, a peasant is found dead; in the second, a displaced family flees; in the third, a masked man threatens peasant youth. Rayuela has also contributed to a repertoire of symbolic resources that "enact embodied memory," drawing heavily on Catholic rituals of mourning (Taylor 2003). These elements include traveling displays of photos of the dead and disappeared and installations in public plazas of religious funeral objects such as crosses, flowers, candles, and funeral invitations on newsprint, of the kind often plastered on street posts and walls, with the name, dates, and family members of those murdered. During marches they cover their mouths with small crosses made of sticks as a sign of being silenced; their uniform at these events is all black, or T-shirts with the slogan, "No más."

The Alliance incorporated many of these elements into its public commemoration of Father Jiménez. In a recent silent march, they held life-sized photos of the priest's face. Later, during a public gathering, they held photos of their dead family members. Along the central street, the *teatro efímero* group had installed empty chairs, shrouded with black tulle, holding small white wooden crosses; thin cement blocks plastered with the death announcements of local residents killed in the violence rested in front of them. Women walked wearing black, carrying crosses and umbrellas draped with white ribbons. The march also featured a moment of street theater, in which women enveloped in white cloth lay down on the street to represent the bodies of the dead and disappeared. Other women kneeled and embraced them, many in tears. These events are not simply cathartic performances of public grieving but also establish new collective histories as well as constitute participants as public political actors.

Many of the priests who studied under Father Jiménez are back in Putumayo, frustrated with the Church hierarchy. Critics of the current bishop point to the focus on implementing government grants for large educational projects rather than community-based projects. They contrast priests from outside the region, who have returned to wearing the cassock, to the previous tradition of native-born priests who worked alongside communities in civilian clothing. They hope to revive the disbanded Peace and Justice Working Group (Mesa de Justicia y Paz) and the Border Mission (Pastoral Fronterizo).

PARISH PRIESTS enjoy a range of political resources they can mobilize during times of crisis. Through their pastoral ministries, they are deeply embedded in local political dynamics as well as intimately connected to individuals' daily lives. Those working in remote rural areas are frequently the only representatives of large institutions to maintain a regular presence. Through the Catholic institutional hierarchy, priests are connected to national and international networks offering funding and educational opportunities. Through these institutional networks, and their local responsibilities and relationships, priests acquire significant political legitimacy before powerful political actors ranging from national and international government bureaucrats to illegal armed actors. Yet their responses to violence and conflict vary. Examination of the experiences of specific parishes, in this case in the southern Colombian state of Putumayo, reveals some of the factors affecting how and why they employ specific political resources, illuminating the opportunities as well as the considerable constraints they face.

At the most immediate level, priests must weigh their pastoral obligations to minister to all—the powerful and the oppressed, the perpetrator and the victim—against their understanding of their particular obligations to the disenfranchised. As in many areas of Latin America, in southern Colombia priests were inspired by the Vatican II reforms and in some cases also the more radical teachings of liberation theology. Just as importantly, as "native sons"—the first generation of priests born in the region, educated in major cities, and then returning—these priests developed ministries focused on marginal migrants, many of whom were involved in coca farming. They were perfectly positioned to take advantage of the paradox of Catholic presence in this jungle lowland border region. The Church in Putumayo was able to play a disproportionate role because of the region's frontier characteristics, including minimal state presence and infrastructure. At the same time, individual priests were granted more latitude because of the relative unimportance of the region in the view of the Church's institutional hierarchy. Thus individual charismatic leaders like Father Jiménez were able to play a critical role.

At the same time, priests working in areas with entrenched illegal armed actors are profoundly vulnerable to attacks. Thus their pastoral calculations also included constant evaluation of the shifting dynamics in the conflict, including troop movements and guerrilla objectives, in relation to their relatively amorphous leverage over such groups. Priests were also forced to evaluate the relative political costs of their distinct pastoral strategies. Supporting efforts for autonomous organizing, independent of armed groups, and publicly denouncing their abuses resulted in lethal retaliation in Putumayo and in other regions around the country. According to the Episcopal Conference of Colombia, between January 1984 and September 2013 two bishops and eighty-four priests were killed in acts of violence, most of them by the paramilitary forces or the FARC.[17]

Many more priests were threatened and managed to escape death by fleeing or being transferred from their parishes, precisely because of the strength of the Church's national and transnational networks. Such relocations weakened the ability of parish priests to intervene with armed commanders on behalf of their parishioners; their legitimacy depended on their established relationships, long-standing trust, and shared histories. Their ability to react was also profoundly transformed as new armed actors moved into conflict zones, such as the paramilitary forces that arrived in southern Colombia. As paramilitaries came to control urban centers, they proved even more brutal, arbitrary, and abusive in their treatment of the local community than the previous generation of guerrilla commanders. Some priests attempted to use their public leadership positions—in security councils, in Mass, and in meetings with public officials—to denounce the violence affecting their parishioners. In other cases, priests chose to respond with private documentation and witnessing as they saw that public protests by their colleagues were ineffective in the face of escalating violence.

Transnational allies such as the U.S. faith-based group Witness for Peace played a critical role in increasing priests' legitimacy with government officials as well as linking them to additional networks. Even as greater U.S. military intervention in the region contributed to escalating violence, it also led to greater transnational solidarity mobilization. The development of faith-based solidarity networks between the United States and Colombia faced many challenges. One of the most important was the limited number of U.S. religious workers in the country. Colombia was a net exporter of priests and religious workers, sending many to other parts of Latin America and Africa, leading to fewer of the connections between religious communities in the United States and Colombia, particularly within Catholic and mainline Protestant denominations that had played a central role in the previous generations of U.S. solidarity movements.

Efforts to develop U.S. solidarity and accompaniment with Putumayo communities were further complicated by the illegal drug trade. Concerns were raised that U.S. activist participation in campaigns in Colombia would imply tolerance of illicit drug abuse and trafficking. Critics of militarized drug policy were also often accused of sympathizing with drug traffickers and guerrillas. For U.S.-based groups attempting to establish institutional relationships with Colombian communities affected by U.S. policies, the extensive criminal activity in the region was extremely difficult to navigate. But local priests, legitimized by their pastoral relationships and institutional ties to the Church, were perfectly positioned to advocate for their parishioners and facilitate efforts by U.S. solidarity groups and activists on their behalf.

Developing projects with Colombian communities and priests rejuvenated some faith-based initiatives that had emerged during the solidarity movement with Central America. Witness for Peace, which played a critical role in Putumayo, is one example. Originally founded in response to U.S. intervention in Nicaragua, during the 1990s the organization went into decline, with a budget reduction of 40 percent. For many in the group, Colombia offered a return to their activist roots, with a focus on political violence directly related to U.S. policy.

A final example of the difference a parish priest can make in local response to violent conflict is the longer-term revival of community organizations inspired by Father Jiménez. Beyond the priests that cite him as a mentor and teacher, the collective work of the Women's Association of Puerto Caicedo, the Women's Alliance of Putumayo, and other peasant organizations demonstrate his ongoing legacy. Their resurgence and resilience—as well as frailty in the face of violence—point to the importance of deep and ongoing histories of such efforts and how the seeds sown bear fruit, long after the initial projects, in unanticipated ways.

Notes

1. This chapter is based on fieldwork carried out during eight research trips to Putumayo between 1999 and 2013, as well as interviews with U.S. and Colombian activists and religious officials conducted in the United States. Many of the Colombians interviewed in Putumayo requested that their identity be concealed because of ongoing security issues in the region. Research travel was supported in part by grants from the U.S. Institute for Peace and the Colby Faculty Development Fund, in addition to the American University Center for Latin American and Latino Studies.

2. Christian base communities are small collectives of laypeople who gather to reflect on spiritual teachings. They frequently evolved into political activism. There is a large literature examining the emergence and decline of liberation theology in Latin America; for some basic history, see Berryman [1987] 2013 and Smith 1991.

3. For more on the religious dimension of U.S. solidarity and accompaniment, see Coy 2012; Smith 1996; and Nepstad 2004. For the religious roots of Colombian human rights groups, see Tate 2007.

4. Plan Colombia initially contained more than US$600 million (of a total of a US$1.3 billion aid package first passed in 2000) for the "Push into Southern Colombia." This aid included military hardware and training for the newly formed counternarcotics battalions of the Colombian army, as well as aid for fumigation and development. These projects were extended over the next five years.

5. Scholars in a number of Latin American contexts have explored the importance of innocence as a fundamental category for solidarity campaigns supporting victims of human rights abuses. In urban Brazil, critics of police brutality have been dismissed by accusations that they care only for the "rights for bandits" (Caldeira 2000) and criminals (Holston 2008). In Peru, the human rights community and local communities in conflict zones engaged in extensive and controversial debates over the importance of innocence for defending victims of abuse (Theidon 2012). Following the imposition of sweeping antiterrorist legislation, NGOs adopted a "campaign for the innocents," defending individuals wrongly imprisoned but refusing to take the cases of members of the Shining Path, even if they suffered torture while incarcerated. During the debate over the reach of the truth and reparations committee, legal advisers discussed what is known as the Clean Hands Doctrine, a legal principle that established eligibility for reparations depending on the degree of criminal involvement. In the Peruvian case, this debate focused on whether to provide reparations to families whose Shining Path relatives had been killed while in government custody (see LaPlante 2007).

6. For more on this history, see Tate 2009.

7. For the early history of this region, see Stanfield 1998; and Taussig 1991.

8. While the Catholic hierarchy is generally characterized as conservative, and hostile to accompaniment projects, revisionist histories of the Colombian Catholic Church have described significant progressive activism since the 1930s. See LaRosa 2000.

9. The national organization includes three hundred entities, among them many of the most important feminist groups in Colombia (e.g., Casa de la Mujer in Bogotá; Vamos Mujer and Mujeres que Crean in Medellín); they also allow individual membership. See Cockburn 2007.

10. The most complete history of this period can be found in Ramírez 2011.

11. The Historical Memory Commission, created by the government as part of the 2003–6 paramilitary demobilization processes, has produced the most

detailed study to date of the impact of the violence on daily life in a Putuamyo hamlet. Ramírez 2012 focuses on the Putumayo hamlet of El Placer; it is available in Spanish at www.centrodememoria historica.gov.co/index.php/informes-gmh/informes-2012/genero-putumayo.

12. Most coca paste, also known as *base*, is the first refining stage in making cocaine, and the peasant families who grow the coca complete the process at home. (On industrial plantations, contract workers carried out a larger-scale version of the same process.) Using a modified weed cutter, they shredded the leaves, mixed them with cement powder, and then soaked them in barrels of gasoline. Hydrochloric acid was added to the liquid squeezed from this mixture to crystallize the alkaloid. The resulting powder, coca base, sold to middlemen in southern Colombia for about US$700 a kilo.

13. For more detail on the coca economy, see the Swedish anthropologist Oscar Jansson's (2008) work.

14. The Office of the United Nations High Commissioner for Human Rights in Colombia reported repeatedly officially informing the Colombian government of links between paramilitary and military forces in the Putumayo region during this period, to no effect. The 2000 annual report, released in February 2001, included this description of the situation:

> This Office also observed that paramilitaries were still operating at the Villa Sandra estate between Puerto Asís and Santa Ana in the same department, a few minutes from the Twenty-Fourth Brigade base. [This Office] was later informed that two raids had been made by the security forces, apparently without result; yet the existence and maintenance of this position are public knowledge—so much so that it has been visited repeatedly by international journalists who have published interviews with the paramilitary commander. Reports received by the Office even speak of meetings between paramilitaries and members of the security forces at the Villa Sandra estate. ("Report of the U.N. High Commissioner for Human Rights on the Human Rights Situation in Colombia," E/CN.4/2001/15, February 8, 2001, par. 134. Available at http://daccess-dds-ny.un.org/doc/UNDOC/GEN/G01/110 /61/PDF/G0111061.pdf?OpenElement.)

15. MINGA facilitated many of these trips and maintained extensive contacts with advocacy and activist organizations in Europe and the United States, sending staff on speaking tours and participating in advocacy campaigns targeting specific legislative initiatives in the United States and the European Union. The growing legitimacy and profile of Colombian activists in Washington was demonstrated when MINGA's executive director and three other activists won the 1998 Robert F. Kennedy Award for human rights and Nancy Sánchez, then MINGA's Putumayo researcher, won the 2003 Letelliet Moffit Award.

16. International Crisis Group, "Colombia: Towards Peace and Justice?," Latin America Report 16, March 14, 2006.

17. "Asesinaron a dos sacerdotes en Roldanillo, Valle," *El Colombiano*, September 28, 2013.

References

Alther, Gretchen. 2006. "Colombian Peace Communities: The Role of NGOs in Supporting Resistance to Violence and Oppression." *Development in Practice* 16, no. 3–4 (June): 278–91.

Berryman, Phillip. [1987] 2013. *Liberation Theology: The Essential Facts about the Revolutionary Movement in Latin America and Beyond.* Toronto: Random House.

Caldeira, Teresa P. R. 2000. *City of Walls: Crime, Segregation, and Citizenship in São Paulo.* Berkeley: University of California Press.

Cockburn, Cynthia. 2007. *From Where We Stand: War, Women's Activism, and Feminist Analysis.* New York: Zed Books.

Coy, Patrick G. 2012. "Nonpartisanship, Interventionism and Legality in Accompaniment: Comparative Analyses of Peace Brigades International, Christian Peacemaker Teams, and the International Solidarity Movement." *International Journal of Human Rights* 16, no. 7: 963–81.

Holston, James. 2008. *Insurgent Citizenship: Disjunctions of Democracy and Modernity in Brazil.* Princeton, NJ: Princeton University Press.

Human Rights Watch. 1998. *War Without Quarter: Colombia and International Law.* New York: Human Rights Watch.

Jansson, Oscar. 2008. "The Cursed Leaf: An Anthropology of the Political Economy of Cocaine Production in Southern Colombia." PhD dissertation, Uppsala Universitet.

Lamberty, Kim Marie. 2012. "Toward a Spirituality of Accompaniment in Solidarity Partnerships." *Missiology: An International Review* 40, no. 2 (April): 181–93.

LaPlante, Lisa. 2007. "The Law of Remedies and the Clean Hands Doctrine: Exclusionary Reparation in Policies in Peru's Political Transition." *American University International Law Review* 23, no. 1: 51–90.

LaRosa, Michael J. 2000. *De la derecha a la izquierda: La Iglesia católica en la Colombia contemporánea.* Santafé de Bogotá: Planeta.

Nepstad, Sharon Erickson. 2004. *Convictions of the Soul: Religion, Culture, and Agency in the Central America Solidarity Movement.* New York: Oxford University Press.

Ramírez, María Clemencia. 2011. *Between the Guerrillas and the State: The Cocalero Movement, Citizenship, and Identity in the Colombian Amazon.* Durham, NC: Duke University Press.

———. 2012. *El Placer: Mujeres, coca y guerra en el bajo Putumayo.* Bogotá: Centro de Memoria Histórica.

Reyes Posada, Alejandro, and Liliana Duica Amaya, eds. 2009. *Guerreros y campesinos: El despojo de la tierra en Colombia.* Bogotá: Grupo Editorial Norma.

Roberts, Kathleen Glenister. 2012. "Universalism in Catholic Social Thought: 'Accompaniment' as Trinitarian Praxis." *Solidarity: Journal of Catholic Social Thought and Secular Ethics* 2, no. 1: article 4.

Smith, Christian. 1991. *The Emergence of Liberation Theology: Radical Religion and Social Movement Theory.* Chicago: University of Chicago Press.

———. 1996. *Resisting Reagan: The U.S. Central America Peace Movement.* Chicago: University of Chicago Press.

Stanfield, Michael Edward. 1998. *Red Rubber, Bleeding Trees: Violence, Slavery, and Empire in Northwest Amazonia, 1850–1933.* Albuquerque: University of New Mexico Press.

Tate, Winifred. 2007. *Counting the Dead: The Culture and Politics of Human Rights Activism in Colombia.* Berkeley: University of California Press.

———. 2009. "U.S. Human Rights Activism and Plan Colombia." *Revista Colombia Internacional* 69: 50–69.

Taussig, Michael. 1991. *Shamanism, Colonialism, and the Wild Man: A Study in Terror and Healing.* Chicago: University of Chicago Press.

Taylor, Diana. 2003. *The Archive and the Repertoire: Performing Cultural Memory in the Americas.* Durham, NC: Duke University Press.

Theidon, Kimberly. 2012. *Intimate Enemies: Violence and Reconciliation in Peru.* Philadelphia: University of Pennsylvania Press.

Torres Bustamente, María Clara. 2011. *Estado y coca en la frontera colombiana: El caso de Putumayo.* Bogotá: Observatorio para el Desarrollo, la Convivencia y el Fortalecimiento Institucional, Centro de Investigación y Educación Popular.

CHAPTER 12

VIOLENCE, RELIGION, AND INSTITUTIONAL LEGITIMACY IN NORTHERN CENTRAL AMERICA

ROBERT BRENNEMAN

The political and cultural landscape of Central America has shifted considerably during the past two decades. In its "Northern Triangle," Guatemala, El Salvador, and Honduras have all emerged from the turbulent 1970s and 1980s, including ugly civil wars in Guatemala and El Salvador, civil and military violence in Honduras, and repeated coups d'état in all three. Each has made considerable gains in establishing a formal representative democracy with open and free presidential elections. Although governmental institutions continue to sputter and creak under the strain of elevated expectations and minimal taxation, only Honduras has experienced the sort of interruption common earlier. Political changes have been accompanied by shifts in the cultural landscape, notably with regard to religious affiliation and practice. The field of religious institutions is far more open today than it was just a few short decades ago, with evangelical Pentecostal churches making by far the largest gains.

Despite these shifts in the political and cultural landscape, Guatemala, El Salvador, and Honduras remain violent and dangerous places for millions of their inhabitants. In 2013 all three posted some of the highest rates of violent death in the world. Yet despite the continuing *presence* of violence, the *nature* of violence—its organization and its motivation—has changed considerably. This chapter examines changes in the dynamics of violence in the Northern Triangle and explores efforts by Central America's religious institutions and leaders to address violence in the past and in the present.

Religious leaders, particularly priests and bishops of the Catholic Church, have made efforts to reduce violence in Central America since at least the 1970s. Typically, they have aimed to use the Church's legitimacy to denounce violent actors and organizations and thus delegitimize them. But as violence has changed in nature in the new century, such direct criticism is less effective than it used to be, since many of today's violent organizations have little need for legitimacy in order to survive. Therefore, although some continuities do exist between the violence of the armed conflicts and that today, I make a distinction between the "state-centered" violence typical of the 1980s and the "private violence" that has flourished since those conflicts ended.

This shift presents religious leaders who want to help reduce violence today with a changed situation. Nevertheless, both Catholic and Evangelical churches have made considerable efforts to address the multifaceted violence of their communities in the new century. Perhaps the most visible and interesting of these are the various urban gang ministries, spearheaded largely by Evangelical pastors, as well as recent efforts by Catholic bishops in El Salvador and Honduras to persuade gang members and leaders to abandon violence. In these cases—from the Pentecostal pastor trying to persuade his neighbors to trust a "transformed" former gang member to the Catholic bishop trying to persuade a skeptical public to support a truce between gang leaders—religious leaders place their considerable legitimacy as trusted, politically neutral spiritual guides on the line in order to "bless" projects of self-reform or truces between gangs. But providing a legitimacy blessing in this way opens up the religious community to criticism from a public that has grown weary of urban violence and distrustful of gang members and anyone who would aid them.[1]

This chapter aims to demonstrate (1) that religious organizations, including Evangelical/Pentecostal churches, continue to lead violence reduction efforts; (2) that such efforts are complicated and risky due to changes in the nature of violence today; and (3) that gang violence has provided Christian churches and leaders with an important proving ground for demonstrating their efficacy in addressing matters of widespread concern. In this context, evangelical Pentecostal churches may hold an advantage insofar as their goals are typically more modest, attainable, and observable.

Violence Transformed

Lethal violence continues in northern Central America and has generally increased to levels that far surpass any of the countries to the nearby north or south. Figure 12.1 shows the homicide rates in these countries in the past two decades. The top three lines in the figure represent the homicide rates of the Northern Triangle beginning in the 1990s.[2] These countries wrestle with lethal violence on a scale well beyond that of any of their neighbors, including Nicaragua.[3]

But the violence today is quite different from that of a few short decades ago. This fact was aptly expressed in the subtitle of a recent report by the Small Arms Survey, which described the violence in Guatemala as a "panorama of a violence transformed" (Restrepo and Tobón García

Figure 12.1. Homicides per 100,000 Inhabitants in Mesoamerica, 1995–2010

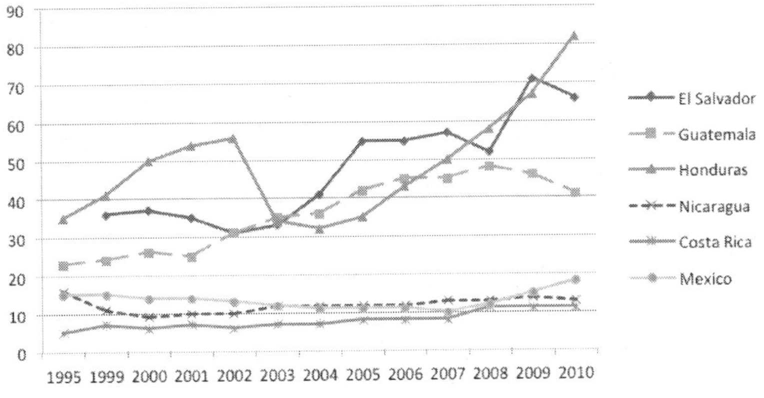

Source: UNODC 2011.

2011). The same could be said of each of the other two nations of the Northern Triangle. Violence has continued, but it has been "transformed" in its aim and its organization. In this section, I explore some of those changes by comparing two "ideal types" of violence. For analytical purposes, I define *state-centered violence* as typifying most of the violence committed in the region in the 1980s. In opposition to this centralized, bureaucratic, and ideologically motivated violence, I employ the term *private violence* to describe most of the violence in the region today. The larger goal is to provide a better picture of changes in the nature of the challenge facing religious institutions wishing to address lethal violence. Many social scientists rightly recognize that violence can take many forms and has many important precursors and consequences, and there is some value in exploring terms such as *structural violence* and *symbolic violence* (Bourdieu 1991). However, for the sake of conceptual clarity my analysis here will remain focused on physical violence: physical aggression resulting in bodily harm to a person or group of persons.[4]

Most of the lethal violence carried out in the 1980s in Central America was political and "state-centered," in the sense that it was committed by actors belonging to organizations seeking to hold on to, or seize, the levers of state power. The institutions of the state, especially its bloated armed forces, were at once sources and objects of violence. Cold War ideologies framed deadly armed conflict between Marxist-inspired guerrilla groups and extremely conservative governments protected by the armed forces, the police, and intelligence units. Meanwhile, the U.S. government, an outside state, sided with national governments in El Salvador and Guatemala, providing direct and indirect support for war and espionage. And although civil unrest in Honduras never rose to the level of open warfare, a swollen military apparatus was willing and able to carry out extrajudicial killings of leaders of popular organizations and anyone suspected of aiding the Salvadoran guerrillas. The army's extensive exercise of influence over elections and elected officials and its lack of accountability for state violence earned Honduras the title *democradura* (Gutiérrez Rivera 2012).

It is worth remembering that guerrilla violence aimed at seizing the power of the state, and that goal necessitated a level of centralized organization and chain of command among the rebel groups. Although multiple rebel organizations existed in Guatemala and El Salvador, by 1980 they had organized themselves into a front, coordinating strategy and co-operating with information in order to achieve a shared goal. That shared goal was national and international recognition as the legitimate representatives of their state. Propaganda, which always argued the need for armed violence against the enemy, was important to both guerrillas and the state. Each side sought to use radio and print media to present its own practice of violence as lamentable but necessary, as distinguished from the illegitimate violence of the enemy.[5] In short, governments no less than guerrilla groups sought to achieve *institutional legitimacy* in a context in which such legitimacy was, at the very least, in question. In light of Max Weber's ([1919] 2004) classic definition of the state as that entity which can lay claim to the "legitimate use of physical violence," the "state-centric" political violence of the period reminds us that it was of crucial importance to convince both the national and international publics of the "necessity" of the use of force. And although both sides endangered their own legitimacy by carrying out atrocities that, when brought to light, undermined their standing in the international community (the military doing so with far greater frequency than the guerrillas), the leaders of these organizations were at pains to make their case as deserving of legitimate recognition within and beyond their own borders.

The nature and motivation of violence have changed dramatically since the 1980s.[6] Central America's most violent organizations today are no longer confined to the state, and guerrilla groups no longer exist. Instead, violence emerges from a multitude of actors belonging to loosely knit organizations like Mexican-based drug cartels, organized criminal groups, *transportistas* (drug couriers), and urban gangs (Arias 2011; Bosworth 2010; Dudley 2010).[7] Lethal violence in northern Central America today has thus been transformed in dramatic ways. Rather than state-centric, the violence of these nations might be described as private violence, carried out by individuals and organizations with minimal ideological attachment. Their key aims are (1) to make money by increasing their organization's profit margin through the expansion and consolidation of their share of illegal markets, and (2) to enhance their own and their group's "respect" by dealing violently with those who disrespect either. Violence is a means to accomplish both of these tasks, through the elimination or intimidation of competitors for money and/or respect. The Mexican-based drug cartels provide the best example of the exercise of such market-motivated violence, but organized crime rings and youth gangs also employ violence to compete for territory and notoriety. Furthermore, rather than having relatively stable, bureaucratic structures, organizations engaging in private violence have loose, provisional structures. The security analysts Douglas Farah and Pamela Phillips Lum (2013, 4) point out that Central American "gangs themselves are in a tremendous state of flux." Elsewhere I describe the gang structure as similar to a franchise that may be adapted by local cell leaders, or "franchisees" (Brenneman 2012). Even the organizations themselves emerge and die with relative frequency, as evidenced by the rise of the Zetas, a major drug cartel that was confined to security operations for the Gulf Cartel less than a decade ago. Already the Zetas appear to have splintered into a number of smaller groups as a result of infighting and external pressure.[8]

For our purposes here, the most important characteristic of private violence is that leaders of these organizations have little or no interest in acquiring institutional legitimacy, in the sense of widespread recognition and acceptance that they possess a right to exercise authority of some kind. Institutional legitimacy is not the same as popularity. A president can be unpopular without being deemed illegitimate precisely because his office is considered a legitimate institution. Governments are especially desirous of institutional legitimacy because of their need to administer authority and distribute resources for a large population, and when their legitimacy is widely questioned, as in the case of Northern Ireland or El Salvador in the 1980s, "governing" through direct violence and fear becomes an attractive temptation. Governments are not the only institutions concerned with legitimacy, though. Other organizations, such as unions, sports leagues, and churches, also administer authority and collect resources and are thus in need of institutional legitimacy.

But with few exceptions, the key actors and producers of today's lethal violence in Central America have made little effort to build institutional legitimacy for the organizations to which they belong. Groups such as gangs, drug cartels, and organized crime rings have little need for widespread recognition or acceptance as *legitimate* institutions. Although some drug cartels have made alliances with local governments, especially in the border towns of El Salvador and Guatemala, these dealings are aimed at ensuring protection and impunity rather than widespread acceptance of or admiration for the organization. Since a great deal of money can be made without acquiring legal status or legitimate recognition, organizations such as drug cartels and *transportistas* are generally content to work from the relative obscurity of their compound or behind other business fronts. Meanwhile, urban gangs—perhaps in part because they are made up largely of youths who have little investment in the social world of adults—are even less interested in social approval and therefore the least careful of offending "traditional" social values (Collins 2007). At least until very recently, institutional legitimacy has ranked very low on their list of priorities, and thus violence that is messy and results in the deaths of bystanders or children is less subject to criticism within the gang and can even enhance the victimizer's standing as a true *loco*.

To contrast the violence of the 1980s and the violence of today in northern Central America, I have introduced two ideal types—state-centered and private violence—in order to gain a conceptual grasp on how lethal violence has changed in recent decades. I am not arguing here that greed was absent as a motive of the "political" violence of the 1980s —clearly, many military officers knew that they would be rewarded rather handsomely for their "service"—or that gang members or drug cartel bosses have no values other than greed. But I believe the ideal types of state-centered and private violence reveal significant differences in the motivations and aims of the violence then and now. Central America's most violent organizations today have, at least until very recently, shown little interest in being recognized as legitimate. As I will show, this aspect of the new violence requires different strategies and approaches from religious institutions and individuals who seek to confront the violence of their communities and their nation.

Religion in Northern Central America Today

Before examining the ways in which Central American churches have addressed the shifting forms of violence in their societies, it is important to consider the religious landscape of the Northern Triangle today, for although Central America teems with religious activity, the nature of that activity has changed considerably. The most important aspect of this change involves the growth of the Protestant evangelical community—a growth that has been dominated by Pentecostal churches. Recent polling, shown in figure 12.2, reveals some of the highest levels of Evangelicals in Latin America.

According to some polls, Honduras, a country in which less than 10 percent of the population self-identified as Evangelical-Protestant in the early 1980s, now has the highest proportion of Evangelical adherents in Central America. In a CID-Gallup Poll conducted in 2012, more Hondurans described themselves as Protestant than as Roman Catholic (Holland 2012).[9] Evangelicals, while still a minority religious tradition, are not far behind Catholics in Guatemala and El Salvador, and in all three countries, only a small minority of the population—about 10 percent or less—professes a faith other than Protestant or Catholic Christianity.

Meanwhile, Catholic Charismatic Renewal movements have been strong in Guatemala and, to a lesser extent, in El Salvador. A significant minority of Central American Catholics now worship in ways that resemble the worship of their Pentecostal counterparts. However, with some exceptions among middle-class Evangelicals, Central American Protestants continue to distinguish themselves from their Catholic neighbors and relatives by lifestyle and behavioral taboos. Evangelical Pentecostals—who typically refer to themselves as *cristianos* as distinguished from *católicos*—tend to avoid alcohol, bars, and dance halls as sources of worldly temptation.[10]

Figure 12.2. Religious Adherents in Northern Central America

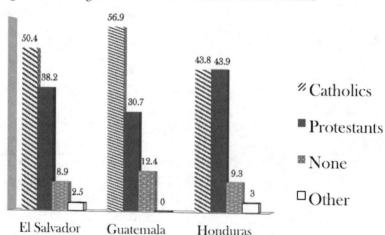

Source: Holland 2012.

Not only do the vast majority of Central Americans continue to profess one form or another of Christianity, most Central Americans hold religious institutions in high regard. Survey research published by Vanderbilt's Latin American Public Opinion Project ranked institutions according to their "legitimacy" by asking a representative sample of citizens to what extent (on a scale of 1 to 7) they trust particular public and cultural institutions.[11] By averaging respondents' scores, researchers constructed a "legitimacy score" for each institution. Despite its diminishing membership, the Catholic Church continues to be at or near the top of the legitimacy rankings among major institutions in each nation. Figure 12.3 shows that in Guatemala and Honduras, survey respondents reported higher trust in the Catholic Church than in any other institution, including the armed forces and the national government (Azpuru 2010; Pérez and Argueta 2010). In El Salvador the Catholic Church did not manage to top the rankings but still scored very high at 63 percent, close behind the armed forces, the national government, and the office of the Human Rights Ombudsman (Macías and Cruz 2010).[12]

Only in Guatemala were respondents polled about their trust in the Evangelical church, which scored an impressive 65 percent—just one

Figure 12.3. "Legitimacy" Scores of Selected Religious and State Institutions

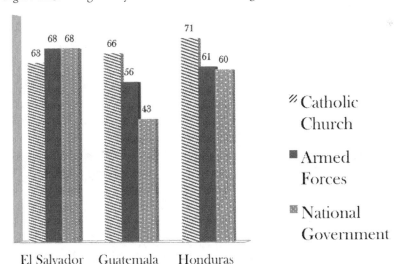

Source: Azpuru 2010; Macías and Cruz 2010; Pérez and Argueta 2010.

point behind the Catholic Church. While it would be a mistake to draw too many conclusions from a comparison of state institutions, which are obliged to make decisions about resources and safety for all citizens, and cultural institutions like the churches, whose policies primarily affect the lives of members, the fact that churches occupy such a high standing in the eyes of most Central Americans is worth noting. At the very least, it reveals that churches have something that politicians want and need—institutional legitimacy. And, comparatively speaking, they have it in spades.

Religion and State-Centric Violence

Data measuring the legitimacy of Central America's religious institutions goes back only as far as 2004. And while it would be difficult to guess at the levels of legitimacy for the Evangelical church in earlier decades, we have little reason to suspect that the high levels of legitimacy enjoyed by the Catholic Church today are a recent phenomenon. It is precisely this context of trust in the Catholic Church and its leaders that helps explain the impact of a key approach by the Catholic leadership when confronting the state-centric violence of that epoch: the withdrawal of legitimacy. Again and again Catholic clergy, including priests and bishops and, in one case, an archbishop, confronted violence by questioning the legitimacy of government-sponsored violence carried out in the name of protecting the state. Public criticism in this context amounted to a kind of *desprestigio*, or discrediting of a state that was supposed to be protecting its citizens rather than attacking them. By questioning the state and its various security apparatuses—and occasionally also questioning guerrilla-induced casualties—the Catholic hierarchy exercised a powerful weapon in the midst of civil war. Such an impact was possible in part because institutional legitimacy was a key concern for both the violent left and the violent right.[13]

This is not the place to catalog such delegitimizing acts and pronouncements. Virginia Garrard-Burnett's chapter in this volume provides a more detailed account of such events, the most famous of which involved the publicly broadcast homily in which Msgr. Óscar Arnulfo Romero appealed directly to the soldiers of the Salvadoran military, imploring them "In the name of God" to "Stop the repression!" (Brockman

1983). By calling state-endorsed force "repression," Romero publicly challenged the claim by Salvadoran authorities that the violence of the armed forces was strategic and necessary. Furthermore, his call to obey the "law of God" rather than the state-sanctioned orders of a superior were accompanied by a letter to then-President Jimmy Carter asking the United States to cease military aid. Such a request was, in effect, a call to the international community to recognize the extent to which the Salvadoran armed forces had lost any legitimacy as guardians of the nation.

That these delegitimizing statements were met with swift and brutal consequences reveals the depth of their impact and the level of threat they posed to the regime. Monsignor Romero was killed one day after delivering his homily. Bishop Juan Gerardi, author of the Recovery of Historical Memory (REMHI) project in Guatemala—sponsored by the Catholic Church—was the target of at least two failed assassination attempts in the early 1980s before he was finally bludgeoned to death just two days after delivering the REMHI Report in 1998. In Guatemala a dozen priests and hundreds of catechists were assassinated during a five-year span at the height of the war. And in El Salvador six Jesuits were brutally killed by the military in 1989 as a result of their efforts to press the state to abandon its policy of repression and engage in peace negotiations. Numerous priests were also targeted by security forces in Honduras, including two foreign priests—a Colombian and a visiting American—killed by a group of landowners and military personnel while participating in a land rights march at Los Horcones in 1975 (Lapper and Painter 1986). Meanwhile, a handful of Protestant leaders, including Episcopal, Lutheran, Presbyterian, and Baptist pastors, also made formal statements questioning the legitimacy of their respective governments (see Garrard-Burnett, this vol.). They were generally treated less brutally, no doubt in part because the Protestant community was then seen as more marginal in Central American society. In any case, critical Protestant and Evangelical leaders were the exception rather than the rule in that community.

Religion and Private Violence

Although the state-centric violence of the 1980s could be effectively confronted (though not eliminated) by religious representatives through public critique and the questioning of institutional legitimacy, the private violence of today is another matter. Private violence, exercised principally by drug cartels, organized crime rings, and street gangs, cannot be addressed in the same way because its key actors are far less interested in obtaining or protecting the institutional legitimacy of their own organization. Only the state can be expected to respond to public critique because its representatives rely on national and international recognition in order to maintain their authority and income. Of course, to the extent that the state has colluded in social cleansing, critical statements or pronouncements of concern by religious leaders can have a useful impact. A number of contemporary Catholic leaders including Bishop Rómulo Emiliani in Honduras as well as leaders of the Institute for Public Opinion at the Jesuit Universidad Centroamericana "José Simeón Cañas" (UCA) in El Salvador, have criticized the state for scapegoating gang youths for all violent crime and for promoting *mano dura* (heavy-handed) approaches to crime that pave the way for social cleansing and the extrajudicial killing of young people and children by off-duty police officers (Aguilar and Miranda 2006).[14] But most of Central America's violent actors today are not embedded in state organizations, and those who are, act outside their official roles. It remains very difficult to have an impact on these organizations by directly confronting or openly criticizing them.

In this context of "illegitimate" actors, some churches, many of them small neighborhood Pentecostal churches with a strong local orientation, have dealt with the violence of their own communities in a very different way—one that is consistent with their conversionist theology and their congregational ecclesiology. Beginning in the late 1990s a not-insignificant number of evangelical Pentecostal congregations began to address the gang violence of their communities through "gang rescue" or "restoration" ministries. In other words, some evangelical Pentecostal pastors and lay leaders have attempted to diminish the gang violence of their communities through evangelization programs that aim to "rescue" individual gang members from the dangerous and often-lethal gang lifestyle (*vida loca*) and bring them into a faith community that prizes a sober, industrious, domestic lifestyle and frequent, deeply emotional worship. Rather than attempt to shame the leaders of organized gangs into reforming themselves (as the Catholic hierarchy sought to do with the repressive regimes of the 1980s), evangelical Pentecostal pastors and gang ministry coordinators have approached gang violence through the lens of individual repentance and reform. By evangelizing individual gang members, gang ministry workers hope to diminish, one by one, the number of violent youths in their neighborhoods and provide them with a pathway to safety, stability, and nonviolent community.[15]

In the past decade, several studies have examined these religious gang ministry efforts (e.g., Gómez and Vásquez 2001; Wolseth 2011; O'Neill 2011). While it would be impossible to gauge the concrete impact of these ministries at the macrolevel, my own investigations at the microlevel in 2007 and 2008 revealed that many former gang members do find in the evangelical gang ministries a welcome means of transforming a violent identity and reestablishing themselves as trustworthy young adults in their community (Brenneman 2012). There are at least three sociological factors contributing to the relative success (at the level of the individual) of such gang ministries. First, most of the rescue or restoration ministries I was able to locate in Honduras, Guatemala, and El Salvador were closely tied to a local congregation with highly committed members and strong, dense social networks readily available to converted or converting former gang members who were in desperate need of nondelinquent social ties. Second, the evangelical Pentecostal congregations spearheading gang ministry tended to seek large time commitments from new converts, who were expected to spend most evenings—especially weekends—in worship at *culto* (church service). Such "time hoarding" appears excessive to outsiders but served deserting gang members especially well, helping them give up criminal activity by separating them from their former networks and haunts. Finally, evangelical Pentecostal congregations and their gang ministries provided a crucial "refuge" from gang reprisals; by the 2000s, local gang leaders had essentially banned members from leaving the gang under most circumstances. Those who dared to desert were subject to a "green light" death sentence, but many leaders provided a special "exemption" to the "morgue rule" if they joined an evangelical Pentecostal church. The only catch was that a profession of conversion had to be demonstrated by an obvious and public change in lifestyle. The former gang member professing to have joined the *hermanos* (brothers and sisters in Christ) had to act like one. A Honduran former gang member reported to me that on informing his leader that he was considering leaving the gang to join a church, the leader told him, "Okay. You know that nobody messes with Curly [*El Colocho*, meaning "God"]. Not with Curly, not with the barrio [gang]. If you're going to change, you'd better do it once and for all" (Brenneman 2012, 159). In addition, a number of former gang members reported that some gang leaders believe *converts* are less likely to compete with the local gang for drug sales and extortion markets when compared to nonreligious gang deserters, who often have difficulty accessing legal income to support family or a lingering drug addiction. Thus the policy of giving a pass to gang leavers who convert probably has at least a certain pragmatic aspect.[16]

Evangelical Pentecostal gang ministries and the churches that support them provide aging gang members with what the sociologist David Kennedy (2011), who has worked on the subject in the United States, might call an "honorable exit" from a violent organization and lifestyle. Furthermore, they provide resources and social networks for individuals whose spoiled identity would make it otherwise impossible to obtain a job and security in a society that has come to fear and loathe them.

Not everyone agrees that providing an "honorable exit" to gang members tired of the *vida loca* is a worthy endeavor. In fact, pastors and other evangelical Pentecostals who participate in gang "restoration" are sometimes criticized for harboring criminals or "terrorists," since many gang members have participated in or authorized unspeakable acts of violence. The popularity of "social cleansing" as a means to reduce the gang population—a practice that 60 percent of Guatemalans approved of according to one poll[17]—is at least a partial result of the inability of police and courts to effectively secure public spaces from gangs, which may act with virtual impunity in their neighborhoods. And yet most gang members are also minors, or were at the time of their decision to join the gang, and many have themselves been victims of extreme abuse or neglect (Medina and Mateu-Gelabert 2007; Rubio 2007). For this reason, I have argued elsewhere (Brenneman 2010) that the risks and expenses taken on by evangelical Pentecostal pastors and gang ministry coordinators might be fruitfully understood as human rights work, even though few if any of its proponents would use such language to describe it.

Gang members are deeply stigmatized and generally vulnerable members of the unprotected and impoverished segments of Central American society. That they are themselves both victims and perpetrators of violence makes working on their behalf far more difficult and complex. But from the perspective of religious gang ministry coordinators, their delinquent actions should not obscure the fact that as human beings they are redeemable by God's love. Gang members also possess rights to life and to due process—rights often ignored by off-duty police and vigilante groups (Moser and Winton 2002; Payne 1999).[18] Providing gang members with a second chance, the goal of evangelical Pentecostal gang ministries, is far from popular. Those who do engage in legitimacy work by giving reforming gang members the protection of their own reputations as religious leaders in the community provide a measure of protection from gang reprisals and the hostility of a skeptical and often angry community.

There are also Catholic gang ministries, but they typically do not employ evangelization or an overtly Christian spiritual component. The Catholic priests and lay workers I interviewed who were involved in this work were wary about vouching for the authenticity of a former gang member reporting to have undergone a transformation. Instead, most Catholic gang ministries assist former gang members in solving very practical problems, such as getting a job or removing the visible tattoos that greatly increase the odds of being targeted by old enemies or for social cleansing.

There are theological reasons for the tendency of evangelical Pentecostals to aim for spiritual transformation and the tendency among Catholics to restrict their ministry to social support. Catholic pastoral practice has not emphasized spiritual rebirth and transformation of individual adults so much as community "accompaniment," which is far more common in the Central American Catholic Church. In addition, as Jon Wolseth (2011) has pointed out, Catholic ministries are more likely to see themselves as representing the needs of the whole community rather than as occupying a unique social space set apart from the rest of the non-Catholic or nonobservant residents of the neighborhood. Thus Central American Catholic congregations cannot provide deserting gang members with refuge by virtue of belonging to a recognizable social group practicing a separate or unique value system. Whereas gang leaders can observe former gang members who profess to be evangelical converts in order to deduce whether or not their postconversion lifestyle fits the teetotaling, domesticated lifestyle of the *hermanos*, no such behavioral indicators exist for professing Catholics. The result is a situation in which evangelical Pentecostal churches, through their maintenance of stricter social taboos, have a more public, visible mechanism available for extending legitimacy to repentant gang members in need of an identity overhaul and the trust of their neighbors and potential employers. Thus whereas the Catholic Church tended to undermine the legitimacy of violent organizations in the 1980s, evangelical Pentecostal congregations engaging in gang ministry have sought to reduce violence by lending their legitimacy to individual actors who are willing to abandon a violent organization but are in need of trust and protection in order to be reintegrated into non-gang society.

The Gang Truce Efforts

Gang members and gang leaders in Central America typically take pride in their ability to flout the values of their surrounding society. Open violation of the most widely accepted social norms is itself a goal, as evidenced by JJ, a former gang leader who described to me what he wanted to make of his own gang cell when making his appeal to become its leader: "As a new *ranflero* I laid out my vision of making my clique the worst of all cliques—the most subversive, the most evil, the most powerful, the most murderous, the one that moved the most drugs and had the most power in prison" (Brenneman 2012, 6). Recently, however, gangs in El Salvador and Honduras have publicly expressed a desire to be taken seriously as youth organizations concerned about the well-being of their respective countries. Their declarations have come as part of a reported truce, first in El Salvador in March 2012 and as of May 2013 in Honduras, between warring factions of the major rival gang franchises. In El Salvador the National Police reported that the homicide rate had been cut in half since the truce went into effect.[19] At least during the initial phase of the truce, the Salvadoran government praised Msgr. Fabio Colindres, a Catholic bishop and chaplain of the armed forces, and credited him with having played a key role in the negotiations. Subsequent investigations revealed that the bishop's role had been almost entirely symbolic, but it had an important impact on public debate over the truce. As Steven

Dudley (2013) observes, the bishop was brought into the process in order to lend an air of legitimacy to the proceedings and provide a bulwark against those who would, predictably, argue that condoning "mediation" among gang leaders was akin to negotiating with terrorists. At the same time in Honduras, Msgr. Rómulo Emiliani, an outspoken defender of the rights of gang members to fair and humane treatment as minors, announced his involvement in a truce between members of the MS-13 and M-18 with vocal support from the Organization of American States, although these efforts were never accompanied by a notable change in the Honduran rate of lethal violence.[20]

By 2014 the Salvadoran truce had largely fallen out of favor with the public and had lost its place as a government-endorsed strategy for dealing with gang violence. Assessing the true impact of the truce in El Salvador—much less the sincerity of its signatories—lies beyond the scope of this chapter. Investigative journalists have provided plenty of reasons to question the primary story of the unfolding truce delivered by the government and its security advisers (Dudley 2013),[21] and research by Jeannette Aguilar (2012) provides reason to suspect that the agreement between gang leaders was accompanied if not overshadowed by an agreement between the government and the Mexican drug cartels. But the truce itself captured the attention of the Salvadoran public, which appears to have changed its mind several times about whether or not the truce (and the government that sanctioned it) ought to be supported.[22] Nevertheless, such national and international attention makes clear that the public blessing of a religious institution can be a valuable commodity in Central America. Salvadoran government officials actively sought a blessing from a Catholic bishop, and when the National Bishops' Conference backed away from supporting the truce—although without issuing a full-throated condemnation—President Mauricio Funes traveled to the Vatican in the hope of convincing a new Latin American pope to publicly support it.[23] Shortly thereafter, in a move that shocked many, Pastor Edgar López Bertrand, also known as "Toby Jr." to tens of thousands of members of a neo-Pentecostal megachurch called the Biblical Baptist Friends of Israel Tabernacle, hosted two prominent gang leaders for a televised interview in his church. In front of thousands of churchgoers and thousands more viewers, Reverend Toby Jr. publicly endorsed the truce and chatted amiably with the two leaders, who had been granted special, highly unusual permission to leave their cells for the interview. "May everyone involved in these proceedings be blessed," said the young pastor, who was enjoying a rare opportunity to lead his church in the absence of his father, the congregation's founding minister, who was recovering from a stroke.[24] The visit created a firestorm of controversy, led to the dismissal of key actors in the government-sponsored truce process, and forced the young reverend to publicly defend his actions and motives.[25] Clearly, stepping into the debate provides religious leaders with both instant attention and the potential for withering criticism from those who question the motives of the government and the gangs.

The shrill debates surrounding the legitimacy of the truce reveal both the political importance of the gang issue and the extent to which Central American politicians crave the "blessing" of religious leaders when embarking on highly controversial policies, especially those that involve deeply stigmatized members of violent organizations like gangs. This reality places the churches in a unique position to influence public opinion and, by extension, public policy on violence and security. But it also opens them up to heated criticism.

The nature of lethal violence in Central America has changed dramatically since the 1980s, and these changes have meant that churches and religious leaders must approach violence and violent organizations in ways wholly distinct from those of an earlier era. While public statements excoriating a repressive military had an important impact as a partial brake on political, state-centered violence in the 1980s, the same efforts are less likely to reduce the private violence of today. Public shaming of criminal organizations will have minimal impact since institutional legitimacy is not vital to their purposes. Thus a key strategy for confronting violence in the past is no longer available to the churches. Nevertheless, individuals in search of an honorable exit from a violent organization like a street gang can find in many evangelical Pentecostal churches a ready and supportive refuge—so long as they are willing to convert and commit to the lifestyle of the *hermanos*.

Truce negotiations between gangs in El Salvador and Honduras opened the door to the participation of the Catholic Church hierarchy, but in contrast to prophetic critique of the state's repressive violence, the Catholic hierarchy has been solicited to extend a "blessing" on a risky and controversial negotiation between youth gang leaders whose motives are far from clear. Meanwhile, it is likely that most Evangelical leaders, the example of Toby Jr. aside, will be reticent to "bless" a process that does not involve the spiritual transformation of once-violent individuals. After all, one of the key attractions of gang ministry for many Evangelical pastors is its potential for demonstrating the spiritual power of conversion to a watching community. I suspect that few Evangelical leaders will go out of their way to follow the example of Toby Jr. in lending their blessing to a highly volatile political truce process. Far more will continue to support spiritual-social gang ministries that target individual gang members or former gang members at the local level.

Nevertheless, it is interesting to note that both the Evangelical and Catholic communities have made efforts to address lethal violence, especially the violence of street gangs. Many Evangelicals, who were typically content to ignore the state-centered violence occurring around them in the 1980s, have taken it upon themselves to demonstrate that their religious goods can be effective in transforming gang members and diminishing gang warfare in their neighborhoods. One likely reason for such engagement is that the violence of recent decades touches the lives of nearly everyone, including "nonpolitical" evangelical Pentecostals in urban barrios. Unlike their predecessors of the 1980s, the evangelical Pentecostal churches of today cannot escape the day-to-day violence of their communities by simply avoiding the discussion of or involvement in politics, social reform movements, or certain "suspect" academic disciplines or universities. Private violence today affects the daily lives of virtually everyone in the Northern Triangle.

Meanwhile, Catholics, who took up the cause of human rights in the 1980s, have tended to promote social ministry aimed at preventing youths from joining gangs, even while a few priests and bishops have recently taken part in truce negotiations among gang leaders, lending the legitimacy of their own institutions to controversial and uncertain processes. In effect, the debate over gang violence has provided the religious community with a proving ground on which to demonstrate the utility and efficacy of their respective religious goods. In such contexts, it is likely that the evangelical Pentecostals approach of offering targeted "rescue" ministries for specific individuals are more apt to be judged successful by onlookers if for no other reason than that they seek much more modest, attainable, and observable results than do the Catholic priests and bishops who engage in gang "prevention" or in negotiations between gang leaders at the national level. In terms of actual impact, however, it is altogether possible, though probably unprovable, that Catholic efforts at gang prevention—often taking the form of vocational-technical training for working-class youths—may keep more youths out of the gangs than evangelical Pentecostal ministries are able to "rescue" from them. In any event, today no less than in the 1980s, it remains difficult if not impossible to discuss violence in Central America without a knowledge of religious actors and their institutions.

Notes

1. It must be noted that the argument here is not that gangs are the only source of violence in northern Central America. They are not even, necessarily, the most lethal contributors to it, although their frequent participation in homicides is indisputable. Furthermore, although Christian churches are involved in various attempts to address violence at the local and national levels, gang ministries are not necessarily the most important of these efforts.

2. Reliable statistics are not available, but homicide rates were probably much higher in Guatemala and El Salvador before 1992.

3. Due to its very small population and its connection to the Caribbean states, I am not including Belize in my analysis here despite a very recent and very alarming spike in the murder rate.

4. I use data on homicides because, though these are far from perfect, sociologists have recognized that such statistics provide the most reliable measures available of physical violence and even crime more generally.

5. Predictably, Gen. Efraín Ríos Montt, in his recent, high-profile court case, employed the well-worn defense of his own administration's exercise of widespread and largely indiscriminate violence as "necessary" given the threat of the guerrillas, who had pitted Guatemalan brother against brother.

6. Honduras presents noteworthy and alarming exceptions here. Especially since the coup of 2009, violence by police and military personnel may have reached a point at which it is difficult to conclude that such acts are random or disconnected to the state.

7. See also Edelberto Torres-Rivas, "La lógica empresarial al servico del crimen," *El Periódico*, January 31, 2010.

8. Randal C. Archibold and Ginger Thompson, "Capture of Mexican Crime Boss Appears to End a Brutal Chapter," *New York Times*, July 16, 2013.

9. As Clifton Holland (2012) points out in his comparison of polling data, there is good reason to take the Honduras poll numbers with a grain of salt since the percentage of self-described Protestants varies considerably by survey company.

10. Recent interview-based research by the author revealed that members of a Catholic Charismatic Renewal group saw their freedom to consume alcohol as the *principal* distinction between their own faith and that of the Pentecostals.

11. In each country, face-to-face surveys were conducted by trained interviewers with respondents in a scientific sample of approximately fifteen hundred homes.

12. Some readers will no doubt be surprised at the high legitimacy ranking of the armed forces, especially in El Salvador, given the bloody history of the military in that country. It should be recalled, however, that crime and criminal violence have provided the military with a means of rehabilitating and elevating its image as a protector of the people. This is especially true in the case of El Salvador, where both the ARENA party and the FMLN have, with great fanfare, launched tough-on-crime policies in which the military figured prominently.

13. One could argue that the Guatemalan and Salvadoran armies committed so many egregious atrocities that "legitimacy" seemed hardly a goal. And yet in almost every case, the armed forces were loath to acknowledge a role in the killing of innocents, knowing well that to do so would itself be a blow to the legitimacy of the army and the government it purported to serve.

14. See also Jill Replogle, "Honduran Catholic Bishop Prepared to Mediate Talks," *Catholic Online*, August 3, 2006.

15. I did find two examples of evangelical gang ministry projects that sought to address community violence by convening negotiations between two warring gang cells in an effort to end the tit-for-tat violence between the two groups. But these efforts—one in Guatemala and the other in Honduras—were exceptional, and even in these cases religious conversion was intended to provide the impetus for gang leaders to participate.

16. Recent reports in the popular press have documented a growing number of cases in which evangelical Pentecostal pastors and laypersons have been the targets of gang violence. It may well be the case that the "Evangelical exemption" observed in the mid-2000s was only sporadically observed in the 2010s.

17. See Rita María Aguilar, "Ven debilidad del estado," *Siglo XXI*, June 28, 2007.

18. See also James C. McKinley Jr., "In Guatemala, Officers' Killings Echo Dirty War," *New York Times*, March 5, 2007.

19. Elyssa Pachico, "100 Days into Gang Truce, El Salvador Sizes Up Security Gains," *InSight Crime*, June 18, 2012.

20. "Honduras: Tregua de maras será de 'cero crímenes,'" *La Prensa*, May 28, 2013.

21. See also José Luis Sanz, "La nueva verdad sobre la tregua entre pandillas," *El Faro*, September 11, 2012.

22. Even some members of the ultraconservative ARENA party were supportive of the truce for a time.

23. "Funes tratará de convencer al papa Francisco de las bondades de la tregua," *El Faro*, May 22, 2013.

24. José Luis Sanz and Carlos Martínez, "Tabernáculo Bíblico bendice la tregua," *El Faro*, May 30, 2013.

25. Alessandra Quiñónez, "Jefes de pandillas fueron invitados al Tabernáculo y 'ardió Troya,'" *La Página*, June 17, 2013.

References

Aguilar, Jeannette. 2012. "La coyuntura actual de las pandillas." Paper presented at the Cátedra de Realidad Nacional, sobre Militarización, Crimen Organizado y Pandillas, Universidad Centroamericana "José Simeón Cañas," November 13. Available at www.contrapunto.com.sv/violencia/la-coyuntura-actual-de-las-pandillas.

Aguilar, Jeannette, and Lissette Miranda. 2006. "Entre la articulación y la competencia: Las respuestas de la sociedad sivil organizada a las pandillas en El Salvador." In *Maras y pandillas en Centroamérica: Las respuestas de la sociedad civil organizada*, edited by José Miguel Cruz, 37–144. San Salvador: Instituto Universitario de Opinion Pública.

Arias, Enrique Desmond. 2011. "State Power and Central American Maras: A Cross-National Comparison." In *Maras: Gang Violence and Security in Central America*, edited by Thomas Bruneau, Lucía Dammert, and Elizabeth Skinner, 123–36. Austin: University of Texas Press.

Azpuru, Dinorah. 2010. "Cultura política de la democracia en Guatemala, 2010." Working Paper Series on Organized Crime in Central America. Vanderbilt University, Nashville, TN. Available at www.vanderbilt.edu/lapop/guatemala/2010-culturapolitica.pdf.

Bosworth, James. 2010. "Honduras: Organized Crime Gaining amid Political Crisis." Working Paper Series on Organized Crime in Central America. Woodrow Wilson International Center for Scholars, Washington, DC. Available at www.wilsoncenter.org/sites/default/files/Bosworth.FIN.pdf.

Bourdieu, Pierre. 1991. *Language and Symbolic Power.* Cambridge, MA: Harvard University Press.

Brenneman, Robert. 2010. "Pentecostal Human Rights Activists? Religious Motives in Gang 'Rescue' Programs in Central America." Paper presented at the annual meeting of the American Sociological Association, Atlanta, GA, August 16.

———. 2012. *Homies and Hermanos: God and the Gang in Central America.* New York: Oxford University Press.

Brockman, James R. 1983. *The Word Remains: A Life of Oscar Romero.* Maryknoll, NY: Orbis Books.

Collins, Randall. 2007. *Violence: A Micro-Sociological Theory.* Princeton, NJ: Princeton University Press.

Dudley, Steven S. 2010. "Drug Trafficking Organizations in Central America: *Transportistas*, Mexican Cartels, and *Maras*." Woodrow Wilson International Center for Scholars, Washington, DC. Available at www.wilson center.org/sites/default/files/Chapter%202-%20Drug%20Trafficking%20 Organizations%20in%20Central%20America%20Transportistas,%20 Mexican%20Cartels%20and%20Maras.pdf.

———. 2013. "The El Salvador Gang Truce and the Catholic Church: What Was the Role of the Catholic Church?" CLALS Working Paper Series No. 1. AU Center for Latin American and Latino Studies, Washington, DC. Available at www.american.edu/clals/Religion-and-Violence-Documents.cfm.

Farah, Douglas, and Pamela Phillips Lum. 2013. "Central American Gangs and Transnational Criminal Organizations: The Changing Relationships in a Time of Turmoil." IBI Consultants, Washington, DC. Available at www .strategycenter.net/docLib/20130224_CenAmGangsandTCOs.pdf.

Gómez, Ileana, and Manuel Vásquez. 2001. "Youth Gangs and Religion among Salvadorans in Washington and El Salvador." In *Christianity, Social Change, and Globalization in the Americas*, edited by Anna L. Peterson, Manuel A. Vásquez, and Philip J. Williams, 165–87. New Brunswick, NJ: Rutgers University Press.

Gutiérrez Rivera, Lirio. 2012. "Geografías de violencia y exclusión: Pandillas encarceladas en Honduras." *Latin American Research Review* 47, no. 2: 167–79.

Holland, Clifton. 2012. "Table of Statistics on Religious Affiliation in the Americas and the Iberian Peninsula." Programa Latinoamericano de Estudios Sociorreligiosos (PROLADES). Available at www.prolades.com/cra/ amertbl06.htm.

Kennedy, David. 2011. *Don't Shoot: One Man, a Fellowship, and the End of Violence in Inner-City America.* New York: Bloomsbury.

Lapper, Richard, and James Painter. 1986. *Honduras: State for Sale.* New York: Monthly Review Press.

Macías, Ricardo Córdova, and José Miguel Cruz. 2010. "Cultura política de la democracia en El Salvador, 2010." Vanderbilt University, Nashville, TN. Available at www.vanderbilt.edu/lapop/es/2010-culturapolitica2.pdf.

Medina, Juanjo, and Pedro Mateu-Gelabert. 2007. *Maras y pandillas, comunidad y policía en Centroamérica: Hallazgos de un estudio integral.* Guatemala City: Demoscopía.

Moser, Caroline, and Ailsa Winton. 2002. "Violence in the Central American Region: Towards an Integrated Framework for Violence Reduction." Overseas Development Institute, London. Available at www.odi.org/sites/odi .org.uk/files/odi-assets/publications-opinion-files/1826.pdf.

O'Neill, Kevin. 2011. "Delinquent Realities: Christianity, Formality, and Security in the Americas." *American Quarterly* 63, no. 2: 333–61.

Payne, Douglas. 1999. *El Salvador: Reemergence of "Social Cleansing" Death Squads.* Washington, DC: INS Resource Information Center.

Pérez, Orlando J., and José René Argueta. 2010. "Cultura política de la democracia en Honduras, 2010." Vanderbilt University, Nashville, TN.

Restrepo, Jorge A., and Alonso Tobón García. 2011. "Guatemala en la encrucijada: Panorama de una violencia transformada." Secretariado de la Declaración de Ginebra, Geneva. www.genevadeclaration.org/fileadmin/docs/ Guatemala_book/GD-Guatemala.pdf.

Rubio, Mauricio. 2007. *De la pandilla a la mara: Pobreza, educación, mujeres y violencia juvenil.* Bogotá: Universidad Externado de Colombia.

United Nations Office on Drugs and Crime (UNODC). 2011. *2011 Global Study on Homicide.* Vienna. Available at www.unodc.org/documents/data-and -analysis/statistics/Homicide/Global_study_on_homicide_2011_web.pdf.

Weber, Max. [1919] 2004. *The Vocation Lectures: Politics as a Vocation; Science as a Vocation.* Translated by R. Livingstone. Indianapolis, IN: Hackett.

Wolseth, Jon. 2011. *Jesus and the Gang: Youth Violence and Christianity in Urban Honduras.* Tucson: University of Arizona Press.

CHAPTER 13

THE POLITICS OF PRESENCE

Evangelical Ministry in Brazilian Prisons

ANDREW JOHNSON

Shortly before noon, Monday, November 9, 2010, authorities lost control of the Pedrinhas Prison Complex in São Luis, capital of the northeastern Brazilian state of Maranhão. A rivalry that had been simmering for weeks between prisoners from two different regions boiled over into a riot. More than a dozen inmates were killed, and law enforcement officials were sent to collect the severed heads of three prisoners that had been thrown over the prison walls. Inside the facility, corpses were piled in a janitor's closet, five prison employees had been taken hostage, and ten inmates had been marked for execution if the rioters' demands were not met. São Luis's police commissioner, Daniel Brandão, needed to act swiftly but did not want to send in the Military Police because that would certainly double or triple the casualties. Brandão made a decision that has become increasingly common among prison officials facing this type of situation: he called on a Pentecostal pastor to negotiate peace.

Marcos Pereira, minister of the Last Days Assembly of God (LDAG) Church in one of the gritty, peripheral neighborhoods of Rio de Janeiro, received the call from the prison marshal that afternoon. The rioting inmates, fearful of being slaughtered if the Military Police invaded the prison, had asked for Pastor Marcos to mediate the situation. Within a couple of hours, the pastor and ten members of the congregation had boarded a plane to São Luis, a city nearly two thousand miles north of their church. The group arrived at midnight and went straight to the prison, by now completely under inmate control. Pastor Marcos spoke with inmate leaders on a cell phone that had been smuggled inside and agreed to return the next morning to start negotiations. On November 10, he and the church members were allowed to enter the prison complex, passing through the lines of heavily armed police officers. The Pentecostal group walked across the prison yard to the cellblocks, where the pastor spoke to the inmates through barred windows. After several tense moments (filmed by a church member with a handheld camera) the door opened and two hostages emerged unharmed. The remaining three hostages were freed an hour later.

Pereira then entered the building to speak with the riot leaders and emerged in less than an hour with three handguns and a collection of knives they had surrendered. The siege was over. Immediately after the pastor turned over the weapons to the prison officials, the LDAG team gathered the inmates in the prison's patio and held a worship service with them. The Last Days Assemblies of God volunteers sang praise songs and prayed over the inmates as the prison officials removed the cadavers from the corridor and started to clean the floors and walls that were still wet with blood.

Pentecostal pastors like Marcos Pereira have become tremendously influential figures inside Brazilian prisons over the past fifteen years, giving them a platform to confront violence in the prison system (Johnson 2012). Their strategy favors direct intervention over traditional political action. Though Pentecostals are becoming increasingly active in Brazilian politics and a number of high-profile Pentecostal politicians now hold office, the Pentecostals I observed in my fieldwork relied on their consistent, physical presence inside Rio's prisons to influence state actors. They chose a "politics of presence" strategy rather than the more traditional political approach of voting for a particular candidate, aligning with a party, or pushing for specific legislation. The Pentecostals' choice to *be there* is a political act because when they stand shoulder to shoulder with the prisoners in the cellblocks they send a powerful message to state authorities and the larger society. Their message is simply that though these prisoners were convicted, or at least accused, of criminal activity, they are citizens, worthy of redemption and deserving of certain rights.

No other group in Brazilian civil society has the sort of intimate contact with prisoners that some Pentecostal leaders and laypersons do. But their presence inside the prisons is complicated because it places them in close proximity not just to prisoners, but to criminal enterprises, specifically the narco-gangs, which are major forces inside the walls. Less than three years after the dramatic events at the Pedrinhas prison, the arrest of Marcos Pereira would demonstrate that while the unique space Pentecostals occupy in prison provides them with an opportunity to respond to potential violence, it may also offer an opportunity to launder money, smuggle contraband, and relay valuable information to criminal leaders.

Methods

I started the fieldwork for this project by living for two weeks in a Brazilian prison as an "inmate." I slept in the same cells as the other inmates, ate the same food, and participated in the daily routines with the men as if I were myself incarcerated. I had initially set out to study nothing more specific than religion in prison, but after those two weeks, it was evident that Pentecostalism is the faith of the prisoner in Brazil. This experience established the trajectory and profoundly shaped the methodology for the rest of the project, which was carried out primarily in one men's jail and one men's penitentiary in Rio de Janeiro. In twelve months, I visited the jail and prison over forty times. I recorded private interviews with fifteen men who were incarcerated, and I participated in countless unrecorded conversations with dozens of inmates. I also collected participant observation data by attending thirty Pentecostal worship services inside the cellblocks. During the year I collected the data for this project, I conducted ethnographic fieldwork in dozens of storefront churches in Rio de Janeiro and interviewed dozens of former inmates who had been released in the previous five years. Throughout, the inmates treated me with the utmost respect. I could not have completed the project without their cooperation and hospitality.

Pentecostalism: The Faith of the Prisoners

Most of the Pentecostal response to violence inside prisons is not as dramatic as the scene described in the opening paragraphs. But these sensational, headline-grabbing interventions are possible because of the influential role that Pentecostalism plays in Rio de Janeiro's prison subculture. The prominence of Pentecostal pastors inside prison did not happen overnight; it is the result of a series of social processes that have been at work in Rio over the past two decades.

Prison culture does not arise in a vacuum but reflects the larger culture (Hunt et al. 1993; Irwin and Cressey 1962). In Rio de Janeiro, the vast majority of inmates are from the city's poor and marginalized neighborhoods (Wacquant 2003). The favelas and the prisons, therefore, are inextricably linked, and prison subculture is an extension of the neighborhoods where the prisoners lived. Pentecostalism's growth inside prison is due in part to the faith's success in the city's favelas and marginalized neighborhoods over the past twenty years. Rio de Janeiro is not the only Latin American city where Pentecostalism has thrived. Social scientists have documented Pentecostalism's resonance with people living on the margins of Latin American societies from the barrios of New York City to indigenous communities in Guatemala to the *villas miserias* of Argentina (Burdick 1999; Garrard-Burnett 1989; Chesnut 1997; Freston 1999; Hallum 2003; Mariz 1994; Miguez 1998). Kimberly Theidon's work (see chap. 15, this vol.) in the Urabá region of Colombia is an excellent example of how the faith is especially attractive to "complicated people," like former combatants in Colombia and, in this case study, prisoners in Brazil.

Reliable sociodemographic data on the number of practicing Pentecostals in Rio de Janeiro are unavailable, as are data that classify religious adherents by more complicated sociodemographic categories. Qualitative evidence of the faith's strength is abundant, however, and can be observed by simply walking through low-income neighborhoods in the city. Rio de Janeiro is primarily a Catholic city, but Catholic churches are noticeably absent in the favelas and peripheral communities located miles away from the city's pristine beaches and iconic urban landscape. Pentecostal churches are everywhere in these spaces. While visiting the hillside home of a former inmate, I asked him how many churches were in his relatively small, very poor neighborhood. He looked out his window and started to name them, pointing at each one as he listed them: "OK, there is one here in front of us, two including my church three with the 'God Is Power.' Then if you go up from the 'God Is Power' there is another, four, five with the 'Community,' six with another 'Assemblies of God,' and seven with the 'God Is Love.' So there are seven Pentecostal churches and one traditional Baptist church."

I asked if there were any Catholic Churches, and he responded, "No. Well, there is one up there, but it is closed and there are a few Macumba centers scattered around."[1] In another much larger favela, I asked a pastor the same question. He replied, "There are about ninety Pentecostal churches here, at least ninety, and a couple of Catholic churches." During the fieldwork, I visited dozens of neighborhoods that had high arrest rates. In all of them, Pentecostalism was the principal faith. So when a pastor told me that "the majority of criminals in Rio are children of Pentecostals," he was illuminating one of the key reasons Pentecostalism is so strong in prison: most inmates were raised in places where Pentecostalism dominates the religious landscape.

One of the defining characteristics of these neighborhoods is a historically weak state presence. What there is of state presence underserves the residents by providing a corrupt and lethal police force, dreadful health care services, and a woefully underfunded educational system (Alves and Evanson 2011; Goldstein 2003; Perlman 2010). In such neighborhoods, the product of decades of deeply rooted social inequality, two institutions now flourish: the criminal gang and the Pentecostal church.[2]

At first glance, these two groups would appear to be natural rivals given their radically different purposes. The Pentecostals preach submission to God, temperance, and interaction with the Holy Spirit; the gangs offer access to a more tangible trinity: money, sex, and power. But surprisingly, the relationship between the church and the gang is not defined by animosity. Pentecostal church members are active in gang-controlled areas, they offer gang members and drug traffickers an exit from criminal life through a faith commitment, but they do not try to wrest power from gang leaders. The Pentecostals' consistent presence in these spaces sends a message to these young men: your life is worth saving. This is a very different message from the one sent by the state through its pitiful provision of services and the city's police force that kills literally hundreds of these young men each year (Instituto de Segurança Pública 2013).

I asked Elizeu dos Santos, a pastor of an Assemblies of God church on the outskirts of Rio de Janeiro, to explain how this counterintuitive relationship plays out in his community. He told me:

> I had a project inside a community, inside a favela, and on the side of the community center there was an open-air drug market. Every time I went there, they transferred the drug market to a different place. They didn't want to endanger the people who were coming to the worship service. They have tremendous respect for us. They actually help us a lot. When we go inside a favela, they open a space for us in the neighborhood. They carry in chairs on their heads, or they give a soda or sandwich for everyone there. The drug traffickers tell me, "Hey, Pastor, whatever you need, it will be there." They bring a sound system, a complete sound system, and we do our work. They really care for us. If there is drug use, they stop it because "the brothers are here." They don't let people smoke, snort cocaine close to us, nobody. Sometimes when we come and they are smoking drugs, they hide it, you can smell it, but they are like, "Hey, the pastor is here; hide that."

The gang-church relationship on the street is crucial to understanding how Pentecostal pastors respond to violence behind bars. Many of the inmates Pastor Elizeu visits were street-level drug dealers, already accustomed to altering their business transactions when Pentecostal teams appear. Other inmates had bought and used drugs in open-air drug markets before they were arrested and were used to hiding their drug use from religious visitors. These cultural norms regarding relations between the criminal factions and Pentecostal groups are even more apparent in prison.

The nature of this relationship was unmistakable when the Pentecostals entered the cellblocks for worship services with the prisoners. Just before they passed through the heavy steel doors that opened into the cellblock corridor, one of the trustees would yell, "The church is coming down!" Immediately, shirtless inmates would disappear into their cells or put on shirts as a sign of respect to the visitors. The inmates who remained in the hallway where the service would take place extinguished their cigarettes and turned down the volume of the television sets and radios that blared nonstop throughout the day. Even the jail's resident tattoo artist would pack up his improvised electric tattoo gun and move to another part of the cellblock when the outside visitors arrived. Some of the inmates may have been annoyed at having to break up a card game or put out a recently lit smoke, but they did it anyway. The part of the prison that hosted the service became a sacred space and was treated as such by the inmates.

I asked one of the pastors who visited the jail each week if he ever felt vulnerable when he was in the cellblock, a space even the prison guards are frightened about entering. He responded, "You have seen it, you have been in there with me, they really respect us. I go in there with the sisters from the church; I go in there with my wife, even my daughter. They really respect us in prison." When the Pentecostal groups passed through the heavy prison doors, they knew full well that they would make excellent hostages if a riot broke out (I was acutely aware of my own value as a potential hostage when I first entered the cells). But the presence of these pastors and their family members and the volunteers from their church was a strong nonverbal way of saying to the inmates, "We trust you." Their presence resonated with the incarcerated men in a way that was much deeper than a verbal pledge of solidarity given at a political rally or another form of traditional political activity like supporting a political candidate who might be sympathetic to the prison population.

The prominence of Pentecostalism in the prison system is more than a reflection of the faith's strength in Rio's poor neighborhoods. Another reason Pentecostal pastors and volunteers are able to intervene and respond to violence in prisons is because of the inmate-led Pentecostal churches that operate autonomously in every penal facility in Rio de Janeiro (Johnson 2012). These inmate-led churches replicate the organizational structure of Pentecostal churches on the outside and adapt it to the prison context. Their members vote for pastors, deacons, worship leaders, and secretaries. In many of the prisons and jails, the members of the church live together in cells they have claimed as their own, and they practice their faith collectively.

Though they share core doctrinal tenets, an expressive worship style, and rituals with the Pentecostal churches outside prison, these inmate churches are independent, autonomous congregations supported by prisoners' donations. They do not report directly to any denomination or ministry on the outside, so they have a structure and character that reflects the realities of the particular jail or prison. These churches are integral parts of the prison subculture and ensure a permanent Pentecostal contingent inside that is not dependent on a pastor, a priest, or a missionary from the outside. The shared Pentecostal identity of inmates and fellow believers, or *crentes*, on the outside contributes to the ability of pastors to intervene in prison matters.

Prisons are places that, generally, people are trying to leave. But one of the problems many jail administrators face is the overwhelming number of Pentecostal churches and volunteers seeking to visit prisons. At the jail where I conducted much of my fieldwork, twelve churches made weekly visits to the cellblocks to hold worship services and sometimes provide medical and material assistance. The jail's warden complained to me that in his previous post he had to deal with seventeen Pentecostal churches making weekly visits to his relatively small jail and that trying to schedule all of them was a major part of his job.

The Pentecostal pastors and volunteers who visit the prisons daily, and at times are called upon to be peacemakers, rarely described their actions as politically motivated. In fact, when asked about their motivations, they gave theological responses that place them squarely within the emergent Progressive Pentecostal movement, a term introduced by Miller and Yamamori (2007, 212) to describe "Christians who claim to be inspired by the Holy Spirit and the life of Jesus and who seek to holistically address the spiritual, physical, and social needs of people in their community." Progressive Pentecostals are not only concerned with saving souls and resisting the temptations of the world; they are on the front lines of efforts to address the consequences of poverty, war, drug addiction, and a host of other social problems.

The primary focus of the groups that visited prisons and jails during my fieldwork was to hold worship services with the inmates. They sang praise songs, preached sermons, allowed inmates to share testimonies, gave altar calls, and prayed for the men and their families. But along with the spiritual services they also offered important material support. In the jails there were absolutely no medical services offered by the state. All of the medical supplies were brought in by family members or donated by individuals or groups that visited the jail. I cannot account for all of the supplies that entered the cellblocks, but outside of family members, I never saw a donation come from anyone not affiliated with a religious organization. It was the volunteers, not the state, that kept the meager supply shelves stocked.

Pastors and Pentecostal volunteers serve the inmates by providing a bridge or a link to their families. After nearly every worship service in prison, inmates passed along scraps of paper to the pastors with the phone numbers of their families or neighbors. There was no access to telephones in the jail, so after the worship services ended pastors stood outside the jail shuffling through the names and phone numbers and calling mothers, uncles, grandmothers, and neighbors to inform them that their loved ones were alive but in jail. Many families depended on the income, often illegal, that abruptly stopped when their son, brother, or father was incarcerated. In response to the acute need, some of the pastors operated ministries aimed at the prisoners' families. I accompanied a number of pastors who visited inmates' families throughout the city, bringing boxes of food, consoling words, and messages from the prisoner to his spouse, child, or parents. Beyond the spiritual goods the volunteers delivered to the jail, the support they offered families earned tremendous respect and trust from the inmates. Miller and Yamamori (2007) argue that this sort of social engagement is one of the reasons Pentecostalism has grown so quickly in Latin America. I would add that it is one of the primary reasons the faith is so rooted in prison life.

The relationship between the gangs and the Pentecostals in Rio de Janeiro may seem out of character for both organizations, especially for the gangs. Over the past twenty years the narco-gangs have relied largely on violence to maintain control of neighborhoods and drug markets in the city. Robert Brenneman's conceptualization of the "free-market" nature of the violence in Central America (see chap. 12, this vol.) is especially helpful for understanding much of the violence in Rio de Janeiro.

This is why even though gang members regularly leave the gang after a Pentecostal conversion, the gang does not see the Pentecostal church as a threat to their power or to their business interests. Pentecostal ministries try to persuade individuals to leave the gang, but I have never heard of a case in Rio de Janeiro where a ministry, pastor, or church has tried to force the gang from their neighborhood. In prison, Pentecostal groups are granted autonomy by the gang, but these inmate-led churches do not interfere with the gang's lucrative drug trade, nor do they try to destabilize the gang's position of power behind bars. Pentecostal inmates remain neutral in intergang conflicts, and in general they do not openly cooperate with the police in their neighborhoods or the guards in the prisons. If the Pentecostals worked with the police, interfered with the gang's drug business, or organized residents against the gang, the relationship between the two organizations would be drastically different.

Responding to Violence inside the Prison

There are many types of violence in Rio's prisons. Inmates murder other inmates, guards are executed during riots, and institutional violence saturates the entire penal system. Not only is the violence in prison diverse, but the responses to it are varied as well. My research focused specifically on state violence, or the potential of state violence, against inmates and how pastors sometimes confront this type of violence by intervening on behalf of individual inmates or entire prisons and by pressuring government officials.

The most common way pastors responded to state violence was by defending individuals like Marcelo,[3] an inmate in his early twenties who was thrown into the gang-controlled wing of the jail with fresh bruises on his face, arms, and torso that he acquired during his arrest. When I met Marcelo I immediately noticed the poorly planned tattoos that covered his shoulders and the very worried look in his bloodshot eyes. He was shirtless, which made the photo of his daughter that hung from his neck by a piece of string even more visible. Whoever gave him the photo had framed it by weaving metallic candy wrappers into a miniature picture frame, which made the smiling face of the four-year-old girl that peeked out of the frame seem out of place in the dismal, dungeonlike conditions of the jail. Over the next six months, I never saw Marcelo without his daughter's photo around his neck, and when he prayed during the daily worship services, he held the photo between the thumbs of his folded hands.

Marcelo had reason to pray. He and three colleagues had been arrested after the police interrupted their armed robbery attempt. In the shootout that ensued, a member of the crew shot and killed a police officer. Marcelo was the only person arrested in the chaotic getaway and sat in jail awaiting trial for the murder.

One afternoon, a group of four police officers arrived at the jail and informed the warden that they were there to transfer Marcelo to another facility. Their arrival came at an odd time of day, and they didn't have an official transport vehicle, so when word reached the cellblocks, Marcelo panicked. He knew instantly that the police officers had arrived as executioners. According to Rio de Janeiro's Institute for Public Security, the city's police force killed 5,435 people between January 2007 and April 2013, nearly one thousand people per year (Instituto de Segurança Pública 2013). The government statistics suggest Marcelo's concern for his life was not exaggerated.

While the police officers were speaking to the jail's warden, Pastor Cicero was in the cellblock leading worship songs by singing over a CD he was playing on a portable stereo. He was in the middle of the chorus when a frantic Marcelo interrupted to pull the pastor aside. Pastor Cicero abruptly ended the service, asked to be let out of the cells, and went directly to the warden. "Please don't do this warden; please don't do this," he begged. "In the name of Jesus, don't give this man to them."

The police officers left the jail without Marcelo, but it is impossible to know exactly what convinced the warden to send them away empty-handed. Maybe the pastor used just the right words to change his mind, or maybe it was as Pastor Cicero told me: "God touched the warden's heart at that moment." Whatever happened, the fact that the pastor was there, standing in front of the warden, the police officers, and the dozens of other people milling about the jail's entrance, was key in influencing the warden's response to this case of potential violence. The pastor's presence in the jail made him a potential witness if something happened to Marcelo, and a witness from civil society can be a powerful deterrent to police violence.

The pastor's action reflects a Pentecostal theology that emphasizes personal salvation. Usually the pastors offer salvation in the afterlife, but saving Marcelo's earthly life from his would-be executioners is consistent with the theology's individualist orientation. I observed a number of Pastor Cicero's worship services in two jails that he visited weekly and in his small church just outside Rio's city limits. The content of the worship services in each location emphasized the lost-to-found narrative common in global Pentecostalism and relied heavily on the pastor's personal conversion story. His jailhouse services ended with invitations to inmates to personally accept Jesus as their lord and savior. When I asked Pastor Cicero about his work, he spoke at length about saving the men in prison from lives of sin but not about improving the prison's conditions. Saving Marcelo's life was the sort of action that fit squarely within a theology that focused on salvation, spiritual and sometimes physical, of individual inmates. Even though Marcelo was an accused cop-killer, the pastor intervened because he thought Marcelo's soul and earthly life were worth saving. But Pastor Cicero did not focus on "saving" the prison system. He focused his work on individual prisoners as opposed to working to achieve a penal system where off-duty police officers could not show up and essentially ask to execute inmates.

Of course, not all Pentecostal responses to violence in prison focused solely on individual inmates; some engaged entire prisons. This chapter opened with a description of a prison riot negotiation by Pastor Marcos Pereira and the members of the Last Days Assembly of God, a church that has been involved in mediating more than a dozen prison riots. Pastor Marcos is a tireless self-promoter and speaks frequently about his peace-keeping abilities during interviews and sermons. A few years ago, church members started to bring video cameras with them wherever they went and published the clips and images in various media outlets. DVDs of Pastor Marcos's "greatest hits" were for sale at more than a dozen informal markets throughout the city. Though the images in these DVDs are powerful, they are also a not so subtle component of his church's propaganda campaign and present a very one-sided version of events.

To get another perspective on the pastor's mediation work in prison riots, I interviewed former inmates who were incarcerated when they occurred. I spoke with João, an active member of Rio's most powerful gang, the Comando Vermelho, when he was incarcerated in Rio de Janeiro's most infamous maximum-security prison. In 2002, João was in the middle of a riot that broke out when a number of gang-affiliated inmates were transferred to another facility. The remaining gang leaders demanded that all inmates in their cellblocks throw their mattresses into the hallways and set them on fire. From João's perspective, the pastor's arrival was a divine intervention in a riot that had gotten out of control.

> The Comando leader ordered us to set fires in the prison, and it was hell in there. I don't know what hell is like, but they say in the Bible that hell is hot, and there is wailing and gnashing of teeth. I'll tell you that things were really ugly there, because the guy in charge of the jail ordered people to set fire to the mattresses and everything. They made a huge bonfire, and the prison doesn't have any ventilation system—it's just a big passage without any outlet for the smoke, so the smoke from the mattresses, reeking, began to fall down, and there wasn't any ventilation system. The smoke kept falling, and if you were walking through the hall, it looked like the roof was caving in with all of that smoke. People were dying from suffocation and people were being trampled. The riot squad arrived, wanting to get in, wanting to get in, and I remember it as if it was today and the only person who was able to get inside to calm the prisoners was Pastor Marcos. That was in 2002. If the riot squad had come in they would have killed everyone, you know? But that didn't happen because Pastor Marcos, that man is a man of God—he doesn't know a lot of things that I'm telling you, but what he—what he did—him passing through there was really important for my life because if the riot squad had gotten in that day, I would be dead, man.

João's account of the prison riot and its peaceful end reveals how grateful some inmates are for this type of response to violence and also how much it relies on a very particular type of authority, charismatic authority in the Weberian sense (Weber 1968). A pastor's ability to respond to violence hinges on his or her identity as a man or woman of God. In certain situations, this sort of authority trumps the authority of a state official, but it is difficult to predict or replicate. I asked João why the active gang members in the prison were so responsive to the pastor given that they were not professing Pentecostals, and he emphasized the importance

of visible displays of power: "Pastor Marcos came in with signs and won-
ders, so the inmates respected him. Pastor Marcos arrived, came into the
building, and started freeing people from the demons that were in the
prison. He prayed during the riot and on that day and the riot ended."

When Pastor Marcos "frees" an inmate from demons, he places his
hands on the head of the individual and prays for him until he falls to the
floor, seemingly unconscious. I observed a worship service in jail that was
led by volunteers from Pastor Marcos's church that concluded with this
type of prayer. The church members started praying for the inmates in
the cellblocks, and within ten minutes there were over a dozen inmates
lying motionless on the jail floor. Many are skeptical of this sort of prayer,
including fellow Pentecostals, and have accused the pastor of employing
a form of hypnosis.[4] Determining what was "really" going on during these
prayers lies beyond the scope of this chapter, but the visual display of
power resonated with some of the inmates and contributed to the pastor's
influence behind bars.

Some pastors' response to prison violence went beyond saving or protecting individual inmates or even entire prison populations from immediate danger to using their influence to pressure the state to improve penal
institutions. Antonio Carlos Costa, a Presbyterian pastor and president of
Rio de Paz, a Rio de Janeiro–based human rights organization, is one example. He not only implored inmates to surrender their souls to the Lord,
but implored the state to transform its prisons. Antonio stood out from
most of the pastors visiting prisons and jails in Rio de Janeiro because his
congregation was largely middle and upper class. He was one of the few
"non-Pentecostal" Protestant pastors I met who was active in the prison
system. The inmates did not make this denominational distinction and
referred to him as well as the Pentecostals ministers as "pastor." Pastor Antonio visited the prison every two weeks and brought a team of dentists,
nurses, and volunteers from his church to provide basic medical attention
to the inmates before and after the worship services. It was a larger, more
organized project than those of the pastors from the storefront churches,
but the worship services were based on the same key components: singing, preaching, and an invitation to make a personal commitment to God.

Pastor Antonio and the volunteers from Rio de Paz addressed medical
needs with supplies and trained medical professionals. But the overcrowding in the cells was a more complicated problem. Generally, two inmates

would sleep head-to-toe on each concrete bed and other detainees would simply curl up on the concrete floor. A few paid a daily fee to cell leaders to spend entire days in an ad hoc hammock system. But no matter what sleeping innovations were implemented, there simply was not enough space to hold the bodies. Some inmates remained standing for much of the night, waiting their turn to squeeze into one of the spaces, or tied themselves to the cell's bars with T-shirts and attempted to sleep while standing.

Pastor Antonio was appalled by the situation and had already petitioned the city government to do something about it. When we were in one of the cells together, he told me, "This is illegal. We don't need new legislation to change this; we need to enforce the laws we already have." After months of stalling and unsatisfactory answers from city police officials, he informed them of his plan to construct an exact replica of a jail cell in the middle of Copacabana Beach, one of the city's most visible spaces. He would then fill it with seventy volunteers so that reporters, journalists, beachgoers, and tourists could see what an overcrowded prison really looks like. The display would juxtapose the iconic beach to a glimpse of the city's dungeonlike jails, providing a stark contrast to the image the city propagated to win the bid for the 2014 World Cup and the 2016 Olympic Games.

When informed of his intentions, police officials became much more attentive to his pleas, and a high-ranking member of the department promised imminent mass inmate transfers that would significantly reduce the number of inmates in each cell. They promised action by a certain date and in return asked for assurances that he would not erect the public display. The inmates were transferred. While the pastor's threat was not the only reason the state acted, it was a key variable in the city's decision. And the pastor's regular presence in the jail was what made his threat credible.

Saints and/or Sinners?

Pastor Marcos Pereira has not mediated any prison riots recently, but he is spending more time in prison than ever before. The pastor was arrested on May 7, 2013, on charges that he raped female members of his congregation. Beyond the rape charges, he is being investigated for laundering drug money and homicide. Rumors floated through the city that Pastor Marcos had clandestine agreements with imprisoned gang leaders. The material wealth he flaunted—a fleet of vintage cars, Rolex watches, and imported electronics—raised suspicions, but when fugitive high-ranking drug traffickers were found hiding in his drug rehabilitation center outside the city, the police started to investigate. Pereira is still awaiting trial, but he serves as a vivid example of how a privileged position inside prison can open a door to illicit activity and personal profit and of the inherent dangers of relying on charismatic authority as a response to violence in prison.

Stories of "corrupt" Pentecostal pastors swirled around Rio de Janeiro during the year I spent collecting data, though none so shocking as the accusations against Pastor Marcos. More common were stories like one I heard from a pastor who had been visiting the prisons in Rio for the past ten years. He told me about an offer made to him by the uncle of an infamous drug trafficker at one of the maximum-security prisons in Rio. After thanking him for the work he had been doing with his nephew and other inmates, the man offered to "bless" the pastor's ministry. The "blessing" was a bit more complicated than dropping an envelope into the offering plate. The uncle offered to open two bank accounts, one in the pastor's name and the other in the church's name, but both accessible by the uncle. He said that at the beginning of each month he would deposit a substantial sum, around 100,000 reais (approximately US$60,000), in each of the two accounts. Using the 10 percent tithing guideline favored in Pentecostal churches, the uncle would withdraw 90 percent of the money at the end of the month and the remaining 10 percent would stay as the "blessing."

When I visited this pastor's church, it was evident that the laundering scheme would have dramatically improved the church's financial situation. The pastor confessed that he was momentarily tempted by the offer but declined in the most delicate terms. The gang leader's uncle did not press the issue further but said he had made this offer to a number of other pastors in the city and very few had refused it. The incident is another example of how the physical presence of the pastors in the prisons is double-edged. It provides opportunities for the pastors to respond to violence, but since it depends so heavily on the charisma of the pastor it can be easily corrupted and lead to participation in very lucrative but illegal arrangements with individuals and criminal organizations connected to the prison.

PENTECOSTAL PASTORS and volunteers who visit Rio de Janeiro's prisons are not organized under a denominational umbrella or a larger "ministry" organization. In fact, I rarely saw pastors from different churches working together in any meaningful way inside the prison. At the jail there were over a dozen independent churches regularly visiting the facility, and though each group had its own style and agenda, there were consistencies in the way they responded to violence. First, the Pentecostal pastors and volunteers stood shoulder to shoulder with the inmates in the cellblocks and trusted the prisoners with their personal safety. Their choice to go to the prisons not only gave weight to their sermons but also provided opportunities to work against violence.

Second, the Pentecostal pastors chose to side with the inmates rather than Rio's police force. They did not condone the inmates' criminal activity (though I spoke with police officers and prison guards who would disagree), but when a crisis emerged they consistently acted on behalf of the inmates. The pastors' "preferential option for the prisoner" mirrored Latin American liberation lheology but was implemented with an unmistakable Pentecostal flavor.

Third, Pentecostal interventions in potentially violent situations relied largely on a charismatic authority that Weber (1968, 241) described as "a certain quality of an individual personality by virtue of which he is considered extraordinary and treated as endowed with supernatural, superhuman, or at least specifically exceptional powers or qualities." This sort of authority holds the potential to challenge traditional legal authority, but it is a combustible type of leadership, difficult to predict and sometimes even more difficult to control.

One component noticeably absent from the Pentecostals' response to violence in Rio de Janeiro's jails and prisons is traditional political action. The pastors I interviewed and observed placed little hope in particular political candidates, legislation, or top-down prison reform. With the exception of Antonio Costa, none of the pastors I met made direct requests to state officials to improve the dreadful conditions in the prisons, to curb illegal detention, or to stop abuse by the guards. Yet in spite of the apparent lack of political participation by the Pentecostals, my argument is that the pastors and volunteers who visit the prisons are engaged in political action—a politics of presence—that has political consequences.

That argument grows out of my own experience inside Rio's prisons. When I first entered the cellblocks with the Pentecostal pastors, I was struck by, and privately critical of, their lack of outrage about the inhumane conditions. There were seventy and eighty men crammed into cells with only fifteen beds, and temperatures reached 134°F in the summer.[5] Some inmates had been detained for nearly a year without formal charges, and others died from wounds incurred during arrest that could easily have been treated. I thought the pastors were turning a blind eye to the gross human rights violations and focusing simply on the spiritual realm. I was critical in part because I thought they were overlooking the political processes and social structures behind the human rights disaster that these prisons represented. In other words, I was critical because they were not looking at the situation as a social scientist would, and they did not seem particularly excited about the social scientist's preferred remedy—traditional political action.

As I continued to visit the prisons, my initial judgments started to soften, and I began to see the Pentecostal pastors' and volunteers' response as a form of political action. One of the reasons my perceptions changed was that as I became more familiar with the jails and prisons through regular visits, I also became acclimated to the environment and less appalled by the overcrowded cells, the intense heat, and the rampant corruption. After a few weeks, I expected my shirt to become heavy with sweat and was not shocked when I had to step over an obviously ill or wounded inmate lying on the concrete floor. If someone had observed my entrance into the cellblocks after I had become accustomed to the conditions, they might think that I too was blind to the social and institutional structures at the root of this injustice.

The criticisms I was so quick to make during the first week of fieldwork were no longer so obvious after personal experience in the jails and prisons. I realized that pastors who had been visiting the jails for five or ten years may have gone through a similar process. Also, for the pastors who led poor congregations located miles away from the glamorous beaches of Copacabana and Ipanema, the failure of the penal institution was not so shocking. It was an extension of the deep state failure in their communities that they knew quite well. In Rio's poorest neighborhoods, the health, education, sanitation, and security institutions are abysmal, and have been for decades. Instead of "missing" or purposefully ignoring the institutional failures and structural inequalities behind the prisons' conditions, as I initially suspected, most of the pastors lived each day in the midst of these injustices and were intimately familiar with them.

Pastors rarely employed social movement rhetoric or terminology from political strategies to describe their prison ministries, but their work achieved some of the same goals that political activists pursue. For example, the pastors were involved in a powerful solidarity movement with the city's most ostracized social group—prisoners. During the sermons in the cells, the Pentecostal pastors rarely framed the prisoners as victims of an unjust society that disproportionately punishes the poor and exonerates the socially connected for a fee. But neither did they subscribe to the dominant narrative in Rio that sees criminals as the source of the city's social problems and tolerates the horrid prison conditions and the police violence directed at them. When the pastors embraced rapists, prayed with murderers, sang worship songs with drug dealers, and treated the inmates as people with inherent worth and value, they were participating in an activity that subverted the social order. They purposefully identified with the most stigmatized population in Rio de Janeiro by calling them *irmão* (brother) instead of *bandido* (bandit) or *vagabundo* (bum). One pastor responded to the inmates' words of gratitude for his visit, "I know that if I am ever in here in the future, you would come to visit me."

The pastors also delivered this same countercultural message to citizens of Rio de Janeiro outside prison, principally the people in their congregations. They recounted the successes and difficulties of their week's work, and they asked the congregation to pray for the inmates and the specific prisons they visited. They also invited members of the congregation to visit the prisons themselves and asked them to get involved in the lives of the struggling families of the incarcerated. These messages were often delivered in the neighborhoods that suffered most from Rio de Janeiro's criminal violence. Even though these messages were delivered inside a church and often in a sermon, the pastors achieved what many political activists try to do: they raised awareness about a particular social issue. I saw the fruits of this message on a small scale when I visited the churches of the pastors who visited the prisons: there were former inmates in the pews.

Though the Pentecostals who visit prisons in Rio de Janeiro and respond to violence in them lack the trappings and rhetoric of traditional politics, I argue that their work can be conceptualized as political action in part because they achieve some of the same goals as political activists. They participate in solidarity campaigns, awareness campaigns, and, in certain cases, they directly influence state officials in charge of the prisons. Pentecostal pastors have used this politics of presence to lobby prison wardens to stop the murder of an inmate, negotiate peace during prison riots, and help reduce overcrowding in the jails in Rio de Janeiro. Though some pastors become active criminals themselves and most of them operate without a comprehensive prison reform strategy, their presence and action inside Rio de Janeiro's prisons and jails have political consequences.

Notes

1. Macumba refers to the Afro-Brazilian religion that is a mix of African spirit worship and Roman Catholic imagery.

2. See Jon Lee Anderson, "Gangland: Who Controls the Streets of Rio de Janeiro?," *New Yorker*, October 5, 2009.

3. None of the inmate's real names are used in this chapter.

4. Danlio Fernandes, "De missionário nas prisões à Pastor Sonic," *Genizah*, July 8, 2010.

5. Antônio Werneck, "'Masmorra medieval': Carceragem da Polinter registra 56,7 graus," *Globo*, February 11, 2010.

References

Alves, Maria Helena Moreira, and Philip Evanson. 2011. *Living in the Crossfire: Favela Residents, Drug Dealers, and Police Violence in Rio de Janeiro*. Philadelphia, PA: Temple University Press.

Burdick, John. 1999. "What Is the Color of the Holy Spirit? Pentecostalism and Black Identity in Brazil." *Latin American Research Review* 34, no. 2: 109–31.

Chesnut, R. Andrew. 1997. *Born Again in Brazil: The Pentecostal Boom and the Pathogens of Poverty.* New Brunswick, NJ: Rutgers University Press.

Freston, Paul. 1999. "'Neo-Pentecostalism' in Brazil: Problems of Definition and the Struggle for Hegemony." *Archives de Sciences Sociales des Religions* 105 (January–March): 145–62.

Garrard-Burnett, Virginia. 1989. "Protestantism in Rural Guatemala, 1872–1954." *Latin American Research Review* 24, no. 2: 127–42.

Goldstein, Donna. 2003. *Laughter Out of Place: Race, Class, Violence, and Sexuality in a Brazilian Shantytown.* Berkeley: University of California Press.

Hallum, Anne Motley. 2003. "Taking Stock and Building Bridges: Feminism, Women's Movements, and Pentecostalism in Latin America." *Latin American Research Review* 38, no. 1 (February): 169–86.

Hunt, Geoffrey, Stephanie Riegel, Tomas Morales, and Dan Waldorf. 1993. "Changes in Prison Culture: Prison Gangs and the Case of the 'Pepsi Generation.'" *Social Problems* 40, no. 3 (August): 398–409.

Instituto de Segurança Pública. 2013. "Estatística oficial de mortes violentas, tentativas de homicídio e casos de desaparecimento no Estado do Rio de Janeiro entre 2007– (junho) 2013." Rio de Janeiro.

Irwin, John, and Donald R. Cressey. 1962. "Thieves, Convicts and the Inmate Culture." *Social Problems* 10, no. 2 (Autumn): 142–55.

Johnson, Andrew. 2012. "If I Give My Soul: Pentecostalism Inside of Prison in Rio de Janeiro." PhD dissertation, University of Minnesota.

Mariz, Cecilia. 1994. *Coping with Poverty: Pentecostals and Christian Base Communities in Brazil.* Philadelphia, PA: Temple University Press.

Miguez, D. 1998. *Spiritual Bonfire in Argentina: Confronting Current Theories with an Ethnographic Account of Pentecostal Growth in a Buenos Aires Suburb.* Amsterdam: Centre for Latin American Research and Documentation.

Miller, Donald E., and Tetsanao Yamamori. 2007. *Global Pentecostalism: The New Face of Christian Social Engagement.* Berkeley: University of California Press.

Perlman, Janice. 2010. *Favela: Four Decades of Living on the Edge in Rio de Janeiro.* New York: Oxford University Press.

Wacquant, Loïc. 2003. "Toward a Dictatorship over the Poor? Notes on the Penalization of Poverty in Brazil." *Punishment and Society* 5, no. 2: 197–206.

Weber, Max. 1968. *Economy and Society.* Vol. 3. Edited by Guenther Roth and Claus Wittich. New York: Bedminister Press.

CHAPTER 14

"FUI MIGRANTE Y ME HOSPEDARON"

The Catholic Church's Responses to Violence against
Central American Migrants in Mexico

AMELIA FRANK-VITALE

Tuve hambre y me dieron de comer, tuve sed y me dieron de
beber, fui migrante y me hospedaron.

[For I was hungry, and you fed me. I was thirsty, and you gave me
drink. I was a migrant, and you invited me into your home.]
—Motto of Hermanos en el Camino,
Ixtepec, from Matthew 25:35

Each year, hundreds of thousands of Central American migrants—mostly
from Guatemala, Honduras, and El Salvador—travel across Mexico in
hopes of reaching the United States. The journey from the Guatemala
border to the U.S. border is an arduous one. In the best-case scenario, a
migrant who knows the route can, with a bit of luck, make it from border
to border in about ten days. For many people it takes weeks or months.
Many migrants make the journey on top of freight trains; the shelters

discussed in this chapter cater primarily to migrants who travel in this fashion. The train, often called *la bestia* (the beast), is extremely dangerous; falls frequently mean the loss of limbs or death. In some areas, migrants are able to board the train before it leaves the railyards, but often they have to grab the ladders and pull themselves up to the roof while the train is already in motion. Once aboard, low-hanging branches, unanticipated bridges and tunnels, and the relentless sun and wind make the journey dangerous and exhausting.

This chapter describes the kind of violence that Central Americans are subjected to as they make their way across Mexico and presents three cases of attempts to protect them. Jacqueline Hagan (2006), in her study of different Christian faiths and their approaches to pastoral care and activism on behalf of migrants, found that the Catholic Church is at the forefront of church-based social justice activities, stemming from its communitarian social theology, whereas Evangelical Protestant churches shy away from political activities with migrants, focusing instead on individual salvation.[1] Her findings hold true in Mexico, where members of the Catholic Church are in the forefront of protecting migrants from violence and defending their human rights. There is a network of over sixty shelters, soup kitchens, and relief centers—all run either directly by the Catholic Church or by devout Catholic laypeople—catering to Central Americans on their way through Mexico.[2] I focus here on three specific examples (from the Mexican states of Coahuila, Mexico, and Oaxaca; see fig. 14.1) to highlight unique theological foundations and evaluate the effectiveness of disparate strategies. I contrast the approaches of two priests who have taken up the cause of defending migrants in Mexico, their distinct theological motivations, the shelters they have developed, their political analyses, and their strategies for protecting both themselves and the migrants they serve. For contrast, I also look at a third, distinct example of a secular attempt at constructing a similar shelter alongside a church-affiliated charity project without an activist orientation.

El Infierno: The Landscape of Violence against Migrants in Mexico

Beyond the physical challenges of freight train travel, migrants on board *la bestia* must contend with various organized crime groups across

Figure 14.1. Map of the Mexican States Coahuila, Mexico, and Oaxaca

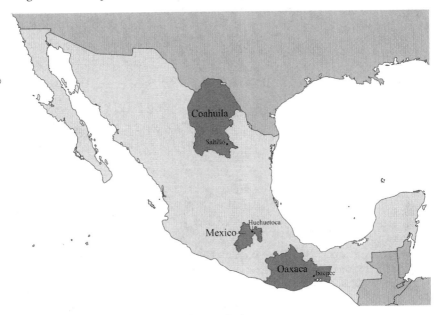

Courtesy of Center for Latin American and Latino Studies.

Mexico.[3] In each region where the trains pass, there are *pandilleros* (local street gangs), *maras* (gangs from Central America that are only loosely affiliated with those infamous organizations), or drug cartels that "tax" the migrants. Many migrants travel with *guías*, or guides, who for a fee manage the journey to the northern border.[4] These *guías* generally work for one of the major trafficking organizations, though they are the lowest rung in the hierarchy of the cartels. They must pay, per person, for the chance to move their people through a given territory. If they fail to pay (or if they are affiliated with a rival organization), they run the risk of being thrown off the moving train or murdered along with their migrant-clients. I met a migrant in Saltillo, Coahuila, in a shelter where migrants wait for weeks or sometimes months as they make arrangements with the people who will take them across the border. When I returned a month later, the migrants who were still there informed me, sadly, that this migrant had been killed. He had gone with a *coyote* who did not pay the Zetas as he was supposed to,[5] and so they killed the *coyote*, the migrant I had met, and the other eleven migrants the *coyote* was attempting to cross.

Controlling the train lines is lucrative business: in December 2012 in Veracruz, a *pandillero* who may have been affiliated with the Zetas demanded US$100 from each migrant aboard the train. A young Guatemalan man did not have that kind of money on him, and the *pandillero*, without hesitating, picked him up and tossed him off the train. The other migrants who recounted this story had no idea if the man lived or died. There are easily between one hundred and five hundred migrants aboard a train at any given time, so at US$100 a head, controlling the rights of passage can bring a criminal organization a great deal of money. The border crossing itself generally requires a payment of US$300 to $500 to the bosses of that territory—in addition to US$3,000 to $4,000 for the actual crossing.[6]

Migrants traveling through Mexico are also subject to robbery, assault, rape, and extortion by corrupt authorities and various unaffiliated criminal actors who prey on their vulnerability (Vogt 2013). Migrants have reported being taken away by immigration officials and federal police officers only to be turned over to kidnappers from the drug cartels. Even when the authorities are not working directly with organized crime, they are known to steal money from migrants during "raids" or to demand a bribe for not deporting them (Coutin 2005, 198). In July 2010, when I first began fieldwork in Ixtepec, Oaxaca, a train arrived that had been assaulted twice. First, criminals had sabotaged the tracks, forcing the train to stop. There they made the migrants get off the train and demanded all the money they had, inflicting blows to show they were serious. The train, with the migrants once again on board, then returned to the nearest town while the train company repaired the damaged tracks. As the migrants were waiting, the federal police arrived, beat up more of them, and stole whatever the first round of assailants had failed to find (Frank-Vitale 2011).

There are two principal starting points for migrants. One involves entering Mexico from Tecún Umán, Guatemala, crossing the Río Suchiate on a raft, and starting out from Ciudad Hidalgo, Chiapas. From there, migrants either walk or take a series of buses to get to Arriaga, Chiapas, the city near the border with Oaxaca where the freight train line begins. Southern Mexico is dotted with immigration checkpoints (*retenes*), so crossing Chiapas in a vehicle involves *rodeando*, or getting out of the bus well before the *retén* and continuing on foot through the countryside, returning to the highway after giving the *retén* a wide berth. One of these places is known as La Arrocera, near Huixtla, Chiapas. In the final two months of 2012, at least four young women were raped by the same man while *rodeando* the *retén*. Yosselin's story is typical:[7] she and her cousin got out of their bus on the prearranged signal from the driver, well ahead of the *retén*. They went into a store and the kind lady suggested they go to a nearby ranch and ask the rancher if they could cut across his land. She told the migrant women that he was a good guy. They followed her advice and went to the ranch, but the owner did not seem to be around. There was another man there, though, whom Yosselin would later recognize as her rapist. She and her cousin continued walking, hoping to find their way back to the highway when the man from the ranch appeared, now masked and accompanied by several others, all armed. The men stole their money and made them remove their clothes, and then the others took the cousin away while the man from the ranch raped Yosselin at gunpoint. They let her and the cousin go after he was finished, and the pair made their way to Arriaga, boarding the freight train there. Days after the attack, when she arrived at the shelter in Ixtepec, Oaxaca, Yosselin met three young women who had nearly identical stories. The four women filed official police complaints, pressed charges, and identified their attacker. Because of their courage and the support of the shelter staff in Ixtepec, their rapist ended up going to jail—an extremely rare outcome for those who commit acts of violence against migrants in Mexico. The shelter staff suspects this man probably raped many other migrant women who were too frightened or too alone to take the steps to bring him to justice.

Perhaps the most harrowing form of violence against Central American migrants in Mexico comes in the form of kidnappings, sometimes en masse. Migrants are picked up while waiting for the train or made to get off the train by heavily armed men with trucks. They are rounded up, at gunpoint, stuffed into the trucks, and taken to a *casa de seguridad* (safe house) where they are typically held, beaten, sometimes raped, and forced to call their family members for ransom. This process can often take months, as in the case of César, a migrant from El Salvador who was kidnapped along with his brother in 2010 by the Zetas. The kidnappers mostly target family members in the United States, but because César and his brother had no relatives there, their sister in El Salvador had to raise the ransom money: US$4,500 each. It took her nearly two months to get the money together, during which time the brothers were barely fed, beaten every day, and made to stay in the same room with the dead bodies of three migrants who had been killed to serve as an example to the rest. The Mexican Human Rights Commission (CNDH) estimated that in a six-month period in 2011 at least ten thousand migrants were kidnapped in Mexico (CNDH 2011). César and his brother were eventually released, but those who cannot pay are either pressed into service or killed. Even in drug-war-torn Mexico where news of murders and beheadings has become almost commonplace, the report of the massacre of seventy-two kidnapped migrants in August 2010 at a ranch in San Fernando, Tamaulipas, shocked the country (Brigden 2012). "San Fernando" and "72" have since become rallying cries to put a stop to the violence against migrants.[8]

The violence and threat of violence that migrants face in Mexico also extend to those who try to protect and defend them. The priests discussed in this chapter have received death threats from organized crime and corrupt police in their respective areas. They have been accused of being people smugglers themselves, and there have been direct acts of violence against their persons and the shelters they operate. Nevertheless, they maintain a commitment to their work with migrants as a necessary expression of their faith. Though they come from different theological perspectives, both Padre Pedro Pantoja Arreola and Padre José Alejandro Solalinde Guerra are fundamentally convinced that their devotion to God requires them to work with and for Central American migrants, facing the same threats, sharing in their suffering, and demanding a stop to the violence they are subjected to in Mexico.

Posada Belén: *Blindaje Social*

The longest-operating shelter for Central Americans in Mexico is in Saltillo, Coahuila, about five hours south of the Texas-Mexico border. Since 2000, Posada Belén has offered a safe haven to migrants in an area heavily controlled by drug cartels. Nuns first began ministering to migrants in Saltillo, but their makeshift shelter needed more institutional support. Saltillo's bishop asked Padre Pedro Pantoja to take over the parish and head the shelter. The priest's first step was to meet with his potential congregants and speak plainly about the implications. He would agree to be their priest if they were prepared to be active in the defense of the migrants passing through their city. They did agree, and their support has been crucial to the longevity and safety of the shelter and the migrants.

Pantoja came to the parish with a long personal history of commitment to the fight for migrants' rights and social justice. He is a tall man with graying hair and immense charisma. He has a charming smile, and, though he is nearly seventy years old, his age barely shows. He is still active, energetic, and an imposing presence. As a young man in a seminary in New Mexico, Pantoja was deeply inspired by the fight for justice for migrant farmworkers led by César Chávez. In 1963 he left the seminary to work with Chávez and the United Farm Workers in the fields. Later he returned to the seminary and became active in the liberation theology movement in Latin America. He explained it to me as follows:

[It] is a radical option of the presence of God among the poor. . . . We considered it a grave social sin to have elaborated theology and theological structures from a great distance from the poor. . . . The challenge then is, how does God speak to me from the poor, how does God speak to me from oppression, from injustice, how can I perceive the language of God through the cry of the poor? . . . That is to say that we do not have another language more faithful to God than to speak from the perspective of the poor. . . . It is a new rereading of the Bible from that as a starting point, and it is consolidated through . . . a profound analysis of social reality. From this theology, one confirms that it is with the poor and from the poor where you ought to find the face of God . . . all those who have the stamp of suffering upon them . . . that only there and from there can church work be oriented, . . . but not just to contemplate [the poor], but to walk with them and struggle alongside them.

In this way, Pantoja places his work with migrants squarely within the preferential option for the poor that is the cornerstone of liberation theology. Migrants are socially excluded and subjected to horrible forms of exploitation and violence; he and the church must be for and with them—"accompany" them in their lives—a pastoral practice also associated with liberation theology. Pantoja risks his life alongside the migrants, standing up to drug cartels and corrupt authorities alike, because that is what he must do to live out his faith. This theological basis combines with his experience as a young man working with César Chávez, not only inspiring him to work with the migrants but also informing *how* he realizes this work.

Posada Belén does not simply provide a safe space for migrants, giving them food, healing their wounds, and offering a place to rest. The shelter also has an *asociación civil* (AC), Frontera con Justicia, which is roughly equivalent to a nonprofit organization. It operates from inside the shelter, but its mission goes beyond providing food and shelter. It addresses the systemic issues that contribute to a context in which violence against migrants is permissible. Staff members conduct strategic litigation, defend migrants accused of crimes, represent migrants who have been victims of crimes, and also develop an analysis of how the corruption and impunity of Mexican authorities allows the violence to continue. In July 2013, for example, Frontera con Justicia released a detailed report on violence and torture of migrants at the hands of police in Saltillo. In a four-month period they documented thirty cases of torture and "cruel, inhumane, and degrading treatment" that included asphyxiation, electric shocks, and sexual and psychological violence (Frontera con Justicia AC 2013).

Though it operates from the shelter, the AC is independent financially from the Catholic Church and from ecclesiastical discipline. The nuns who started working with the migrants before the shelter was entrusted to Pantoja consciously set up the AC in this way to guard against any change in Church leadership that might jeopardize their mission. Pantoja supports this kind of vision. As he says, in Belén they are not just there to give food and shelter; they are also fomenting social change by creating an alternative social space. We do not *give* workshops, he often says, but we live them together with the migrants. And, he adds, when migrants leave the shelter, they should be the best defenders of the human rights of other migrants.

Human rights have come to form an important part of Pantoja's thinking, in fact. Whereas the concept of human rights was at one time distant and in some ways contrary to the liberation theology movement, Pantoja seamlessly weaves them together. He explains this trajectory:

> From liberation theology we overflowed from the Church, and we incorporated ourselves into a social, philosophical body [with] an aggressive, provocative thinking . . . in the fight for the liberation of victims. . . . As we transcend the traditional ecclesiastical, theological, and social world of the seminaries . . . we form ourselves in another context wholly from the real world, from the world of social struggle. . . . The theme of human rights is in constant evolution. It is a very strong liberating whirlwind that can take many faces. We have to go forward following these faces, working together, to be faithful to this struggle. . . . For us the language, the expression, and the struggle of human rights is the experience of God. . . . [A]nd it is the same, that away from these faces [of the poor] we cannot [find God] and away from human rights we cannot find another stronger social methodology.

The concept of human rights, for Pantoja, is the secular expression of the commitment to the poor and liberation that, for him, comes from his Catholic theology. It offers a field of communication and a language for dialogue with actors outside the Church that liberation theology on its own cannot necessarily achieve. Here, Pantoja coincides with Solalinde (whose work is discussed below) in an important way. Though their theological foundations differ, each man has come to embrace human rights as a doctrine that coincides with his theology and supports the work of protecting migrants. Their examples demonstrate the evolution of rights-based thinking for Church actors and of the continuation in the early twenty-first century of the trajectory of the theory and practice of rights that Daniel H. Levine details from the 1960s to the 1990s (see chap. 1, this vol.).

In part because of Pantoja's status as a parish priest, in part because of an approach to priesthood informed by liberation theology and human rights, and in part because of his experience with social justice community organizing, his relationship with the community in Saltillo is markedly different from that of priests who work with migrants elsewhere. He understands that the safety of the migrants, the shelter, and his own person are directly tied to the extent to which the community supports him, the migrants, and the mission. He calls this *blindaje social*, or social armor. He maintains that he is still alive today as a direct result of the strong *blindaje social* he has developed around Posada Belén. The shelter's deep ties with different actors in the community are reflected in the kinds of programs found there. Nearly every day, community members from different churches, organizations, schools, or businesses come to the shelter and interact with the migrants. Dinners are often served by a local family or an evangelical Christian congregation. Regardless of denomination, the shelter opens its doors (and its kitchen) to these volunteer groups that come to serve the migrants for an evening. Once a month, students from a Saltillo beauty school come to give free haircuts. Local university students complete their service requirement for graduation there. A pair of teachers comes weekly to engage the migrants in physical activities and exercises to provoke thoughtful reflection. Another woman teaches English. There are "know your rights" workshops and self-esteem building sessions. Local businesses donate goods to the shelter on a regular basis. This kind of community engagement is almost entirely absent in Ixtepec, the next case to which I turn, save for a few exceptions, and the hostility to migrants that is almost palpable in Ixtepec is much less evident in Saltillo.

This is not to say that there is no anti-immigrant feeling in Saltillo, but it is less ubiquitous than in Ixtepec and the shelter is far less isolated from the community. The shelter and its staff, however, receive threats just like those working in Ixtepec do. Saltillo is in the heart of territory controlled by the Zetas, whose influence extends to the police forces and politicians in the area. While the mere existence of the shelter may not pose a threat to the criminal organizations, the work of Frontera con Justicia, Pantoja's public speeches about corruption, impunity, and violence against the migrants, and the shelter's political posture do constitute a threat. So, while members of the community have not come to Belén with torches, like their counterparts in Ixtepec, prepared to burn the shelter to the ground (as we shall see below), computers have been stolen during break-ins and members of the team, including Pantoja and the executive director of Frontera con Justicia, have received death threats.

Hermanos en el Camino: A Fundamental Option for the Human Being

The Hermanos en el Camino shelter in Ixtepec, Oaxaca, and its founder, Padre José Alejandro Solalinde Guerra, stand in clear contrast to Posada Belén and Pantoja in a few important ways. Solalinde is a slight man, in his mid-sixties. His thinning hair contrasts with the boyish enthusiasm he exhibits. He dresses all in white, with a simple wooden cross around his neck. He does not have the booming voice of Pantoja; it is often hard to hear him celebrating Mass over the din of the shelter, but he has a quiet charisma.

Solalinde is officially a *clérico vago*, a priest without a parish. When he mentioned his concern for the increasing numbers of Central Americans appearing near the town's railroad tracks, the Ixtepec parish priest was wholly uninterested. Solalinde was stunned. He thought, "These are sheep without a shepherd. Isn't that our duty?" The parish priest, however, like many longtime residents of Ixtepec, was essentially numb to the flow of Central Americans through the small city. Solalinde, already in his sixties at the time, had found his calling. He petitioned the diocese to allow him to work full-time with migrants. Despite doubts, the diocese eventually agreed, and Solalinde abandoned the traditional relationship between a parish priest and his parishioners and dedicated himself entirely to attending to migrants on their way through Ixtepec. In 2007 he opened Hermanos en el Camino, which was at first just a large plot of dirt and a few folding chairs and tables next to the train tracks.

The second feature unique to Solalinde and his shelter is the relationship he has developed with outside actors. Given that he was not the parish priest and that the parish priest was uninterested in his ministry, he could not rely on parishioner support to run the shelter or to keep it safe, as Pantoja has done with Posada Belén. The shelter-community relationship in Ixtepec has improved over the years, but it is still contentious, and Solalinde certainly does not enjoy the local *blindaje social* fostered in

Saltillo. This is fueled in part by bitterness among people who are struggling economically themselves and receive little support from the state or
the Church. I have heard people complain that in Ixtepec "un migrante
vale más que un mexicano" (a migrant is worth more than a Mexican).
The tension is exemplified by an incident during the shelter's early years
when a mob wielding rocks, sticks, and cans of gasoline, led by the municipal president and including members of the police force, came to the
shelter intending to burn it to the ground. Solalinde put himself between
the crowd and the shelter and, spreading his arms wide and lowering his
head, told the mob if they were going to burn the shelter, they should
start with him. He thinks his Christ-like posture in that moment deterred
the crowd, or maybe it was just that they were unprepared to burn a
human being that day. Whatever the case, the mob backed down.

With community and local institutional opposition to his project,
Solalinde turned outward, all but ignoring any kind of relationship with
his immediate neighbors in order to develop his profile and that of the
shelter at the international level. He forged relationships with Amnesty
International, Doctors Without Borders, Peace Brigades International,
the International Organization for Migration, and the United Nations'
High Commission on Refugees, among other international organizations
and foundations. He also adopted a firm policy to welcome the press. He
granted every interview asked of him, and nothing seen at or heard about
the shelter was off the record. His strategy was clear and effective: if the
local community could not be counted on to support the shelter's mission, he would turn to the international community to keep himself, the
shelter, and the migrants from harm. It worked: he found *blindaje* from
the international community. While locals had been prepared to burn the
shelter down, Amnesty International would respond to threats against
Solalinde with a letter-writing campaign.[9]

Over the years there has been some movement toward cooperation
with the local people, but Solalinde's very high international profile remains crucial. He has been nominated for and received numerous human
rights awards and peace prizes, and his personal safety is now protected
by a team of armed bodyguards and police who serve as security for the
shelter. The Inter-American Commission on Human Rights, concerned
for Solalinde's safety, mandated that Mexico provide him with a security

detail. He has been invited to form part of the Council on the Role of Faith for the World Economic Forum, and he has met with the United Nations Human Rights head, Navi Pillay. The international strategy has also brought the shelter significant resources. Its funding, beyond a small monthly allowance provided by Solalinde's family, comes from donations, the bulk of them international. European foundations have funded construction projects; the International Organization for Migration has provided, among other things, the bunk beds where migrants sleep; and Doctors Without Borders financed the enclosure of the shelter's kitchen. Though smaller in scale, this echoes the successful strategy of the Jesuits in the Magdalena Medio in Colombia who, unable to count on the state or the Church hierarchy for support, secured funding from high-profile international organizations and foreign NGOs for their community-based peace-building initiatives (see Pachico, this vol.).

In 2012, the diocese of Tehuantepec, where Ixtepec is located, informed Solalinde of its decision to move him from the shelter, citing the standard practice of rotating priests. Solalinde immediately talked to members of the press with whom he had built a solid relationship over the years. An article even appeared in *USA Today*, reporting his claim that the proposed assignment to parish duties was meant to "smother" his work as an advocate for migrants.[10] Soon the bishop of the diocese said publicly that it had all been a misunderstanding; he had never intended to make Solalinde leave his work with the migrants.[11] Solalinde once said to me ironically, "I used to be the black sheep of the diocese. Now I'm the diamond."

The third defining feature of Solalinde and his shelter is related to the previous two: Solalinde lives at the shelter in Ixtepec. He does not have a home elsewhere; there is no rectory associated with a church. He has a room at the shelter, but his room is often used as storage or office space. Frequently Solalinde sleeps on a mattress on the concrete, covered by a white sheet, in the open air. Living with the migrants gives him a particular kind of closeness that other priests who have duties to a parish may not achieve. He shares their meals, generally a simple plate of rice and black beans. He bathes as the migrants do when they stay at the shelter, *a la jícara*, using buckets of cold water. He lives with the migrants, putting into practice one of the primary tenets of liberation theology, even though his personal experience made him critical of how that theology might be applied in practice.

In the 1980s Solalinde was intrigued by the idea of liberation theology. After years of comfortable life as a parish priest in Toluca, outside Mexico City, he felt called by God to shed his comforts and seek out a more meaningful ministry. In the early 1980s, he went to the Isthmus of Tehuantepec, where he became the priest for small villages in the mountains of Oaxaca. His reception in Tehuantepec soured him to what liberation theology could mean in practice. He was treated like a bourgeois outsider (which he readily admits he was), and new colleagues did not respect his good intentions and desire to learn and change. He came to believe the preferential option for the poor had become an exclusionary idea rather than a liberating one, and that it spoke only about the evils of the rich and the virtues of the poor but rarely mentioned the teachings of Jesus. As a result, he said, the Church was losing a lot of followers to evangelical Christianity.

Liberation theology, he explained, came from a time when the Church and Marxists were learning from each other. However, it has not proven a dynamic theology, he believed, because it was limited by its rigid ideas about class warfare.

> I think that liberation theology had a certain liberating sense, but [it should be] for everyone, . . . not just for the poor. They [focused] a lot on the poor, . . . but before that there wasn't a premise that went toward the human being. [It must start with] a fundamental option for the human being. Then the poor. This goes afterwards. You can have a preferential option for the poor, but if you don't make first the fundamental option for the human being it becomes ideology. . . . Today we don't need class war, but we need consciousness-raising of the classes. . . . You don't need to fight for a class. You have to fight for all. So that there are equal conditions for everyone. Without excluding anyone.

For Solalinde, liberation theology lacks a universality that recognizes the fundamental dignity of all people, regardless of their class position. The rich should not be rejected or despised simply for being rich but rather loved and treated with the dignity and respect all human beings merit. For this reason he rejects the preferential option for the poor as interpreted in liberation theology. Whereas Pantoja finds the concept of human rights consistent with his interpretation of liberation theology, Solalinde believes that human rights are an answer to the flaws he sees in it. He finds in the concept of human rights the universality he thought missing in liberation theology. "I think that human rights are the same and go totally for the human being because of the dignity that he has. And this goes universally for all," Solalinde explains. "In this sense I think that the culture of full human rights for all guarantees liberty and freedom from oppression. This is equivalent to the objective of liberation theology."

Solalinde turned away from liberation theology and instead embraced an alternative human rights–centered theology. Human rights have clear Christian roots, he maintains, even though Jesus did not mention them as such.

> In the Bible it is the love of God toward human beings. [Jesus] tells us, as my father loved me, I love you. For this reason, love one another. In the time of Jesus, [there was a group] that idolatrized purity. They said that the temple was contaminated, corrupt. . . . [T]heir solution was to preserve themselves from it, to distance themselves from it, and they encapsulated themselves. Jesus says, no. It's not about isolating yourself from the human being but about healing the human being. [Even the oppressor] is a human being, and the solution is not to exterminate him but to convert him, so that both he and I are made free and happy. . . . He doesn't mention them as human rights explicitly, but he is planting the idea of human rights for all. Everything comes together in a way to provide the solid foundation for human rights.

Solalinde sees a philosophy of human rights, based on the love Jesus demonstrated for all people, as a more faithful manifestation of divine teachings than the exclusive preference for the poor taught by liberation theology. For Solalinde, the Church is wrong to ignore the poor, the marginalized, the migrant, but it is also wrong not to acknowledge the fundamental human dignity of even those who are rich, who exploit, and who visit violence on the migrants he defends. In accordance with this view, Solalinde regularly prays for the Zetas, and all those who assault, extort, and kidnap migrants, when he celebrates Mass. Moving from prayer to politics, he once even asked for forgiveness from the Zetas, recognizing that they too are victims of a corrupt government.[12]

The embrace of human rights as the basis for Solalinde's commitment to protecting migrants and his distancing from Marxist-related liberation theology in Latin America fit with his strategy of fostering international *blindaje*. He has developed a particularly close relationship with Amnesty International; they speak the same language. When Solalinde or other shelter staff members are threatened, they count on Amnesty International to immediately release an action alert, and Amnesty has always come through. The shelter has also worked with Amnesty International and Gael García Bernal to make a series of short films documenting the violence migrants face traversing Mexico. Since human rights are also less controversial as a philosophy than Marxist-linked liberation theology, Solalinde cannot be easily dismissed by Church leaders and government officials.[13] Though Solalinde has come to this position only in the past eight years of working with migrants, his thinking makes him an intellectual heir to the "full-throated theological and activist" embrace of human rights that Patrick Kelly (this vol.) identifies as beginning in the Church in the 1970s.

Ultimately, Solalinde's internationalist, human rights–centered strategy has been largely successful. I mentioned earlier a train that was assaulted twice en route to Ixtepec. For years this was a common occurrence—shelter staff said they could almost count on an assault like this every two months. By 2013, however, Oaxaca had become one of the safer zones migrants pass through, in large part because of Solalinde's work and the international attention he has garnered. In late 2010 Oaxaca's new governor, Gabino Cué Monteagudo, for example, immediately sought to work with Solalinde on migrant issues, knowing that he could be a valuable ally. Cué also opened a new *fiscalía*, an office associated with the *procuraduría* (roughly equivalent to a district attorney's office), dedicated to investigating crimes against migrants. In late 2012 the head of the *fiscalía* told me that his office had not had a single case of aggression against migrants in Oaxaca since it was opened earlier that year. All the cases that reached his office were of migrants who had been victims of violence in Chiapas, before reaching Oaxaca. While it seems doubtful there was no violence at all against migrants in Oaxaca at that time, it is telling that all the migrants who brought charges cited attacks in Chiapas.

Solalinde came to this work out of humanitarian conviction and a sense that the people he saw along the train tracks needed someone to take care of them. Through his work, he has developed a political analysis of why migrants suffer, why corrupt officials are able to keep operating, and how economic policy, security strategy, and the drug war contribute to the situation migrants encounter in Mexico. He has become a voice of political pressure beyond the moral authority of his status as a priest. He now calls for a regional solution to the migration issue, to be developed together by Central America, Mexico, and the United States; the complete dismantling of the INM, Mexico's immigration authority; and a transit visa for all migrants entering Mexican territory. During Mass, he often calls for an end to the neoliberal capitalist system that creates the push and pull factors associated with migration. He also frequently blames the Mérida Initiative for funding and supporting the violent crackdown on migration in Mexico.[14] He and his staff have turned the shelter into a base for advocacy; they encourage migrants, like Yosselin, to press charges against their attackers and stay to see the case to the end. Hundreds of migrants have filed *denuncias* with the support of the shelter in Ixtepec, and though convictions are rare, this constant pressure plays no small part in making the region safer for migrants.

Initially Solalinde envisioned himself as a shepherd tending an abandoned flock. His closeness to migrants who had suffered assaults, extortion, and traumatizing violence, however, led him to question why they were subjected to violence. Through reading, a constant dialogue with international human rights organizations, and an evolving interpretation of the scripture that inspires him, he has developed an astute political analysis to answer that question. His defense of migrants has evolved from providing them with temporary shelter to fighting for their rights in the international political arena. He blames the neoliberal capitalist system for expelling migrants from their home countries, for obligating them to migrate, and for taking advantage of the cheap labor force that those who make it to the United States provide.

Huehuetoca: Committed Secularists and Traditional Church Charity

The success Pantoja and Solalinde have achieved protecting migrants from violence, with very different strategies but similar levels of personal commitment, is brought into sharp relief by a more problematic example from the town of Huehuetoca in the state of Mexico, just outside Mexico City. For about a year, from summer 2012 to summer 2013, there were two migrant aid facilities in the town, one run by the Catholic Church, the other by secular civil society organizations. Neither succeeded in guaranteeing safety for Central American migrants passing through the area.

All freight train lines carrying migrants north converge in Lechería, on the northern fringe of Mexico City. Since different train companies move cargo from Lechería to northern Mexico, migrants must change trains—no easy task. Lechería is heavily patrolled by police and *garroteros*, the railroad companies' private security guards, so many migrants make the forty-kilometer trek to Huehuetoca and climb aboard the northbound trains there. In summer 2012, the Church-run shelter that had tended to migrants in Lechería since 2009 was closed after pressure from the local population (possibly with political backing).[15] The bishop of the Diocese of Cuautitlán, to which both Lechería and Huehuetoca belong, approved the closure and oversaw the opening of a supposed replacement shelter in Huehuetoca, despite complete lack of interest by the local parish priest. The new Albergue San Juan Diego consisted of a large tent, a row of port-a-potties, folding chairs, and thin mattresses, all enclosed by a high wire fence. It received support from both the diocese and the municipal government.

Earlier that summer, a group of civil society activists, unaffiliated with any one organization or church, had opened the Albergue San José shelter in Huehuetoca. It was run by a collective with representatives from a handful of Mexico City–based activist groups that took turns staffing the shelter each day. Many were students from Mexico City's universities, others were loosely affiliated with human rights groups, and some were veteran migrants' rights activists with experience in other shelters. Together they collected the funds and goods necessary to run a shelter. Once the Church shelter in Lechería closed, traffic through Huehuetoca increased substantially, and the Albergue San José became an extremely important stopping point for migrants. Many preferred it to the Albergue San Juan Diego, run by the Church and municipality, where, they complained, they felt like prisoners, the food was not hot, and their stays were limited to twenty-four hours.

However, about six months later the Albergue San José, the civil society–run shelter, ran into security problems. The same *mareros, pandilleros*, and narco networks that posed problems for shelters elsewhere in Mexico appeared, as expected, in Huehuetoca. Wherever migrants congregate, those who make a profit from providing a service (such as the *guías*) or robbing and extorting tend to gather as well. Security concerns increased for the migrants and for the staff and volunteers at the shelters. On the tracks in front of the shelter, *polleros* affiliated with different organized crime groups started charging migrants for the right to pass through the area. They were not in the least concerned about the police who passed by from time to time or the staff inside the shelter.

In December 2012 the Albergue San José shut its doors because it could no longer protect the migrants who came there for refuge. The closure was intended to be temporary; those involved were well aware that the permanent closure of the only civil society–run shelter in Mexico would set a dangerous precedent. In February 2013 the *albergue* reopened as a *comedor*, providing food to the migrants passing through during the day but no longer offering overnight shelter. For that, migrants were directed to San Juan Diego, the tent shelter a few miles down the train tracks.

The commitment to the human rights of the migrants evident in the shelters run by Pantoja and Solalinde is notably absent at San Juan Diego. The services provided are basic (food, a thin mattress to sleep on, first aid, and access to toilets and showers), the priest nominally in charge is rarely seen, and the shelter is not involved in denouncing aggression against migrants. As a result, its presence does little to mitigate the violence migrants face in the area. In fact, some migrants reported that the police now "guarding" the shelter include officers who had robbed them previously. Following the closure of the San José shelter, there have been numerous reports of migrant kidnappings in the Huehuetoca area, and at least two migrants have fallen to their deaths while attempting to board the train.

Meanwhile, the bishop of Cuautitlán, Guillermo Ortiz Mondragón, who decided to shutter the shelter in Lechería and relocate to the remote outskirts of Huehuetoca, has been named the Church's new head of its Pastoral de la Movilidad Humana, its office for migration issues.[16] A statement he made after a particularly brutal assault on migrants on May 1, 2013, in Veracruz, raises questions about his commitment to the fight for migrants' rights and his compassion for their suffering. Central American migrants are not children, he said. They are aware of the dangers they might face in Mexico. It is their responsibility, whatever happens to them.[17] Consistent with the bishop's views, the new shelter in his diocese does not protect migrants in the ways the two others analyzed here do. Migrants are not noticeably safer as they pass through Huehuetoca.

A telling example of the difference between Saltillo and Ixtepec, on the one hand, and Huehuetoca, on the other, is an immigration raid in Huehuetoca in June 2013. Municipal police entered the *comedor* San José and removed migrants who were having breakfast. With immigration officials waiting outside, they then rounded up migrants along the train tracks, beating many of them in the process, and loaded them into their trucks. There are conflicting reports about what happened in the Church-run Albergue San Juan Diego. Some migrants claim that authorities also entered the *albergue* and removed some individuals. Staff deny that but admit that the officials did round up migrants on the tracks in front of the shelter.[18]

This incident is important for three reasons. First, under Mexican immigration law, municipal police are not allowed to participate in immigration actions; entering the *comedor* and rounding up migrants along the track were therefore illegal acts. They were not looking for specific individuals but simply picking up all the migrants they encountered. Second, under Mexican law, the *comedores* and *albergues* are designated sanctuary spaces where immigration raids are not permitted. Third, whereas the activists associated with the *comedor* immediately sent out statements expressing outrage and met with the human rights commission, the *albergue* was completely silent. In fact, based on the testimony of one migrant who was inside the *albergue*, it is possible that the raid was the result of a call made by the priest in charge of San Juan Diego. The priest reportedly objected to migrants asking for money at street corners and called immigration to clean up the town. Even if this is not true, the priest seemed indifferent to the raid. He made no public statements denouncing the illegal actions of the municipal police and the immigration authorities. And the complaints of the civil society groups from the *comedor* had little impact. About a week later a similar raid took place in the next town along the train route, Bojay, Hidalgo.

The events suggest that neither the civil society–run shelter nor the Church-run one without a committed leader provides the same deterrent against violence and the repression of migrants that Pantoja and Solalinde have achieved. The conviction and moral authority of an individual priest coupled with the backing of the Catholic Church, the local community, and international organizations combine to create an environment in which violence against migrants is reduced. The Church alone is not enough, nor is the commitment of civil society activists, without social *blindaje* from another source.

In Ixtepec, Solalinde developed a theology and praxis that incorporate the concept of human rights to protect migrants from violence. He used his moral authority as a priest to bring media attention to his mission, keeping Hermanos en el Camino operating safely through support from international agencies and human rights groups. In Saltillo, Pantoja, a parish priest with deep ties to the community, a commitment to liberation theology, and personal experience and knowledge of movement building, has kept Posada Belén operating safely with the full support of his bishop. Both shelters continue to operate despite recurrent threats. The civil society–run shelter in Huehuetoca, however, lacked reliable backing when similar threats and security concerns arose and had little choice but to change from a shelter to a *comedor*, significantly limiting the protection they could provide to migrants. Without Church pressure on municipal police and local organized crime groups, or international support, the civil society shelter found itself particularly vulnerable to criminal elements.

The distinct Church-shelter dynamic in each area studied has an impact on the levels of violence against migrants in each shelter's vicinity. In Ixtepec, Solalinde's presence and mission helped turn the area into one of the safer points along the route for migrants. In Saltillo, Posada Belén is a legitimate sanctuary, even though nearby Monterrey is among the most dangerous places to be a migrant and the border is even worse. In Lechería, attacks against migrants have increased since the closure of the shelter there. Migrants report demands for money from the municipal police, and the *garroteros*, the private security guards that work for the train companies, are known to steal from and shoot at migrants. A few migrants who arrived in Huehuetoca told me that in Lechería the *garroteros* had shot at them aboard the train, hitting one man in the leg. They then forced the other migrants to get down and refused to let them assist the wounded man. The train left the yard with the bleeding migrant alone on top. As far as the migrants knew, he died there. The violence is so bad in Lechería and Huehuetoca today that many *guías* avoid the area entirely, taking their migrant-clients on buses from Mexico City to the state of Hidalgo directly, preferring to risk a surprise immigration *retén* than deal with the violence in the state of Mexico.

These three case studies of migrant shelters and their founders are only a small sample of the more than sixty *albergues*, soup kitchens, and relief centers across Mexico today and can only begin to suggest some of the factors that may affect success or failure in addressing the larger issue of violence against migrants. They do demonstrate, however, how committed priests have been able to combat the violence against migrants. In Saltillo, Coahuila, a long-term activist priest with a liberation theology background runs a shelter with the full backing of the diocese. Relying on carefully fostered *blindaje social*, it offers migrants sanctuary and empowerment in the midst of Zeta territory. In Ixtepec, Oaxaca, a *clérico vago* relies on international and media pressure to calm the violence against migrants and keep both his shelter and himself safe. In Huehuetoca, in contrast, the presence of two shelters is not enough to have any substantial impact on the violence. Although the people from civil society organizations who ran the shelter and later the *comedor* have a commitment comparable to Solalinde's and Pantoja's, it has not been enough to make immigration authorities or the police respect the law, let alone cease aggression toward migrants. Meanwhile, the neighboring Church-run shelter offers simple assistance without a willingness to tackle the landscape of violence that migrants face.

Notes

In Spanish, the last phrase of Matthew 25:35, the passage adopted by Hermanos en Camino, usually reads, "fui forastero [stranger]" or "fui extranjero [stranger]," but many in the migrants' rights movement in Mexico have taken the liberty of substituting "fui migrante." See the shelter's website www.hermanosenel camino.org/.

1. Hagan finds mainline Protestants in the United States more willing to engage politically on immigration issues than their Evangelical or Pentecostal counterparts.

2. There is one initiative in Tapachula, Chiapas, run by the evangelical Hermano Ramón called Todo Por Ellos, dedicated to helping street children, many of whom are Central American. It is the exception in the migrants' rights movement in Mexico.

3. Regarding this section's head, migrants and migrant rights' advocates in Mexico regularly refer to what migrants endure while crossing Mexico as *el infierno* (hell).

4. *Guías* are also colloquially referred to as *polleros* or *caminadores*. I employ the term *guía* here because it is the most neutral and generic.

5. Although *coyote* has a variety of meanings in Mexican Spanish, it is commonly used to refer to a person who moves migrants across the border into the United States.

The Zetas are one of the dominant cartels in Mexico, controlling northern and eastern parts of the country. They are notorious for their brutality and, as they control the smuggling routes in their territories, the migrants passing through must deal with them.

6. The *coyote* who leads the migrant across the border receives a fraction of this money. Most of the fee goes to the cartel higher-ups.

7. Yosselin, like the names of all migrants identified in the chapter, is a pseudonym.

8. The migrant shelter in Tenosique, Tabasco, which is not one of the examples explored in this chapter, is named "La 72" to honor those killed in San Fernando. It is run by a Franciscan friar, Tomás González Castillo, who is a relative newcomer to the field, beginning his work with migrants in 2011. I chose to focus here on the priests who have developed their positions over longer periods. In the future, Fray Tomás could provide another illuminating example of Catholic theology and human rights commitment expressed in the defense of Central American migrants.

9. See www.amnesty.ie/node/1768.

10. Mark Stevenson, "Church Wants to Reassign Mexico Activist Priest," *USA Today*, August 8, 2012.

11. Rodrigo Vera, "Niega bispo que ordenara renuncia de Solalinde," *Proceso*, August 8, 2012.

12. Jesús Lastra, "Solalinde pide perdón a los Zetas: 'Son víctimas de un gobierno corrupto,'" *La Jornada*, July 30, 2011.

13. Pantoja has the fortune of serving in the diocese of Bishop Raúl Vera, the only current bishop in Mexico to have been inspired by liberation theology.

14. Signed in 2008, the Mérida Initiative promised US$1.6 billion in aid to Mexico (and Central America) to fight drug traffickers, strengthen the rule of law and government and judicial institutions, and develop a "twenty-first-century border" and support communities alongside it. It also dedicated funding to strengthen government institutions, the rule of law, and the court system. This support came in the form of training, equipment, and technology to enable the Mexican military and other government forces to undertake its war against the cartels. It also funded the training of immigration agents and the building of new immigration facilities.

15. The closure of the Lechería shelter occurred after a relatively calm period in shelter-community relations. Seemingly out of nowhere, a neighborhood group staged a symbolic closure of the shelter, and the Church leadership acquiesced, closing the shelter permanently. Many are suspicious of the real motivations, however, as the sudden activity occurred right after elections that returned the former ruling Partido Revolucionario Institucional (PRI) to power in Mexico. By closing the shelter in Lechería and opening a new one in a remote area, the PRI could claim at once to be listening to residents' demands and to be concerned about the safety of migrants. Closing the shelter in Lechería, more than appeasing the locals, though, opened up the area to those corrupt agents who prey on the migrants' vulnerabilities. The actual decision making behind these developments, however, remains opaque.

16. Ortiz Mondragón replaced Hermana Leticia Gutiérrez as the head of the Pastoral de la Movilidad Humana. Gutiérrez is from the Scalabrini order of nuns, whose core mission is to work with migrants. Gutiérrez's term was up, and the position was set to rotate to someone else in accordance with the Church's standard practice. The choice of Ortiz Mondragón as head, however, instead of appointing another Scalabriniana or one of the many priests or nuns who work with migrants, is seen as largely political. Ortiz Mondragón is viewed as a close ally of the state's former governor and Mexico's current president, Enrique Peña Nieto.

17. Juan Manuel Barrera, "Migrantes de CA conocen peligros que enfrentan," *El Universal*, May 3, 2013.

18. The municipal police did not release an official statement about the incident. Under any circumstances, however, police entering a shelter and/or *comedor* is illegal.

References

Brigden, Noelle K. 2012. "'Like a War': The New Central American Refugee Crisis." *NACLA Report on the Americas* 45, no. 4 (Winter): 7–11.

Comisión Nacional de los Derechos Humanos (CNDH). 2011. "Informe especial sobre secuestros de migrantes en México." Mexico City. Available at www.cndh.org.mx/sites/all/fuentes/documentos/informes/especiales/2011 _secmigrantes_0.pdf.

Coutin, Susan Bibler. 2005. "Being En Route." *American Anthropologist* 107, no. 2 (June): 195–206.

Frank-Vitale, Amelia. 2011. "Guerreros del Camino: Central American Migration through Mexico and Undocumented Migration as Civil Disobedience." MA thesis, American University.

Frontera con Justicia AC. 2013. "Saltillo, Coahuila. México un lugar de tortura a personas migrantes." Casa del Migrante de Saltillo.

Hagan, Jacqueline. 2006. "Making Theological Sense of the Migration Journey from Latin America: Catholic, Protestant, and Interfaith Perspectives." *American Behavioral Scientist* 49, no. 11 (July): 1554–73.

Vogt, Wendy. 2013. "Crossing Mexico: Structural Violence and the Commodification of Undocumented Central American Migrants." *American Ethnologist* 40, no. 4: 764–80.

CHAPTER 15

FROM GUNS TO GOD

Mobilizing Evangelical Christianity in Urabá, Colombia

KIMBERLY THEIDON

In *el monte*, forget about the seven plagues. Out there? There must be fourteen! And the commanders always warned us the only way out was dead.
　—Former combatant, Bloque Bananero, Turbo, January 2013

What we're searching for is forgetting. I say let's go for it because if we don't forget we aren't doing anything. Well, it's not that we're going to forget what we learned because a person doesn't forget. But you need to get the war out of your mind. You need to leave the war behind, know that you're not stuck in this war—that you have a new life.
　—"Juan," former combatant, the FARC, December 2006

A key component of peace processes and postconflict reconstruction is the disarmament, demobilization, and reintegration (DDR) of former combatants. Since 1989, more than sixty DDR processes have been implemented in countries around the world (CCDDR 2009). As I have argued elsewhere, DDR programs entail multiple transitions: the combatants who lay down their weapons, the governments that seek an end to armed conflict, the communities that receive—or vehemently reject—these demobilized warriors (see Theidon 2007, 2009). At each level, these transitions involve complex debates about balancing the demands of peace with those of justice, reparations, and social repair. And yet traditional (or "first-generation") approaches to DDR focused almost exclusively on military and security objectives, which resulted in these programs being developed in relative isolation from the growing field of transitional justice and its concerns with historical clarification, justice, reparations, and reconciliation (see Theidon 2007, 2009). By reducing DDR to "dismantling the machinery of war," these programs failed to adequately consider how to move beyond demobilizing combatants to facilitating social repair and coexistence (Knight and Özerdem 2004, 2).

A growing awareness of the limitations of a one-man-one-weapon approach to DDR—with its myopic focus on the individual (male) combatant—led the United Nations Department of Peacekeeping Operations (UNDPKO) to rethink best practice standards in 2010. As the UNDPKO (2010, 3) notes, "Whereas traditional DDR focuses mainly on combatants that are present within military structures, the focus of Second Generation programmes shifts away from military structures towards the larger communities that are affected by armed violence." With this shift in focus, "second-generation" DDR programs must grapple with community involvement and the social reintegration of former combatants (UNDPKO 2010). One way to think of this shift is in terms of introducing a politics of scale: from negotiating macrolevel peace accords to disarming and demobilizing armed groups to rebuilding the intimate spheres of social relationships and individual subjectivities.[1] It is this last sphere—that of social reconstruction or social repair—that I explore in this chapter.

In the same document outlining Second Generation DDR practices, the UNDPKO encourages DDR practitioners to design and implement psychosocial interventions that "help individuals to regain their capacity for resilience, while restoring social capital and contributing to a greater sense of national unity," acknowledging that "efforts will be most effective when utilizing indigenous and local resources to develop, translate and communicate positive psycho-social messages" (UNDPKO 2010, 27–28). In keeping with the new focus on community-based approaches, these psychosocial interventions should address "trauma to both perpetrators and victims, recognizing that the experience of many individuals and communities lies somewhere in between" (28).

The nod to psychosocial interventions is laudable, albeit vague. What exactly does the "psychosocial" entail? Who are its agents, and where does this psychosocial work occur? While reading the UNDPKO document, I recalled many former combatants who assured me they were "*totalmente psicosocializado*" (totally psychosocialized), an assurance they offered in a tone vacillating between cynicism and lament. They had attended the mandatory psychosocial sessions, involving techniques that can range anywhere from an appointment with a psychologist to attending a bake sale in a parking lot. They were thoroughly "psychosocialized," yet were still searching for ways to construct "*una nueva vida*" (a new life). My research makes clear that former combatants, and those around them, are searching for tools with which to make individual and collective life a bit easier, to make living with both self and others more bearable.

This chapter draws on field research with former combatants from the paramilitaries Fuerzas Armadas Revolucionarias de Colombia (FARC) and Ejército de Liberación Nacional (ELN). Since January 2005 I have been conducting anthropological research on the individual and collective demobilization programs.[2] To date my Colombian colleague Paola Andrea Betancourt and I have interviewed 236 male and 53 female former combatants. In addition, we have interviewed representatives of state entities and nongovernmental organizations (NGOs) as well as the military, the Catholic and Evangelical churches, and various sectors of the "host communities" to which former combatants are sent or to which they return. I sought to understand the local dynamics between victims and victimizers and the experiences of those individual and communities the UNDPKO rightly describes as lying somewhere in between.

This chapter focuses in particular on several neighborhoods located on the outskirts of Apartadó and Turbo in the Urabá region of Colombia (fig. 15.1). I followed a group of former combatants back home, if you will, to explore everyday life and its challenges. Following in their steps often led me to the doors of the Evangelical churches that have multiplied throughout this conflictive region of the country. It is the proliferation of these churches, as well as the centrality of religious referents in many conversations with former combatants, that convinces me that local religious leaders—in this case, evangelical pastors—are performing crucial "psychosocial work" in the sermons they deliver each day in *culto* (church service). In these *cultos*, they also confront the complex debates with which this chapter began: how to balance the demands of peace with those of justice, reparations, and social repair.

I begin with an overview of Colombia's current DDR program and its impact on Urabá, located in the region with the highest concentration of demobilized combatants. I then explore how evangelical pastors manage memory and the past, issues of great relevance in the lives of former combatants and those around them. This leads to a discussion of repertoires of justice and the elaboration of local theologies of redemption and reconciliation. I conclude by analyzing the role these churches play in providing a space for the development of alternative masculinities and the much-desired personal transformations that may allow these former combatants to forge *una nueva vida*.

Urabá: The Perpetual Frontier

Urabá is rich in natural resources and man-made woe. The region has historically been a zone of colonization. The departmental government in Antioquia sponsored "civilizational campaigns" during the early 1900s, in which *paisas* were encouraged to homestead the region and "civilize" the Afro-Colombian population.[3] The dominance of *paisas* in the region marks present-day identity politics and tensions, and the association of the Catholic Church hierarchy with *paisas* and the state is one factor my interviewees cited in the growth of evangelical churches in the region. Indeed, until the 1940s the Catholic Church was quite conservative and a significant landholder.[4] In addition, as María Teresa Uribe (1992, 11) has argued, lengthy and successful migrations to the region have resulted in "permanent colonization" and subsequently contributed to the multiethnic and multiregional demographics of Urabá. This in turn has led to the lack of a cohesive regional identity, and to friction among successive migrant groups struggling over land and other resources.

Figure 15.1. Map of Urabá, Colombia

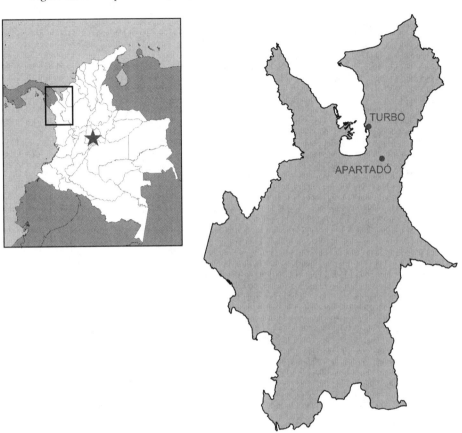

Courtesy of Jorge Saldarriaga.

In addition to the complicated ethnic composition of the region, Urabá has been a zone of refuge and clandestinity. During the slaveholding era, *cimarrones* (people of African descent) arrived fleeing brutal servitude; more recently, other Colombians traveled to the region in hopes of escaping poverty; still other migrants came because they were wanted for sundry legal infractions elsewhere in the country (Uribe 1992, 42). Invoking the lawlessness associated with frontier regions—an association with both literal and metaphorical dimensions—Urabá has thus been constructed as a perpetual frontier in which the state has never consolidated its presence. Importantly, Urabá is a region in which justice has long been administered by private forces and regional strongmen, or caciques (Ortiz Sarmiento 2007, 173).

Among those competing for control of this resource-rich part of Colombia were national and international companies, which have amassed great wealth via the extraction of wood and the cultivation of bananas. These industries were key actors in a land grab that would be further exacerbated by the drug traffickers and paramilitary commanders who engaged in a "counter agrarian reform."[5] Magnifying the strategic importance of the region is the border with Panama, which serves as the thin line through which drugs are smuggled out and arms smuggled in. These resources, combined with the Atrato River and the port at Turbo, made control of this region desirable to international businesses and local elites, as well as to the paramilitaries and the FARC who engaged in a struggle for control of the region during the 1990s and early 2000s.

In Urabá the paramilitaries in alliance with local elites and their military connections controlled the towns and cities, and the guerrillas dominated the countryside.[6] In 1994 the infamous Castaño brothers forged an alliance among various paramilitary units under the name Autodefensas Campesinas Unidas de Córdoba y Urabá (ACCU), which in 1997 merged with paramilitary units from other regions to form the Autodefensas Unidas de Colombia (AUC). From that date forward the region became the site of an intense armed struggle between the AUC and the FARC. The paramilitaries pursued a depopulation strategy as part of their military offensive, and when the violence escalated dramatically in the mid-1990s thousands of peasants were displaced, leaving abandoned villages in their wake. Crowding into the small towns along the Atrato as well as the larger cities of Turbo and Apartadó, peasants endured several years *"andando en tierra ajena"* (wandering in foreign land). By 1997 there were an estimated seventeen thousand refugees in Urabá alone.

The displacement prompted these peasant farmers to begin organizing, motivated by their desire to return to land many of them had worked since the time of their great-grandparents, with both land and communal histories passed down across several generations. They decided to return as Peace Communities, declaring themselves residents of neutral zones in the midst of the armed conflict, and sought support from the Catholic Church—one of the few institutions in the region with some capacity to mediate between the various parties to the conflict. Under the guidance of Fr. Leonidas Moreno—a progressive priest with more than twenty-five years of experience in the region—these peasants carved out precarious "territories of life" along the sinewy banks of the ríos Sucio and Atrato.

The struggle to maintain neutrality was constant, especially against the backdrop of *paramilitarismo*—the transformation of paramilitary groups into an economic, social, and political force that infiltrated Colombian society. Beyond the individual combatants who collectively organized into armed and lethal groups, *paramilitarismo* became a corrosive and insidious institution. In addition, there was the complicated and ambiguous relationship these groups had with the state. As Garcia-Peña (2005, 59) has noted, "A principal characteristic of *paramilitarismo* is its relationship with the state. For some, *paramilitarismo* is a policy of state terrorism, while for others it is the response of desperate citizens confronted with guerrilla abuses due to an absent state: curiously, for both sides the state's responsibility is central, rather by action or omission" (my translation).

By the presidential elections of 2002, an increasing number of Colombians were demanding peace. The debacle of earlier peace processes readied many sectors of Colombian society for someone who would take a "hard-line" approach to the violence. Álvaro Uribe promised to be that man. President Uribe was not inclined to attempt dialogue with the FARC, which he considered a "terrorist threat." Rather, Uribe cautiously explored the possibility of negotiating with the paramilitaries while simultaneously promising to rein in the guerrillas. There is a certain irony in these negotiations. In part the paramilitary demobilization was an attempt to "deparamilitarize" the Colombian state. Clearly earlier government initiatives to fill its absence with civilian defense committees went beyond the state's control. Thus at some juncture the government was destined to find itself negotiating peace not only with the guerrillas but with the paramilitaries as well. As García-Peña (2005, 66) has observed, "The most innovative ingredient in the current administration's peace policy is the negotiations with the AUC, which break the stance maintained by every government since 1989 when President Barco declared the self-defense groups illegal. With this, the analytical frame changes radically: it was always thought that the paramilitary demobilization would be the result of peace with the insurgency—either simultaneously or subsequently—because the paramilitaries themselves claim to be a consequence of the guerrilla."

Thus in August 2002 the government began negotiations with the paramilitaries. The Uribe government promoted the demobilization of individual combatants from all armed groups and began negotiations for the collective demobilization of the AUC.[7] The government named Luis Carlos Restrepo High Commissioner for Peace and gave him the task of negotiating peace. The signing of the Santa Fe de Ralito I agreement on July 15, 2003, marked the beginning of formal talks between the AUC-linked paramilitary groups and the government, and priests from the Diócesis of Apartadó played an important role as mediators at the negotiating table. The terms of the agreement included the demobilization of all combatants by the end of 2005, with provisions for concentrating the leadership and troops in specified locations. The negotiations also obligated the AUC to suspend its lethal activities and maintain the unilateral ceasefire, as well as aid the government in its anti-drug-trafficking efforts.

The Sante Fe de Ralito II agreement, signed on May 13, 2004, set up a 368-square-kilometer "concentration zone" (*zona de ubicación*) in Tierralta, Córdoba.[8] The concentration zone was created to facilitate and consolidate the process between the government and the AUC, to improve verification of the ceasefire, and to establish a timetable for the demobilization process. The Accords also established the Mission in Support of the Peace Process of the Organization of American States (MAPP-OEA), which was placed in charge of the verification process in regard to the disarmament and demobilization of combatants. Since 2002, 30,151 AUC combatants have collectively demobilized, and almost 12,000 combatants from the FARC, ELN, and certain paramilitary *bloques* have individually demobilized.[9]

In addition to the above initiatives, on July 22, 2005, President Uribe signed Law 975, the Justice and Peace Law. The law embodies the competing tensions of peace and justice, and victim-survivor's organizations succeeded in challenging certain key aspects of the law on the grounds that it failed to provide sufficient assurance of their right to truth, justice, and reparations.[10] Under pressure from victim-survivor's organizations and domestic and international human rights organizations, the Colombian government was forced to modify the law; although still imperfect when measured by absolute human rights standards, the Colombian Constitutional Court ruling of May 2006 did serve to strengthen the law in response to these challenges. If at one time states wielded their sovereign prerogative to issue amnesties in the name of political expediency, stability, and peace—prerogatives that characterized past demobilization efforts in Colombia—changes in international norms increasingly place limits on the granting of leniency to perpetrators, forcing governments to address transitional issues of truth, justice, and redress. Thus the Uribe administration was forced to implement DDR on the terrain of transitional justice, which presented both opportunities and challenges (Laplante and Theidon 2006; Theidon 2007).

Central to social dynamics in Urabá was the demobilization of the paramilitary units Bloque Bananero and Bloque Élmer Cárdenas. On November 25, 2004, the Bloque Bananero formally demobilized in Corregimiento El Dos, located outside of Turbo. Under the command of Éver Veloza García (aka H.H., or "El Mono Veloza"), 447 combatants demobilized and began the process of reincorporation into civilian life. The Bloque Élmer Cárdenas, under the command of Freddy Rendón Herrera (aka "El Alemán," the German) also demobilized in three phases during 2006.[11] These two paramilitary units account for approximately 2,000 former combatants, combined with another 1,200 demobilized combatants from other paramilitary units that operated throughout the country.[12] In addition, there are several hundred former FARC combatants, leading to the highest concentration of demobilized combatants anywhere in Colombia.[13]

These numbers speak to an underlying racial issue that bears on this discussion. Urabá was known as a *zona exportadora de paramilitares* (a paramilitary export zone), and the ways in which racial imaginaries articulated with the paramilitary project is understudied. Without denying the strategic importance of the region and thus the interest elites and their paramilitary allies had in controlling Urabá, I am convinced the region became a recruitment zone in part because of racist stereotypes about Afro-Colombians. Throughout my years of working in the region, *paisas* have warned me about the voracious sexual appetites, proclivity to violence, and reckless amorality of the Afro-Colombian inhabitants of Urabá. These stereotypes both reflect and reinforce racial hierarchies across social fields. For example, in his analysis of the earlier Ejército Popular de Liberación (EPL) demobilization, Ortiz Sarmiento (2007, 52) found that the guerrilla commanders were primarily *paisas*. This resonates with numerous interviews I conducted with former combatants from the region, who complained about the racist treatment they suffered at the hands of their *paisa* commanders. This racial imaginary influenced recruitment patterns and led *paisa* paramilitary and guerrilla leaders to seek out darker-skinned recruits to serve as the foot soldiers who would "*poner el pecho a la guerra*" (do the heavy lifting of war).

The Black Box of DDR

Throughout Colombia's lengthy internal armed conflict, each successive president has attempted some sort of military victory or, in the face of that impossibility, peace negotiations.[14] While it is beyond the scope of this chapter to present an exhaustive review of these previous efforts, there are certain key features that warrant our attention and allow us to understand both the great challenges and the possibilities that the current demobilization process poses.

In the glossary of postconflict reconstruction and peace building, three terms are omnipresent: *disarmament, demobilization,* and *reintegration* (UNDPKO 1999). As the United Nations Department of Peacekeeping Operations (UNDPKO) defines it, disarmament in the context of peace processes consists of the collection, control, and elimination of small arms, ammunition, explosives, and light and heavy weapons from the combatants and, depending on the circumstances, the civilian population. Demobilization is the process by which armed organizations (which may consist of government or opposition forces) decrease in size or are dismantled as one component of a broad transformation from a state of war to a state of peace. Generally demobilization involves the concentration, quartering, disarming, management, and licensing of former combatants, who may receive some form of compensation or other assistance to motivate them to lay down their weapons and reenter civilian life. Finally, reinsertion or reintegration consists of those measures directed at former combatants that seek to strengthen the capacity of these individuals and their families to achieve social and economic reintegration in society. The reinsertion programs may include economic assistance or some other form of monetary compensation, as well as technical or professional training or instruction in other productive activities.

Reflecting the limitations of traditional DDR programs, the Colombian Agency for Reintegration (ACR, formerly the High Commissioner for Reintegration) was created in 2006 in an effort to move beyond the one-man-one-gun focus to a more community-oriented vision of reintegration. The ACR works throughout Colombia, sponsoring community-based activities and reconciliation initiatives. In one of my early interviews with a director of the ACR office responsible for Urabá, I asked if the staff coordinated with the Catholic Church given the high-profile role of priests from the Diócesis of Apartadó in the Peace Communities and in the demobilization negotiations in Santa Fe de Ralito. The director shook his head and replied, "We don't coordinate with them because they just focus on the victims. They are always talking about the victims and, well, you know these *muchachos* [referring to former combatants] are much more complicated!" We both laughed at the euphemism, but he certainly set me thinking about how and where religious actors might be working with these "complicated individuals."

"Ellos que tienen pasados": Those Who Have a Past

When someone has killed another person, God can forgive him. Some people may forgive him, but many others won't. And if you killed a member of their family . . . well, that's really hard.

—"Manuel," demobilized combatant, Apartadó, January 2013

[The paramilitary commanders]—oh, they've threatened me so many times. When their men convert, they accuse me of taking away their men. I've had to explain to them that they convert because they owe God something, because God has touched them.

I say, "Yes, before they chose guns, but now they choose God."
I try to explain it to them so they understand.
— Pastor "Filomeno," United Pentecostal Church of Colombia,
Turbo, January 5, 2013

My questions regarding how and where religious actors might be working with "complicated people" led me to the Evangelical churches that have multiplied throughout Urabá over the past ten years. Although the *evangélicos* have a lengthy history in the region, their massive increase during the past decade is striking.[15] No matter how small the town, a walk through its streets will send one's head pivoting in an attempt to count all the Evangelical temples. Attending *cultos* and speaking with pastors helped me understand why.

Pastor José is a slender Afro-Colombian man with close-cropped hair and a fierce preaching style. The first time I attended *culto* at the Iglesia Pentecostal Unida Universal, I sat toward the front of the church for fear that I might not catch everything being said. This ill-fated strategy positioned me close to the washing machine–sized speakers that began to vibrate with religious conviction. He was being sworn in as pastor, and this was the first sermon he delivered to the forty *hermanos* and *hermanas* gathered together that night.[16] José roared until the veins on his neck bulged and the tendons grew taut. He paced back and forth, exhorting his congregation to remember that Jesus had given his blood for them. Although other blood could stain or taint, the blood of Christ cleansed the body and purified the soul. The blood of Christ can wash us clean, wash away all of our sins. I was struck by the number of young men in the congregation, jaws clenched and eyes closed as they swayed to the cadence of José's voice.

I visited José the following afternoon at his home, located right above the church. Urabá's heat baked the wooden walls and floor of his house, and my nose registered the burn of a dry sauna set a few notches too high. His wife generously brought out a fan and cold orange soda pop, and I willed the sweat to stop dripping down my face and back. In contrast, José was immaculate in his pressed dress shirt and slacks, with shoes that seemed to effortlessly repel the dust.

After several years spent "*caminando veredas*" throughout Chigorodó and Currulao, José, his wife, and four daughters would be settling down in Apartadó. I mentioned that he must be looking forward to the relative calm of Apartadó after having worked through some difficult times in the countryside. José smiled broadly and assured me that although he had crossed paths with many armed groups, they had allowed him to preach, and he had never received a threat. "God was protecting us, *hermana*," he added.

I explained the nature of my research, and José nodded even before I had finished my brief introduction.

> *Hermana*, we live in a country at war, and the state can't do anything—the state is very corrupt. So much pain, so many loved ones dead! These young men live in armed groups, so how to take them out of the conflict? *There has to be a way out.* The government thinks about getting them to leave their weapons behind, but they come to us. This is our work. We are concerned about this problem. In our work, we seek to influence, to transform the person. We reach out to the person right where they are, we understand a person. We work so that they are no longer aggressive—instead of being filled with hate, they are filled with love. All sorts of people arrive at our church, drug addicts, criminals. *Hermana, ellos han tenido un pasado.*

The skinny young man fidgeting at José's side momentarily distracted me. I had noticed him the evening before in *culto*, a bit unnerved by the fervor of his worship. Diego's religious frenzy was almost frightening, somehow ferocious. I glanced at him as he sat peeling off layers of his discolored fingernails as José and I spoke. He suddenly shifted his pale Malamute eyes my way, staring unblinkingly. I shifted back to José but sensed Diego was one of those people with a past.

José continued to explain how he saw the role of the church. "The capacity to change, to change ourselves and our country, is important. Violence is not a change—from violence only comes more violence. We seek psychological changes, and we're seeing results. We don't have a peace project as such, but we are always looking for the mental transformation of each person."

I nodded and asked him about the topic of reconciliation. "Oh yes, we touch on that theme. We are all human beings, *la raza humana*. Such tremendous violence to the human race! We must speak of the Word and stop this hatred. People have rancor, they feel it in their heart, but we must stop the cycle of revenge."

José then turned to the example of Jesús Crucificado, who cried out, "Forgive them for they know not what they do." "It's from ignorance, so we must share the Word. Each of us must say, 'I will not pay this back the same way. I am leaving the past behind.'"

Diego eagerly chimed in, suggesting each of us must turn the other cheek.

José nodded, and insisted on the importance of restoring souls in order to live in a peaceful country. "We work psychologically, *hermana*."

I realized the afternoon was coming to a close and thanked José, adding that I imagined he needed some time to prepare his sermon for that evening. He shook his head. "I don't write out my sermons." Picking up my glass of orange soda, he added, "I'm like this glass. The Spirit fills me in the moment."

A KEY COMPONENT of Evangelical religious practice is the construction of a new "sacred self." As Joel Robbins (2004) has noted, Pentecostal Christianity has both world-breaking and world-making facets, which introduce their own cultural logics while being organizationally local and responsive to local concerns. Via rituals of rupture—confession, repentance, atonement—converts leave their old identities behind. The emphasis on rupture shares the temporalizing functions of transitional justice in that it constructs a "before" and "after" with regard to violent events and actors; however, the logics also diverge. One aspect of contemporary memory politics is the incitement to memory as a deterrent to future violence, and as a pillar of the rights enshrined in "guarantees of nonrepetition." In this formula, forgetting is assigned an almost uniformly negative connotation, and is considered to be both a failure of memory and a dangerous opening for the relentless repetition of a violent past. This article of faith may be summed up by an oft-repeated aphorism: "He who forgets the past is condemned to repeat it." I am not so sure, and neither are the Evangelicals with whom I have spoken.

Pastor José was not alone in insisting that many members of his congregation "have a past" and that they are looking for a way to leave it behind. For many former combatants, life in *el monte* was difficult, exhausting, and they wish to "get the war out of their minds." The theme of change and transformation is central to their desires and to Evangelical practice. Just as the weight of one's own past may be unbearable, I think of the broader history in which these people are situated. In Urabá, unless one is at least seventy years old, there is no lived memory of a time "before all this began"—of a time when there was not ongoing lethal and intimate violence. While the past can obviously be a resource in the (re)construction of social life, it can also be a dead weight that continues to poison the present. I suspect that one appeal of *evangelismo* is the management of individual memory and the social containment of the violent past.

Moreover, for combatants who have been continuously assured that the only way out is in a casket—and for those who live fearing retaliation from former comrades still actively participating in armed groups—finding an "exit strategy" is no easy matter. Pastor José emphasized that offering people a way out is beyond the capability of state-sponsored DDR programs, and indeed the number of former combatants who have been assassinated following demobilization is alarming.[17] Several pastors described their role in negotiating safe passage for combatants who were looking for a way out. Striking is the pastors' insistence that God has chosen these men, touched them in some way. The displacement of agency onto God himself is a powerful means of deflecting reprisals and of locating accountability for desertion in a serious moral authority. In his work with former gang members in Central America, Robert Brenneman (2012, 16) found that "many gang leaders extend a 'pass' to members who report a conversion or have joined a church, though the self-described convert will be observed to make sure his conversion was not simply a ruse to escape the morgue rule."[18] One way to signal the sincerity of conversion is via the adherence to strict behavioral guidelines and an emphasis on the domestic sphere (Brenneman 2012, 17).[19]

These signals of conversion are abundant in Urabá. I found most pastors are as likely to preach about the "here and now" as they are to preach about the world beyond. While there is certainly a concern with salvation, one aspect of achieving that goal is by living in such a way as to make one's life "a living testament to His word."[20] This involves a moral recalibration, as well as changes in speech, dress, bodily praxis—a transformation of oneself. In his critique of how religion has been constructed by Western social scientists, Talal Asad (1993, 46) has noted that "religion has been constructed as an object of study, and reduced to an internalized state of belief rather than powerful action in this world, as a site for producing disciplined knowledge and personal discipline." The importance of discipline combines with the aforementioned mnemonic readjustments to result in *evangelismo* constituting powerful activity in *this* world.

Repertoires of Justice: Theology in the Vernacular

Justice, like beauty, is in the eye of the beholder and can be interpreted in a variety of ways.

—Eric Stover and Harvey M. Weinstein,
My Neighbor, My Enemy

The women in the focus group in Turbo arrived one by one, their spirits lifted by the bottles of chilled soda pop awaiting them. In the midst of a busy, sweltering afternoon they had accepted my invitation to talk about the demobilization process that was reconfiguring life in their communities. With each sip, the heat ceded to a bit more openness. As I would learn, many of them had fathers, husbands, partners, sons, and daughters in the guerrillas, the army, the police, the paramilitary—in some cases, all at once. Several of the women shook their heads as they listed their family members and the armed groups to which they had belonged in the course of this interminable war. Slowly the conversation wound around to my central questions: "What do you think the government should do? I know this process is so controversial. What do you think of all this?" They murmured among themselves, some looking at bit uncomfortable. Finally one woman stood and spoke on behalf of the group: "Well, if they come here and round up all the men who've ever held a gun and put them in jail— *bueno*, there'd be no men left around here [*nos quedamos en pueblos sin hombres*]."[21]

One component of this research involves repertoires of justice. I am interested in the forms of justice people imagine and demand. Evangelical Christians may have tremendous influence on the course of the violence and its potential aftermath. While Catholic priests from the Diócesis of Apartadó have played important roles in macrolevel peace negotiations between armed groups, and between armed groups and the state, these negotiations involved the leadership of both state and nonstate actors. In her comparative analysis of zones of peace in Colombia, Catalina Rojas (2007, 75) urges her readers to attend to the regional differences of the conflict and to regional forms of resistance to the war: "These regional practices are questioning two assumptions: first, that 'dialogues' should only be held at the national level; and second, that negotiations should be exclusively between armed actors and the government." The variation she found illustrates the need to complement the formal negotiation process between elites, and between the leadership of armed groups and the government, with "bottom up" processes involving locally situated people with particular histories of the war. Based on my previous research in Peru, I am convinced that when we look beyond conflict resolution or peace-building writ large to the micropolitics of social reconstruction, religious actors play a vital role (see Theidon 2013).

Transitional justice imports many elements from the liberal justice and human rights traditions, with their foundations in Enlightenment principles of individual freedom; the autonomous individual and the social contract; the public sphere of secular reason; the rule of law; and the centrality of retributive justice with its emphasis on punishment, particularly in the form of trials. Some have referred to this as the "liberal peace-building consensus" and acknowledge the many contributions this approach has made to postwar reconstruction. However, when we look to the daily work of social repair, the limitations of secular justice to address profound moral injuries may in part explain people's faith in divine justice. Confronted with the burden of unpunished crime and the need to break cycles of revenge, divine justice is not simply "fatalism," but an alternative conception of justice and reckoning that lies outside the liberal legal approach to these issues. My conversation with Pastor Abiathar helps explain why.[22]

When I called Pastor Abiathar to see if he might have time to talk, he replied by telling me to wait for him right outside the church. He arrived on a motorcycle, looking even younger than his thirty-two years. Short black hair framed his smooth round face and big smile. He is from the region, proudly Afro-Colombian, and his preaching style includes a great deal of gentle humor, leaving the fire of hell and the acrid odor of brimstone to others. His church is one that explicitly provides outreach and accompaniment to demobilized combatants and to children at risk of being recruited into an armed group. When he spoke about their community-based programs, Abiathar emphasized, "The church is like a big family, with affection and acceptance. Here there are no differences in class, race, ethnicity, or status. We're all equal."

The equality message was one I heard in several *cultos* and from the pastors with whom I spoke. In light of the racism mentioned earlier, the emphasis that Afro-Colombian religious leaders place on *la raza humana* and equality is noteworthy. Although the local Catholic Church has had some progressive priests who engaged in extensive outreach to poor communities, the Church hierarchy has retained a conservative profile that reflects its historical association with regional elites—and its own status as a large landholder. Besides, even the progressive priests were and are "outsiders." In his history of Urabá, Ortiz Sarmiento (2007, 90) notes, "The relationship of these [Catholic] leaders, although being of a different nature than that of the caciques and political party leaders, is still a vertical relationship and not necessarily the product of internal processes of cohesion or the internal organization of communities" (my translation).

Catholic priests are not only visiting outsiders; they are also overwhelmingly *paisas*. In contrast, when Afro-Colombians take their seats amid the rows of plastic chairs carefully arranged for *culto*, at the front of the church they see someone who not only looks like them, but who may be from their own or a nearby community. One young man, clearly a former combatant, although he chose not to talk about it directly, denounced the "racism" of the Catholic Church. He noted that with the exception of two Afro-Colombian priests he had *heard* of, every priest he has *seen* is paisa. "The Catholic Church belongs to the *paisas*," he insisted. "For them, the black person must be a peon." He was drawn to *evangelismo* in part because the pastors are Afro-Colombian, and he admired the fact that "they go places even the army doesn't reach."[23]

In reflecting on this material, I returned to John Burdick's (1998) work on evangelical Christianity, identity, and race in Brazil. In tracing the arc of his research, he began to understand that many of those who were passionate about evangelical Christianity "found liberation theology too abstract to heal the wounds of their everyday lives" (1998, vii). Among those wounds was the centrality of race and racism to people's lived experience, including their religious experience. In asking what complex connections might in fact exist in Brazil between evangelical and black identities, he draws his readers into a sustained analysis of race and religion (6). His central argument is that Christianity is an important and viable idiom for imagining and articulating black ethnic identity and antiracism (21). From the revindication of black ideals of beauty and self-worth to the forging of new sacred selves, the Evangelical churches offered a site for reworking daily and historical experiences of oppression.

When we turn to Urabá, we find that in addition to sharing a "racial" background, there are Evangelical pastors who share a past with "those who have a past." As Abiathar explained, throughout the region there are pastors who are demobilized combatants from the AUC, their leadership providing an example to many others. "With conversion, they are firm in their faith. Their *ex-compañeros* pressure them to return to their previous life [*vida anterior*], but they insist they will not go back. They insist, 'I would rather die. I am a new person now.'"

Abiathar paused for a moment before leaning forward to emphasize his words: "The demobilized need access to social life, to a new life. They live under the shadow of the past. Because of their guilt, and because they are rejected by others, they also reject themselves. They need to forgive themselves and remake themselves as people." His church has been working on these themes for the past seven years. "The demobilized were agents of destruction," he continued, "but now they can help repair the damage done. We look at both preventive and curative processes, and in both we focus on the centrality of the heart. It's not enough to disarm their hands; you must disarm their hearts."

Abiathar mentioned various encounters the church had organized, in which the pastors invited demobilized combatants from the left and the right to come and talk. "These encounters? *Hermana*, what I've lived with them is true Christianity. They shed their previous life. And do you think they don't also have things to forgive? Uuufff! They live knowing they have family members who were killed because of the options they took and the decisions they made. Their loved ones were killed because of the choices they made. They need to learn to reincorporate themselves in the family, feel they are lovable. They need to find acceptance. You know, they were children conceived in violence."

I told him how powerful his last sentence was. He smiled, before adding, "The history of our parents is violence."

Abiathar was speaking about his history as well. He was only fourteen years old in 1995, and several pastors had been killed for protesting forced recruitment. As he named the dead, he noted they were symbols of "the suffering church, the persecuted church. This is a church that suffers, that contributes. The church is not just these four walls. No! The church is daily life, and it reaches far beyond these four walls."

The persecution also reached into his own home. Abiathar's father was a pastor who had preached throughout Urabá, and it turns out that he was one of the pastors killed, there in the same church in which the two of us sat talking that afternoon. Right in the midst of *culto*, a group of paramilitaries entered and shot his father dead in front of the stunned congregation. "They came into the church and killed him in front of everyone." His father's death hit him very hard, but he took some comfort from the fact that his death was quick; the other pastors the paramilitaries killed were hauled off and chopped into pieces over a period of several days.

In the aftermath of his father's murder, Abiathar contemplated what to do. "Some of my friends offered to kill the person who did it. He was someone we all knew." He and his family were forced to flee, and he remembers sleeping atop a cardboard box, enduring things he had never imagined. "They took away something so valuable. But you know what? My contribution lies in not seeking revenge for my father's death."

"What do you mean?," I asked.

"Forgiveness is the key. It all begins with forgiveness. I understand that my father was assassinated, and no one judged [the killers], there was no trial—nothing. But Jesus already paid. He suffered the sentence [*condena*]. Justice was done in Jesus, Jesus paid for our guilt. Based upon this justice, I can forgive. I don't have to look for the killer because justice was done in Christ. This was the burden of Christ."[24]

I pushed back a bit, suggesting that it is not so easy for people to accept this and live with a sense of being grievously wronged. Abiathar acknowledged that but said waiting for God to do justice means continuing to live with "something vengeful." "It means the person still wants revenge, but by means of an intermediary. The sense of a vengeful God, of wishing for the death of another person, is still a sin." Abiathar then turned again to his own experience with death and rancor. He prayed a great deal, and declined the repeated offers to kill his father's murderer. He explained to me, "*Hermana,* a desire for revenge is part of the cycle that keeps fueling these armed groups. There is so much recruitment among people who just want to settle accounts."

Staying the Hand of Vengeance

Abiathar raised an issue that came up in many conversations with former combatants across the political spectrum: revenge. In 2007 I published preliminary findings from the first phase of this project on DDR in Colombia. At that point, my research assistant and I had spoken with 112 former combatants; 64 were from a guerrilla group (the ELN or the FARC), and 48 were from the AUC. Of the 112, 14 were women, all of whom had been guerrillas. We asked why they had joined an armed group. Among guerrillas, the primary reasons were (1) an acquaintance convinced them to join (21 percent); (2) they lived in a zone controlled by an armed group and entering the ranks was almost "natural" (36 percent); (3) they were recruited by force or threat (9 percent); or they were motivated by economic concerns (9 percent). Among AUC members, the primary reasons were (1) an acquaintance convinced them to join (29 percent); (2) they lived in a zone under paramilitary control and joining was "just what you did" (17 percent); (3) they were recruited by force or threat (14 percent); or they were motivated by economic concerns (27 percent) (see Theidon 2007).

However, beyond the "reasons at a glance" statistics, what emerged in our lengthy conversations was the burning desire to avenge the death of loved ones. Justice as *lex talionis*—the proverbial eye for an eye—dominated all our conversations. I offer a quick review of the most common answers: "Everyone should do justice as he sees fit"; "Justice is . . . well, if someone kills my father, I'll kill him"; "Justice? The word makes no sense to me"; "I don't think justice exists. What you gotta do is take revenge." Even those who did mention that justice should be administered "by God" qualified their statements by adding that "helping him out" was not necessarily a bad thing (see Theidon 2007).

In one particularly powerful response to the question why he had joined the FARC and fought for eight years, "Juan" shook his head as he searched for an answer. "That's the most difficult thing for someone to understand about Colombia. The reason why all of us from the same country—between families, friends, neighbors, you name it—why we have to have a war. In the end, we don't know why we have it. Before we had it clear—people fought for a town, for a party, against poverty, for I don't know what all. Ta ta ta—for thousands of things. But right now we don't have it clear why there's this war. The war right now just goes from revenge to revenge—that's how this war goes."[25]

What was striking across the board was the absence of the state in former combatants' discussions of justice. The state as an actor, an intermediary, a protagonist in the administration of justice simply was not mentioned. One factor that contributes to the desire for revenge that so many of these former combatants expressed is precisely the lack of legal alternatives for dispute resolution and the climate of impunity that continues to reign in many regions of Colombia. In her work on postconflict processes, Martha Minow (1998, 14) has argued, "Finding some alternative to vengeance—such as government-managed prosecutions—is a matter, then, not only of moral and emotional significance. It is urgent for human survival." Criminal justice and prosecutions are one way of staying the hand of vengeance, but they are not exhaustive. In the aftermath (or in the midst) of massive violence, the sheer number of low-level perpetrators may exceed the capacity of the judicial system to mount a timely response. In addition, a focus on prosecutions may preclude a discussion of the other forms of justice that animate people's lives and legal consciousness. For example, the focus group with women in Turbo offers more than an anecdote: when the women state that rounding up every man who ever held a gun would result in *"pueblos sin hombres,"* they are opening up a conversation about alternative forms of justice that can satisfy people's demands for accountability and reckoning. Among those alternative forms is divine justice, which draws on Christian compassion and righteous wrath.

My research in Peru and Colombia illustrates the need to grasp people's long-standing, abiding faith that God judges and settles accounts—and to grasp this as something more than fatalism, false consciousness, resignation, or *ressentiment*. All of these approaches are too dismissive, and suggest that adherents are somehow the dupes of history (see Theidon 2013, 312–13). Nigel Biggar, a Christian moral theologian, offers a sustained reflection on divine justice in his book *Burying the Past: Making Peace and Doing Justice after Civil Conflict* (2003). Departing from a certain acceptance of the limits of human justice—an acknowledgment that echoes throughout my research—he suggests we consider "eschatological hope." Although such hope acknowledges the impossibility of proportionality in the face of grave harm, it is not inimical to secular forms of seeking justice, nor does it mean sinking into despairing inertia. Rather, eschatological hope "is necessary to render rational and possible an acceptance of the severe limits of secular justice that is not acquiescent but expectant, not resigned but resolute" (Biggar 2003, 19). It is the steadfast faith that victims will be vindicated, and it captures best what I have seen and heard repeatedly in my research. This faith is a resource in the face of irreparable loss, offering hope to those who feel they are victims. This same hope may hang over the heads of the perpetrators who enter Evangelical churches in an effort to make amends with their fellow beings in the here and now, and with God in the realm that lies beyond. Eschatological hope may in part quench the thirst for earthly vengeance.

"Una hoja de vida dañada": Scripting a Future

I return now to my conversation with Pastor Abiathar, and his insistence that former combatants can shed their previous lives. Part of evangelical practice is testimonial and involves speaking about one's past life and one's "rebirth" in Christ. Conversion involves giving one's testimony publicly, in front of other *hermanos* and *hermanas*, as a sign of "being right with the Lord" and of demonstrating the power of the Lord to effect change in one's life. These testimonies invariably include references to a past life of sin and suffering, but they are also stories of superation and movement, not stasis. Thinking about *this* incitement to speech reveals an interesting twist.

I shared with Abiathar my ambivalence about some of the human rights and transitional justice mechanisms, which not only rely on asking people to produce stories about their painful pasts but also at times oblige them to do so—repeatedly. I mentioned an experience that occurred during the Truth and Reconciliation Commission in Peru. A mobile team from the commission arrived at a village in Ayacucho, and an older woman shrugged wearily when informed they were there to collect testimonies: "Oh, why should I remember all of that again? From the top of my head to the bottom of my feet, from the bottom of my feet to the top of my head—I've told what happened here so many times. And for what? Nothing ever changes." I worried that this practice could lead to "the tyranny of total recall," in which people are incited to keep remembering and reproducing narratives of their painful pasts in the elusive hope of obtaining some form of justice.[26]

Abiathar nodded emphatically. "We don't ask people to endlessly recount the past. One can leave the past behind. We tell them, 'You are people with a future. Let's keep looking ahead.' We treat people as they are, not as they were before. They are new people. There is no need to keep looking back." He thought for a moment and then explicitly contrasted the "human rights approach" with what is practiced in the Evangelical churches. "Think of how many times people are asked to tell what happened, over and over again, and for what? We have almost total impunity here." His concern, however, was not simply that the seemingly endless production of painful narratives was futile. Rather, he emphasized, "What comes of recounting the wound so many times? At times the wound itself becomes the person's identity."

What *are* the consequences of conflating a person with his or her injury? Of reducing a human being to his or her wound? In her critique of liberalism and justice, Wendy Brown (1993) cautions against "wounded attachments" as a means of "doing politics." As she argues, an identity politics based on a logic of pain—one in which politicized identity is founded on a wounded character—has limited emancipatory potential because it tethers the individual to ontological claims of suffering, which breeds a politics of recrimination and rancor. It can also give rise to a politics of victimhood in which narration serves to solidify injury as the core of a person's subjectivity rather than a means of scripting a new self, a new future.

Time and again former combatants lamented the challenges of living with "*una hoja de vida dañada.*" This roughly translates as having a damaged resumé or CV, but the literal meaning is "a damaged page of life." This "*hoja de vida dañada*" can make it difficult to obtain legal employment because of the stigma attached to being a former combatant. However, something more is being invoked. If an individual is held to one tainted version of his life, what options does he have to change? Freezing people in fixed categories—be it victim or perpetrator—can result in that "damaged page" becoming an entire life history. This is narrative as idée fixe rather than as a means of transforming one's fate, and contrasts starkly with the former combatants who insist they are striving for "*una nueva vida.*"

La Nueva Vida: Becoming a New Man

I always dreamed of holding a gun. I wanted to know what it felt like—what it would feel like in my hands. To feel like a man.
                —Oscar, twenty-five years old, former combatant
                of the ELN, at a shelter in Bogotá

When I first began research on the DDR program, I was struck by the lack of attention to the links between weapons, masculinity, and violence. Constructing certain forms of masculinity is not incidental to militarism; rather, it is essential to its maintenance. Militarism and armed conflict require a sustaining gender ideology as much as they need guns and bullets. I suggested that DDR practitioners think of ways to "disarm masculinity" after armed conflict. [27] Of particular interest is militarized masculinity—that fusion of certain practices and images of maleness with the use of weapons, the exercise of violence, and the performance of an aggressive and frequently misogynist masculinity (see Goldstein 2003).

Without denying the diversity that exists among former combatants, there is a hegemonic masculinity that these men have in common.

Connell (2005, 84) approaches the concept of masculinities as a "configuration of practice[s] within a system of gender relations." This practice approach allows the researcher to capture how individuals practice an embodied politics of masculinity that draws on a diverse cultural repertoire of masculine behavior, which in turn is informed by one's class, ethnic, racial, religious, and other identities. While emphasizing the relational aspects of gendered identities and their malleability, Connell also draws attention to the unequal field of power in which all genders are forged. Thus in any given context there is a "hegemonic masculinity"— "the masculinity that occupies the hegemonic position in a given pattern of gender relations, a position always contestable" (Connell 2005, 76). Hegemonic masculinity obscures alternatives—not only the alternative masculinities that exist in any given cultural context, but also within each individual. To more effectively further the goals of DDR and of transitional justice, researchers and practitioners should explore the connections between men, weapons, and the use of violence and design strategies for changing the configuration of practices that signify not only what it means to be a man but also what it means *to be good at being a man*.[28] One site for forging alternative masculinities is in the Evangelical churches.[29]

Alternative Masculinities: "El solo mando es Jesucristo"[30]

God did not give us a wife so that we could make her our slave. We need to value her, help her, and make the way we live our lives our best testimony.

—Pastor, Seventh-Day Adventist church, Turbo, January 2013

The Seventh-Day Adventist church on the outskirts of Turbo was two-thirds full, and the number of young men in the congregation was striking. An older pastor welcomed us but quickly ceded the floor to an energetic young preacher. The sermon came as a surprise; it was a sustained exhortation to remember that religion begins at home, with how one treats his wife and children. "What did you do as you prepared for church today? Were you so busy getting ready that you left feeding the children to your wife? Did you help make the breakfast? Wash some of the dishes? Dress the children? If not, then you are not living the Word. We are letters to be read [*Somos cartas leídas*]. What do our lives tell others about us? Are we living *el Evangelio*?" Amens rippled across the room, and a couple of young men rose to their feet to praise the Lord.

Following *culto*, I asked if perhaps some of the men would be willing to speak with me, and a few days later we sat in a circle as nine *evangélicos* spoke with me about being men. Several began by talking about their lives before joining the church, and one constant was how hard those lives had been. One man had become so desperate he wished for death: "I was sick and tired of myself. I looked up and said, 'God, if you do exist, please kill me.'" Another nodded and added, "To have lived through such awful times is like being given a vaccination against ever going back to that life!" More nods. "We all have scars, we all have pasts."

There are two key themes that bear on my discussion. At various points, the former combatants in the group emphasized that the demobilization agreement was negotiated between the state and leaders of the armed groups: "The commanders made a pact, not those of us who fought. The government never signed any agreement with me. No one consulted us." We can again reflect on the difference between macrolevel processes and their logics and the more intimate spaces of daily life, which in turn may illuminate why these men are in an Evangelical church rather than attending a Catholic Mass. As we have seen, Catholic priests played an important intermediary role at Santa Fe de Ralito, as they had in prior peace negotiations in Urabá. At the institutional level the Catholic Church has a high profile; at the community or neighborhood level, however, it is the *evangélicos* who are performing this mediation between family members and neighbors. The theology of redemption and reconciliation that echoes throughout *cultos* intervenes in the micropolitics of the everyday. One of the men in the focus group waved his hand around the room: "Look at all of us sitting here, from the *autodefensas*, the guerrilla, soldiers. Where else would you see this?" Another added, "A pact between leaders can't bring peace. Here we each make a pact with ourselves."

A general trend in the literature on *evangelismo* in Latin America suggests it is overwhelmingly women who join these churches and then convert their men in an effort to limit their drinking, curb their "woman-izing," and thus direct more of the men's resources into the household economy.[31] Something different is occurring in these churches, many of whose congregations include unaccompanied young men; evidently, they are their own "masculinity projects." Indeed, conversion and transform-ing one's life are configured as manly projects of struggle. Men in the focus group emphasized this point: "We are fighters, entrepreneurs. Dying is easy—it's living that is difficult."[32] From this perspective, it takes cour-age to change one's life, strength to make the transformation: it takes a "real man" to become a new one.[33]

Conclusion

> The circumstances of civil war make it supremely difficult for people threatened by the violence to leave and find sanctuary in non-involved countries or societies. This frequently leaves them with the sole option of creating their own sanctuaries, physically within the territory where the war is being fought.
> —Christopher Mitchell, "The Theory and Practice of Sanctuary"

I want to conclude with an admission regarding my own ambivalence, which I imagine some readers may share. I am not issuing a blanket en-dorsement of *evangelismo* as an antidote to armed conflict. There is noth-ing intrinsically peaceful about Christianity; history is rife with examples of the Christian capacity to do violence to others. Rather, I am drawing attention to the ways in which historically situated individuals and groups appropriate evangelical Christianity, in this case in the midst of ongoing violence and insecurity. Mitchell (2007) notes that the circumstances of civil war mean that many people will continue to live with those they re-sent, hate, or fear; others will confront those same emotions as they con-tinue to live with themselves and the things they have done. Tools that make social life a bit easier, and that help people find ways of effecting change at the personal and interpersonal levels, warrant further study. Co-existence is forged and practiced locally, and in Urabá the *evangélicos* have an important role to play.

Notes

I thank Alex Wilde and Eric Hershberg for the opportunity to participate in this edited volume. I also thank the participants of the Religion and Violence in Latin America workshop, held at the American University, March 26–27, 2012, for many helpful comments on this research project. My gratitude goes to Paola Andrea Betancourt for her able research assistance in Colombia.

1. The 2006 United Nations Integrated DDR Standards (UNIDDRS) underscored the deficiency of reintegration efforts and insisted on "the need for measures to be conducted in consultation and collaboration with all members of the community and stakeholders engaged in the community, and that [DDR programs] make use of locally appropriate development incentives" (UN 2006, II.2.4).

2. Although the individual and collective demobilization processes vary in detail, I have interviewed former combatants in both programs because I am interested in the reintegration phase and the experiences of both these demobilized combatants and their families and host communities.

3. *Paisa* refers to Antioqueños who trace their ancestry to European settlers. Within the complex ethnic categories in Urabá, *paisas* are also lighter-skinned people.

4. During the 1940s, Protestants moved into the region and began to have success converting people. This led to a concern about the "invasion of the sects" and an initial phase of tension between the Catholic and the Protestant Churches. This friction seems to have largely dissipated, and I did not find open hostility between these organizations during my fieldwork.

5. For details on the "counter agrarian reform," see Cubides 2005; Molano 2005.

6. In 1991 in Urabá, there was the largest guerrilla demobilization to date in the country. Members of the Ejército Popular de Liberación were "reinserted" in civil life in 1990, morphing into the political group Esperanza, Paz y Libertad. Many of the former combatants were subsequently assassinated by the paramilitaries as well as the FARC. Thus the latest demobilization process in the region occurred against this backdrop of bad faith negotiations and fear.

7. For a detailed analysis of the legal framework for this process and the ensuing debates, see Laplante and Theidon 2006.

8. Implemented through Resolution 092 of 2004. This resolution suspended the arrest warrants for the members of the AUC who are within the perimeters of its 368-square-kilometer area during the period it was in effect, in principle until December 1, 2004. The agreement provided that the zone would

be in force for six months, which could be extended, depending on the needs of the process, and that in the event that the zone ceased to be in force due to a coordinated decision or unilaterally, the members of the Autodefensas Unidas de Colombia would have a period of five days to evacuate the zone. The OAS Mission to Support the Peace Process (MAPP/OAS) verified compliance with this guarantee, with the accompaniment of the Church.

9. See Ministerio de la Defensa Nacional, *Programa de Atención Humanitaria al Desmovilizado*, Colombia, 2006.

10. See Laplante and Theidon 2006 for a detailed discussion of the challenges to the law.

11. According to a report from the High Commissioner for Reintegration, in the first part of 2007, 2,704 people from thirty different paramilitary blocks were living in Urabá, representing 29 percent of the total number of demobilized in the department of Antioquia and 8.4 percent of the total demobilized in the country (see Mejía Walker 2012).

12. See Mejía Walker 2012 for an overview of the DDR process in Urabá.

13. The Agencia Colombiana para la Reintegración provides aggregate statistics by department and capital city. In Antioquia, as of early 2013 there were 529 demobilized combatants from the FARC. See www.reintegracion.gov.co/Reintegracion/cifrasacr/Documents/regiones/antioquia.pdf.

14. I have referred to the black box of DDR in my previous work, drawing on Bruno Latour's (1987) analysis of science and the ways in which the production of knowledge is mystified, erased, or placed beyond question, reducing the function of the black box to providing only input and output data. In the case of DDR, on one side enters the combatant, and on the other emerges the civilian. In between, the "psychosocial" evidently works its magic.

15. In his history of *evangélicos* in Urabá, Ríos Molina (2002, 24) found that the oldest Protestant denomination in Colombia was the Presbyterian Church, dating to the arrival of missionaries in 1852 from the British and Foreign Bible School who funded the Colombian Biblical Society. Bastian (1994, 122) argues in his history of Protestantism in Latin America that Colombia was one of the countries in which they established their earliest presence. For the purposes of this chapter, I draw attention to the 1940s as a period of increased evangelization and the growth of Pentecostalism in the region. Thus I am not constructing a "before" and "after" story with regard to the *evangélicos* but rather one of accelerated growth over the past ten to twelve years.

16. It is a common practice among evangelical Christians to call one another *hermano* (brother) and *hermana* (sister).

17. Given the sensitivity of the topic, tracing these homicides is difficult. However, apart from any reality that statistics might establish, the fear of lethal

reprisals against oneself or loved ones echoes throughout the interviews we conducted with former combatants.

18. Kevin O'Neill (2010) reports similar findings in his research among prison chaplains in Guatemala.

19. Also see Brenneman's chapter, "Violence, Religion, and Institutional Legitimacy in Northern Central America," in this volume.

20. *Culto*, Seventh-Day Adventists, unnamed community, June 2013.

21. Corregimiento El Dos, Turbo, Colombia, September 2005. This is the same *corregimiento* in which the Bloque Bananero demobilized.

22. Interview, June 21, 2013. In this case, I have changed the name of the pastor (which I routinely do) and do not use the name of the church because it is well known and the information shared with me was in confidence.

23. This was one of numerous conversations about race and religion. Another pastor insisted he was alienated from Catholicism because it was too formulaic, resulting in masses that are excessively formalized and in which priests must carefully follow a given script. He contrasted this with Evangelical pastors, who speak as the Spirit so moves them, allowing for improvisation. The pastor added, "We [Afro-Colombians] threw off one form of servitude! Why would we choose to accept another?"

24. I include these lines in Spanish because of their resonance and the challenge of adequately capturing the meaning. "El perdón es clave. Es desde el perdón. Entiendo que mi padre fue asesinado. Nadie juzgó, ni juicio, nada. Pero Jesús ya pagó. Jesús sufrió la condena. La justicia hizo en Jesús; nuestra culpa Jesús pagó. Sobre esta justicia puedo perdonar. No tengo que buscar el culpable por que se hizo justicia en Cristo. Ésta fue la carga de Cristo."

25. "Juan," former combatant, the FARC, December 2006.

26. See Theidon 2013, 285: "There is an equation that infuses the work of truth commissions: more memory = more truth = more healing = more reconciliation. I am not certain why we believe this, but it is the logic that guides these commissions and the politics of memory that characterize our historic époque. I question the tyranny of total recall, an idea that has been converted into an article of faith within the discourse of human rights. My fieldwork makes me reflect on the complex alchemy of memory and forgetting that functions at the local level—on the role of forgetting (which can consist of remembering something else) in the reconstruction of coexistence after years of intimate violence."

27. I draw here on Theidon 2009.

28. See Herzfeld 1985 for a discussion of manhood and "performative excellence."

29. Both Brenneman (2012) and O'Neill (2011) have also found that evangelical Christianity was one route men took to exit gangs and to forge new understandings of masculinity.

30. "The only commander is Jesus Christ."

31. For a Colombia-based example, see Brusco 1995.

32. "Somos luchadores, emprendedores. Morir es fácil; vivir es difícil."

33. In no way do I deny the contradictory gender messages across the Evangelical churches writ large. Indeed, during my research in Peru I frequently heard pastors promoting very traditional messages about gender in which women's roles were in the home, dedicated to reading to children and such. This is why I find the message in Urabá so striking. This resonates with what Brenneman (2012) and O'Neill (2011) have found in Central America.

References

Asad, Talal. 1993. *Genealogies of Religion: Discipline and Reasons of Power in Christianity and Islam.* Baltimore, MD: Johns Hopkins University Press.

Bastian, Jean-Pierre. 1994. *Protestantismos y modernidad latinoamericana: Historia de unas minorías activas en América Latina.* Mexico City: Fondo de Cultura Económica.

Biggar, Nigel, ed. 2003. *Burying the Past: Making Peace and Doing Justice after Civil Conflict.* Washington, DC: Georgetown University Press.

Brenneman, Robert. 2012. *Homies and Hermanos: God and Gangs in Central America.* New York: Oxford University Press.

Brown, Wendy. 1993. "Wounded Attachments." *Political Theory* 21, no. 3 (August): 390–410.

Brusco, Elizabeth E. 1995. *The Reformation of Machismo: Evangelical Conversion and Gender in Colombia.* Austin: University of Texas Press.

Burdick, John. 1998. *Blessed Anastácia: Women, Race, and Popular Christianity in Brazil.* New York: Routledge.

CCDDR. 2009. *The Cartagena Contribution to Disarmament, Demobilization and Reintegration.* Cartagena: CCDDR.

Connell, Raewyn. 2005. *Masculinities.* Berkeley: University of California Press.

Cubides, Fernando. 2005. "Narcotráfico y paramilitarismo: ¿Matrimonio indisoluble?" In *El poder paramilitar*, edited by Alfredo Rangel, 205–59. Bogotá: Fundación Seguridad y Democracia and Planeta.

García-Peña, Daniel. 2005. "La relación del estado Colombiano con el fenómeno paramilitar: Por el esclarecimiento histórico." *Análisis Político* 52: 53–76.

Goldstein, Joshua. 2003. *War and Gender: How Gender Shapes the War System and Vice Versa.* New York: Cambridge University Press.

Herzfeld, Michael. 1985. *The Poetics of Manhood: Contest and Identity in a Cretan Mountain Village.* Princeton, NJ: Princeton University Press.

Knight, Mark, and Alpaslan Özerdem. 2004. "Guns, Camps and Cash: Demobilization and Reinsertion of Former Combatants in Transitions from War to Peace." *Journal of Peace Research* 41, no. 4 (July): 499–516.

Laplante, Lisa J., and Kimberly Theidon. 2006. "Transitional Justice in Times of Conflict: Colombia's *Ley de Justicia y Paz*." *Michigan Journal of International Law* 28, no. 1 (Fall): 49–108.

Latour, Bruno. 1987. *Science in Action*. Cambridge, MA: Harvard University Press.

Mejía Walker, Carlos Alberto. 2012. "Urabá, los escenarios locales de la desmovilización, el desarme y la reinserción." In *Ensayos sobre conflicto, violencia y seguridad ciudadana en Medellín, 1997–2007*, edited by Manuel Alberto Alonso Espinal, William Fredy Pérez Toro, and Juan Carlos Vélez Rendón, 351–83. Medellín: Instituto de Estudios Políticos, Universidad de Antioquia.

Minow, Martha. 1998. *Between Vengeance and Forgiveness: Facing History after Genocide and Mass Violence*. Boston: Beacon Press.

Mitchell, Christopher. 2007. "The Theory and Practice of Sanctuary: From Asylia to Local Zones of Peace." In *Zones of Peace*, edited by Landon Hancock and Christopher Mitchell, 1–28. Bloomfield, CT: Kumarian Press.

Molano, Alfredo. 2005. *The Dispossessed: Chronicles of the Desterrados of Colombia*. New York: Haymarket Books.

O'Neill, Kevin Lewis. 2010. "The Reckless Will: Prison Chaplaincy and the Problem of Mara Salvatrucha." *Public Culture* 22, no. 1: 67–88.

———. 2011. "Delinquent Realities: Christianity, Formality, and Security in the Americas." *American Quarterly* 63, no. 2 (June): 333–65.

Ortiz Sarmiento, Carlos Miguel. 2007. *Urabá: Pulsiones de vida y desafíos de muerte*. Medellín: La Carreta Editores.

Ríos Molina, Carlos Andrés. 2002. *Identidad y religión en la colonización en el Urabá antioqueño*. Bogotá: Comunican.

Robbins, Joel. 2004. "The Globalization of Pentecostal and Charismatic Christianity." *Annual Review of Anthropology* 33: 117–43.

Rojas, Catalina. 2007. "Islands in the Stream: A Comparative Analysis of Zones of Peace within Colombia's Civil War." In *Zones of Peace*, edited by Landon Hancock and Christopher Mitchell, 71–89. Bloomfield, CT: Kumarian Press.

Stover, Eric, and Harvey M. Weinstein. 2004. *My Neighbor, My Enemy: Justice and Community in the Aftermath of Mass Atrocity*. New York: Cambridge University Press.

Theidon, Kimberly. 2007. "Transitional Subjects? The Disarmament, Demobilization and Reintegration of Former Combatants in Colombia." *International Journal of Transitional Justice* 1, no. 1: 66–90.

———. 2009. "Reconstructing Masculinities: The Disarmament, Demobilization and Reintegration of Former Combatants in Colombia." *Human Rights Quarterly* 31, no. 1 (February): 1–34.

———. 2013. *Intimate Enemies: Violence and Reconciliation in Peru.* Philadelphia: University of Pennsylvania Press.

United Nations. 2006. *Integrated Disarmament, Demobilization and Reintegration Standards.* New York.

United Nations Department of Peacekeeping Operations (UNDPKO). 1999. *Disarmament, Demobilization and Reintegration of Ex-Combatants in a Peacekeeping Environment: Principles and Guidelines.* New York.

———. 2010. *Second Generation Disarmament, Demobilization and Reintegration (DDR) Practices in Peace Operations.* New York.

Uribe, María Teresa. 1992. *Urabá: ¿Region o territorio?* Medellín: Corpourabá-Iner, Universidad de Antioquia.

AFTERWORD

In July 2013 I took part in a three-day meeting in Guatemala City about how the Christian churches of Latin America are addressing the problem of violence.[1] It was not an academic seminar but a gathering of some thirty-five clergy and lay activists with social pastoral ministries on the front lines. They spoke from personal experience very close to the human realities of violence on the ground. They brought with them a palpable sense of urgency about their work and how it related to their faith. They were intensely interested in the work of other participants. And they wanted to understand connections—the links, for example, between violence against Central American migrants in Mexico and drug trafficking and youth gangs in Guatemala, Honduras, and El Salvador. For many, Colombian religious activists for peace illuminated a whole new landscape. Participants knew what they were up against and yet were deeply dedicated and hopeful. They seemed to draw strength from being there, part of something larger than themselves.

They came from different countries and faced different forms of violence, but they found much common ground in how they perceived the challenges and what sustained them in their work. They also drew from a range of Christian faith traditions. Those from Evangelical and Pentecostal churches were an active presence in the gathering, belying conventional belief that their theology of individual conversion and spirituality precludes wider concern for "social" matters. Catholics inspired by teaching tracing back to the Second Vatican Council and participants from "peace churches" such as the Mennonites spoke from their own perspectives about living out one's faith on the ground. The meeting seemed to me a new kind of ecumenism, I commented to a priest one night at dinner. Reproving me gently for my "antiquated theology," he said, "*Somos todos de una sola iglesia aquí*"—"We are all of one church here."

This volume catches something of the spirit animating that gathering. Its different chapters bring us voices that speak from direct knowledge of violence and its challenges to religious faith. They give us insights particularly into activism guided by belief in defending inherent human dignity and awakening human agency. We can see that these values are shared by activists in both Evangelical and Catholic churches but may lead to many different approaches to the problems violence presents—about, for example, how to engage violent actors, or whether it is better to remember or forget past violence. By the nature of their religious mission, the churches will always raise moral questions about violence, and readers will find rich resources in this volume to consider them. They remind us that we must understand the moral dimensions of violence if we are to have any hope of coping with it.

This volume also helps us understand better the unique qualities of religion as a social force against violence. It examines the remarkable vitality and presence of the churches, Catholic and Evangelical, in dangerous places, among marginalized populations where trust in official institutions is low and violent actors establish their own forms of rule. Here the churches may possess a certain legitimacy and offer a measure of protection from the dynamics of local violence. In some circumstances their presence may give them a distinctive role in "accompanying" and catalyzing other forces, as they did historically in the human rights movement and as they are doing in various places in Latin American democracies today. Various chapters also make us aware that violence is often woven into the life of parishes and congregations themselves. Their members may be victims or, conversely, have violent pasts, but where they know each other violence becomes more immediate and personal in ways that make concrete demands on faith.

These studies of religion and violence over a half century should engender a sense of proportion—and perhaps of humility—about the difficulties, duration, and unpredictability of the processes of social change. They illuminate how the manifestations of violence have changed and also how its underlying causes have not changed enough. They help us rethink the place of religion among other forces driving change and give us deeper understanding of the forces *within* religion that have shaped its responses. We cannot know now if pedophilia, financial scandals, and cover-up in the Catholic Church will overwhelm the hopeful pastoral emphasis of Pope Francis. And we can only speculate whether Evangelical ministries directly addressing violence, like those examined in this book, might become more common in churches with different spiritual traditions. But as we see in these pages, religious activism against violence is a reality in Latin America, facing heavy odds but carried by the belief that it is necessary and possible to struggle against the violence inherent in the human condition.

Alexander Wilde
October 2014

Note

1. Claudia Dary Fuentes, "Las Iglesias ante las violencias en Latinoamérica" (Center for Latin American and Latino Studies, American University, Washington, DC, 2013). A working paper downloadable at www.american.edu/clals/Religion-and-Violence-Documents.cfm.

ABOUT THE CONTRIBUTORS

Robert Albro is a sociocultural anthropologist at American University whose research and publications have concentrated on urban and indigenous politics and cultural policy making.

Javier Arellano-Yanguas is on the faculty at the Universidad de Deusto in Spain and studies the interaction of local governments, mining companies, and local social movements in Peru.

Robert Brenneman, a sociologist, is the author of *Homies and Hermanos* (2011), which examines former gang members and Evangelical churches in the Northern Triangle.

María Soledad Catoggio teaches at the University of Buenos Aires. Her work focuses on churches under authoritarian rule in the Southern Cone and questions of legitimacy.

Amelia Frank-Vitale, a doctoral student in anthropology at the University of Michigan, is researching the violence faced by Central American migrants transiting Mexico en route to the United States.

Virginia Garrard-Burnett, University of Texas, is the author of *Terror in the Land of the Holy Spirit* (2010) and has published widely on Latin American religious history.

Andrew Johnson, Princeton Center for the Study of Religion, has examined Pentecostal Christianity among inmate populations in Brazilian prisons.

Patrick William Kelly received his PhD in history in 2015 from the University of Chicago. He is currently the A. W. Mellon Postdoctoral Fellow in the Humanities and Humanistic Sciences at the University of Wisconsin–Madison, where he is completing his book manuscript on the centrality of Latin America to the rise of global human rights politics in the 1970s.

Daniel H. Levine, Professor of Political Science Emeritus at the University of Michigan, is the author of more than a dozen books on religion, politics, and democracy in Latin America.

Gustavo Morello, S.J., Boston College, researches the relationship between Catholics, politics, and the idea of the secular in Argentina's recent history.

Elyssa Pachico is a researcher for InSight Crime based in Medellín, Colombia.

Rafael Mafei Rabelo Queiroz, a professor at the University of São Paulo Law School, is writing on the legal profession and human rights in Brazil.

Winifred Tate, an anthropologist at Colby College, is the author of the award-winning *Counting the Dead: The Culture and Politics of Human Rights Activism in Colombia* (2007).

Kimberly Theidon, an anthropologist at Tufts University, is the author of *Intimate Enemies* (2012), on Peru's internal armed conflict, and also writes about contemporary Colombia.

Alexander Wilde, a political scientist and research fellow at CLALS, American University, formerly directed WOLA and the Ford Foundation's regional office in Chile.

INDEX